Marriages & Families

a **Transaction/Society** reader

Marriages & Families

edited by

Helena Z. Lopata
Loyola University of Chicago

**D. Van Nostrand Company**
New York • Cincinnati • Toronto • London • Melbourne

D. Van Nostrand Company Regional Offices:
New York   Cincinnati   Milbrae

D. Van Nostrand Company International Offices:
London   Toronto   Melbourne

Published by D. Van Nostrand Company
450 West 33rd Street, New York, N. Y. 10001

Published simultaneously in Canada by
Van Nostrand Reinhold Ltd.

10 9 8 7 6 5 4 3 2 1

Acknowledgments

"Portnoy's Mother's Complaint" by Pauline Bart: This investigation was supported in part by a pre-doctoral research training fellowship from the National Institute of Mental Health.

"Kapluna Daughter" by Jean Briggs: Reprinted from Peggy Golde, editor, *Women in the Field* (Chicago: Aldine Publishing Company, 1970). Copyright © Aldine Publishing Company. Reprinted by permission of the author and Aldine Atherton, Inc.

"Children and Their Caretakers" by Norman K. Denzin: An earlier version of this article was commissioned by the Work Group on Self-Concept of the Social Science Research Council Subcommittee on Learning and the Educational Process, 1970.

"Young Intelligentsia in Revolt" by Richard Flacks: Reprinted with the permission of The Macmillan Company from *The New American Revolution*, edited by Rod Aya and Norman Miller, 1971. Copyright © by The Free Press, a division of The Macmillan Company.

"The Social Construction of the Second Sex" by Jo Freeman: Excerpted from *Roles Women Play: Readings Toward Women's Liberation*, edited by Michele Hoffnumn Garskof, published by Brooks Cole Publishing Company. Copyright © 1971 by Jo Freeman.

"Roots of Black Manhood" by Ulf Hannerz: Reprinted with the permission of The Macmillan Company from "What Ghetto Males Are Like" in *Afro-American Anthropology: Contemporary Perspectives*, edited by Norman E. Whitten and John Swed. Copyright © by The Free Press, a division of The Macmillan Company.

"Child Convicts" by Paul Lerman: An earlier version of this article was commissioned by the Work Group on Self-Concept of the Social Science Research Council Subcommittee on Learning and the Educational Process, January 1970.

"Even the Saints Cry" by Oscar Lewis: Excerpted from *La Vida* by Oscar Lewis, published by Random House, 1968.

"Future Family" by Margaret Mead: This article is based upon an edited transcript of an address given by the author to Barnard students and their parents, February 12, 1970.

"The Relief of Welfare" by Frances Fox Piven and Richard A. Cloward: From *Regulating the Poor: The Functions of Public Relief* by Frances Fox Piven and Richard A. Cloward, published by Pantheon Books, 1971.

"Post-1984 America" by Lee Rainwater: Copyright © 1972 by the author.

"The Brutality of Modern Families" by Richard Sennett: From *The Uses of Disorder: Personal Identity and City Life* by Richard Sennett. Copyright © 1970 by Richard Sennett. Reprinted by permission of Alfred A. Knopf, Inc.

"Genteel Backlash" by Richard Sennett: From *Nineteenth-Century Cities: Essay in the New Urban History*, edited by Stephan Thernstrom and Richard Sennett (New Haven and London: Yale University Press, 1969). Copyright © 1969 by Yale University.

"Day Care Centers" by Gilbert Y. Steiner: Excerpted from *The State of Welfare* by Gilbert Y. Steiner. Copyright © 1971 by The Brookings Institution, Washington, D. C.

"Anatomy of a Chicago Slum" by Gerald D. Suttles: Reprinted from *The Social Order of the Slum* by Gerald D. Suttles. Copyright © 1968, The University of Chicago Press.

Foreword

The blunt truth is that there is no such thing as a trade book or a text book—but much more to the point, good books and bad books. It is with that in mind that this collection of articles, based on work previously published in the magazine *trans-Action/Society*, is being made available for the college and university communities.

It is our feeling at Transaction, shared by D. Van Nostrand Company and hopefully by readers of this book as well, that these analyses of marriage and the family which first appeared in article form in *trans-Action/Society* are of sufficient interest and value to hold up over time and can become both part of the permanent learning experience of the student and, beyond that, part of the permanent corpus of solid materials by which the best of any field is deservedly judged. The text that has resulted from this compilation clearly demonstrates, we believe, the superiority of starting with real world problems, and searching out practical solutions. That the essays fall into generally established patterns of professional disciplines is more an accident than a necessity; it also demonstrates a growing awareness on the part of the basic areas of social science of their larger commitment to the amelioration of the human condition.

The demands upon scholarship and scientific judgment are always stringent—especially so in an era of booming scientific information, to the point of overload. The advantage of these studies is that in every essay there has been an effort to communicate the experience of the crisis of current social living. Yet, despite the sense of urgency these contributions exhibit, the editor has chosen them because they match, if not exceed, in durable interest the best of available social science literature, and because they have withstood the test of time. This collection, then, attempts to address fundamental issues and in so doing add to the basic insights derived from a classical literature in the various fields of the social sciences.

Because of the concreteness of these writings, the editor has seen fit to develop at considerable length a theoretical scaffold that links the specific essays themselves. As a result, the text can serve as a valuable series of core readings or as an adjunct anthology. There was nothing slap-dash or random about the selection process, the editing process, or the ideological process that went into this volume. It is our feeling that these essays represent the best in social science thinking and deserve the permanence granted by republication in book form.

The social scientists involved, both as editor and authors of this reader, have gone beyond observation, and have entered into the vital and difficult tasks of explanation and interpretation. The text has defined issues in a way that makes solutions possible. It has provided answers as well as asked the right questions. Thus, this book is dedicated not simply to highlighting social problems for students already inundated with such an awareness but, far more important, establishing guidelines for social solutions based on the social sciences.

Irving Louis Horowitz
Editor-in-Chief
trans-Action/Society

Contents

Preface

I have had a great deal of pleasure preparing this volume of essays on a subject that has recently come of age in America. The book presents an interdisciplinary view of marriage and the family, with emphasis on the family in contemporary society. I undertook the project in response to the expanding enrollments in college courses on courtship, marriage, and family life, as well as the increasing interest in this field on the part of many social scientists from a wide variety of disciplines. It is apparent today not only that the family is a rich subject for study but also that the study benefits greatly from the contributions of anthropology, economics, education, women's studies, sexology, ecology, and gerontology; no less than those of sociology and psychology.

The book is organized so as to highlight changes in marriage, family composition, social relations and roles, as well as the mutual interdependence between these and other institutions of society. We begin with the traditional pre-industrial or pre-urban family, showing how and why it began changing at a rapid rate and exploring the problems of transitional phases. The present family, with its middle-class ideals, is then examined closely. Finally, several trends in modern families are identified and some tentative predictions about future families made.

The articles included within this framework have been selected on the basis of readability, good reporting, and their pertinence to issues of widespread concern today. Each touches upon some fundamental dynamic of marriage, family, or a related sphere of social life. Each raises significant questions for an understanding of marriage and the family in our present period of great change.

My own comments throughout the book focus on the seeds of change that have influenced and continue to influence the patterns of marriage and family life. We shall look closely, for example, at what appears to be a shift in values away from the economic institution to that of the family and its various alternatives. We shall trace a conscious and repercussive reexamination of basic American values which has brought new pressures to bear upon other societal institutions—pressures to adapt to the desires and values of people *in families* rather than in, say, vocations. This shift of focus seems visible everywhere today but is especially strong among young people, who express deep concern over their interpersonal relationships. It is no coincidence that sensitivity training and transactional analysis have become so popular and that American bestseller lists and college reading lists are crowded with books on open marriage and self-awareness.

In addition to promoting insights into the family as a social institution, I hope this book will serve three other functions. For one, it can illuminate social roles other than those entailed in marriages and families. Understanding any major institution in a society inevitably increases our insight on other fronts. If, as we have suggested, the values, relations, and roles of the family and its alternatives become a major source of change for the total society, then knowledge of family change provides a head start toward understanding the future of all aspects of life in America. Later sections of the book, in particular, affirm that the interrelationships between the family institution and education, economic and political structures, religion, and recreation are manifold.

A second function I hope the book will serve is that of supplying the reader with an abstract of alternate life styles. Because the essays collected here present lively, descriptive analyses of the many ways people relate to each other within marriages and families, they may well suggest alternatives which the reader will want to ponder. More than prior generations, today's students are being educated to gain knowledge vicariously as well as through concrete experience. They are adept at rehearsing alternate ways of doing things in imagination rather than using time, energy, and often psychic health to experiment. We know it is not necessary to become a juvenile delinquent in order to understand the dynamics and consequences of delinquency: vicarious knowledge can help us act in a nondelinquent manner ourselves and, hopefully, bring up our children so that they will not become delinquent. For although tradition is still very much with us and the strains of change can be painful, people today must routinely make more life choices than previous generations did. To the extent that some alternatives can be weighed in imagination, the individual is less likely either to follow current fashion unthinkingly or to fall back upon established patterns which may be dysfunctional.

Thus, true freedom of thought and action is based on information and scientific insight—on vicarious knowledge such as the essays in this book can provide. The reader may say to himself during the study of this book: "That sounds like an interesting way to live," or, "There but for luck (and the awareness I'm gaining through this article) goes *my* family!"

Finally, being a student of the family myself, I hope that this collection may direct some readers toward a similar career choice. For I feel sure that the field will offer great challenges and rewards in coming years.

Most literature dealing with American families (and therefore most of the material in this volume) focuses on the middle class, although *trans-Action/Society* has been better than average at publishing analyses of other life styles. Doubtless, future researchers will broaden the scope of this inquiry. But it is also true that "the action" today is in the middle classes. Americans are now approaching, or already settling into, that middle-class model which contains what our American creed has long defined as "ideal." Many studies of lower-class families show that they hold middle-class notions of what is desirable, even though they may be prevented by a host of factors from achieving a middle-class life style.

Whether this pattern of aspiration will persist now that the middle class appears to be redefining its ideal is but one of many absorbing questions likely to occur to anyone reading the essays that follow. They illuminate the variety of ways that social scientists study marriage and the family, the tools they use, and some of the conclusions they draw.

Helena Z. Lopata

Editor's Acknowledgments

This book is clearly the product of many people. The authors of the articles are responsible for the quality of their pieces, as are the editors of *trans-Action/Society* who reviewed and published them. Credit must also go to the many gifted photographers whose work accompanies the text. Photography is becoming an increasingly important tool of the social sciences, and the pictures which here appear consistently capture the symbolic quality of the analysis. Eileen Markeley Znaniecki edited my sections, as she has helped me for years. Thanks also go to Pamela Rose, Monica Velasco and Frank Steinhart of the Center for the Comparative Study of Social Roles at Loyola University of Chicago, to Mary E. Curtis for her editorial direction, and to the staff of *trans-Action/Society*.

HZL

Before analyzing American marriage and family, past, present and future, we should answer two basic questions: What is marriage? And what is the family? The definitions are not easy to arrive at. To learn what the family is and does throughout the world we must discover the universal composition of the unit and the roles each member plays. One way of settling the matter is to state that the *family* is the social unit responsible for carrying on the family institution. Now we are in smoother waters, for sociologist Robin Williams, through his analysis of American society has already suggested that the family institution consists of all those ways of thinking, doing and having (ideas, norms and objects) which focus upon the functions of mate selection, the marital bond, social roles within the nuclear unit of a married couple and their children, and the relations they have with their extended kin. Now we are back to the need to define *marriage*, and this we can do by stating simply that marriage involves an officially sanctioned entrance of one or more men with one or more women into the roles of husband and wife. The relation they have with each other, and with everyone else who is involved in their social circles within these roles, is based on their setting up a household and functioning as a "living unit" with the potential to expand through the birth of young members. The basic family, then, consists of people united through marriage or birth, who share a common household and carry out activities which make living together possible.

Families are recognized by the community as forming a unit bound together. Thus, in America, the *nuclear* family contains people functioning in the roles of husband, wife, father, mother, son and daughter. The term *extended family* is generally used to indicate a larger unit consisting of people defined as related by birth, adoption or marriage, even though they do not live together in the same

Prologue

household or housing complex and do not form a basic unit for interaction. The extended family, also called the kin group, may include, in American urban society, any of the following: grandparents, grandchildren, adult children and their spouses, aunts, uncles, nieces, nephews and first cousins. It may even include a fourth generation of great-grandparents. Each person belongs to a family of orientation, into which he was born or officially adopted as a son or daughter, and most adults have a family of procreation which they form with a mate and children.

Now that we have defined both marriage and the family, we need to point out that, although the nuclear and extended units mentioned above are the normal or usual way in which people are organized on the basis of marriage and birth, this does not mean that every American is in fact a member of an extended kin group, a family of orientation and a family of procreation. Some babies are born out of wedlock or illegitimately, that is, they have not been legitimized by the prior marriage of their mother and father. Some people performing the roles traditionally associated with marriage are not married. Similarly, persons can assume the role of parent by adoption rather than by childbearing. The term "family" has been used at times to include all the nuns in a convent, everyone living in a commune, members of both sexes and their children sharing a home, members of sororities or fraternities, all the people identified with a social movement (as in a "sisterhood") and even all human beings because of their supposed descent from Adam and Eve. However, everyone applying the concept "family" to such social organizations is aware that these are imitations, extensions or "deviations" from the "normal" family. Other people may call themselves a family and may even perform many of the functions carried on by the traditional family, such as reproduction and child rearing, but, strictly speaking, they are not carrying out the *social roles* of husband, wife, parent, child and sibling unless they have the cooperation of the community in which they live. This is important, for in speaking of societally established families, we are speaking of people involved in social roles containing duties and rights within a wide social circle. Giving birth to a baby does not ensure one the social role of mother. Modern society is so constructed that it is virtually impossible for a girl to act as a mother without the cooperation of many other people who recognize her in that role and who grant her rights and facilities. She needs food, protection, people to care for the child when she is not present, educators and so forth. Society insists on its right to take the baby away from her and prevent her from performing the role of mother, if it does not approve of her qualifications for the role or her actions within it. One of the qualifications may be to have a man legally or at least socially present and active in the role of father. If society allows her to perform her role, it may provide a father substitute, in the form of a social worker or money to take the place of the breadwinner. People in this society picture the normal family as containing one (and only one) husband, one (and only one) wife and their young biological children. In other societies, the term means something else, in that it includes other social roles. We do not consider boarders, servants, unmarried siblings or anyone else living with the basic unit as really being part of it. They are outsiders. We practice monogamy (and we are one of the few societies of the world to insist on it), in that we marry only one husband or wife at a time.

What we have established thus far are the following characteristics of the family:

1. It is a social unit, in that the members consider themselves and are considered by the community to be socially related, with definite boundaries and patterned social roles and identities.

2. It is a social unit which has all the characteristics of a social group: a name or symbol of identity, a set of functions, a division of labor by which these are carried out, a hierarchy of status, a method of entry which is publicly recognized, common property, and some norms or ways of doing things. Each family is a complicated social group and is unique in the way it combines these characteristics.

3. At least until now, the "complete family" has consisted of people intertwined by societally recognized social roles, including husband and wife, father and mother, son, daughter, sister and brother. The "extended family" has provided additional roles such as grandfather, eldest son, other sons, the women they marry, etc., but all of these are considered secondary roles in our society.

4. The modern family unit has its foundation in the processes of mate selection and the establishment of a marriage, followed by the birth of one or more children. The married couple themselves are not considered a complete family, by American standards, because of the traditional assumption that they become "fulfilled" only by having children. Thus, the bond between husband and wife is still assumed to be grounded in the bond that these two people will develop later as parents.

5. This family unit has a relatively short life span, being considered complete only when both spouses are present, and before the last child has left home to start its own household and family unit.

6. The family lives together in that they share a household, manage it through a division of labor, function as a production-, distribution- and consumption-unit, and carry out basic activities including sexual intercourse, reproduction, socialization of the young, emotional interaction, identity maintenance, and so forth. The family performs more life-sustaining functions than any other social group, but it receives help—in varying degrees, depending on its social structure—from other families and other types of social groups.

Three Models of Family Organization

Agricultural societies of the past and the present are likely to have an extended family system in which the structure of the unit living and working together is complex. Most of these units are based on a consanguine relation, which is considered more basic than that established by marriage. Usually, the consanguine, or blood, line followed is patrilineal, in which case the basic unit consists of a man, his eldest son, his other sons, his grandsons and the women they marry. The family is patriarchal in that authority is transmitted and delegated along the male descent line, and it is age-stratified in that the oldest living male has the right to assign and define social roles and relations until he retires, at which time he will delegate that right to the next in line. Mate selection tends to be a matter for the whole family, or its specially designated representatives. A wife is chosen for her potential contribution to the whole family; romantic love between spouses is unexpected and is even discouraged as interfering with basic loyalties. The matchmakers balance the candidate's assets, such as an assumed or proven ability to bear many offspring, her contribution of economic goods, her strength for work, her status-enhancing qualities, such as beauty or an ability to play the piano, and the likelihood of her fitting into the group, against what the groom's family can offer. Her family is also concerned that she gain proper status in marriage, because her position reflects on them. In addition, when the girl's family is assumed to be losing a valuable worker, it is often compensated by economic goods, called a brideprice. If she is regarded as a liability, on the other hand, her family may have to offer the equivalent of a bribe to the other group in order to take her off their hands. The dowry with which a girl enters marriage is either kept by her as her own property or absorbed into the husband's family wealth. The amount of independence a woman has within her husband's family depends, therefore, upon whether residence is patrilocal and upon the rights obtained from marriage. Especially important are her right of control over the property she brings with her or earns in marriage, and her right of inheritance from her husband. Both of these rights vary according to whether the bride is the direct recipient of property or whether she holds it in trust for her male children. Most patrilineal and strongly patriarchal families prohibit their women from inheriting property and provide family male guardians whenever the heirs are too small to manage their inheritance.

If the family is so patrilocal that sons bring their wives home to the household or nearby, the wife may lose her identification as a member of her own family of orientation. Her degree of subservience to the already-established family members of her husband's unit varies from society to society. His allegiance and focal relations, in any case, are not with her, but with his male relatives. Statistics indicate that young brides in traditional southeastern China were so badly treated and worked so hard by their mothers-in-law that many committed suicide. The child brides of India generally fared better, as long as their husbands remained living, but the lot of the Indian widow in the past and even now in rural areas has been recorded as miserable. In parts of Africa, where women have generally had the right to keep anything they earned through trading or selling products, the status of the wife seems to be better. There are great variations by social class the world over.

The pre-industrial family, furthermore, fits the new bride into the women's tasks within the family work system, while her husband continues his participation in the male labor. The power wielded by head of the family over all its members is strong, since he controls the economic resources, occupational tools, job training and assignments. However, he is not the sole *owner* of these properties, only holding and working them in trust for future generations. The concept of individuated ownership is foreign to traditional extended families, who are tied to a defined piece of land. Familism is their basic ideology, and it is so pervasive as to affect not only relations but identities. A person is born or gradually absorbed into a family continuing through generations and is socialized into certain norms of behavior which are followed to the letter. The world contains spirits of deceased family members who observe and judge, insuring that no change or harm is done to what is communally owned and transmitted to future generations. Property is held, used and contributed to *in continuum*—each generation taking it from the prior and passing it on to the next. The ancestral home is symbolic of this attitude; it is not redecorated by each new owner, but the old pieces are retained as receptacles for the essence of the family. It is on this land and in this home that their ancestors toiled and died; it is here that birth and death form a continuous cycle of existence.

Social units strongly infused with the familistic ethic usually grant the husband and his relatives strong rights over the wife. According to the anthropologist Paul J. Bohannan (1962), the husband's rights may include those of: setting up a household with the wife and sharing the work of maintaining it; the economic right to what she brings or produces; the right of sexual access and the *in genetricem* rights. The last-named prerogatives guarantee that all children born to the wife be identified as his and joined to his family. This may include the right to any children she bears after his death. In times when death rates were very high and men married women much younger than they, the probability of a woman's becoming a widow while still in childbearing years was great. Simultaneously, the infant mortality was such that a man wishing either family continuity or offspring who would protect his spirit after death was reassured by the guarantee that one of his male agnates (relatives from his father's side) would enter into a relation with the widow, having sexual intercourse with her in order to "raise up his seed." This "levirate" system has been practiced in many societies and there is frequent reference to it in the Bible. Other ways of insuring continued reproduction by a widow include her remarriage or her being inherited by a male member of the husband's family. Since most societies have allowed polygamy, widow inheritance has been an accepted way of solving the problem of early widowhood. An additional advantage of these customs has been the insurance of a male protector for a woman and her children in societies in which she had not been trained, or allowed, to maintain herself independently. An alternative solution provided a male guardianship relation that lacked sexual rights. This pattern was particularly prevalent when the widow was too old to bear more offspring and lacked an adult son to take over management of the family. Thus, in traditional and non-industrial situations where the family was the main economic unit, the production of new members and participation in the division of labor were so important that marriage was viewed as having these functions above all others. Sentiments interfering with such a marriage—romantic love or jealousy, for example—were devalued and discouraged.

In his delightful *Centuries of Childhood*, Phillipe Ariès (1962) describes households of an intermediary type between the agriculturally based extended unit and its industrialized, urbanized counterpart. His analysis of paintings and other works by European artists of the Middle Ages reveals that the very concepts of family and of childhood did not exist in Europe prior to the sixteenth century. The household contained many people: adults, miniature adults, manor heads, workers, guests, tutors and people performing diverse roles. Of course, he is describing the manor home, not the peasant's. The house was open for entrance and activity at all hours of day and night, and the life of the society flowed through it constantly. Sleeping, eating, even giving birth and dying, were public events, and the common rooms witnessed a whole range of activities simultaneously and in time sequence. People living in such households also had free access to others in the village, the town or the estate; the streets were filled with people talking, walking and playing.

Ariès found that the death rate was so high in those centuries before the discoveries of modern medicine that people invested little emotion in their offspring. Children were portrayed as little adults in paintings and were considered able to work in economically productive roles by the age of seven. They were often apprenticed to other households. "Boy" meant servant, and boys served not only as helpers to craftsmen but as domestic workers. The service lasted for years, the youth returning home only much later. The English, for example, felt that apprenticing their children to other families was good for them, since they could thus learn better manners than they would acquire at home. "Children were not kept at home; they were sent to another house, with or without a contract, to live there and start their life there, or to learn the good manners of a knight, or a trade, or even go to school and learn Latin. In this apprenticeship we see a custom common to all classes of society." (Ariès, 1962:366).

Thus, family life as currently idealized was not part of medieval upper-class Europe, boundaries of the unit and social roles being very indefinite and flexible. Ariès links the development of the idea of a private family with the movement of work away from home and the expansion of the school system, because the latter began to differentiate the generations by separating the child from the adult. Children became increasingly important to parents as a source of emotional rather than economic investment. Life of a public nature, economically, politically and socially, began simultaneously with withdrawal from the home. People went to public places to work, organize power, recreate, pray and do any number of social things. The home became a private place, to which family members withdrew after involvement in the specialized and often difficult or dangerous world outside. The household shrank in importance as societal life moved out of it. Extra members of the household withdrew into separate quarters, and the role of servant became socially distant to the extent that children of servants did not play with the lord's offspring. The prior free association among classes and varieties of persons decreased. The family ate alone and slept away from nonfamily members. Visiting and business activities became limited to a few well-defined hours and individuals, while contact with others usually took place in buildings other than the home.

Thus, gradually, evolved the modern nuclear, conjugal family. In terms of daily life, the structure and functions of this family differ in many ways from those of the extended unit. Boys and girls in American society leave their homes for the major part of their waking day to enter schools where, for years, they are educated to live in a complex society. Their families simply cannot provide them with sufficient knowledge to warrant their being kept home. The daughter marries at an average age of 20.8 years, the son almost two years later. At that time, still in school or working, they set up their own home, usually an apartment in an urban center. Although they receive gifts from both sets of parents, they are expected to be economically independent. The identification units are bilineal in that both the husband's and the wife's families are assumed to have equal rights and duties to the new family unit, although the patriarchal tradition is evident in the fact that the husband does not change his name or official designation as Mr. John Brown, while the wife ceases to be Miss Susan Owsiak and becomes Mrs. John Brown. The couple has complete rights over their housing unit, within the limits of the rental agreement, without interference from either family of orientation. This arrangement is very different from one in which the bride entered the husband's ancestral home which was dominated by his mother. The wife continues working until nearly the end of her first pregnancy (at an average age of about 22) and then stays home to take care of her small children, unless poverty forces her out into the labor market again. The couple often buys a home in urban fringes or suburbs. The wife returns to work when the children are in school for most of the day or are judged old enough to use mother-substitutes. After age 46, the mother is generally left without children in the home. She lives another fifteen years with her husband as the only other occupant of the house. They may sell their home at that time or, after the husband retires, move to smaller quarters—if they have the money, to a southern climate. The wife becomes widowed and lives the last fifteen years of her life alone. Seldom does she move in with married children to form a three-generation household, but she may share a residence with adult unmarried, divorced or widowed offspring at one time or another.

The factors which have changed the extended family unit to the essentially nuclear one described above are many, but, according to the eminent sociologist Max Weber (1958), they stem mainly from the Protestant Reformation. Weber, who studied many societies and periods of human association, found that Western Europeans changed their focal institutions from the religious to the economic, due to the development of a Protestant ethic which justified strong personal and societal concentration of thought and energy on economic activity. As Melville Herskowitz (1955), an anthropologist, has pointed out, each society is built around a focal institution, one special area of its life. Not all societies have the same focal institution; nor do all institutions experience change in the same manner or at the same rate. In fact, Far Eastern societies have, until very recently, retained an emphasis on religious institutions. Australian aborigines focus on the family institution to such an extent as to prevent any change in the economic aspects of their life—so that they have a very simple material culture which they refuse to modify, while their family structure is extremely complicated. Some societies are focused on the military establishment, forcing other sets of relations and styles of life to conform to its demands. Whatever the focal institution, all other value systems, social roles and knowledge systems must conform to it. If there is a conflict, it is resolved so as to protect the central institution. Its representatives, be they priests, generals, fathers or business tycoons, are accorded the greatest prestige and have the most power. Max Weber was saying that the Protestant Reformation made possible a shift of attention from the religious sphere of life to the economic.

The scientific and commercial revolutions which accompanied this turning of attention to material goods in Western culture provided techniques, technologies and secularized orientation which welcomed experimentation and change. Societies and social classes which had previously been tied to an agricultural subsistence source began to industrialize and urbanize rapidly. Material culture grew by leaps and bounds, while earlier forms of social relations and identities which interfered with this sudden wealth were pushed into the background. Past sources of prestige (as in family name) and power (as in patriarchies) lost their influence and were replaced by individual achievement and mobility. According to sociologist Robert Winch (1968), world history shows that agricultural societies, in which mobility was lacking and the family was the basic work-group, enabled the extended family to exist and control life. Industrialization and urbanization freed people from the domain of the extended family by providing training and jobs independent of the patriarch, the manor lord and class constraints. Freedom from the past was afforded by the new emphasis on the material culture: freedom from starvation, from autocratic leadership, from the patriarch, from the restrictive kin group, even from the all-knowing and omnipotent God who punished any signs of self-indulgence (Fromm, 1941). Pleasure was to be derived from life on earth, not hereafter; but it had to be won, and the price was high: constant work and upward mobility. Each step of proving one's worth was rewarded by increasing time for "re-creation" and material comfort, preparing the person for the next step up.

Clearly, the older family could not remain unchanged. Its form and role content changed dramatically under pressure of the economic revolution bringing urbanization, industrialization and increased societal complexity. A person could change life styles not just once, or once in a while, but frequently. The changes were often painful, but were always justified by the reassurance that life was becoming better and that all problems would be solved when the goals of economic change and expansion were reached.

The movement of vital areas of life away from the home to segmentalized centers focusing on specialized activities, such as factories, and the uneven rate of industrialization and urbanization in the world resulted in the migration of different peoples into centralized areas. Services, transportation and distribution were standardized. Money became an important common denominator and source of measurement, a means for comparing the value of different items in the ever-shifting culture. Man began measuring himself in terms of what he could command on the open market for his skills and talents. Societal changes were so dramatic that socialization and education, despite the introduction of mass schooling, could not keep up with them. The burgeoning cities filled with former village and small-town residents who did not understand the complex within which they functioned on a minimal level, huddled together and fearful of their surroundings. Even now the urban villager is more typical of city residents than is the "cosmopolitan" who can analyze the city's resources and use them to fill self-defined needs. Although industrializing, urbanizing and technologically complex societies are based on voluntaristic participation of competent and flexible human beings, the family, the school, the neighborhood and most of the social groups which are responsible for developing multidimensional and self-motivating participants have failed to prepare people for urban lives, as evidenced by personal and family disorganization indices.

What are the indices which point to strains in human life resulting from the "cultural lag" or the decrystallization of past life styles and norms without the creation of alternative styles more fitting the economically focused urban and industrial world? Broadly, they are the actions of individuals and groups which prevent them and others from using their own and society's potential to the fullest: psychosis, or the complete inability to function in a society as realistically given; neurosis, or the disproportionate use of energy and emotion in building defenses against others and the broader world; alcoholism or drug abuse, which stop personal development and social involvement; aggression against self or others; prejudice and discrimination, inhibiting one's own progress in order to delay that of others; the inability to form deeply satisfying social relations; resorting to action which brings societal punishment, as in delinquency, rape, prostitution, theft; the ultimate of withdrawal in suicide. These are but a few of the more dramatic ways in which people restrict their opportunities to live fully in the modern world. The statistics of divorce, desertion, separation and family conflict are high in urbanizing and industrializing nations. The poor, the old, the young whose parents do not function efficiently in their roles, the native American, the ghetto black, the immigrant and his child—many people suffer from the rapidity of change from agricultural and rural background to urban culture.

The tremendous emphasis on the economic sphere of life so typical of the past decades of American society has not escaped sociological attention. William Ogburn (1922) observed it and concluded that social change always begins with inventions or diffusion of technological improvements in economic aspects of culture. Subsequently, other social institutions or patterns of procedure experience secondary waves of change, much like the waves in water after a stone has disrupted its surface stillness. The family institution, according to Ogburn, is the last to change, always lagging behind innovations produced by technology. This explanation of change in ideologies and styles of life is not surprising when generalized from what was happening in

America in the 1920s, when Ogburn was doing research on social change. Nevertheless, it is quite possible that changes are now emanating from other aspects of the American culture which may result in a shift of emphasis *away from* economic institutions directly *toward* the family or perhaps even to recreational institutions. Let us first examine in greater detail the consequences of historical changes upon the family, as well as some attempts to purposely initiate modifications that will solve problems produced by the cultural lag.

The decrease in the power of the extended family which we have traced has had important repercussions on the mate-selection system. When boys and girls started mixing freely in schools, participating in many activities together, their new freedom of contact away from the family home gradually evolved into a dating and self-selection mating scheme. The romantic love current in the age of chivalry and described in the literature dealing with kings and their mistresses began to be attached to modern marriage. Now youth can test their own personalities and those of potential husbands and wives, as they date, engage in leisure-time activities, and even share work or study. They fall in and out of love until they are finally ready to settle down in marriage. Parents have no power to prevent a marriage, once their child has passed the age when parental consent is necessary. Actually, marriages generally do involve the cooperation of the parents, and most young people select the kind of partner that the parents would have selected had traditional methods been followed. This means that most young people do not marry outside of their social class and major identity group. Few black girls marry white boys. But assimilation does bring cross-ethnic marriages; as the process goes on, being a Pole decreases so much in importance that a youth of Polish extraction can feel just as comfortable with people of different backgrounds as with fellow Polish-Americans.

In falling-in-love situations, popularity and personal characteristics have replaced older criteria for the selection of a mate. Observers of the American scene often criticize this as a "romantic fallacy," instead of a rational base for picking a mate with whom one is to share the rest of one's life. But "falling in love" is the accepted base for marriage now, and few people marry without claiming to be so infatuated. The fallacy contains, according to the critics, the assumption that the romantic love will turn into marital love automatically. What often happens, however, is that the marital partners continue to seek the excitement of romantic love in relations outside of marriage, leading to extramarital affairs or serial marriages, since the initial feeling does not usually last beyond the "honeymoon is over" stage. Those who stay married value this changed relationship more than its alternatives. But divorce is becoming easier, so that a choice between remaining married and ending the relationship is always available.

Although the patriarchal tradition is still evident in many American marriages, as we have noted, there is a trend toward egalitarianism between husband and wife as the result of several factors. For one, the mate selection system tends to allow greater equality than the traditional system. Also, since the new husband and wife are the only adults in the household, they must rely on each other in a cooperative division of labor. Girls today lead lives more similar to boys than at any other time and the relation between sexes is increasingly open.

However, the changes in family lives, including neolocal residence and even democratization, have had some negative effects on both husband-wife and parent-child relationships. As marriage increased in personal importance with its emphasis on love, other relationships become less important. The husband is expected to turn away from the male friendship clique of his past, because society sees it as interfering with the development of a good marriage. The demands on the marital partners to be each other's primary companion in leisure-time games, co-member in many groups, lover, and recipient of all the sentiments of liking, sexual attraction, and romantic infatuation which are subsumed under the general umbrella of "love" are heavy. Their weight is not often felt as strongly in the early years of marriage, when husband and wife are involved in roles outside the home, usually in jobs which provide an opportunity to utilize aspects of the personality that the family situation does not tap. The problems arise when the wife leaves her multi-dimensional life with the birth of her first child. At that time the husband-wife relation changes in significance for her, acquiring almost stifling importance because the mate is the only other adult with whom she has daily contact—and that for only a few hours at a time. Unless the young mother has a group with whom she can exchange problems and solutions, conversation and services, in the form of neighbors or easily available relatives, she is likely to make new emotional demands upon her husband. Even marriages which were stable during the initial period may become disorganized at this time. Divorce, desertion, even marital homicide rates of urban Americans indicate that the strain of attempting to restrict all primary relations and significant sentiments to the mate is tremendous.

The burdens of parenthood have also grown, while the facilities available for alleviating them remain inadequate. Today's developmental approach to childrearing, coupled with the current awareness of the open nature of human potential, make the responsibility of rearing the child within the isolated home a heavy one. The village, with its homogeneous culture and extended family group, is no longer available to assist with the task. Nor is the traditional cultural standard that condoned blind obedience from children and allowed strong forms of punishment. Studies of American urbanites indicate that parents of all but the lower classes have modified the disciplinary roles of mother and father dramatically, attempting to develop rather than restrict their children. Children used to be an economic asset, motivating parents to give birth in order to insure a comfortable old age. Today's child is no longer an economic investment. Indeed, the average offspring costs approximately $30,000 to $40,000 to rear to adulthood—more, if the income which the mother lost by staying at home is counted. The main motive for having children is now love. But this only intensifies the burden of being a mother, because love involves ego projections and strong sentiments of identification. The mother holds herself, and is held by society, as the only person really accountable for how her child turns out and for his behavior on the way. Yet she cannot control the larger environment, so she is powerless to do the job that society demands of her. The father is not held so strongly accountable for the actions of his children, since he is absent from home during most of their waking hours. In traditional cultures, people assumed that personality was inherited and that what parents do was not important. The mother bore her child, nursed it and turned it over to older offspring or other adults within the household. Child-rearing was everybody's business, not just the mother's. So was care of the handicapped, the aged and others who would be excessively burdensome to a single household. Now the nuclear family must care for all of its own problems or depend on charity. Although this unit is not isolated from their kin, who help in emergencies and maintain contact, such assistance is not sufficiently systematic, because of distance and involvement in competing roles. A daughter cannot care for an aged mother with a broken hip when she must be in her own home caring for her husband and small children.

Middle years are difficult for the modern family, since people live longer and have more energy today than in previous generations. Our culture is still geared for mothers who become old rapidly and die before the last child leaves home. It offers no role to the 46-year-old woman who has thirty more years to live after her major functions of reproduction and caring for children are over. That is a long time to be retired and functionless. The same problem faces the still virile 65-year-old man who is abruptly cut off from his work habits, associates and income through retirement. Even death has become a problem in the modern, medicine-oriented world, so that it is ignored or carried out in hiding.

Although many aspects of modern life are difficult because the family institution has lagged behind the urbanizing and industrializing spheres of culture and social structure, significant new movements are afoot which may help solve the problems and perhaps even modify other institutions in relation to the demands of the family unit.

The women's movement is bringing the ideology of equality, long taken for granted but very inconsistently applied, to society's attention in a more integrated package of values and behavior. The same is true of the third world people's movement. Youth is questioning the established emphasis on the economic institution and demanding that other values, primarily personal worth and human dignity, be incorporated into the focal institution of the culture. Various social groups are experimenting with solutions to the problems produced by the isolation of the family in its own household. Cooperative babysitting pools and housecleaning projects are developing, providing social contact and work teams that prevent a duplication of effort. Sewing and canning "bees," cooking get-togethers and similar cooperative efforts decrease the isolation of the wife-mother from society. The home is again becoming a center of social life, with people and ideas flowing in and out of it. The husband brings his working associates, often with their wives, into the home for leisure-time couple-companionate activities; children play there instead of using the street as a common meeting place; the PTA and other community groups gather in homes as well as in public places; and television, radio, newspapers and magazines pipe in fresh ideas which are experimentally tried by increasingly competent family members. Furniture reupholstering, room paneling, weaving, interior decorating of great complexity are being carried out by family members, often with tools borrowed from other households. Neighborhoods work together to solve problems and exchange ideas. Thus, the privacy-demanding, closed-off and withdrawn household, managed by a limited "housewife" who is uninvolved in the world and confined to a continuous round of repetitious tasks and formula actions, is becoming dramatically reformulated into a center uniting many segmentalized institutions through family members. Children and, increasingly, adults are educated both in the home and outside of it, and each family member brings home the consequences of his or her participation in the knowledge expansion. Production has partially returned to the home, as energy and time are freed by industrial efficiency; choice includes the freedom to be a gourmet cook or clothes designer, artisan or private carpenter. Freed from rigid cultural prescriptions of what is right and wrong, natural or beautiful, taught to analyze situations competently and gather resources to meet self-defined goals, the American family is experimenting not only with solutions to problems but, more important, with new joys and experiences. Marriages founded on inadequate bases, which have not yielded happiness, or marriages failing because of changed life circumstances, are being dissolved, but new ones are being built more carefully, with more regard to individual personalities than to strict rules. The games people play in families have not vanished, but there is movement toward greater honesty and respect for human dignity. Thus, the disorganization brought about by changing technology has provided a new impetus for increased health, energy, understanding and a reexamination of assumptions about human nature. Positive plans for increasing human well-being in general and for making family roles more dynamic and relevant to developing personalities are being developed, although the complete absence of guidelines and the complexity of the situation often result in less than satisfactory effects. It is probable that family institutions, as a set of procedures by which people marry and establish close heterosexual relations, have children and socialize them, provide economic and household units, gratify interpersonal needs—in short, the procedures by which people live together—will become the focal institution of our future society, replacing the economic focus.

The trends point away from economics and toward interpersonal relationships as the Protestant ethic comes into question, as the society of scarcity changes to one of abundance, as people become socialized to choose, and as the number of choices expands. For some Americans, the integrative character of the family and the home already provides the new emphasis. For many others, the majority in fact, these trends are only for future generations. Reared in rigid, authoritarian families and communities, they restrict themselves and others in spite of an outward belief in the freedom of choice. As society strives to work itself out of the dilemma produced by following an ideology ill-suited to implementation—by the cultural lag carried over from times when women, children, workers, students, ethnic minorities and other marginal categories of people were expected to leave the thinking, decision-making and problem-solving to the elite—by socialization practices completely outdated in the great cities—new behaviors begin to emerge and new alternatives are tested. It will take many years before the youth, third world and women's movements free portions of the population to build their own lives—and we have not yet even begun a mass social movement in which groups such as the above unite toward a common goal. Men are still forced to decide before one quarter of their life is over what they want to do during its next three quarters, locking the remainder of their life into place.

While the general direction of change involves gradual reformulation, some experiments are very revolutionary. Divorce is still such a painful process and sign of failure that some of the young refuse to enter marriage. Communal living, involving several adults sharing house-maintenance and parental roles, is emerging as one form of experimentation—a practice with a long history, but still without societal approval. Homosexual unions, delayed marriage, adoption of children in the absence of either mother or father, the refusal to add to the population explosion by having children, the serious occupational or career involvements of wives, career shifts by middle-aged husbands, foster grandparenthood, cohabitation of the elderly who are unwilling to lose the benefits of pensions and Social Security through marriage, same-age communities isolated from the problems of the other generations, leisure focus rather than work motivation—all these experiments indicate a decision by some people to break with the past in terms of heterosexual and family roles.

The family revolution is not the first one that Americans have undertaken. This society is inhabited by the descendants of early revolutionaries who rejected the social structures into which they had been born and moved to another continent. Leaving behind the authoritarian village, the elders, the ascribed leaders, they came to a new land and created a new culture. Their progeny rebelled again in the post-World War II period, leaving ethnic community and elders, to build the "other-directed" life in modern suburbia (Riesman, 1950). That generation turned to each other, to the peer group with whom they were on equal terms, in order to build a new set of life styles. Their children, and some of the parents themselves, are now revolting, once again. But they are reorganizing their identities and social relations on their home territory. There is no new geographical frontier to which they can move. The revolution must go on where they are, agricultural communes not being a logical choice for most of them. Today's attempt to discard the vestiges of tradition with its restrictions on personality and human growth is as revolutionary as were earlier movements. Each purposeful ideological and behavioral reform breaks with aspects of the past and tries to tie together a new package. Knowing this, we must turn our attention to the past, to see what are the traditions against which the new trends are moving. We must also seek to understand the reasons for the problems produced by the fact that change in the family institution has been, until now, an adaptive, lagging mechanism, while the society focused on its economic institution and devalued any social roles which stood in the way of material and technological "progress."

The child born into a farm, village or small town of pre-industrial character grew up in a homogeneous culture. People around him acted in ways which were integrated with each other. They shared the same view of the world, understood each other's roles and fitted their actions into it without questioning its foundation. Children were reared publicly, by everyone who came into contact with them. Seldom, if ever, did strangers enter the community to bring new ways of doing things or to throw a different light on traditional beliefs. An experimentation in behavior on the child's part was immediately noticed and stopped by an adult or an older child. Growth into adulthood progressed through a series of regimented steps, for which models were always available. Questions concerning life had set answers, and unexpected questions were immediately squelched as immoral, unnatural or sacrilegious. By the time the child grew up, he or she was familiar with the culture, as organized into appropriate roles; only the handicapped were unable to act, think and handle objects in customary ways. The family made sure that children learned to behave in ways fitting their age and sex, and little privacy was afforded throughout the life cycle. Education into skills and the knowledge needed for everyday life were acquired at home and in the village. Often there were no specialized teacher roles, except for transmitting religious rituals and beliefs. Children learned to hunt and fish by practicing with miniature spears from their early years, so that the eye and the hand were coordinated by the time they were allowed to go out with the elders.

Although the world is going through a revolution in life styles, due to urbanization, industrialization and increased societal complexity, and although this has strongly affected the family as an interacting unit and its relations to other kinds of units, the revolution is not being experienced to the same extent everywhere.

Part One

Pre-Industrial Families

Even in the United States there are pockets in which the effects of these processes of social change are not felt as deeply as they are in urban centers and sprawls. Anthropologists, sociologists and occasional psychiatrists have gone into the still-rural areas to study in detail their family systems. They have provided us with knowledge of alternative ways in which family life is still functioning. Their research results remind us of our own distant past, when our ancestors lived on many continents. The four essays in this first Part illustrate some of the prevalent patterns of family life in the past.

Jean L. Briggs, author of the first essay, is an anthropologist, reared in the modern American family system. In order to study an Eskimo group intensively, she lived for many months with a partially nomadic community (not fully nomadic, because they rotate residences to the same two locations each fall and spring). Like several other anthropologists, she decided that she could best accomplish her goal of studying the Eskimos if she became a participant-observer and was adopted as a daughter by one of the major families. Such a technique for gaining insight into the life of a people has many advantages, since the scientist learns to understand the symbolic meaning of life by being involved in daily interchanges. That is, as the "Kapluna Daughter: Living with Eskimos," she could, over time, develop insights into, and detailed knowledge of, the family and community life of this group so different from the one in which she had been socialized. On the other hand, adoption into a particular position in a particular family has disadvantages, as she points out, because it immediately restricts behavior and relations with everyone else. The strain between being a "proper daughter" and an objective anthropologist, who must investigate all aspects of a culture, is recorded in this article which can provide a useful understanding of the extent of personality differences arising out of differences in family systems. The socialization Dr. Briggs had received, and her education as an anthropologist, made her quite unfit to live as a real daughter among a patriarchal, patrilineal and patrilocal family of Eskimos.

Although the essay focuses on the strains between two, or really three, cultural systems—the one Dr. Briggs was socialized into, that of an anthropologist, and the one in which she was temporarily living—it contains much information about the family life of the Eskimo. Of immediate interest is the rigidity of social roles within the system. The daughter must be obedient. The wife must be passive, waiting for orders from her husband. She is not responsible

for heating the igloo, so she sits in the cold. She cooks for her husband, not for herself, and does not make tea until he asks for it. Education of the young begins early, as evidenced by the fact that the adult Dr. Briggs was unable to develop the muscles required for chewing skins or sewing them together. The culture does not provide for privacy, and the Eskimos could not understand her need for it. The strength of the whole socialization system was shown in the Eskimos' many attempts to make the anthropologist into a "decent" woman. But in a group in which anger, irritation or similar sentiments could not be expressed, and ideally were never felt, she was simply uneducable. No matter how much her adopted father tried to teach her by example or through proverbs, stories, "lessons" and other means by which his biological children had been successfully socialized, he was unable to make a good Eskimo woman out of her. Her very behavior made her into a eunuch, sexless as far as the males of the community were concerned.

The fact that a rigid, internally integrated family system such as that of the Eskimos can be perpetuated through generations even in American society is evidenced by Robert Coles' portrayal of a pre-industrial group, in the following essay, "Life in Appalachia—The Case of Hugh McCaslin." Dr. Coles is a research psychiatrist who functioned in this study much like an anthropologist, though his training provided him with a different set of insights. In this piece, his contribution as a social scientist is threefold: 1) the questions he asks, the areas of life he observes and probes; 2) his faithful accounting, as seen through Hugh McCaslin's mind, of what Hugh actually thinks and feels about the world; 3) his trained understanding of the psychological reasons for—and the consequences of—what Hugh feels and thinks about his way of life.

Hugh McCaslin's ideas about the world are derived from his experiences and his culture. These ideas and beliefs influence his actions and restrict his view of alternative styles of life. He, like his father before him, tried to escape from the bare subsistence-level economy of "the hollow" by moving away and getting a job as a coal miner. Being uneducated and unskilled for the modern industrialized and urbanized world, he was forced to return to the valley when an injury terminated his ability to perform in that occupational role. His attitudes towards the world and his relations with his family are traditional, for he was not "modernized" by his stay in the mining community. He does not function in terms of long-range plans based on a careful investigation of societal resources, a selection of goals and mobilization of resources. Those are middle-class and rationalized ways of approaching life, and Hugh McCaslin was not trained to function that way. A father is a patriarch and his roles are the traditional ones, although modified by his physical incapacity. Someone else must do his "chores" when he is unable to carry them out, but he retains control. Frustration over dependency and not being able to do the things men are "supposed to do" is inevitable for this man reared in a traditional style of life which makes few alternatives available or acceptable to him.

McCaslin's social life space is contained within a very small geographical area and set of relations. He is surrounded by lifelong friends and kin members, operating out of separate households but within easy contact distance. The psychiatrist, Coles, is the only stranger. The world outside of the hollow exerts an indirect influence because kin members do leave and the youth dream of getting out. Escape would not be possible if the outside world were not already industrialized and independent economic maintenance was available. The one-room schoolhouse, however, does not prepare villagers for that outside world; in spite of TV images, the only bridges leading to it are the army and the coal mine.

The brief description of "Ila Slavery" which follows the Coles piece was also written by an anthropologist, Arthur Tuden. It provides details about complex extended families, the population in this case being Zambia. The Zambians are agriculturists, growing foodstuffs and raising cattle. Unlike the Eskimos who exist on a bare subsistence level because of their dependency on hunting and gathering, they are able to maintain an extensive kinship system because of their means of self-support. Like the feudal system of Europe during the Middle Ages, this kinship system includes roles and members who are not biologically affiliated with the main family. Slaves, descendants of slaves and people of mixed background are the marginal members of society. Their place in the extended kinship system resembles the apprenticeship customs of the English, except that the former are lifelong positions and are also inheritable. The importance of the family as the basic unit for production, distribution and consumption is indicated by the name given to slaves dependent on villagers with whom they are not biologically affiliated: the slaves are people who "had no other place to go." In contrast to the Appalachian hollow, the Zambian locale offers no effective alternative location. One must belong to a village, in a semi-kinship adoption. The only place of escape is another village. The kinship group, with its extension through slaves, also functions as the main political unit, since no outside unit exists

in the daily lives of members and the village itself contains no independent and specialized political group. All these factors produce a strong familistic system, with each member attached to a group through ties of marriage, birth, adoption or slavery.

A patriarchal authority base and extended kinship system are also illustrated by Lawrence Rosen's essay, "I Divorce Thee," with its interesting insights into economically based marital relations and the influence of external power groups. Although many readers will undoubtedly be shocked by the economic manipulations involved in the Moroccan marriage, they should remember that traditional American marriages are arranged in a similar fashion. In the Moroccan society of which Rosen writes, economic dependence has resulted in complicated "games people play" in order to keep households together. Social pressure, including that of kinfolk, is frequently resorted to as a means of shaming a spouse into remaining in the family. The system described by Rosen also illustrates some of the effects of urbanization. The young man in the case study is no longer dependent upon his family for economic survival, having obtained sufficient education to hold a job outside of it. Even the law is now introducing change, in that a son is allowed to set up a household away from his parents. We can imagine what changes will occur in this family in the future, as the traditionally restricted wife becomes educated and economically independent. The whole set of relations reflects the complexities of grafting new behaviors onto traditional norms. Marriages are still arranged, and may be dissolved at the will of the male, but the marriage partners are also embedded in many other social roles, with each member having duties and rights toward kin members and the rest of the community. These are used to jockey for power within the marriage unit, and the results have repercussions outward again. The very system by which the wife has no assurance of stability in her marriage and no ability to prevent divorce necessitate a web of mechanisms for making it unprofitable for the husband to desire a separation. Concern over the distribution and shifts of power is inevitable under the basic framework of bride-price, dowry and easy divorce. The family system, therefore, is affected not only by the content of the traditional culture, but by cultural aspects which are codified into more formal laws and by the complexity of the society itself. The more the society interferes, through its political and economic activities, with the authority structure of the family (be it in the kinship group, the elders or the patriarch), the more that family system begins to break down, historically to be replaced by a more egalitarian system.

13

14

Kapluna Daughter
Living with Eskimos

Jean L. Briggs

"It's very cold down there—*very cold*. If I were going to be at Back River this winter, I would like to adopt you and try to keep you alive."

My Eskimo visitor, Uunai, dramatized her words with shivers as we sat drinking tea in the warm nursing station in Gjoa Haven. It was only mid-August, but already the wind that intruded through the cracks in the window frame was bitter, and the ground was white with a dusting of new snow. Last winter's ice, great broken sheets of it, still clogged the harbor, so that the plane I was waiting for was unable to get through to us. I was on my way to spend a year and a half with the Utkuhikhalingmiut, a small group of Eskimos who lived in Chantrey Inlet at the mouth of the Back River on the northern rim of the American continent. They were the most remote group of Eskimos that I could find on the map of the Canadian Arctic, a people who in many ways lived much as they had in the days before *kaplunas* (white men) appeared in the north. They were nomadic; they lived in snowhouses in winter, in tents in summer; and their diet consisted very largely of fish—trout and whitefish—supplemented now and again by a few caribou.

Uunai's words presaged the most important influence on the course of my life at Back River, namely my adoption as a "daughter" in the household of an Utkuhikhalingmiut family. I want to describe an aspect of that relationship here, with the aim of illustrating some of the difficulties that a host community or family may encounter in its hospitable efforts to incorporate a foreigner.

I arrived in Chantrey Inlet at the end of August 1963 on a plane that the Canadian government sent in once a year to collect the three or four schoolchildren who wished to go to Inuvik. I had with me letters of introduction from the Anglican deacon and his wife in Gjoa Haven. Nakliguhuktuq and Ikayuqtuq were Eskimos from the eastern Arctic who served as missionaries not only to the Anglican Eskimos in Gjoa Haven, but also to the Utkuhikhalingmiut. The letters—written in the syllabic script in which the Utkuhikhalingmiut, like most other Canadian Eskimos, are literate—noted that I would like to live with the Utkuhikhalingmiut for a year or so, learning the Eskimo language and skills: how to scrape skins and sew them, how to catch fish and preserve them or boil the oil out of them for use in lighting and heating the winter iglus. They asked the Eskimos to help me with words and fish and promised that in return I would help them with tea and kerosene. They told the people that I was kind and that they should not be shy and afraid of me—"She's a little bit shy herself"—and assured them that they need not feel (as they often do feel toward kaplunas) that they had to comply with my every wish. They said, finally, that I wished to be adopted into an Eskimo family and to live with them in their iglu as a daughter.

Choosing a Father

I had a number of reasons for wishing to be adopted, and there were several precedents for adoption as well: four other kaplunas of my acquaintance, both scholars and laymen, who had wintered with Eskimos had done so as "sons," sharing the iglus of their Eskimo families. Living in the iglu would be warmer than living alone, I thought (Ikayuqtuq and Nakliguhuktuq agreed); and I thought vaguely that it might be "safer" if one family had specific responsibility for me. The idea had romantic appeal too; I saw it as a fulfillment of a childhood wish to "be" an Eskimo, and I expected no rapport problems, since on two previous trips to the Alaskan Arctic I had identified strongly with the Eskimo villagers with whom I had lived. To be sure, there were also arguments against adoption: I had qualms concerning the loss of an "objective" position in the community, drains on my supplies that would result from contributing to the maintenance of a family household and loss of privacy with resultant difficulties in work-·ing. Still, when the moment of decision came, the balance lay.in favor of adoption.

There were two suitable fathers among the Utkuhikhalingmiut (that is, two household heads who had wives alive and at home), and these two were both more than eager to adopt me. One, however—an intelligent, vigorous man named Inuttiaq—far outdid the other in the imagination and persistence with which he "courted" me as a daughter. Not only were he and his family extremely solicitous, but

he was also a jolly and ingenious language teacher. Most gratifying of all, both he and his wife, Allaq, were astonishingly quick to understand my halting attempts to communicate. There was no question which family I preferred. Fortunately, Inuttiaq also occupied a much more central position among the Utkuhikhalingmiut than did Nilak, the other possible father. He had many more close kin and was also the Anglican lay leader of the group. I was convinced that both anthropology and I would benefit more if I were adopted by Inuttiaq.

Winter

From the moment that the adoption was settled, I was "Inuttiaq's daughter" in the camp. Inuttiaq and his relatives with much amusement drilled me in the use of kin terms appropriate to my position, just as they drilled his three-year-old daughter, who was learning to speak. They took charge of my material welfare and of my education in language and skills. Allaq also to some extent took charge of my daily activities, as it was proper that a mother should. She told me what the day's job for the women of the family was going to be: gathering birch twigs for fuel, scraping caribou hides in preparation for the making of winter clothing or skinning the fish bellies out of which oil was to be boiled. The decision to participate or not was left to me, but if I did join the women—and I usually did—she made sure that my share of the work was well within the limits of my ability and stamina. "We will be walking very far tomorrow to get birch twigs," she would say. "You will be too tired." If I went anyway, it was always silently arranged that my load should be the lightest, and if I wandered out of sight of the other women in my search for birch bushes, someone always followed behind—sent by Allaq, as I discovered months later—to make sure that I didn't get lost.

I felt increasingly comfortable with my family and found their solicitude immensely warming. At the same time, I dreaded the loss of privacy that the winter move into their iglu would bring. Curiously, the effect of the move when it came in October was the opposite of what I had expected. I basked in the protectiveness of Inuttiaq's household; and what solitude I needed I found on the river in the mornings, when I jigged for salmon trout through the ice with Inuttiaq, or, to my surprise, in the iglu itself in the afternoons, when the room was full of visitors and I retired into myself, lulled and shielded by the flow of quiet, incomprehensible speech.

Behaving

The family's continuing graciousness was very seductive. I came to expect the courtesies that I received and even to resent it a bit when they were not forthcoming, though at the same time I told myself that such feelings were shameful. However, as time passed and I became an established presence in the household, I was less and less often accorded special privileges, except insofar as my ineptitude made services necessary. Allaq still mended my skin boots for me and stretched them when they shrank in drying; my stitches were not small enough and my jaws not strong enough. She continued to fillet my fish when it was frozen nearly as hard as wood. But in other respects Allaq, and especially Inuttiaq—who was far less shy than his wife—more and more attempted to assimilate me into a proper adult parent-daughter relationship. I was expected to help with the household work to the best of my ability—to make tea or bannock and to fetch water—and I was expected to obey unquestioningly when Inuttiaq told me to do something or made a decision on my behalf.

Unfortunately, I found it impossible to learn to behave in every respect like an Utkuhikhalingmiut daughter. Inuttiaq lectured me in general terms on the subject of filial obedience, and once in a while I think he tried to shame me into good behavior by offering himself as a model of virtue—volunteering, for example, to make bannock for me if I were slow in making it for him—but to little avail. Sometimes I was genuinely blind and deaf to his lessons, unaccustomed as I was to Utkuhikhalingmiut subtlety. At other times I saw what was wanted but resisted for reasons I will describe in a moment. Inevitably, conflicts, covert but pervasive, developed, both regarding the performance of household chores and regarding the related matter of obedience to Inuttiaq.

Assumptions in Conflict

The causes of the conflicts were three. First was the fact that some feminine skills were hard for me to learn. Overtly my Utkahikhalingmiut parents were very tolerant of the lack of skill that they rightly attributed to kapluna ignorance and perhaps also to kapluna lack of intelligence, or *ihuma*. However, perhaps because of an assumption that kaplunas were unable to learn, if I was at all slow to understand Allaq's instructions and demonstrations, she easily gave up trying to teach me, preferring instead to continue to serve me. And though she stretched my boots and cut my fish in the most cheerful manner, after a while her added chores may well have been burdensome to her.

A second cause of the conflicts was that some of Inuttiaq's and Allaq's assumptions about the nature of parental and daughterly virtue were at variance with mine; in consequence not only did I have to learn new patterns, I also had to unlearn old ones. Hardest of all to learn was unquestioning obedience to paternal authority. Sometimes I could not help resisting, privately but intensely, when Inuttiaq told me to "make tea," to "go home," "to hurry up" or to "pray." I was irritated even by the fact that after the first weeks of gracious formality had passed he began to address me in the imperative form, which is often used in speaking to women, children and young people. Rationally I knew that I should have welcomed this sign of "acceptance," but I could not be pleased. My irritation was due partly to the fact that subordination threatened my accustomed—and highly valued—independence, but it was aggravated by a fear that the restrictions placed on me interfered with my work.

And herein lay the third cause of the conflicts: I found it hard sometimes to be simultaneously a docile and helpful daughter and a conscientious anthropologist. Though Allaq appeared to accept my domestic clumsiness as inevitable, she may have felt less tolerant on the occasions when it was not lack of skill that prevented me from helping her, but anxiety over the pocketful of trouser-smudged, disorganized field notes that cried out to be typed. A number of times, when I could have helped to gut fish or to carry in snow to repair the sleeping platform or floor or could have offered to fetch water or make tea, I sat and wrote instead or sorted vocabulary—tiny slips of paper spread precariously over my sleeping bag and lap. It was sometimes professional anxiety that prompted me to disobey Inuttiaq too; and I am sure that on such occasions, as on others, he must have found my insubordination not only "bad," but completely incomprehensible. My behavior at moving time is an example. My gear, minimal though it was by kapluna standards, placed a severe strain on Inuttiaq when we moved camp. Whereas the sleds of others were loaded to little more than knee height, the load on Inuttiaq's sled was shoulder-high. From his point of view it was only reasonable that he should instruct me to leave my heavy tape recorder and my metal box of field notes on the top of a small knoll, as the Utkuhikhalingmiut cached their own belongings, while we moved downstream, not to return until after the flood season. I, however, questioned whether the water might rise over the knoll, and Inuttiaq's silent scrutiny seemed to say that he considered my inquiry a reflection on his judgment.

I do not mean to create the impression that life in Inuttiaq's household during that first winter was continuous turmoil. There were many days, even weeks, when I, at least, felt the situation to be very peaceful and enjoyable. I was grateful for the warmth of my parents' company and care; it was good to feel that I belonged somewhere, that I was part of a family, even on a make-believe basis. But the rewards of my presence for Inuttiaq and his real family were of a different, and probably of a lesser, order. Because Inuttiaq's purchases in Gjoa Haven were supplemented by mine, our household was richer than others in store goods: tea, tobacco, flour, jam, dry milk, raisins and kerosene. But apart from these material benefits, and at first perhaps the novelty (and prestige?) of having a kapluna daughter, it is hard to see what Inuttiaq's family gained in return for the burden they carried. I played "Tavern in the Town" and "Santa Lucia" on my recorder; Inuttiaq enjoyed that and once in a while asked me to play for guests. I helped inefficiently in the mornings to remove the whitefish from the family nets and to drag them home, harnessed with Allaq to the sled. I assisted—erratically, as I have mentioned—with the other domestic chores; and in late winter, when the sun returned and Inuttiaq began again to jig for salmon trout, I usually fished with him. That is all that occurs to me, and a trivial contribution it must have been from my family's point of view.

Satan and Self-control

It was hard for me to know at the time, however, just what their reactions to me were, because the tensions that existed were nearly all covert. Hostility among Utkuhikhalingmiut is ignored or turned into a joke; at worst it becomes the subject of gossip behind the offender's back. I, too, did my best to smother my annoyance with frustration, but my attempts were not wholly successful. My training in self-control was less perfect than theirs, and at the same time the strains were greater than those I was accustomed to dealing with in my own world. Moreover, the most potentially gratifying of the outlets utilized by the Utkuhikhalingmiut—gossip—was not open to me as an anthropologist. I did my best to learn with the children when they were taught to turn annoyance into amusement, but laughter didn't come easily.

The Utkuhikhalingmiut are acutely sensitive to subtle indications of mood. They heard the coldness in my voice when I said, "I don't understand," noted the length of a solitary walk I took across the tundra or the fact that I went to bed early and read with my back turned to the others.

Later, Inuttiaq might give me a lecture—phrased, as always, in the most general terms—about the fate of those who lose their tempers: Satan uses them for firewood. Or he might offer me an especially choice bit of fish—whether to shame me or to appease me I don't know. The contrast between my irritability and the surface equanimity of others gave me many uncomfortable moments, but I persuaded myself that the effects of my lapses were short-lived. When I laughed again and heard others laugh with me, or when they seemed to accept the generous gestures with which I tried to make amends, I was reassured that no damage had been done. I was wrong. But it was only when I returned to Gjoa Haven on my way home a year later that I learned how severe the tensions had become between November and January of that first winter. Then the deacon's wife, Ikajuqtuq, told me of the report Inuttiaq had made of me in January when he went in to Gjoa Haven to trade: "She is not happy. She gets angry very easily, and I don't think she likes us anymore." Shortly after Inuttiaq's return from Gjoa Haven in January, conflict erupted into the open.

"The Iglus Are Cold"

The two weeks of Inuttiaq's absence in Gjoa Haven had been an especially trying period for me. I had looked forward to them as a much needed interlude in which to type and organize my swelling pile of penciled notes. When Inuttiaq was at home, it was often difficult to maintain the iglu temperature within the range of 27 to 31 degrees at which typing was feasible. If I tried to type during the daylight hours of the morning, when the outdoor work was done, my fingers and carbon paper froze as a result of Inuttiaq's drafty comings and goings at jobs that seemed to necessitate propping the door open. But in the sociable afternoon and evening hours the snow dome dripped in the heat and occasionally deposited lumps of slush into my typewriter, and the iglu steamed so that my work was lost in a wet fog as a result of Inuttiaq's demands for tea, boiled fox, bannock and soup in rapid succession. Many were the frustrated moments when I heartily wished him gone; but it was only when he *was* gone that I discovered how completely our comfort depended on his presence. "When the men are away the iglus are cold," the women said; and it was true. The morning drafts that had plagued me before were nothing compared with the chill that resulted when nobody came and went at all. It was partly, of course, that Inuttiaq had taken with him one of our two primus stoves and one of the two kerosene storm lanterns, which ordinarily heated the iglu. But Allaq's behavior during her husband's absence intensified the cold. She never boiled fish, rarely brewed tea and never lit the lamp to dry clothes—any of which activities would have warmed the iglu. She merely sat in her corner of the sleeping platform, blew on her hands and remarked that the iglu was cold. It was; it was 20 degrees colder than when Inuttiaq was at home. I fretted and fumed in silent frustration and determined that when he came back I would take drastic steps to improve my working conditions.

I broached the subject to Inuttiaq a few days after his return to camp. He listened attentively to my explanation. I told him that I had thought about going to live for a while in the empty wooden building that stood on a peninsula a few miles from camp. The government had built it as a nursing station, but it had never been used except by me as a cache for my useless belongings. It had a kerosene stove, which would make it luxuriously comfortable—unless the stove was as erratic as the one in the similar nursing station in Gjoa Haven, with which I had once had an unfortunate experience. Inuttiaq agreed that the stove was unpredictable. Instead, he suggested that he take me to the nursing station every morning and fetch me again at night, so that I would not freeze. As often before, he reassured me: "Because you are alone here, you are someone to be taken care of." And, as often before, his solicitude warmed me. "Taking me to the nursing station every day will be a lot of work for you," I said. The round trip took an hour and a half by dog sled, not counting the time and effort involved in harnessing and unharnessing the team. He agreed that it would be a lot of work. "Could you perhaps build me a small iglu?" I asked. It would take only an hour or two to build a tiny iglu near our own, which I could use as an "office"; then he need concern himself no further. Lulled by the assurance he had just given me of his desire to take care of me and by the knowledge that the request I made was not time-consuming, I was the more disagreeably startled when he replied with unusual vigor, "I build no iglus. I have to check the nets."

A Daughter's Tent

The rage of frustration seized me. He had not given me the true reason for his refusal. It only took two hours to check the nets every second or third day; on the other days, Inuttiaq did nothing at all except eat, drink, visit and repair an occasional tool. He was offended, but I could not imagine why. Whether Inuttiaq read my face I do not know, but he softened his refusal immediately: "Shall Ipuituq or Tutaq"—he named two of the younger men—"build an iglu for you?" Perhaps it would be demeaning for a man of Inuttiaq's status, a mature householder, to build an iglu for a mere daughter. There was something in Inuttiaq's reaction that I did not understand, and a cautioning voice told me to contain my ethnocentric judgment and my anger. I thought of the small double-walled tent that I had brought with me for emergency use. It was stored in the nursing station. "They say my tent is very warm in winter," I said. Inuttiaq smoked silently. After a while he asked, "Shall they build you an iglu tomorrow?" My voice shook with exasperation: "Who knows?" I turned my head, rummaging—for nothing—in my knapsack until the intensity of my feeling should subside.

Later, when Inuttiaq was smoking his last pipe in bed, I raised the subject again, my manner, I hoped, a successful facsimile of cheerfulness and firmness. "I would like to try the tent and see whether it's warm, as I have heard. We can bring it here, and then if it's not warm, I won't freeze; I'll come indoors." Allaq laughed, Inuttiaq accepted my suggestion, and I relaxed with relief, restored to real cheer by Inuttiaq's offer to fetch the tent from the nursing station the following day—if it stormed—so that he could not go on the trapping trip he had planned.

My cheer was premature. Two days later the tent had still not been fetched, though Inuttiaq had not gone trapping. I decided to walk to the nursing station. I had no intention of fetching the tent myself—it would have been impossible; but I needed a few hours alone, and vaguely I knew that the direction of my walk would be to Inuttiaq a sign, however futile, that I was in earnest about my tent.

But I did not dream that he would respond as charitably as he did. I had just arrived at the nursing station and was searching among my few books for a novel to comfort me in my frustration when I heard the squeak of sled runners on the snow outside and a familiar voice speaking to the dogs: *Hoooo* [whoa]. Inuttiaq appeared in the doorway. I smiled. He smiled. "Will you want your tent?"

Gratitude and relief erased my anger as Inuttiaq picked up the tent and carried it to the sled. "You were walking," he said, in answer to my thanks. "I felt protective toward you."

It was a truce we had reached, however, not a peace, though I did not realize it at once. Since it was nearly dark when we reached camp, Inuttiaq laid the tent on top of the iglu for the night, to keep it from the dogs. Next morning I went with Inuttiaq to jig for trout up-river, and when we returned I thought that finally the time was ripe for setting up the tent. Not wanting to push Inuttiaq's benevolence too far, and remembering the force of his response to my query about iglu-building, I asked, "Shall I ask Ipuituq to help me put up my tent?" "Yes," said Inuttiaq. There was no warmth in his face; he did not smile, though he did tell me to keep my fur trousers on for warmth while I put up the tent. I obeyed, but the wind had risen while we drank our homecoming tea, so that even in fur trousers tent-raising was not feasible that day or the next.

When the wind died two days later, Inuttiaq and I went fishing again, most companionably. Relations seemed so amicable, in fact, that this time on our return I was emboldened to say directly, without mention of Ipuituq, "I would like to put up my tent."

Naïvely I thought that Inuttiaq would offer to help. He did not. His face was again unsmiling as he answered, "Put it up."

My anger was triggered again. "By myself?" I inquired rudely.

"Yes," said Inuttiaq, equally rudely.

"Thank you very much." I heard the coldness in my voice but did not try to soften it.

Inuttiaq, expressionless, looked at me for a moment then summoned two young men who were nearby and who came, with a cheer that was in marked contrast to his own manner, to help me set up the tent.

Although Inuttiaq thought it ridiculous anyway to set up a tent in winter, I think now that he was also personally affronted by my request. One clue to his reaction I find in a question that I hardly heard at the time: he had wanted to know, after the tent was up, whether I planned to sleep in it or only to work there, and I think he may have felt that my demand for a tent was a sign that I was dissatisfied with him as a father, with his concern for my welfare.

In any case, his behavior was a curious blend of opposites. He chose the site for my tent with care, correcting my own choice with a more practiced eye to prowling dogs and prevailing wind. He offered advice on heating the tent, and he filled my primus stove so that it would be ready for me to use when my two assistants and I had finished setting up the tent. And when I moved my writing things out of his iglu, he told me that if I liked, I might write instead of going fishing. "If I catch a fish, you will eat," he assured me. But he turned his back on the actual raising of the tent and went home to eat and drink tea.

Never in Anger

On the following day I saw his displeasure in another form. It was Sunday morning and storming; our entrance was buried under drifting snow. Since there could be no church service, Inuttiaq and Allaq had each, separately and in mumbling undertones, read a passage from the Bible. Then Inuttiaq began to read from the prayer book the story of creation, and he asked if I would like to learn. I agreed, the more eagerly because I feared that he had perceived my skepticism toward his religious beliefs and that this was another hidden source of conflict between us. He lectured me at length. The story of creation was followed by the story of Adam and Eve (whose sin was responsible for the division of mankind into kaplunas and Eskimos), and this story was in turn followed by an exposition of proper Christian behavior: the keeping of the Sabbath— and of one's temper. "God is loving," said Inuttiaq, "but only to believers. Satan is angry. People will go to heaven only if they do not get angry or answer back when they are scolded." He told me that one should not be attached to earthly belongings, as I was: "One should devote himself only to God's word." Most striking of all was the way Inuttiaq ended his sermon to me. "Nakliguhuktuq made me king of the Utkuhikhalingmiut," he said. "He wrote that to me. He told me that if people—including you— don't want to believe what I tell them and don't want to learn about Christianity, then I should write to him, and he will come quickly and scold them. If people don't want to believe Nakliguhuktuq either, then . . . a bigger leader, a kapluna, the king in Cambridge Bay [the government center for the central Arctic], will come in a plane with a big and well-made whip and will whip people. It will hurt a lot."

Much of this I had heard before, but this version was more dramatic than previous ones. It made me see more clearly than I had before something of Inuttiaq's view of kaplunas generally. I heard the hostility directed against myself as well, but again he had softened the latter by blending it with warmth, in the manner that I found so confusing. He knew that I believed in God, he said, because I helped people, I gave things to people—not just to one or two, which God doesn't want, but to everybody.

The rest of the winter passed more peacefully, at least on the surface. I spent much of the time working in my tent, and there was no more overt hostility. But I am no longer sure that my peace of mind was justified. In retrospect, it seems possible that the warm and solicitous acts my family continued to perform were neither rewards for improved behavior on my part nor evidence of a generous willingness to accept me in spite of my thorny qualities, but, rather, attempts to extract or blunt some of the thorns. If I knew I was cared for, I might not get angry so easily. I thought I heard similar logic in the admonition Inuttiaq once in a while gave his six-year-old daughter when she sulked: "Stop crying, you are loved." Another possible motive may have been a desire to shame me, by virtuous example, into reforming. Perhaps these kind acts even had the effect of nullifying Inuttiaq's and Allaq's own prickly feelings, permitting them to prove to themselves that—as Inuttiaq once said—they didn't get angry, only I did.

Incorrigible

But whatever the interpretation of these incidents, it is clear to me now that there existed more of an undercurrent of tension in my relationship with Inuttiaq and Allaq than I perceived at the time. I began to suspect its presence in the spring, when our iglu melted and I moved—at Inuttiaq's order—back into my own tent; Allaq almost never visited me, as she had done the first days after my arrival in Chantrey Inlet. More important, these winter tensions, I think, added their residue of hostility to a crisis situation that developed at the end of the summer. This introduced a new phase in my relations, not merely with Inuttiaq and Allaq, but with all the other Utkuhikhalingmiut as well —a phase in which I ceased to be treated as an educable child and was instead treated as an incorrigible offender, who had unfortunately to be endured but who could not be incorporated into the social life of the group.

The crisis was brought about by the visit to Chantrey Inlet of a party of kapluna sports fishermen. Every July and August in recent years Chantrey Inlet has been visited by sportsmen from the provinces and from the United States who charter bush planes from private sports airlines and fly up to the Arctic for a week's fishing. Every year the sportsmen ask permission to borrow the Eskimos' canoes, which were given to them by the Canadian government after the famine of 1958 and are indispensable to their economy. In 1958 the disappearance of the caribou herds from the Chantrey Inlet area forced the Eskimos to begin to rely much more completely on fish than they had formerly done. This meant accumulating and storing quantities of fish during seasons when they were plentiful, and to facili-

tate this, the government introduced fish nets and canoes. Originally there had been six canoes, one for each of the Utkuhikhalingmiut families, but by the time I arrived in Chantrey Inlet only two of these remained in usable condition.

In Anger

The first parties that came asked, through me, if they might borrow both canoes, and the Utkuhikhalingmiut, who for various reasons rarely, if ever, refuse such requests, acquiesced, at some cost to themselves. They sat stranded on the shore, unable to fish, unable to fetch the occasional bird that they shot on the water, unable to fetch a resupply of sugar for their tea from the cache on the nearby island and worst of all, perhaps, unable to visit the odd strangers who were camped out of sight across the river. Ultimately these kaplunas left and were replaced by another group, which asked to borrow only one canoe. But relief was short-lived; trolling up and down the unfamiliar river in the late twilight, the kaplunas were unfortunate enough to run the canoe on a rock and tear a large hole in the canvas, whereupon they returned the canoe and announced to the men through sign language that since that craft was unusable they were now obliged to borrow the other—Inuttiaq's. When I arrived on the scene, the kaplunas were attaching their outboard to the canoe as Inuttiaq and the other Utkuhikhalingmiut men watched.

I exploded. Unsmilingly and in a cold voice I told the kaplunas' guide some of the hardships that I foresaw if his men damaged the second canoe. Then, armed with the memory that Inuttiaq had earlier, before the arrival of this party of kaplunas, instructed me in vivid language never again to allow anyone to borrow his canoe, I told the kaplunas that the owner of that second canoe did not wish to lend it.

The kapluna guide was not unreasonable; he agreed at once that the loan of the boat was the owner's option: "It's his canoe, after all." Slightly mollified, I turned to Inuttiaq who stood nearby, expressionless like the other Utkuhikhalingmiut. "Do you want me to tell him you don't want to lend your canoe?" I asked in Eskimo. "He will not borrow it if you say you don't want to lend it."

Inuttiaq's expression dismayed me, but I didn't know how to read it. I knew only that it registered strong feeling, as did his voice, which was unusually loud: "Let him have his will!"

"We Wish She Would Leave"

That incident brought to a head months of uneasiness on the part of the Utkuhikhalingmiut concerning my volatility. I had spoken unbidden and in anger; that much the Eskimos knew. The words they couldn't understand, but it didn't matter; the intrusion and the anger itself were inexcusable. The punishment was so subtle a form of ostracism that I would have continued to think that my difficulties were all of my own imagining had I not come into possession of a letter that Allaq's father, Pala, had written to the deacon, Nakliguhuktuq, the day after the kaplunas left. Pala had intended to send it out on the plane that was daily expected to come and pick up the schoolchildren; he had kept it for a time, but then—fearing that when the plane finally came, he would forget the letter—he had given it to me to hold along with my own correspondence. The letter was in syllabics, of course; in an amoral spirit I decided to read it, to test my skill in reading Eskimo. I did not anticipate the contents: "Yiini [that was my name] lied to the kaplunas. She gets angry very easily. She ought not to be here studying Eskimos. She is very annoying; because she scolds and one is tempted to scold her. She gets angry easily. Because she is so annoying, we wish more and more that she would leave."

But it was not until October, when the autumn iglus were built, that the change in the Eskimos' feelings really became apparent. I was not at all sure that Inuttiaq would invite me to move in with his family again as he had done the year before, but I need not have worried; his hostility did not take such a crass form. However, the quality of life in the iglu was in striking contrast with the previous year. Whereas then Inuttiaq's iglu had been the social center of the camp, now family and visitors congregated next door, in Allaq's father's iglu. Inuttiaq and Allaq—the children too—spent the better part of every day at Pala's. Even in the early mornings, when the family awoke, and at night when we were preparing for bed, I was isolated. It was as though I were not there. If I made a remark to Inuttiaq or Allaq, the person addressed responded with his usual smile, but I had to initiate almost all communication. As a rule, if I did not speak, no one spoke to me. If I offered to fetch water or make tea (which I seldom did), my offer was usually accepted, but no one ever asked me to perform these services. The pointedness of this avoidance was driven home one day when we were cooking. I do not recall what was being made or who had initiated the cooking; I think it likely that I had done so, since the primus stood on the floor in front of me, instead of in its usual place near Al-

laq. Nevertheless, when the pressure began to run down, unnoticed by me, Inuttiaq turned not to me but to Allaq to order her to pump up the primus. And she had to get up and come over to my side of the iglu to pump up the stove! Had he spoken to me, I would only have had to lean over to do it. Too late I realized the dignity inherent in the Utkuhikhalingmiut pattern of authority, in which the woman is obedient to the man. I envied Allaq the satisfaction of knowing that she was appreciated because she did well and docilely what Inuttiaq told her to do.

One day, about a week after we had moved into the autumn iglus, Inuttiaq suggested that when we moved into winter iglus later on, I should be physically walled off to a degree. Often when Utkuhikhalingmiut build their permanent winter iglus, they attach to one side a small chamber, called a *hiqluaq,* in which to store the fish they net. The hiqluaq opens into the interior of the iglu by way of a hole just big enough to crawl through. Inuttiaq's idea was to build such a chamber for me to live in; after I left, he would use it in the orthodox manner, for fish storage.

But in spite of all these tensions, I was still treated with the most impeccable semblance of solicitude. I was amazed that it should be so—that although my company was anathema, nevertheless people still took care to give me plentiful amounts of the foods I liked best, to warn me away from thin ice and to caution me when my nose began to freeze. The Utkuhikhalingmiut saw themselves—and wanted me to see them—as virtuously solicitous, no matter what provocations I might give them to be otherwise. Allaq's sister expressed this ethos of concern explicitly in a letter to Ikayuqtuq in Gjoa Haven: "Because she is the only kapluna here and a woman as well, we have tried to be good to her . . . and though she is sometimes very annoying . . . we still try to help her."

It was at the end of August that the incident with the kapluna fishermen occurred, and it was the end of November before I was finally able to explain myself to the Utkuhikhalingmiut. I had wanted from the beginning, of course, to confront them with an explanation of my behavior, but I had feared that such un-Eskimo directness would only shock them the more. Instead, I had written my version of the story to Ikayuqtuq, had told her about my attempt to protect the Utkuhikhalingmiut from the impositions of the kaplunas and had asked her if she could help to explain my behavior to the Eskimos. My letter went out to Gjoa Haven, along with Pala's, when the school plane came in September. Unfortunately there was no way in which Ikayuqtuq could reply until the strait froze in November, enabling the men to make the long trip out to Gjoa Haven to trade. But when Inuttiaq, accompanied as usual by Allaq's brother, Mannik, finally went out, they brought back from the deacon and his wife a response that surpassed my most sanguine expectations. Inuttiaq reported to his family: "Nakliguhuktuq says that the kaplunas almost shot us when Yiini wasn't there." The exaggeration was characteristic of Inuttiaq's lurid style of fantasy. He turned to me: "Did you write that to Nakliguhuktuq?" I denied it—and later, in Gjoa Haven, Nakliguhuktuq denied having made such a statement to Inuttiaq—but I did confirm the gist of Inuttiaq's report: that I had tried to protect the Eskimos. I described what it was that I had written to Ikayuqtuq, and I explained something of the reasons for my anger at the kaplunas.

Wall of Ice

The effect was magical. The wall of ice that had stood between me and the community suddenly disappeared. I became consultant on the moral qualities of fishing guides; people talked to me voluntarily, offered me vocabulary, included me in their jokes and in their anecdotes of the day's activities; and Inuttiaq informed me that the next day he and I were going fishing. Most heartwarming of all is the memory of an afternoon soon after the men had returned. The iglu was filled with visitors, and the hum of the primus on which tea was brewing mingled with the low voices of Inuttiaq and his guests. I knew every detail of the scene even as I bent over my writing, and I paid no attention until suddenly my mind caught on the sound of my name: "I consider Yiini a member of my family again." Was that what Inuttiaq had said? I looked up, inquiring. "I consider you a family member again," he repeated. His diction was clear, as it was only when he wanted to be sure that I understood. And he called me "daughter," as he had not done since August.

Not that I had suddenly become a wholly acceptable housemate; that could never be. I was not and could never become an Utkuhikhalingmiutaq, nor could I ever be a "daughter" to Inuttiaq and Allaq as they understood that role. Inuttiaq made this quite clear one day about this time when we were both sitting, silently working, in the iglu. "I think you're a leader in your country," he said suddenly. The remark had no obvious context; it must mean, I thought, that he had never reconciled himself to my intractable behavior. There was also the slightly wild look that I caught in his eye when I said I thought that I might someday return to Chantrey Inlet. The look vanished

when Allaq explained that I meant to return after I had been to my own country, not merely to Gjoa Haven. "Yes," he said then, "We will adopt you again, or others may want to—Nilaak, perhaps, or Mannik, if he marries." And later, when we were talking about the possibility of other "learners" coming to Chantrey Inlet, Inuttiaq said, "We would be happier to have a woman come than a man—a woman like you, who doesn't want to be a wife. Maybe *you* are the only acceptable kapluna."

But it was the letters that Allaq and Inuttiaq wrote me when I left Chantrey Inlet in January that expressed most vividly and succinctly what it meant to them to have a kapluna daughter. They both said, "I didn't think I'd care when you left, but I did."

Stranger, Child, Simpleton

I observed three more or less distinct phases in the Utkuhikhalingmiut's view of me. During the first period I was a stranger and a guest, and I was treated with the formal courtesy and deference that the Utkuhikhalingmiut ordinarily accord to such persons. I was referred to as a kapluna, a white person, and addressed by my personal name —"Yiini" in the Eskimos' speech. Much of the time during this period the Eskimos must have been at a loss what to make of my behavior, and often when I did something that under other circumstances they might have defined as reprehensible—when I went to bed early, nursing a bad humor, or when I was silent in depression—they gave me the benefit of the doubt; they asked me if I were tired and considerately lessened my work load or withdrew so that I might "sleep."

Gradually, however, this first phase gave way to a second, in which my immediate family (though not others in the community) treated me in some respects as a daughter and a child. My parents replaced the name "Yiini" with the term "daughter" when speaking, and sometimes when referring to me; and my two small sisters called me "elder sister." Inuttiaq—though never Allaq—also began to use the imperative forms of speech that he used in addressing his other daughters and his wife. Even an appropriate age was invented for me: I had to be younger than Allaq—if only by one season—though all the evidence pointed to my being in fact slightly older than she was. Both parents directed my daily activities, and I was expected to obey them as a daughter should. When I did not, efforts were made to teach me better behavior through lecturing or shaming, the former a technique that was otherwise only used in teaching small children. My moodiness was no longer interpreted charitably, and efforts were made to educate me out of that behavior too.

Categorization of me as a "child" was probably determined by a combination of factors: I had introduced myself as one who wanted to "learn" from the Utkuhikhalingmiut, and I had asked to be adopted as a "daughter"; I was also obviously ignorant of Utkuhikhalingmiut proprieties and skills. The fact that I am a woman may also have facilitated my categorization as a child in several respects. For one thing, among the Utkuhikhalingmiut a woman's technical skill—skin-sewing—is very difficult to learn. I never mastered more than the most rudimentary, clumsy stitching; my work was so poor that when I mended my skin boots, Allaq considered it necessary to redo the job. Moreover, in order to be considered properly adult, a woman must have children, and I had none. For these reasons the role of an adult woman was virtually closed to me, whereas had I been a man, I might have earned an adult role as a fisherman and hunter, as some male kaplunas who have lived among Eskimos appear to have done. Finally, the fact that I am physically weaker than a man and thus unthreatening may have made it easier for the Utkuhikhalingmiut to view my ill temper, as I think they did, like that of a child. Had I been a man, I think they might have seen my temper as dangerous, even potentially lethal—anything but childish.

The third phase, in which I was treated as an incorrigible offender, replaced the "child" phase, I think, when it became apparent to the Utkuhikhalingmiut that I was uneducable. Inuttiaq no longer lectured me or used any other method to teach me. I was called "Yiini" again instead of "daughter," and daughterly services were no longer asked of me. In fact, nothing at all was demanded of me. Though my physical needs for warmth, food and protection from danger were still taken care of, socially I was simply "not there." There was one other person in the community who was similarly ostracized: a woman of about my age, who appeared to be of subnormal intelligence. Almost all of her personal qualities—her imperfect speech, clumsy gestures and domestic incompetence—were subject to comment behind her back, but hostility in her case, as in mine, centered on her volatility—the fact that she was easily upset and was unable to exercise proper restraint in the expression of her feelings. She too was considered uneducable, and I am sure that, like her, I was privately labeled simpleminded.

Hosts and Anthropologists

In more general terms the sequence of judgments passed on me seemed to be: strange; educable; uneducable in important ways. And each phase, each judgment, was associated with a role familiar to the Utkuhikhalingmiut: stranger; child; simpleton—each role being identifiable in terms of the way I was addressed, the kinds of behavior that were expected of me, the interpretations that were placed on my misbehavior and the methods that were used to control that misbehavior.

Although an anthropologist must have a recognized role or roles in order to make it possible to interact with him sensibly and predictably, nevertheless it will be evident from what I have described of my own case that the assignment of a role may create as many problems as it solves for both the anthropologist and his hosts. When Inuttiaq undertook to adopt me, I think he assumed that I would naturally behave as he was accustomed to having daughters behave. He knew, of course, that as a kapluna I was ignorant of the Eskimo skills that adult daughters have usually mastered, but it is easier to recognize cross-cultural differences in technology and language than differences in the structuring of interpersonal relations; one is far more inclined to think of the latter as given in "human nature."

He was wrong, of course, in assuming that my behavior would be that of an Utkuhikhalingmiut daughter. Consequently his first hypothesis was replaced by a second: that kaplunas don't (or Yiini doesn't) know how to behave correctly but can learn. For various reasons, none of which were, I think, recognized by Inuttiaq, I didn't learn easily. The first reason why learning must be difficult is that the intruder faces a double task. On the one hand he must discover what has to be learned—that is, what exactly is wrong with his "normal" behavior and what the proper behavior should be. And on the other hand he must overcome resistance to doing what is required—resistance caused by the interference of his old patterns of role behavior. Such interference may be expected to be particularly marked when the role to be learned bears the same name ("daughter") as a role one is accustomed to playing in one's own culture.

Learning will also be difficult and imperfect because the anthropologist is not completely committed to the role he is playing vis-à-vis his hosts. For one thing, he must try to learn all kinds of facts about the community, many of which it may be inappropriate for someone in his assumed native role to know. He must try to maintain sufficient distance from the culture he is studying and from himself so that he can record "objectively" and, hopefully, use his reactions to his experiences as sources of data. And he must try to record and participate simultaneously. The latter problem has been amply illustrated in my case as I have described it above.

It was because of these difficulties and others that Inuttiaq's second hypothesis—that I was educable—proved to a large extent wrong. And so he arrived at his third hypothesis (shared, as I have said, by the rest of the community), to the effect that I was a defective person: "bad" and "simpleminded."

This analysis of the relationship between my Eskimo family and me is, of course, far from complete. It is obvious that difficulties of conceptualization are only one of the problems that beset relationships of any kind. It is obvious also that most relationships—and the one described here is no exception—have strongly positive features as well, or they would cease to exist. Nevertheless, the account that I have presented here may serve as a basis for discussion of the general issues of anthropological role-playing.

Life in Appalachia— the Case of Hugh McCaslin

Robert Coles

Hugh McCaslin is unforgettable. He has red hair and, at 43, freckles. He stands six feet four. As he talked to me about his work in the coal mines, I kept wondering what he did with his height down inside the earth.

Once he must have been an unusually powerful man; even today his arms and legs are solid muscle. The fat he has added in recent years has collected in only one place, his waist, both front and back.

"I need some padding around my back; it's hurt, and I don't think it'll ever get back right. I broke it bad working, and they told me at first they'd have it fixed in no time flat, but they were wrong. I don't know if they were fooling themselves, or out to fool me in the bargain. It's hard to know *what's* going on around here—that's what I've discovered these last few years.

"I'll tell you, a man like me, he has a lot of time to think. He'll sit around here, day upon day, and what else does he have to keep his mind on but his thoughts? I can't work, and even if I could, there's no work to do, not around here, no sir. They told me I'm 'totally incapacitated,' that's the words they used. They said my spine was hurt, and the nerves, and I can't walk and move about the way I should. As if I needed them to tell me!

"Then they gave me exercises and all, and told me I was lucky, because even though I wasn't in shape to go in the mines, I could do anything else, anything that's not too heavy. Sometimes I wonder what goes on in the heads of those doctors. They look you right in the eye, and they're wearing a straight face on, and they tell you you're sick, you've been hurt digging out coal, and you'll never be the same, but you're really not so bad off, because your back isn't so bad you can't be a judge, or a professor, or the president of the coal company or something like that, you know."

Once Hugh McCaslin (not his real name) asked

me to look at an X-ray taken of his back and his shoulders—his vertebral column. He persuaded the company doctor to give him the X-ray, or so he said. (His wife told me that he had, in fact, persuaded the doctor's secretary to hand it over, and tell her boss—if he ever asked—that somehow the patient's "file" had been lost.) He was convinced that the doctor was a "company doctor"—which he assuredly was—and a "rotten, dishonest one." Anyway, what did *I* see in that X-ray? I told him that I saw very

little. I am no radiologist, and whatever it was that ailed him could not be dramatically pointed out on an X-ray, or if it could I was not the man to do it. Well, yes he did know that, as a matter of fact:

"I got my nerves smashed down there in an accident. I don't know about the bones. I think there was a lot of pressure, huge pressure on the nerves, and it affected the way I walk. The doctor said it wasn't a fracture on a big bone, just one near the spine. He said it wasn't 'too serious,' that I'd be O.K., just not able to go back to work, at least down there.

"Then, you see, they closed down the mine itself. That shows you I wasn't very lucky. My friends kept telling me I was lucky to be alive, and lucky to be through with it, being a miner. You know, we don't scare very easy. Together, we never would talk about getting hurt. I suppose it was somewhere in us, the worry; but the first time I heard my friends say anything like that was to me, not to themselves. They'd come by here when I was sick, and they'd tell me I sure was a fortunate guy, and God was smiling that day, and now He'd be smiling forever on me, because I was spared a *real* disaster, and it was bound to come, one day or another. It kind of got me feeling funny, hearing them talk like that *around my bed,* and then seeing them walk off real fast, with nothing to make *them* watch their step and take a pain pill every few hours.

"But after a while I thought maybe they did have something; and if I could just recover me a good pension from the company, and get my medical expenses all covered—well, then, I'd get better, as much as possible, and go fetch me a real honest-to-goodness job, where I could see the sun all day, and the sky outside, and breathe our air here, as much of it as I pleased, without a worry in the world.

"But that wasn't to be. I was dumb, real dumb, and hopeful. I saw them treating me in the hospital, and when they told me to go home I thought I was better, or soon would be. Instead, I had to get all kinds of treatments, and they said I'd have to pay for them, out of my savings or somewhere. And the pension I thought I was supposed to get, that was all in my mind, they said. They said the coal industry was going through a lot of changes, and you couldn't expect them to keep people going indefinitely, even if they weren't in the best of shape, even if it did happen down in the mines.

"Well, that's it, to make it short. I can't do hard work, and I have a lot of pain, every day of my life. I might be able to do light work, desk work, but hell, I'm not fit for anything like that; and even if I could, where's the work to be found? Around here? Never in a million years. We're doomed here, to sitting and growing the food we can and sharing our misery with one another.

"My brother, he helps; and my four sisters, they help; and my daddy, he's still alive and he can't help except to sympathize, and tell me it's a good thing I didn't get killed in that landslide and can see my boys grow up. He'll come over here and we start drinking. You bet, he's near 80, and we start drinking, and remembering. My daddy will ask me if I can recollect the time I said I'd save a thousand dollars for myself by getting a job in the mines and I say I sure can, and can he recollect the time he said I'd better not get too greedy, because there's bad that comes with good in this world, and especially way down there inside the earth."

He will take a beer or two and then get increasingly angry. His hair seems to look wilder, perhaps because he puts his hands through it as he talks. His wife becomes nervous and tries to give him some bread or crackers, and he becomes sullen or embarrassingly direct with her. She is trying to "soak up" his beer. She won't even let it hit his stomach and stay there a while. She wants it back. He tells her, "Why don't you *keep* your beer, if you won't let it

do a thing for me?"

They have five sons, all born within nine years. The oldest is in high school and dreams of the day he will join the army. He says he will be "taken" in, say, in Charleston or Beckley—in his mind, any "big city" will do. He will be sent off to California or Florida or "maybe New York" for basic training; eventually he will "land himself an assignment—anywhere that's good, and it'll be far away from here, I do believe that." Hugh McCaslin becomes enraged when he hears his son talk like that; with a few beers in him he becomes especially enraged:

"That's the way it is around here. That's what's happened to us. That's what they did to us. They made us lose any honor we had. They turned us idle. They turned us into a lot of grazing sheep, lucky to find a bit of pasture here and there. We don't *do* anything here anymore; and so my boys, they'll all want to leave, and they will. But they'll want to come back, too—because this land, it's in their bones going way back, and you don't shake off your ancestors that easy, no sir.

"My daddy, he was born right up the road in this here hollow, and his daddy, and back to a long time ago. There isn't anyone around here we're not kin to somehow, near or far. My daddy was the one supposed to leave for the mines. He figured he could make more money than he could dream about, and it wasn't too far to go. He went for a while, but some years later he quit. He couldn't take it. I grew up in a camp near the mine, and I'd still be there if it wasn't that I got hurt and moved back here to the hollow. Even while we were at the camp we used to come back here on Sundays, I remember, just like now they come here on weekends from Cincinnati and Dayton and those places, and even from way off in Chicago. I can recall the car we got; everybody talked about it, and when we'd drive as near here as we could—well, the people would come, my grandparents and all my uncles and aunts and cousins, and they'd look and look at that Ford, before they'd see if it was *us,* and say hello to us. I can recollect in my mind being shamed and wanting to disappear in one of those pockets, where my daddy would keep his pipes. My mother would say it wasn't they didn't want to see us, but the Ford, it was real special to them, and could you blame them for not looking at us?

"That was when things were really good. Except that even then I don't think we were all that contented. My mother always worried. Every day, come 3 or so in the afternoon, I could tell she was starting to worry. Will anything happen? Will he get hurt? Will they be coming over soon, to give me some bad news? (No, we had no telephone, and neither did the neighbors.) It got so we'd come home from school around 2 or so, and just sit there with her, pretending—pretending to do things, and say things. And then he'd come in, every time. We could hear his voice coming, or his steps, or the door, and we'd all loosen up—and pretend again, that there was nothing we'd worry about, because there wasn't nothing *to* worry about.

"One day—I think I was seven or eight, because I was in school, I know that—we had a bad scare. Someone came to the school and told the teacher something, whispered it in her ear. She turned into a sheet, and she looked as though she'd start crying. The older kids knew what had happened, just from her looks. (Yes, it was a one-room schoolhouse, just like the one we have here, only a little bigger.) They ran out, and she almost took off after them, except for the fact that she remembered us. So she turned around and told us there that something bad had happened down in the mines, an explosion, and we should go home and wait there, and if our mothers weren't there—well, wait until they got home.

"But we wanted to go with her. Looking back at it, I think she worried us. So she decided to take us, the little ones. And I'll tell you, I can remember that walk with her like it was just today. I can see it, and I can tell you what she said, and what we did, and all. We walked and walked, and then we came through the woods and there they were, all of a sudden before our eyes. The people there, just standing around and almost nothing being said between them. It was so silent I thought they'd all turn around and see us, making noise. But, you see, we must have stopped talking, too, because for a while they didn't even give us a look over their shoulders. Then we come closer, and I could hear there was noise after all: The women were crying, and there'd be a cough or something from some of the miners.

"That's what sticks with you, the miners wondering if their buddies were dead or alive down there. Suddenly I saw my father, and my mother. They were with their arms about one another—real unusual—and they were waiting, like the rest.

"Oh, we got home that night, yes, and my daddy said they were gone—they were dead and we were going away. And we did. The next week we drove here in our Ford, and I can hear my daddy saying it wasn't worth it, money and a car, if you die young, or you live but your lungs get poisoned, and all that, and you never see the sun except on Sundays.

"But what choice did he have? And what choice did I have? I thought I might want to do some farming, like my grandfather, but there's no need for me, and my grandfather couldn't really keep more than himself going, I

mean with some food and all. Then I thought it'd be nice to finish school, and maybe get a job someplace near, in a town not a big city. But everything was collapsing all over the country then, and you'd be crazy to think you were going to get anything by leaving here and going out there, with the lines standing for soup—oh yes, we heard on the radio what it was like all over.

"It could be worse, you say to yourself, and you resolve to follow your daddy and be a miner. That's what I did. He said we had a lousy day's work, but we got good pay, and we could buy things. My daddy had been the richest man in his family for a while. In fact, he was the only man in his family who had any money at all. After the family looked over our Ford, they'd give us that real tired and sorry look, as though they needed some help real bad, and that's when my daddy would hand out the dollar bills, one after the other. I can picture it right now. You feel rich, and you feel real kind."

Hugh McCaslin's life wouldn't be that much better even if he had not been seriously hurt in a mine accident. The miners who were his closest friends are now unemployed, almost every one of them. They do not feel cheated out of a disability pension, but for all practical purposes he and they are equally idle, equally bitter, equally sad. With no prompting from my psychiatric mind he once put it this way:

"They talk about depressions in this country. I used to hear my daddy talk about them all the time, depressions. It wasn't so bad for my daddy and me in the thirties, when the Big One, the Big Depression, was knocking everyone down, left and right. He had a job, and I knew I was going to have one as soon as I was ready, and I did. Then when the war come, they even kept me home. They said we were keeping everything going over here in West Virginia. You can't run factories without coal. I felt I wouldn't mind going, and getting a look at things out there, but I was just as glad to stay here, I guess. I was married, and we were starting with the kids, so it would have been hard. My young brother, he went. He wasn't yet a miner, and they just took him when he was 18, I think. He come back here and decided to stay out of the mines, but it didn't make much difference in the end, anyway. We're all out of the mines now around here.

"So, you see it's *now* that *we're* in a depression. They say things are pretty good in most parts of the country, from what you see on TV, but not so here. We're in the biggest depression ever here: We have no money, and no welfare payments, and we're expected to scrape by like dogs. It gets to your mind after a while. You feel as low as can be, and nervous about everything. That's what a depression does, makes you dead broke, with a lot of bills and the lowest spirits you can ever picture a man having. Sometimes I get up and I'm ready to go over to an undertaker and tell him to do something with me real fast."

I have spent days and nights with the McCaslin family, and Hugh McCaslin doesn't always feel that "low," that depressed, that finished with life. I suppose it can be said that he has "adapted" to the hard, miserable life he faces. At times he shouts and screams about "things," and perhaps in that way keeps himself explicitly angry rather than sullen and brooding. His friends call him a "firebrand," and blame his temper on his red hair. In fact, he says what they are thinking, and need to hear said by someone. They come to see him, and in Mrs. McCaslin's words, "get him going." They bring him home-made liquor to help matters along.

The McCaslins are early risers, but no one gets up earlier than the father. He suffers pain at night; his back and his legs hurt. He has been told that a new hard mattress would help, and hot baths, and aspirin. He spends a good part of the night awake —"thinking and dozing off and then coming to, real sudden-like, with a pain here or there." For a while he thought of sleeping on the floor, or trying to get another bed, but he could not bear the prospect of being alone:

"My wife, Margaret, has kept me alive. She has some of God's patience in her, that's the only way I figure she's been able to last it. She smiles when things are so dark you'd think the end has come. She soothes me, and tells me it'll get better, and even though I know it won't I believe her for a few minutes, and that helps."

So he tosses and turns in their bed, and his wife has learned to sleep soundly but to wake up promptly when her husband is in real pain. They have aspirin and treat it as something special—and expensive. I think Hugh McCaslin realizes that he suffers from many different kinds of pain; perhaps if he had more money he might have been addicted to all sorts of pain-killers long ago. Certainly when I worked in a hospital I saw patients like him—hurt and in pain, but not "sick" enough to require hospitalization, and in fact "chronically semi-invalids." On the other hand, such patients had tried and failed at any number of jobs. We will never know how

Hugh McCaslin might have felt today if he had found suitable work after his accident, or had received further medical care. Work is something a patient needs as he starts getting better, as anyone who works in a "rehabilitation unit" of a hospital well knows. Hugh McCaslin lacked medical care when he needed it, lacks it today, and in his own words needs a "time-killer" as much as a pain-killer. His friends despair, drink, "loaf about," pick up a thing here and there to do, and "waste time real efficiently." So does he—among other things, by dwelling on his injured body.

He dwells on his children, too. There are five of them, and he wants all of them to leave West Virginia. Sometimes in the early morning, before his wife is up, he leaves bed to look at them sleeping:

"I need some hope, and they have it, in their young age and the future they have, if they only get the hell out of here before it's too late. Oh, I like it here, too. It's pretty, and all that. It's peaceful. I'm proud of us people. We've been here a long time, and we needed real guts to stay and last. And who wants to live in a big city? I've been in some of our cities, here in West Virginia, and they're no big value, from what I can see, not so far as bringing up a family. You have no land, no privacy, a lot of noise, and all that. But if it's between living and dying, I'll take living; and right here, right now, I think we're dying—dying away, slow but sure, every year more and more so."

He worries about his children in front of them. When they get up they see him sitting and drinking coffee in the kitchen. He is wide-awake, and hungrier for company than he knows. He wants to learn what they'll be doing that day. He wants to talk about things, about the day's events and inevitably a longer span of time, the future: "Take each day like your life hangs on it. That's being young, when you can do that, when you're not trapped and have some choice on things." The children are drowsy, but respectful. They go about dressing and taking coffee and doughnuts with him. They are as solicitous as he is. Can they make more coffee? They ask if they can bring him anything—even though they know full well his answer: "No, just yourselves."

Mrs. McCaslin may run the house, but she makes a point of checking every decision with her husband.

He "passes on" even small matters—something connected with one of the children's schoolwork, or a neighbor's coming visit, or a project for the church. She is not sly and devious; not clever at appearing weak but "manipulating" all the while. She genuinely defers to her husband, and his weakness, his illness, his inability to find work—and none of those new medical, social, or psychological "developments" have made her see fit to change her ways. Nor is he inclined to sit back and let the world take *everything* out of his hands. As a matter of fact, it is interesting to see how assertive a man and a father he still is, no matter how awful his fate continues to be. He is *there,* and always there—in spirit as well as in body. I have to compare him not only with certain Negro fathers I know, who hide from welfare workers and flee their wives and children in fear and shame and anger, but also with a wide range of

The Ironies of Appalachia

Appalachia is full of ironies, but nothing is more ironic than the fact that America's oldest ethnic group, its white Anglo-Saxon Protestants, live there in poverty as desperate as that experienced by any other impoverished people. It took courage and enterprise to settle the region—and now the region's people are called inert, apathetic, and unresourceful. The region has experienced the severest kind of unemployment as a result of technological change, and yet side by side one sees an almost primitive economy. If ever there was a section of America that needed planned capital investment, federally sustained—as indeed this country has done in other regions of the world with its money—then indeed Appalachia is that region.

In my experience the people of Appalachia do not fit the usual sociological and anthropological descriptions applied to them. By that I mean that their apparent inertia and apathy are reasonable responses to a lack of opportunity and a lack of employment. Given jobs, real jobs, jobs that are not substitutes for work, Appalachian men and women work well and hard. They also can be open, friendly, and generous—even to an outsider like me. What they do not want is a kind of patronizing and condescending sympathy. They are proud and stubborn people who want from this country a share of its wealth. Given that, I don't think we would have any "psychological problems" with the region's citizens.   R.C.

white middle-class fathers who maintain a round-the-clock absence from home (for business reasons, for "social" reasons), or else demonstrate a much-advertised "passivity" while there. Hugh McCaslin, as poor as one can be in America, not at all well-educated, jobless, an invalid, and a worried, troubled man, nevertheless exerts a strong and continuing influence upon everyone in his family. He is, again, *there*—not just at home, but very much involved in almost everything his wife and children do. He talks a lot. He has strong ideas, and he has a temper. He takes an interest in all sorts of problems—not only in those that plague Road's Bend Hollow:

"My daddy was a great talker. He wasn't taken in by the big people who run this country. He didn't read much, even then when he was young, but he had his beliefs. He said we don't give everyone a break here, and that's against the whole purpose of the country, when it was first settled. You know, there are plenty of people like him. They know how hard it is for a working man to get his share—to get *anything*. Let me tell you, if we had a chance, men like me, we'd vote for a different way of doing things. It just isn't right to use people like they're so much dirt, hire them and fire them and give them no respect and no real security. A few make fortunes and, the rest of us, we're lucky to have our meals from day to day. That's not right; it just isn't.

"I tell my boys not to be fooled. It's tough out there in the world, and it's tough here, too. We've got little here except ourselves. They came in here, the big companies, and bled us dry. They took everything, our coal, our land, our trees, our health. We died like we were in a war, fighting for those companies—and we were lucky to get enough money to bury our kin. They tell me sometimes I'm bitter, my brothers do, but they're just as bitter as I am—they don't talk as much, that's the only difference. Of course it got better here with unions and with some protection the workers got through the government. But you can't protect a man when the company decides to pull out; when it says it's got all it can get, so goodbye folks, and take care of yourselves, because we're moving on to some other place, and we just can't do much more than tell you it was great while it lasted, and you helped us out a lot, yes sir you did."

He does not always talk like that. He can be quiet for long stretches of time, obviously and moodily quiet. His wife finds his silences hard to bear. She doesn't know what they will "lead to." Every day she asks her husband whether there is anything "special" he wants to eat—even though they both know there isn't much they can afford but the daily mainstays—bread, coffee, doughnuts, crackers, some thin stew, potatoes, homemade jam, biscuits. Mrs. McCaslin defers to her husband, though; one way is to pay him the courtesy of asking him what he wants. I have often heard them go back and forth about food, and as if for all the world they were far better off, with more choices before them:

"Anything special you want for supper?"
"No. Anything suits me fine. I'm not too hungry."
"Well, if that's it then I'd better make you hungry with something special."
"What can do that?"
"I thought I'd fry up the potatoes real good tonight and cut in some onions. It's better than boiling, and I've got some good pork to throw in. You wait and see."
"I will. It sounds good."

He hurts and she aches for him. His back has its "bad spells," and she claims her own back can "feel the pain that goes through his." They don't touch each other very much in a stranger's presence, or even, I gather, before their children, but they give each other long looks of recognition, sympathy, affection, and sometimes anger or worse. They understand each other in that silent, real, lasting way that defies the gross labels that I and my kind call upon. It is hard to convey in words—theirs or mine—the subtle, delicate, largely unspoken, and continual *sense of each other* (that is the best that I can do) that they have. In a gesture, a glance, a frown, a smile they talk and agree and disagree:

"I can tell what the day will be like for Hugh when he first gets up. It's all in how he gets out of bed, slow or with a jump to it. You might say we all have our good days and bad ones, but Hugh has a lot of time to give over to his moods, and around here I guess we're emotional, you might say."

I told her that I thought an outsider like me might not see it that way. She wanted to know what I meant, and I told her: "They call people up in the hollow 'quiet,' and they say they don't show their feelings too much, to each other, let alone in front of someone like me."

"Well, I don't know about that," she answered quickly, a bit piqued. "I don't know what reason they have for that. Maybe they don't have good ears. We don't talk *loud* around here, but we say what's on our mind, straightaway, I believe. I never was one for mincing on words, and I'll tell anyone what's on my mind, be he from around here or way over on the other side of the world. I do believe we're cautious here, and we give a man every break we can, because you don't have it easy around here, no matter who you are; so maybe that's why they think we're not given to getting excited and such. But we do."

I went back to Hugh. Did she think he was more "emotional" than others living nearby?

"Well, I'd say it's hard to say. He has a temper, but I think that goes for all his friends. I think he's about ordinary, only because of his sickness he's likely to feel bad more than some, and it comes out in his moods. You know, when we were married he was the most cheerful man I'd ever met. I mean he smiled all the time, not just because someone said something funny. His daddy told me I was getting the happiest of his kids, and I told him I believed he was right, because I'd already seen it for myself. Today he's his old self sometimes, and I almost don't want to see it, because it makes me think back and remember the good times we had.

"Oh, we have good times now, too; don't mistake me. They just come rare, compared to when times were good. And always it's his pain that hangs over us; we never know when he'll be feeling right, from day to day.

"But when he's got his strength and there's nothing ailing him, he's all set to work, and it gets bad trying to figure what he might do. We talk of moving, but we ask ourselves where we'd go to. We don't want to travel a thousand miles only to be lost in some big city and not have even what we've got. Here there's a neighbor, and our kin, always. We have the house, and we manage to scrape things together, and no one of my kids has ever starved to death. They don't get the food they should, sometimes, but they eat, and they like what I do with food. In fact they complain at church. They say others don't brown the potatoes enough, or the biscuits. And they like a good chocolate cake, and I have that as often as I can.

"When Hugh is low-down he doesn't want to get out of bed, but I make him. He'll sit around and not do much. Every few minutes he'll call my name, but then he won't really have much to say. I have those aspirin, but you can't really afford to use them all the time.

"When he feels good, though, he'll go do chores. He'll make sure we have plenty of water, and he'll cut away some wood and lay it up nearby. He'll walk up the road and see people. He has friends, you know, who aren't sick like him, but it doesn't do them much good around here to be healthy. They can't work any more than Hugh can. It's bad, all the time bad.

"We find our own work, though, and we get paid in the satisfaction you get. We try to keep the house in good shape, and we keep the road clear all year round. That can be a job come winter.

"A lot of the time Hugh says he wished he could read better. He'll get an old magazine—the *Reader's Digest,* or the paper from Charleston—and he'll stay with it for hours. I can see he's having a tough time, but it keeps him busy. He tells the kids to remember his mistakes and not to make them all over again. Then they want to know why he made them. And we're off again. He talks about the coal companies and how they bribed us out of our 'souls,' and how he was a fool, and how it's different now. When they ask what they'll be doing with their reading and writing, it's hard to give them an answer without telling them to move. You don't want to do that, but maybe you do, too. I don't know.

"Hugh fought the television. He said it was no good, and we surely didn't have the money to get one. You can get them real cheap, though, secondhand, and there's a chance to learn how to fix it yourself, because some of the men who come back from the army, they've learned how and they'll teach you and do it for you if you ask them. We had to get one, finally. The kids, they said everyone else didn't have the money, any more than we did, but somehow they got the sets, so why couldn't we? That started something, all right. Hugh wanted to know if they thought we could manufacture money. So they wanted to know how the others got their sets. And Hugh said he didn't know, but if they would go find out, and come tell him, why then he'd show them that each family is different, and you can't compare people like that. Well, then they mentioned it to their uncle—he works down there in the school, keeping it in order, and he's on a regular salary, you know, and lives as good as anyone around here, all things told, I'd say. So he came and told us he'd do it, get a set for us, because the kids really need them. They feel left out without TV.

"That got Hugh going real bad. He didn't see why the radio wasn't enough, and he wasn't going to take and take and take. He wanted help, but not for a TV set. And then he'd get going on the coal companies, and how we got that radio for cash, and it was brand-new and expensive, but he was making plenty of money then. And he didn't want to go begging, even from kin. And we could just do without, so long as we eat and have a place to sleep and no one's at our door trying to drive us away or take us to jail.

"Finally I had to say something. I had to. It was one of the hardest things I've ever had to do. He was getting worse and worse, and the kids they began to think he was wrong in the head over a thing like TV, and they didn't know why; they couldn't figure it out. He said they wouldn't see anything but a lot of trash, and why should we let it all come in here like that? And he said they'd lose interest in school, and become hypnotized or something, and he'd read someplace it happens. And he said gadgets and machines, they came cheap, but you end up losing a lot more than you get, and that was what's happening in America today.

"Now, the kids could listen for so long, and they're respectful to him, to both of us, I think you'll agree. They'd try to answer him, real quiet, and say it wasn't so important, TV wasn't, it was just there to look at, and we would all do it and have a good time. And everyone was having it, but that didn't mean that the world was changing, or that you'd lose anything just because you looked at a picture every once in a while.

"And finally, as I say, I joined in. I had to—and I sided with them. I said they weren't going to spend their lives looking at TV, no sir, but it would be O.K. with me if we had it in the house, that I could live with it, and I think we could all live with it. And Hugh, he just looked at me and didn't say another word, not that day or any other afterwards until much later on, when we had the set already, and he would look at the news and listen real careful to what they tell you might be happening. He told me one day, it was a foolish fight we all had, and television wasn't any better or worse than a lot of other things. But he wished the country would make more than cheap TVs. 'We could all live without TV if we had something more to look forward to,' he said. I couldn't say anything back. He just wasn't feeling good that day, and to tell the truth TV is good for him when he's like that, regardless of what he says. He watches it like he used to listen to his radio, and he likes it better than he'd ever admit to himself, I'm sure."

On Sundays they go to church. Hugh says he doesn't much believe in "anything," but he goes; he stays home only when he doesn't feel good, not out of any objection to prayer. They all have their Sunday clothes, and they all enjoy getting into them. They become new and different people. They walk together down the hollow and along the road that takes them to a Baptist church. They worship vigorously and sincerely, and with a mixture of awe, bravado, passion, and restraint that leaves an outside observer feeling, well—skeptical, envious, surprised, mystified, admiring, and vaguely nostalgic.

I think they emerge much stronger and more united for the experience, and with as much "perspective," I suppose, as others get from different forms of contemplation, submission, and joint participation. Hugh can be as stoical as anyone else, and in church his stoicism can simply pour out. The world *is* confusing, you see. People have *always* suffered, good people. Somewhere, somehow, it is not all for naught—but that doesn't mean one should raise one's hopes too high, not on this earth.

After church there is "socializing," and its importance need not be stressed in our self-conscious age of "groups" that solve "problems" or merely facilitate "interaction." When I have asked myself what "goes on" in those "coffee periods," I remind myself that I heard a lot of people laughing, exchanging news, offering greetings, expressing wishes, fears, congratulations and condolences. I think there is a particular warmth and intensity to some of the meetings because, after all, people do not see much of one another during the week. Yet how many residents of our cities or our suburbs see one another as regularly as these "isolated" people do? Hugh McCaslin put it quite forcefully: "We may not see much of anyone for a few days, but Sunday will come and we see everyone we want to see, and by the time we go home we know everything there is to know." As some of us say, they "communicate efficiently."

There is, I think, a certain hunger for companionship that builds up even among people who do not feel as "solitary" as some of their observers have considered them. Particularly at night one feels the woods and the hills close in on "the world." The McCaslins live high up in a hollow, but they don't have a "view." Trees tower over their cabin, and the smoke rising from their chimney has no space at all to dominate. When dusk comes there are no lights to be seen, only their lights to turn on. In winter they eat at about 5 and they are in bed about 7:30 or 8. The last hour before bed is an almost formal time. Every evening Mr. McCaslin smokes his pipe and either reads or carves wood. Mrs. McCaslin has finished putting things away after supper and sits sewing—"mending things and fixing things;

there isn't a day goes by that something doesn't tear." The children watch television. They have done what homework they have (or are willing to do) before supper. I have never heard them reprimanded for failing to study. Their parents tell them to go to school; to stay in school; to do well in school—but they aren't exactly sure it makes much difference. They ask the young to study, but I believe it is against their "beliefs" to say one thing and mean another, to children or anyone else.

In a sense, then, they are blunt and truthful with each other. They say what they think, but worry about how to say what they think so that the listener remains a friend or—rather often—a friendly relative. Before going to bed they say good-night, and one can almost feel the reassurance that goes with the greeting. It is very silent "out there" or "outside."

"Yes, I think we have good manners," Hugh McCaslin once told me. "It's a tradition, I guess, and goes back to Scotland, or so my daddy told me. I tell the kids that they'll know a lot more than I do when they grow up, or I hope they will; but I don't believe they'll have more consideration for people—no sir. We teach them to say hello in the morning, to say good morning, like you said. I know it may not be necessary, but it's good for people living real close to be respectful of one another. And the same goes for the evening.

"Now, there'll be fights. You've seen us take after one another. That's O.K. But we settle things on the same day, and we try not to carry grudges. How can you carry a grudge when you're just this one family here, and miles away from the next one? Oh, I know it's natural to be spiteful and carry a grudge. But you can only carry it so far, that's what I say. Carry it until the sun goes down, then wipe the slate clean and get ready for another day. I say that a lot to the kids."

Once I went with the McCaslins to a funeral. A great-uncle of Mrs. McCaslin's had died at 72. He happened to be a favorite of hers and of her mother. They lived much nearer to a town than the McCaslins do, and were rather well-to-do. He had worked for the county government all his life—in the Appalachian region, no small position. The body lay at rest in a small church, with hand-picked flowers in bunches around it. A real clan had gathered from all over, as well as friends. Of course it was a sad occasion, despite the man's advanced age; yet even so I was struck by the restraint of the people, their politeness to one another, no matter how close or "near kin" they were. For a moment I watched them move about and tried to block off their subdued talk from my brain. It occurred to me that, were they dressed differently and in a large manor home, they might very much resemble English gentry at a reception. They were courtly people; they looked it and acted it. Many were tall, thin, and close-mouthed. A few were potbellied, as indeed befits a good lusty duke or duchess. They could smile and even break out into a laugh, but it was always notice-able when it happened. In general they were not exactly demonstrative or talkative, yet they were clearly interested in one another and had very defi-nite and strong sentiments, feelings, emotions, what-ever. In other words, as befits the gentry, they had feelings but had them under "appropriate" control. They also seemed suitably resigned, or philosophical —as the circumstances warranted. What crying there was, had already been done. There were no out-bursts of any kind, and no joviality either. It was not a wake.

A few days later Hugh McCaslin of Road's Bend Hollow talked about the funeral and life and death:

"He probably went too early, from what I hear. He was in good health, and around here you either die very young —for lack of a doctor—or you really last long. That's the rule, though I admit we have people live to all ages, like anywhere I guess. No, I don't think much of death, even being sick as I am. It happens to you, and you know it, but that's O.K. When I was a boy I recall my people bury-ing their old people, right near where we lived. We had a little graveyard, and we used to know all our dead people pretty well. You know, we'd play near their graves, and go ask our mother or daddy about who this one was and what he did, and like that. The other way was through the Bible: Everything was written down on pieces of paper inside the family Bible. There'd be births and marriages and deaths, going way back, I guess as far back as the beginning of the country. I'm not sure of the exact time, but a couple of hundred years, easy.

"We don't do that now—it's probably one of the biggest changes, maybe. I mean apart from television and things like that. We're still religious, but we don't keep the records, and we don't bury our dead nearby. It's just not that much of a *home* here, a place that you have and your kin always had and your children and theirs will have, until the end of time, when God calls us all to account. This here place—it's a good house, mind you—but it's just a place I got. A neighbor of my daddy's had it, and he left it, and my daddy heard and I came and fixed it up and we have it for nothing. We worked hard and put a lot into it, and we treasure it, but it never was a *home,* not the kind I knew, and my wife did. We came back to the hollow, but it wasn't like it used to be when we were kids and you felt you were living in the same place all your ancestors did. We're *part* of this land, we were here to start and we'll probably see it die, me or my kids will, the way things are going. There will be no one left here and the stripminers will kill every good acre we have. I thought of that at the funeral. I thought maybe it's just as well to die now, if everything's headed in that direction. I guess that's what happens at a funeral. You get to thinking."

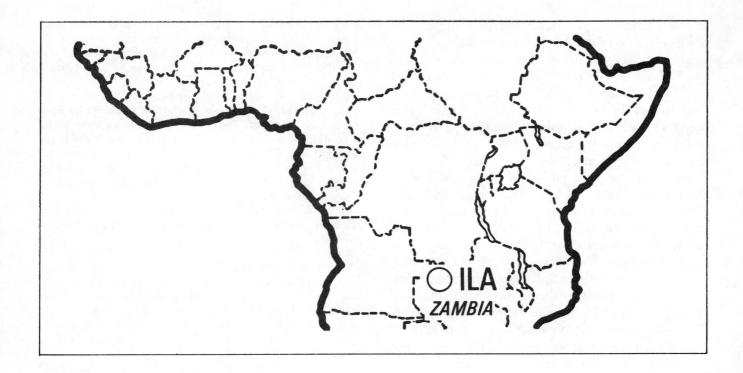

Ila Slavery in Zambia

Arthur Tuden

Among the Ila of Rhodesia there were three sources of slaves: raids, payment of debt, and purchase.

Relatively few were obtained from raids. A larger source were those individuals, usually children, who were accepted as payment for debts or fines. But the majority of slaves were purchased from nearby groups culturally similar to the Ila. Cattle, salt, leopard skins, hoes, or grain were the standard media of exchange. Characteristics most eagerly sought by purchasers were youth and absence of deformities.

There were no preferences in sex; both males and females were avidly purchased. Males were used as workers and fighters, while females added cattle to the family herds when they married or, if they did not marry, they produced children for the family and worked in the fields.

The ambiguous and indeterminate positions of Ila slaves are reflected in the terms used to describe them, and the attitudes about them. No elaborate stereotype existed; slaves were represented primarily as people who "didn't know where their ancestors came from" or "women who did not receive property in marriage"—there was no invidious connotation. Direct reference to their being slaves was considered insulting. A joking name, kinship term or spirit name, or the customary term of address for a free person were accepted procedures for addressing slaves.

The relationship between a slave and his owner was clearly not that of superior and subordinate. It was phrased in kinship terms. As soon as slaves were brought to the village, they became part of their owner's kin group. During a communal ritual a kin member informed the ancestral spirits of the slaves' entrance into the group and asked them to recognize and protect the new members. The slave called his owner by a kin term as well, and this genealogical function was adopted and extended to other relatives.

In outward appearance, the treatment and condition of a young slave was indistinguishable from that of the free Ila child. Both free and slave children lived within the village and aided in cattle herding, running errands, and doing minor tasks. Subtle preferences were perhaps shown to actual kinsmen in choice of foods or presents; but impartiality was the general rule, and the fact of slave status or ancestry was minimized.

Slave children were consciously raised as Ila and kinsmen. They underwent the same initiation rites as the free Ila with full ceremonies. During a slave's youth, his owner presented him with cattle from the family herds, further establishing kinship. These animals became the slave's property and represented the nucleus of his private herd. He acquired the same privileges and responsibilities in regard to them and the family herd as direct descendants did. The owner assumed responsibility for his slaves' debts and fines, and fines for slaves and non-slaves were the same.

There were times, however, when the position of a slave was clear, and the fictitious kinship was ignored. At these times young slaves were regarded primarily as property. At the death of an owner, young slaves could be inherited by the creditors of their deceased master or be distributed within the kin group like other property. Older slaves were not inherited in this fashion, but the Ila were vague about the exact age at which a slave was assured of continuity of residence and stability of relations. They did insist, however, that if a slave had lived in one village for a greater portion of his life he was a quasi-kinsman and was not considered property.

The differences between adult slaves and non-slaves was of degree rather than kind. Older slaves were used as labor, thus relieving the owner and his kinsmen of unpleasant tasks. Slaves did most of the work. Further, those slaves (a minority) who did not possess fields of their own, worked exclusively in their owner's fields or herded his cattle. But physical punishment was not common, and the methods used to control slaves were similar to those applied to free men.

Female slaves were absorbed into the kinship system with more difficulty than the males, and their condition reflected the real discrepancies between verbalized and actual kinship affiliation. The *nabutema* (divorced or older unmarried slave women) lived in the center of the village in small huts of inferior quality; they cleared the fields,

planted the crops, and gathered wood. If desired, they were assigned to visitors for their sexual pleasure. Of all slaves, they suffered the greatest exploitation.

Slave ancestry presented no definite barrier to intermarriage with free Ila. Ila free women married male slaves, slave women married free men, and interslave unions took place. However, the most common status for a slave woman was that of a secondary wife (junior wife in a polygynous household). Slave women were sometimes given in marriage to sons or kinsmen of their owner. Thus they served as an extra supply of wives for the kin group.

The children of a marriage between a slave and a free man further served to blur the distinction between slave and non-slave. Slavery, among the Ila, implied a lack of extended kinship affiliations, but second-generation slaves established such affiliations through marriage and residence, since they had more opportunity to establish kinship relations. The Ila summarized this fact by stating that anyone born within a village is a kinsman. Thus, slaves began to incorporate into the Ila kin groups after one generation.

Slave status or ancestry did not hamper the slaves in the Ila economic system for they owned property—including other slaves. Former slaves who had acquired property could establish their own lineage units by purchasing other slaves or by persuading the dissatisfied relatives of a deceased headman to transfer allegiance to them.

Crucial to an understanding of the role of slavery was the fact that slaves contributed cattle to the bride-wealth of their adopted kinsmen, and in return they shared its distribution within the group. (Bride-wealth refers to a payment, or series of them, made by the groom and his kinship unit to the bride's kinship group upon the inception of a marriage.) In addition, upon the death of a headman, slaves or those of slave ancestry inherited a portion of the cattle held in the name of the lineage group. Conversely, the slave's owner, and his immediate kin, were the major recipients of a slave's property after he died. Yet with all these distributions and contributions, the fact remains that the economic activity of the slave was generally restricted to that one section of the total social structure; first-generation slaves did not inherit from or participate in exchanges with any larger kin groups.

Free members of the community maintained multiple ties and relationships through the various kinship groups of their mothers and grandmothers. These relationships, although providing economic aid and support for participants, resulted in conflicting loyalties and responsibilities for non-slaves. As a result, the position of a *musolozhi* (headman) was measurably strengthened by the presence in his village of a number of individuals who "had no other place to go"—that is, primarily, slaves.

Since centralized leadership was lacking, there was a continual struggle among kinship units for political power. Authority was diffused; power did not automatically devolve upon anybody. The authority of the kinship head was based upon the number of dependents he could control, so that a large number of slaves living in a village would be very useful, politically. Since slaves, like kinsmen, were necessary for defense and for support in the constant maneuvering for property and the regulation of village life, a slave who had been unfairly treated could run away from his village, and a neighboring village would accept him gladly. The new owner or the runaway slave himself would reimburse the previous owner, and the slave would be incorporated into the village on a quasi-kinship basis.

It appears that slavery among the Ila did not produce fixed social classes with an unequal distribution of wealth or authority. Those that did exist did not affect the slave permanently, and within a short time slaves were truly incorporated into the kinship system on a basis similar to non-slaves.

"I Divorce Thee"
Lawrence Rosen

There is probably no better example of a stereotype that springs from wish-fulfillment than the widespread notion that Moslem men have only to intone "I divorce thee" three times in order to be rid of the harridan that plagues their married years. To be sure, it's getting a lot easier these days, almost everywhere in the West, to get a divorce; but for sheer simplicity and ease the Moslem practice seems unbeatable.

Unfortunately, like many stereotypes of the nonwestern world, this one too is a mixture of half-truth and complete misunderstanding. It is true that in most Moslem countries men still retain the right to repudiate their spouses unilaterally. But it is equally true that there is a host of social, economic and indeed legal means through which a woman and her family may effectively check her husband's ability to do anything with his seemingly unlimited legal powers. In a modern Islamic nation like Morocco the law codes alone offer only the narrowest view of husband-

wife relations in such a society. One must look closely at a number of social and economic factors associated with divorce to get a more sophisticated view.

Moreover, a study of this sort reveals various social and legal problems that are of considerable importance to several aspects of contemporary sociological theory. For if it is indeed true, as we shall argue, that Moroccan society is not composed of a series of fixed groupings whose members relate to one another on the basis of very narrowly defined roles such as "husband" and "wife," then it becomes necessary to consider the situational contexts of these relationships and the ways in which contractual ties and personal manipulations may modify relationships that would seem to be defined simply on the basis of status.

Morocco presents a good example of the interplay of social and legal factors associated with divorce in the contemporary Moslem world. As embodied in the Code of Personal Status adopted two years after national independence in 1956, the Moroccan laws of divorce reflect fewer significant changes from the traditional rules of the Malikite school of Islamic law than do the codes of, say, Algeria, Tunisia or even Egypt, which were heavily influenced by French and Swiss legal codes. The Moroccan husband's rights of divorce remain very considerable. Indeed, the first time a man repudiates his wife, the courts will not only uphold his right to do so, they will also sanction his power to call her back to his bed and board at any time during a three-month period. If the three months go by without a reconciliation—and any pregnancy on the woman's part will be attributed to the husband— the divorce will be declared final. If, however, the husband exercises the right to call his wife back, and then for some reason thinks better of the idea, he can repudiate her a second time. But if he changes his mind again, he must have the wife's consent in order to bring her back. Moreover, the husband will have to give her some gift as a sign of their reconciliation. If, finally, the husband repudiates his wife for a third time, the law will not permit them to take up residence together once again even if both parties desire it. Only after the expiration of the waiting period and the formation and dissolution of a marriage with another man would the woman be eligible to remarry her first husband.

One Moroccan characterized the differences between these three forms of divorce as being similar to the situation of a man who holds a small bird in his hand. To repudiate a woman for the first time would be like releasing the bird with a string attached to one of its legs: provided the bird does not get three months distant the captor can reel it back whenever he chooses. In a second repudiation, however, the bird has been released completely unfettered and will only return to its master if properly enticed. And after a third repudiation the bird will fly away altogether to seek a new and more congenial source of sustenance.

In each of these cases, then, the legal powers of the husband are indeed absolute, but there are several other forms of divorce in which the initiative actually lies with the wife and the officials of the local court. If, for example, a woman can prove to the court that her husband has failed to fulfill one of the defining duties of the marital contract—if, say, he fails to support her or mistreats her excessively—she can petition the court for a judicial decree of separation. In another instance the woman may secure a divorce by getting her husband to agree to accept some form of remuneration for releasing her. Acceptance of such an arrangement by the husband carries with it an

inherent and irrevocable repudiation. Clearly such an arrangement places a great deal of power—verging at times on extortion—in the hands of the husband, but the bride and her family may have hedged against such an eventuality when the marital contract itself was drawn up.

At the time a marital contract is agreed upon, representatives for the woman may have certain stipulations written into the document which are intended to strengthen the position of the woman and her family against the husband. Among the most common stipulations not directly concerned with property are, for example, the understanding that the woman need never move more than a specified distance away from her family of origin, or that her husband may never take an additional wife without first granting her a divorce. The woman's family may even stipulate that the marriage will actually be subject to termination at the pleasure of the wife herself. Court officials rationalize this apparent breach of the Koranic law (which grants the power of repudiation to the husband alone) by saying that the woman has actually contracted a situation similar to that in which she gains release from her husband through some form of remuneration. But here the "payment" is with the words the husband himself agreed to have placed in the contract rather than with a sum of money, custody of a child or some other form of consideration.

The most common stipulation found in marital contracts, however, refers to the payment of the brideprice. In Islamic law and custom every marriage requires as its fundamental defining act the payment to the bride or her marital guardian of a sum of money or goods whose value may vary from that of a simple token to any sum agreed upon by the representatives of the bride and groom. However, not all of the brideprice need actually be paid at the time the marriage itself is contracted. Rather, a portion of the brideprice may remain to be paid at the time of any subsequent divorce or at any time the woman herself chooses to demand it. Clearly this condition gives a woman considerable leverage in curbing her husband's right to summarily dismiss her. Any man who has contracted a marriage with this provision in it will think twice before arbitrarily exercising his right of divorce or indeed of provoking his wife in any way that might move her to demand the outstanding portion of her brideprice.

The extent to which a man may find himself obliged to acquiesce in the inclusion of such contractual provisions as these is, for the most part, a function of the relative power of each of the parties concerned, particularly economic power. If a man is attempting to marry up socially or economically, and if at the same time the bride's family suspects that the prospective husband may mistreat his wife or try to make life for her so miserable that she will pay any sum to secure her freedom, the family of the bride may leave part of the brideprice unpaid or require certain other rights for the bride. In some parts of the countryside whole communities customarily use the deferred brideprice clause as a means of insuring some degree of marital stability. There will often be considerable haggling over the terms of a marital contract and the sums involved. The outcome will vary according to such considerations as the intangible prestige value of one's descent, the present market in potential mates and the conflicting motives of various members of both families.

There are several other factors associated with the laws of brideprice payments and divorce that may give women and their families considerable power to modify the husband's legal privileges. In recent years, there has been a substantial increase in brideprices paid in Morocco, particularly by members of the urban upper classes. Where ten years ago a well-to-do man may have paid several hundred dollars as a brideprice, a man of comparable circumstances today may have to spend as much as $1,000. People sometimes speak of this as brideprice competition, and there is little doubt that brideprice payments may be one way to establish social standing in a heterogeneous and highly mobile society lacking in any all-pervasive system of group stratification. But insofar as only the closest friends and relatives will know exactly what sums or conditions are involved, there is reason to suspect that the competition is, in point of fact, not for brideprices per se but for the dowries associated with each brideprice payment.

Upon receipt of a brideprice for his daughter or marital ward, a man will add a substantial sum of his own and use the combined amount to purchase a dowry for the bride. This dowry itself is called, quite significantly, "the furnishings of the household." It is these goods, whether actual furnishings, items of personal jewelry or raw wool, which will be considered the personal property of the woman and will leave the marriage with her in the event of divorce or widowhood. In addition to their security value these goods, rather than the brideprice itself, are made clearly visible to the entire community as well as to those who later visit the couple's home. Indeed, on the day a bride moves to her husband's home the goods comprising her dowry are paraded around the streets of the city to the accompaniment of oboists and drummers, chanting relatives and screaming children. Poorer families carry the goods in

their hands and on their heads while wealthier people will lay out the entire dowry—down to the last fragile teacup—on the beds of several pickup trucks. It is for these goods, which represent both the status of the bride and a real source of her personal security, for which the competition directly expressed in brideprices is being carried on. The mother of the bride is usually the most insistent that her daughter's dowry should be as substantial as possible. She will nag her husband to increase the brideprice demanded, while he, seeking both respite from the nagging and a vehicle for emphasizing his own social standing, will increase the brideprice accordingly.

In addition to setting up an index of relative social status, it is also important to note that the law automatically assumes that all of the "household furnishings" except for the most personal possessions of the husband (such as his clothing and tools) are the sole property of the woman and may be taken away by her when she leaves. Since the woman's family generally doesn't allow the precise content of the dowry itself to be entered into the marriage contract, this legal fiction gives the wife a potentially powerful lever to use against her husband. Indeed, insofar as they can do so without creating an unbearable strain on the marriage itself, Moroccan women frequently try to pressure their husbands into buying them as many things as possible in order to insure themselves against a sudden divorce. Everyone is well aware that the more a man has to lose financially by divorce, the less likely he will be to exercise his legal powers arbitrarily. And if such a divorce means not only the loss of those goods bought during the marriage and any outstanding portion of the brideprice, but also means incurring a whole new set of social and financial debts associated with the collection of a new brideprice, a man will certainly hesitate before making use of his power of instant repudiation. The extent, then, to which a husband may be put at an economic disadvantage by a wife who is herself at a clear legal disadvantage will be a function of the relative power of the persons involved, particularly their respective financial positions.

In addition to the legal prerogatives and economic pressures affecting marital relations, there is a host of ways in which different social ties may be utilized by the parties involved. We have already seen how the bride's mother may cajole and conspire to elicit from her husband the largest dowry possible for her daughter, and how a husband may be reluctant to divorce his wife because of the degree of personal independence he may have to give up in seeking help with a new brideprice from his relatives and acquaintances. Similarly a wife who wants to get her husband to abandon his plan to divorce her may turn to commonly shared friends and relatives, neighbors or some individual "in whose presence her husband feels shame." For example, if a husband and wife are first paternal cousins, which is quite common in Moslem societies, the wife may utilize the position of her father as the husband's uncle rather than simply as his father-in-law to constrain the husband to act as a nephew properly should. Or by galvanizing the opinion of neighbors or threatening a public court action a woman may hope to induce her husband to give her more substantial support, abstain from occasional beatings or spend less of his time at a nearby café. Again the success of her endeavors will vary tremendously with the social, economic and legal positions of all those involved. What remains constant in this system, however, is neither the forms of behavior associated with certain relationships nor the groupings that are crystallized at any given moment to accomplish an ad hoc task but simply the ways in which persons can indeed relate to one another without overstepping "the bounds of permissible leeway" as they pursue their individually and pointedly defined goals.

Mohamed's Case

As an example of the subtle interplay of social, legal and economic factors associated with divorce in Morocco, take the case of a young friend of mine who was experiencing some difficulty with his wife. Mohamed was a clerk in the local administrator's office who had married a girl from his home town of Fez and settled down to live with her in his father's house. Almost from the start, however, his wife and mother began fighting with one another as each tried to maintain the greater degree of influence over Mohamed's actions. The situation created great strains among the members of Mohamed's own family and between all of them and his wife's kinsmen. Mohamed finally decided to move away altogether in the hope that setting up house for himself in a nearby town would solve the basic problem. But his wife continued to nag him and demand his complete attentiveness to her every wish. Mohamed tried gobetweens from his wife's family and from neighbors, but in each case his wife's agreement to behave herself was quickly followed by a renewal of her bossy and nagging attitude. Mohamed was hesitant to divorce her since he would then have to pay a very substantial sum remaining from the brideprice and begin all over again to collect money for a

new wife of the standing he deemed appropriate for a man of his background and position. He thought that having children might make her more tractable but was equally afraid that if this did not settle the problem and he still had to divorce her he would then have the additional burden of long-term child support. Quite literally, he said, he could neither live with his wife nor without her. He finally decided that since it was an independent identity of her own and an ability to have a say in her own future that was at the root of his wife's problem the only workable solution was to allow her to finish enough of her education so that she could find some work outside of their home. Although he had the power and even the desire to repudiate his wife forthwith, Mohamed recognized that he was effectively constrained from doing so by the social and financial implications of such an act.

Nonlegal Powers

In more general terms, then, Mohamed's marital difficulties point up several important aspects of the law and practice of divorce in Morocco. Unlike many other societies in the world, in which an individual's actions are almost wholly determined by the ways he is expected to behave towards his various kinds of relatives, in Morocco a person is usually free to manipulate these relationships in a wide variety of ways. One can play on the different interests of family members, the control one has over the family's property, the aid one can expect from having done favors for non-kinsmen, and indeed the implications of the existing laws to establish a position of relative power vis-à-vis the other people in one's family. Because so many different interests can be brought to bear in the arrangement or dissolution of a marriage, even the strong legal position of a husband may be undercut by the economic and social forces available to his wife and her family.

During the course of a marriage a woman and her family will, therefore, try to balance their social and legal obligations with the demands that can be made on a husband in the hope of giving the wife the greatest degree of security possible under the circumstances. And the husband and his family, in turn, will seek to use their properties and relationships to maintain the husband's ability to exercise his legal powers without incurring a significant loss of money or personal independence. When divorce does occur, then, it is less because of a division of loyalties between one's family and one's spouse than because of the numerous tensions that develop from this constant personal struggle for economic, social or legal superiority.

The Moroccan government is itself aware of the fact that these tensions are at the root of the country's high divorce rate and it has tried to take certain legal steps to ease the situation. The law does, therefore, recognize the woman's right to demand that her husband find living quarters for the couple outside his parent's home and in an area sufficiently well populated with respectable people to enable the woman to call upon the necessary witnesses to substantiate any case she might bring alleging misconduct on the part of her husband. With full recognition that husbands may act without due consideration, in moments of great stress, the law also denies the husband the right to divorce his wife three times all at once. And, recognizing that fear of financial loss is the greatest dissuader of hasty action, the law also requires the husband make a "conciliatory payment" of unspecified amount to his wife upon divorcing her. But insofar as local courts generally fix this sum at roughly one-third of the registered brideprice with a ceiling of less than $100, it is clear that this relatively insignificant sum has not greatly affected divorce rates, though it may have increased the frequency with which a husband and wife use this payment in maneuvering for positions of greater strength in a marital dispute.

Consideration of the laws of divorce alone, then, give only a partial and truncated view of the nature of divorce as it is actually practiced in an Islamic state like Morocco. A woman's legal rights, though limited, can be supplemented with significant economic and social powers. This is so because of the maleability of various relationships each of which contains wide behavioral alternatives that can be developed into divers patterns.

Families Do Not Define Persons

But to say this means that we will have to reconsider certain features of contemporary sociological theory. For it would appear that one's inherent positions in this society do not define the whole person or the whole range of one's possible associations. Rather, one constantly uses both the ideal forms of behavior associated with any inherent position and the wide range of ambiguous behavior permitted within such role relations to establish ties centered on the individual and capable of being developed into a host of distinctive and often ephemeral associations. One cannot, as some present-day students of nonwestern legal processes do, argue with Sir Henry Maine that in such societies "all the relations of Persons are summed up in the relations of Family." The norm of behavior is not so rigidly fixed nor the sanctions on that behavior so narrowly confined that one cannot arrange certain ties with more distant kinsmen or outsiders in such a way as to place one in closer alliance with these persons than with the members of one's own immediate family. And one can also utilize these same contractual ties and manipulated alliances of kinsmen and others to strenghten one's own position in situations where one's legal rights may actually be rather limited.

Although the legal rights of women in many Islamic countries have been substantially increased in recent years, a true picture of the actual relations between husbands and wives—as well as an appreciation of the repercussions any changes in the law might have—requires a careful consideration of the social and economic means through which these legal powers are sustained, amended, or significantly undermined. The Moroccan case thus reflects not only the law and practice of divorce in one modern Islamic state but the dynamic interplay of family law and social structure characteristic of a number of the developing nations.

Rapid urbanization and industrialization throughout the world, with an accompanying growth in societal size and complexity, have introduced many changes into people's lives, but at uneven rates and with variations influenced by diverse factors. Some have remained where their ancestors lived for generations, while the environment changes around them: villages grow into towns and towns expand dramatically to become cities. Others have moved their families to a new location, in search of a job, a better way of life, a set of promised freedoms. Societal changes have brought the need for a different kind of population, for a nation of cosmopolites to replace the traditional structure of a small, educated elite controlling 95 percent of society's members; but education and socialization institutions have not been able to keep up with the demands. Although the middle classes have grown considerably, changing the rather flat social class pyramid (△) into a structure resembling a fat wine bottle (◁▷), the movement up from a peasant background has usually been accompanied by strains and major problems.

Nor is the status of most Americans, let alone that of people in other parts of the world, crystallized at any level. Elements of lower-class culture are woven into their lives with items of more middle-class style and even with some diffusions from the upper-class world. The hodgepodge does not add up to a consistent pattern. Profound changes, in the society at large, in the lives of different families and in the personality of each individual, have removed past sources of comfort and knowledge, of identity and cooperation, without providing viable alternatives.

Some groups or participants in the urban-industrial world have been particularly hard hit by the rapidity of social change. This section is devoted to the strains and problems created by it in the lives of those Americans. The villagers and the farmers who abandoned their way of doing things to move to a nearby city, across the

Part Two
Families in Transition

Courtesy Chicago Historical Society

45

nation, or even to societies with entirely different cultures, faced disorganization of their social world. Sometimes they were able to delay the process of acculturation and assimilation, with its inevitable stresses, by huddling together in communities with people from "back home" or "the old country." Ethnic communities emerged in all American cities, like the Italian *Urban Villagers* of Boston, described by sociologist Herbert Gans. W. I. Thomas and Florian Znaniecki studied *The Polish Peasant in Europe and America*, and Louis Wirth wrote about the Jews who created anew *The Ghetto*. Patterns of family life in these ethnic enclaves had many similarities. Much of what is true of the modern American family, its traits and problems, is understandable because most of our population consists of immigrants or of descendants of rural and agricultural lower-class European, Chinese, African, Mexican, Puerto Rican and other people who are trying to build completely new lives.

The early ethnic communities and those which still survive in urban ghettos arose during periods when many people followed the migration chains forged by early "pioneers" from their families and villages. Settlement in urban America was not random, but involved coming to stay with a friend or relative who helped the newcomer find a job or an apartment for his family, participation in the newly formed mutual-aid society which guaranteed a "nice funeral" in the strange land, membership in a church in which the language of the old country was spoken and so forth. The ethnic community developed its own stores and services, so that a Polish-American could (and some did) spend his or her whole life in "Polonia," without learning a word of English. If the size of the migrant group were large enough and its methods insulating itself from the dominant culture strong enough, it could perpetuate its culture, transmitted to the young with some changes due to new life circumstances, for generations. Jews and Chinese were the ethnic groups who were the most successful of all immigrant Americans in developing relatively self-sufficient communities, but the processes of change so dominant in American society have eroded even their self- and other-imposed social isolation. The forcible removal of the Japanese from their settlements and ways of life in this country during World War II, for example, contributed to the rapid Americanization of that group.

As the younger members of these communities of urban villagers started to leave their relatively homogeneous confines, they faced the very problems of disorganization which their forebears had tried to alleviate by creating such communities in the first place. Mass education, occupational choice and economic success have been utilized by youth as means of moving to new areas and starting new styles of life. Their personalities have undergone a corresponding change in one or several generations, with an intermediary period of being marginal men and women.

Moving away from the farm, the village, the small town, the ethnic neighborhood or the subcommunity within which relations and identities had been formed means a loss or modification of those relations and support systems (compare the situation of college graduates in the city-singles areas, in Part Three). As Oscar Lewis points out, in the essay immediately following, there is quite a difference between being surrounded by people who have known you from childhood, who developed a bond with your family even before you were born, who remain your neighbors and your teachers, who provide friends of your own age with whom you communicate easily and who offer interpersonal exchanges which treat you as a familiar person—and being a stranger in a new neighborhood of a rapidly urbanizing center. By the same token, social and geographical mobility can provide a new start in life. The migrant can leave behind the constraints of a tight little group with its preconceptions and demands for conformity. Mobility provides new choices and chances for establishing new personalities.

Thus, movement out of a prior life requires establishing oneself in a new one: coming into contact with new people and new ideas, being tested and testing, developing new actions and social relations. The ease with which this is done, and the consequences of a change in social roles or the creation of a new life style, depend to a great extent upon the competence of the mover and that of the people among whom he settles. The personality of the villager and that of the cosmopolitan member of the upper class are completely different. The upper classes of most Western European and American societies have settled in many places the world over, with resources and self-assurance, knowing that they will be able to change the environment or their own behavior sufficiently to prevent a restriction in their social life space. Even in relatively isolated situations they have retained a cosmopolitan interest and communication.

The villager, in contrast, often does not know how to convert strangers into acquaintances, and then into friends; to organize segmentalized roles into personality wholes; to maintain privacy, yet develop deep emotional attachments; to enjoy the resources of the modern world without feeling discouraged by a lack of skills in some sector of life. The urban scene requires expanded selves in a variety of societal dimensions. Unfortunately, most of the first, second and even later generations of migrants suffered in the process of introducing change in themselves and in their social relations, because of restrictions imposed on their abilities by their backgrounds. The point is not that mobility and urban life are of themselves difficult or "unnatural," as some observers of modern societies prejudicially claim, but that the ease of such experiences is dependent upon knowledge and skills developed through socialization and education aimed at identification with a large, complex and changing world.

Socialized by parents still rooted in village-like cultures, and lacking extensive formal education—in short, only partially prepared for the modern urban world—descendents of migrants often possess conflicting beliefs and habits of acting and relating which make many aspects of their lives difficult. Women want to be independent, yet protected from the consequences of decision-making. Upwardly mobile men want ethnic background memories, but not current identifications, even being ashamed of association with their less successful siblings. Both sexes want the warmth of an extended kinship group, yet resent its attempt to control their lives. Parents want their sons to be "successful" in the outside world, yet fear the very success that would remove the next generation from the close family group.

Thus the family in transition experiences myriad stresses, extending far deeper than the surface points at which the family interacts with society. Marian Morris points out that the women who undergo "psychological miscarriage" are incapable of coping with the demands of the mother role. They fear their own babies, whom they delivered in alienating circumstances and for whom they feel an overwhelming responsibility. Their rejection of their children involves lack of initiating interaction with the baby, inability to understand the child's needs and unwillingness to meet its demands. Feelings of incompetence and of being overwhelmed are particularly strong if there is no group to which the young mother can turn with confidence and expectations of acceptance. Morris' essay, as well as those by Richard Sennett which appear later in this Part, indicate that the modern family experiences serious problems as the result of its withdrawal from an extended family in favor of a privacy-stressing, isolated household during the difficult years when the child must be cared for and socialized.

The experiences of a person who becomes socialized into a world in which he or she can no longer satisfactorily function, for whatever reason, are also illustrated by Merwyn Garbarino's "Seminole Girl," except that this is a more unusual situation of reversed mobility. The girl moves away from her family of orientation and its community to become educated into a completely different culture. She internalizes its values and behavior patterns sufficiently to become really changed, unfit to interact satisfactorily with the people "back home." When she returns, she is judged as no longer acting "like a woman," so that she is rejected as a marital candidate, much as was the anthropologist living among the Eskimos, in Part One. The same type of community criticism was directed towards both women: they are bossy, mean, stubborn and they refuse to reformulate themselves so as to fit into the group, thus remaining strangers. Not even native Seminole birth can offset the effects of education into another culture or ease her strains in social relations.

People socialized into homogeneous and restricted communities often find it difficult to live in heterogeneous neighborhoods or cities. The growth of an urban center inevitably brings together not one, but many, different kinds of people who do not share similar styles of life and who are often feared by one another. The migrants have their problems, as already mentioned, but so do the already established residents who have only recently "made it" a few steps up the socioeconomic ladder. Richard Sennett shows how the fear of foreigners and of what goes on in city streets leads the new middle class to withdraw from the public world into the privacy of the home, preferably in a homogeneous neighborhood. His "Genteel Backlash: Chicago 1886" describes the fears and inadequacies of new lower middle-class families in late nineteenth-century industrial America. The "white backlash" of the "hardhats" is similar in that both sets of people are saying, "Leave us alone, we have made a life for ourselves. Those people 'out there' should be prevented from coming too close." This reaction to strangers—to alien people who try to live next door and who diminish hard-won achievements by their very presence, let alone by their actions—is one of high anxiety and self-protectiveness. The inadequate, uncrystallized socialization of the new middle class in a cosmopolitan urban center is evidenced more quietly by their withdrawal into a homogeneous, smaller suburb which isolates the resident from "those people." Sennett's second essay, "The Brutality of Modern Families," explains some of the factors which have pushed the new middle-class family into isolation in a homogeneous suburb. This author, however, decries the movement, believing it to be detrimental to the health of society and of the family which so isolates itself.

Thus, modern technology and an emphasis on the economic institution have created an urban sprawl and a voluntaristic society demanding the ability to achieve social roles and relations at a level deemed satisfactory by each person. Yet there are many evidences that the family institution and its assisting agencies such as the school have not yet changed sufficiently to help its members to enjoy all the new opportunities and resources. The rapidity of change has left the migrants, their more urbanized descendents and the still uncrystallized middle classes holding many peasant-like beliefs and anxieties, including a fear of strangers and of "the big city" outside their isolated homes.

Even the Saints Cry
Oscar Lewis

"You cannot take people out of an old-fashioned slum, where reality has been giving them a grim, distorted education for years, place them in a project, and expect them to exhibit all kinds of gentle, middle-class virtues."

Michael Harrington

This article describes the experiences of a young Puerto Rican mother, Cruz Rios, who moved from La Esmeralda—one of the oldest slums in San Juan only a short distance from the governor's palace—about four miles east to Villa Hermosa, a new government housing project in a middle-class section of Rio Piedras. Cruz' story illustrates the difficult problems of adjustment in her new environment and helps us understand why, in spite of the efforts of well-intentioned governments and the spending of huge sums of money on public housing, the positive effects hoped for by social planners are not always forthcoming.

When I began my study of Cruz in 1963, she was just 17 and living alone on relief with her two children. She lived in a small, dark, one-room apartment for which she paid a rental of eight dollars a month. Her kitchen was a tiny corner alcove equipped with a three-burner kerosene stove and a water faucet jutting out from the wall. She shared a run-down hall toilet with two other families and paid a neighbor $1.50 a month for the privilege of an extension cord which supplied her with electricity.

Cruz, a crippled, mulatto girl with reddish brown kinky hair and a pretty face, was lame since early childhood. She left school after the fifth grade, set up house with her sweetheart at 14 and gave birth to her first child at 15. Two years later, before the birth of her second child, she separated from her husband, Emilio, who refused to recognize the baby as his own.

49

Part I gives the reader a glimpse of living conditions in the slum; part II, recorded five months after Cruz had moved, gives her reactions to the housing project. (Names of all places and people in this tape-recorded narrative have been changed to guarantee the anonymity of the narrator.)

I

Here in La Esmeralda, the only thing that disturbs me are the rats. Lice, bedbugs, and rats have always been a problem in my room. When I moved in here a year ago, the first thing I found were little baby rats. "Kill them!" my friend Gloria said. *"Ay Bendito!* I can't do it. Poor little things—they look like children," I said, and I left them there in a hole. The next day they were gone. I didn't kill them, they just disappeared. I cleaned up the house and about a month later they were going back and forth through the room from one hole to another, with me just looking at them.

When Alejandro was living with me, more rats came because there was a hen with eggs under the house. A rat had given birth and had eaten some of the chicks.. The owner took the hen and 29 chicks out of there because there were baby rats underneath the hen too. The man threw them out but a week later they came back and were all over the place, even getting into the pan with the baby's milk and eating up whatever I left around.

One Sunday my *mamá* said, "Let's buy a rat trap and see if we can't get rid of some of them." Well, we tried it and that day between us and the next-door neighbor we caught 29 little rats. After a while, more came. Anita used to chase them across the room to see if she could catch them, and the boys who came to the house would say, "Look, a rat."

I would tell them, "Let it be, it's one of the family. They keep me company, now that I'm all by myself. I'm raising them for soup."

So I left them alone, but before I knew it, there were great big rats here. One Sunday I said to Catín, who had just eaten a breaded cutlet, "Catín, you'd better go bathe or the rats will eat you up." Then I forgot about it and she lay down. Later I took a bath and went to bed. About midnight, Catín screamed, *"Ay, ay, ay,* it bit me!" The first thing that came to my mind was that it was a snake or a scorpion. "What bit you?" I asked and when I turned on the light, she said, "Look, look!" and I could see a rat running away.

She had been bitten on the arm and I could see the little teeth marks. I squeezed out the blood and smeared urine and bay rum on it.

Then I said, "Catín, you'd better come into my bed with me. God knows whether it was because the crib is dirty or you are dirty." I was wearing only panties, Chuito and Anita were naked, but Catín was wearing a jacket and pants. Well, later that same rat came and bit her again on the other arm. I sprinkled bay rum all over the bed where she was sleeping and rubbed it on her and nothing else happened that night.

The next day I went to the church and told the Sister that the girl had been bitten by a rat. She told me that if Catín didn't start running a fever, to leave her alone, and if she did, to take her to the hospital. Then I said to Catín, "You see? That's what happens when you don't bathe." She took a bath every day after that.

At the end of the year, Anita got a rat bite on the lip. I squeezed it out for her and it dried up and she didn't get a fever or anything. A few days after that, I was sitting in a chair with my arm hanging down when a rat came and *pra!* it tried to take off my finger. It wanted human flesh. I lifted my hand, and the rat ran to a hole and disappeared.

Then I said to myself, "These rats have to be finished off. I can't live like this with so many blessed rats. There are more rats than people." And I bought a trap from the man next door. I fixed the bacon myself and put it in the trap. First I caught a real big rat, then another, and another. Three in all that same night. But there were still more left.

The next morning, I heard screams coming from Rosa Maria's room up above. I said, "Rosa, what's wrong?" Her little boy was crying and shaking his hand, with a rat hanging from it. "Kill it," I said, but he answered, "I can't. Its teeth are stuck in my finger." Finally he got if off by dragging it along the floor. Rosa Maria attended him but the next day the child had a fever which kept going up. The doctor said that the boy was getting tetanus and had to go to the hospital.

The people upstairs leave a lot of rotting clothes piled there, and cans of food and rice. If they don't get rid of that filth, the rats won't leave. I asked the landlord to cover the holes because the rats keep coming in and out as if they were in a bus terminal. He said he didn't live here and I should do it myself.

There are lots of cockroaches in my room too. And new fleas have come in, I don't know from where, except probably from the rats themselves. There are also crickets and lizards. These houses are hollow underneath, and below the floor there's a lot of old boards and filth and all kinds of garbage that has accumulated, and at night the animals come crawling up.

I've noticed that it's on Thursday nights that the rats give us the most trouble. Every other Thursday, before the social worker comes, I clean my house from top to bottom so there are no crumbs on the floor for the rats to eat and no dirty dishes for them to clean. I've learned that unless I leave something for them, the rats come closer and closer to us. When the house is clean, we are in more danger of getting bitten.

II

The social worker told me it would be a good idea to get the children out of La Esmeralda because there's so much delinquency there. My moving to the housing project was practically her idea; she insisted and insisted. Finally one day she came to me and said, "Tomorrow you have to move to the *caserío* in Villa Hermosa." I didn't want to upset her because she's been good to me, so I said okay.

You should have seen this place when I moved in. It was bursting with garbage and smelling of shit, pure shit. Imagine, when the social worker opened the door that first day, a breeze happened to blow her way. She stepped back and said, "Wait, I can't go in. This is barbarous." I had to go outside with her. I tell you, the people who lived here before me were dirtier than the dirtiest pig. When I moved out of my little room in La Esmeralda, I scrubbed it so clean you could have eaten off the floor. Whoever moved in could see that a decent person had lived there. And then I came here and found this pig-sty, and the place looked so big I felt too little and weak to get it clean. So, fool that I am, instead of sending out for a mop and getting right down to work, I just stood in a corner and cried. I locked the door and stayed in all day, weeping. I cried floods.

And this place isn't like La Esmeralda, you know, where there's so much liveliness and noise and something is always going on. Here you never see any movement on the street, not one little domino or card game or anything. The place is dead. People act as if they're angry or in mourning. Either they don't know how to live or they're afraid to. And yet it's full of shameless good-for-nothings. It's true what the proverb says, "May God deliver me from quiet places; I can defend myself in the wild ones."

Everything was so strange to me when I first moved here that I was scared to death. I hated to go out because it's hard to find your way back to this place even if you know the address. The first couple of times I got lost, and I didn't dare ask anybody the way for fear they would fall on me and beat me. If anyone knocked on my door I thought four times before deciding to open it. Then when I did, I took a knife along. But I'm not like that any more. I've made my decision: if someone wants to kill me, let him. I can't live shut in like that. And if anybody interferes with me it will be the worse for them. I have a couple of tricks up my sleeve and can really fuck things up for anybody when I want to.

After a few days, I finally started cleaning up the place. I scrubbed the floors and put everything in order. I even painted the whole apartment, although I had to fight tooth and nail with the man in charge of the buildings in order to get the paint. That old man wanted to get something from me in return, but I wouldn't give it to him. I never have been attracted to old men.

The apartment is a good one. I have a living room, bedroom, kitchen, porch and my own private bathroom. That's something I never had in La Esmeralda. I clean it every morning and when the children use it I go and pull the chain right away.

I never had a kitchen sink in La Esmeralda either, and here I have a brand new one. It's easy to wash the dishes in these double sinks because they're so wide and comfortable. The only trouble is the water, because sometimes it goes off and the electricity, too—three times since I've been here.

I still don't have an ice-box or refrigerator but the stove here is the first electric one I've ever had in my life. I didn't know how to light it the day I moved in. I tried everything I could think of, backward and forward. Luckily, the social worker came and she lit it for me, but even so I didn't learn and Nanda had to show me again that afternoon. She has worked for rich people so long that she knows all those things. I really miss my own little kerosene stove, but Nanda wanted it, so what could I do? She's my *mamá* and if she hankered after a star I would climb up to heaven to get it for her if I could.

The main advantage of the electric stove is that when I have a lot of work to do and it gets to be ten or eleven o'clock, I just connect the stove and have lunch ready in no time. In La Esmeralda I had to wait for the kerosene to light up well before I could even start to cook. And this stove doesn't smoke and leave soot all over the place, either. Still, if the power fails again or is cut off because I don't pay my bill, the kids will just have to go hungry. I won't even be able to heat a cup of milk for them. In

La Esmeralda, whenever I didn't have a quarter to buy a full gallon of kerosene, I got ten cents worth. But who's going to sell you five or ten cents worth of electricity?

I haven't seen any rats here, just one tiny little mouse. It doesn't bother me much because it lives down below, in a hole at the bottom of the stairs. There's no lack of company anywhere, I guess—rats in La Esmeralda and lots of little cockroaches here.

This apartment is so big that I don't have to knock myself out keeping it in order. There's plenty of room for my junk. I even have closets here, and lots of shelves. I have so many shelves and so few dishes that I have to put a dish here and a dish there just to keep each shelf from being completely empty. All the counters and things are no use at all to me, because I just cook a bit of oatmeal for the children and let them sit anywhere to eat it since I have no dishes with which to set a table. Half of my plates broke on the way from La Esmeralda. I guess they wanted to stay back there where they weren't so lonely.

Here even my saints cry! They look so sad. They think I am punishing them. This house is so big I had to separate the saints and hang them up in different places just to cover the empty walls. In La Esmeralda I kept them all together to form a little altar, and I lit candles for them. In La Esmeralda they helped me, but here I ask until I'm tired of asking and they don't help me at all. They are punishing me.

In La Esmeralda I never seemed to need as many things as here. I think it is because we all had about the same, so we didn't need any more. But here, when you go to other people's apartment and see all their things . . . It's not that I'm jealous. God forbid! I don't want anyone to have less than they have. It's only that I would like to have things of my own too.

What does bother me is the way people here come into my apartment and furnish the place with their mouths. They start saying, "Oh, here's where the set of furniture should go; you need a TV set in that corner and this one is just right for a record-player." And so on. I bite my tongue to keep from swearing at them because, damn it, I have good taste too. I know a TV set would look fine in that corner, but if I don't have the money to buy one, how can I put it there? That's what I like about La Esmeralda—if people there could help someone, they did; if not, they kept their mouths shut.

I really would like a TV though, because they don't have public sets here, the way they do in La Esmeralda. I filled in some blanks for that program, Queen for a Day, to see if I can get one as a gift. It was Nanda's idea and she's so lucky that maybe I will get it. If I do, then at least I could spend the holidays looking at TV. And the children might stay home instead of wandering around the neighborhood so much.

The traffic here really scares me. That's the main reason I don't like this place. Cars scud by like clouds in a high wind and, I'm telling you, I'm always afraid a car will hit the children. If something should happen to my little penguins, I'd go mad, I swear I would. My kids are little devils, and when I bring them in through the front door, they slip out again by climbing over the porch railing. Back in La Esmeralda, where our house was so small, they had to play out in the street whenever people came over, but here there is plenty of room to run around indoors.

Maybe I was better off in La Esmeralda. You certainly have to pay for the comforts you have here! Listen, I'm jittery, really nervous, because if you fail to pay the rent even once here, the following month you're thrown out. I hardly ever got behind on my payments in La Esmeralda, but if I did, I knew that they wouldn't put me out on the street. It's true that my rent is only $6.50 a month here while I paid $11.50 in La Esmeralda, but there I didn't have a water bill and I paid only $1.50 a month for electricity. Here I have already had to pay $3.50 for electricity and if I use more than the minimum they allow in water, I'll have to pay for that too. And I do so much washing!

It's a fact that as long as I lived in La Esmeralda I could always scare up some money, but here I'm always broke. I've gone as much as two days without eating. I don't play the races at El Comandante any more. I can't afford to. And I can't sell *bolita* numbers here because several cops live in this *caserío* and the place is full of detectives. Only the other day I almost sold a number to one of them, but luckily I was warned in time. I don't want to be arrested for anything in the world, not because I'm scared of being in jail but because of the children.

Since I can't sell numbers here, I sell Avon cosmetics. I like the pretty sets of china they give away, and I'm trying to sell a lot so that they'll give me one. But there's hardly any profit in it for me.

In La Esmeralda I could get an old man now and then to give me five dollars for sleeping with him. But here I haven't found anything like that at all. The truth is, if a man comes here and tries to strike up a conversation I usually slam the door in his face. So, well, I have this beautiful, clean apartment, but what good does it do me?

Where am I to get money? I can't dig for it.

In La Esmeralda we used to buy things cheap from thieves. They stole from people who lived far away and then they came to La Esmeralda through one of the side entrances to sell. And who the hell is going to go looking for his things down there? Not a chance! You hardly ever saw a rich person in La Esmeralda. We didn't like them, and we scared them off. But so far as I can tell, these dopes around here always steal from the *blanquitos,* the rich people, nearby. Suppose one of them took it into his head to come here to look for the missing stuff? What then?

Since I've moved I'm worse off than I have ever been before, because now I realize all the things I lack and, besides, the rich people around here are always wanting everything for themselves. In La Esmeralda you can bum a nickel from anyone. But with these people, the more they have, the more they want. It's everything for themselves. If you ask them for work, they'll find something for you to do fast enough, but when it's time to pay you'd think it hurt them to pull a dollar out of their pocket.

Listen, to get a few beans from some people who live in a house near here I had to help pick and shell them. People here are real hard and stingy. What's worse, they take advantage of you. The other day I ironed all day long for a woman and all I got for it was two dollars and my dinner. I felt like throwing the money in her face but I just calmly took it. I would have been paid six dollars at the very least for a whole day's ironing in La Esmeralda. At another lady's house near here I cooked, washed the dishes, even scrubbed the floor, and for all that she just gave me one of her old dresses, which I can't even wear because it's too big for me.

Right now, I don't have a cent. The lady next door lets me charge the food for breakfast at her husband's *kiosko.* She's become so fond of me, you can't imagine. Her husband won't sell on credit to anybody, but there's nothing impossible for the person who is really interested in helping you out. She trusts me, so she lets me write down what I take and keep the account myself.

I buy most of my food at the Villa Hermosa grocery. It's a long way from here and I have to walk it on foot every time I need something, like rice or tomato sauce. It's a supermarket, so they don't give credit, but everything is cheaper there, much cheaper. A can of tomato sauce costs seven cents there and 10 cents in La Esmeralda. Ten pounds of rice costs $1.25 in La Esmeralda and 99 cents here. The small bottles of King Pine that cost 15 cents each in La Esmeralda are two for a quarter here.

Sometimes Public Welfare gives me food, but not always, and I don't like most of the things they give. That long-grained rice doesn't taste like anything. It's like eating hay. The meat they give has fat on top and it comes in a can and it's real dark. They say it's corned beef but I don't know. The same goes for that powdered milk. Who could drink the stuff? In La Esmeralda I saved it until I was really hard up and then I sold it to anybody who was willing to shell out a quarter for it to feed it to their animals or something. But I don't dare do that here because it's federal government food, and it's against the law to sell it. I could get into trouble that way in a place like this, where I don't know anybody. I might try to sell that stuff to a detective without realizing who he was and I'd land in jail.

I haven't been to La Esmeralda often since I moved here, because I can't afford it. Every trip costs 40 cents, 20 cents each way. I want to pay off all my debts in La Esmeralda so that I can hold my head high and proud when I go there. I want people to think I've bettered myself because one can't be screwed all one's life. Even now when I visit, still owing money as I do, I put on my best clothes and always try to carry a little cash. I do this so Minerva, Emilio's aunt, won't get the idea I'm starving or anything like that. She really suffers when she sees me in La Esmeralda, and I do all that just to bother her. I dress up the kids real nice and take them to call on everybody except her.

When I first moved out of La Esmeralda, nobody knew that I was leaving, in the first place because it made me sad and in the second place because that old Minerva had gone around telling everybody she hoped I'd clear out. She even said it to my face. I'd yell back at her, "What right do you have to say that? Did you buy La Esmeralda or something?"

Another reason why I hardly ever go to La Esmeralda is because Emilio spies on me. He has come after me in the *caserío* just the way he did in La Esmeralda, though not as often. He likes to use the shower in my new apartment when he comes. When I start home after visiting La Esmeralda, he gets into his car and drives along behind me, offering to give me a lift. But, listen, I wouldn't get into that car even if I had to walk all the way from San Juan to Villa Hermosa. I put a curse on that car, such a tremendous curse that I'm just waiting to see it strike. I did it one day when Anita had asthma and I had no money to take her to the hospital. I happened to glance out of the window and I saw Emilio stretched out in his car, relaxed as could be, as if he deserved nothing but the best. I let go and yelled with all the breath in my chest, "I hope to God someday you'll wear that car as a hat. I hope it turns to dust with you all fucked up inside it." Now I can't ride in the car, because I'm afraid the curse will come true some time when both of us are in it.

You can't imagine how lonely I feel here. I have friends, but they're sort of artificial, pasted-on friends. I couldn't confide in them at all. For example, I got pregnant a little while ago, and I had to have an abortion. I nearly went crazy thinking about it. Having a baby is nothing, it's the burden you have to take on afterwards, especially with a cowardly husband like mine who takes the easiest way out, denying that the child is his. So there I was, pregnant and, you know, I was ashamed. I was already out of La Esmeralda, see? Well, I know that my womb is weak, so I took two doses of Epsom salts with quinine and out came the kid. You can't imagine how unpleasant that is. In La Esmeralda you can tell everybody about it, and that sort of eases your heart. But here I didn't tell anybody. These girls I know here are *señoritas,* mere children, and something like that . . . *ay, bendito!*

But, to tell you the truth, I don't know what they call a *señorita* here in Villa Hermosa. The way it is in La Esmeralda, a girl and boy fall in love. For a few months they control themselves. Then they can't any more, and the boy does what he has to do to the girl. The hole is bigger than the full moon and that's that. They tell everybody and become husband and wife in the eyes of all the world. There's no trying to hide it. But here you see girls, who by rights should already have had a couple of kids, trying to keep from being found out. They'll go to a hotel with their sweethearts and let them stick their pricks into every hole in their body except the right one. And then they're so brazen as to come out of that hotel claiming they're still *señoritas.* It's plain shameless.

There are some policemen here who make love like this to some girls I know. Well, the policeman who did it to my friend Mimi came and told me that if I loaned him my bed for a little while he would give me three pesos. As that money wouldn't be bad at all and as he wasn't going to do it to me, I rented him the bed and grabbed the three pesos. Let them go screw! They locked themselves in the bedroom for a little while and then they went away. It was none of my business. If they didn't do it here, they would go do it somewhere else. And she didn't lose her virginity or anything here. So my hands are clean.

Sometimes I want to go back to La Esmeralda to live and other times I don't. It's not that I miss my family so much. On the contrary, relatives can be very bothersome. But you do need them in case you get sick because then you can dump the children on them. Sometimes I cry for loneliness here. Sometimes I'm bored to death. There's more neighborliness in La Esmeralda. I was used to having good friends stop by my house all the time. I haven't seen much of this neighborhood because I never go out. There's a Catholic church nearby but I've never been there. And I haven't been to the movies once since I've been living here. In La Esmeralda I used to go now and then. And in La Esmeralda, when nothing else was going on, you could at least hear the sea.

In La Esmeralda nobody ever made fun of my lameness. On the contrary, it was an advantage because everyone went out of his way to help me: "Let me help the lame girl. Let me buy *bolita* numbers from Lame Crucita, because cripples bring luck." But it isn't like that here, where people just laugh. That's why I'd like to live in La Esmeralda again or have Nanda move in here with me.

The social worker told me that I could go to the hospital and have an operation to fix my back. But who could I leave my little baby crows with? And suppose what they do is take my guts out in order to make me look right? Still, now that I live in a place like Villa Hermosa, I would like to have an operation to make me straight.

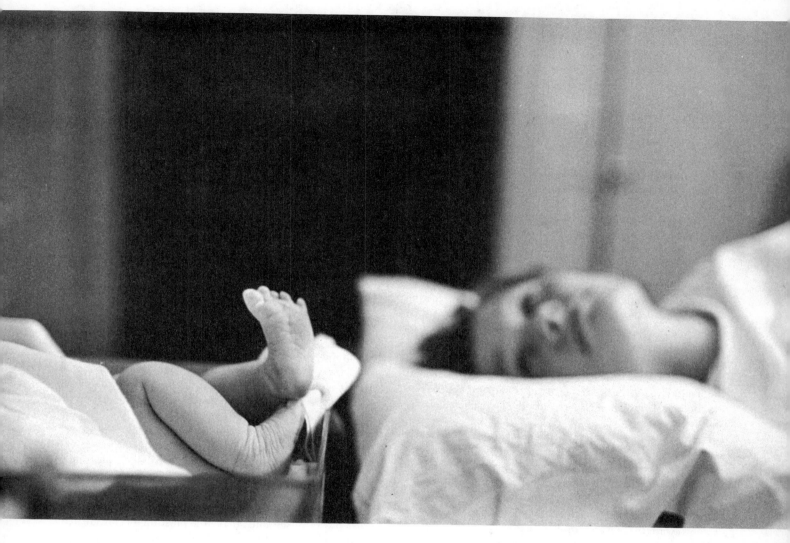

Psychological Miscarriage
An End to Mother Love

Marian Gennaria Morris

Not long ago a mother in the Midwest, while giving her baby its bath, held its head underwater until it drowned. She said that there was something wrong with the child. Its smell was strange and unpleasant; it drooled; it seemed dull and listless. It reminded her of a retarded relative, and the thought of having to spend the rest of her life caring for such a person terrified her. Her husband was out of work, and she was pregnant again. She said she "felt the walls closing in." When, in her confused and ignorant way, she had asked her husband, a neighbor, and a doctor for help, she got promises, preachments, and evasions. So she drowned the baby.

This mother said she had felt "so all alone." But, unfortunately, she had plenty of company. Many thousands of American women do not love or want their babies. Although few actually kill their infants, the crippling effects of early maternal rejection on children can hardly be exaggerated—or glossed over. The number directly involved is large. The social harm, for everybody, is great. An idea of the size of the problem can be gained from the following figures, taken from federal, state, and local sources:

> 50-70,000 children neglected, battered, exploited annually;
> 150,000 children in foster homes for these reasons;
> over 300,000 children in foster care altogether;
> 8 to 10 percent of all school children in one twenty-county study in need of psychiatric examination and some type of treatment for their problems.

But even these figures can hardly begin to describe the violence, deprivation, and dehumanization involved.

Recently we concluded a study of thirty rejecting mothers and their children, who can serve as examples. Our findings are supported by a number of other studies of parents and their children who have various physical and psychological disorders. Although the poor are hardest hit by family and emotional problems it should be noted that the majority of these families were not poverty-stricken. Psychological miscarriage of motherhood attacks all classes and levels.

Twenty-one of the thirty mothers demonstrated clearly from the time of delivery that they could not properly mother or care for their babies—could not even meet their basic needs. Yet no one who had had contact with them—neither doctors, nurses, nor social workers—had apparently been able to help, effectively, any one of them, nor even seemed aware that severe problems existed.

The entire population of mothers was characterized by old troubles and hopelessness, stretching back to the previous generation—and in one-third of the cases, back to the third generation. Half the children were illegitimate, or conceived before marriage. Sixty percent of the families had been in juvenile, criminal or domestic courts at some earlier time. Two-thirds of the children were either first-borns, or first-borns of their sex—and lack of experience with children increased their mothers' insecurities.

All thirty children needed intensive psychiatric treatment. Only two of the thirty were "well" enough—from homes that were "stable" enough—for out-patient care to even be considered. The remaining twenty-eight were headed for institutions. Their prognoses are grave, their chances doubtful. They will cost us a great deal in the years to come

and their problems will be with us a long time. Some will never walk the streets as free men and women.

Actually, the children were so disturbed that they could not be diagnosed with great accuracy. For instance, it was impossible to tell how intelligent most really were because they were in such emotional turmoil that they could not function properly on tests, and seemed retarded. A fifth of them had been so beaten around the head that it is quite possible their brains were damaged. (One baby had been thrown across the room and allowed to stay where it fell.) Women who feel neglected and less than human in turn neglect their children and treat them as less than human.

FEAR AND REALITY

In our supposedly interdependent society, we are close together in violence, but apathetic to each other's needs. But apathy to their needs constitutes a violence to women facing labor, delivery, and the early and bewildering adjustments of motherhood. And it is in these days and weeks that psychological miscarriage occurs.

During pregnancy, labor, and delivery the basic fears of childhood—mutilation, abandonment, and loss of love—are vividly revived for a woman, and with double force—for herself and the baby. Nor are these fears simply fantasies: mothers *are* frequently cut, torn, and injured, babies *are* born with congenital defects.

The entire pregnancy period, with its lowering of defenses, makes the mother more capable of loving and feeling for her baby. But whether she finds his needs pleasing or threatening depends on what happened to her in the past, and the support she gets in the present.

After delivery, still in physical and emotional stress, under great pressure, she must make the most important, difficult adjustments of all. She must "claim" her baby. That is, she must make it, emotionally, part of herself again; identify it with the qualities and values in herself and her life that she finds good, safe, reassuring, and rewarding. After all the dreams and fears of pregnancy, she now must face and cope with the reality—the baby and his needs. If she miscarries now and rejects the child as something bad that cannot be accepted, then the child cannot grow to be normal. Nor can its society be normal, since the mothers must hand down to each generation the values by which society survives.

In older days, when most women had their babies at home, these adjustments were made in familiar surroundings, with such family support as was available. Now they are made largely in the hospital. What actually happens to mothers in today's hospitals?

Childbirth, once a magnificent shared experience, has increasingly become a technical event. Administrative and physical needs get priority. Emotional needs and personalities tend to get in the way of efficiency. Administrators and medical personnel, like everyone else, respond most readily to those pressures which affect them. Since they are in charge, they pass them down to the patient, whether they help the patient or not.

The mothers of the poor in particular arrive faceless, knowing no one on the ward, with little personal, human contact from before birth until they leave. Increasingly, they arrive already in labor, so that the hospitals cannot turn them away. They also come at this late stage so that they can avoid the constant procession of doctors and the three and four-hour clinic waits, during which they are called "mother" because their names have been lost in the impersonal clinic protocols. In the wards, they may be referred to simply by their bed numbers.

Birth itself may be subordinated to the schedule: some doctors schedule their deliveries, and induce labor to keep them on time. Even "natural" labor may be slowed down or speeded up by drugs for convenience.

A PUBLIC EVENT

Mothers say that they are allowed little dignity or modesty. Doctors strange to them may, and do, examine them intimately, with little attempt at privacy. They say that without their permission they are often used as live lecture material, giving birth before interested audiences of young interns and students while the obstetrician meticulously describes each step and tissue. How apathetic we have become to the routine dehumanization of mothers is well illustrated by the story of an upper-middle-class woman I know. She was in labor, almost hidden by drapes preparatory to vaginal examination, light flooding her perineum (but not her face). Approached by a nurse and gloved physician she suddenly sat up in her short-tailed hospital gown and said, "I don't know who *you* are, doctor, but *I* am Mrs. Mullahy." Good for Mrs. Mullahy! She has a strong sense of personal identity, and is determined to preserve it.

Mothers say they are isolated and humiliated. They say that in addition to their own anxieties they must worry about what their doctors think, and be careful to please and propitiate the staff members, who may have power of life and death over them and their babies.

They say that they are kept in stirrups for hours—shackled in what reduces them to something sub-human—yet afraid to complain.

Is it increasingly true, as mothers say, that babies are not presented to them for from four to twelve hours after birth? Social histories show that prompt presentation is necessary for the mental health of the mothers; studies of other mammals indicate that such delay interrupts mothering impulses and may bring on rejection of the young. Is this happening to human mothers and babies? How necessary, medically, is such a delay? Is it worth the price?

Many women become deeply depressed after childbirth. Is this at least partly a reaction to hospital experiences? Is it an early distress signal of psychological miscarriage? There is very little research that attempts to assess early maternal adaptation, and we need such research badly. Are the violent mothers, so brutal to their children, violent at least in part because of our faceless and impersonal birth practices? Clinical studies show that the less sense of identity and personal worth a mother has, the more easily she displaces her aggressions onto others—*any* others. Are we scapegoating our children?

STAKING A CLAIM

To a mother, the birth of her baby is not a technical event. It starts in intimate contact with the father, and has deep roots in her feelings for and relationship with him, whether positive or negative. It reflects her personality, her state of maturity, the experiences of her most intimate anxieties and special hopes, and her associations with the adults who have had most influence on her. She enters the hospital prey to childhood insecurities, and stripped alike of defenses and clothes. Attitudes and cues from the hospital personnel, and from others, strongly affect her self-respect and her feelings about her own and her baby's worth.

It is difficult to observe most normal claiming behavior in a hospital. But some of it can be observed. Most mothers, for example, do find ways to make contact with their babies' bodies—touching and examining them all over delightedly, even to the tiny spaces between fingers and toes—cooing and listening to them, inhaling their odors, nuzzling and kissing them.

Socially, a major way to claim a child is to name it. Names suggest protective good magic; they establish identity and suggest personality; they emphasize masculinity or femininity; they affirm family continuity and the child's place in it.

Nevertheless, it is usually difficult to follow claiming behavior for two reasons. First, because hospital routines and tasks interfere. To the staff, the process of mothers becoming acquainted with infants is seen as merely cute, amusing, or inconvenient. Babies are presented briefly, pinned and blanketed tightly, making intimate fondling—for women who have carried these infants for months—difficult and sometimes even guilt-producing.

The second reason is related to the nature of normal motherhood. The well-adjusted mother is secure within herself, content to confine her communications mostly to her baby, rather than project them outward. As Tolstoy said of marriage, all happy ones tend to be happy in the same way, and relatively quiet. But the unhappy ones are different and dramatic—and it is by observing unhappy mothers that the pathological breakdown of maternal claiming can be most easily traced.

Let us consider a few examples:

Tim—Breakdown in Early Infancy

When Tim's mother first felt him move in her, and realized then that all evasion and doubt about her pregnancy was past, she blacked out (she said) and fell down a flight of stairs.

Tim was her second child. Her first pregnancy was difficult and lonely and, she had been told, both she and the baby had almost died during delivery. She suffered from migraine headaches, and was terrified of a second delivery.

For the first four months of Tim's life, she complained that he had virulent diarrhea and an ugly odor, and took him from doctor to doctor. Assured by each one that there was nothing wrong with the child (in the hospital the diarrhea cleared up in one day), she took this to mean that there was something wrong with *her*—so she sought another doctor. She took out thirteen different kinds of cancer insurance on Tim.

During an interview, she told a woman social worker that it was too bad that doctors could not look inside a baby and know he was *all* O.K.

The social worker decided to probe deeper: "You would have a hard time convincing me that you *deliberately* threw yourself down those stairs."

"Who, me? Why I told my mother all along that I would never *willingly* hurt a hair of one of my children's heads."

But suppose you had, unwillingly. Would you blame someone else for doing it, under the circumstances?"

"No! I was sick and don't even know how it happened."

After that, the demon that had haunted her was in the open, and recovery began. She had felt that she was both criminal and victim, with the child as the instrument of her punishment. (Only a "good" mother deserves a good baby;

a "bad" mother deserves a "bad"—damaged or sick—baby.) The implied criticisms of her mother and doctor had aggravated these feelings. She identified Tim not with the good in her but the "evil"—he was something faulty, something to be shunned.

Under treatment she learned to accept herself and re-own her role of mother. She was not really the bad little girl her critical mother and doctor had implied; neither, therefore, was Tim bad—she could accept him. It was no longer dangerous to identify with her. She let Tim see her face; she held him comfortably for the first time; she did not mention his "ugly" smell; she stayed by his bed instead of restlessly patrolling the corridors. She referred to our hospital as the place she had "got him *at*." instead of the hospital, ninety miles away, where he had actually been born.

Jack—Effects on an Older Child

Shortly after Jack was born, his mother asked her obstetrician whether Jack's head was all right. Gently touching the forceps marks, he said, "*These* will clear up." Thinking that she had been told delicately that she had a defective child, she did not talk to Jack for five-and-a-half years—did not believe he could understand speech.

At five-and-a-half, approaching school, he had never spoken. A psychologist, thinking that the child was not essentially retarded, referred the mother to a child guidance clinic, where the social worker asked whether she had ever found out if the obstetrician had meant the *inside* of Jack's head. For the first time in all the years it occurred to her that there might have been a misunderstanding. Three months later Jack was talking—though many more months of treatment were still necessary before he could function adequately for his age.

Behind this, of course, was much more than a misunderstanding. Behind it was Jack's mother's feelings of guilt for having caused her own mother's death. Guilt went back many years. During an auto ride long ago, she had an accident in which her mother suffered a mild blow on the head. In the early months of pregnancy with Jack, she had found her mother dead in the tub. The cause was cancer, which had nothing to do with the bump. But deep down she could not believe this, and she developed the fear that Jack's head, too, was damaged—a fitting punishment for a woman who feared she had killed her mother. When her obstetrician seemed to confirm it, she did not question further.

For almost six years Jack was not so much an infant or

child as a damaged head. Like her mother he was silent—from "brain injury." It was only under treatment that she accepted the possibility that she might have "misunderstood."

Babs—Hell Revisited

Babs was fourteen months old when she was flown to our hospital from South America, physically ill with diarrhea and dehydration, and emotionally badly withdrawn. In South America, her mother had trouble getting proper drugs and talking effectively with Spanish-speaking doctors—and when she had had to face Babs' pleading eyes with little relief to offer, she had gone into acute panic. She hadn't been able to comfort her child, but had drawn away and could hardly look at her or touch her. From this rejection Babs had in turn withdrawn, and a mutual vicious cycle of rebuff and retreat had come about.

The mother felt that she had lived through all this before in her own childhood. When she was five, she had had a little brother, aged three. Her sick mother often left him in her charge. ("He was *my* baby.") One day both ate sprayed peaches from a tree. Both came down with severe diarrhea. She survived. She remembers vividly seeing him in "his little white coffin."

The pregnancy period with Babs had been stormy, full of family crises; she felt guilty about "not feeding Babs right." She could not accept the reassurances of her obstetrician. After Babs was born she was over-meticulous about cleaning her after bowel movements.

During treatment she shook visibly when asked whether Babs resembled her in any way. But when asked: "Could you have been Jim's *real* mother when you were only five?" she relaxed, and grew radiant. Later she said: "I know *now* that I couldn't have known that the peaches were poisoned."

"Nor that Babs would get sick with diarrhea if you went to South America to live with your husband?"

"No. I know now that the *place* is not good for any of us. I didn't know that before."

In a few days she was admiring in Babs the very qualities she had said she admired in herself—her sense of fun, and her determination. The positive identification between them had been made.

MOTHERS AS PATIENTS

How can we prevent such psychological miscarriages—and how can we limit their ravages once they have already occurred?

The dynamics of maternal rejection are not completely known—we need far more research, far more detailed and orderly observation of each maternal behavior. Nevertheless, enough is known already about the symptoms (detailed in the box) for us to be able to work up a reliable profile of the kind of woman who is most likely to suffer damage, and to take steps to make sure that help is offered in time. After all, the ultimate cause of maladaptation is lack of human sympathy, contact, and support, even though the roots may go back for more than one generation. We must, therefore, offer that support. We may not be able completely to heal old, festering wounds, but we can palliate their worst effects, and keep them from infecting new babies.

Mothers in our study identified the periods of greatest danger as just before and after delivery. It is then—and swiftly—that intervention by a psychiatric team should occur. What can be done?

> We must have early recognition of trouble. Early signs of maternal maladaptation are evident in the mutual aversion of mother and child. But these signs have to be watched for—they cannot be ignored because of hospital routine that is "more important."
>
> Let the mother have enough time to see and become acquainted with the hospital personnel with whom she will experience birth. Length of hospital stay is geared to technical requirements—five days for middle-class mothers, down (in some places) to twenty-four hours or less for the poor. Therefore, acquaintance should start before birth, at least with the physician, so that when delivery comes the mother will not be faced with a stranger in cap and gown, but a human being she already knows. Nurses and social workers should also be included. (The Hahnemann Medical College and Hospital in Philadelphia already assigns resident physicians to the pre-natal clinics to provide this continuity.)
>
> Mothers of young infants suffer from geographical and psychological isolation. Services should work toward reducing both of these isolations. Ideally such services should come from a team, including not only the doctor and nurses, but a sympathetic pediatrician, psychiatric and medical social workers, of both sexes, who could also act as substitute parents. This help should be as available to the middle-class as to the poor (middle-class patients are sometimes denied hospital social services).
>
> Help should carry over into home care. *Make sure that each mother has someone to care for her at home.* After their too brief hospital stay, poverty-stricken women, many without husband or family, are often

Patterns of Rejection

There are several criteria that can be used to assess the adequacy of a mother's behavior during the early weeks of an infant's life. Mother-infant unity can be said to be *satisfactory* when a mother can:

find pleasure in her infant and in tasks for and with him;

understand his emotional states and comfort him;

read his cues for new experience, sense his fatigue points.

Examples: she can receive his eye contact with pleasure; can promote his new learnings through use of her face, hands and objects; does not overstimulate him for her own pleasure.

In contrast, there are specific signs that mothers give when they are *not adapting* to their infants:

See their infants as ugly or unattractive.

Perceive the odor of their infants as revolting.

Are disgusted by their drooling and sucking sounds.

Become upset by vomiting, but seem fascinated by it.

Are revolted by any of the infants' body fluids which touch them, or which they touch.

Show annoyance at having to clean up infants' stools.

Become preoccupied with the odor, consistency and numbers of infants' stools.

Let infants' heads dangle, without support or concern.

Hold infants away from their own bodies.

Pick up infants without warning by touch or speech.

Juggle and play with infants, roughly, after feeding, even though they often vomit at this behavior.

Think infants' natural motor activity is unnatural.

Worry about infants' relaxation following feeding.

Avoid eye contact with infants, or stare fixedly into their eyes.

Do not coo or talk with infants.

Think that their infants do not love them.

Believe their infants expose them as unlovable, unloving parents.

Think of their infants as judging them and their efforts as an adult would.

Perceive their infants' natural dependent needs as dangerous.

Fear death at appearance of mild diarrhea or cold.

Are convinced that infants have defects, in spite of repeated physical examinations which prove negative.

Often fear that infants have diseases connecting with "eating": leukemia, or one of the other malignancies; diabetes; cystic fibrosis.

Constantly demand reassurance that no defect or disease exists, cannot believe relieving facts when they are given.

Demand that feared defects be found and relieved.

Cannot find in their infants any physical or psychological attribute which they value in themselves.

Cannot discriminate between infant signals of hunger, fatigue, need for soothing or stimulating speech, comforting body contact, or for eye contact.

Develop inappropriate responses to infant needs: over or under-feed; over or under-hold; tickle or bounce the baby when he is fatigued; talk too much, too little, and at the wrong time; force eye contact, or refuse it; leave infant alone in room; leave infant in noisy room and ignore him.

Develop paradoxical attitudes and behaviors.

---

more helpless and lost at home than in the hospital.

Mothers should not be left alone for long periods, whether under sedation or not. Schedules should and must be modified to allow them to have normal family support as long as possible. If they have none, substitutes—volunteers—should be found. Isolated mothers, cut off from support or even contact with their physicians, and treated as objects, much too often displace their loneliness, depression, resentment, bitterness, humiliation, rage, and pain onto their babies.

Get rid of the stirrups—and the practice of using them to hang mothers' legs in the air for hours! Find some other way to hold women on the delivery table until the last moments. Women often spend months recovering from backaches caused by stirrups.

Present the baby as soon as possible. The most frequent comment from mothers who remain conscious in the delivery room is, "The doctor gave him to me." This is psychologically very sound; when the father-image (doctor) presents the baby with the obvious approval of the mother-image (nurse), latent feelings of guilt about having a baby and about the acceptability of the baby—and of motherhood—are lulled and dispelled. Too often, however, the nurse is cast, or casts herself, in the role of unwilling, stingy, critical giver of the baby—in fact the whole institution lends itself to this. Presentation should precede and not depend on feeding; it should be made gladly and willingly; it should allow time and ease of access for the mother to examine her baby's body.

Doctors, nurses, and aides should understand and come to know pregnancy, labor, delivery, and early growth as a continuing process, rather than in bits and pieces, a series of techniques. They need to understand and see it from the mothers' viewpoint, as well as in terms of bottles, diapers, rooms, instruments, and procedures.

Reassure mothers about their infants. This includes understanding the real meanings of their questions. If a mother continually discounts good reports, rejection may be underway, and psychological miscarriage imminent.

First-born children, and the first-borns of each sex, are the ones most commonly rejected; their mothers need special care—as do the mothers of the poor and those without family, husband, or outside human supports.

None of these proposals are radical—even administratively.

Most are quite simple, and could be done directly in the wards and the private rooms.

Overall, we need more research. We do not know enough about the earliest signals of psychological miscarriage; we have not trained ourselves, nor taken the trouble, to watch for these early signs. Nor do we know enough about the long-term effects of maladaptation. Are the older children completely lost? Is the process irreversible? Cannot something be done to bring them back to productive life?

There is nothing more important in a maternity pavilion, nor in a home, then the experiences with which life begins. We must stop the dehumanization of mothers. We must give all children a chance for life.

Seminole
Girl
Merwyn S. Garbarino

ONE HUNDRED and thirty miles of circuitous road and 250 years of history separate the city of Miami from the four federal reservations that lock the Seminole Indians into the Florida swamplands known as Big Cypress Swamp. A new road is under construction that will trim in half the traveling distance between the city and the reservations scattered along the present winding U.S. Highway 41 or Tamiami Trail as it is called by the Indians. But the new road will only draw the two communities closer on the speedometer; it will not alter the vastly different lifeways it links; it may only make more apparent the historical inequities that brought the two areas into existence.

• • •

SOMEWHERE along the Tamiami Trail, Nellie Greene —a pseudonym of course—was born a Seminole, raised in a chickee, and learned the ways of her people. Her father was a frog hunter and could neither read nor write; her mother was a good Seminole mother who later had troubles with tuberculosis and drinking. No one Nellie knew had much more education than her father and mother. Yet, despite the ignorance and illiteracy on the reservation, Nellie Greene wanted and was encouraged to get a good education. As it does for most Indians in the United States, this meant leaving her "backward" people, mixing with whites who at best patronized her.

I first met Nellie Greene when she had graduated from college and was living in an apartment in Miami where she worked as a bank clerk. I knew her background from having spent three summers in the middle sixties, thanks to the National Science Foundation, on the Seminole res-

ervations of Florida. In September of 1966 Nellie wrote me that she had been offered a job as manager in the grocery store back on the reservation. If she didn't take it, a white person would, for she was the only native with the necessary knowledge of bookkeeping. She had accepted the job, she said, but since she had once told me (in Miami) that she could never give up the kind of life she had grown accustomed to there, I was curious to find out why she had returned to the reservation.

She herself said that she took the job to help her people, but she added that it had not been an easy decision; in fact it had been quite a struggle. I could have guessed that this was so; many Indian tribes that offer educational grants to their younger members do so only with the stipulation that the recipients later return to the reservation. The stipulation is a measure of the difficulty in getting their educated members to come back to the tribe. In any event, I wanted to hear Nellie Greene tell her own story. I went to see her, and this is what she told me.

Nellie Greene's Story

I was born in a Miami hospital on February 6, 1943. At that time my parents were living on the (Tamiami) Trail, and my daddy was making his living frog hunting. He owned an air boat and everything that goes along with frog hunting. It was during the war, and at that time I guess it was hard to get gas. When it was time for me to be born, my father had to borrow gas from a farmer to get to Miami. But the tail light was broken, so my father took a flashlight and put a red cloth over it and tied it on to the truck and went to the hospital. My daddy often told me about that.

I had an older sister and an older brother. We lived in a chickee until 1961 when my daddy bought a CBS (a cement block structure, "hurricane proof" according to state standards) at Big Cypress, and we moved into it. When I was little, my daddy had to be out in the Everglades a lot, so he would take all of us out to a hummock, and we would make camp there and stay there while he went off to hunt for frogs. When he got back, he'd take the frog legs into the hotels and sell them. Then he would bring back something for each of us. When he would ask us what we wanted, I always asked for chocolate candy.

About all I remember of the Everglades is that it was a custom when you got up to take a bath or go swimming early in the morning. My mother says they always had to chase me because I didn't like to get wet in winter when it was cold. We were there four or five years, and then we moved near .the Agency at Dania (renamed Hollywood in 1966). I had never been to school until then. We were taught at home, the traditional things: to share with each other and with children of other families, to eat after the others—father and grandfather first, then mothers and kids. But lots of times us kids would climb up on our father's knees while they were eating. They didn't say anything, and they'd give us something. It just wasn't the custom for families to eat the way we do today, everybody sitting together around the table.

Folktales, too, we learned; they were like education for us, you know. The stories told about someone doing something bad, and then something bad happened to him. That was the way of teaching right and wrong.

When we were growing up we broke away from some family customs. My parents spanked us, for instance, not my mother's brother, who would have been the right person to punish his sister's children—one of the old ways. But they were not close to my mother's family because my daddy was a frog hunter, and we wandered around with him. My parents were chosen for each other by their families. I guess they learned to love each other in some ways, but I have heard my mother say that it is not the same kind of love she would have had if she had chosen her own husband. It was respect, and that was the custom of the Indians.

Most parents here show so little affection. Even if they love their kids, maybe they don't think they should show love. I know a lot of parents who really care, but they don't tell their kids how they feel. We always knew how our parents felt about us. They showed us affection. Sometimes I hear kids say, "My mother doesn't care whether I go to school or not." These kids have seen how others get care from their parents, like the white children at school. And that kind of concern doesn't show up here. A lot of parents don't even think of telling their children that they want them to succeed. They don't communicate with their children. You never see an Indian mother here kiss and hug children going to school. But white parents do that, and when Indian children see this in town or on TV, it makes them think that Indian parents just don't care. Kids are just left to go to school or not as they wish. Often the mothers have already left to work in the fields before the school bus comes. So no one sees whether children even go to school.

I felt loved. My parents never neglected us. We have never gone without food or clothes or a home. I have always adored my mother. She has made her mistakes, but I still feel the same about her as when I was a child.

We moved to Big Cypress around 1951 or 1952. I had been in first grade at Dania. I remember I didn't understand English at all when I started first grade. I learned it then. We moved around between Big Cypress and Dania, visiting, or because my father was doing odd jobs here and there.

Both my parents wanted me to go to school because they had wanted to go to school when they were kids. I can remember my mother telling me that she and her sister wanted to go to school. But the clan elders—their uncles—wouldn't let them. The uncles said they would whip the two girls if they went.

One of my father's greatest desires was to go to school when he was a boy. He said that he used to sneak papers and pencils into the camp so that he could write the things he saw on the cardboard boxes that the groceries came in, and figures and words on canned goods. He thought he would learn to read and write by copying these things. My daddy adds columns of figures from left to right, and he subtracts the same way. His answers will be correct, but I don't know how. Almost everything he knows he learned on his own. He can understand English, but he stutters when he talks. He has a difficult time finding the right word when he speaks English, but he understands it.

When my parents said no, they meant no. That was important to me. They could be counted on. The other thing that was important in my childhood schooling was that my daddy always looked at my report card when I brought it home from school. He didn't really know what it meant, and he couldn't read, but he always looked at my report card and made me feel that he cared how I did in school. Other parents didn't do this. In fact, most of the kids never showed their parents their report cards. But my daddy made me feel that it was important to him. I told him what the marks stood for. It was rewarding for me because he took the time.

"Nothing for Me to Do"

Public school was hard compared to what I'd had before, day school on the reservation and a year at Sequoyah Government School. I almost flunked eighth grade at the public school, and it was a miracle that I passed. I just didn't know a lot of things, mathematics and stuff. I survived it somehow. I don't know how, but I did. The man who was head of the department of education at the Agency was the only person outside of my family who helped me and encouraged me to get an education. He understood and really helped me with many things I didn't know about. For a long time the white public school for the Big Cypress area would not let Indian children attend. A boy and I were the first Big Cypress Indians to graduate from that school. He is now in the armed forces.

After I graduated from high school I went to business college, because in high school I didn't take courses that would prepare me for the university. I realized that there was nothing for me to do. I had no training. All I could do was go back to the reservation. I thought maybe I'd go to Haskell Institute, but my mother was in a TB hospital, and I didn't want to go too far away. I did want to go on to school and find some job and work. So the director of education said maybe he could work something out for me so I could go to school down here. I thought bookkeeping would be good because I had had that in high school and loved it. So I enrolled in the business college, but my English was so bad that I had an awful time. I had to take three extra months of English courses. But that helped me. I never did understand why my English was so bad—whether it was my fault or the English I had in high school. I thought I got by in high school; they never told me that my English was so inferior, but it was not good enough for college. It was *terrible* having to attend special classes.

"I Learned How to Dress"

At college the hardest thing was not loneliness but schoolwork itself. I had a roommate from Brighton (one of the three reservations), so I had someone to talk to. The landlady was awfully suspicious at first. We were Indians, you know. She would go through our apartment, and if we hadn't done the dishes, she washed them. We didn't like that. But then she learned to trust us.

College was so fast for me. Everyone knew so much more. It was as though I had never been to school before. As soon as I got home, I started studying. I read assignments both before and after the lectures. I read them before so I could understand what the professor was saying, and I read them again afterwards because he talked so fast. I was never sure I understood.

In college they dressed differently from high school, and I didn't know anything about that. I learned how to dress. For the first six weeks, though, I never went anywhere. I stayed home and studied. It was hard—real hard. (I can imagine what a real university would be like.) And it was so different. If you didn't turn in your work, that was just your tough luck. No one kept at me the way they did in high school. They didn't say, "OK, I'll give you another week."

Gradually I started making friends. I guess some of them thought I was different. One boy asked me what part of India I was from. He didn't even know there were Indians in Florida. I said, "I'm an American." Things like that are kind of hard. I couldn't see my family often, but in a way that was helpful because I had to learn to adjust to my new environment. Nobody could help me but myself.

Well, I graduated and went down to the bank. The president of the bank had called the agency and said he would like to employ a qualified Indian girl. So I went down there and they gave me a test, and I was interviewed. And then they told me to come in the following Monday. That's how I went to work. I finished college May 29, and I went to work June 1. I worked there for three years.

In the fall of 1966, my father and the president of the Tribal Board asked me to come back to Big Cypress to manage a new economic enterprise there. It seemed like a dream come true, because I could not go back to live at Big Cypress without a job there. But it was not an easy decision. I liked my bank work. You might say I had fallen in love with banking. But all my life I had wanted to do something to help my people, and I could do that only by leaving my bank job in Miami. Being the person I am, I had to go back. I would have felt guilty if I had a chance to help and I didn't. But I told my daddy that I couldn't give him an answer right away, and I knew he was upset because he had expected me to jump at the chance to come back. He did understand though, that I had to think about it. He knew when I went to live off the reservation that I had had a pretty hard time, getting used to a job, getting used to people. He knew I had accomplished a lot, and it wasn't easy for me to give it up. But that's how I felt. I had to think. At one time it seemed to me that I could never go back to reservation life.

But then really, through it all, I always wished there was something, even the smallest thing, that I could do for my people. Maybe I'm helping now. But I can see that I may get tired of it in a year, or even less. But right now I'm glad to help build up the store. If it didn't work out, if the store failed, and I thought I hadn't even tried, I would really feel bad. The basic thing about my feeling is that my brothers and sisters and nieces and nephews can build later on in the future only through the foundation their parents and I build. Maybe Indian parents don't always show their affection, but they have taught us that, even though we have a problem, we are still supposed to help one another. And that is what I am trying to do. Even when we were kids, if we had something and other kids didn't, we must share what we had with the others. Kids grow up the way their parents train them.

By the age of nine, girls were expected to take complete care of younger children. I too had to take care of my little brother and sister. I grew up fast. That's just what parents expected. Now teen-agers don't want to do that, so they get angry and take off. Headstart and nurseries help the working mothers because older children don't tend the little ones any more. The old ways are changing, and I hope to help some of the people, particularly girls about my age, change to something good.

There are people on the reservation who don't seem to like me. Maybe they are jealous, but I don't know why. I know they resent me somehow. When I used to come in from school or from work back to the reservation, I could tell some people felt like this. I don't think that I have ever, ever, even in the smallest way, tried to prove myself better or more knowing than other people. I have two close friends here, so I don't feel too lonely; but other people my age do not make friends with me. I miss my sister, and I miss my roommate from Miami. My two friends here are good friends. I can tell them anything I want. I can talk to them. That's important, that I can talk to them. That's what I look for in a friend, not their education, but for enjoyment of the same things, and under-

standing. But there are only two of them. I have not been able to find other friends.

The old people think I know everything because I've been to school. They think it is a good thing for us to go to school. But the old people don't have the kind of experience which allows them to understand our problems. They think that it is easy somehow to come back here. They think there is nothing else. They do not understand that there are things I miss on the outside. They do not understand enough to be friends. They are kind, and they are glad that I am educated, but they do not understand my problems. They do not understand loneliness.

It was hard for me to get used again to the way people talk. They have nothing interesting to talk about. They are satisfied to have a TV or radio, but they don't know anything about good books or good movies or the news. There is almost no one I have to talk to about things like that. Here people don't know what discussion is. That's something I found really hard. They gossip: they talk about people, not ideas.

And it was hard getting used to what people think about time. You know, when you live in the city and work, everything is according to time. You race yourself to death, really. But I got used to that and put myself on a schedule. But here, when you want something done, people take their time. They don't come to work when they should, and I just don't want to push them. I would expect it of the older people, but the younger generation should realize how important time is. When you go to school, you just eat and study and go to school, and not worry too much about time; but on a job, you must keep pace. You are being paid for a certain performance. If you do not do what you are supposed to, you do not get paid. But how do I get that across to my people?

"I Don't Know Why . . ."

I was lonely when I first came back here. I was ready to pack up and go back to Miami. People hardly talked to me —just a few words. I don't know why. I've known these people all my life. I don't know why they didn't know me after just three years. I couldn't carry on a conversation with anyone except my own family. I was working all day at the store, and then I had nothing to do but clean the house, or go fishing alone, or with someone from my family.

Coming back to the reservation to live did not seem to be physically hard. At first I lived in a house with a girl friend because I did not want to stay with my family. I wanted to be sure of my independence. I think this hurt my father. But later, when more of my friend's family moved back to the reservation, I decided it was too crowded with her and went back to live in my old home with my father and family. My father's CBS is clean and comfortable. It is as nice as an apartment in Miami.

My idea was that, being raised on the reservation and knowing the problems here, I could hope that the Indian girls would come to me and ask about what they could do after they finished high school: what they could do on the reservation, what jobs they could get off the reservation. I hoped they would discuss their problems with me, what their goals should be. I'd be more than happy to talk with them. But I can't go to them and tell them what to do. Just because I've worked outside for three years doesn't give me the right to plan for other people. But I thought I had something to offer the girls here, if only they would come for advice.

"They Say I'm Mean . . ."

I would like to see the financial records at the store so well kept that an accountant could come in at any time and check the books, and they would be in perfect order. It is difficult because only Louise and I can run the store, and if either of us gets sick, the other one has to be at the store from 7 AM to 9 PM, or else close the store. At first I had to be very patient with Louise and explain everything to her. She had no training at all. Sometimes I started to get mad when I explained and explained, but then I'd remember that she can't help it. People do not know some of the things I know, and I must not get irritated. But if things go wrong, I am responsible, and it is a big responsibility. The younger people are not exactly lazy; they just don't know how to work. I want them to work and be on time. If they need time off, they should tell me, not just go away or not appear on some days.

So some of them start calling me bossy. But that is my responsibility. I tried to talk to them and tell them why I wanted them to come to work on time, but still they didn't. I want them to realize that they have to work to earn their money. It is not a gift. They were supposed to do something in return for their wages. They are interested in boys at their age, and that's why they aren't good workers. But still, the National Youth Corps, operating in Big Cypress, gives kids some idea of how it is to work, to have a job. If I don't make them do the job, they're really not earning their money. That is one thing I had to face. I know that they are going to say I'm mean and bossy. I ex-

pect that. But if I'm in charge, they're going to do what they're supposed to do. That's the way I look at it. Everybody talks here. I know that, but I've been away, and I can take it.

I think people my own age are jealous. It is not shyness. Before I left, they were all friendly to me. I came back, and they all look at me, but when I go to talk to them, they just turn around, and it is so hard for me. They answer me, but they don't answer like they used to, and talk to me. That has been my main problem. It is hard for someone to come back, but if he is strong enough, you know, he can go ahead and take that. Maybe some day people will understand. There is no reason to come back if you really think you are better than the people. They are wrong if that is what they believe about me. There is not enough money here, and if I didn't really care about the people, then I would have no reason to return.

I am worried about my mother, and I want to stay where I can help her (my parents are now divorced). It is best to come back and act like the other people, dress like they dress, try to be a part of them again. So even if a person didn't have kinfolk here, if he wanted to help, he could. But he must not show off or try to appear better.

If I didn't have a family here, it would be almost like going to live with strangers. I have to work now. It has become a part of my life. People here just don't understand that. I can't just sit around or visit and do nothing. If there were no work here, I could not live here. It would be so hard for me to live the way the women here do, sewing all the time or working in the fields, but if I had to take care of my family and there was nothing else to do, I guess I would stay here for that. My aunt has taught me to do the traditional sewing, and how to make the dolls, so I could earn money doing that; but I wouldn't do it unless I had to stay here to take care of my family.

I think the reason almost all the educated Indians are girls is because a woman's life here on the reservation is harder than the man's. The women have to take all the responsibility for everything. To go to school and get a job is really easier for a woman than staying on the reservation. The men on the reservation can just lay around all day and go hunting. They can work for a little while on the plantations if they need a little money. But the women have to worry about the children. If the women go away and get jobs, then the men have to take responsibility.

A woman and a man should have about the same amount of education when they marry. That means there is no one at Big Cypress I can marry. The boys my age here do not have anything in common with me. If a girl marries an outsider, she has to move away, because the Tribal Council has voted that no white man can live on the reservation. A woman probably would miss the closeness of her family on the reservation. I would want to come back and visit, but I think I could marry out and make it successful. I would expect to meet and know his family. I would like to live near our families, if possible. I will always feel close to my family.

"I Think About the City . . ."

Sometimes I think about the city and all the things to do there. Then I remember my mother and how she is weak and needs someone who will watch over her and help her. You know my mother drinks a lot. She is sick, and the doctors want her to stop; but she herself cannot control her drinking. Well, I guess us kids have shut our eyes, hoping things will get better by themselves. I know you have not heard this before, and I wish I was not the one to tell you this sad story, but my move back to the reservation was partly brought on because of this. She has been to a sanitarium where they help people like her. It has helped her already to know that I want to see her get help and be a better person. I am having a chickee built for her, and I must stay here until she is well enough to manage alone.

ECONOMIC opportunity has been severely limited on the reservation until recently. Employment for field hands or driving farm machinery has been available on ranches in the area, but the income is seasonal. Both men and women work at crafts. The products are sold either privately or through the Arts and Crafts Store at the tribal agency on the coast but the income is inadequate by itself. Some of the men and one or two Indian women own cattle, but none of these sources of income would appeal to a person with higher education. Until the opening of the grocery store, there was no job on the reservation which really required literacy, let alone a diploma.

Examining these possibilities and the words of Nellie Greere, what would entice an educated Indian to come back to work and live on the reservation? A good paying job; a high status as an educated or skilled person; to be back in a familiar, friendly community; a desire to be with his family and to help them. Perhaps for the rare individual, an earnest wish to try to help his own people. But income from a job on the reservation must allow a standard of living not too much lower than that previously enjoyed as a member of outer society. Nellie never gave any consideration to returning to the reservation until there was the possibility of a job that challenged her skills and promised a comparable income. The salary she receives from managing the store is close to what she had made at the bank in Miami. In Miami, however, she worked 40 hours a week, while on the reservation she works nearly 60 hours a week for approximately the same pay, because there are no trained personnel to share the responsibility. Given the isolation of Big Cypress, there is not enough time, after she has put in her hours at the store, to go anywhere off the reservation. It is not merely a question of total pay; it is a problem of access to a way of life unattainable on the reservation. Economic opportunity alone is not sufficient.

It is quite apparent from Nellie's interviews and from observation of the interaction between Nellie and other Indians, both in the store and elsewhere on the reservation, that her status is very low. Her position appears to vary: from some slight recognition that her training places her in a category by herself, to distinct jealousy, to apparent puzzlement on the part of some of the old folks as to just what her place in the society is. Through the whole gamut of reaction to Nellie, only her proud family considers her status a high one.

The primary reason Nellie gave for returning to the reservation was to help her people, but the reservation inhabitants did not indicate that they viewed her activities or presence as beneficial to them. Older Indians, both male and female, stated that it was "right" that she returned because Indians should stay together, not because she might help her people or set an example to inspire young Indians who might otherwise be tempted to drop out of school. Younger people regard her as bossy and trying to act "white." She does not even have the status of a marriageable female. There is no Indian man on the reservation with the sort of background that would make him a desirable marriage partner, from her standpoint; in their traditional view of an ideal wife, she does not display the qualities preferred by the men. At the same time, there is a council ordinance which prohibits white men from living on the reservation, and therefore marriage to a white man would mean that she would have to leave the reservation to live. There is no recognized status of "career woman," educated Indian, or marriageable girl, or any traditional status for her.

Obviously, with an inferior status, it is unlikely that a person would perceive the community as a friendly, familiar environment. From the point of view of the reservation people, who have had contacts with her, she is no longer truly "Indian," but rather someone who has taken over so much of the Anglo-American ways as to have lost her identity as an Indian woman. Nearly all of Nellie's close acquaintances are living off the reservation. The only two girls she considers friends on the reservation are, like herself, young women with more than average contact with outside society, although with less formal education.

Nellie may have rationalized her decision to return by stressing her determination to help the people, but her personal concern for her mother probably influenced her decision to return more than she herself realized. Nellie was the only person in the family who had the ability, knowledge and willingness to see that her mother received the proper supervision and help.

THE BUREAU of Indian Affairs is attempting to increase the economic opportunities on the reservations, but I believe their efforts at holding back the "brain drain" of educated Indians will not be effective. Retraining the reservation people who do not have an education is certainly desirable. But, as the story of Nellie Greene points out, it takes more than good pay and rewarding work to keep the educated Indians down on the reservations. If the educated Indian expects to find status with his people, he is going to be disappointed. White people outside are apt to pay more attention to an educated Seminole than his own Indian society will. If the Indian returns from college and expects to find warm personal relationships with persons of his own or opposite sex, he is going to find little empathy, some distrust and jealousy because of his training and experiences outside the reservation. For Nellie Greene there was a personal goal, helping her sick mother. She was lucky to find a job that required her skills as an educated person, and which paid her as well as the bank at Miami. Her other goal, to help her own people, was thwarted rather than helped by her college education.

A bomb exploded in Chicago's Haymarket Square on May 4, 1886, killing seven people and setting off what may have been the first police riot in that city's history. The neighborhood in which this violence broke out was hardly what one would call a high crime area today. The quiet residential district adjacent to the Haymarket was considered so nondescript, so ordinary, that it had never even been given a special name. Richer and poorer neighborhoods had names; Union Park, as I shall call it here, was anonymous, like most other middle- and lower middle-class communities in the industrial cities of nineteenth century America.

The people of Union Park were the forgotten men of that era, neither poor enough to be rebels like the Socialist workingmen who assembled that day in Haymarket Square, nor affluent enough to count in the affairs of the city. For a quarter of the century, from 1865 to 1890, Union Park epitomized that tawdry respectability of native-born, lower middle-class Americans that Dreiser was to capture in *Sister Carrie,* or that Farrell would later rediscover in the bourgeois life of Catholic Chicago.

The beginnings of Union Park, when Chicago was a commercial town rather than a diverse manufacturing city, were much grander. In the 1830s and 1840s it was a fashionable western suburb, separated by open land from the bustle of the business district and the noisome unhealthy river at the heart of the city. Then, in the years after the Civil War, a change in the pattern of commercial land investment, the filling in of a swamp on the edge of Lake Michigan by Potter Palmer and the growth of a manufacturing district to the south of Union Park led fashionable people to desert the old suburb for newer, more magnificent residences along the lake shore of Chicago. In their place, in the 1870s, came people of much lesser means, seeking a respectable place to live where rents and land were becoming cheap. Union Park for these new people was a neighborhood where they could enjoy the prestige of a once-fashionable address, and even pretend to be a little grander than they were. "The social Brooklyn of Chicago," Mayor Harrison called it; "a place where modest women become immodest in their pretentions," wrote another contemporary observer. For 25 years the old holdings were gradually divided up into little plots, and native-born Americans—who were the bulk of the migrants to the cities of the Midwest before the 1880s—rented small brick houses or a half floor in one of the converted mansions.

Genteel Backlash
Chicago 1886

Richard Sennett

It was here, in this modest, cheerless community, that a series of unexpected events took place in the late 1880s, beginning with the bloody encounter between police and workingmen in nearby Haymarket Square. That riot was followed 18 months later by a series of highly expert robberies in the community, a crime wave that culminated in the murder of a leading Union Park resident. The striking feature of all this violence lay not in the events themselves but in the reaction of shopkeepers, store clerks, accountants and highly skilled laborers to the disorder suddenly rampant among their sedate homes. Their reaction to the violence was impassioned to an extent that in retrospect seems unwarranted by events; the character of their reaction will,

PROCLAMATION

TO THE PEOPLE OF CHICAGO:

MAYOR'S OFFICE, Chicago, May 5, 1886.

WHEREAS, Great excitement exists among the people of this good city, growing out of the **LABOR TROUBLES**, which excitement is intensified by the open defiance of the guardians of the peace by a body of lawless men, who, under the pretense of aiding the laboring men, are really endeavoring to destroy all law. And Whereas, last night these men, by the use of weapons never resorted to in **CIVILIZED LANDS, EXCEPT IN TIMES OF WAR or for REVOLUTIONARY PURPOSES, CAUSED GREAT BLOODSHED AMONG CITIZENS AND AMONG OFFICERS of the MUNICIPALITY** who were simply in the performance of their duties. And Whereas, the **CITY AUTHORITIES PROPOSE TO PROTECT LIFE AND PROPERTY AT ALL HAZARDS,** and in doing so will be compelled to break up all unlawful or dangerous gatherings; and

WHEREAS, Even when men propose to meet for lawful purposes, bad men will attempt to mingle with them, armed with cowardly missiles, for the purpose of bringing about bloodshed, thus endangering innocent persons;

THEREFORE, I, Carter H. Harrison,

MAYOR OF THE CITY OF CHICAGO, DO HEREBY PROCLAIM THAT GATHERINGS OF PEOPLE IN CROWDS OR PROCESSIONS IN THE STREETS and PUBLIC PLACES OF THE CITY ARE DANGEROUS AND CANNOT BE PERMITTED, AND ORDERS HAVE BEEN ISSUED TO THE POLICE TO PREVENT ALL SUCH GATHERINGS and TO BREAK UP and DISPERSE ALL CROWDS, TO PREVENT INJURY TO INNOCENT PERSONS.

I urge all law-abiding people to quietly attend to their own affairs, and not to meet in crowds. If the police order any gatherings to disperse, and they be not obeyed, all persons so disobeying will be treated as law-breakers, and will surely incur the penalty of their disobedience.

I further assure the good people of Chicago that I believe the police can protect their lives and property and the good name of Chicago, and WILL do so.

CARTER H. HARRISON, Mayor.

The ____ & JEFFERY Printing and Engraving Co. Chicago

however, seem familiar to students of urban backlash in our own time. The forgotten men of Union Park responded to violence by holding a whole class—the poor, and especially the immigrant poor—responsible for the course of these violent eruptions. For a modern observer, the puzzle is what made them react this way.

The Haymarket Bombing

Certain people, mostly foreigners of brief residence among us, whose ideas of government were derived from their experience in despotic Germany, sought by means of violence and murder to inaugurate a carnival of crime. *F. H. Head, official orator at the unveiling of the Haymarket Square Statue for policemen slain in the riot, reported in the* Chicago Daily Tribune, *May 31, 1889.*

Chicago's haymarket constituted the dividing line between the residences and neighborhood stores of Union Park and the warehouses of the growing central city. Haymarket Square itself was enclosed by large buildings and the Des Plaines Street Police Station was just off the Square. It was hardly a place to engage in clandestine activity, but, for a peaceful meeting, the Square was an ideal forum, since it could accommodate roughly 20,000 people.

The common notion of what happened on May 4, 1886, is that a group of labor unionists assembled in Haymarket Square to listen to speeches and that, when the police moved in to break up the meeting, someone in the crowd

Despite the call to arms posted by the Socialists (right) the turnout at the Haymarket was meager. But following the riot, police Captain Schaak (opposite) kept "respectable" people's fears alive with lurid stories of other "anarchist" plots.

threw a bomb, killing and wounding many policemen and bystanders. This account is true as far as it goes, but explains little of what determined the event's effect on the community and city in the aftermath.

The people who came to the meeting were the elite of the working class, those who belonged to the most skilled crafts; they were hardly the "dregs" of society. The crowd itself was small, although it had been supposed that events in Chicago during the preceding days would have drawn a large gathering. On May 3, demonstrations had been organized in the southwestern part of the city against the McCormick Works, where a lockout of some union members had occurred. The police had responded with brutal force to disperse the crowd. Later that same night, at a number of prescheduled union meetings, it was resolved to hold a mass meeting at some neutral place in the city.

A small group of Socialist union leaders, led by August Spies and Albert Parsons, decided the time was ripe for a mass uprising of laboring men; the moment seemed perfect for an expression of labor solidarity, when large numbers of people might be expected to rally to the cause as Spies and Parsons understood it—the growth of Socialist power. Haymarket Square was the obvious choice for a neutral site. Posters were printed in the early hours of the next day and spread throughout the city.

When Parsons and Spies mounted the speakers' rostrum the next night in Haymarket Square, they must have been appalled. Instead of vast crowds of militants, there were only a thousand or so people in the Square, and as speaker after speaker took his turn the crowd dwindled steadily. The audience was silent and unmoved as the explanations of the workers' role in socialism were expounded, though there was respect for the speakers of the kind one would feel for a friend whose opinions grew out of a different sphere of life. Yet as the meeting was about to die out, a phalanx of policemen suddenly appeared on the scene to disperse the crowd.

Why the police intruded is the beginning of the puzzle we have to understand. Their reaction was totally inappropriate to the character of what was occurring before their eyes; they ought rather to have breathed a sigh of relief that the meeting was such a peaceful fiasco. But, as the civil riots of a later chapter in Chicago's history show, it is sometimes more difficult for the police to "cool off" than it is for the demonstrators. In any event, just as the Haymarket meeting was falling apart, the police moved in to disperse it by force, and thus brought back to life the temporary spirit of unity and of outrage against the violence at McCormick Works that had drawn the crowd and orators together.

The knots of men moved back from the lines of police advancing toward the speaker's stand, so that the police gained the area in front of the rostrum without incident. Then, suddenly, someone in the crowd threw a powerful bomb into the midst of the policemen, and pandemonium broke loose. The wounded police and people in the crowd dragged themselves or were carried into the hallways of buildings in the eastern end of Union Park; drugstores, like Ebert's at Madison and Halstead and Barker's on West Madison, suddenly became hospitals with bleeding men stretched out on the floors, while police combed the residences and grounds of Union Park looking for wounded members of the crowd who had managed to find shelter under stoops or in sheds from the police guns booming in the Square.

As the news spread, small riots with aimless energy broke out in the southwestern part of the city, but they were soon dispersed. By the morning of May 5, the working-class quarters were quiet, though the police were not. They, and the middle-class people of Chicago, especially those living in Union Park, were in a fever, a fever compounded of fear, a desire for vengeance, and simple bewilderment.

REVENGE!

Workingmen, to Arms!!!

Your masters sent out their bloodhounds — the police —; they killed six of your brothers at McCormicks this afternoon. They killed the poor wretches, because they, like you, had the courage to disobey the supreme will of your bosses. They killed them, because they dared ask for the shortenin of the hours of toil. They killed them to show you, "Free American Citizens", that you must be satisfied and contended with whatever your bosses condescend to allow you, or you will get killed!

You have for years endured the most abject humiliations; you have for years suffered unmeasurable iniquities; you have worked yourself to death; you have endured the pangs of want and hunger; your Children you have sacrificed to the factory-lords — in short: You have been miserable and obedient slave all these years: Why? To satisfy the insatiable greed, to fill the coffers of your lazy thieving master? When you ask them now to lessen your burden, he sends his bloodhounds out to shoot you, kill you!

If you are men, if you are the sons of your grand sires, who have shed their blood to free you, then you will rise in your might, Hercules, and destroy the hideous monster that seeks to destroy you. To arms we call you, to arms!

Your Brothers.

Rache! Rache!

Arbeiter, zu den Waffen!

Arbeitendes Volk, heute Nachmittag mordeten die Bluthunde Eurer Ausbeuter 6 Eurer Brüder draußen bei McCormick's. Warum mordeten sie dieselben? Weil sie den Muth hatten, mit dem Loos unzufrieden zu sein, welches Eure Ausbeuter ihnen beschieden haben. Sie forderten Brod, man antwortete ihnen mit Blei, eingedenk der Thatsache, daß man damit das Volk am wirksamsten zum Schweigen bringen kann! Viele, viele Jahre habt Ihr alle Demüthigungen ohne Widerspruch ertragen, habt Euch vom frühen Morgen bis zum späten Abend geschunden, habt Entbehrungen jeder Art ertragen, habt Eure Kinder selbst geopfert — Alles, um die Schatzkammern Euer Herren zu füllen, Alles für sie! Und jetzt, wo Ihr vor sie hintretet, und sie ersucht, Eure Bürde etwas zu erleichtern, da hetzen sie zum Dank für Eure Opfer ihre Bluthunde, die Polizei, auf Euch, um Euch mit Bleikugeln von der Unzufriedenheit zu kuriren Sklaven, wir fragen und beschwören Euch bei Allem, was Euch heilig und werth ist, rächt diesen scheußlichen Mord, den man heute an Euren Brüdern beging, und vielleicht morgen schon an Euch begeben wird. Arbeitendes Volk, Herkules, Du bist am Scheideweg angelangt. Wofür entscheidest Du Dich? Für Sklaverei und Hunger, oder für Freiheit und Brod? Entscheidest Du Dich für das Letztere, dann säume keinen Augenblick; dann, Volk, zu den Waffen! Vernichtung den menschlichen Bestien, die sich Deine Herrscher nennen! Rücksichtslose Vernichtung ihnen — das muß Deine Losung sein! Denk' der Helden, deren Blut den Weg zum Fortschritt, zur Freiheit und zur Menschlichkeit gebahnt — und strebe, ihre würdig zu werden!

Eure Brüder.

It is this reaction that must be explored to gauge the true impact of the Haymarket incident on the Union Park community. The first characteristic of this reaction was how swiftly an interpretation, communally shared, was formed; the middle-class people of Union Park, and elsewhere in Chicago, were immediately moved by the incident to draw a clearly defined picture of what had happened, and they held onto their interpretation tenaciously. Today it is easy to recognize, from the location of the meeting next to a police station, from the apathy of the crowd, from the sequence of events that preceded the bombing, that the Haymarket incident was not a planned sequence of disorder or a riot by an enraged mob, but rather the work of an isolated man, someone who might have thrown the bomb no matter who was there. But the day after the bombing, these objective considerations were not the reality "respectable" people perceived. Middle-class people of Chicago believed instead that "the immigrant anarchists" were spilling out of the slums to kill the police, in order to destroy the security of the middle classes themselves. "Respectable" people felt some kind of need to believe in the enormity of the threat, and in this way the community quickly arrived at a common interpretation of what had happened.

The enormity of the threat was itself the second characteristic of their reaction. The color red, which was taken as a revolutionary incitement, was "cut out of street advertisements and replaced with a less suggestive color." On the day after the riot a coroner's jury returned a verdict that all prisoners in the hands of the police were guilty of murder, because Socialism as such led to murderous anarchy, and anyone who attended the meeting must have been a Socialist. Yet this same jury observed that it was "troublesome" that none of those detained could be determined to have thrown the bomb. Anarchism itself was generalized to a more sweeping scope by its identification with foreign birth; the "agitators" were poor foreigners, and this fact could explain their lawlessness. For example, the *Tribune* reported that on the day after the Haymarket Riot police closed two saloons

that were the headquarters of the foreign-speaking population, which flaunts and marches under the red flag, and heretofore they were the centers of a great throng of men who did little but drink beer and attend the meetings in the halls above.

On May 5 and 6, the police were engaged in a strenuous effort to determine where the "anarchist" groups lived, so that the population as a whole might be controlled. On May 7, and this was the view to prevail henceforth, they announced that the residences of most anarchists must be in the southwestern portion of the city, the immigrant, working-class area.

In Union Park the assigning of the responsible parties to the general category of "foreigner" excited even more panic. The *Tribune* of May 7 reported that the community was gripped by a fear that lawless marauders would again erupt out of the proletarian sector of the city and terrorize people in the neighborhood of the riot. These fears were sustained by two events in the next week.

First were reports of the deaths, day after day, of policemen and innocent bystanders who had been seriously wounded by the bomb on May 4, coupled with a massive newspaper campaign to raise money for the families of the victims. Second, and by far more important, fear of renewed bombing was kept alive by the fantasies of a Captain Schaack of the Chicago police who day by day discovered and foiled anarchist plots, plans to bomb churches and homes, attempts on the lives of eminent citizens. Such were the scare stories with which the middle-class people of Chicago horrified themselves for weeks.

The same deep communal force that immediately led the people of Union Park to interpret an objectively confused event in a very similar and very simplistic fashion also led them to use increasingly horrific metaphors to describe the nature of the threat and challenge. But as events a year later were to show, this force also prevented the men of Union Park from being able to deal effectively with the future violence.

Crime in the Streets

On Thursday, February 9, 1888, the *Chicago Tribune* gave its lead space to the following story:

Amos J. Snell, a millionaire who lived at the corner of Washington Boulevard and Ada Street, was shot to death by two burglars who entered his house and made off with $1,600 worth of county warrants and $5,000 in checks. The murder was committed at about 2 A.M. and discovered by a servant at about 6:30 A.M.

Snell had been a resident of the area since 1867, when he built a home in Union Park and bought up many blocks of desirable real estate around it.

The murder of Snell climaxed a tense situation in Union Park that had existed since the beginning of the year 1888. Since New Year's Day, "between forty and fifty burglaries

have been committed within a radius of half a mile from the intersection of Adams and Ashland Avenues," the editor of the *Tribune* wrote the day after Snell's death. Though the police counted half this number, it appears that the burglars had a simple and systematic scheme: to loot any household goods, such as furs, silver plate, jewelry or bonds left in unlocked drawers. Occasionally some of the property was recovered, and occasionally a thief was arrested who seemed to have been involved, but the operation itself was remarkably smooth and successful.

How did people in Union Park react to these burglaries, and what did they do to try to stop them? The reaction of the community was much like their reaction to the Haymarket bombing: they felt caught up at once in a "reign of terror," as the *Tribune* said, "that was none of their doing —they didn't know when the danger would strike again or who would be hurt. Most of all, they didn't know how to stop it." Once again, community fear was escalated to a general, sweeping and impersonal terror.

Before the Snell murder, the citizens of the community had tried two means of foiling the robbers, and so of quieting the fears of their families. One was to make reports to the police, reports which the editor of the *Tribune* claimed the police did not heed. The citizens then resorted to fortifying their homes, to hiring elderly men as private guards but the thieves were professional enough to deal with this: "somehow or other the burglars evaded all the precautions that were taken to prevent their nocturnal visits."

The Neighborhood as Garrison State

The Snell murder brought public discussion of the robberies, and how to stop them, to a high pitch. Especially in Union Park, the vicinity of Snell's residence, the community was "so aroused that the people talked of little else than vigilance committees and frequent holdings of court . . . as a panacea for the lawless era that had come upon them." Gradually, the small-town vigilante idea gave way to a new attitude toward the police, and how the police should operate in a large city. "It is no use," said one member of the Grant Club, the West Side club to which Snell himself had belonged, "to attempt to run a cosmopolitan city as you would run a New England village." He meant that the police had up to that time concentrated on closing down gambling houses and beer parlors as a major part of their effort to keep the town "respectable" and "proper." Thus they didn't deal effectively with serious crimes like robbery and murder because they spent too much time trying to clean up petty offenses; the main thing was to keep the criminal elements confined to their own quarters in the city. In all these discussions, the fact of being burglarized had been forgotten. The search turned to a means of separatism, of protection against the threatening "otherness" of the populace outside the community.

Such views were striking, considering the position of Union Park. The community's own physical character, in its parks and playgrounds, was nonurban, designed in the traditions of Olmstead and Vaux; the people, as was pointed out repeatedly in the newspaper account, were themselves among the most respectable and staid, if not the most fashionable in the city. Yet here were the most respectable among the respectable arguing for abandoning the enforcement of a common morality throughout the city. The petty criminals outside the community's borders ought to be left in peace, but out of sight. Union Park existed in a milieu too cosmopolitan for every act of the lower classes to be controlled; the police ought to abandon attempts to be the guardians of all morality and instead concentrate on assuring the basic security of the citizens against outbursts of major crime.

What Union Park wanted instead, and what it got, was a garrison of police to make the community riotproof and crimeproof. For the police did indeed abandon the search for the killers, and concentrated on holding the security of Union Park, like an area under siege. In this way, the original totally suburban tone of the parks and mansions was transformed; this respectable neighborhood felt its own existence to be so threatened that only rigid barriers, enforced by a semimilitary state of curfew and surveillance, would permit it to continue functioning.

The characteristics of their reaction to violence could only lead to such a voluntary isolation: everyone "knew" immediately what was wrong; and what was wrong was overwhelming: it was nothing less than the power of the "foreigner," the outsider who had suddenly become dominant in the city. Isolation, through garrisons and police patrols, was the only solution.

Union Park held onto its middle-class character until the middle of the 1890s; there was no immediate desertion by respectable people of the area in the wake of the violence: where else in a great city, asked one citizen, was it safe to go? Everywhere the same terror was possible.

The contrast between the limited character of civil disturbance and the immediate perception of that disturbance as the harbinger of an unnameable threat coming from a generalized enemy is a theme that binds together much research on urban disorders.

Until a few years ago, riots were taken to be the expression of irrational and directionless aggression. "Irrationality of crowds" and similar explanations of crowd behavior as an innate disorder were first given a cogent interpretation in the industrial era in the writings of Le Bon, for whom the irrational brutality of crowds was a sign of how the "psychology" of the individual becomes transformed when the individual acts in concert with other people. This image of crowds was as congenial to many of the syndicalists on the Left as it was to the fears of bourgeois people like those in Union Park. The difficulty with the image is that, for the nineteenth century at least and for the Haymarket Riots certainly, it does not seem to fit the facts of crowd behavior.

Nevertheless, expecting "seething passions" to erupt hysterically, the middle-class people of Chicago and their police were somehow blind to a spectacle they should have enjoyed, that of the workers' increasing boredom with the inflammatory talk of their supposed leaders. The expectations of a seething rabble had somehow to be fulfilled, and so the police themselves took the first step. After the shooting was over, the respectable people of Chicago became inflamed. This blind passion in the name of defending the city from blind passion is the phenomenon that needs to be explained. A similar contradiction occurred in the series of robberies 18 months later as well. As in the riot, the facts of the rationality of the enemy and his limited purpose, although acknowledged, were not absorbed; he was felt to be something else—a nameless, elusive terror, all-threatening—and the people reacted with a passion equal to his.

This mystifying condition, familiar now in the voices heard from the "New Right," is what I should like to explain, not through a sweeping theory that binds the past to the present, but through a theory that explains this peculiar reaction in terms of strains in the family life of the Union Park people. What I would like to explore—and I certainly do not pretend to prove it—is how, in an early industrial city, the fears of the foreign masses held by a middle-class group may have reflected something other than the actual state of interaction between bourgeoisie and proletariat. These fears may have reflected instead the impact of family life on the way the people like those in Union Park understood their places in the city society.

If it is true that in the character one ascribes to one's enemy lies a description of something in one's own experience, the nature of the fear of lower-class foreigners among Union Park families might tell something about the Union Park community itself. The Union Park men, during the time of the riot and robberies, accused their chosen enemies of being lawless anarchists whose base passions pushed them outside the bounds of acceptable behavior, which finally, sent them emotionally out of control. If the poor were reasonable, if they were temperate, ran the argument, these violent things would not have come to pass.

What about the Union Park people themselves, then? Were they masters of themselves? A study I have recently completed on the family patterns of the Union Park people during the decades of the 1870s and 1880s may throw some light on the question of stability and purposefulness in their lives: it is the dimension of stability in these family patterns, I believe, that shaped their reaction to violence in their city.

A Close and Happy Home?

In 1880, on a 40-square-block territory of Union Park, there lived 12,000 individuals in approximately 3,000 family units. The latter were of three kinship types: single-member families, where one person lived alone without any other kin; nuclear families, consisting of a husband and wife and their unmarried children; and extended families, where to the nuclear unit was added some other relative—a brother or sister of the parents, a member of a third generation, or a son or daughter who was married and lived with his spouse in the parental home. The most common form of the extended family in Union Park was that containing "collateral kin," that is, unmarried relatives of the same generation as the husband or wife.

The dominant form of family life in Union Park was nuclear, for 80 percent of the population lived in such homes, with 10 percent of the population living alone in single-member families, and the remaining 10 percent living in extended family situations. A father and mother living alone with their growing children in an apartment or house was the pervasive household condition. There were few widowed parents living with their children in either nuclear or extended homes, and though the census manuscripts on which my study of the year 1880 is based were inexact at this point, there appeared to be few groups of related families living in the same neighborhood but in separate dwellings.

Family Sizes

The size of the Union Park family was small. Most families had one or two children; it was rare for a family to have more. And, the size of poorer families was in its contours similar to the size of the wealthier ones: few families were larger than six members.

Over the course of time internal conditions of family structure and of family size tended to lead to similar family histories. Nuclear families had characteristic histories similar to the experience of smaller families having from two to four kin members in the 1870s and 1880s. Extended families, on the other hand, had histories similar to the experience of the minority of families with four to six kin members during these decades. What made this process subtle was that nuclear families did not tend to be smaller, or extended larger. Family size and family kinship structure seemed rather to be independent structures with parallel internal differences in functioning.

Why and how this was so can be understood by assessing the patterns of the generations of the dominant group.

The nuclear, small-size families during the year 1880 were very cohesive in relations between husbands and wives, parents and children. Whether rich or poor—and about 25 percent of the community fell into a working class category—the young men and women from such homes rarely broke away to live on their own until they themselves were ready to marry and found families, usually when the man was in his early thirties. The families of Union Park, observers of the time noted, were extremely self-contained, did little entertaining, and rarely left the home even to enjoy such modest pleasures as a church social or, for the men, a beer at the local tavern. The small family, containing only parents and their immediate children, resisted the diverse influences either of other relatives or extensive community contacts. These intensive families would seem to epitomize stability among the people of Union Park.

Mobility and Family Stability

Nevertheless, my study of intergenerational mobility in work and residence from 1872 to 1890 did reveal a complicated, but highly significant pattern of insecurity in the dominant intensive families as compared to the smaller group of less intensive families.

The first insecurity of these families was in the rate of desertion. While divorce was rare—it was an act carrying a terrible stigma a hundred years ago—practical divorce in the form of desertion did occur. In Union Park, the rate of desertion was twice as high as that of *poorer* communities—in nearly one out of ten families husband or wife had deserted. A more subtle pattern of insecurity was at work as well.

In the nuclear-family homes and in the smaller families the fathers were stable job holders, as a group, over the course of the 18 years studied; roughly the same proportions of unskilled, skilled and white-collar workers of various kinds composed the labor force of these nuclear fathers in 1890 as in 1872. Given the enormous growth of Chicago's industrial production, its banking and financial capital, retail trade volume, as well as the increase of the population (100 percent increase each ten years) and the greatly increasing proportion of white-collar pursuits during this time, such stability in job distribution is truly puzzling.

But equally puzzling is the fact that this pattern of job holding among the fathers of intensive families was not shared by the fathers in extended families or fathers of larger families living in Union Park. For, unlike their neighbors, fathers of these more complex and extensive families were mobile up into exclusively bureaucratic, white-collar pursuits—so much so that by 1890 virtually none of these fathers worked with their hands. They gradually concentrated in executive and other lesser managerial pursuits and decreased their numbers in shopkeeping, toward which, stereotypically, they are supposed to gravitate.

Even more striking were the differences between fathers and sons in each of these family groups. The sons in the dominant family homes were, unlike their fathers, very unstable in their patterns of job holding. As many moved down into manual pursuits over the course of the 18 years as moved up into the white-collar occupations. One is tempted to explain this simply as a regression toward the mean of higher status groups in time. But the sons of extended and large families did not move in this mixed direction. Rather, they followed the footsteps of their fathers into good white-collar positions, with almost total elimination of manual labor in their ranks as well. This pattern occurred in small-family sons versus large-family sons and in nuclear-family sons versus extended-family sons. The difference in the groups of sons was especially striking in that the starting points of the sons in the occupational work force had virtually the *same* distribution in all types of families. Stephan Thernstrom has pointed out that economic aid between generations of workers is more likely to manifest itself at the outset of a young person's career than when the older generation has retired and the young have become the principal breadwinners. But the fact is that in Union Park, both extended-family and nuclear-family sons, both large- and small-family sons, began to work in virtually the same pursuits as their fathers, then became distinctively different in their patterns of achievement. This strongly suggests that something *beyond*

monetary help was at work in these families to produce divergences in the work experiences of the different groups of sons.

The residence patterns of the generations of the intensive and less intensive families also bears on the issues of stability and instability in the lives of the people of Union Park. Up to the time of violence in the Union Park area, the residence patterns of the two kinds of families, in both the parents' and the sons' generations, were rather similar. In the wake of the violence, however, it appears that within the parents' generation there was significant movement back into the Union Park area, whereas for the half decade preceding the disturbances there was a general movement out to other parts of Chicago. It is in the generation of the sons that differences between the two family groups appeared. In the wake of the violence, the sons of large families and of extended families continued the exodus from Union Park that began in the early 1880s. The sons from intensive families did not; in the years following the violence they stopped migrating beyond the boundaries of the community they had known as children, and instead kept closer to their first homes.

Family Background and Making It

These observations have an obvious bearing on an important debate over what form of bourgeois family life best nurtures the kind of children who can cope with the immensely dynamic and risky world of the industrial city. Talcott Parsons has argued that the small nuclear family is a kinship form well adapted to the industrial order; the lack of extensive kin obligations and a wide kin circle in this family type means, Parsons has contended, that the kinship unit does not serve as a binding private world of its own, but rather frees the individual to participate in "universalized" bureaucratic structures that are urban-wide and dynamic.

The cultural historian Phillippe Aries, in *Centuries of Childhood,* has challenged this theory by amassing a body of historical evidence to show that the extended kinship relationships in large families, at least during an earlier era, were actually less sheltering, more likely to push the individual out into the world where he would have to act like a full man on his own at an early age, than the intense, intimate conditions of the nineteenth-century home. In intensive homes, the young person spent a long time in a state of dependence under the protection and guidance of his elders. Consequently, argues Aries, the capacity of the young adult from small nuclear homes to deal with the world about him was blunted, for he passed from a period of total shelter to a state in which he was expected to be entirely competent on his own.

The data I collected on Union Park clearly are in line with the argument made by Aries. The young from homes of small scale or from homes where the structure of the family was nuclear and "privatistic," in Aries' phrase, had an ineptness in the work world, and a rootedness to the place of their childhood not found to the same degree among the more complex, or larger-family situations. (I have no desire to argue the moral virtues of this rootedness to community or failure to "make it" in the city; these simply happened to be the conditions that existed.) But the conditions that faced Union Park families in a new kind of city, a city at once disorganized and anarchic, set the stability of the family against adaptation to city life. For it is clear that the nineteenth-century, privatistic, sheltering homes Aries depicts, homes that Frank Lloyd Wright describes in his *Autobiography* of his early years in Chicago, homes that observers of the time pointed to as a basic element in the composition of the "dull respectability" of Union Park, could themselves have easily served as a refuge from the confusing, dynamic city that was taking shape all around the confines of Union Park.

And what is more natural than that middle-class people should try to hold onto the status position they had in such a disrupting, growing milieu, make few entrepreneurial ventures outside their established jobs, and withdraw into the comfort and intimacy of their families. Here is the source of that job "freeze" to be seen in the mobility patterns of fathers in intense-family situations; the bourgeois intensive family in this way became a shelter from the work pressures of the industrial city, a place where men tried to institute some control and establish some comforting intimacies in the shape of their lives, while withdrawing to the sidelines as the new opportunities of the city industries opened up. Such an interpretation of these middle-class families complements Richard Hofstadter's interpretation of middle-class political attitudes in the latter part of the nineteenth century. He characterizes the middle-class as feeling that the new industrial order had passed them by and left them powerless. It is this peculiar feeling of social helplessness on the part of the fathers that explains what use they made of their family lives.

But the late nineteenth century was also the world of Horatio Alger, of "luck and pluck"; it was no time for withdrawal. The idea of seizing opportunities, the idea of instability of job tenure for the sake of rising higher and higher, constituted, as John Cawelti has described it, the commonly agreed-upon notion among respectable people of the road to success. One should be mobile in work, then, for this was the meaning of "opportunity" and "free enterprise," but in fact the overwhelming dislocations of the giant cities seem to have urged many men to retreat into the circle of their own families, to try simply to hold onto jobs they knew they could perform.

Conditions of privacy and comfort in the home weakened the desire to get ahead in the world, to conquer it; since the fathers of the intensive families were retreating from the confusions of city life, their preparation of their sons for work in Chicago became ambiguous, in that they wanted, surely, success for their sons, yet shielded the young, and did not themselves serve as models of successful adaptation. The result of these ambiguities can be seen directly in the work experience of the sons, when contrasted to the group of sons from families which, by virtue either of family form or size, were more complex or less intense. Overlaid on these family patterns was a relatively high rate of hidden marital breakdown in Union Park—one in every ten homes—while the expectation was, again, that such breakdowns must not occur, that they were a disgrace.

Because the goals of these middle-class people were bred of contradictory desires to escape from and succeed in the city, the possibility of a wholly satisfying pattern of achievement for them was denied. The family purposes were innately contradictory. A family impulse in one direction inevitably defeated another image of what was wanted. This meant that the sources of defeat were nameless for the families involved; surely these families were not aware of the web of self-contradictions in which in retrospect they seem to have been enmeshed; they knew only that things never seemed to work out to the end planned, that they suffered defeats in a systematic way. It is this specific kind of frustration that would lead to a sense of being overwhelmed, which, in this community's family system, led easily to a hysterical belief in hidden, unknown threats ready to strike at a man at almost any time.

What I would like to suggest is that this complex pattern of self-defeat explains the character of the Union Park reaction to violence. For the dread of the unknown that the middle classes projected onto their supposed enemies among the poor expressed exactly the condition of self-instituted defeat that was the central feature of the family system in Union Park. And this dread was overwhelming precisely because men's own contradictory responses to living in such a city were overwhelming. They had defined a set of conditions for their lives that inevitably left them out of control. The fact that in Union Park there was a desire to destroy the "immigrant anarchists" or to garrison the neighborhood against them, as a result of the incidents of violence, was important in that it offered an outlet for personal defeats, not just for anger against lawbreakers. This response to violence refused to center on particular people, but rather followed the "path of hysterical reaction," in Freud's phrase, and centered on an abstract class of evildoers. The fear of being suddenly overwhelmed from the outside was really a sign that one was in fact in one's own life being continually overwhelmed by the unintended consequences of what one did.

The terrible fear of attack from the unbridled masses was also related to the fear of falling into deep poverty that grew up in urban middle-class families of this time. To judge from a wide range of novels in the latter half of the nineteenth century there was a dread among respectable people of suddenly and uncontrollably falling into abject poverty; the Sidwells in Thackeray's *Vanity Fair* plummet from wealth to disorganized penury in a short space of time; In Edith Wharton's *Age of Innocence,* Lily Bart's father is similarly struck down by the symbol of entrepreneurial chance in the industrial city, the stock market. This feeling of threat from the impersonal, unpredictable workings of the city economy was much like the sense of threat that existed in the Union Park families, because the dangers encountered in both cases were not a person or persons one could grapple with, but an abstract condition, poverty, or family disorder that was unintended, impersonal and swift to come if the family should once falter. Yet what one *should* do was framed in such a self-contradictory way that it seemed that oneself and one's family were always on the edge of survival. In this way, the growth of the new industrial city, with its uncertainties and immense wastes in human poverty, not all victims of which were easily dismissed as personal failures, could surely produce in the minds of middle-class citizens who were uneasy about their own class position and lived out from the center of town, the feeling that some terrible force from below symbolized by the poor, the foreigner, was about to strike out and destroy them unless they did something drastic.

The reaction among most of the families to the eruption of violence bears out this interpretation of events. With the exception of the upwardly mobile, extended-family sons, most family members did not try to flee the community as a response to the threats of riot and the organized wave of crime. There was a renewed feeling of community solidarity in the face of violence, a solidarity created by fear and a common dread of those below.

The relations between family life and the perception of violence in this Chicago community could be formed into the following general propositions. These were middle-class families enormously confused in what they wanted for themselves in the city, both in terms of their achievements in the society at large and in terms of their emotional needs for shelter and intimacy. Their schema of values and life goals was in fact formed around the issues of stability and instability as goals in a self-contradictory way. The result of this inner contradiction was a feeling of frustration, of not really being satisfied, in the activities of family members to achieve *either* patterns of stability or mobility for themselves. The self-defeat involved in this process naturally led these families to feel themselves threatened by overwhelming, nameless forces they could not control, regardless of what they did. The outbreak of violence was a catalyst for them, giving them in the figure of the "other," the stranger, the foreigner, a generalized agent of disorder and disruption.

It is this process that explains logically why the people of Union Park so quickly found a communally acceptable villain responsible for violence, despite all the ambiguities perceived in the actual outbreaks of the disorders themselves. This is why the villain so quickly identified, was a generalized, nonspecific human force, the embodiment of the unknown, the outside, the foreign. This is why the people of Union Park clung so tenaciously to their interpretation, seemed so willing to be terrorized and distraught.

Then and Now

If the complex processes of family and social mobility in Union Park are of any use in understanding the great fear of disorder among respectable, middle-class urbanites of our own time, their import is surely disturbing. For the nature of the disease that produced this reaction to violence among the industrial middle classes was not simply a matter of "ignorance" or failure to understand the problems of the poor; the fear was the consequence, rather, of structural processes in the lives of the Union Park families themselves. Thus for attitudes of people like the Union Park dwellers to change, and a more tolerant view of those below to be achieved, nothing so simple as more education about poor people, or to put the matter in contemporary terms, more knowledge about

Negroes, would have sufficed. The whole fabric of the city, in its impact on staid white-collar workers, would have to have been changed. The complexity and the diversity of the city itself would need to have been stilled for events to take another course. But were the disorder of the city absent, the principal characteristic of the industrial city as we know it would also have been absent. These cities were powerful agents of change, precisely because they replaced the controlled social space of village and farm life with a kind of human settlement too dense and too various to be controlled.

And it comes to mind that the New Right fears of the present time are as deeply endemic to the structure of complex city life as was the violent reaction to violence in Union Park. Perhaps, out of patterns of self-defeat in the modern middle classes, it is bootless to expect right-wing, middle-class repression to abate simply through resolves of goodwill, "education about Negroes," or a change of heart. The experience of bourgeois people of Chicago 100 years ago may finally make us a great deal more pessimistic about the chances for reason and tolerance to survive in a complex and pluralistic urban society.

The Brutality of Modern Families

Richard Sennett

In the past ten years many middle-class children have tried to break out of the communities, the schools and the homes that their parents had spent so much of their own lives creating. If any one feeling can be said to run through the diverse groups and life styles of the youth movement, it is a feeling that these middle-class communities of the parents were like pens, like cages keeping the young from being free and alive. The source of the feeling lies in the perception that while these middle-class environments are secure and orderly regimes, ·people suffocate there for lack of the new, the unexpected, the diverse in their lives.

There is an irony in this accusation for it seems to run counter to widely held beliefs that, far from being more secure, the lives of metropolitans have become almost intolerably complex, wildly out of control. Yet what the kids have touched on in an oblique way is that what Lewis Mumford calls the "technics" of city life—the means by which people communicate with each other, work together or exchange services with each other, aided by machines and complex bureaucratic rules—are a cornucopia of

tools with which metropolitan man is brutalizing his social relations into ever more simple, ever more controllable, ever less anarchic forms. In the process, the civilizing possibilities that a metropolis uniquely can offer are disappearing. The possibilities for unexpected and unplanned social encounter, the coexistence of diverse communities, the eccentricity and human variety that flourish when masses of people live without rules together—all these urbane qualities of community are on the wane. It is this urbanity the young are searching for but cannot find.

Indeed, it may appear in the future that men of this era balanced their energies in a peculiar way. The enthusiasm with which they invented machines for quick communication, rapid transport between communities and so on was balanced by a refusal to be social: all the labor-saving devices somehow left each man more and more alone.

This transformation of metropolitan life is profound and mystifying. It has taken a revolt of the children of middle-class affluence to awaken us to the fact that order and security can be destructive. Yet I fear we have much more to learn about the dimensions of this paradox before we will be able to understand why we have willfully excluded a healthy disorder from our lives.

This paradox poses a question: is there a standard of urbanity by which we can judge metropolitan living today? It is not a utopian dream but history that affords us that standard, I believe, and history of a most ordinary sort. The life styles of civility and sophistication to which modern affluent urban life can be compared were found in the "low culture" of ethnic ghettos in our cities more than 70 years ago. For in those ethnic enclaves of the late nineteenth century, there were hidden threads of cooperation and communal association that gave people who lived there regions of identity beyond the fact of their own poverty.

On Halstead Street

Let us take a tour down Halstead Street, the center of Chicago's great immigrant ghetto, around 1900. The street was 22 miles long, most of it teeming with people. Were we to start at its northern end and move south, we would see that most of these people were "foreigners," but at any given point different kinds of foreigners, all mixed together. A native might tell us that a certain few blocks were Greek or Polish or Irish, but were one actually to look at particular houses or apartment buildings, one would find the ethnic groups jumbled together. Even on the Chinese blocks of the street—for the Chinese are supposed at this time to have been the most closed of ethnic societies—there would be numerous families from Ireland or eastern Europe.

The functioning of all these groups on Halstead Street would appear hopelessly tangled to modern observers. The apartments would be mixed in with the stores, the streets themselves crowded with vendors and brokers of all kinds; even factories, as we moved to the southern end of Halstead Street, would be intermixed with bars, brothels, synagogues, churches and apartment buildings. In the midst of this jumble, there were some hidden threads of a structured social existence.

Were we to follow one of the residents of Halstead Street through a typical day, the experience would be something like this: up at six in the morning, a long walk or streetcar ride to the factory and then ten or 11 hours of grueling work. With this much of his day we would be familiar. But when the whistle to stop work blew at six in the evening, his life would take on a dimension that is perhaps not immediately recognizable. The path back home from the factory might be broken by an hour's relaxation at a tavern or coffeehouse. Halstead Street was crammed in 1900 with little cafés where men would come after work to let the tension drain out, talking to friends or reading a newspaper. Dinner would usually be at home, but after dinner the man, sometimes with his wife, would be out of the house again, attending a union meeting, caring for a sick member of a mutual-aid society to which he belonged or just visiting the apartment of friends. Occasionally, when the family needed some special help, there would be a glass of beer shared with the local political boss and a plea for assistance—a soft job for an infirm relative, help with a naturalization form, some influence in getting a friend out of jail. Religious responsibilities also pulled the man and woman out of the house, particularly if they were Jewish or practicing Catholics. Synagogues and churches had to be built in this strange city, and the money and organization to build them could come only from the little men who were their members.

The life of a child on Halstead Street in 1900 would also seem odd to us, not to say frightening. The child of ten or 11 would be wakened early in the morning, scrubbed and sent off to school. Until three in the afternoon he would sit at a high desk reciting and memorizing. This experience is not strange to us, but again, his life after school would be. For if he did not come home to work, and many did not, he would be out on Halstead Street selling or hawking in the stall of someone much older, who sold and cajoled the passing traffic just as he did. It is amazing to see in old photographs of Halstead Street the young and old, shoulder to shoulder in these stalls, shouting out the prices and the virtues of their wares. Many youths would, with the tacit consent of their parents, enter into the more profitable after-school activity of stealing—we read, for instance, in the letters of one Polish family of great religious piety, of the honor accorded to a little son who had stolen a large slab of beef from a butcher on the corner. Life was very hard, and everyone had to fight for his needs with whatever weapons were at hand.

This life on Halstead Street required an urbanity of outlook, and multiple, often conflicting points of social contact, for these desperately poor people to survive. They *had* to make this diversity in their lives, for no one or two or three institutions in which they lived could provide all their needs. The family depended on political favors, the escape valve of the coffee shops and bars, the inculcation of discipline of the *shuls* and churches and so forth. The political machines tended in turn to grow along personal lines, to interact with the shifting politics of church and synagogue. This necessary anarchy took the individuals of the city outside the ethnic "subcultures" that supposedly were snugly encasing them. Polish people who belonged to steel unions often came into conflict with Polish people who had joined the police. It is the mark of a sophisticated life style that loyalties become crossed in conflicting forms, and this sophistication was the essence of these poor people's lives.

This condition has been carefully described by the great Chicago urbanist, Louis Wirth, in his essay "Urbanism as a Way of Life." He tried to show how the city of necessity broke apart the self-contained qualities of the various ethnic groups. The groups were not like little villages massed together in one spot on the map; rather they penetrated into each other, so that the daily life of an individual was a journey through various kinds of group life, each one different in its function and character from the others.

The subtlety of this idea can be seen by comparing a city subculture, as Wirth observed it, to the structure of village culture from which the ethnic groups came. In the small towns of southern Italy, in the *shtetl* of eastern Europe or the settlements of Anatolia, one finds what Robert Redfield has called a "village ethic": the accessibility of all village activities to all members of the village community. The village ethic is a web of cohesion: there are no disconnected or isolated social regions because, though different people might hold different rank or perform specialized activities, the character of the separate activities is known to everyone, and the differences add up to one organic whole. What made areas like Halstead Street in Chicago, New York's Lower East Side or London's East End seem so different to writers like Wirth was that the separate activities, or the different groups, depended on one another but were not harmoniously related. Each piece of the city mosaic had a distinct character, but the pieces were free of each other, they were not organically bound, they did not dovetail neatly. Individuals had to enter into a number of social regions in the course of daily life, even though the regions were not fluently organized and may even have been warring.

The Decline of Civility

It is the popular stereotype about "working-class" or "ethnic" culture that prohibits us from seeing the kind of density and sophistication that the city life of ordinary peo-

ple possessed in the past. Writers such as William Whyte make that life into an image of a village when in fact it was more complex, less unitarily organized. No easy myth of solidarity could develop out of Halstead Street, no simplicity of the sort "I am who I am by what I do and what I believe." Nevertheless, this civility was bought at the price of much strain and economic anxiety; to recognize the

"They still fear the City."

complexity in these people's lives is not to glorify poverty —that would be a stroke of romantic cruelty—but to try to learn what strengths it is possible for city men to achieve.

In the last half-century, a majority of the ethnic groups in the city have achieved a state of prosperity for themselves far beyond what the first immigrants ever dreamed of. In the process, this necessary anarchy, this necessary sophistication, has died out; in its stead, social activities have become more coherent, more simple, and the social bond itself has become less compelling. The reason for this change is to be uncovered, I believe, in the transformation that family life has undergone as a majority of white urban Americans have achieved relative affluence. It is in the family lives of urban men today that one finds the expression of those forces that eroded the urbanity of city life in the past, eroded the necessary anarchy of the city and the complexities of feeling it exacted in ordinary experience.

When I first began to do research on the structure of city family life, I encountered over and over a popular stereotype: the idea that city conditions somehow contribute to the instability of the home. Evidently, the assumption is that the diversity of the city threatens the security and attachment family members feel for each other. Especially as suburban community life has come to dominate cities, there has grown up a mythological family image of affluent homes where Dad drinks too much, the kids are unloved and turn to drugs, divorce is rampant and breakdowns are routine. The good old rural families, by contrast, were supposedly loving and secure.

The trouble with this popular image is that it simply isn't true. Talcott Parsons has amassed evidence to show that the rate of divorce and desertion was much higher "in the good old days" at the turn of the century than it is now. William Goode has taken the idea a step further by showing how divorce is *less* frequent in affluent homes than in working-class homes. There may still be a great deal of unrest and tension in these suburban families, but it cannot be allied to their structural instability. In fact, we shall see, it is the juncture of great formal stability with deep and unresolved tension that now marks these families.

The idea of the city weakening the family has also come to express itself in the popular perversions of the Moynihan report on the family lives in the black ghettos. The phenomenon this document actually describes is the impact of unemployment on family structure. It has been misread, however, as a description of how northern city life has broken apart the black family, and, in its most distorted form, as a sign that there is something too "weak" in black culture to enable it to withstand the terrors of the city. What Moynihan describes occurs wherever unemployment or intermittent employment is a long-term family experience; one therefore finds a much higher rate of female-headed households, with shifting male partners and "illegitimate" children, among persecuted rural Catholics in Northern Ireland than among the blacks of New York City. But the myth remains: somehow it is the city that is the destroyer.

There is an important history to this stereotype of the city's threat to the home. At the turn of the century, the bulk of the population of American cities was working-class, people whose origins and urban experience was of a piece with the residents of Halstead Street. But there was a numerically smaller group of middle-class families in cities like Chicago whose family patterns were very different, much closer to the narrowness of the life of the affluent middle class in today's metropolitan areas. In *Families Against the City* I explored the lives of one such middle-class community and what the history of these people revealed was that the common stereotype of the city's impact on the family has to be reversed for middle-class homes. For the disorder and vigor of city life in the first decade of this century frightened middle-class families, but, unlike working-class people, they had the means to do something about their fears. They drew in upon themselves: there was little visiting outside the confines of home; voluntary groups like churches and political clubs claimed few bourgeois participants; in America, unlike France or Germany, the urban middle class shunned public forms of social life like cafés and banquet halls. The home became for these early middle-class city dwellers a sanctuary against the confusions of the outside world.

Family Intensity

That kind of family isolation has abated in modern times, particularly when a family is in crisis. But there was something about such urban middle-class families at the opening of the twentieth century that has survived over time. These families possessed a character that now typifies families in middle-class suburbs as well as the middle-class islands within the central city; it is a quality of living that unites newly middle-class families whose parents were immigrants with the native-born urban middle-class families that have always lived in large cities. This characteristic of family life is the intensity of family relations. It links the variety of groups and backgrounds of people lumped together as middle-class, and the reach of this phenomenon extends beyond the city proper into the suburb and the town.

What is meant by an "intense" family life? There are, I think, a state of mind and a style of living that define the family intensity now found in many if not most segments of the urban population. The state of mind is that family members believe the actions and feelings that transpire in the family are in fact a microcosm of the whole range of "meaningful" actions and feelings in the world at large. The belief is, as one middle-class mother in Queens explained to an interviewer recently, that nothing "really important" in human relationships occurs that cannot be experienced within the boundaries of the home. People who think in this way can therefore conceive of no reason for making social forays or social contacts that cannot be ultimately reconciled or absorbed in family life.

The style of living that makes for an intense family life is the reduction of family members to levels of equality. This characteristic is much more pronounced in American urban families than in European ones. The feeling consists, most vulgarly, in fathers wanting to be "pals" to their sons and mothers wanting to be sisters to their daughters; there is a feeling of failure and dishonor if the parents are excluded from the circle of youth, as though they were tarnished by being adult. A good family of this sort is a family whose members talk to each other as equals, where the children presume to the lessons of experience and the parents try to forget them. That the dignity of all the family members might lie exactly in mutual respect for separateness and uniqueness is not conceived; dignity is conceived to lie in treating everyone equally. This brings the family members into a closer relation to each other— for there are taken to be, ideally, no unbridgeable gaps.

Both the state of mind and the life style have become in fact structures for limiting the sophistication and tolerance of the people who live in such homes.

The conviction that a family is the whole social arena in microcosm stifles parents and children both in an obvious and in a subtle way. Clearly, no band of four or five people represents the full spectrum of attitudes and human traits to be found in the wider society. The family as a world of its own can therefore become highly exclusive. Studies of intense family attitudes toward strangers reveal that the outsiders are judged to be "real," to be important and dealt with, only to the extent to which they reflect the particular attitudes and personalities found within a family circle. The most striking form of this can be seen in situations where middle-class neighborhoods have been successfully integrated racially. The black families have been accepted to the extent that people feel they are after all "just like us," or as a respondent in one study put it: "You wouldn't know from the way the Jones family acts they were Negroes." Accepting someone ineradicably different is not what occurs under these conditions.

Conflict Is a "No-No"

The subtle way in which families, feeling themselves a microcosm of the society, become self-limiting has to do with the base of stability on which such families rest. This base is the existence, or the belief in the existence, of long-term trust. For families to believe they are all-important there has to be the conviction that no betrayal and breakup will occur. People do not concentrate all their energies in one place and simultaneously believe it may one day shatter or betray them. Yet long-term situations of trust and reliability are rare in the larger social world. Not only in work but also in a variety of human affairs there are experiences of power and significance that cannot depend on a mutual commitment or trust for a long period. An intense family life must refuse to grant worth to that which is shifting, insecure or treacherous, and yet this is exactly what the diversity in society is built of.

When people in a family believe they must treat each other as equal in condition, the same self-blinding, the same limitation, occurs. A recent project made psychiatric interviews in homes of "normal," "just average" families in a modest suburb outside a large city. Over and over again in these interviews adults expressed a sense of loss, sometimes amounting to feelings of annihilation, in the things in their lives they had wanted to do and could afford to do but refrained from doing for fear of leaving out the children. These sacrifices were not dictated by money; they were much more intimate, small-scale, yet important things: establishing a quiet spot in the day after work when a man and his wife were alone together, taking trips or vacations alone, eating dinner after the children were put to bed. In another frame, fathers spoke again and again of how they had failed their sons by not being able to understand them. When the interviewers asked what they meant, the response usually came as a version of "he doesn't open up to me the way he does to his friends." Such burdens are acquired, so many daily chances for diversity and change of routine are denied, out of the belief in the rightness of treating children as much as equals as possible, especially in early and middle adolescence.

In one way, the belief in the family as a microcosm of the world leads to this will to believe the family members all alike, all "pals." For if the family is a whole world, then somehow the conditions of friendship and comradeship must be established within its borders, and this can only be done by treating all the family members as comrades who can understand each other on the same grounds.

The idea just advanced may seem untrue to the experience of many—an experience of family tension and estrangement unlike what previous generations seemed to have known. But there is a perverse, hidden strain to this family intensity that may make sense of the phenomenon.

Islands of Freedom lights and air.

Perhaps I can illustrate this from some professional work now being done by family researchers.

A few students of the family have recently been at pains to unravel what is awkwardly called "the guilt-over-conflict syndrome." This syndrome appears in the attitudes of many intense family members toward their families. The syndrome is simple to state, but not simple to overcome by people painfully caught up in it: to most people it appears that good families, upright families, ought to be happy, and it also appears that happy families ought to be tranquil, internally in harmony. What happens then when conflict or serious fights erupt? For many people, the emergence of conflict in their family lives seems to indicate some kind of moral failure; the family, and by reflection the individual, must be tarnished and no good. Until recently many therapists, too, thought family fighting was morally destructive. Like their clients, they imagined a healthy family to be one where differences were "resolved" without emotional heat. But a body of evidence about conflict and mental illness in families has accumulated sufficiently to make this middle-class notion untenable; the facts indicate that families in which abrasive conflicts are held down turn out to have much higher rates of deep emotional disorders than families in which hostilities are openly expressed, even though unresolved.

But the guilt-over-conflict syndrome is significant because it is so deeply held a presupposition about family life: people look, for example, at conflicts between generations as an evil, revealing some sort of rottenness in the familial social fabric, rather than as an inevitable and natural process of historical change. Sharp personality differences within the children's generation, leading to estrangements between brothers and sisters, are viewed as a sign of bad parental upbringing, and so on. Put another way, anxiety and guilt over family conflict really express the wish that for the sake of social order, diversity and ineradicable differences should not exist in the home.

Islands in Metropolis

But this guilt about conflict, produced by the desire for intense family relations, helps explain a much broader social phenomenon: the ways in which the family group brutalizes its members, both young and old, in their dealings with the larger society. The link between family life of this kind and the society beyond it can be understood by posing this question: is there any reason to call an intense family life, fearful of conflict, an "urban" condition? Could it not simply be the way in which families live today in America, and since most families live in urban areas, be an "urban" family trait by location only?

There is an intimate relation between the desire for family intensity, the guilt it produces over conflict or disorder in intimate affairs and the social structure of a city. For, as the intensity of family relations grows, freshening of one's perceptions through diverse experience in the outside world diminishes. Intense families wall in the consciousness men have of "significant" or "important" experiences in their lives. One special social institution—the family group—becomes the arena of what is real. Indeed, the guilt that family intensity produces about experiences of disorder or conflict makes this absorption into the home appear as a moral or healthy act. The diversity of the city world beyond, as an older generation of immigrants or blacks knew it, never fit together in an orderly way; men were continually becoming involved in messy situations or having to change the face they presented to the world. In the new order of affluence, significant social life can be more proper, more dignified, by virtue of a more narrow order. One affluent working-class father told me recently, "When I was a kid, I had to be on my toes all the time, see, because in the slums of Boston you couldn't take anything for granted if you wanted to survive. Now that I've got some money, I can live respectably, you know, take care of the house and kids and not worry about what's hap-

Fights are bad?

pening outside. Maybe I'm not as sharp, but I've got more respect."

The essence of intense family life is this absorptive capacity, a power to collect the interests and attention of the individual in the tight-knit band of kin. Historically, the last half-century of city life has been marked exactly by such intimacy-making. This spells a decline in the sophisticated anarchy of association for most city men and the rise of an urban isolationism for the masses—an isolationism once encircling only the small, native-born, middle class.

Suburban Closeness

The vehicle for replacing the sophistication of an older urban life by the suffocation in the family today is the growth of middle-class suburbs in this country. The shrinking of diverse community life into the family is the hidden history of suburban places—which seem so empty of secrets; this history makes sense of their simplicity and their great appeal to Americans.

The classic pattern of industrial city-suburb arrangements up to the Second World War was the pattern still extant in Turin or Paris. Cities were arranged in rings of socio-economic wealth, with the factories at the outskirts of town, workers' suburbs or quarters next to them and then increasingly more affluent belts of housing as one moved closer to the center of the city. There were exceptions to this pattern, to be sure, like Boston or Lyons, but the pattern seemed to apply to most of the great urban centers in the United States; New York, Philadelphia and Chicago showed in general such a pattern at the opening of the present century.

When the flight to the suburbs first began in massive numbers after the Second World War, it was commonly thought that its causes were related to the depression and to the population dislocation of the war. But this explanation is simply inadequate to explain the persistence of the event over the course of time.

Nor, in the United States, can the movement to the suburbs cannot be explained by the growing presence of Negroes in the urban centers after the Second World War. For one thing, these Negroes seldom moved close to areas where young middle-class people had lived; those poorer people whose neighborhoods were gradually taken over by

Fights are good?

Negroes did not move to far-lying suburbs but relocated only slightly farther away from the urban core. There are some exceptions to this latter pattern; there are some people in outer Queens who moved to avoid blacks, but few in Darien, Connecticut, did.

The historical circumstances of depression, war, land value and racial fear all have played a role, but they are offshoots of a more central change in the last decades that has led to the strength of suburban life. This deeper, more hidden element is a new attitude about the conduct of family life within and without the city.

A variety of recent books on suburbs, like Herbert Gans' *The Levittowners* or John Seeley's *Crestwood Heights,* reveal that people who now live in suburbs value their home settings because they feel that closer family ties are more possible there than in the city center. The closeness is not so much a material one—after all, families in city apartments are extremely close physically. Rather, as is now being learned, it is the simplification of the social environment in the suburbs that accounts for the belief that close family life will be more possible there than in the confusion of the city.

In most American suburbs, physical space has been rigidly divided into homogeneous areas: there are wide swatches of housing separated from swatches of commercial development concentrated in that unique institution, the shopping center; schools are similarly isolated, usually in a parklike setting. Within the housing sectors themselves, homes have been built at homogeneous socioeconomic levels. When critics of planning reproach developers for constructing the environment in this way, the developers reply truthfully that people want to live with people just like themselves; people think diversity in housing will be bad for social as well as economic reasons. In the new communal order made possible by affluence, the desire of people is for a functionally separated, internally homogeneous environment.

Homogenous Zones

I believe this homogeneous-zones idea in suburbs is a brutalizing community process, in contrast to the urban situation that preceded it in time. For the homogeneous zones of function in a suburb prohibit an overlay of different activities in the same place; each place has its own predefined function. What therefore results is a limitation on the chance combination of new situations, of unexpected events, of unlikely meetings between people that create diversity and a sense of complexity in individual lives. People have a vision of human variety and of the possibility of living in a different and better way only when they are challenged by situations they have not encountered before, when they step beyond being actors in a preordained, unchanging routine. This element of surprise is how human growth is different from the simple passage of time in a life; but the suburb is a settlement fitted only to muffle the unknown, by separating the zones of human activity into neat compartments.

This prohibition of diversity in the arrangement of suburban areas permits, instead, the intensity of family relations to gather full force. It is a means for creating that sense of long-term order and continuity on which family intensity must be based. In a stable family, where long-term trust between pretend-equals exists, the "intrusions" of the outside must be diminished, and such is the genius of the suburban mode. The hidden fear behind this family life in the suburbs is that the strength of the family bond might be weakened if the individual family members were exposed to a richer social condition, readily accessible outside the house.

When the suburbs began to grow rapidly after the Second World War, some observers, such as David Riesman, were moved to criticize them for an aimlessness and emptiness in communal relations. But there was and is a peculiar kind of social bond made possible by this very emptiness, this lack of confusion. The bond is a common determination to remain inviolate, to ensure the family's security and sanctity through exclusionary measures of race, religion, class.

Involved here was a new event in the idea of a "neighborhood," for such a place became much more definable in becoming more homogeneous. Social scientists used to spend a great deal of time fighting with each other about the meaning of "neighborhood" in cities, one of the principal points being that there was such a multiplicity of social contact that individuals could not be neatly categorized by where they lived. Now they can. The growth of intensive family life in the suburb has brought into being a metropolitan region where each neighborhood is all too identifiable in socioeconomic, racial and ethnic terms. Now people really are getting to know who their neighbors are: they are just like themselves.

This kind of family living in the suburbs surely is a little strange. Isn't the preference for suburbia as a setting for family life in reality an admission, tacit and unspoken to be sure, that the parents do not feel confident of their own human strengths to guide the child in the midst of an environment richer and more difficult than that of the neat lawns and tidy supermarkets of the suburbs? If a close, tight-knit family emerges because the other elements of the adult and child world are made purposely weak, if parents assume their children will be better human beings for being shielded or deprived of society outside the home and homelike schools, surely the family life that results is a forced and unnatural intimacy.

Of course there are many similar criticisms one could make of suburbs, all centered in some way on the fact that suburbanites are people who are afraid to live in a world they cannot control. This society of fear, this society willing to be dull and sterile in order that it not be confused or overwhelmed, has become as well a model for the rebuilding of inner-city spaces. It is often said that the differences are disappearing between the suburbs and such central-city developments as Lefrak City in New York or the urban renewal projects of inner Boston or the South Shore of Chicago. It would be more accurate to say that these inner-city, middle-class communities are becoming suburbanized in a historical sense: rigidly planned usage of space,

an emphasis on security and warding off intrusions from the outside—in short, a simplification of the contacts and the environment in which the family lives. In the name of establishing the "decencies" of life as regnant, the scope of human variety and freedom of expression is drastically reduced. The emotions shaping the rebuilding of inner-city living-places run much deeper than protection from the blacks or from crime; the blacks and the criminals are a symbolic cover under which the family can turn inward, and the family members withdraw from dealing with the complexities of people unlike themselves.

The Morality of Being Passive

This urban transformation has now a frightening impact on the social and political life of adult city men as citizens. In the collapsing of multiple, interwoven points of social contact as the majority of city families have come to live in intense situations, lies an urban crisis as important as the crises of life faced by city people who are still oppressed and without economic power.

It is common for "slum romantics" to bemoan the loss of intimate social space and small scale in modern city life. But from the vantage point of what has been set forth so far, the issue would appear to be the reverse. There has not been a loss of intimate small scale per se, but rather a loss of multiple foci of small scale. The urban family of this affluent era has developed a power to absorb activities and interests that were once played out in a variety of settings in the city. Indeed, it might best be said of city life during the past 25 years that the scale of life has become too intimate, too intense.

There has therefore grown up a change in the "morality" of participation in urban affairs. If one looks back to the ethnic ghettos of the turn of the century, one finds men and women forced to deal with each other, forced to deal with diverse and often strange social situations, in order to survive. In the suburbanized cities of our time men are not forced into association; each family has the means and the desire to provide for all its perceived needs within the borders of kin relations. But the ethos of intense family life works in a more forceful manner as well to make men passive in the larger society of the city.

This new configuration of polarized intimacy in the city provides the individual with a powerful moral tool in shutting out new or unknown social relations for himself. For if the suburbanized family is a little world of its own, and if the dignity of that family consists in creating bases of long-term stability and concord, then potentially diversifying experiences can be shut out with the feeling of performing a moral act. For the sake of "protecting the home" a man refuses to wander or to explore: this is the meaning of that curious self-satisfaction men derive in explaining what they gave up "for the sake of the children." It is to make impotence a virtue.

The glorification of passivity makes clearer the willful indifference or the hostility that most middle-class urbanites show toward programs aimed at eradicating conditions of poverty in the city. For this hostility, as people give voice to it, is more than a feeling of simple class interest or class conflict. I once interviewed a suburban mother about a school bussing program between her community and a part of the Brownsville ghetto in New York; she tried to explain her anger at the program by saying finally, "What I don't understand is why they don't let us alone; I didn't make them poor, they live totally different from me; why should I have to see their kids in my school?" It isn't that the poor are black that rankles so much, it isn't even that they are poor; what hurts is that middle-class people are asked by programs such as school bussing to be more than passive onlookers in the social process, they are asked to interact with people who are different, and that kind of interaction they find too painful. It is this same inner-turning little world of family affairs, unused to the daily shocks of confrontation and the expression of ineradicable differences, that reacts with such volatility when oppressed groups in the city become disorderly. It is a short step from concentrating on one's own home affairs to sanctioning terrible repression of disturbances from below: if the poor are silenced, then there need be no intrusions on the "meaningful" circle of one's own life, the intimate relationships between Pop, Mom and the kids.

In these ways, affluent city life has created a morality of isolationism. The new virtue, like the religious puritanism of old, is a ritual of purifying the self of diverse and conflicting avenues of experience. But where the first puritans engaged in this self-repression for the greater glory of God, the puritans of today repress themselves out of fear—fear of the unknown, the uncontrollable. The intense family is the *via regia* by which this fear operates: such a family creates in men's intimate lives the necessity for known functions and well-worn routines. It is this kind of family life that explains, I believe, why so many white Americans can accept with equanimity the remaining injustices and oppressive poverty faced by blacks and Puerto Ricans in our cities.

However rural and agricultural the foundation of the American family institutions may be, and however lower class the background of its families, the life styles which have emerged are predominantly urban and middle class. Variations exist, by class and by choice, but the basic model, the "ideal-typical" family, bears many new traits of middle-class nature. Studies of this country's urbanites show that the majority identify with the middle stratum, even when their actual behavior contains traces or even major segments of their lower-class past. Though many descendants of European migrants have given themselves coats-of-arms and nobility-encrusted ancestors, in actuality the upper classes of Europe in past centuries were proportionately small in size and were unlikely to migrate to new areas, unless they could be guaranteed all the privileges of their current status. Alexis de Tocqueville, writing *Democracy in America* after having toured this country in 1831, explained much of what he observed as the inevitable consequence of democracy, not realizing that it was rather the consequence of a striving for middle-class status by people unaccustomed to such. The great push toward the middle stratum ignored the presence of the upper classes and, for centuries, of blacks, who were assumed to belong forever on the bottom. The "melting pot" theory anticipated that, eventually, the ignorant masses would be blended and lifted upward after they had lost their idiosyncratic peasant ways.

The "American dream" became getting a good job, saving money, buying a house, giving the kids a good education and gathering as much material wealth as possible. Maybe the streets weren't paved with gold, but hard work would pay off in a better life than the old country could offer. Few parents expected to make it to the top themselves, but their children and grandchildren really believed the Horatio Alger stories. Children got better jobs than their parents had ever held and moved out of

Part Three

Families of the 1970s

the ethnic cultures of their childhood. The big move to the suburbs helped them build middle-class lives. Husbands and wives became increasingly egalitarian in their relations with each other and with their children, as all cooperated in the attempt to change life styles.

What, then, is this middle-class model and what are its variations? One way of studying the families of the 1970s is to view them at different stages of their life cycle. Clearly, the cycle repeats itself continuously as societal life proceeds, and we can begin its examination at any stage. A good starting point is with a young child: following it through socialization, dating and mating, procreation, life in the middle years, old age and death. Let us, then, begin our analysis with socialization, that process by which the young learn how to be human beings in general and specific individuals in particular. In this way we can observe the parental generation and surrounding social environment supplying the new generation with tools and resources that will help develop the kinds of people who can undertake appropriate societal roles and interpersonal relations at each stage of their own life cycles.

(Before we proceed, however, I would like to mention a problem with American English which bothers me— and many others. Our language has certain limitations which make it difficult to deal with childhood and socialization, as well as other subjects. The term "child" may be treated as sexually neutral, which is unrealistic since "it" is assigned a sexual role the minute of birth. Or it may be masculine—"he" being the common generic term, just as "mankind" is supposed to cover all human beings. I realize that some readers may find the whole issue insufficiently important but several essays collected here indicate, and a growing literature affirms, that it is of significance to an increasing number of people. Several writers have recently experimented with de-sexing our vocabulary. I tried to write the following section using some suggested new forms but found the process too confusing and gave up in despair. Our thought patterns are so ingrained that having to focus constantly on terms foreign to my vocabulary interfered with my writing and would, I suspect, contribute to confusion in reading. So, please forgive me if I compromise and use the dual "he or she" which has become more acceptable, as have "chairperson" or "Ms." for the sexist "chairman" or "Miss" or Mrs.")

After exploring the life cycle of families in the 1970s, we will turn to an analysis of the relations between these units and their members, and between the family and other institutions of society.

1. socialization in the family life cycle

Socialization is a social-science concept summarizing the complicated process by which an infant, born with tremendous potentialities for thought, communication, understanding, planning and building flexible behavior, learns to function as a human being—as a unique person who nevertheless can relate successfully to others in social roles and in the social groups which comprise his or her society. The infant must learn to be a boy or a girl, a potential man or woman, a son or daughter, a brother or sister, a friend, a student, a member of a team, an employee and so forth. The infant must also develop several vital human actualities in the interplay between his or her acting/experiencing self and other people and objects. The developing child must learn to talk and think, to organize sounds in such a way that they constitute significant symbols, evoking in his or her mind, and in the minds of others with whom the communication is taking place, the same object.

This activity involves several components. The child must be able to select out of the environment certain characteristics which he or she organizes into *objects* for potential or actual action. Perceiving a "thing," he or she must decide what kind of an object to make of it. If the thing is to be called a chair, those characteristics which are selected for attention must facilitate sitting. The same object could be conceptually organized into a piece of firewood, a building block, a decorator's item, a piece of furniture with which to fill an empty space, a relic of a recently dead father and so forth. In order to demonstrate to other people the type of object he or she makes of it, the child can either sit on it or refer to it by a commonly used name. But in order to do the latter, the child must combine sounds in such a way that they connote the object he or she has in mind. It is with the help of socializing agents that one's perceptions, the objects one makes of them, and the words one uses to designate them develop into the great reservoirs of knowledge and activity a human being needs in order to function in a symbolically shared world. It is one of the responsibilities of socializing agents to insure that the small child, constantly exploring and trying to organize his or her world of impressions into meaningful wholes, learns to create the "right" objects and to designate them with the "right" words to make cooperative action possible.

There are other abilities which the child must develop with the help of (sometimes in spite of hindrances provided by) socializing agents. At first, these agents are parents and other household residents, those who enter the home or with whom the child comes in contact outside the home. Later, they include peers and everyone significant who is used as a reference person or as part of a reference group.

Probably the most important object which a child must learn to formulate is a self. He or she must feel an identity: a set of selves which are intertwined and which involve a realistic appraisal of what he or she is to others or what he or she can do, feel and "be." This identity extends into the past, present and future—in space and in relation to others. The child must be able to "take the role of the other" with whom he or she interacts. The child must see the self as being an object of his or her own thought and action, in addition to being an object of the thought and action of others. The developing self must understand the world from the point of view of others so as to anticipate their behavior, not only toward the self, but toward other objects.

There are several stages in the development of the self, all closely tied to stages in the development of language and thought. The child observes and realizes him- or herself, seeing that self act, affect other things and respond to itself. He or she pokes and pulls on parents and on the self, obtaining different results that are gradually organized into direct and reflective feelings. The child watches the expressions of others, mimics them, and gradually learns to feel what others are feeling. The first essay in this Part, John S. Watson's "Why Is a Smile?", discusses some of the early interactions between a baby and socializing agents.

An important phase in the child's growing awareness of the self and others is his or her ability to "play the role of the other." This usually starts with playing at being "mother." Acting like the mother acts, and reproducing in him- or herself the sentiments sensed in the mother, the child makes an object of him- or herself—the object of the mother's feeling and actions. The child may pretend that a doll or some other symbol is the self, while he or she is the mother, thereby learning to understand the mother's behaviors and sentiments toward not only the child but also toward other objects. Gradually, the child begins to "generalize the other," to compare and to abstract from the concrete situations certain general principles which serve to classify things and actions. Other mothers are observed, and there develops a generalized image of "what mothers do." The final process of generalization discards individuated models and becomes a set of principles. A child learns the rules of a baseball game in general, not merely what actions a player must perform as shortstop when playing that position. He or she can imagine the game played anywhere—can even imagine the set of rules without actual players. Other rules of action are internalized and depersonalized, based on moral beliefs, religion, sexual roles, going to school, etc. The child may break these rules, but always knows what they are—not because mother said so but because "that's the way things are" or because that is how they "should be."

According to social scientists who have studied the development of human nature through the socialization process, such as George Herbert Mead and Jean Piaget, the ability to generalize and abstract frees the acting person from repeating behavior instinctively or through a direct or conditioned response to stimuli, both of which restrict choices for other animals. The whole complex of self—the ability to take the role of the other, thought based on created objects from selective perception and communication of them symbolically—is what makes the human being unique. Some animals have rudimentary aspects of certain of these abilities, but not the whole package. A self lends facility in planning for the future as well as remembering and reformulating the past. A self makes it possible to weave one's actions into those of other people, so that one can perform complex social roles. With the tools the child acquires through the socialization process, she or he can progress through the educational system, learning segments of the culture by formal procedures. The school as we know it—the classroom, the teacher, this book—would not be possible without our ability to think abstractly, to organize our resources and to utilize the fantastically large and complex store of knowledge we have already acquired and are building upon. The socialization process provides not only knowledge and beliefs, but sentiments. We must be able to feel the "normal" sentiments of our society, to control our feelings to fit the situation and to understand the sentiments of others. We must be able to fall in love, since that is the basis of marriage in this society and both we and people around us would consider us deviants if we did not feel that sentiment when we marry. We are expected to love our children, but not our employers. For the latter we need to be motivated to work. According to how others define us and act toward us, we must want to be a girl or a boy, but not both. Finally, we must internalize motivation, be willing to accept normatively valued goals as our own and mobilize our resources in order to achieve these. Thus, what the child acquires at home and from every source to which he or she attends, are the tools for living in this culture.

Not every child acquires the same wealth of tools during socialization. In the first place, not all the immediate environments into which children are born are equally complex and able to develop these abilities. Parents and others in the environment vary in their ability to think and in the content of the culture with which they are familiar. They cannot teach reading if they do not know how to read. Secondly, parents and other socializing agents vary in the means by which they socialize the child. Some means are less suited to developing the child's potential than others. Elliot Aronson, in "Threat and Obedience," demonstrates the complications of using a threat of severe punishment as a means of teaching children to follow rules. Harsh punishment—behavior indicating to the child his complete rejection, an unloving atmosphere, absence of positive communication with the child—such characteristics in the environment restrict the normal growth process. The offspring can become afraid to experiment or to build a world of his or her own objects; he or she can become convinced that he or she is "bad" or "stupid." Neurotic anxiety can keep the child so busy defending the ego that there is little desire or energy available to explore and play at roles and games. The child may be worked so hard that he or she simply repeats each day's action the next day, and does not picture any alternative actions even in fantasy. The child may fear to fantasize because it is judged by the family as "bad" or "dangerous," or because no occasions for doing so occur. Girls are often discouraged from experimenting with behavior and ideas and are forced to be passive and unimaginative because the ideal presented to them lacks any other qualities, while their brothers are seen as adventurous, temperamental, difficult, always in trouble and so forth. "Boys will be boys."

Socialization is transmitted to youth in a variety of ways, ranging from direct teaching to indirect "tales and stories" with morals; from examples to the presence of models which can be imitated; through action and mood, verbally, or through a whole variety of signals, such as eye movements. The child, surrounded by a moving and acting world, must fit into that world and be in constant interplay with it, carrying on his or her own roles. The world of symbols is organized, more or less consistently, in the minds and actions of the people with whom the child interacts. This is an important point. No child is born into an unstructured environment which waits passively for him or her to start initiating action, then mobilizing to help him or her accomplish goals, or at least to prevent him or her from injury until he or she can organize behavior to carry out a life plan. The parents to whom a baby is born or who adopt one into their family have definite attitudes toward the infant even before official entrance into parental roles. Attitudes, in sociological terms, depend on definitions of the situation in which an event is taking place, sentiments about the circumstances and the event and the social relations involved in them. Behavior involves all these ingredients and is planned in anticipatory socialization prior to entrance into the role. After a baby is born, responses between it and the people around it become organized into interactional scenes which gradually become stabilized and woven into social relations and social roles. This does not mean, of course, that the relations between child and parents remain stable throughout the life cycle. The child changes, and so do people in the environment. The child learns more and more about the world and about him- or herself. As he or she acquires more tools for thought and action, the child assumes the roles of many others, begins to understand their worlds, and absorbs some of their definitions, objects and generalized rules of association among objects. These objects always include the self, since others act toward that self in patterned ways or differently, depending on whether they are friend Sue, or boyfriend Jim, mother, father, sister and so forth. Change occurs in the structure of a child's set of identities whenever he or she enters new social relations or more complex social roles, whenever he or she exits from such interactions, or when surrounding others change so much that he or she must modify what would otherwise be done. The death of a significant other, the birth of a new member of the family, exit from school, classification as a bully—all these events and uncountable others affect people's behavior, thought and sentiments throughout life. The early years are the ones when the greatest change occurs, because it is purposely undertaken by the socialization agents, because the child is so active and because everything is so new to him or her.

Gradually, the socialization content and the education process begin to restrict young people's lives, by channeling them into a certain direction, and life becomes patterned and less flexible. The older generation lives in its own social world, whose content it learned years ago, and to which most are adding new content at diminishing rates, while the new generation learns a different content, particularly in a society whose culture is rapidly changing. The more years that separate the young from the old, the more probability that they are learning and living in different symbolic worlds containing different beliefs, actions and objects. Thus, the greater the age gap and the faster the culture is changing, the more probable is a "generation gap." It is not inevitable, because some adults still learn and change their store of ideas constantly. Unless they are experts in the youth culture, however, what they learn may be different from what is being learned by their children or grandchildren. Of course, the young generation may be learning what the older ones are creating as artists and writers!

Organization of the world by parents and other significant others, and the way this system influences the child, are apparent when we examine the basic social roles imposed upon people. The minute that parents are officially declared to be responsible for a particular child, he or she is registered as having a name. The "last name," as we call it, identifies the infant as belonging to a patrilineal descent line, while the first name identifies him or her as a unique person within that unit—though the name may be that of a previous living or dead member in the descent line whom the child is expected to replace. In spite of the supposed "egalitarianism" of the urban American sex roles, the last name given to the child still ignores its mother's line. Simultaneously the male descent name is only a temporary source of identification for some children, since if the fetus is labeled a girl, her future identity will depend on the males with whom she is related. She carries the family name of her father until she marries; then she must change her whole public and private identity to that of her husband's wife. She has an individual identity in her family of orientation, but that is wiped out with marriage, as women trying to obtain charge-plates with major department stores under their own name soon find out. Only men can be responsible for bills incurred by married women, even in this modern age. The patrilineal and patriarchal forefathers from whom we inherited our family institution must often sigh with relief that things have not changed too much. They would approve of the means used to make girls "act like girls" described by Jo Freeman.

Sexual role is not the only role assigned the child at birth. The family is already identified in society by other labels implying social roles or at least differentiated relations. The identities which the child inherits socially include race, religion, social class, ethnic subculture, type of residence inhabited, and so forth. All these locating identities, insure that the child learns what "we do" and what "we do not do." Thus, the socializing world is organized into identities which the socializing agents transmit to children.

The assumption in modern America that the socialization process requires a "complete" family with husband present is contained in Ulf Hannerz' "Roots of Black Manhood," a careful analysis of the models available to growing boys. This essay shows how people pick up from the social situation models and cues which actually contradict what is officially presented as the ideal personality.

All the essays following provide insights into how adults select and organize the world for themselves and, thus, to a great extent for their children. We select out of the total culture only certain things to "know," believe, value positively or negatively, trust, define clearly or assume haphazardly, want, reject, do, refuse to do, love, hate, fear, accept unquestionably, touch, avoid, see, dream about.

Of course, the fact that a home may contain a certain organization of objects and thoughts, does not mean that the child is restricted to these in building his or her own world. Many other sources of knowledge, feeling, belief and action are available. If the culture is homogeneous and limited in content, there will be limits to the alternatives available to the socializing youth. But American culture is heterogeneous, communicating and complex. It is impossible for parents to isolate their children from the rest of society, unless the children are virtually chained to beds in rooms lacking cultural dissemination media. This means that modern society presents many difficulties to the socialization process. In fact, the inability, the mobility ideology, and often the unwillingness of parents to demand that their sons be just like their fathers have made it difficult to raise children today. This is particularly true in life areas where the community within which the family functions has a culture or cultures which are different from the one into which the parents try to socialize and educate their children. Ethnic cultures are not easy to transmit in a heterogeneous neighborhood. Some of the patterns of behavior available to youth, even to adults, are deemed deviant by the community. Parents whose offspring choose these deviations are apt to be very unhappy, unless they themselves are already doing the same thing. Such terms as "queer," "crazy," "dope fiend" are some of the labels placed by society on people who act in deviant ways.

Sometimes a deviation of behavior from a norm which the family tries to transmit may become accepted by such a large segment of the population as to evolve into a cultural alternative. Despite horror expressed by older and many not-so-old Americans about the similarity in outward appearance of boys and girls in the late 1960s and early 1970s, in pants and long hair, now even the children of the upper and middle classes sport that look. Interestingly enough, a counterrevolution seems to be spreading, as evinced by the popularity, not only among youth but among adult men, of beards, mustaches and sideburns. After all, although girls may wear pants and boys may grow hair, girls still cannot compete in facial hair arrangements. This may be a movement back to the "vive la différence" emphasis or it may simply be another manifestation of the desire for freedom and experimentation in the presentation of self, so new in the fashion of modern American men.

This Part, then, deals with the first stage of what we can call the family life cycle: the socialization of the young as human beings, in the type defined at birth, by sex and other identities, such as race, ethnicity, social class and individual personality.

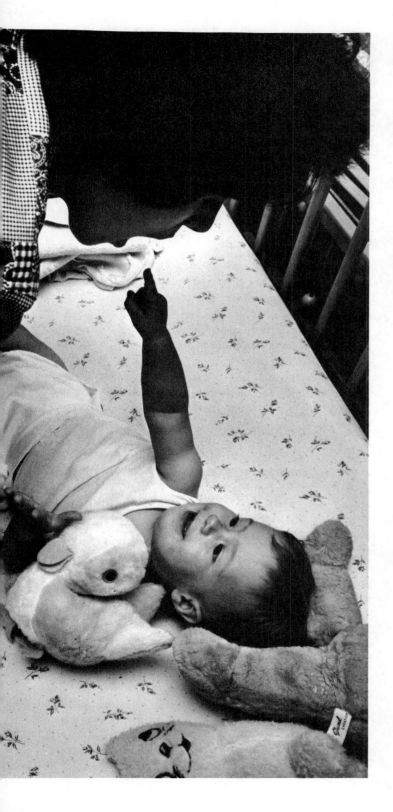

Why is a Smile?

John S. Watson

If I claimed I had a beautiful daughter and to prove it produced a picture showing only her feet (or arms or part of her torso), I would quickly acquire a reputation as being rather odd. But if the picture showed only her face, then the viewers—whether or not they agreed with me about her beauty—would at least be satisfied that they had *seen* my daughter and were in a position to judge her attractiveness. Whatever else we include in a "portrait"—head, bust, or full-length—a substantial portion of the face must be present.

Only among human beings is the sight of the face so important a social stimulus. In lower species, various non-visual stimuli (olfactory, auditory) often play the primary roles in the evocation and maintenance of social behavior.

Why do we respond so quickly to faces—especially smiling ones? Is this an acquired characteristic related perhaps to the fact that faces are generally exposed and closer to our eye level? Does it come perhaps from association with the feelings of pleasure, satisfaction, and security we got as babies while watching the hovering faces of those who tended and fed us? Or could it be something innate, a response we were born with and that is necessary, like the sucking reflex, to our survival?

Studies indicate that the face is uniquely attractive to the human infant in his early months—even as early as two to four days after birth. They also show that this interest will increase and then decline during the first six months of life.

But how do we know with certainty that the baby really sees a face? By this seemingly strange question I mean the following: Does an infant's interest in faces depend on the angle at which the face (or a drawing of a face) is perceived by the child—that is, whether he sees it aligned with his face, partially aligned, or upside down? Does he respond to the face *per se* or to something associated with a face?

Experimental Smiles

In order to find out, we have conducted four studies that shed light on the question. The first two experiments used real smiling faces presented to the baby at different angles; his own smile was considered to be a response. The third study used drawings rather than real faces, presenting them too at different orientations; response was measured by how long the baby kept his gaze fixed on them. The fourth experiment concentrated on mothers and how they, in fact, tend to orient their faces when caring for or playing with their infants.

The subjects for the first three experiments were 68 babies (20 in the first, 48 in the second and third). They were from 7 to 26 weeks old, all of them white, all the offspring of college students or college graduates—a rather homogeneous group.

In the first two studies each infant was tested while reclining on his back. (In the second study a special bassinet was constructed with a viewing porthole directly above the infant's head.) The experimenter leaned over, holding his face about 15 inches away. After a short period (20 seconds in the first experiment, 30 in the second) he withdrew, to appear again about 15 seconds later from a different angle.

The angles were 0°, 90°, and 180°—that is, from the baby's view, face to face, sideways (from the left), and upside down. (See illustration.) At all times the experimenter's face was smiling but silent and unresponsive. Different stimuli were also used to check whether the baby would smile at *any* stimulus. In one experiment it was a multi-colored card, in the other a three-dimensional mask worn by the experimenter.

The third experiment differed in that, instead of a real live face, schematic "face forms" (as shown in the illustration) were substituted and the duration of the baby's "fixation" on it, rather than his smile, was measured.

It was hoped that these three experiments would help answer three questions:

■ Do babies show greater responsiveness to faces than non-faces? Prior findings had said yes; and the results of these experiments agree.

■ Does this responsiveness vary according to the angle at which the baby sees the face? In all three studies the infants showed significantly greater response for the face-to-face orientation (0°) than any of the others. There was, however, no particular difference in response between the sideways (90°) and upside-down (180°) orientations.

Therefore, responsiveness to faces *does* vary with orientation for infants under six months old.

■ Does the observed growth and waning of responsiveness during the first six months vary with the baby's angle of view? Analysis of the data is rather complicated, but the answer is yes. Further, they indicate that the growth and decline of interest occurs with the face-to-face orientation. The other angles show little change in effect across the two- to six-month age period.

Enough evidence has accumulated to justify the conclusion that smiling at a face is an almost universal response in normal babies. These experiments further indicate that a smile is only elicited to any appreciable degree face to face.

Smiles to Make You Happy

Could this general pattern of responsive smiling be *necessary* for adequate human development? If so, why? There are two primary ways it could be explained:

■ It could be viewed as a sign of satisfaction.

■ It could be a method of controlling adult behavior—that is, adults might be more pleased by, and thus reward and love, a smiling baby.

If smiling is a sign of satisfaction, then what kind is it? Infants, we find, do not always smile in response to being

Facial Orientations

fed, watered, or changed, if at all. But they are likely to smile at a face almost any time when not in distress.

But what could the mere sight of a face satisfy? One possibility is that babies have needs to receive social stimuli —just as they have the needs to receive food and water— and a face represents the earliest digestible form of social stimulation. The fact that responsiveness declines with time does not contradict this possibility—tastes in food also change. If this view should be true, then seeing faces would have a significant role in the formation of the human social personality. Personality growth itself, therefore, might to some degree depend on the early and frequent opportunity to see faces.

Two independent studies would seem to support this viewpoint. First, Richard Walters and Ross Parke of the University of Waterloo have recently compiled an impressive review of research literature which indicates that early emotional attachment is more dependent on sheer frequency of visual and auditory contact—from anybody— than on any primitive appreciation by the child of who, precisely, is providing for his physical needs. Second, research among emotionally deprived children in institutions has shown that their smiling response is frequently delayed when compared to children who are raised at home. Could it be that institutionalized children simply do not get as much chance, or time, for face-to-face contact with adults? And is it not also probable that in relatively impersonal and shorthanded nurseries the greatest emphasis must be on meeting the baby's physical needs—usually from the side? There is no fond mother available to talk and play with the child face to face. We know that children raised in institutions more often have difficulties in social adjustment. What role does lack of facial stimulation play?

Of course, smiling may not be a sign of satisfaction. Since the baby cannot speak, we cannot know. But even if it were not, the fact is that his smiles make adults feel happy, flattered, and gratified—and this has important and pleasant consequences for the infant. Smiling, therefore, would at least be "social currency"; when the child smiles in response to the faces above him, he tends to reinforce actions that are pleasant and necessary to him, and this, in turn, will reinforce his tendency to smile. The very young human infant is utterly dependent and has little else to offer in exchange. It is not difficult to imagine that in earlier, harsher times the more delightful child who gratified the adults around him might have had an easier chance for survival. In fact, Jacob Gewertz of the National Institute of Mental Health has proposed that we should try to teach institutionalized infants to smile more readily at faces—simply as a practical means of getting better care and more affection for them.

To briefly summarize then: We know that very young infants will attend and smile at faces; that this will increase and then diminish during the first six months of life, usually reaching its peak at about 14 weeks; and that this response is primarily associated with a face-to-face exposure, rather than one from the side or upside down. And, finally, this response may well have some survival value for the infant, either as a necessary factor in personality development or because it may help him secure more nurture, love, and care.

Where's Mother?

But an important question remains: From what angle do modern mothers present their own faces to their infants while caring for them?

This brings us to the fourth experiment—a preliminary study in which 30 mothers and their infants were observed in caretaking activities at the Merrill-Palmer Infant Laboratory. All babies were 9 to 10 weeks old—a good age for this research, since this is the period in which the smiling response is presumably on the rise.

Is the smile of the baby associated with the pleasures and satisfactions of feeding—and with the orientation of the mother's face as she feeds him? Without revealing entirely what our purpose was, we suggested that the mothers—who were waiting for another test—feed their babies since "this should help eliminate fussiness due to hunger during the observational session." Observations of how each mother held her face, relative to her baby's face, were recorded every five seconds for a maximum of five consecutive minutes by an observer behind a one-way mirror in an adjoining room. In 28 of 34 cases it was possible to obtain at least one minute of continuous feeding. The results are in Table I. Only about one-fifth of the time did mothers look at their babies in a face-to-face

Table I: Facial orientations of mothers during first minute of feeding	
0°	21%
45°	28
90°	20
Profile	31
Number of observations—336	

manner while feeding; sideways and profile accounted for almost 60 percent. Quite obviously, therefore, the smiling response, which we know is tied in very strongly with the face-to-face position, cannot come simply from association with the satisfactions of feeding and of being held.

Following the feeding, each infant was placed in a crib, and the mother was asked from time to time to go to her baby and (in different orders for the different mothers) to check three things: the diaper, the baby's eyes to see if they were clear, and to note whether the baby would smile. To do each of these, of course, the mother would have to bring her face somewhere close to her baby, in one orientation or another. Table II shows the results. The evidence is strong that when a mother attends her baby's face, she orients her own face in the 0° position;

Table II: Facial orientations of mothers in response to three requests

Request	0°	45°	90°	Total	No. of Observations
Check diaper	18%	23%	59%	100%	34
Check eyes	70	15	15	100	34
Check smile	79	12	9	100	34

this is not true when she attends the baby's bottom. One conclusion I would draw from these data is that some maternal activities may well be highly associated with face-to-face presentation—even though they may not be of the kind we usually consider caretaking.

Speak to Me of Love

What understanding can these studies give us? First, sheer familiarity—the most common position of the adult face—is not the answer. If it were, the sideways position would have brought many more smiles than the upside-down orientation, and yet they brought about the same. Moreover, visual complexity can not explain the infant's interest in faceness. The face-to-face position, which brought the most smiles, is no more or less complex than the sideways and upside-down orientations. The question sometimes arises: Will non-smiling or fierce expressions produce a different result? In this experiment the smiling face was used for its value to the infant's mother. However, in a few past studies which used non-smiling faces the infants made no fewer smiling responses.

The fourth experiment provides a potential lead to understanding why babies smile. If the baby's smile develops because of something that mothers do, it must be something that is uniquely done from a face-to-face position. Since we have evidence that feeding is not a face-to-face activity, it must be something that is not primarily, or entirely, associated with taste, smell, or touch. What is left? Hearing.

We have some indication that a mother when talking to her baby is most likely to align herself face to face. She seems more apt to speak to him from that position than from a sideways position, or while facing his profile or his bottom. If so, speaking thus would become associated with the face-to-face position.

Because of this association, the 0° face would continue to have a special significance: Even when the mother is not speaking, the baby will smile. And since that smile gives the mother pleasure, she would herself tend to line up in the face-to-face orientation to get it.

But if this is so, then why does the smiling response eventually wane? Some investigators have suggested that as the infant matures he learns to discriminate between his mother's face and others, to respond only to hers. But that obviously means that response to her face would not decline—and yet we have found the mother's face obtains the same growth and waning pattern as the unfamiliar face of the experimenter.

The very factor that most limited our experiments is the one that might give us a special clue. All faces or face drawings that we presented to the child in the first three experiments were silent. If, however, the initial attraction of the 0° face was its association with speech, then the more mature, more sophisticated infant might learn to distinguish between the two and become progressively less interested in a 0° face that did not speak. We are now beginning a systematic study of the effect of speech combined with familiar and unfamiliar faces.

So while it seems clear that an adult can be charmed by a silent face, we may yet discover that a baby's initial social responses cannot grow on face alone.

Threat and Obedience

Elliot Aronson

Most psychologists, parents, and employers have learned that if one wants a rat, a pigeon, a four-year-old child, a college sophomore, or a factory worker to do something, good results can usually be attained by rewarding "good" behavior or by threatening to punish "bad" behavior. Ice cream cones, spankings, food pellets, electric shocks, ridicule, flunking grades, high salaries—these have all been used successfully to control the behavior of children, laboratory animals, or adult humans. Generally, the larger the reward or the more severe the threat of punishment, the greater the likelihood of compliance.

But to induce compliance by rewards and punishments is terribly inefficient, because in order to ensure continued compliance, rewards or punishment must also be continued indefinitely—and often in increasing doses. The indulgent mother must keep doling out candy, the tough foreman can never relax. It would be much more efficient and desirable if society could somehow induce people to enjoy doing things that must be done, and refrain from doing those things that society considers undesirable. For example, few people would run a stop sign if a policeman always stood alongside, pencil conspicuously poised, ready to issue a costly ticket. But it would be more efficient if all drivers could be persuaded to quit running through stop signs, policeman or no.

Such a technique of persuasion—or self-persuasion—is quite possible. It can be derived from Leon Festinger's theory of "cognitive dissonance" which states, briefly, that when a person simultaneously holds two incompatible ideas (cognitions), dissonance occurs. This creates internal tension. Such tension is unpleasant, and the individual tries to diminish it by reducing the dissonance. This can be done by changing one idea (cognition) or the other to bring them closer together and make them more compatible.

For example, suppose one man lies to another. He knows there is a great disparity between what he believes true and what he has said. If he considers himself to be a basically truthful person, dissonance is set up. One way for him to reduce it is to rationalize—to convince himself that it wasn't such a big lie after all, and therefore closer to the truth than it seemed. This involves changing prior attitudes and beliefs. An even better technique to diminish dissonance is to justify the lie, since the amount of dissonance depends on the strength of his motives (what caused him to lie in the first place?). The greater the pressure and need to lie, the less the dissonance. For example, if he told a small lie to save a life, or to become very wealthy, he will experience little dissonance—the consequences help justify the act. "All right," he can say in effect, "so I told a lie—but it was worth it." His basic attitudes have not changed; he still sees himself as the same truthful person, adapting to exceptional circumstances.

But if he receives little or no reward for lying, he will have a great deal of dissonance, and will much more likely change his prior attitudes ("It wasn't such a big lie") to cut down the tension.

Several experiments in the last few years support this idea: people who tell a lie—say things they do not think right—and get only *small* rewards for them, undergo *greater* changes in attitude than those who tell the *same* lies for *large* rewards.

TO BEAT OR NOT TO BEAT

A few years ago (1963), Merrill Carlsmith and I applied dissonance theory to the problem of punishment, in an attempt to understand the relationship between degree of punishment and extent of attitude change. We reasoned that if you threaten to punish a person for a particular action, the more severe the threat, the greater the likelihood that he will refrain from the activity—while you are there watching him. But if you reduced the threat, you might succeed in producing a more permanent change in behavior through inducing a dislike of that activity.

For example, suppose you have a young child who likes to beat up his little brother and you want him to stop. Probably the best way to get him to stop is to threaten to hit him and hit him hard. The more severe the threat, the greater likelihood that he will stop, at that moment, *while you're watching him*. However, he may very well hit his brother again as soon as you turn your back.

But suppose instead that you threaten him with a very mild punishment—a punishment which is just barely se-

vere enough to get him to stop aggressing at that time. In either case—under threat of severe punishment or of mild—the child is experiencing dissonance—he is aware that he is not beating up on his little brother while also aware that he wants to. When the little brother is present, the child has the urge to beat him up and, when he refrains, he asks himself in effect, "How come I'm not beating up my little brother?" Under severe threat he has a ready answer: "I know damn well why I'm not beating up my little brother. I'm not beating him up because if I do, that giant standing over there (my father) is going to knock the hell out of me." In effect, the severe threat of punishment has provided the child with justifications for not beating up his brother, *at that moment, while he's being watched*.

But consider the child in the mild threat situation; he experiences dissonance too. He asks himself, in effect, "How come I'm not beating up my little brother?" But the difference is that he doesn't have a good answer—because the threat (loss of candy, for example) was so mild that it does not provide complete justification for staying stopped. In this situation he continues to experience dissonance. There is no simple way for him to reduce it by blaming his inaction on a severe threat. He must, therefore, find reasons consonant with not hitting his little brother. He can, for instance, try to convince himself that he really doesn't like to beat his brother up, that he didn't want to do it in the first place.

In sum, Carlsmith and I suggested that one way to get a person to inhibit an activity is to get him to devalue it—and one way to get him to devalue it is to stop him in the first place with a mild threat rather than a severe one.

In our experiment, for ethical reasons, we did not try to manipulate basic values like aggression (beating up brothers). Instead, we chose a much more mundane value—toy preference. We first asked children to rate the attractiveness of several toys; then we chose one that a child considered to be quite attractive, and we told him he couldn't play with it. With one experimental group we threatened mild punishment for transgression—"I would be a little annoyed"; with the other, we threatened severe punishment—"I would be very angry. I would have to take all of my toys and go home and never come back again. I would think you were just a baby." After that, we left the room and allowed the children to play with the other toys—and perhaps to resist the temptation to play with the forbidden one. On returning to the room, we remeasured the attractiveness of all of the toys. We found that those children who were forbidden to play with a toy under a threat of mild punishment now derogated the toy. Those children under a severe threat did not derogate it.

Subsequent experiments have confirmed and extended our conclusion. In one recent experiment, Elizabeth Anne Turner and John C. Wright (1965) have confirmed our finding. In addition, they have shown clearly that derogation of the crucial toy occurs in the mild threat (high dissonance) situation in spite of a strong general tendency for children to overemphasize the attractiveness of a toy with which they have had little experience. That is, while they refrained from playing with the crucial toy, they *were* playing with other toys. The crucial toy was rated as less attractive (relative to the others) in spite of the fact that they tended to become satiated with the others. In a control situation where no threats were used, but the crucial toy was simply concealed from the children, they rated it *more* attractive than the others. Thus, not only did Turner and Wright show that a mild threat induces children to derogate the toy, they also showed that this dissonance effect is a very powerful one—powerful enough to overcome the appeal of that toy's novelty.

THE EFFECTIVE THREAT

Carlsmith and I originally reasoned that dissonance through insufficient threat of punishment would produce a long-lasting effect—because the individual *himself* was induced to derogate the activity. The child ceased playing with a toy, not because someone told him it was not fun, but because he convinced *himself* that it was not fun. But we did not design our experiment to provide for a thorough test of derogation over time. However, Jonathan L. Freedman has recently (1965) produced striking evidence confirming our speculations about the long-lasting effect of a mild threat. In his experiment, he repeated our procedure with minor changes. The crucial toy was by far the most attractive to all the children; it was one of those super-duper battery powered robots which hurls bombs against a child's enemies. The other toys were trivial by comparison. Freedman forbade the children to play with the mechanical robot, using mild threats for some and severe for others.

After some twenty-three to sixty-four days had elapsed, different experimenters came to the classroom under totally unrelated circumstances to administer a psychological test. They tested the students in the same room that was used by Freedman—the original toys were rather carelessly strewn about. After each experimenter had administered one test to a child, she told him that she would have to score it and might want to ask him some questions about it later—and while he was waiting, if he wanted to, he could amuse himself by playing with some of the toys lying around. The second experimenters, of course, did not know what part each child had played in Freedman's study.

The results were clear and exciting. Of twenty-one children under mild threat, only six played with the crucial toy; of the twenty-one under severe threat, fourteen played with it. The results are highly significant. The effect of a *single mild threat* was not only strong enough to lower the attractiveness of a preferred toy (as in the Aronson-Carlsmith experiment), it also was powerful enough to inhibit their playing with that toy as much as sixty-four days later!

The effects demonstrated in these experiments may very well apply beyond mere toy preference, to more basic and important values. For example, a parent might have more success in controlling aggressiveness in a child if he used threats of mild rather than severe punishment. By doing this, he might help the child convince himself that aggression is undesirable and so bring about a lasting change in his behavior. Studies in child development suggest clearly that parents who use severe punishment to stop a child's aggression do not succeed in curtailing it. In fact, aggressiveness in children increases directly with the severity of parental punishment. The more harshly a parent treats a child, the more aggressive he becomes, at least outside of the home.

On the other hand, although there appears to be no obvious reason why the results of these experiments cannot be replicated using more important value systems, caution is dictated in generalizing beyond the actual data until such replications are forthcoming. Moreover, the practical application of these results hinges upon the subtle problem of finding precisely the correct amount of threatened punishment—a threat which is severe enough to induce momentary compliance and yet mild enough to provide inadequate justification for that compliance. In the experiments described here, 100 percent compliance was achieved with the use of a very mild threat. My guess is that this high degree of compliance was aided by the fact that the experimenters were strangers; children are known not to comply as readily to the requests of their parents as to those of strangers.

Clearly, more research is needed before we can determine whether these techniques can bring about either a more efficient, more civilized society or an Orwellian nightmare.

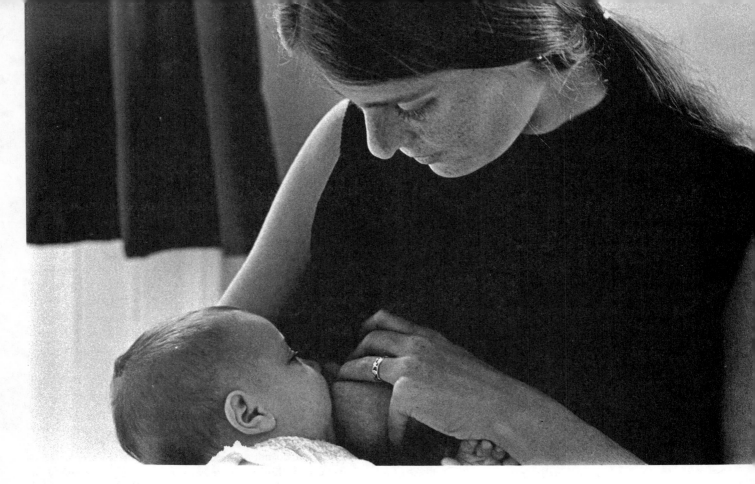

The Social Construction of the Second Sex

Jo Freeman

The passivity that is the essential characteristic of the "feminine" woman is a trait that develops in her from the earliest years. But it is wrong to assert a biological datum is concerned; it is in fact a destiny imposed upon her by her teachers and by society.

Simone de Beauvoir

During the last 30 years social science has paid scant attention to women, confining its explorations of humanity to the male. Research has generally reinforced the popular mythology that women are essentially nurturant, expressive, passive and men instrumental, active, aggressive. Social scientists have tended to justify these stereotypes rather than analyze their origins, their value or their effect.

The result of this trend has been a social science that is more a mechanism of social control than of social inquiry. Rather than trying to analyze why, it has only described what. Rather than exploring how men and women came to be the way they are, it has taken their condition as irrevocably given and sought to explain this on the basis of "biological" differences.

Nonetheless, the assumption that psychology recapitulates physiology has begun to crack. William Masters and Virginia Johnson shattered the myth of woman's natural sexual passivity—on which her psychological passivity was claimed to rest. Research is just beginning in other areas, and while evidence is being accumulated, new interpretations of the old data are being explored. What these new interpretations say is that women are the way they are because they've been trained to be that way—their motivations as well as their alternatives have been channelled by society.

This motivation is controlled through the socialization process. Women are raised to want to fill the social roles in which society needs them. They are trained to model themselves after the accepted image and to meet as individuals the expectations that are held for women as a group. Therefore, to understand how most women are socialized we must first understand how they see themselves and are seen by others. Several studies have been done on this.

One thorough study asked men and women to choose out of a long list of adjectives those that most closely applied to themselves. The results showed that women strongly felt that they could accurately be described as uncertain, anxious, nervous, hasty, careless, fearful, dull, childish, helpless, sorry, timid, clumsy, stupid, silly and domestic. On the more positive side women felt they were understanding, tender, sympathetic, pure, generous, affectionate, loving, moral, kind, grateful and patient. This is not a very favorable self-image, but it does correspond fairly well to the myths about what women are like. The image has some "nice" qualities, but they are not the ones normally required for the kinds of achievement to which society gives its highest rewards.

Gross Distortions

Now, one can justifiably question both the idea of achievement and the qualities necessary for it, but this is not the place to do so. The fact remains that these standards are widely accepted and that women have been told they do not meet them. My purpose here, then, is to look at the socialization process as a mechanism to keep them from doing so. All people are socialized to meet the social expectations held for them, and only when this process fails to work (as is currently happening on several fronts) is it at all questioned.

When we look at the *results* of female socialization we find a strong similarity between what our society labels, even extols, as the typical "feminine" character structure and that of oppressed peoples in this country and elsewhere. In his classic study on *The Nature of Prejudice*, Gordon Allport devotes a chapter to "Traits Due to Victimization." Included are such personality characteristics as sensitivity, submission, fantasies of power, desire for protection, indirectness, ingratiation, petty revenge and sabotage, sympathy, extremes of both self and group hatred and self and group glorification, display of flashy status symbols, compassion for the underprivileged, identification with the dominant group's norms and passivity. Allport was primarily concerned with Jews and Negroes, but his characterization is disturbingly congruent with the general profile of girls that Lewis Terman and Leona Tyler draw after a very thorough review of the literature on sex differences among young children. For girls, they listed such traits as sensitivity, conformity to social pressures, response to environment, ease of social control, ingratiation, sympathy, low levels of aspiration, compassion for the underprivileged and anxiety. They found that girls compared to boys were more nervous, unstable, neurotic, socially dependent, submissive, had less self-confidence, lower opinions of themselves and of girls in general, and were more timid, emotional, ministrative, fearful and passive.

Girls' perceptions of themselves were also distorted. Although girls make consistently better school grades than boys until late high school, their opinion of themselves grows progressively worse with age and their opinion of boys and boys' abilities grows better. Boys, however, have an increasingly better opinion of themselves and worse opinion of girls as they grow older.

These distortions become so gross that, according to Phillip Goldberg in an article in this magazine, by the time girls reach college they have become prejudiced against women. He gave college girls sets of booklets containing six identical professional articles in traditional male, female and neutral fields. The articles were identical, but the names of the authors were not. For example, an article in one set would bear the name John T. McKay, and in another set the same article would be by-lined Joan T. McKay. Each booklet contained three articles by "women" and three by "men." Questions at the end of each article asked the students to rate the articles on value, persuasiveness and profundity and the authors for style and competence. The male authors fared better on every dimension, even such "feminine" areas as art history and dietetics. Goldberg concluded that "women are prejudiced against female professionals and, regardless of the actual accomplishments of these professionals, will firmly refuse to recognize them as the equals of their male colleagues."

This combination of group self-hate and a distortion of perceptions to justify that group self-hate is precisely typical of a minority group character structure. It has been noted time and time again. Kenneth and Mamie Clark's finding of the same pattern in Negro children in segregated schools contributed to the 1954 Supreme Court decision that outlawed such schools. These traits, as well as the others typical of the "feminine" stereotype, have been found in the Indians under British rule, in the Algerians under the French and in black Americans. It would seem,

105

then, that being "feminine" is related to low social status.

This pattern repeats itself even within cultures. In giving Thematic Apperception Tests to women in Japanese villages, George De Vos discovered that those from fishing villages, where the status position of women was higher than in farming communities, were more assertive, not as guilt-ridden and were more willing to ignore the traditional pattern of arranged marriages in favor of love marriages.

In Terman's famous 50-year study of the gifted, a comparison of those men who conspicuously failed to fulfill their early promise with those who did, showed that the successful had more self-confidence, fewer background disabilities and were less nervous and emotionally unstable. But, he concluded, "the disadvantages associated with lower social home status appeared to present the outstanding handicap."

Sexual Characteristics

The fact that women do have lower social status than men in our society and that both sexes tend to value men, and male characteristics, values and activities more highly than those of women, has been noted by many authorities. What has not been done is to make the connection between this status and its accompanying personality. The failure to analyze the effects and the causes of lower social status among women is surprising in light of the many efforts that have been made to uncover distinct psychological differences between men and women to account for the tremendous disparity in their social production and creativity. The Goldberg study implies that even if women did achieve on a par with men it would not be perceived or accepted as such and that a woman's work must be of a much higher quality than that of a man to be given the same recognition. But these circumstances alone, or the fact that it is the male definition of achievement which is applied, are not sufficient to account for the relative failure of women to achieve. So research has turned to male-female differences.

Most of this research, in the Freudian tradition, has focused on finding the psychological and developmental differences supposedly inherent in feminine nature and function. Despite all these efforts, the general findings of psychological testing indicate only that individual differences are greater than sex differences. In other words, sex is just one of the many characteristics that define a human being.

An examination of the work done on intellectual differences between the sexes discloses some interesting patterns, however. First of all, the statistics themselves show some regularity. Most conclusions of what is typical of one sex or the other are founded upon the performances of two-thirds of the subjects. For example, two-thirds of all boys do better on the math section of the College Board Exam than they do on the verbal section, and two-thirds of the girls do better on the verbal than the math. Robert Bales' studies show a similar distribution when he concludes that in small groups men are the task-oriented leaders and women are the social-emotional leaders. Not all tests show this two-thirds differential, but it is the mean about which most results of the ability tests cluster. Sex is an easily visible, differentiable and testable criterion on which to draw conclusions; but it doesn't explain the one-third that do not fit. The only characteristic virtually all women seem to have in common, besides their anatomy, is their lower social status.

Secondly, girls get off to a very good start. They begin speaking, reading and counting sooner. They articulate more clearly and put words into sentences earlier. They have fewer reading and stuttering problems. Girls are even better in math in the early school years. Consistent sex differences in favor of boys do not appear until high school age. Here another pattern begins to develop.

During high school, girls' performance in school and on ability tests begins to drop, sometimes drastically. Although well over half of all high-school graduates are girls, significantly less than half of all college students are girls. Presumably, this should mean that a higher percentage of the better female students go on to higher education, but their performance vis-a-vis boys' continues to decline.

Only Men Excel

Girls start off better than boys and end up worse. This change in their performance occurs at a very significant point in time. It happens when their status changes or, to be more precise, when girls become aware of what their adult status is supposed to be. It is during adolescence that peer group pressures to be "feminine" or "masculine" increase and the conceptions of what is "feminine" and "masculine" become more narrow. It is also at this time that there is a personal drive for conformity. And one of the norms of our culture to which a girl learns to conform is that only men excel. This was evident in Beatrice Lipinski's study on *Sex-Role Conflict and Achievement Motivation in College Women* which showed that thematic pictures depicting males as central characters elicited significantly more achievement imagery than those with females in them. One need only recall Asch's experiments to see how peer group pressures, armed only with our rigid ideas about "feminity" and "masculinity" could lead to a decline in girls' performance. Asch found that some 33 percent of his subjects would go contrary to the evidence of their own senses about something as tangible as the comparative length of two lines when their judgements were at variance with those made by the other group members. All but a handful of the other 67 percent experienced tremendous trauma in trying to stick to their correct perceptions.

When we move to something as intangible as sex role behavior and to social sanctions far greater than the displeasure of a group of unknown experimental stooges we can get an idea of how stifling social expectations can be. A corollary of the notion that only men can excel is the cultural norm that a girl should not appear too smart or surpass boys in anything. Again, the pressures to conform, so prevalent in adolescence, prompt girls to believe that the development of their minds will have only negative results. These pressures even affect the supposedly unchangeable IQ scores. Corresponding with the drive for social acceptance, girls' IQs drop below those of boys during high school, rise slightly if they go to college and go into a steady and consistent decline when and if they become full-time housewives.

These are not the only consequences. Negative self-conceptions have negative effects. They stifle motivation and channel energies into areas more likely to get some positive social rewards. The clincher comes when the very people (women) who have been subjected to these pressures are condemned for not having striven for the highest rewards society has to offer.

A good example of this double bind is what psychologists call the "need for achievement." Achievement motivation in male college sophomores has been studied extensively. In women it has barely been looked at. The reason for this is that women didn't fit the model social scientists set up to explain achievement in men. Nonetheless, some theories have been put forward which suggest that the real situation is not that women do not have achievement motivation but that this motivation is directed differently than that of men. In fact, the achievement orientation of both sexes goes precisely where it is socially directed—educational achievement for boys and marriage achievement for girls.

After considerable research on the question James Pierce concluded that "girls see that to achieve in life as adult females they need to achieve in non-academic ways, that is, attaining the social graces, achieving beauty in person and dress, finding a desirable social status, marrying the right man. This is the successful adult woman . . . Their achievement motivations are directed toward realizing personal goals through their relationship with men . . . Girls who are following the normal course of development are most likely to seek adult status through marriage at an early age."

Achievement for women is adult status through marriage, not success in the usual use of the word. One might postulate that both kinds of success might be possible, particularly for the highly achievement-oriented woman. But in fact the two are more often perceived as contradictory; success in one is seen to preclude success in the other.

Matina Horner recently completed a study at the University of Michigan from which she postulated a psychological barrier to achievement in women. She administered a test in which she asked undergraduates to complete the sentence, "After first term finals Anne finds herself at the top of her medical school class," with a story of their own. A similar one for a male control group used a masculine name. The results were scored for imagery of fear of success and Horner found that 65 percent of the women and only 10 percent of the men demonstrated a definite "motive to avoid success." She explained the results by hypothesizing that the prospect of success, or situations in which success or failure is a relevant dimension, are perceived as, and in fact do, have negative consequences for women.

While many of the choices and attitudes of woman are determined by peer and cultural pressures, many other sex differences appear too early to be much affected by peer groups and are not directly related to sex role attributes.

Analytic Children

One such sex difference is spatial perception, or the ability to visualize objects out of their context. This is a test in which boys do better, though differences are usually not discernible before the early school years. Other tests, such as the Embedded Figures and the Rod and Frame Tests, likewise favor boys. They indicate that boys perceive more analytically while girls are more contextual. Again, however, this ability to "break set" or be "field independent" also does not seem to appear until after the fourth or fifth year.

According to Eleanor Maccoby, this contextual mode of perception common to women is a distinct disadvantage for scientific production: "Girls on the average develop a somewhat different way of handling incoming information—their thinking is less analytic, more global, and more perservative[sic]—and this kind of thinking may serve very well for many kinds of functioning but it is not the kind of thinking most conducive to high-level intellectual productivity, especially in science."

Several social psychologists have postulated that the key

107

developmental characteristic of analytic thinking is what is called early "independence and mastery training," or as one group of researchers put it, "whether and how soon a child is encouraged to assume initiative, to take responsibility for himself, and to solve problems by himself, rather than rely on others for the direction of his activities." In other words, analytically inclined children are those who have not been subject to what Urie Bronfenbrenner calls "oversocialization," and there is a good deal of indirect evidence that such is the case. D.M. Levy has observed that "overprotected" boys tend to develop intellectually like girls. Bing found that those girls who were good at spatial tasks were those whose mothers left them alone to solve the problems by themselves while the mothers of verbally inclined daughters insisted on helping them. H.A. Witkin similarly found that mothers of analytic children had encouraged their initiative while mothers of nonanalytic children had encouraged dependence and discouraged self-assertion. One writer commented on these studies that "this is to be expected, for the independent child is less likely to accept superficial appearances of objects without exploring them for himself, while the dependent child will be afraid to reach out on his own, and will accept appearances without question. In other words, the independent child is likely to be more active, not only psychologically but physically, and the physically active child will naturally have more kinesthetic experience with spatial relationships in his environment."

The qualities associated with independence training also have an effect on IQ. I.W. Sontag did a longitudinal study in which he compared children whose IQs had improved with those whose IQs had declined with age. He discovered that the child with increasing IQ was competitive, self-assertive, independent and dominant in interaction with other children. Children with declining IQs were passive, shy and dependent.

Maccoby commented on this study that "the characteristics associated with a rising IQ are not very feminine characteristics." When one of the people working on the Sontag study was asked about what kind of developmental history was necessary to make a girl into an intellectual person, he replied, "The simplest way to put it is that she must be a tomboy at some point in her childhood."

However, analytic abilities are not the only ones that are valued in our society. Being person-oriented and contextual in perception are very valuable attributes for many fields where, nevertheless, very few women are found. Such characteristics are also valuable in the arts and some of the social sciences. But while women do succeed here more than in the sciences, their achievement is still not equivalent to that of men. One explanation of this, of course, is the study by Horner which established a "motive to avoid success" among women. But when one looks further it appears that there is an earlier cause here as well.

Sons and Daughters

The very same early independence and mastery training which has such a beneficial effect on analytic thinking also determines the extent of one's achievement orientation. Although comparative studies of parental treatment of boys and girls are not extensive, those that have been made indicate that the traditional practices applied to girls are very different from those applied to boys. Girls receive more affection, more protectiveness, more control and more restrictions. Boys are subjected to more achievement demands and higher expectations. In short, while girls are not always encouraged to be dependent per se, they are usually not encouraged to be independent and physically active. As Bronfenbrenner put it, "Such findings indicate that the differential treatment of the two sexes reflects in part a difference in goals. With sons, socialization seems to focus primarily on directing and constraining the boys' impact on the environment. With daughters, the aim is rather to protect the girl from the impact of environment. The boy is being prepared to mold his world, the girl to be molded by it."

Bronfenbrenner concludes that the crucial variable is the differential treatment by the father, and "in fact, it is the father who is especially likely to treat children of the two sexes differently." His extremes of affection and of authority are both deleterious. Not only do his high degrees of nurturance and protectiveness toward girls result in "oversocialization" but "the presence of strong paternal . . . power, is particularly debilitating. In short, boys thrive in a patriarchal context, girls in a matriarchal one."

Bronfenbrenner's observations receive indirect support from Elizabeth Douvan who noted that "part-time jobs of mothers have a beneficial effect on adolescent children, particularly daughters. This reflects the fact that adolescents may receive too much mothering."

Anxiety

The importance of mothers, as well as mothering, was pointed out by Kagan and Moss. In looking at the kinds of role models that mothers provide for developing daughters, they discovered that it is those women who are looked upon as unfeminine whose daughters tend to achieve intellectually. These mothers are "aggressive and competitive women who were critical of their daughters and presented themselves to their daughters as intellectually competitive and aggressive role models. It is reasonable to assume that the girls identified with these intellectually aggressive women who valued mastery behavior."

To sum up, there seems to be some evidence that the sexes have been differentially socialized with different training practices, for different goals and with different results. If David McClelland is right in all the relationships he finds between child-rearing practices, in particular independence and mastery training, achievement motivations scores of individuals tested, actual achievement of individuals and, indeed, the economic growth of whole societies, there is no longer much question as to why the historical achievement of women has been so low. In fact, with the dependency training they receive so early in life, the wonder is that they have achieved so much.

But this is not the whole story. Maccoby, in her discussion of the relationship of independence training to analytic abilities, notes that the girl who does not succumb to overprotection and develop the appropriate personality and behavior for her sex has a major price to pay—a price in anxiety. Some anxiety is beneficial to creative thinking, but high or sustained levels of it are damaging. Anxiety is particularly manifest in college women, and of course they are the ones who experience the most conflict between their current—intellectual—activities and expectations about their future—unintellectual—careers.

Maccoby feels that "it is this anxiety which helps to account for the lack of productivity among those women who do make intellectual careers." The combination of social pressures, role expectations and parental training together tells "something of a horror story. It would appear that even when a woman is suitably endowed intellectually and develops the right temperament and habits of thought to make use of her endowment, she must be fleet of foot indeed to scale the hurdles society has erected for her and to remain a whole and happy person while continuing to follow her intellectual bent."

The reasons for this horror story must by now be clearly evident. Traditionally, women have been defined as passive creatures, sexually, physically and mentally. Their roles have been limited to the passive, dependent, auxiliary ones, and they have been trained from birth to fit these roles. However, those qualities by which one succeeds in this society are active ones. Achievement orientation, intellectuality, analytic ability all require a certain amount of aggression.

As long as women were convinced that these qualities were beyond them, that they would be much happier if they stayed in their place, they remained quiescent under the paternalistic system of Western civilization. But paternalism was a pre-industrial scheme of life, and its yoke was partially broken by the industrial revolution. With this loosening up of the social order, the talents of women began to appear.

In the eighteenth century it was held that no woman had ever produced anything worthwhile in literature with the possible exception of Sappho. But in the first half of the nineteenth century, feminine writers of genius flooded the literary scene. It wasn't until the end of the nineteenth century that women scientists of note appeared and still later that women philosophers were found.

Lords at Home

In pre-industrial societies, the family was the basic unit of social and economic organization, and women held a significant and functional role within it. This, coupled with the high birth and death rates of those times, gave women more than enough to do within the home. It was the center of production, and women could be both at home and in the world at the same time. But the industrial revolution, along with decreased infant mortality, increased life span and changes in economic organization, has all but destroyed the family as the economic unit. Technological advances have taken men out of the home, and now those functions traditionally defined as female are being taken out also. For the first time in human history women have had to devote themselves to being full-time mothers in order to have enough to do.

Conceptions of society have also changed. At one time, authoritiarian hierarchies were the norm, and paternalism was reflective of a general social authoritarian attitude. While it is impossible to do retroactive studies on feudalistic society, we do know that authoritarianism as a personality trait does correlate strongly with a rigid conception of sex roles, and with ethnocentrism. We also know from ethnological data that, As W.N. Stephens wrote, there is a "parallel between family relationships and the larger social hierarchy. Autocratic societies have autocratic families. As the king rules his subjects and the nobles subjugate and exploit the commoners, so does husband tend to lord it over wife, father rule over son."

According to Roy D'Andrade, "another variable that appears to affect the distribution of authority and deference between the sexes is the degree to which men rather than women control and mediate property." He presented evidence that showed a direct correlation between the extent to which inheritance, succession and descent-group membership were patrilineal and the degree of subjection of women.

Even today, the equality of the sexes in the family is often reflective of the economic quality of the partners. In a Detroit sample, Robert Blood and D.M. Wolfe found that the relative power of the wife was low if she did not work and increased with her economic contribution to the family. "The employment of women affects the power structure of the family by equalizing the resources of husband and wife. A working wife's husband listens to her more, and she listens to herself more. She expresses herself and has more opinions. Instead of looking up into her husband's eyes and worshipping him, she levels with him, compromising on the issues at hand. Thus her power increases and, relatively speaking, the husband's falls."

William J. Goode also noted this pattern but said it varied inversely with class status. Toward the upper strata wives are not only less likely to work but when they do they contribute a smaller percentage of the total family income than is true in the lower classes. Reuben Hill went so far as to say "Money is a source of power that supports male dominance in the family . . . Money belongs to him who earns it not to her who spends it, since he who earns it may withhold it." Phyllis Hallenbeck feels more than just economic resources are involved but does conclude that there is a balance of power in every family which affects "every other aspect of the marriage—division of labor, amount of adaptation necessary for either spouse, methods used to resolve conflicts, and so forth." Blood feels the economic situation affects the whole family structure. "Daughters of working mothers are more independent, more self-reliant, more aggressive, more dominant, and more disobedient. Such girls are no longer meek, mild, submissive, and feminine like 'little ladies' ought to be. They are rough and tough, actively express their ideas, and refuse to take anything from anybody else . . . Because their mothers have set an example, the daughters get up the courage and the desire to earn money as well. They take more part-time jobs after school and more jobs during summer vacation."

Sex and Work

Herbert Barry, M.K. Bacon and Irvin Child did an ethno-historiographic analysis which provides some further insights into the origins of male dominance. After examining the ethnographic reports of 110 cultures, they concluded that large sexual differentiation and male superiority occur concurrently and in "an economy that places a high premium on the superior strength and superior development of motor skills requiring strength, which characterize the male." It is those societies in which great physical strength and mobility are required for survival, in which hunting and herding, or warfare, play an important role, that the male, as the physically stronger and more mobile sex, tends to dominate.

Although there are a few tasks which virtually every society assigns only to men or women, there is a great deal of overlap for most jobs. Virtually every task, even in the most primitive societies, can be performed by either men or women. Equally important, what is defined as a man's task in one society may well be classified as a woman's job in another. Nonetheless, the sexual division of labor is much more narrow than dictated by physical limitations, and what any one culture defines as a woman's job will seldom be performed by a man and vice versa. It seems that what originated as a division of labor based upon the necessities of survival has spilled over into many other areas and lasted long past the time of its social value. Where male strength and mobility have been crucial to social survival, male dominance and the aura of male superiority have been the strongest. The latter has been incorporated into the value structure and attained an existence of its own.

Thus, male superiority has not ceased with an end to the need for male strength. As Goode pointed out, there is one consistent element in the assignment of jobs to the sexes, even in modern societies: "Whatever the strictly male tasks are, they are defined as *more honorific* [emphasis his] . . .Moreover, the tasks of control, management, decision, appeals to the gods—in short the higher level jobs that typically do not require strength, speed or traveling far from home—are male jobs."

He goes on to comment that "this element suggests that the sexual divisions of labor within family and society, come perilously close to the racial or caste restrictions in some modern countries. That is, the low-ranking race, caste, or sex is defined as not being able to do certain types of prestigious work, but it is also considered a violation of propriety if they do. Obviously, if women really cannot do various kinds of male tasks, no moral or ethical prohibition would be necessary to keep them from it."

Companionship

These sex role differences may have served a natural function at one time, but it is doubtful that they still do so.

The characteristics we observe in women and men today are a result of socialization practices developed for the survival of a primitive society. The value structure of male superiority is a reflection of the primitive orientations and values. But social and economic conditions have changed drastically since these values were developed. Technology has reduced to almost nothing the importance of muscular strength. In fact, the warlike attitude that goes along with an idealization of physical strength and dominance is coming to be seen as dreadfully dangerous. The value of large families has also come to be questioned. The result of all these changes is that the traditional sex roles and the traditional family structures have become dysfunctional.

To some extent, patterns of child rearing have also changed. Bronfenbrenner reports that at least middle-class parents are raising both boys and girls much the same. He noted that over a 50-year period middle-class parents have been developing a "more acceptant, equalitarian relationship with their children." With an increase in the family's social position, the patterns of parental treatment of children begin to converge. He likewise noted that a similar phenomenon is beginning to develop in lower-class parents and that equality of treatment is slowly working its way down the social ladder.

These changes in patterns of child rearing correlate with changes in relationships within the family. Both are moving toward a less hierarchical and more egalitarian pattern of living. As Blood has pointed out, "today we may be on the verge of a new phase in American family history, when the companionship family is beginning to manifest itself. One distinguishing characteristic of this family is the dual employment of husband and wife . . . Employment emancipates women from domination by their husbands and, secondarily, raises their daughters from inferiority to their brothers . . . The classic differences between masculinity and femininity are disappearing as both sexes in the adult generation take on the same roles in the labor market . . . The roles of men and women are converging for both adults and children. As a result the family will be far less segregated internally, far less stratified into different age generations and different sexes. The old asymmetry of male dominated, female-serviced family life is being replaced by a new symmetry."

Leftover Definitions

All these data indicate that several trends are converging at about the same time. Our value structure has changed from an authoritarian one to a more democratic one, though our social structure has not yet caught up. Social attitudes begin in the family; only a democratic family can raise children to be citizens in a democratic society. The social and economic organization of society which kept women in the home has likewise changed. The home is no longer the center of society. The primary male and female functions have left it, and there is no longer any major reason for maintaining the large sex role differentiations that the home supported. The value placed on physical strength, which reinforced the dominance of men, and the male superiority attitudes that this generated have also become dysfunctional. It is the mind, not the body, that society needs now, and woman's mind is the equal of man's. The pill has liberated women from the uncertainty of childbearing, and with it the necessity of being attached to a man for economic support. But our attitudes toward women, and toward the family, have not changed. There is a distinct "cultural lag." Definitions of the family, conceptions of women and ideas about social function are left over from an era when they were necessary for social survival. They have persisted into an era in which they are no longer viable. The result can only be called severe role dysfunctionality for women.

The necessary relief for this dysfunctionality must come through changes in the social and economic organization of society and in social attitudes that will permit women to play a full and equal part in the social order. With this must come changes in the family, so that men and women are not only equal but can raise their children in a democratic atmosphere. These changes will not come easily, nor will they come through the simple evolution of social trends. Trends do not move all in the same direction or at the same rate. To the extent that changes are dysfunctional with each other they create problems. These problems will be solved not by complacency but by conscious human direction. Only in this way can we have a real say in the shape of our future and the shape of our lives.

Roots of Black Manhood

Ulf Hannerz

Some 5.7 million people were simply not counted in the 1960 census, and most of them, it now appears, were Negro men living in northern cities. This statistical oversight, if that is what it was, is not unique to the government's census takers. Ever since the beginnings of the scholarly study of black people in the Americas, there has been an interesting fascination with the differences between the family life of Negroes and that of their white counterparts, the chief difference being seen as the dominant, not to say dominating, role of women in black families.

From E. Franklin Frazier's pioneering 1932 study of *The Negro Family in Chicago* through Melville Herskovits' *The Myth of the Negro Past* in 1941 to the so-called Moynihan Report of 1965, social scientists have been repeatedly rediscovering, analyzing and worrying over the crucial role of the mother (or grandmother) in the family structure of blacks in the New World. Herskovits saw the centrality of the mother as an African vestige, typical of the polygynous marriage in which every woman, with her offspring, formed a separate unit. Frazier is generally regarded as the first to ascribe to the institution of slavery itself the strongest influence in undermining the stability of marriage, an influence that was later reinforced when blacks encountered what Frazier perceived as the peculiarly urban evils of anonymity, disorganization and the lack of social support and controls. Moynihan, like Frazier, sees the matriarchal family as being practically without strengths, at least in the context of the larger American society, but his Report emphasizes the ways in which employer discrimination and, more recently, welfare policies have contributed to the breaking up (or foreclosure) of the male-dominated family unit among blacks.

In all of these studies, however, the black *man*—as son, lover, husband, father, grandfather—is a distant and shadowy figure "out there somewhere" . . . if only because his major characteristic as far as the household is concerned is his marginality or absence.

I do not mean to suggest that the black man is undiscovered territory. Obviously he is not. His popular image was fixed for one (long) era in *Uncle Tom's Cabin* and prophetically fashioned for our own time in Norman Mailer's essay "The White Negro." Here is Mailer's Hipster, modeled on the Negro: "Sharing a collective disbelief in the words of men who had too much money and controlled too many things, they knew almost as powerful a disbelief in the socially monolithic ideas of the single mate, the solid family and the respectable love life." And here is Mailer's black man:

> Knowing in the cells of his existence that life was war, nothing but war, the Negro (all exceptions admitted) could rarely afford the sophisticated inhibitions of civilization, and so he kept for his survival the art of the primitive, he lived in the enormous present, he subsisted for his Saturday night kicks, relinquishing the pleasures of the mind for the more obligatory pleasures of the body, and in his music he gave voice to the character and quality of his existence, to his rage and the infinite variations of joy, lust, languor, growl, cramp, pinch, scream and despair of his orgasm.

Certainly there is poetic exaggeration in Mailer's description, and perhaps a conscious effort to mythicize his subject; and certainly too there is a great deal of stereotyping in the general public's imagery of the people of the black ghetto. But hardly anyone acquainted with life in the ghetto can fail to see that Mailer's portrait captures much of the reality as well. Lee Rainwater's sketch of the "expressive life-style" of the black male shows a trained social scientist's analysis that is remarkably similar to Mailer's. And undoubtedly there *is* a sizable segment of the black male population that is strongly concerned with sex, drinking, sharp clothes and "trouble"; and among these men one finds many of those who are only marginally involved with married life. Of course, ghetto life styles are heterogeneous, and there are many men who live according to "mainstream" values; but it is to the ones who do not that we should turn our attention if we want to understand what kinds of masculinity go with the female-dominated family.

This essay is an attempt to outline the social processes within the ghetto communities of the northern United States whereby the identity of street-corner males is established and maintained. To set the stage and state the issues involved in this essay, I'd like to look at the views of two other observers of the ghetto male. One is Charles Keil, whose *Urban Blues* (1966) is a study of the bluesman as a "culture hero." According to Keil, the urban blues singer, with his emphasis on sexuality, "trouble" and flashy clothes, manifests a cultural model of maleness that is highly valued by ghetto dwellers and relatively independent of the mainstream cultural tradition. Keil criticizes a number of authors who, without cavilling at this description of the male role, tend to see it as rooted in the individual's anxiety about his masculinity. This, Keil finds, is unacceptably ethnocentric:

Any sound analysis of Negro masculinity should first deal with the statements and responses of Negro women, the conscious motives of the men themselves and the Negro cultural tradition. Applied in this setting, psychological theory may then be able to provide important new insights in place of basic and unfortunate distortions.

Keil, then, comes out clearly for a cultural interpretation of the male role we are interested in here. But Elliot Liebow in *Tally's Corner* (1967), a study resulting from the author's participation in a research project that definitely considered ghetto life more

in terms of social problems than as a culture, reaches conclusions which, in some of their most succinct formulations, quite clearly contradict Keil's:

Similarities between the lower-class Negro father and son . . . do not result from "cultural transmission" but from the fact that the son goes out and independently experiences the same failures, in the same areas, and for much the same reasons as his father.

Thus father and son are "independently produced look-alikes." With this goes the view that the emphasis on sexual ability, drinking and so forth is a set of compensatory self-deceptions which can only unsuccessfully veil the streetcorner male's awareness of his failure.

Keil and Liebow, as reviewed here, may be taken as representatives of two significantly different opinions on why black people in the ghettos, and in particular the males, behave differently than other Americans. One emphasizes a cultural determinism internal to the ghetto, the other an economic determinism in the relationship between the ghetto and the wider society. It is easy to see how the two views relate to one's perspective on the determinants of the domestic structure of ghetto dwellers. And it is also easy to see how

these perspectives have considerable bearing on public policy, especially if it is believed that the ghetto family structure somehow prevents full participation by its members in the larger American society and economy. If it is held, for example, that broad social and economic factors, and particularly poverty, make ghetto families the way they are—and this seems to be the majority opinion among social scientists concerned with this area—then public policy should concentrate on mitigating or removing those elements that distort the lives of black people. But if the style of life in the ghetto is culturally determined and more or less

independent of other "outside" factors, then public policy will have to take a different course, or drop the problem altogether *qua* problem.

Admittedly, the present opportunity structure places serious obstacles in the way of many ghetto dwellers, making a mainstream life-style difficult to accomplish. And if research is to influence public policy, it is particularly important to point to the wider structural influences that *can* be changed in order to give equal opportunity to ghetto dwellers. Yet some of the studies emphasizing such macrostructural determinants have resulted in somewhat crude conceptualizations that

are hardly warranted by the facts and which in the light of anthropological theory appear very oversimplified.

First of all, let us dispose of some of the apparent opposition between the two points of view represented by Keil and Liebow. There is not necessarily any direct conflict between ecological-economic and cultural explanations; the tendency to create such a conflict in much of the current literature on poverty involves a false dichotomy. In anthropology, it is a commonplace that culture is usually both inherited and influenced by the community's relationship to its environment. Economic determinism and cultural determinism can go hand in hand in a stable environment. Since the ecological niche of ghetto dwellers has long remained relatively unchanged, there seems to be no reason why their adaptation should not have become in some ways cultural. It is possible, of course, that the first stage in the evolution of the specifically ghetto life-style consisted of a multiplicity of identical but largely independent adaptations from the existing cultural background—mainstream or otherwise—to the given opportunity structure, as Liebow suggests. But the second stage of adaptation—by the following generations—involves a perception of the first-stage adaptation as a normal condition, a state of affairs which from then on can be expected. What was at first independent adaptation becomes transformed into a ghetto heritage of assumptions about the nature of man and society.

Yet Liebow implies that father and son are independently produced as streetcorner men, and that transmission of a ghetto-specific culture has a negligible influence. To those adhering to this belief, strong evidence in its favor is seen in the fact that ghetto dwellers —both men and women—often express conventional sentiments about sex

115

and other matters. Most ghetto dwellers would certainly agree, at times at least, that education is a good thing, that gambling and drinking are bad, if not sinful, and that a man and a woman should be true to each other. Finding such opinions, and heeding Keil's admonition to listen to the statements and responses of the black people themselves, one may be led to doubt that there is much of a specific ghetto culture. But then, after having observed behavior among these same people that often and clearly contradicts their stated values, one has to ask two questions: Is there any reason to believe that ghetto-specific behavior is cultural? And, if it *is* cultural, what is the nature of the coexistence of mainstream culture and ghetto-specific culture in the black ghetto?

To answer the first question, one might look at the kinds of communications that are passed around in the ghetto relating to notions of maleness. One set of relationships in which such communications occur frequently is the family; another is the male peer group.

Deficient Masculinity?

Much has been made of the notion that young boys in the ghetto, growing up in matrifocal households, are somehow deficient in or uncertain about their masculinity, because their fathers are absent or peripheral in household affairs. It is said that they lack the role models necessary for learning male behavior; there is a lack of the kind of information about the nature of masculinity which a father would transmit unintentionally merely by going about his life at home. The boys therefore supposedly experience a great deal of sex-role anxiety as a result of this cultural vacuum. It is possible that such a view contains more than a grain of truth in the case of some quite isolated female-headed households. Generally speaking, however, there may be less to it than meets the eye. First of all, a female-headed household without an adult male in residence but where young children are growing up—and where, therefore, it is likely that the mother is still rather young—is seldom one where adult males are totally absent. More or less steady boyfriends (sometimes including the separated father) go in and out. Even if these men do not assume a central household role, the boys can obviously use them as source material for the identification of male behavior. To be sure, the model is not a conventional middle-class one, but it still shows what males are like.

Furthermore, men are not the only ones who teach boys about masculinity. Although role-modeling is probably es-

sential, other social processes can contribute to identity formation. Mothers, grandmothers, aunts and sisters who have observed men at close range have formed expectations about the typical behavior of men which they express and which influence the boys in the household. The boys will come to share in the women's imagery of men, and often they will find that men who are not regarded as good household partners (that is, "good" in the conventional sense) are still held to be attractive company. Thus the view is easily imparted that the hard men, good talkers, clothes-horses and all, are not altogether unsuccessful as men. The women also act more directly toward the boys in these terms—they have expectations of what men will do, and whether they wish the boys to live up (or down) to the expectations, they instruct them in the model. Boys are advised not to "mess with" girls, but at the same time it is emphasized that messing around is the natural thing they will otherwise go out and do—and when the boys start their early adventures with the other sex, the older women may scold them but at the same time point out, not without satisfaction, that "boys will be boys." This kind of maternal (or at least adult female) instruction of young males is obviously a kind of altercasting, or more exactly, socialization to an alter role—that is, women cast boys in the role complementary to their own according to their experience of man-woman relationships. One single mother of three boys and two girls put it this way:

> You know, you just got to act a little bit tougher with boys than with girls, 'cause they just ain't the same. Girls do what you tell them to do and don't get into no trouble, but you just can't be sure about the boys. I mean, you think they're OK and next thing you find out they're playing hookey and drinking wine and maybe stealing things from cars and what not. There's just something bad about boys here, you know. But what can you say when many of them are just like their daddies? That's the man in them coming out. You can't really fight it, you know that's the way it is. They know, too, But you just got to be tougher.

This is in some ways an antagonistic socialization, but it is built upon an expectation that it would be unnatural for men not to turn out to be in some ways bad—that is fighters, drinkers, lady killers and so forth. There is one thing worse than a no-good man—the sissy, who is his opposite. A boy who seems weak is often reprimanded and ridiculed not only by his peers but also by adults, including his mother and older sisters. The combination of role-modeling by peripheral fathers or temporary boyfriends with altercasting by adult women certainly provides for a measure of male role socialization within the family.

And yet, when I said that the view of the lack of models in the family was too narrow, I was not referring to the observers' lack of insight into many matrifocal ghetto families as much as I was to the emphasis they placed on the family as *the* information storage unit of a community's culture. I believe it is an ethnocentrism on the part of middle-class commentators to take it for granted that if information about sex roles is not transmitted from father to son within the family, it is not transmitted from generation to generation at all. In American sociology, no less than in the popular mind, there is what Ray Birdwhistell has termed a "sentimental model" of family life, according to which the family is an inward-turning isolated unit, meeting most of the needs of its members, and certainly their needs for sociability and affection. The "sentimental model" is hardly ever realistic even as far as middle-class American families are concerned, and it has even less relevance for black ghetto life. Ghetto children live and learn out on the streets just about as much as within the confines of the home. Even if mothers, aunts and sisters do not have streetcorner men as partners, there is an ample supply of them on the front stoop or down at the corner. Many of these men have such a regular attendance record as to become quite familiar to children and are frequently very friendly with them. Again, therefore, there is no lack of adult men to show a young boy what men are like. It seems rather unlikely that one can deny all role-modeling effect of these men on their young neighbors. They may be missing in the United States census records, but they are not missing in the ghetto community.

Much of the information gained about sex roles outside the family comes not from adult to child, however, but from persons in the same age-grade or only slightly higher. The idea of culture being stored in lower age-grades must be taken seriously. Many ghetto children start participating in the peer groups of the neighborhood at an early age, often under the watchful eye of an elder brother or sister. In this way they are initiated into the culture of the peer group by interacting with children—predominantly of the same sex—who are only a little older than they are. And in the peer-group culture of the boys, the male sex role is a fairly constant topic of concern. Some observers have felt that this is another consequence of the alleged sex role anxiety of ghetto boys. This may be true, of course, at least in that it may have had an important part in the development of male peer-group life as a dominant element

of ghetto social structure. Today, however, such a simple psychosocial explanation will not do. Most ghetto boys can hardly avoid associating with other boys, and once they are in the group, they are efficiently socialized into a high degree of concern with their sex role. Much of the joking, the verbal contests and the more or less obscene songs among small ghetto boys, serve to alienate them from dependence on mother figures and train them to the exploitative, somewhat antagonistic attitude toward women which is typical of streetcorner men.

"Mother!"

This is not to say that the cultural messages are always very neat and clear-cut. In the case of the kind of insult contest called "playing the dozens," "sounding" or (in Washington, D. C.) "joning," a form of ritualized interaction which is particularly common among boys in the early teens, the communication is highly ambiguous. When one boy says something unfavorable about another's mother, the other boy is expected either to answer in kind or to fight in defense of his honor (on which apparently that of his mother reflects). But the lasting impression is that there is something wrong about mothers—they are not as good as they ought to be ("Anybody can get pussy from your mother"), they take over male items of behavior and by implication too much of the male role ("Your mother smokes a pipe"). If standing up for one's family is the manifest expected consequence of "the dozens," then a latent function is a strengthening of the belief that ghetto women are not what they ought to be. The other point of significance is that the criteria of judgment about what a good woman should be like are apparently like those of the larger society. She should not be promiscuous, and she should stick to the mainstream female role and not be too dominant.

The boys, then, are learning and strengthening a cultural ambivalence involving contradictions between ideal and reality in female behavior. I will return to a discussion of such cultural ambivalence later. But the point remains that even this game involves continuous learning and strengthening of a cultural definition of what women are like that is in some ways complementary to the definition of what men are like. And much of the songs, the talk and the action—fighting, sneaking away with girls into a park or an alley or drinking out of half-empty wine bottles stolen from or given away by adult men—are quite clearly preparations for the streetcorner male role. If boys and men show anxiety about their masculinity, one may suspect that this is induced as much by existing cultural standards as by the alleged nonexistence of models.

This socialization within the male peer group is a continuing process; the talk that goes on, continuously or intermittently, at the street corner or on the front steps may deal occasionally with a football game or a human-interest story from the afternoon newspaper, but more often there are tales from personal experience about adventures of drinking (often involving the police), about women won and lost, about feminine fickleness and the masculine guile (which sometimes triumphs over it), about clothing, or there may simply be comments on the women passing down the street. "Hi ugly . . . don't try to swing what you ain't got."

This sociability among the men seems to be a culture-building process. Shared definitions of reality are created out of the selected experiences of the participants. Women are nagging and hypocritical; you can't expect a union with one of them to last forever. Men are dogs; they have to run after many women. There is something about being a man and drinking liquor; booze makes hair grow on your chest. The regularity with which the same topics appear in conversation indicates that they have been established as the expected and appropriate subjects in this situation, to the exclusion of other topics.

■ Mack asked me did I screw his daughter, so I asked: "I don't know, what's her name?" And then when I heard that gal was his daughter all right, I says, "Well, Mack, I didn't really have to take it. 'cause it was given to me." I thought Mack sounded like his daughter was some goddam white gal. But Mack says, "Well, I just wanted to hear it from you." Of course, I didn't know that was Mack's gal, 'cause she was married and had a kid, and so she had a different name. But then you know the day after when I was out there a car drove by, and somebody called my name from it, you know, "hi darling," and that was her right there. So the fellow I was with says, "Watch out, Buddy will shoot your ass off." Buddy, that's her husband. So I says, "Yeah, but he got to find me first!"

■ Let me tell you fellows, I've been arrested for drunkenness more than two hundred times over the last few years, and I've used every name in the book. I remember once I told them I was Jasper Gonzales, and then I forgot what I had told them, you know. So I was sitting there waiting, and they came in and called "Jasper Gonzales," and nobody answered. I had forgotten that's what I said, and to tell you the truth, I didn't know how to spell it. So anyway, nobody answered, and there they were calling "Jasper Gonzales.

Jasper Gonzales!" So I thought that must be me, so I answered. But they had been calling a lot of times before that. So the judge said, "Mr. Gonzales, are you of Spanish descent?" And I said, "Yes, your honor, I came to this country thirty-four years ago." And of course I was only thirty-five, but you see I had this beard then, and I looked pretty bad, dirty and everything, you know, so I looked like sixty. And so he said, "We don't have a record on you. This is the first time you have been arrested?" So I said, "Yes, your honor, nothing like this happened to me before. But my wife was sick, and then I lost my job you know, and I felt kind of bad. But it's the first time I ever got drunk." So he said, "Well, Mr. Gonzales, I'll let you go, 'cause you are not like the rest of them here. But let this be a warning to you." So I said, "Yes, your honor." And then I went out, and so I said to myself, "I'll have to celebrate this." So I went across the street from the court, and you know there are four liquor stores there, and I got a pint of wine and next thing I was drunk as a pig.

■ Were you here that time a couple of weeks ago when these three chicks from North Carolina were up here visiting Miss Gladys? They were really gorgeous, about 30-35. So Charlie says why don't we step by the house and he and Jimmy and Deekay can go out and buy them a drink. So they say they have to go and see this cousin first, but then they'll be back. But then Brenda (Charlie's wife) comes back before they do, and so these girls walk back and forth in front of the house, and Charlie can't do a thing about it, except hope they won't knock on his door. And then Jimmy and Deekay come and pick them up, and Fats is also there, and the three of them go off with these chicks, and there is Charlie looking through his window, and there is Brenda looking at them too, and asking Charlie does he know who the chicks are.

Groups of one's friends give some stability and social sanction to the meanings that streetcorner men attach to their experiences—meanings that may themselves have been learned in the same or preceding peer groups. They, probably more than families, are information storage units for the ghetto-specific male role. At the same time, they are self-perpetuating because they provide the most satisfactory contexts for legitimizing the realities involved. In other words, they suggest a program for maleness, but they also offer a haven of understanding for those who follow that program and are criticized for it or feel doubts about it. For of course all streetcorner males are more or less constantly exposed to the definitions and values of the mainstream cultural apparatus, and so some cultural ambivalence can hardly be avoided. Thus, if a man is a dog for running after women —as he is often said to be among ghetto dwellers—he wants to talk about it with other dogs who appreciate that this is a fact of life. If it is natural for men to drink, let it happen among other people who understand the nature of masculinity. In this way the group maintains constructions of reality, and life according to this reality maintains the group.

It is hard to avoid the conclusion, then, that there is a cultural element involved in the sex roles of streetcorner males, because expectations about sex are manifestly shared and transmitted rather than individually evolved. (If the latter had been the case, of course, it would have been less accurate to speak of these as roles, since roles are by definition cultural.) This takes us to the second question stated above, about the coexistence of conventional and ghetto-specific cultures. Streetcorner men certainly are aware of the male ideal of mainstream America—providing well for one's family, remaining faithful to one's spouse, staying out of trouble, etc.—and now and then every one of them states it as his own ideal. What we find here, then, may be seen as a bicultural situation. Mainstream culture and ghetto-specific culture provide different models for living, models familiar to everyone in the ghetto. Actual behavior may lean more toward one model or more toward the other, or it may be some kind of mixture, at one point or over time. The ghetto-specific culture, including the streetcorner male role, is adapted to the situation and the experience of the ghetto dweller; it tends to involve relatively little idealization but offers shared expectations concerning self, others and the environment. The mainstream culture, from the ghetto dweller's point of view, often involves idealization, but there is less real expectation that life will actually follow the paths suggested by those ideals. This is not to say that the ghetto-specific culture offers no values of its own at all, or that nothing of mainstream culture ever appears realistic in the ghetto; but in those areas of life where the two cultures exist side by side as alternative guides to action (for naturally, the ghetto-specific culture, as distinct from mainstream culture, is not a "complete" culture covering all areas of life), the ghetto-specific culture is often taken to forecast what one can actually expect from life, while the mainstream norms are held up as perhaps ultimately more valid but less attainable

under the given situational constraints. "Sure it would be good to have a good job and a good home and your kids in college and all that, but you got to be yourself and do what you know." Of course, this often makes the ghetto-specific cultural expectations into self-fulfilling prophecies, as ghetto dwellers try to attain what they believe they can attain; but, to be sure, self-fulfilling prophecies and realistic assessments may well coincide.

"Be Yourself"

On the whole, one may say that both mainstream culture and ghetto-specific culture are transmitted within many ghetto families. I have noted how socialization into the ghetto male role within the household is largely an informal process, in which young boys may pick up bits and pieces of information about masculinity from the women in the house as well as from males who may make their entrances and exits. On the other hand, when adult women —usually mothers or grandmothers—really "tell the boys how to behave," they often try to instill in them mainstream, not to say puritanical norms—drinking is bad, sex is dirty and so forth. The male peer groups, as we have seen, are the strongholds of streetcorner maleness, although there are times when men cuss each other out for being "no good." Finally, of course, mainstream culture is transmitted in contacts with the outside world, such as in school or through the mass media. It should be added, though, that the latter may be used selectively to strengthen some elements of the streetcorner male role; ghetto men are drawn to Westerns, war movies and crime stories both in the movie house and on their TV sets.

Yet, even if the nature of men's allegiance to the two cultures makes it reasonably possible to adhere, after a fashion, to both at the same time, the bicultural situation of streetcorner males involves some ambivalence. The rejection of mainstream culture as a guide to action rather than only a lofty ideal is usually less than complete. Of course, acting according to one or the other of the two cultures to a great extent involves bowing to the demands of the social context, and so a man whose concerns in the peer-group milieu are drinking and philandering will try to be "good" in the company of his mother or his wife and children, even if a complete switch is hard to bring about. There are also peer groups, of course, that are more mainstream-oriented than others, although even the members of these groups are affected by streetcorner definitions of maleness. To some extent, then, the varying allegiance of different peer groups to the two cultures is largely a difference of degree, as the following statement by a young man implies.

Those fellows down at the corner there just keep drinking and drinking. You know, I think it's pretty natural for a man to drink, but they don't try to do nothing about it, they just drink every hour of the day, every day of the week. My crowd, we drink during the weekend, but we can be on our jobs again when Monday comes.

However, although where one is or who one is with does bring some order into this picture of bicultural ambivalence, it is still one of less than perfect stability. The drift between contexts is itself not something to which men are committed by demands somehow inherent in the social structure. Ghetto men may spend more time with the family, or more time with the peer group, and the extent to which they choose one or the other, and make a concomitant cultural selection, still appears to depend much on personal attachment to roles, and to changes in them. The social alignments of a few men may illustrate this. One man, Norman Hawkins, a construction laborer, spends practically all his leisure time at home with his family, only occasionally joining in the streetcorner conversations and behavior of the peer group to which his neighbor, Harry Jones, belongs. Harry Jones, also a construction worker, is also married and has a family but stays on the periphery of household life, although he lives with his wife and children. Some of the other men in the group are unmarried or separated and so seldom play the "family man" role which Harry Jones takes on now and then. Harry's younger brother, Carl, also with a family, used to participate intensively in peer group life until his drinking led to a serious ailment, and after he recuperated from this he started spending much less time with his male friends and more with his family. Bee Jay, a middle-aged bachelor who was raised by his grandmother, had a job at the post office and had little to do with street life until she died. Since then, he has become deeply involved with a tough, hard-drinking group and now suffers from chronic health problems connected with his alcoholism. Thus we can see how the life careers of some ghetto men take them through many and partly unpredictable shifts and drifts between mainstream and ghetto-specific cultures, while others remain quite stable in one allegiance or another.

Two Cultures

The sociocultural situation in the black ghetto is clearly complicated. The community shows a great heterogeneity of life-styles; individuals become committed in some degree to different ways of being by the impersonally-enforced structural arrangements to which they are subjected, but unpredictable contingencies have an influence, and their personal attachments to life-styles also vary. The socioeconomic conditions impose limits on the kinds of life ghetto dwellers may have, but these kinds of life are culturally transmitted and shared as many individuals in the present, and many in the past, live or have lived under the same premises. When the latter is the case, it is hardly possible to invent new adaptations again and again, as men are always observing each other and interacting with each other. The implication of some of Frazier's writings, that ghetto dwellers create their way of life in a cultural limbo —an idea which has had more modern expressions—appears as unacceptable in this case as in any other situation where people live together, and in particular where generations live together. The behavior of the streetcorner male is a natural pattern of masculinity with which ghetto dwellers grow up and which to some extent they grow into. To see it only as a complex of unsuccessful attempts at hiding failures by self-deception seems, for many of the men involved, to be too much psychologizing and too little sociology. But this does not mean that the attachment to the ghetto-specific culture is very strong among its bearers.

The question whether streetcorner males have mainstream culture or a specific ghetto culture, then, is best answered by saying that they have both, in different ways. There can be little doubt that this is the understanding most in line with that contemporary trend in anthropological thought which emphasizes the sharing of cultural imagery, of expectations and definitions of reality, as the medium whereby individuals in a community interact. It is noteworthy that many of the commentators who have been most skeptical of the idea of a ghetto-specific culture, or more generally a "culture of poverty," have been those who have taken a more narrow view of culture as a set of values about which an older generation consciously instructs the younger ones in the community.

Obviously, the answer to whether there is a ghetto-specific culture or not will depend to some extent on what we shall mean by culture. Perhaps this is too important a question to be affected by a mere terminological quibble, and perhaps social policy, in some areas, may well proceed unaffected by the questions raised by a ghetto-specific culture. On the other hand, in an anthropological study of community life, the wider view of cultural sharing and transmission which has been used here will have to play a part in our picture of the ghetto, including that of what ghetto males are like. ■

2. dating, mating, and procreating in the family life cycle

One of the basic functions of the socialization process is to establish sexual identities and behaviors. It teaches those children designated as girls to act like girls, in relation to other girls and in relation to boys. The same means are used to convert infants into boys and, later, men. As we saw in the last section, the socialization process is intricate and it is usually successful in separating the two sexes in identity and interest as well as preparing them for the traditionally important functions of mating and procreating. However, the rate and direction of changes within urbanizing, industrializing, increasingly complex societies are such that these functions, the persons who attempt to fulfill them and the mating-procreating sequences have become *decrystallized.* When families selected mates for their children, through a complex, but known, bargaining system, few aspects of the mating and procreating package were left to chance. Women were protected from becoming emotionally attached to the wrong kind of men or from succumbing to sexual advances at inappropriate times. Men were saved by social norms from marrying women with whom they would not wish to raise a family or who could not fit into their consanguine group. Personal preference interfered with the process only in extreme situations; legends and fairy tales warned the youth of its tragic consequences.

But loss of kinship control over mating and procreating has brought about some strains and problems, while simultaneously adding new dimensions to relations between men and women. Each girl must now insure her own marriage, as each boy must "win" his mate. There are no guaranteed arrangements, no matchmakers insuring that the appropriate people get married. Each person must make him- or herself selectable by modern criteria of desirability. The society may be less worried about survival through reproduction than it used to be in days of high mortality, but it still desires the preservation of its internal divisions by preventing the birth of children to cross-category couples. American society has developed (as have other societies the whole world over) direct and inobtrusive means of preventing three situations thus far deemed dysfunctional to

its life style: 1) the socialization of members in a manner making them unfit for, or unwilling to enter, the mating and procreating sequences; 2) mating with the "wrong" person, i.e. selection of a mate from a racial or socioeconomic category considered outside the "marriageable" limits; and 3) alteration of the proper sequence of mating and procreating. The ideal middle-class sequence is: dating several people—falling in love (preferably several times with increasing seriousness)—selection of a future mate—engagement—marriage—birth of first child (preferably two years after marriage).

Any decrystallization of the mating and procreating pattern, however, is not likely to occur at the early stages of socialization into same- and other-sex identities and behaviors, not only because of the efforts of adult socializing agents but also thanks to peer group influences. Parents and other significant adults continually remind boys and girls which actions are appropriate to their sex. The inevitable effect of being told "don't be a sissy, only girls play with dolls," turns the boy to children of his own kind who play in a different way. The status hierarchy of the two sexes in American society is evident by efforts made to prevent boys from playing girls' games at an age earlier than girls are made to cease being "tomboys." It appears more natural to parents that a girl covets the freedom outside the home that is afforded her brother, and that she tags along after his play group, than that he stays home in the company of her friends.

It is interesting to note that, although girls have close friendships and cliques with same-sex colleagues, they generally lack the complex, organized "gangs" of boys. Groups like the "White Gangs" described by Walter B. Miller, of predominantly lower class families hang around on street corners and experiment with criminal behavior. Their upper and middle-class counterparts follow similar patterns of male association with different activities, and their territory is the home or a club area. Some male gangs have "sister" branches, but these are regarded as peripheral to the main unit. There are girl "hangers-on" in boys' gangs, but they are just that—nonmembers who provide diversion from the serious business of male activity. Even the actions leading to a labeling of "juvenile delinquent" vary by sex early in life. Girls get into trouble with the society for their relations with boys, while boys commit antisocial acts as members of same-sex gangs or cliques.

Not being admitted to male association, not wishing to organize groups of girls into activity having its own vitality, girls turn finally to popularity competition among each other and vis-à-vis boys. By the time of high school, according to a team of social scientists under the leadership of James Coleman, as described in *Adolescent Society*, girls have accentuated their sexual potential, gaining attention by being different from boys rather than like them. The boys, in the meantime, have diversified their interests, becoming achievement oriented in school, in sports, in "maleness." They have gradually replaced their sisters as the darlings of the classroom.

Same-sex and opposite-sex (interesting word, opposite) interaction during the teen years usually results in an increasing division of the world into *his* and *hers*, a division judged as necessary if mating and procreating are to take place. Dating assists the process by filling many functions, allowing opportunities for the testing of personality: for trying on "new faces," for learning new styles of behavior from other teenagers in "double" and "clique" pairing. It creates sets of mutually shared recreational activities. It crystallizes preferences for certain types of people and actions. In the long run, the ultimate purpose of dating is to find a spouse and a parent for future children. It is this function which draws societal attention—and methods preventing "inappropriate" mating. Residential segregation through law or "gentlemen's agreements" not to sell or rent to members of outside groups isolates young children, as long as their activities can be restricted to the local area. Gunner Myrdal, a Swedish sociologist, long ago described the complex mechanisms developed in America to keep black and white girls and boys away from each other. Of course, the most effective means is prejudice. Children are taught to look on members of other social, racial, religious, ethnic, class and even some community groups as unacceptable marital partners, even as unacceptable dates. Standards of beauty, a major means of eliminating others from social and sexual contact, place the ideal within one's own group. As a result, people with different color, hair, features, clothing, etc., appear ugly and undesirable.

Frank Petroni describes other pressures applied to the young, by the community at large and by their own peer groups, to prevent "Interracial Dating" among teenagers. The techniques are generally effective, and continue even in college, where there is often greater heterogeneity and an absence of parents functioning as observers and critics. College substitutes for the family appear in the form of sororities and fraternities, which take it upon themselves to insure restrictive mate selection. John Finley Scott's essay on "Sororities and the Husband Game" documents that tendency. The peer groups Scott examines arrange encounters with the "right" partners and discourage those with persons deemed inferior by background or current

identification, as determined by obvious signs, such as skin color, or more subtle ones, such as residence on campus. These various techniques insure that most people who marry in college, or marry someone they met there, chose spouses with a similar composite of past, present and future statuses. Small private schools even go further by providing homogeneity of the whole student body through various means, money being a major one, but religion and color selection having played an important part in the past.

By the time women and men are out of college and on their own, they are so well indoctrinated to choose associates of their own status that they avoid encounters which might result in a meaningful relation with an "inappropriate" person. Of course, most people do not mind marrying someone of slightly higher background, as such a match could help in their move up the prestige pyramid and in their acquisition of all the other things which come with better life styles. This is another reason that people are leery of those below them. As Joyce Starr and Donald Carns found out, boys are more willing than girls to have sexual intercourse with someone "inferior" because their whole subculture has provided methods for getting out of entanglements that might lead to a marriage outside the ideal match. Girls, taught to "fall in love" and to use sex as a means for developing stronger relations, are often caught in the consequences of such actions.

Fearful of unwanted marriage or pregnancy, of being used, or exploited sexually, financially and/or emotionally, young single people in high-density urban areas lead lives that fail to measure up to glamorous "swinging singles" stereotypes, according to Starr and Carns. Lacking the protection of home and school, which shielded them from unwelcome encounters or provided excuses for not venturing outside the familiar world for same-sex or other-sex interaction, these singles mistrust their own judgment of people met casually at bars and fear to develop close relations with those for whom they are easily available on home territory. The workplace then becomes a substitute for the school of the past, for continued encounters for business reasons are guaranteed, allowing opportunities for screening out undesirables and building relationships without immediately needing to "jump into bed." The as yet not-so-"modern" generation still experiences many of the past's "hang-ups" with casual sex, due to the traditional tie between sexual relations, love, marriage and reproduction. Refusing to turn their sexual encounters into promiscuous scenes lacking sentimental attachment, the young today are working out and evolution rather than a revolution of sexual values and sentiments. According to Ira Reiss, in "How and Why

America's Sex Standards Are Changing," they are doing so without behavior that is dramatically different from that of their parents.

Although socialization into sexual identities and mate selection according to traditional in-group lines have not been subject to strong decrystallization as of the early 1970s, the sequences of mating and procreating have undergone some dramatic changes. The whole of American culture is infused with a sexual theme, accompanied by a hangover from the past, in the form of a "machismo" or "maleness" complex in which the boy proves his virility by "seducing" the girl, even by making her pregnant. Dating interaction or even more casual contact becomes a struggle, culminating often in the "victory" of his sexual advances over her defensive practices. There are few reports of girls bragging that they have conquered a boy, even in modern times, but the opposite is frequent. Changing sexual standards are modifying this conquest scene in that people "in love" are now more expected to be "making love" together.

The result of some of these changes is that an increasing proportion of girls are becoming pregnant before, or even without, marriage. In the past, it was mostly the lower-class girl who became pregnant while still unmarried. In recent years, pre-marital pregnancy has expanded in frequency among the upper- and middle-class youth.

Many societies refuse to allow an unmarried women to keep her child because of the assumption that she cannot take care of it adequately. According to traditional social roles, such assumptions are somewhat justified unless father substitutes are found, because of a division of labor among parents. It is hard for a woman to be housewife and breadwinner, mother and father. However, despite certain complications, divorced and widowed women have managed to solve such problems in one way or another. Therefore, it seems that the middle-class world refuses the unwed girl the right to be a mother, partly because of moral judgments and partly because of anxiety that the traditional family will disintegrate and family lines will lose their meaning if this becomes a popular custom. The legitimacy of an infant born in the 1970s still depends on the mother's being married to a man willing to perform the role of father and give the child his name. It is possible, however, that, in the far future, a baby will be deemed legitimate if a woman alone claims it as her own, assigns it a name and enters into the role of mother, performing the duties and receiving the rights of that role, even in the absence of a father. Society's current method in dealing with women who have illegitimate children or with homes where the father is absent has been judged unsatisfactory by the parties concerned. Welfare attitudes and procedures are demeaning to all. The women's liberation movement is pushing society toward a change in these practices.

In view of the rejection of unmarried mothers by American society, several solutions to pre-marital pregnancy have evolved. The most common is abortion. As Alice Rossi shows, in her essay on "Abortion Laws and Their Victims" later in this chapter, lower-class girls, both black and white, have no chance to solve their pregnancy problems by the medically induced abortions which are used by wealthier classes with better physician contacts. Most states still have laws forbidding abortion in other than unusual circumstances, although the appeals used recently by medical men and feminists are changing attitudes and, gradually, laws. Many abortions are induced through home remedies which often damage the health of the girl. A second method of solving the problem of premarital pregnancy is through adoption of the baby by a couple who, for one reason or another, want to enter such a relationship. One of the major differences in the situation of white and black unwed mothers, however, is that white babies are in much greater demand on the adoption market than nonwhites. The black community has evolved a third solution to premarital pregnancies, and that is the absorption of the illegitimate children within the matrifocal unit, with the help of several relatives, and even of men who are not the father or husband.

The most frequent resolution of premarital pregnancy in a society demanding both a mother and a father for child rearing is marriage. At the present time, estimations as to the frequency of pregnancy prior to marriage run as high as one in every three brides. There are two possible sequences of events behind this fact: a couple deciding on marriage only after conception, or a couple adding sexual intercourse to their relation only after beginning preparation for marriage.

Regardless of whether the bride is pregnant, most Americans do marry, within the established ceremonials surrounding this event. Tradition calls for newlyweds to go away for a honeymoon, thereby breaking past residential and relational ties so that they can, upon return, be re-engaged on a different level and establish an independent residence. The honeymoon itself, idealized as a period of beginning sexual relations immediately achieving intense pleasure and adjustment, has often been found to be problematic. Too-high expectations of self and the other, within strange surroundings and an artificial atmosphere, have repeatedly been a source of privately held disappointment for one or both partners. Changing attitudes toward sexual experiences, including sensitivity to the other's feelings and an openness of communication, may solve some of these problems.

Traditionally, a couple did not marry unless they were either assured of full support in the ancestral home or patrilocal farm, to which the couple contributed their share of the work, or until they had accumulated, individually or with the help of kin members, sufficient goods to start a household and keep it functioning until a steady source of goods was assured. Americans have generally worked out a compromise that varies by family. Lacking any *rites de passage* or formal initiation rites to mark the passage from childhood to adulthood, American society uses marriage as their equivalent. Most parents are willing to support their children for years, even with no economic contribution in return, provided they are obtaining training for their future independence—but only so long as they are not married. A child's entrance into marriage frees the parents from their obligation to support them. This is true even of offspring who marry while in school, making it necessary for one or both spouses to drop out in order to support the new unit economically. It is usually the bride who goes to work in such marriages, since it is assumed that she will not need higher education in the future. Her husband is expected to support her for the rest of her life, in spite of the high probability of widowhood and of a variety of events which may necessitate or make desirable her occupational involvement.

There are some reports, however, of families of the bride and groom agreeing to support their own offspring or the unit during schooling. And many sociologists who study the family have discovered that most young couples are helped by their parents, in the form of gifts rather than steady support. Kin members and friends arrange for "bridal showers," which replace the hope chest as a source of goods needed for day-to-day life, or they help with special events such as entertaining. The couple becomes established in its own apartment or home with furniture donated or bought by the family. Downpayments on a house, car, appliances, vacations are means by which kin members help the young couple before an income sufficient to maintain the household is available.

Although young marrieds often report increased maturity, mostly because of the need to support and maintain their independent housing unit, their relationship often continues to be somewhat similar to that of the engagement period. They spend as much time together as possible under the circumstances of their both being involved for many hours in roles outside of the home. They modify their friendship group gradually to other marrieds, as a strain develops with single associates or as the change in interests and finances shifts their attention to new people. They continue to be recreationally active and to use their apartment as a home base for venturing out. However, during this time, and for the rest of the wife's fertile years, the couple is always aware of the possibility of pregnancy. Attitudes toward pregnancy and childbirth become complicated, not only with the first baby but later. The desire for children varies with factors such as competition from other roles (having to give up a job or a life of "fun"), economic constraints, unwillingness to change the relation between the marital partners, timing of the pregnancy (too soon after marriage or too late in life), number of children already in the family, desire for a child of a sex different than the existing children (especially a son to carry on the family name), proof of femininity or masculinity, social pressure, feelings about the spouse and so forth. Attitudes toward the process of conception, childbearing and delivery have had an interesting history in Western culture, as described by Una Stannard in "Adam's Rib, or the Woman Within." Both men and women have given different interpretations and assigned different sentiments to the vital processes of procreation over time and in different societies. Each society holds many beliefs as to the origin of reproduction, what is actually transmitted biologically, what should be done to guarantee pregnancy, the best circumstances under which pregnant women should live, the effect of the father on the birth process (as in couvade, when the man instead of the woman takes to bed with labor pains), and the immediate needs of the newborn.

That women become pregnant without careful plans or strong desires for the pregnancy is a known but often misunderstood fact. Sociologist Lee Rainwater, having studied contraception and conception among lower-class American women, reported in *And the Poor Get Children* that pregnancies occur because of a whole complex of attitudes and life realities which make their prevention difficult in these strata. Males, for example, often resent or refuse to allow the woman to use contraceptives and will not use them themselves, feeling their masculinity threatened. Then too, the methods most often used by lower-class women are the least effective. Further, the subculture is impulsive and thus discourages long-range planning. Finally, the cultural attitudes toward premarital pregnancy are not so clearly rejective of the girl as in the middle-class world. Ruth B. Dixon explains why even the availability of the contraceptive pill does not guarantee the end of unwanted pregnancies and why it will be some time before decisions to have a particular pregnancy are a matter of real choice (see "Hallelujah the Pill?").

Whether a pregnancy is planned, or not, and whatever the attitudes toward it by the future mother and father, they have time to get accustomed to the idea and to work out anticipatory plans for welcoming the baby. However, many observers of the American scene are very critical of the extreme privatization of the whole conception and birth process.

Sexual intercourse is only now being discussed in public and, except in the rare cases of "group sex," is undertaken in extreme isolation from other people—even hidden from the partners themselves, as evidenced by the frequent absence of any light. The pregnant woman is not generally regarded as a symbol of beauty, as she has been at other times and in other cultures. Our society is not only youth-centered, but beauty-centered, and the stretch-marks from bearing children are not considered beauty marks. As Marian Gennaria Morris concluded in "Psychological Miscarriage: An End to Mother Love" in Part Two, the whole delivery process is alienating, in that the mother is isolated from her world in a strange place, treated as an object of medical care rather than as a person. All these factors, including fear of misshapen breasts, result in a frequent refusal or inability of the mother to nurse the baby. Sterilized bottles are preferred; some mothers even prop up the bottle so that they do not have to hold the infant, and changing diapers is judged an unpleasant task.

The husband is alienated from the whole process of childbirth and from his wife and baby. He is forbidden to have sexual intercourse with her for a number of weeks before and after pregnancy. He does not understand the changes she is experiencing. Excluded from the delivery room, he is a stranger in the whole hospital scene, even more than the unconscious mother is. It is only recently that the LaMaze and similar movements are trying to make the whole situation more meaningful through "self-directed childbirth," involving the active cooperation of both mother and father. There is even an increase in the home delivery of babies, not by accident but by choice. There is, in short, an active revolt of young couples against the dehumanizing and alienating aspects of pregnancy, child delivery and child care as they have evolved in recent decades.

The life of most couples in urban America changes dramatically with the birth of a baby. The infant needs constant care, usually undertaken by the mother. This means, as we noted in the Prologue, that she withdraw from her multidimensional involvement in society, keeping to her household, in isolation from other adults for most of the day. Modern American women are not prepared for being alone, having been surrounded by people ever since their own infancy. The multiple identities which they developed in various social relations and roles are suddenly unrelated to daily life. Thus, a new mother often reports that her "mind is vegetating." The baby demands her attention to the extent of wearing her out physically, so that she is unable to interact even with her husband on the level of prior exchanges. Her world becomes limited to four walls. This dilemma of wanting multidimensional involvement, yet being unable to attend to what goes on outside the home is a real one for mothers of young children. Feelings of isolation, of tremendous responsibility, of incompetence in solving many problems of child care, and of personality change in an undesirable direction are very disquieting to the person who previously functioned with competence in a complex group with shared responsibilities. In fact, since most women take jobs that are essentially dependent, they are often unaccustomed to being the sole solvers of problems. Caring for a child is also an emotionally trying experience, because of crises and the very volatility of the offspring itself. Parents trained to "keep their cool" become very disturbed when they catch themselves screaming at a small child or feeling completely depressed. Unfortunately, it is only recently that these sentiments have been understood as a natural consequence of the circumstances of parenthood in a changing family system among an unprepared population—not as a proof of Freudian psychopathology!

There is an interesting contrast in how the lower and middle classes view the change in their marriages which parenthood brings about. Lower-class women, who tend to live in a sex-segregated world, feel that they have, at last, a bond with their husbands beyond intercourse and house-sharing. The child is considered a bridge between the man's world and the woman's world. They now have something in common to talk about and to occupy their attention. Middle-class women, however, report some negative consequences in their relations with their husbands, from the very presence of the child and from the need to care for and socialize her or him. The strain in marriage becomes intensified by the addition of each new child, as the home situation becomes more complex, requiring more work and "patience." In the first place, the wife has less time for her husband, and less energy. Secondly, she places new demands on him, which often produce irritation. The husband has been busy, interacting away from the home, and wants peace and quiet when he returns to it. The wife has been without adult companionship, eagerly awaiting the minute he enters the home because he can relieve her of some of the work and tension, and keep her company. She wants to talk, to tell him everything about her world, and to hear about his. Their worlds, in other words, suddenly become different, while in the past they were similar. She has, by the act of having a baby, withdrawn into the traditional woman's world, from which most housewives do not emerge until much later in life, if ever.

Certain mothers are unable to cope with the burdens of caring for their children in an isolated nuclear household. Some of the dangers that result were documented in the essay, "Psychological Miscarriage: An End to Mother Love" in Part Two. Indeed, the "battered child" is a subject of considerable interest to social scientists today. Additional symptoms of strain are seen in the high suicide rate of young mothers, in alcoholism, in psychosis displayed in other ways, and in other indices of personal disorganization. Family dissolution through divorce, separation and desertion often results when too much strain is placed on people who are immature or who have too few resources to handle the responsibilities and frustrations of adjusting to marital and parental roles.

Those families which survive physical dissolution must develop some *modus operandi* for getting through the daily routine and surmounting its crises in a manner satisfactory to their members, or at least better than the alternatives. Several types of marriages emerge over time. Some couples—usually lower-class couples, but not always—develop a traditional division of worlds into his and hers, with home and child being more important to her. Such couples run their lives on parallel, though close, tracks. A second type of marriage gradually grows apart as interests spread and rarely converge. A third type of marriage ritualizes into a set of routines, undertaken either together or separately, seldom involving deep commitment. Many couples, however, aware of what is happening now that parenthood has been added to their relations, attempt to build the whole family into a dynamic unit, affording each member personality expression and change, meeting individual needs through flexible action and sentiment rather than through rigid roles. Such marriages do not necessarily have an easy time of it, as strains and conflicts are not removed, only understood and dealt with creatively. Several studies have concluded that, regardless of how much conflict comes between a husband and a wife from cultural and personality differences, or from the strains of everyday life at home and outside of it, what keeps the unit together is creativity in problem solving. This means that the problems are faced, alternative solutions examined cooperatively, individual needs at that particular moment recognized, and a pattern of action developed. Difficulties arise when the psychological needs of more than one member are at a high point of demand but resources are limited, so that the family becomes organized primarily around one person. Dynamic families try to prevent such situations from occurring. If people consistently receive love, attention and acceptance, they are able to tolerate even neglect temporarily in order to meet a crisis situation. As long ago as the Depression, Mirra Komarowsky found that the difference between families with unemployed fathers which became completely disorganized and those which continued as a cooperative unit despite the unemployment stemmed from the degree of their integration into a dynamic unit. Some families never develop into such a unit, each member functioning to satisfy his or her needs without trying to understand and freely interact with the other members.

As new knowledge and newly vitalized ideals of human dignity and openness in social relations impregnate the American family institution, thanks to the youth and women's movements, and to the not yet visible men's movement, it is possible that more marriages and more parent-child relations will become dynamic and viable.

White Gangs Walter B. Miller

If one thinks about street corner gangs at all these days, it is probably in the roseate glow of *West Side Story,* itself the last flowering of a literary and journalistic concern that goes back at least to the late 40's. Those were the days when it seemed that the streets of every city in the country had become dark battlefields where small armies of young men engaged their honor in terrible trials of combat, clashing fiercely and suddenly, then retiring to the warm succor of their girl cohorts. The forward to a 1958 collection of short stories, *The Young Punks,* captures a bit of the flavor:

These are the stories behind today's terrifying headlines—about a strange new frightening cult that has grown up in our midst. Every writer whose work is included in this book tells the truth. These kids are tough. Here are knife-carrying killers, and thirteen-year-old street walkers who could give the most hardened call-girl lessons. These kids pride themselves on their "ethics": never go chicken, even if it means knifing your own friend in the back. Never rat on a guy who wears your gang colors, unless he rats on you first. Old men on crutches are fair game. If a chick plays you for a sucker, blacken her eyes and walk away fast.

Today, the one-time devotee of this sort of stuff might be excused for wondering where they went, the Amboy Dukes - and all those other adolescent warriors and lovers who so excited his fancy a decade ago. The answer, as we shall see, is quite simple—nowhere. The street gangs are still there, out on the corner where they always were.

The fact is that the urban adolescent street gang is as old as the American city. Henry Adams, in his *Education,* describes in vivid detail the gang fights between the Northsiders and Southsiders on Boston Common in the 1840's. An observer in 1856 Brooklyn writes: " . . . at any and all hours there are multitudes of boys . . . congregated on the corners of the streets, idle in their habits, dissolute in their conduct, profane and obscene in their conversation, gross and vulgar in their manners. If a female passes one of the groups she is shocked by what she sees and hears. . . . " The Red Raiders of Boston have hung out on the same corner at least since the 1930's; similarly, gang fighting between the Tops and Bottoms in West Philadelphia, which started in the 30's, is still continuing in 1969.

Despite this historical continuity, each new generation tends to perceive the street gang as a new phenomenon generated by particular contemporary conditions and destined to vanish as these conditions vanish. Gangs in the 1910's and 20's were attributed to the cultural dislocations and community disorganization accompanying the mass immigration of foreigners; in the 30's to the enforced idleness and economic pressures produced by the Great Depression; in the 50's to the emotional disturbance of parents and children caused by the increased stresses and tensions of modern life. At present, the existence of gangs is widely attributed to a range of social injustices: racial discrimination, unequal educational and work opportunities, resentment over inequalities in the distribution of wealth and privilege in an affluent society, and the ineffective or oppressive policies of service agencies such as the police and the schools.

There is also a fairly substantial school of thought that holds that the street gangs are disappearing or have already disappeared. In New York City, the stage of so many real and fictional gang dramas of the 50's and early 60's, *The Times* sounded their death-knell as long ago as 1966. Very often, the passing of the gang is explained by the notion that young people in the slums have converted their gang-forming propensities into various substitute activities. They have been knocked out by narcotics, or they have been "politicized" in ways that consume their energies in radical or reform movements, or their members have become involved in "constructive" commercial activities, or enrolled in publicly financed education and/or work-training programs.

As has often been the case, these explanations are usually based on very shaky factual grounds and derived from rather parochial, not to say self-serving, perspectives. For street gangs are not only still widespread in United States cities, but some of them appear to have again taken up "gang warfare" on a scale that is equal to or greater than the phenomenon that received so much attention from the media in the 1950's.

In Chicago, street gangs operating in the classic formations of that city—War Lords, High Supremes, Cobra Stones—accounted for 33 killings and 252 injuries during the first six months of 1969. Philadelphia has experienced a wave of gang violence that has probably resulted in more murders in a shorter period of time than during any equivalent phase of the "fighting gang" era in New York. Police estimate that about 80 gangs comprising about 5,000 members are "active" in the city, and that about 20 are engaged in combat. Social agencies put the total estimated number of gangs at 200, with about 80 in the "most hostile" category. Between October 1962 and December 1968, gang members were reportedly involved in 257 shootings, 250 stabbings and 205 "rumbles." In the period between January 1968 and June 1969, 54 homicides and over 520 injuries were attributed to armed battles between gangs. Of the murder victims, all but eight were known to be affiliated with street gangs. The assailants ranged in age from 13 to 20, with 70 percent of them between 16 and 18 years old. Most of these gangs are designated by the name of the major corner where they hang out, the 12th and Poplar Streeters, or the 21 W's (for 21st and Westmoreland). Others bear traditional names such as the Centaurs, Morroccos and Pagans.

Gangs also continue to be active in Boston. In a single 90-minute period on May 10, 1969, one of the two channels of the Boston Police radio reported 38 incidents involving gangs, or one every 2½ minutes. This included two gang fights. Simultaneous field observation in several white lower-class neighborhoods turned up evidence that gangs were congregating at numerous street corners throughout the area.

Although most of these gangs are similar to the classic types to be described in what follows, as of this summer the national press had virtually ignored the revival of gang violence. *Time* magazine did include a brief mention of "casual mayhem" in its June 27 issue, but none of the 38 incidents in Boston on May 10 was reported even in the local papers. It seems most likely, however, that if all this had been going on in New York City, where most of the media have their headquarters, a spate of newspaper features, magazine articles and television "specials" would have created the impression that the country was being engulfed by a "new" wave of gang warfare. Instead, most people seem to persist in the belief that the gangs have disappeared or that they have been radically transformed.

This anomalous situation is partly a consequence of the problem of defining what a gang is (and we will offer a definition at the end of our discussion of two specific gangs), but it is also testimony to the fact that this enduring aspect of the lives of urban slum youth remains complex and poorly understood. It is hoped that the following examination of the Bandits and the Outlaws—both of Midcity—will clarify at least some of the many open questions about street corner gangs in American cities.

Midcity, which was the location of our 10-year gang study project (1954-64), is not really a city at all, but a portion of a large one, here called Port City. Midcity is a predominantly lower-class community with a relatively high rate of crime, in which both criminal behavior and a characteristic set of conditions—low-skill occupations, little education, low-rent dwellings, and many others—appeared as relatively stable and persisting features of a developed way of life. How did street gangs fit into this picture?

In common with most major cities during this period, there were many gangs in Midcity, but they varied widely in size, sex composition, stability and range of activities. There were about 50 Midcity street corners that served as hangouts for local adolescents. Fifteen of these were "major" corners, in that they were rallying points for the full range of a gang's membership, while the remaining 35 were "minor," meaning that in general fewer groups of smaller size habitually hung out there.

In all, for Midcity in this period, 3,650 out of 5,740, or 64 percent, of Midcity boys habitually hung out at a particular corner and could therefore be considered members of a particular gang. For girls, the figure is 1,125 out of 6,250, or 18 percent. These estimates also suggest that something like 35 percent of Midcity's boys, and 80 percent of its girls, did *not* hang out. What can be said about them? What made them different from the approximately 65 percent of the boys and 20 percent of the girls who did hang out?

Indirect evidence appears to show that the practice of hanging out with a gang was more prevalent among lower-status adolescents, and that many of those who were not known to hang out lived in middle-class or lower-class I (the higher range of the lower-class) areas. At the same time, however, it is evident that a fair proportion of higher-status youngsters also hung out. The question of status, and its relation to gang membership and gang behavior is very complex, but it should be borne in mind as we now take a closer look at the gangs we studied.

The Bandit Neighborhood

Between the Civil War and World War II, the Bandit neighborhood was well-known throughout the city as a colorful and close-knit community of Irish laborers. Moving to a flat in one of its ubiquitous three-decker frame tenements represented an important step up for the impoverished potato-famine immigrants who had initially settled in the crowded slums of central Port City. By the 1810's the second generation of Irish settlers had produced a spirited and energetic group of athletes and politicos, some of whom achieved national prominence.

Those residents of the Bandit neighborhood who shared in some degree the drive, vitality and capability of these famous men assumed steady and fairly remunerative positions in the political, legal and civil service world of Port City, and left the neighborhood for residential areas whose green lawns and single houses represented for them what Midcity had represented for their fathers and grandfathers. Those who lacked these qualities remained in the Bandit neighborhood, and at the outset of World War II made up a stable and relatively homogeneous community of low-skilled Irish laborers.

The Bandit neighborhood was directly adjacent to Midcity's major shopping district, and was spotted with bars, poolrooms and dance halls that served as meeting places for an active neighborhood social life. Within two blocks of the Bandits' hanging-out corner were the Old Erin and New Hibernia dance halls, and numerous drinking establishments bearing names such as the Shamrock, Murphy and Donoghue's, and the Emerald Bar and Grill.

A number of developments following World War II disrupted the physical and social shape of the Bandit community. A mammoth federally-financed housing project sliced through and blocked off the existing network of streets and razed the regular rows of wooden tenements. The neighborhood's small manufacturing plants were progressively diminished by the growth of a few large establishments, and by the 1950's the physical face of the neighborhood was dominated by three large and growing plants. As these plants expanded they bought off many of the properties which had not been taken by the housing project, demolished buildings, and converted them into acres of black-topped parking lots for their employees.

During this period, the parents of the Bandit corner gang members stubbornly held on to the decreasing number of low-rent, deteriorating, private dwelling units. Although the Bandits' major hanging corner was almost surrounded by the housing project, virtually none of the gang members lived there. For these families, residence in the housing project would have entailed a degree of financial stability and restrained behavior that they were unable or unwilling to assume, for the corner gang members of the Bandit neighborhood were the scions of men and women who occupied the lowest social level in Midcity. For them low rent was a passion, freedom to drink and to behave drunkenly a sacred privilege, sporadic employment a fact of life, and the social welfare and law-enforcement agencies of the state, partners of one's existence.

The Bandit Corner was subject to field observation for about three years—from June 1954 to May 1957. Hanging out on the corner during this period were six distinct but related gang subdivisions. There were four male groups: The Brigands, aged approximately 18 to 21 at the start of the study period; the Senior Bandits, aged 16 to 18; the Junior Bandits, 14 to 16, and the Midget Bandits, 12 to 14. There were also two distinct female subdivisions: The Bandettes, 14 to 16, and the Little Bandettes, 12 to 14.

The physical and psychic center of the Bandit corner was Sam's Variety Store, the owner and sole employee of which was not Sam but Ben, his son. Ben's father had founded the store in the 1920's, the heyday of the Irish laboring class in the Bandit neighborhood. When his father died, Ben took over the store, but did not change its name. Ben was a stocky, round-faced Jew in his middle 50's, who looked upon the whole of the Bandit neighborhood as his personal fief and bounden responsibility—a sacred legacy from his father. He knew everybody and was concerned with everybody; through his store passed a constant stream of customers and noncustomers of all ages and both sexes. In a space not much larger than that of a fair-sized bedroom Ben managed to crowd a phone booth, a juke box, a pinball machine, a space heater, counters, shelves and stock, and an assorted variety of patrons. During one 15-minute period on an average day Ben would supply $1.37 worth of groceries to 11-year-old Carol Donovan and enter the sum on her mother's page in the "tab" book, agree to extend Mrs. Thebodeau's already extended credit until her A.D.C. check arrived, bandage and solace the three-year-old Negro girl who came crying to him with a cut forefinger, and shoo into the street a covey of Junior Bandits whose altercation over a pinball score was impeding customer traffic and augmenting an already substantial level of din.

Ben was a bachelor, and while he had adopted the whole of the Bandit neighborhood as his extended family, he had taken on the 200 adolescents who hung out on the Bandit corner as his most immediate sons and daughters. Ben knew the background and present circumstances of every Bandit, and followed their lives with intense interest and concern. Ben's corner-gang progeny were a fast-moving and mercurial lot, and he watched over their adventures and misadventures with a curious mixture of indignation, solicitude, disgust, and sympathy. Ben's outlook on the affairs of the world was never bland; he held and freely voiced strong opinions on a wide variety of issues, prominent among which was the behavior and misbehavior of the younger generation.

This particular concern was given ample scope for attention by the young Bandits who congregated in and around his store. Of all the gangs studied, the Bandits were the most consistently and determinedly criminal, and central to Ben's concerns was how each one stood with regard to "trouble." In this respect, developments were seldom meager. By the time they reached the age of 18, every one of the 32 active members of the Senior Bandits had appeared in court at least once, and some many times; 28 of the 32 boys had been committed to a correctional institution and 16 had spent at least one term in confinement.

Ben's stout arm swept the expanse of pavement which fronted his store. "I'll tell ya, I give up on these kids. In all the years I been here, I never seen a worse bunch. You know what they should do? They should put up a big platform with one of them stocks right out there, and as soon as a kid gets in trouble, into the stocks with 'im. Then they'd straighten out. The way it is now, the kid tells a sob story to some soft-hearted cop or social worker, and pretty soon he's back at the same old thing. See that guy just comin' over here? That's what I mean. He's hopeless. Mark my word, he's gonna end up in the electric chair."

The Senior Bandit who entered the store came directly to Ben. "Hey, Ben, I just quit my job at the shoe factory. They don't pay ya nothin', and they got some wise guy nephew of the owner who thinks he can kick everyone around. I just got fed up. I ain't gonna tell Ma for awhile, she'll be mad." Ben's concern was evident. "Digger, ya just gotta learn you can't keep actin' smart to every boss ya have. And $1.30 an hour ain't bad pay at all for a 17-year-old boy. Look, I'll lend ya 10 bucks so ya can give 5 to ya Ma, and she won't know."

In their dealings with Ben, the Bandits, for their part, were in turn hostile and affectionate, cordial and sullen, open and reserved. They clearly regarded Ben's as "their" store. This meant, among other things, exclusive possession of the right to make trouble within its confines. At least three times during the observation period corner boys from outside neighborhoods entered the store obviously bent on stealing or creating a disturbance. On each occasion these outsiders were efficiently and forcefully removed by nearby Bandits, who then waxed indignant at the temerity of "outside" kids daring to consider Ben's as a target of illegal activity. One consequence, then, of Ben's seigneurial relationship to the Bandits was that his store was unusually well protected against theft, armed and otherwise, which presented a constant hazard to the small-store owner in Midcity.

On the other hand, the Bandits guarded jealously their own right to raise hell in Ben's. On one occasion, several Senior Bandits came into the store with a cache of pistol bullets and proceeded to empty the powder from one of the bullets onto the pinball machine and to ignite the powder. When Ben ordered them out they continued operations on the front sidewalk by wrapping gunpowder in newspaper and igniting it. Finally they set fire to a wad of paper containing two live bullets which exploded and narrowly missed local residents sitting on nearby doorsteps.

Such behavior, while calculated to bedevil Ben and perhaps to retaliate for a recent scolding or ejection, posed no real threat to him or his store; the same boys during this period were actively engaged in serious thefts from similar stores in other neighborhoods. For the most part, the behavior of the Bandits in and around the store involved the characteristic activities of hanging out. In warm weather the Bandits sat outside the store on the sidewalk or doorstoops playing cards, gambling, drinking, talking to one another and to the Bandettes. In cooler weather they moved into the store as the hour and space permitted, and there played the pinball machine for such cash payoffs as Ben saw fit to render, danced with the Bandettes to juke box records, and engaged in general horseplay.

While Ben's was the Bandits' favorite hangout, they did frequent other hanging locales, mostly within a few blocks of the corner. Among these was a park directly adjacent to the housing project where the boys played football and baseball in season. At night the park provided a favored locale for activities such as beer drinking and lovemaking,

neither of which particularly endeared them to the adult residents of the project, who not infrequently summoned the police to clear the park of late-night revellers. Other areas of congregation in the local neighborhood were a nearby delicatessen ("the Delly"), a pool hall, and the apartments of those Bandettes whose parents happened to be away. The Bandits also ran their own dances at the Old Erin and New Hibernia, but they had to conceal their identity as Bandits when renting these dance halls, since the proprietors had learned that the rental fees were scarcely sufficient to compensate for the chaos inevitably attending the conduct of a Bandit dance.

The Bandits were able to find other sources of entertainment in the central business district of Port City. While most of the Bandits and Bandettes were too young to gain admission to the numerous downtown cafes with their rock 'n' roll bands, they were able to find amusement in going to the movies (sneaking in whenever possible), playing the coin machines in the penny arcades and shoplifting from the downtown department stores. Sometimes, as a kind of diversion, small groups of Bandits spent the day in town job-hunting, with little serious intention of finding work.

One especially favored form of downtown entertainment was the court trial. Members of the Junior and Senior Bandits performed as on-stage participants in some 250 court trials during a four-year period. Most trials involving juveniles were conducted in nearby Midcity Court as private proceedings, but the older Bandits had adopted as routine procedure the practice of appealing their local court sentences to the Superior Court located in downtown Port City. When the appeal was successful, it was the occasion for as large a turnout of gang members as could be mustered, and the Bandits were a rapt and vitally interested audience. Afterwards, the gang held long and animated discussions about the severity or leniency of the sentence and other, finer points of legal procedure. The hearings provided not only an absorbing form of free entertainment, but also invaluable knowledge about court functioning, appropriate defendant behavior, and the predilections of particular judges—knowledge that would serve the spectators well when their own turn to star inevitably arrived.

The Senior Bandits

The Senior Bandits, the second oldest of the four male gang subdivisions hanging out on the Bandit corner, were under intensive observation for a period of 20 months.

At the start of this period the boys ranged in age from 15 to 17 (average age 16.3) and at the end, 17 to 19 (average age 18.1). The core group of the Senior Bandits numbered 32 boys.

Most of the gang members were Catholic, the majority of Irish background; several were Italian or French Canadian, and a few were English or Scotch Protestants. The gang contained two sets of brothers and several cousins, and about one third of the boys had relatives in other subdivisions. These included a brother in the Midgets, six brothers in the Juniors, and three in the Marauders.

The educational and occupational circumstances of the Senior Bandits were remarkably like those of their parents. Some seven years after the end of the intensive study period, when the average age of the Bandits was 25, 23 out of the 27 gang members whose occupations were known held jobs ordinarily classified in the bottom two occupational categories of the United States census. Twenty-one were classified as "laborer," holding jobs such as roofer, stock boy, and trucker's helper. Of 24 fathers whose occupations were known, 18, or 83 percent, held jobs in the same bottom two occupational categories as their sons; 17 were described as "laborer," holding jobs such as furniture mover and roofer. Fathers even held jobs of similar kinds and in similar proportions to those of their sons, e.g., construction laborers: sons 30 percent, fathers 25 percent; factory laborers: sons 15 percent, fathers 21 percent. Clearly the Senior Bandits were not rising above their fathers' status. In fact, there were indications of a slight decline, even taking account of the younger age of the sons. Two of the boys' fathers held jobs in "public safety" services—one policeman and one fireman; another had worked for a time in the "white collar" position of a salesclerk at Sears; a fourth had risen to the rank of Chief Petty Officer in the Merchant Marine. Four of the fathers, in other words, had attained relatively elevated positions, while the sons produced only one policeman.

The education of the Senior Bandits was consistent with their occupational status. Of 29 boys whose educational experience was known, 27 dropped out of school in the eighth, ninth, or tenth grades, having reached the age of 16. Two did complete high school, and one of these was reputed to have taken some post-high-school training in a local technical school. None entered college. It should be remarked that this record occurred not in a backward rural community of the 1800's, nor in a black community, but in the 1950's in a predominantly white neighborhood of a metropolis that took pride in being one of the major educational centers of the world.

Since only two of the Senior Bandits were still in school during the study, almost all of the boys held full-time jobs at some time during the contact period. But despite financial needs, pressure from parents and parole officers and other incentives to get work, the Senior Bandits found jobs slowly, accepted them reluctantly, and quit them with little provocation.

The Senior Bandits were clearly the most criminal of the seven gangs we studied most closely. For example, by the time he had reached the age of 18 the average Senior Bandit had been charged with offenses in court an average of 7.6 times; this compared with an average rate of 2.7 for all five male gangs, and added up to a total of almost 250 separate charges for the gang as a whole. A year after our intensive contact with the group, 100 percent of the Senior Bandits had been arrested at least once, compared with an average arrest figure of 45 percent for all groups. During the 20-month contact period, just about half of the Senior Bandits were on probation or parole for some period of time.

Law Violation, Cliques and Leadership

To a greater degree than in any of the other gangs we studied, crime as an occupation and preoccupation played a central role in the lives of the Senior Bandits. Prominent among recurrent topics of discussion were thefts successfully executed, fights recently engaged in, and the current status of gang members who were in the process of passing through the successive states of arrest, appearing in court, being sentenced, appealing, re-appealing and so on. Although none of the crimes of the Senior Bandits merited front-page headlines when we were close to them, a number of their more colorful exploits did receive newspaper attention, and the stories were carefully clipped and left in Ben's store for circulation among the gang members. Newspaper citations functioned for the Senior Bandits somewhat as do press notices for actors; gang members who made the papers were elated and granted prestige; those who did not were often disappointed; participants and non-participants who failed to see the stories felt cheated.

The majority of their crimes were thefts. The Senior Bandits were thieves *par excellence,* and their thievery was imaginative, colorful, and varied. Most thefts were from stores. Included among these was a department store theft of watches, jewelry and clothing for use as family Christmas presents; a daylight raid on a supermarket for food and refreshments needed for a beach outing; a daytime burglary of an antique store, in which eight gang members, in the presence of the owner, stole a Samurai sword and French duelling pistols. The gang also engaged in car theft. One summer several Bandits stole a car to visit girl friends who were working at a summer resort. Sixty miles north of Port City, hailed by police for exceeding speed limits, they raced away at speeds of up to 100 miles an hour, overturned the car, and were hospitalized for injuries. In another instance, Bandits stole a car in an effort to return a drunken companion to his home and avoid the police; when this car stalled they stole a second one parked in front of its owner's house; the owner ran out and fired several shots at the thieves, which, however, failed to forestall the theft.

The frequency of Senior Bandit crimes, along with the relative seriousness of their offenses, resulted in a high rate of arrest and confinement. During the contact period somewhat over 40 percent of the gang members were confined in correctional institutions, with terms averaging 11 months per boy. The average Senior Bandit spent approximately one month out of four in a correctional facility. This circumstance prompted one of the Bandettes to remark, "Ya know, them guys got a new place to hang—the reformatory. That bunch is never together—one halfa them don't even know the other half. . . ."

This appraisal, while based on fact, failed to recognize an important feature of gang relationships. With institutional confinement a frequent and predictable event, the Senior Bandits employed a set of devices to maintain a high degree of group solidarity. Lines of communication between corner and institution were kept open by frequent visits by those on the outside, during which inmates were brought food, money and cigarettes as well as news of the neighborhood and other correctional facilities. One Midcity social worker claimed that the institutionalized boys knew what was going on in the neighborhood before most neighborhood residents. The Bandits also developed well-established methods for arranging and carrying out institutional escape by those gang members who were so inclined. Details of escapes were arranged in the course of visits and inter-inmate contacts; escapees were provided by fellow gang members with equipment such as ropes to scale prison walls and getaway cars. The homes of one's gang fellows were also made available as hideouts. Given this set of arrangements, the Bandits carried out several

highly successful escapes, and one succeeded in executing the first escape in the history of a maximum security installation.

The means by which the Senior Bandits achieved group cohesion in spite of recurrent incarcerations of key members merit further consideration—both because they are of interest in their own right, and because they throw light on important relationships between leadership, group structure, and the motivation of criminal behavior. Despite the assertion that "one halfa them guys don't know the other half," the Senior Bandits were a solidaristic associational unit, with clear group boundaries and definite criteria for differentiating those who were "one of us" from those who were not. It was still said of an accepted group member that "he hangs with us"—even when the boy had been away from the corner in an institution for a year or more. Incarcerated leaders, in particular, were referred to frequently and in terms of admiration and respect.

The system used by the Senior Bandits to maintain solidarity and reliable leadership arrangements incorporated three major devices: the diffusion of authority, anticipation of contingencies, and interchangeability of roles. The recurring absence from the corner of varying numbers of gang members inhibited the formation of a set of relatively stable cliques of the kind found in the other gangs we studied intensively. What was fairly stable, instead, was a set of "classes" of members, each of which could include different individuals at different times. The relative size of these classes was fairly constant, and a member of one class could move to another to take the place of a member who had been removed by institutionalization.

The four major classes of gang members could be called key leaders, standby leaders, primary followers, and secondary followers. During the intensive contact period the gang contained five key leaders—boys whose accomplishments had earned them the right to command; six standby leaders—boys prepared to step into leadership positions when key leaders were institutionalized; eight primary followers—boys who hung out regularly and who were the most dependable followers of current leaders; and 13 secondary followers—boys who hung out less regularly and who tended to adapt their allegiances to particular leadership situations.

Predictably, given the dominant role of criminal activity among the Senior Bandits, leadership and followership were significantly related to criminal involvement. Each of the five key leaders had demonstrated unusual ability in criminal activity; in this respect the Senior Bandits differed from the other gangs, each of which included at least one leader whose position was based in whole or in part on a commitment to a law-abiding course of action. One of the Senior Bandits' key leaders was especially respected for his daring and adeptness in theft; another, who stole infrequently relative to other leaders, for his courage, stamina and resourcefulness as a fighter. The other three leaders had proven themselves in both theft and fighting, with theft the more important basis of eminence.

Confinement statistics show that gang members who were closest to leadership positions were also the most active in crime. They also suggest, however, that maintaining a system of leadership on this basis poses special problems. The more criminally active a gang member, the greater the likelihood that he would be apprehended and removed from the neighborhood, thus substantially diminishing his opportunities to convert earned prestige into operative leadership. How was it possible, then, for the Senior Bandits to maintain effective leadership arrangements? They utilized a remarkably efficient system whose several features were ingenious and deftly contrived.

First, the recognition by the Bandits of five key leaders—a relatively large number for a gang of 32 members—served as a form of insurance against being left without leadership. It was most unlikely that all five would be incarcerated at the same time, particularly since collective crimes were generally executed by one or possibly two leaders along with several of their followers. During one relatively brief part of the contact period, four of the key leaders were confined simultaneously, but over the full period the average number confined at any one time was two. One Bandit key leader expressed his conviction that exclusive reliance on a single leader was unwise: " . . . since we been hangin' out [at Ben's corner] we ain't had no leader. Other kids got a leader of the gang. Like up in Cornerville, they always got one kid who's the big boss . . . so far we ain't did that, and I don't think we ever will. We talk about 'Smiley and his boys,' or 'Digger and his clique,' and like that. . . . "

It is clear that for this Bandit the term "leader" carried the connotation of a single and all-powerful gang lord, which was not applicable to the diffuse and decentralized leadership arrangements of the Bandits. It is also significant that the gangs of Cornerville which he used as an example were Italian gangs whose rate of criminal involvement was relatively low. The "one big boss" type of leadership found in these gangs derives from the "Caesar" or "Il Duce"

pattern so well established in Italian culture, and it was workable for Cornerville gangs because the gangs and their leaders were sufficiently law-abiding and/or sufficiently capable of evading arrest as to make the removal of the leader an improbable event.

A second feature of Bandit leadership, the use of "standby" leaders, made possible a relatively stable balance among the several cliques. When the key leader of his clique was present in the area, the standby leader assumed a subordinate role and did not initiate action; if and when the key leader was committed to an institution, the standby was ready to assume leadership. He knew, however, that he was expected to relinquish this position on the return of the key leader. By this device each of the five major cliques was assured some form of leadership even when key leaders were absent, and could maintain its form, identity and influence vis-a-vis other cliques.

A third device that enabled the gang to maintain a relatively stable leadership and clique structure involved the phenomenon of "optimal" criminal involvement. Since excellence in crime was the major basis of gang leadership, it might be expected that some of those who aspired to leadership would assume that there was a simple and direct relationship between crime and leadership: the more crime, the more prestige; the more prestige, the stronger the basis of authority. The flaw in this simple formula was in fact recognized by the actual key leaders: in striving for maximal criminal involvement, one also incurred the maximum risk of incarceration. But leadership involved more than gaining prestige through crime; one had to be personally involved with other gang members for sufficiently extended periods to exploit won prestige through wooing followers, initiating noncriminal as well as criminal activities, and effecting working relationships with other leaders. Newly-returned key leaders as well as the less criminally-active class of standby leaders tended to step up their involvement in criminal activity on assuming or reassuming leadership positions in order to solidify their positions, but they also tended to diminish such involvement once this was achieved.

One fairly evident weakness in so flexible and fluid a system of cliques and leadership was the danger that violent and possibly disruptive internal conflict might erupt among key leaders who were competing for followers, or standby leaders who were reluctant to relinquish their positions. There was, in fact, surprisingly little overt conflict of any kind among Bandit leaders. On their release from confinement, leaders were welcomed with enthusiasm and appropriate observances both by their followers and by other leaders. They took the center of the stage as they recounted to rapt listeners their institutional experiences, the circumstances of those still confined, and new developments in policies, personnel and politics at the correctional school.

When they were together Bandit leaders dealt with one another gingerly, warily and with evident respect. On one occasion a standby leader, who was less criminally active than the returning key leader, offered little resistance to being displaced, but did serve his replacement with the warning that a resumption of his former high rate of crime would soon result in commitment both of himself and his clique. On another occasion one of the toughest of the Senior Bandits (later sentenced to an extended term in an adult institution for ringleading a major prison riot), returned to the corner to find that another leader had taken over not only some of his key followers but his steady girl friend as well. Instead of taking on his rival in an angry and perhaps violent confrontation, he reacted quite mildly, venting his hostility in the form of sarcastic teasing, calculated to needle but not to incite. In the place of a direct challenge, the newly returned key leader set about to regain his followers and his girl by actively throwing himself back into criminal activity. This course of action—competing for followers by successful performance in prestigious activities rather than by brute-force confrontation—was standard practice among the Senior Bandits.

The Junior Bandits

The leadership system of the Junior Bandits was, if anything, even farther removed from the "one big boss" pattern than was the "multi-leader power-balance" system of the Seniors. An intricate arrangement of cliques and leadership enabled this subdivision of the gang to contain within it a variety of individuals and cliques with different and often conflicting orientations.

Leadership for particular activities was provided as the occasion arose by boys whose competence in that activity had been established. Leadership was thus flexible, shifting, and adaptable to changing group circumstances. Insofar as there was a measure of relatively concentrated authority, it was invested in a collectivity rather than an individual. The several "situational" leaders of the dominant clique constituted what was in effect a kind of ruling council, which arrived at its decisions through a process of extended collective discussion generally involving all concerned. Those who were to execute a plan of action thereby took part in the process by which it was developed.

A final feature of this system concerns the boy who was recognized as "the leader" of the Junior Bandits. When the gang formed a club to expedite involvement in athletic activities, he was chosen its president. Although he was an accepted member of the dominant clique, he did not, on the surface, seem to possess any particular qualifications for this position. He was mild-mannered, unassertive, and consistently refused to take a definite stand on outstanding issues, let alone taking the initiative in implementing policy. He appeared to follow rather than to lead. One night when the leaders of the two subordinate factions became infuriated with one another in the course of a dispute, he trailed both boys around for several hours, begging them to calm down and reconcile their differences. On another occasion the gang was on the verge of splitting into irreconcilable factions over a financial issue. One group accused another of stealing club funds; the accusation was hotly denied; angry recriminations arose that swept in a variety of dissatisfactions with the club and its conduct. In the course of this melee, the leader of one faction, the "bad boys," complained bitterly about the refusal of the president to take sides or assume any initiative in resolving the dispute, and called for a new election. This was agreed to and the election was held—with the result that the "weak" president was re-elected by a decisive majority, and was reinstated in office amidst emotional outbursts of acclaim and reaffirmation of the unity of the gang.

It was thus evident that the majority of gang members, despite temporary periods of anger over particular issues, recognized on some level the true function performed by a "weak" leader. Given the fact that the gang included a set of cliques with differing orientations and conflicting notions, and a set of leaders whose authority was limited to specific areas, the maintenance of gang cohesion required some special mechanisms. One was the device of the "weak" leader. It is most unlikely that a forceful or dominant person could have controlled the sanctions that would enable him to coerce the strong-willed factions into compliance. The very fact that the "weak" leader refused to take sides and was noncommittal on key issues made him acceptable to the conflicting interests represented in the gang. Further, along with the boy's nonassertive demeanor went a real talent for mediation.

The Outlaw Neighborhood

The Outlaw street corner was less than a mile from that of the Bandits, and like the Bandits, the Outlaws were white, Catholic, and predominantly Irish, with a few Italians and Irish-Italians. But their social status, in the middle range of the lower class, was sufficiently higher than that of the Bandits to be reflected in significant differences in both their gang and family life. The neighborhood environment also was quite different.

Still, the Outlaws hung out on a classic corner—complete with drug store, variety store, a neighborhood bar (Callahan's Bar and Grill), a pool hall, and several other small businesses such as a laundromat. The corner was within one block of a large park, a convenient locale for card games, lovemaking, and athletic practice. Most residents of the Outlaw neighborhood were oblivious to the deafening roar of the elevated train that periodically rattled the houses and stores of Midcity Avenue, which formed one street of the Outlaw corner. There was no housing project in the Outlaw neighborhood, and none of the Outlaws were project residents. Most of their families rented one level of one of the three-decker wooden tenements which were common in the area; a few owned their own homes.

In the mid-1950's, however, the Outlaw neighborhood underwent significant changes as Negroes began moving in. Most of the white residents, gradually and with reluctance, left their homes and moved out to the first fringe of Port City's residential suburbs, abandoning the area to the Negroes.

Prior to this time the Outlaw corner had been a hanging locale for many years. The Outlaw name and corner dated from at least the late 1920's, and perhaps earlier. One local boy who was not an Outlaw observed disgruntledly that anyone who started a fight with an Outlaw would end up fighting son, father, and grandfather, since all were or had been members of the gang. A somewhat drunken and sentimental Outlaw, speaking at a farewell banquet for their field worker, declared impassionedly that any infant born into an Outlaw family was destined from birth to wear the Outlaw jacket.

One consequence of the fact that Outlaws had hung out on the same corner for many years was that the group that congregated there during the 30-month observation period included a full complement of age-graded subdivisions. Another consequence was that the subdivisions were closely connected by kinship. There were six clearly differentiated subdivisions on the corner: the Marauders, boys in their late teens and early twenties; the Senior Outlaws, boys between 16 and 18; the Junior Outlaws, 14 to 16; and the Midget Outlaws, 11 to 13. There were also two girls groups, the Outlawettes and the Little Outlawettes.

The number of Outlaws in all subdivisions totalled slightly over 200 persons, ranging in age, approximately, from 10 to 25 years.

The cohesiveness of the Outlaws, during the 1950's, was enhanced in no small measure by an adult who, like Ben for the Bandits, played a central role in the Outlaws' lives. This was Rosa—the owner of the variety store which was their principal hangout—a stout, unmarried woman of about 40 who was, in effect, the street-corner mother of all 200 Outlaws.

The Junior Outlaws

The Junior Outlaws, numbering 24 active members, were the third oldest of the four male subdivisions on the Outlaw Corner, ranging in age from 14 to 16. Consistent with their middle-range lower-class status, the boys' fathers were employed in such jobs as bricklayer, mechanic, chauffeur, milk deliveryman; but a small minority of these men had attained somewhat higher positions, one being the owner of a small electroplating shop and the other rising to the position of plant superintendent. The educational status of the Junior Outlaws was higher than that of the Bandit gangs, but lower than that of their older brother gang, the Senior Outlaws.

With regard to law violations, the Junior Outlaws, as one might expect from their status and age, were considerably less criminal than the lower-status Bandits, but considerably more so than the Senior Outlaws. They ranked third among the five male gangs in illegal involvement during the observation period (25 involvements per 10 boys per 10 months), which was well below the second-ranking Senior Bandits (54.2) and well above the fourth-ranking Negro Kings (13.9). Nevertheless, the two-and-a-half-year period during which we observed the Juniors was for them, as for other boys of their status and age group, a time of substantial increase in the frequency and seriousness of illegal behavior. An account of the events of this time provides some insight into the process by which age-related influences engender criminality. It also provides another variation on the issue, already discussed in the case of the Bandits, of the relation of leadership to criminality.

It is clear from the case of the Bandits that gang affairs were ordered not by autocratic ganglords, but rather through a subtle and intricate interplay between leadership and a set of elements such as personal competency, intra-gang divisions and law violation. The case of the Junior Outlaws is particularly dramatic in this regard, since the observation period found them at the critical age when boys of this social-status level are faced with a serious decision—the amount of weight to be granted to law-violating behavior as a basis of prestige. Because there were in the Junior Outlaws two cliques, each of which was committed quite clearly to opposing alternatives, the interplay of the various elements over time emerges with some vividness, and echoes the classic morality play wherein forces of good and evil are locked in mortal combat over the souls of the uncommitted.

At the start of the observation period, the Juniors, 13-, 14- and 15-year-olds, looked and acted for the most part like "nice young kids." By the end of the period both their voices and general demeanor had undergone a striking change. Their appearance, as they hung out in front of Rosa's store, was that of rough corner boys, and the series of thefts, fights and drinking bouts which had occurred during the intervening two-and-one-half years was the substance behind that appearance. When we first contacted them, the Juniors comprised three main cliques; seven boys associated primarily with a "good boy" who was quite explicitly oriented to law-abiding behavior; a second clique of seven boys associated with a "bad boy" who was just starting to pursue prestige through drinking and auto theft; and a third, less-frequently congregating group, who took a relatively neutral position with respect to the issue of violative behavior.

The leader of the "good boy" clique played an active part in the law-abiding activities of the gang, and was elected president of the formal club organized by the Juniors. This club at first included members of all three cliques; however, one of the first acts of the club members, dominated by the "good boy" leader and his supporters, was to vote out of membership the leader of the "bad boy" clique. Nevertheless, the "bad boy" leader and his followers continued to hang out on the corner with the other Juniors, and from this vantage point attempted to gain influence over the uncommitted boys as well as members of the "good boy" clique. His efforts proved unsuccessful, however, since during this period athletic prowess served for the majority of the Juniors as a basis of greater prestige than criminal behavior. Disgruntled by this failure, the "bad boy" leader took his followers and moved to a new hanging corner, about two blocks away from the traditional one.

From there, a tangible symbol of the ideological split within the Juniors, the "bad boy" leader continued his campaign to wean away the followers of the "good boy" leader, trying to persuade them to leave the old corner for the new. At the same time, behavior at the "bad boy" corner became increasingly delinquent, with, among other things, much noisy drinking and thefts of nearby cars. These incidents produced complaints by local residents that resulted in several police raids on the corner, and served to increase the antagonism between what now had become hostile factions. Determined to assert their separateness, the "bad boy" faction began to drink and create disturbances in Rosa's store, became hostile to her when she censured them, and finally stayed away from the store altogether.

The antagonism between the two factions finally became sufficiently intense to bring about a most unusual circumstance—plans for an actual gang fight, a "jam" of the type characteristic of rival gangs. The time and place for the battle were agreed on. But no one from either side showed up. A second battle site was selected. Again the combatants failed to appear. From the point of view of intragang relations, both the plan for the gang fight and its failure to materialize were significant. The fact that a physical fight between members of the same subdivision was actually projected showed that factional hostility over the issue of law violation had reached an unusual degree of bitterness; the fact that the planned encounters did not in fact occur indicated a realization that actual physical combat might well lead to an irreversible split.

A reunification of the hostile factions did not take place for almost a year, however. During this time changes occurred in both factions which had the net effect of blunting the sharpness of the ideological issue dividing them. Discouraged by his failure to win over the majority of the Outlaws to the cause of law-violation as a major badge of prestige, the leader of the "bad boy" clique began to hang out less frequently. At the same time, the eight "uncommitted" members of the Junior Outlaws, now moving toward their middle teens, began to gravitate toward the "bad boy" corner—attracted by the excitement and risk of its activities. More of the Juniors than ever before became involved in illegal drinking and petty theft. This trend became sufficiently pronounced to draw in members of the "good boy" clique, and the influence of the "good boy" leader diminished to the point where he could count on the loyalty only of his own brother and two other boys. In desperation, sensing the all-but-irresistible appeal of illegality for his erstwhile followers, he increased the tempo of his own delinquent behavior in a last-ditch effort to win them back. All in vain. Even his own brother deserted the regular Outlaw corner, although he did not go so far as to join the "bad boys" on theirs.

Disillusioned, the "good boy" leader took a night job that sharply curtailed the time he was able to devote to gang activities. Members of the "bad boy" clique now began a series of maneuvers aimed at gaining control of the formal club. Finally, about two months before the close of the 30-month contact period, a core member of the "bad boy" clique was elected to the club presidency. In effect, the proponents of illegality as a major basis of prestige had won the long struggle for dominance of the Junior Outlaws. But this achievement, while on the surface a clear victory for the "bad boy" faction, was in fact a far more subtle process of mutual accommodation.

The actions of each of the opposing sides accorded quite directly with their expressed convictions; each member of the "bad boy" faction averaged about 17 known illegal acts during the observation period, compared to a figure of about two per boy for the "good boy" faction. However, in the face of these sharp differences in both actions and sentiments respecting illegality, the two factions shared important common orientations. Most importantly, they shared the conviction that the issue of violative behavior as a basis of prestige was a paramount one, and one that required a choice. Moreover, both sides remained uncertain as to whether the choice they made was the correct one.

The behavior of both factions provides evidence of a fundamental ambivalence with respect to the "demanded" nature of delinquent behavior. The gradual withdrawal of support by followers of the "good boy" leader and the movement toward violative behavior of the previously "neutral" clique attest to a compelling conviction that prestige gained through law-abiding endeavor alone could not, at this age, suffice. Even more significant was the criminal experience of the "good boy" leader. As the prime exponent of law-abiding behavior, he might have been expected to serve as an exemplar in this respect. In fact, the opposite was true; his rate of illegal involvement was the highest of all the boys in his clique, and had been so even before his abortive attempt to regain his followers by a final burst of delinquency. This circumstance probably derived from his realization that a leader acceptable to both factions (which he wanted to be) would have to show proficiency in activities recognized by both as conferring prestige.

To Be a Man

It is equally clear, by the same token, that members of the "bad boy" faction were less than serenely confident in their commitment to law-violation as an ideal. Once they had won power in the club they did not keep as their leader the boy who had been the dominant figure on the "bad boy" corner, and who was without question the most criminally active of the Junior Outlaws, but instead elected as president another boy who was also criminally active, but considerably less so. Moreover, in the presence of older gang members, Seniors and Marauders, the "bad boy" clique was far more subdued, less obstreperous, and far less ardent in their advocacy of crime as an ideal. There was little question that they were sensitive to and responsive to negative reactions by others to their behavior.

It is noteworthy that members of both factions adhered more firmly to the "law-violation" and "law-abiding" positions on the level of abstract ideology than on the level of actual practice. This would suggest that the existence of the opposing ideologies and their corresponding factions served important functions both for individual gang members and for the group as a whole. Being in the same orbit as the "bad boys" made it possible for the "good boys" to reap some of the rewards of violative behavior without undergoing its risks; the presence of the "good boys" imposed restraints on the "bad" that they themselves desired, and helped protect them from dangerous excesses. The behavior and ideals of the "good boys" satisfied for both factions that component of their basic orientation that said "violation of the law is wrong and should be punished;" the behavior and ideals of the "bad boys" that component that said "one cannot earn manhood without some involvement in criminal activity."

It is instructive to compare the stress and turmoil attending the struggle for dominance of the Junior Outlaws with the leadership circumstances of the Senior Bandits. In this gang, older and of lower social status (lower-class III), competition for leadership had little to do with a choice between law-abiding and law-violating philosophies, but rather with the issue of which of a number of competing leaders was *best* able to demonstrate prowess in illegal activity. This virtual absence of effective pressures against delinquency contrasts sharply with the situation of the Junior Outlaws. During the year-long struggle between its "good" and "bad" factions, the Juniors were exposed to constant pressures, both internal and external to the gang, to refrain from illegality. External sources included Rosa, whom the boys loved and respected; a local youth worker whom they held in high esteem; their older brother gangs, whose frequent admonitions to the "little kids" to "straighten out" and "keep clean" were attended with utmost seriousness. Within the gang itself the "good boy" leader served as a consistent and persuasive advocate of a law-abiding course of action. In addition, most of the boys' parents deplored their misbehavior and urged them to keep out of trouble.

In the face of all these pressures from persons of no small importance in the lives of the Juniors, the final triumph of the proponents of illegality, however tempered, assumes added significance. What was it that impelled the "bad boy" faction? There was a quality of defiance about much of their delinquency, as if they were saying—"We know perfectly well that what we are doing is regarded as wrong, legally and morally; we also know that it violates the wishes and standards of many whose good opinion we value; yet, if we are to sustain our self-respect and our honor as males we *must,* at this stage of our lives, engage in criminal behavior." In light of the experience of the Junior Outlaws, one can scarcely argue that their delinquency sprang from any inability to distinguish right from wrong, or out of any simple conformity to a set of parochial standards that just happened to differ from those of the legal code or the adult middle class. Their delinquent behavior was engendered by a highly complex interplay of forces, including, among other elements, the fact that they were males, were in the middle range of the lower class and of critical importance in the present instance, were moving through the age period when the attainment of manhood was of the utmost concern.

In the younger gang just discussed, the Junior Outlaws, leadership and clique structure reflected an intense struggle between advocates and opponents of law-violation as a prime basis of prestige.

The Senior Outlaws

Leadership in the older Senior Outlaws reflected a resolution of the law-conformity versus law-violation conflict, but with different results. Although the gang was not under direct observation during their earlier adolescence, what we know of the Juniors, along with evidence that the Senior Outlaws themselves had been more criminal when younger, would suggest that the gang had in fact undergone a similar struggle, and that the proponents of conformity to the law had won.

In any case, the events of the observation period made it clear that the Senior Outlaws sought "rep" as a gang primarily through effective execution of legitimate enterprises such as athletics, dances, and other non-violative activities. In line with this objective, they maintained a consistent concern with the "good name" of the gang and with "keeping out of trouble" in the face of constant and ubiquitous

temptations. For example, they attempted (without much success) to establish friendly relations with the senior priest of their parish—in contrast with the Junior Outlaws, who were on very bad terms with the local church. At one point during the contact period when belligerent Bandits, claiming that the Outlaws had attacked one of the Midget Bandits, vowed to "wipe out every Outlaw jacket in Midcity," the Senior Outlaws were concerned not only with the threat of attack but also with the threat to their reputation. "That does it," said one boy, "I knew we'd get into something. There goes the good name of the Outlaws."

Leadership and clique arrangements in the Senior Outlaws reflected three conditions, each related in some way to the relatively low stress on criminal activity: the stability of gang membership (members were rarely removed from the area by institutional confinement), the absence of significant conflict over the prestige and criminality issue, and the importance placed on legitimate collective activities. The Senior Bandits were the most unified of the gangs we observed directly; there were no important cleavages or factions; even the distinction between more-active and less-active members was less pronounced than in the other gangs.

But as in the other gangs, leadership among the Senior Outlaws was collective and situational. There were four key leaders, each of whom assumed authority in his own sphere of competence. As in the case of the Bandit gangs there was little overt competition among leaders; when differences arose between the leadership and the rank and file, the several leaders tended to support one another. In one significant respect, however, Outlaw leadership differed from that of the other gangs; authority was exercised more firmly and accepted more readily. Those in charge of collective enterprises generally issued commands after the manner of a tough army sergeant or work-gang boss. Although obedience to such commands was frequently less than flawless, the leadership style of Outlaw leaders approximated the "snap-to-it" approach of organizations that control firmer sanctions than do most corner gangs. Compared to the near-chaotic behavior of their younger brother gang, the organizational practices of the Senior appeared as a model of efficiency. The "authoritarian" mode of leadership was particularly characteristic of one boy, whose prerogatives were somewhat more generalized than those of the other leaders. While he was far from an undisputed "boss," holding instead a kind of *primus inter pares* position, he was as close to a "boss" as anything found among the direct-observation gangs.

His special position derived from the fact that he showed superior capability in an unusually wide range of activities, and this permitted him wider authority than the other leaders. One might have expected, in a gang oriented predominantly to law-abiding activity, that this leader would serve as an exemplar of legitimacy and rank among the most law-abiding. This was not the case. He was, in fact, one of the most criminal of the Senior Outlaws, being among the relatively few who had "done time." He was a hard drinker, an able street-fighter, a skilled football strategist and team leader, an accomplished dancer and smooth ladies' man. His leadership position was based not on his capacity to best exemplify the law-abiding orientation of the gang, but on his capabilities in a variety of activities, violative and non-violative. Thus, even in the gang most concerned with "keeping clean," excellence in crime still constituted one important basis of prestige. Competence as such rather than the legitimacy of one's activities provided the major basis of authority.

We still have to ask, however, why leadership among the Senior Outlaws was more forceful than in the other gangs. One reason emerges by comparison with the "weak leader" situation of the Junior Bandits. Younger and of lower social status, their factional conflict over the law-violation-and-prestige issue was sufficiently intense so that only a leader without an explicit commitment to either side could be acceptable to both. The Seniors, older and of higher status, had developed a good degree of intragang consensus on this issue, and showed little factionalism. They could thus accept a relatively strong leader without jeopardizing gang unity.

A second reason also involves differences in age and social status, but as these relate to the world of work. In contrast to the younger gangs, whose perspectives more directly revolved around the subculture of adolescence and its specific concerns, the Senior Outlaws at age 19 were on the threshold of adult work, and some in fact were actively engaged in it. In contrast to the lower-status gangs whose orientation to gainful employment was not and never would be as "responsible" as that of the Outlaws, the activities of the Seniors as gang members more directly reflected and anticipated the requirements and conditions of the adult occupational roles they would soon assume.

Of considerable importance in the prospective occupational world of the Outlaws was, and is, the capacity to give and take orders in the execution of collective enterprises. Unlike the Bandits, few of whom would ever occupy other than subordinate positions, the Outlaws belonged to that sector of society which provides the men who exercise direct authority over groups of laborers or blue collar workers. The self-executed collective activities of the gang—organized athletics, recreational projects, fund-raising activities—provided a training ground for the practice of organizational skills—planning organized enterprises, working together in their conduct, executing the directives of legitimate superiors. It also provided a training ground wherein those boys with the requisite talents could learn and practice the difficult art of exercising authority effectively over lower-class men. By the time they had reached the age of 20, the leaders of the Outlaws had experienced in the gang many of the problems and responsibilities confronting the army sergeant, the police lieutenant and the factory foreman.

The nature and techniques of leadership in the Senior Outlaws had relevance not only to their own gang but to the Junior Outlaws as well. Relations between the Junior and Senior Outlaws were the closest of all the intensive-contact gang subdivisions. The Seniors kept a close watch on their younger fellows, and served them in a variety of ways, as athletic coaches, advisers, mediators and arbiters. The older gang followed the factional conflicts of the Juniors with close attention, and were not above intervening when conflict reached sufficient intensity or threatened their own interests. The dominant leader of the Seniors was particularly concerned with the behavior of the Juniors; at one point, lecturing them about their disorderly conduct in Rosa's store, he remarked, "I don't hang with you guys, but I know what you do. . . . " The Seniors did not, however, succeed in either preventing the near-breakup of the Junior Outlaws or slowing their move toward law-breaking activities.

The Prevalence of Gangs

The subtle and intricately contrived relations among cliques, leadership and crime in the four subdivisions of the Bandits and Outlaws reveal the gang as an ordered and adaptive form of association, and its members as able and rational human beings. The fascinating pattern of intergang variation within a basic framework illustrates vividly the compelling influences of differences in age and social status on crime, leadership and other forms of behavior—even when these differences are surprisingly small. The experiences of Midcity gang members show that the gang serves the lower-class adolescent as a flexible and adaptable training instrument for imparting vital knowledge concerning the value of individual competence, the appropriate limits of law-violating behavior, the uses and abuses of authority, and the skills of interpersonal relations. From this perspective, the street gang appears not as a casual or transient manifestation that emerges intermittently in response to unique and passing social conditions, but rather as a stable associational form, coordinate with and complementary to the family, and as an intrinsic part of the way of life of the urban low-status community.

How then can one account for the widespread conception of gangs as somehow popping up and then disappearing again? One critical reason concerns the way one defines what a gang is. Many observers, both scholars and non-scholars, often use a *sine qua non* to sort out "real" gangs from near-gangs, pseudo-gangs, and non-gangs. Among the more common of these single criteria are: autocratic one-man leadership, some "absolute" degree of solidarity or stable membership, a predominant involvement in violent conflict with other gangs, claim to a rigidly defined turf, or participation in activities thought to pose a threat to other sectors of the community. Reaction to groups lacking the *sine qua non* is often expressed with a dismissive "Oh, them. That's not a *gang*. That's just a bunch of kids out on the corner."

On the Corner Again

For many people there are no gangs if there is no gang warfare. It's that simple. For them, as for all those who concentrate on the "threatening" nature of the gang, the phenomenon is defined in terms of the degree of "problem" it poses: A group whose "problematic" behavior is hard to ignore is a gang; one less problematic is not. But what some people see as a problem may not appear so to others. In Philadelphia, for example, the police reckoned there were 80 gangs, of which 20 were at war; while social workers estimated there were 200 gangs, of which 80 were "most hostile." Obviously, the social workers' 80 "most hostile" gangs were the same as the 80 "gangs" of the police. The additional 120 groups defined as gangs by the social workers were seen as such because they were thought to be appropriate objects of social work; but to the police they were not sufficiently troublesome to require consistent police attention, and were not therefore defined as gangs.

In view of this sort of confusion, let me state our definition of what a gang is. A gang is a group of urban adolescents who congregate recurrently at one or more nonresidential locales, with continued affiliation based on self-defined criteria of inclusion and exclusion. Recruitment, customary places of assembly and ranging areas are based in a specific territory, over some portion of which limited use and occupancy rights are claimed. Membership both in the gang as a whole and in its subgroups is determined on the basis of age. The group maintains a versatile repertoire of activities, with hanging out, mating, recreational and illegal activity being of central importance; and it is internally differentiated on the basis of authority, prestige, personality and clique-formation.

The main reason that people have consistently mistaken the prevalence of gangs is the widespread tendency to define them as gangs on the basis of the presence or absence of one or two characteristics that are thought to be essential to the "true" gang. Changes in the forms or frequencies or particular characteristics, such as leadership, involvement in fighting, or modes of organization, are seen not as normal variations over time and space, but rather as signs of the emergence or disappearance of the gangs themselves. Our work does not support this view; instead, our evidence indicates that the core characteristics of the gang vary continuously from place to place and from time to time without negating the existence of the gang. Gangs may be larger or smaller, named or nameless, modestly or extensively differentiated, more or less active in gang fighting, stronger or weaker in leadership, black, white, yellow or brown, without affecting their identity as gangs. So long as groups of adolescents gather periodically outside the home, frequent a particular territory, restrict membership by age and other criteria, pursue a variety of activities, and maintain differences in authority and prestige—so long will the gang continue to exist as a basic associational form.

Teen-age Interracial Dating

Frank A. Petroni

Early in the still unfolding story of school desegregation, many observers were saying that what white opponents of integration were most afraid of was interracial sex. People who had been comforting themselves with such abstractions as "Negroes are OK, but I wouldn't want my daughter to marry one," now, with desegregation, had suddenly to cope (they thought) with a real possibility, not a farfetched hypothesis.

Be this as it may, I doubt there are many Americans who have not, at one time or another had to cope with the question of interracial sex, either in imagination—"what would happen if . . ."—or in fact. Interracial dating and interracial marriage are social realities, however much white racists and black nationalists may deplore it.

A few years ago, while I was with the Menninger Foundation in Topeka, Kansas, my wife and I had an opportunity to study the extent of, and students' feelings about, interracial dating at a desegregated high school. Our procedure was rather unorthodox. Instead of trying to gather a 5 percent random sample of the 3,000-member student body, we began slowly by letting our initial student contacts tell us what they considered to be the principal "types" of student in the school. They distinguished 12 such types: middle-class whites, hippies, peaceniks, white trash, "sedits" (upper-class blacks), elites, conservatives, racists, niggers, militants, athletes and hoods. Then, and again through our initial contacts, we brought in other students and roughly classified them according to "type." In this way, I believe we got a representative cross section of the social world of this high school. We interviewed the boys and girls in groups of three or four, and in time 25 groups came to our house for these conversations. We had two refusals: a black girl canceled her appointment after Martin Luther King was killed, and a boy told us he wouldn't talk to white people.

Few topics demonstrate the multiple pressures students are subject to better than interracial dating. These pressures come from parents, teachers, counselors, school administrators and peers. However, mixed dating is emphatically not a barometer of the amount of "integration" in a desegrated school; that is not the reason we chose to study it.

Needless to say, the students did not all share the same point of view on interracial dating. Yet, most of them—independent of race—did feel that it was none of the school's business: if students wanted to date interracially, the school had no right to stop them.

White Boys and Black Girls

Not one student knew of a case of interracial dating involving a white boy and a black girl. There was considerable speculation about why. A conservative white girl said that white boys are too proud to date blacks. The two white boys with her disagreed: both said that it's because black girls aren't as pretty as white girls. One of the two also suggested that blacks and whites have little in common and so he would not consider dating a black. Note the popular stereotypes in this answer:

Well, there are cultural differences, and their attitudes are different. I think that's what makes the difference. They're easygoing. They like to have a lot of fun. They don't think about the future, about things that are important like getting a job, or supporting a family. They don't try for grades. They're just out to have a good time.

Even when black girls met an individual's standard of physical attractiveness, however, white boys spoke of other obstacles: where to go, how to ignore community disapproval and what to do about family and friends who disapprove. These conflicts are cogently summarized in the response of a white boy who considered dating a black:

I think if you dated a Negro, you would lose a lot of so-called friends. But you would probably gain some Negro friends. I contemplated asking this Negro girl for a date, but I chickened out. I thought, where would I take her? The only place where people wouldn't stare at me would be a drive-in movie, and I don't have a car. If you went to a restaurant, you would get dirty looks from people. I couldn't take her home and introduce her to my mom; she'd probably kill me.

Social obstacles apart, there is some doubt in my mind whether a black girl, in the school we studied, would go out with a white boy even if asked. Each black girl we

143

interviewed was asked, "Suppose a white boy asked you out, how easy would it be for you to accept?" One girl answered: "Any white boy who asked me out, I would know what he wants. For a Negro boy to have a white girl is some sort of status symbol, but if a white boy asked me out, it would be a step down for him. I would think he wants something I'm not about to give him."

Other black girls spoke of the double standard between boys and girls, and how girls were less free to date interracially because their reputations would be ruined. Fear for one's reputation was also a factor among white girls. The students associated interracial dating with sex; and girls, be they black or white, stood to lose the most. Yet sex was not always associated with dating. There was no reference to sex when respondents talked about dating within one's race. Sometimes the reference to sex in interracial dating was subtle, but nonetheless it was present. A white girl's comment demonstrates this: "When you think of mixed dating, you always think of a colored boy with a white girl. And you always think it is the white girl who is low. If it was a white boy with a colored girl, then it would be the white boy who was low."

When asked for the meaning of low, another white girl said: "Well, generally the public thinks that the girl has low standards and low morals, if she's willing to go out with a Negro."

Particularly among "elite" blacks, parental disapproval of interracial dating also stood between black young women and dates with white boys. Most of the black students in this strata stated that their parents would not tolerate interracial dating. The parents expected their children to compete with white students academically, for school offices, and in extracurricular activities; socially, however, they expected them to stay with blacks.

Still other respondents saw the white boys' reluctance to date blacks as essentially a matter of status considerations. If the belief that *all* whites are better than *all* blacks is general in this society (and it showed up among some of the blacks in our sample as well), then the response of an 18-year-old black girl, who was given the highest academic award the school has to offer, makes sense:

White boys would be scared to ask us out anyway. The Negro boys will ask white girls out, but white boys will never ask Negro girls out. For a Negro boy, going out with a white girl is an accomplishment; it raises his status, even if the white girl is lower-class. All white kids are supposed to be better than Negro kids. If a white boy dated a Negro, even if the white boy was one of the "trashy" kind, and the girl was, say me, his status would drop. They would ask him if he was hard-up or something. White boys would be stepping down if they asked Negro girls for dates.

Aside from the black girl's fear of parental disapproval and loss of her reputation, we were told that few blacks would accept a date from a white boy because of pressures from black young men, who would object if black girls dated whites. However, this pressure doesn't appear to count for much with the elite, college-bound black girl; it was the athletic girl who gave us this answer. Unlike her elite counterpart, the athletic black girl was not preoccupied with achieving what the white man prized for whites: academic achievement, social popularity and a svelte figure. The reference group for these girls was the black community. A star on the girl's track team said:

No Negro girls that I know of have ever been dated by a white guy. There are some that wish they could. In fact, I know some white guys, myself, I wouldn't mind going out with, but the Negro girls are mostly afraid. Even if a white guy asked them out, they wouldn't go out with them. Negro boys don't like for Negro girls to date white guys. Sometimes I see white guys who look nice, and I stop and talk to them. The Negro boys get upset. They are real screwy. They can date white girls, but we can't date white guys.

The Reaction of Black Males

The black young men in our sample at times disagreed on how they would react to dating between white boys and black girls, but in general their answers fell into one of the categories predicted by the black girls. A boy, who has dated white girls, admitted to the double standard alleged by the girl athlete. He told us:

You know, I think that Negro boys would detest having a Negro girl go out with a white boy. They don't want Negro girls to date white boys. They don't like it. I feel like that, and I think I'm a hypocrite. I've been out with white girls, but I don't like it if a Negro girl goes out with a white boy. If I see a colored girl with a white boy, I think, why didn't she date me, or another Negro? What's he got that I ain't got?

Not all blacks who date whites felt this way. The young man whom we just quoted identified positively with the black community. But another young man, with a steady white girl friend, and who prized white over black, had this to say: "I don't think most of the white boys would ask Negro girls out. Maybe I shouldn't say this, but I think any Negro girl would consider it a privilege to have a white boy ask her out. I feel if a colored girl is good enough to get a white boy, they should go out together."

It was easier for most of the students, white or black, to talk about interracial dating in which the girl is white. This is the kind of dating most of them have seen. Some students, however, had seen black girls with white boys at the state university and in larger communities. One black spoke frankly of his reactions when he first saw a white man with a black woman:

You see this at the colleges [white boys with Negro girls]. You know, it's a funny thing now that you mention it, you never see Negro girls with white boys here. I was in New York once. It was kind of funny; I saw this Negro girl with a white guy. I was shocked. You know, I looked, and it seemed kind of funny to me. I mean you see white girls with Negro boys, but you never see a Negro girl with a white guy; it kind of shocks you at first.

Black Males and White Girls

The pressures from parents, teachers, counselors, peers and the community are also brought to bear on the black boy and white girl who cross the barrier against interracial dating. As one student poignantly put it, "For those who violate this convention, the tuition is high." Just how high is exemplified by the white girl in the most talked about relationship involving an interracial couple.

Around Christmas time, I got to know this colored guy real well and wanted to date him. There was a big mix-up; my parents didn't like it. My parents put a lot of pressure on me not to go out with him. They are the type people, like Dad, who says he's not prejudiced. He even has *them* working in his office, but he wants them to stay in their place. At school there was a lot of talking behind my back and snickering when I walked down the hallway. I tried to tell myself it didn't matter what people thought, but it still hurt. It hurt an awful lot. My parents made me feel so guilty. They made me feel so cheap. They were worried about what people would say. They made me feel like two pieces of dirt. You know, I never thought interracial dating was a good idea, but when I met this colored guy, it changed me. I never went with anyone I really liked before. I think this changes your outlook. It gives you hope, when you find someone you really like.

Sex and Dating

That sexual intercourse is associated with interracial dating is indicated by the fact that one reaction to such dating is to question the girl's moral standards. We heard this frequently from both white girls and boys, but particularly the latter. Prior to dating a black, however, the girl's personal conduct is rarely mentioned. It seems as if the disbelief among the white community that a white girl would date a black is softened by the rationalization that she "'must be immoral." One white girl found it hard to accept this student reaction: "I got kind of sick of the kids throwing her to the dogs. There were times when you had to take a stand. You either turned the other cheek, or you

fought back for her. They thought she was cheap, and they said nasty things about her. Even the guy I'm dating, he's that way, too."

However, a white girl doesn't have to date a black to have others question her morality. Just talking to a black student can result in the same labeling process. A liberal white girl, identified as a hippie, told us: "One day we were talking to some black power students in front of school. Some adults going by in cars made some filthy remarks. You can imagine what they think of white women, hanging around talking to Negroes. They shot it right out as they drove by. These are the good, white middle-class people."

A very articulate black youth described a similar incident in which he was talking to a white girl: "One time I was walking down the stairs outside school. I was standing with this white girl, and we were talking. About six white kids drove by and yelled, 'White trash, you're nothing but white trash.' I guess because she was white and I'm black, and we were talking, she was white trash."

Other blacks, aware of the white community's reaction to white girls who date or talk in public with blacks, were prevented from asking white girls out because they did not want to ruin the girls' reputations. The son of a prominent black professional, who was a football letterman, in the student government and extremely popular, refused to date a white girl for this reason.

In general, I would say that just the fact that I was taking out a white girl, the imaginations would go wild. They think the moral standards are lower in interracial dating. There's this one white girl I goofed around with a lot. It's gone beyond the friendship stage, but we never dated. If I did go out with a white girl, it would be hard to take her anyplace. I would have to think about it for a while before I took out a white girl, because I feel she would be downgraded. I wouldn't want to ruin her reputation.

White girls who date across the color line find themselves unacceptable to white boys. Most of the students agreed that to date interracially limited a girl's field of potential dates. For many white girls, knowledge of this reaction on the part of white boys served as a deterrent to interracial dating. Nevertheless, a number of white girls told us they were attracted to certain black young men. One of the girls who did defy her society reported this also. She said, "When I was dating him, I was surprised at how many girls wanted to date colored guys. They would come up to me and ask me things. They really wanted to date colored guys, but they were afraid."

White "Boycott"

We found, too, that the white boycott (as it were) persisted after the interracial couple no longer dated, albeit only among white boys still in school. Girls who broke off their relationship with blacks were dated by older whites in the community. But to regain admission as an acceptable date among the high school boys, a girl would have to move to a new community to lose the pejorative label, which is part of the price for dating interracially.

The black male who dates a white girl does not escape criticism from his own race, particularly the black girls. Part of their disapproval is motivated, again, by the lack of reciprocity: black girls were not dated by whites. When a high status black, generally an athlete, dated a white girl, he was replaced by neither a high status nor low status white. The black girls' resentment is summarized in the answer of one of our respondents, identified as a "militant."

Well, in junior high, the Negro girls resented the fact that I went out with a white girl, and they really got onto me. They feel inferior. The white girls get all the guys. Some hostility between the Negro girls and white girls comes from this. The Negro girls kind of feel left out. She doesn't have white guys to date, and she doesn't have Negro guys to date. She says, "Hey, gal, you dating that Negro, and I can't get a date with him." This kind of builds up a resentment in her.

Pressure on the black male comes in two forms. First, his racial identification may be questioned. Often he is accused of thinking he is white. Second, retaliation by black girls can be more direct and swift. There were reports of boys physically beaten for dating a white girl. However, this response was the exception; it was more common for girls to spread the rumor that a boy is an "Uncle Tom."

Parental Pressures

The double threat of losing one's reputation and losing favor among the white boys prevented many white girls from dating blacks. Yet the pressures do not end there. Interracial dating is a test of the white liberal's commitment to civil rights—a test that few have passed. A number of white students spoke of their disappointment in their parents who gave lipservice to "liberalism" but in the final analysis were prejudiced. White girls reported this more often than white boys. However, white girls *tested* their parents more often. A white girl who sensed this in one of her parents said:

This Negro friend of mine gets along beautifully with my mother, but not my father. He senses this, too. After meeting my father, he said my father didn't like him. This is something new for me because my father and mother have always been liberal. Now that he has been over to my house a couple of times, my father is acting strange. I guess I'm learning something about him I didn't know before.

Sometimes the parental reaction isn't as subtle as the feeling that one's father doesn't approve of interracial dating. A rather tough black girl, who admitted that at one time she was a hood, told us what happened to a white girl, who used to date her ex-boy friend:

For many Negro boys, dating white girls is their way of showing their superiority, their way of trying to hurt the white man. This boy I used to date went with a white girl once. She went through hell with her parents and everyone else to go out with him. But he didn't really care. He was just showing off. Her father even spit in her face. Her parents attacked her; they beat her and called her a slut.

Parental disapproval of interracial dating is not restricted to whites. The blacks reported a generation gap between themselves, their parents and their grandparents on this issue. In general, they reported that the intensity of the disapproval varied directly with age. Thus, grandparents showed more disapproval than parents. By and large, however, the black students agreed that the mixed couple that chooses to go out together should have that choice without interference from members of the adult community, be they parents, teachers, counselors, school administrators or anonymous members of the community.

The sample included few Mexican-Americans; those interviewed, however, reported the same phenomenon: Mexican parents, like white and black parents, objected to interracial dating. An outspoken Mexican-American girl related the Mexican parents' position. Her answer reveals the confusion parental inconsistencies can create for a young person.

Mom always said have your fun as long as you're young, and as long as you marry a Mexican. I don't feel that way. If I fall in love with a Negro, I'll marry him. If I fall in love with a white, I'll marry a white. My parents would frown on us dating a Negro, even if he has higher standards than the Mexicans we date now: even if the Negro's father was a lawyer or a doctor, and he was a better person than many of the lower-class Mexicans we date now. I don't understand it. They would rather see us go out with white people, who aren't as good, just because of skin color. They say they want the best for us; if the best meant going out with a Negro, they would say no!

The School

As if the pressures of peers, parents and community were not enough, those who try to break down the barrier against interracial dating, or who ignore it, must also cope with teachers, counselors and school administrators, who, by and large, are united on this issue. In a word, boy-girl relationships should be white-white, or black-black, but not black-white.

It became apparent to us that when we discussed the school's position on interracial dating, the students' objections to interference became more emotionally charged. This suggested to us that the students perceived the school and its functionaries as having less legitimacy than either parents or peers in attempting to control and dictate norms for their social life.

The hostility was increased by the fact that both black and white students perceived a selective interference by the school. The teachers, counselors and school administrators did not interfere with interracial dating per se. Their interference increased in direct proportion to the white girl's social status. A black girl described this selective process to us.

I think it's their business, not the school's. She was crazy about him, and he was crazy about her. They went to school to get an education, and that's what the school should be concerned with: giving them an education. Instead, they threatened him, they said he wouldn't get an athletic scholarship. I felt this was entirely wrong for the school to interfere. It's not the school's affair to concern itself with whether or not the students have companionship. It's their business to teach. These kids aren't the only couple at school. But she was somebody. With some of the other couples, the girls aren't important. In fact, one of the other girls is just white "trash." They don't say too much to these others; it's the important ones they want to save.

Another girl left little doubt of the painful slur implicit in this attitude of the school functionaries: "If you're a low white person, the administration could care less, but if you're a higher white person, they're worried that you might be dragged down by a Negro."

Although we cannot be certain, there is a possibility that the school's policy in these matters is dictated by the reality of the situation. There was little that the school could do to low status students who dated across the color line; the school did not have an effective lever to stop them from continuing except to inform the parents, and most parents already knew. The only other course open to them was to expel the students for the slightest infraction of the rules. Among high status students, however, the school could threaten removal from the very positions the students worked to achieve. Black athletes were called in and ordered to desist or forfeit their chances for an athletic

scholarship; others were threatened with removal from the team. And white girls were told they could not run for a school office, they were not eligible to become cheerleaders and they would receive no assistance in obtaining a scholarship.

Summary and Conclusions

Interracial dating was one of the most emotionally charged subjects in our discussions with these young people. Although we have not cited all our respondents in this brief presentation, all of them had opinions on the issue. There was complete agreement on the type of interracial dating that occurred. In no case was the male white and the female black. Generally the black male, who dated a white girl, was a high status athlete; however, by high status we are not referring to his father's socioeconomic position in the community. This may, or may not, have been high; in most cases it was not.

The fact that black students with prestige took up with white girls was a source of tension between black and white girls. More than her male counterpart, the black girl preached black separatism. Some students felt that this was because the girls did not share a sports experience such as that shared by black and white boys. On the surface, that may appear to be right. However, since there was little camaraderie between black and white athletes off the field or court, direct competition for high status blacks in the dating-mating complex seems to be a more plausible explanation for the friction between white and black girls.

While interracial dating was not commonplace, it did exist, and those who did it paid a heavy price. Payment was exacted from peers, parents, the community, teachers, counselors and other school administrators. In short, the entire social world of these teen-agers was united against them. There was no citadel to protect them. When school and peers were allied against them, there was no comfort from their parents. The couple had each other, and a small enclave of "friends," but even among the latter, the attrition rate was high.

Join this to the implication that their moral standards were lower if they dated interracially, and it is small wonder that few felt strong enough to weather all these assaults.

Sororities
and the
Husband
Game

John Finley Scott

Marriages, like births, deaths, or initiations at puberty, are rearrangements of structure that are constantly recurring in any society; they are moments of the continuing social process regulated by custom; there are institutionalized ways of dealing with such events.

A. R. Radcliffe-Brown
African Systems of Kinship and Marriage

In many simple societies, the "institutionalized ways" of controlling marriage run to diverse schemes and devices. Often they include special living quarters designed to make it easy for marriageable girls to attract a husband: the Bontok people of the Philippines keep their girls in a special house, called the *olag,* where lovers call, sex play is free, and marriage is supposed to result. The Ekoi of Nigeria, who like their women fat, send them away to be specially fattened for marriage. Other peoples, such as the Yao of central Africa and the aborigines of the Canary Islands, send their daughters away to "convents" where old women teach them the special skills and mysteries that a young wife needs to know.

Accounts of such practices have long been a standard topic of anthropology lectures in universities, for their exotic appeal keeps the students, large numbers of whom are sorority girls, interested and alert. The control of marriage in simple societies strikes these girls as quite different from the freedom that they believe prevails in America. This is ironic, for the American college sorority is a pretty good counterpart in complex societies of the fatting houses and convents of the primitives.

Whatever system they use, parents in all societies have more in mind than just getting their daughters married; they want them married to the *right* man. The criteria for defining the right man vary tremendously, but virtually all parents view some potential mates with approval, some with disapproval, and some with downright horror. Many ethnic groups, including many in America, are *endogamous,* that is, they desire marriage of their young only to those within the group. In *shtetl* society, the Jewish villages of eastern Europe, marriages were arranged by a *shatchen,* a matchmaker, who paired off the girls and boys with due regard to the status, family connections, wealth, and personal attractions of the participants. But this society was strictly endogamous—only marriage within the group was allowed. Another rule of endogamy relates to social rank or class, for most parents are anxious that their children marry at least at the same level as themselves. Often they hope the children, and especially the daughters, will marry at a higher level. Parents of the *shtetl,* for example, valued *hypergamy*

—the marriage of daughters to a man of higher status—and a father who could afford it would offer substantial sums to acquire a scholarly husband (the most highly prized kind) for his daughter.

The marriage problem, from the point of view of parents and of various ethnic groups and social classes, is always one of making sure that girls are available for marriage with the right man while at the same time guarding against marriage with the wrong man.

THE UNIVERSITY CONVENT

The American middle class has a particular place where it sends its daughters so they will be easily accessible to the boys—the college campus. Even for the families who worry about the bad habits a nice girl can pick up at college, it has become so much a symbol of middle-class status that the risk must be taken, the girl must be sent. American middle-class society has created an institution on the campus that, like the fatting house, makes the girls more attractive; like the Canary Island convent, teaches skills that middle-class wives need to know; like the *shtetl,* provides matchmakers; and without going so far as to buy husbands of high rank, manages to dissuade the girls from making alliances with lower-class boys. That institution is the college sorority.

A sorority is a private association which provides separate dormitory facilities with a distinctive Greek letter name for selected female college students. Membership is by invitation only, and requires recommendation by former members. Sororities are not simply the feminine counterpart of the college fraternity. They differ from fraternities because marriage is a more important determinant of social position for women than for men in American society, and because standards of conduct associated with marriage correspondingly bear stronger sanctions for women than for men. Sororities have much more "alumnae" involvement than fraternities, and fraternities adapt to local conditions and different living arrangements better than sororities. The college-age sorority "actives" decide only the minor details involved in recruitment, membership, and activities; parent-age alumnae control the important choices. The prototypical sorority is not the servant of youthful interests; on the contrary, it is an organized agency for controlling those interests. Through the sorority, the elders of family, class, ethnic, and religious communities can continue to exert remote control over the marital arrangements of their young girls.

The need for remote control arises from the nature of the educational system in an industrial society. In simple societies, where children are taught the culture at home, the family controls the socialization of children almost completely. In more complex societies, education becomes the province of special agents and competes with the family. The conflict between the family and outside agencies increases as children move through the educational system and is sharpest when the children reach college age. College curricula are even more challenging to family value systems than high school courses, and children frequently go away to college, out of reach of direct family influence. Sometimes a family can find a college that does not challenge family values in any way: devout Catholic parents can send their daughters to Catholic colleges; parents who want to be sure that daughter meets only "Ivy League" men can send her to one of the "Seven Sisters"—the women's equivalent of the Ivy League, made up of Radcliffe, Barnard, Smith, Vassar, Wellesley, Mt. Holyoke, and Bryn Mawr—if she can get in.

The solution of controlled admissions is applicable only to a small proportion of college-age girls, however. There are nowhere near the number of separate, sectarian colleges in the country that would be needed to segregate all the college-age girls safely, each with her own kind. Private colleges catering mostly to a specific class can still preserve a girl from meeting her social or economic inferiors, but the fees at such places are steep. It costs more to maintain a girl in the Vassar dormitories than to pay her sorority bills at a land-grant school. And even if her family is willing to pay the fees, the academic pace at the elite schools is much too fast for most girls. Most college girls attend large, tax-supported universities where the tuition is relatively low and where admissions policies let in students from many strata and diverse ethnic backgrounds. It is on the campuses of the free, open, and competitive state universities of the country that the sorority system flourishes.

When a family lets its daughter loose on a large campus with a heterogenous population, there are opportunities to be met and dangers to guard against. The great opportunity is to meet a good man to marry, at the age when the girls are most attractive and the men most amenable. For the girls, the pressure of time is urgent; though they are often told otherwise, their attractions are in fact primarily physical, and they fade with time. One need only compare the relative handicaps in the marital sweepstakes of a 38-year old single male lawyer and a single, female teacher of the same age to realize the urgency of the quest.

The great danger of the public campus is that young girls, however properly reared, are likely to fall in love, and—in our middle-class society at least—love leads to marriage. Love is a potentially random factor, with no regard for class boundaries. There seems to be no good way of preventing young girls from falling in love. The only practical way to control love is to control the type of men the girl is likely to encounter; she cannot fall dangerously in love with a man she has never met. Since kinship groups are unable to keep "undesirable" boys off the public campus entirely, they have to settle for control of counter-institutions within the university. An effective counter-institution will protect a girl from the corroding influences of the university environment.

There are roughly three basic functions which a sorority can perform in the interest of kinship groups:
- It can ward off the wrong kind of men.
- It can facilitate moving-up for middle-status girls.
- It can solve the "Brahmin problem"—the difficulty of proper marriage that afflicts high-status girls.

Kinship groups define the "wrong kind of man" in a variety of ways. Those who use an ethnic definition support sororities that draw an ethnic membership line; the best examples are the Jewish sororities, because among all the ethnic groups with endogamous standards (in America at any rate), only the Jews so far have sent large numbers of daughters away to college. But endogamy along class lines is even more pervasive. It is the most basic mission of the sorority to prevent a girl from marrying out of her group (exogamy) or beneath her class (hypogamy). As one of the founders of a national sorority artlessly put it in an essay titled "The Mission of the Sorority":

> There is a danger, and a very grave danger, that four years' residence in a dormitory will tend to destroy right ideals of home life and substitute in their stead a belief in the freedom that comes from community living . . . culture, broad, liberalizing, humanizing culture, we cannot get too much of, unless while acquiring it we are weaned from home and friends, from ties of blood and kindred.

A sorority discourages this dangerous weaning process by introducing the sisters only to selected boys; each sorority, for example, has dating relations with one or more fraternities, matched rather nicely to the sorority on the basis of ethnicity and/or class. (A particular sorority, for example, will have dating arrangements not with all the fraternities on campus, but only with those whose brothers are a class-match for their sisters.) The sorority's frantically busy schedule of parties, teas, meetings, skits, and exchanges keeps the sisters so occupied that they have neither time nor opportunity to meet men outside the channels the sorority provides.

MARRYING UP

The second sorority function, that of facilitating hypergamy, is probably even more of an attraction to parents than the simpler preservation of endogamy. American society is not so much oriented to the preservation of the *status quo* as to the pursuit of upward mobility.

In industrial societies, children are taught that if they study hard they can get the kind of job that entitles them to a place in the higher ranks. This incentive actually is appropriate only for boys, but the emphasis on using the most efficient available means to enter the higher levels will not be lost on the girls. And the most efficient means for a girl—marriage—is particularly attractive because it requires so much less effort than the mobility through hard work that is open to boys. To the extent that we do socialize the sexes in different ways, we are more likely to train daughters in the ways of attracting men than to motivate them to do hard, competitive work. The difference in motivation holds even if the girls have the intelligence and talent required for status climbing on their own. For lower-class girls on the make, membership in a sorority can greatly improve the chances of meeting (and subsequently marrying) higher-status boys.

Now we come to the third function of the sorority—solving the Brahmin problem. The fact that hypergamy is encouraged in our society creates difficulties for girls whose parents are already in the upper strata. In a hypergamous system, high status *men* have a strong advantage; they can offer their status to a prospective bride as part of the marriage bargain, and the advantages of high status are often sufficient to offset many personal drawbacks. But a *woman's* high status has very little exchange value because she does not confer it on her husband.

This difficulty of high status women in a hypergamous society we may call the Brahmin problem. Girls of Brahmin caste in India and Southern white women of good family have the problem in common. In order to avoid the horrors of hypogamy, high status women must compete for high status men against women from all classes. Furthermore, high status women are handicapped in their battle by a certain type of vanity engendered by their class. They expect their wooers to court them in the style to which their fathers have accustomed them; this usually involves more formal dating, gift-giving, escorting, taxi-ing, etc., than many college swains can afford. If upper-stratum men are allowed to find out that the favors of lower class women are available for a much smaller investment of time, money, and emotion, they may well refuse to court upper-status girls.

In theory, there are all kinds of ways for upper-stratum families to deal with surplus daughters. They can strangle them at birth (female infanticide); they can marry several to each available male (polygyny); they can offer money to any suitable male willing to take one off their hands (dowries, groom-service fees). All these solutions have in fact been used in one society or another, but for various reasons none is acceptable in our society. Spinsterhood still works, but marriage is so popular and so well rewarded that everybody hopes to avoid staying single.

The industrial solution to the Brahmin problem is to corner the market, or more specifically to shunt the eligible bachelors into a special marriage market where the upper stratum women are in complete control of the bride-supply. The best place to set up this protected marriage-market is where many suitable men can be found at the age when they are most willing to marry—in short, the college campus. The kind of male collegians who can be shunted more readily into the specialized marriage-market that sororities run, are those who are somewhat uncertain of their own status and who aspire to move into higher strata. These boys are anxious to bolster a shaky self-image by dating obviously high-class sorority girls. The fraternities are full of them.

How does a sorority go about fulfilling its three functions? The first item of business is making sure that the girls join. This is not as simple as it seems, because the values that sororities maintain are more important to the older generation than to college-age girls. Although the sorority image is one of membership denied to the "wrong kind" of girls, it is also true that sororities have quite a problem of recruiting the "right kind." Some are pressured into pledging by their parents. Many are recruited straight out of high school, before they know much about what really goes on at college. High school recruiters present sorority life to potential rushees as one of unending gaiety; life outside the sorority is painted as bleak and dateless.

A membership composed of the "right kind" of girls is produced by the requirement that each pledge must have the recommendation of, in most cases, two or more alumnae of the sorority. Membership is often passed on from mother to daughter—this is the "legacy," whom sorority actives have to invite whether they like her or not. The sort of headstrong, innovative, or "sassy" girl who is likely to organize a campaign inside the sorority against prevailing standards is unlikely to receive alumnae recommendations. This is why sorority girls are so complacent about alumnae dominance, and why professors find them so bland and uninteresting as students. Alumnae dominance extends beyond recruitment, into the daily life of the house. Rules, regulations, and policy explanations come to the house from the national association. National headquarters is given to explaining unpopular policy by any available strategem; a favorite device (not limited to the sorority) is to interpret all non-conformity as sexual, so that the girl who rebels against wearing girdle, high heels, and stockings to dinner two or three times a week stands implicitly accused of promiscuity. This sort of argument, based on the shrewdness of many generations, shames into conformity many a girl who otherwise might rebel against the code imposed by her elders. The actives in positions of control (house manager, pledge trainer or captain) are themselves closely supervised by alumnae. Once the right girls are initiated, the organization has mechanisms that make it very difficult for a girl to withdraw. Withdrawal can mean difficulty in finding alternative living quarters, loss of pre-paid room and board fees, and stigmatization.

Sororities keep their members, and particularly their flighty pledges, in line primarily by filling up all their time with house activities. Pledges are required to study at the house, and they build the big papier-mache floats (in collaboration with selected fraternity boys) that are a traditional display of "Greek Row" for the homecoming game. Time is encompassed completely; activities are planned long in advance, and there is almost no energy or time available for meeting inappropriate men.

The girls are taught—if they do not already know—the behavior appropriate to the upper strata. They learn how to dress with expensive restraint, how to make appropriate conversation, how to drink like a lady. There is some variety here among sororities of different rank; members of sororities at the bottom of the social ladder prove their gentility by rigid conformity in dress and manner to the stereotype of the sorority girl, while members of top houses feel socially secure even when casually dressed. If you are born rich you can afford to wear Levi's and sweatshirts.

PRELIMINARY EVENTS

The sorority facilitates dating mainly by exchanging parties, picnics, and other frolics with the fraternities in its set. But to augment this the "fixer-uppers" (the Ameri-

can counterpart of the *shatchen*) arrange dates with selected boys; their efforts raise the sorority dating rate above the independent level by removing most of the inconvenience and anxiety from the contracting of dates.

Dating, in itself, is not sufficient to accomplish the

GLOSSARY OF MARRIAGE TERMS

Endogamy: **A rule or practice of marriage within a particular group.**

Exogamy: **A practice or rule of marriage only between persons who are *not* members of a well-defined group, such as one based on family or locality.**

Hypergamy: **The movement of a woman, through marriage, to a status *higher* than that to which she was born.**

Hypogamy: **The movement of a woman, through marriage, to a status *lower* than that to which she was born.**

Polygyny: **The marriage of one husband to two or more wives. It is not the same as *polygamy*, which simply means a plurality of mates irrespective of sex.**

---

sorority's purposes. Dating must lead to pinning, pinning to engagement, engagement to marriage. In sorority culture, all dating is viewed as a movement toward marriage. Casual, spontaneous dating is frowned upon; formal courtship is still encouraged. Sorority ritual reinforces the progression from dating to marriage. At the vital point in the process, where dating must be turned into engagement, the sorority shores up the structure by the pinning ritual, performed after dinner in the presence of all the sorority sisters (who are required to stay for the ceremony) and attended, in its classic form, by a choir of fraternity boys singing outside. The commitment is so public that it is difficult for either partner to withdraw. Since engagement is already heavily reinforced outside the sorority, pinning ceremonies are more elaborate than engagements.

The social columns of college newspapers faithfully record the successes of the sorority system as it stands today. Sorority girls get engaged faster than "independents," and they appear to be marrying more highly ranked men. But what predictions can we make about the system's future?

All social institutions change from time to time, in response to changing conditions. In the mountain villages of the Philippines, the steady attacks of school and mission on the immorality of the *olag* have almost demolished it. Sororities, too, are affected by changes in the surrounding environment. Originally they were places where the few female college students took refuge from the jeers and catcalls of men who thought that nice girls didn't belong on campus. They assumed their present, endogamy-conserving form with the flourishing of the great land-grant universities in the first half of this century.

ON THE BRINK

The question about the future of the sorority system is whether it can adapt to the most recent changes in the forms of higher education. At present, neither fraternities nor sororities are in the pink of health. On some campuses there are chapter houses which have been reduced to taking in non-affiliated boarders to pay the costs of running the property. New sorority chapters are formed, for the most part, on new or low-prestige campuses (where status-anxiety is rife); at schools of high prestige fewer girls rush each year and the weaker houses are disbanding.

University administrations are no longer as hospitable to the Greeks as they once were. Most are building extensive dormitories that compete effectively with the housing offered by sororities; many have adopted regulations intended to minimize the influence of the Greeks on campus activities. The campus environment is changing rapidly: academic standards are rising, admission is increasingly competitive and both male and female students are more interested in academic achievement; the proportion of graduate students seriously training for a profession is increasing; campus culture is often so obviously pluralist that the Greek claim to monopolize social activity is unconvincing.

The sorority as it currently stands is ill-adapted to cope with the new surroundings. Sorority houses were built to provide a setting for lawn parties, dances, and dress-up occasions, and not to facilitate study; crowding and noise are severe, and most forms of privacy do not exist. The sorority songs that have to be gone through at rushing and chapter meetings today all seem to have been written in 1915 and are mortifying to sing today. The arcane rituals, so fascinating to high school girls, grow tedious and sophomoric to college seniors.

But the worst blow of all to the sorority system comes from the effect of increased academic pressure on the dating habits of college men. A student competing for grades in a professional school, or even in a difficult undergraduate major, simply has not the time (as he might have had in, say, 1925) to get involved in the sorority forms of courtship. Since these days almost all the "right kind" of men *are* involved in demanding training, the traditions of the sorority are becoming actually inimical to hypergamous marriage. Increasingly, then, sororities do not solve the Brahmin problem but make it worse.

One can imagine a sorority designed to facilitate marriage to men who have no time for elaborate courtship. In such a sorority, the girls—to start with small matters—would improve their telephone arrangements, for the fraternity boy in quest of a date today must call several times to get through the busy signals, interminable paging, and lost messages to the girl he wants. They might arrange a private line with prompt answering and faithfully recorded messages, with an unlisted number given only to busy male students with a promising future. They would even accept dates for the same night as the invitation, rather than, as at present, necessarily five to ten days in advance, for the only thing a first-year law student can schedule that far ahead nowadays is his studies. Emphasis on fraternity boys would have to go, for living in a fraternity and pursuing a promising (and therefore competitive) major field of study are rapidly becoming mutually exclusive. The big formal dances would go (the fraternity boys dislike them now); the football floats would go; the pushcart races would go. The girls would reach the hearts of their men not through helping them wash their sports cars but through typing their term papers.

But it is inconceivable that the proud traditions of the sororities that compose the National Panhellenic Council could ever be bent to fit the new design. Their structure is too fixed to fit the changing college and their function is rapidly being lost. The sorority cannot sustain itself on students alone. When parents learn that membership does not benefit their daughters, the sorority as we know it will pass into history.

Singles
in the
City
Joyce R. Starr
and Donald E. Carns

In increasing numbers the young college graduate has come to expect more from life than immediate security. For many, social and financial independence and career mobility have replaced early marriage as immediate postgraduation goals. Since the romantic image of the city as the place of flourishing ambitions has changed little during the past century, the urban setting has a magnetic pull on young people of all persuasions. Such has been the function of the city in a tradition which has held from Theodore Dreiser's nineteenth-century innocent *Sister Carrie* to the jaded twentieth-century heroine of *Darling*.

But never before has the city seemed so organized in its readiness to accommodate the young. Most cities appear to have an abundance of singles bars; some have co-ed singles apartment houses. Ads for singles weekends and excursions pad out the travel sections of big city newspapers. All this would seem to suggest an unprecedented institutionalization of this new life style in cities. But does it become a reality? Or is it just another media-created fantasy profitable only to those businessmen involved in its promotion? The question is significant in the same way any challenge to or test of a stereotype is socially meaningful, whether it relates to blacks, women, students, Communists or whomever. The question has further meaning since a large proportion of these elite middle-class singles are the product of our advanced educational system. The degree to which preurban socialization (in school, at home and so forth) prepared them for the realities of urban living—or conversely for its image—is crucial because it provides a partial test of the efficacy of these institutions, Are these people fulfilled, hopeful, nostalgic, sad, lonely or what?

Finally, since this population will in a few years help swell the familiar ranks of married, middle-class suburbanites, to what degree do men and women anticipate this probable future state? What are their attitudes toward marriage, monogamy, security, responsibility?

It is not possible in this brief article to address all these issues. Our discussion will focus on the three major (basic) tasks involved in successful urban adjustment: finding and maintaining a place to live; finding, keeping or changing jobs; and meeting friends, dates and potential mates (whether legal or consensual).

Our findings are based upon approximately 70 face-to-face interviews which are structured but essentially open-ended. Our subjects are never-married college graduates of both sexes who are in their early- to mid-twenties, who have not done graduate work and who have opted to come to or remain in Chicago to work. We conducted our interviews during 1970 and the first half of 1971 and are still interviewing. Ruling out the feasibility of a sampling method, we substituted a "snowball" technique (one contact leading to the next), attempting to include a variety of occupations, living arrangements, locations and other aspects of urban life style.

Chicago's Singles Community

Chicago's North Side singles community extends approximately eight miles north of the Loop, roughly two-and-one-half miles to the west and is bounded on the east by Lake Michigan. This general area encompasses four fairly distinct subareas, each of which is home to a wide range of life styles. The Near North, which lies closest to the Loop, is a city planner's horror—a patchwork of 20-story apartment buildings and renovated brownstones seeded with a number of stand-up style singles bars in the Rush Street area.

Moving farther north we find Chicago's Old Town, a subarea characterized by aging brownstones, occasional duplexes and a few high rises, whose alarmingly rapid encroachment on the scene is altering the fundamental character of the neighborhoods. Wells Street, one of the Old Town's major arteries, is a potpourri of fun houses, ice cream palaces, "head-shops" and strip joints to which tourists and teeny-boppers gravitate and which singles generally avoid.

Old Town merges into the Mid-North—a dense concentration of back-to-back high rises and four-plus-ones (cheaply built four-story apartment buildings—four stories plus a parking level—that took advantage of a loophole in Chicago's otherwise stringent building code and are now illegal).

The Mid-North has only a smattering of night spots and retail establishments. At the loosely defined boundaries of the Mid-North, New Town begins. This subarea managed without a specific name until the advent of the commercial boom that began to move north along Broadway and Clark streets. In its wake it spawned a profusion of easy-entry stores and boutiques purveying antiques, waterbeds and ethnic cuisine. There are also a number of sit-down bars ("that give you a chance to talk") and a small sprinkling of Chicago's own "off-Broadway" and out-of-the-Loop playhouses. An area of mixed housing types—four-plus-ones, brownstones and occasional high rises in the vicinity of Lake Michigan—New Town also contains Homo-Heights, which is exactly what the name implies.

The proportion of young college graduates is by no means equally distributed among these areas but it tends to increase as one moves northward to the lower rental sections of the Mid-North and New Town. The young, unattached graduates, contrary to the mass media's image of the "singles scene," are clearly outnumbered by other kinds of people living in the area. Older persons, particularly widows, comprise a significant proportion of this less newsworthy population. There are also a number of married couples (with or without children), who have either returned to the city after an unsuccessful brush with the suburbs or who are unwilling to leave it. Other residents include divorcées, bachelors over 30 and students. The bond among these disparate groups is neither age nor life style but expedience—the desire to live close to the city's central business district.

The typical graduate arriving in Chicago has little or no awareness of Chicago's singles scene. The decision to move to Chicago after finishing college, then, is rarely a function of informed expectations concerning social life in the city. For the majority of those who were raised in Chicago or its environs, their return is usually based on no more substantial criteria than "it seemed like the natural thing to do." The decision of other graduates appears even more haphazard. "I wanted to get away from home and Chicago is the nearest big city." "A few of my close friends from college were coming here, and I had no place else to go, so . . ." "My boy (or girl) friend had decided to move here." "I figured the job market would be better here than New York or San Francisco." "The job I was offered just happened to be based in this city." Women typically offer one of the first three responses while men are more likely to respond with one of the last two.

Governed by such social motives, a woman moves only to that city where friends and/or family may serve her needs. Because the man's decision is more often work related, he will frequently move to a city where he has neither family nor friends. He therefore is more likely to find an apartment by himself, to live alone when he first comes into the city. Also contributing to this pattern, of course, is the fact that male graduates, earning higher salaries, can better afford to live alone.

The out-of-town female, on the other hand, tends to establish living arrangements with one or two college friends. Having no car at her disposal, the typical woman is primarily concerned that her new living quarters be close to transportation and involve a reasonably short commute to her place of work. Her second concern is for safety, both in terms of the building itself and the surrounding area. Many women consequently restrict their apartment hunt to buildings equipped with doormen or buzzer systems; they are more likely than men to move initially into a high rise or four-plus-one.

By contrast, the typical male graduate moving to Chicago usually has access to a car and is largely unconcerned with safety. Faced with high expenses and automobile payments (not to mention astronomical urban insurance costs), he generally chooses to economize on rent and therefore tends to seek an older building. Moreover, because of these different considerations, men frequently seek apartments in blue-collar and migrant neighborhoods along the western border of Chicago's singles community.

Both men and women soon learn that desirable apartments are at a premium. With their search usually limited to the span of one weekend, most out-of-town graduates settle on a building (and consequently on a neighborhood) merely because "the apartment was available." Chicago's tradition of May-to-October leasing periods exacerbates the shortage by making relatively fewer apartments available at other times of the year. Furthermore, many graduates never suffer the rigors of apartment hunting; they either move in with a friend (or a friend of a friend) who already has an apartment or they let their roommate(s)-to-be do the hunting and deciding.

Neighbors Avoided

Unlike cities in California and some other states, Chicago has few, if any, "singles only" buildings or complexes; there are none in the North Side (this area does contain one megacomplex which rose from the rubble of urban blight under the rubric and financing of "middle-income housing," but which has actually done little to serve that population. Housing about six thousand people, it bears a reputation as a miniature "swingle's city"—an undeserved reputation in that the majority of its residents are not under 25 and single.)

Our data suggest that the majority of graduates, especially the men, prefer not to live in a building that fabricates and formalizes the meeting and dating process. To be sure,

many have fond recollections of the communal type of living arrangements of their college years. "I knew 90 percent of the people living in my building; here I don't even know my next-door neighbor." But the kind of living situations they seek is exemplified by such key terms as spontaneous, casual and not forced. The majority of those interviewed were uncomfortable or openly disdainful about living arrangements that focus on or exploit their single status. However, given a climate that permits year-round outdoor facilities (such as swimming pools and tennis courts) this population would probably find such arrangements more acceptable in natural settings, such as California. (The party rooms and mixing lounges that abound in cold-climate buildings bent on attracting single populations are anathema to them. Clearly this climate variable merits future research.)

It should be kept in mind that the college student spends the bulk of his day alone whether in classes or studying. In classrooms even when surrounded by peers, the student is not actually interacting with anyone in an active and meaningful way; nor is college performance dependent upon such interactions. Although unlikely, it is quite possible to complete four years of college successfully and earn a bachelor's degree without ever having spoken to a fellow student or, sad to say, to a professor.

The world of work, on the other hand, places a high premium on interpersonal skills—a fact that graduates soon discover. (Ironically, when asked how, if at all, college prepared them for the experience of working, the typical response is "it taught me how to get along with people.") Because the average working graduate in this sample finds himself (or herself) interacting with people eight or more hours per day, frequently in pressure situations which could hardly be characterized as purely social, his need for privacy and solitude is a real one. While the modal graduate laments the city's coldness and unfriendliness, nostalgically recalling his school days, the majority sheepishly admit that they have in fact expended little effort to alter the situation; few have ever overtly initiated a friendship and most have not followed through on overtures made by others. Clearly, they cherish their house as a haven of privacy in an environment of functional and personal interaction.

Averted Eyes

The home-as-haven concept persists in the face of neighborhoods with strong concentrations of people with similar ages and educational backgrounds. We must seriously question whether such homogeneity is a sufficient condition for meaningful social interaction. Our data suggest that neighborhood- and housing-based interactions

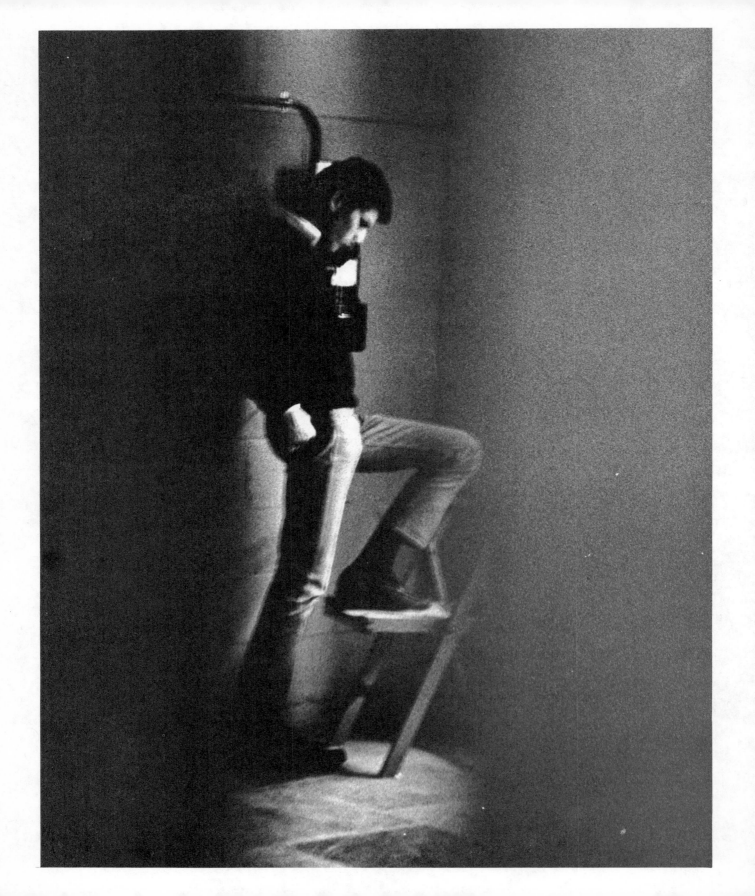

do not significantly contribute to the formation of friendships and dating relationships.

Several reasons are offered for this lack of neighborhood-based interaction. Some blame themselves, but with little remorse: "I just never think about it" or "I know enough people." Others cite lack of time rather than a lack of interest. But the majority attribute it to the hostile, impersonal and secondary nature of the big city milieu where "everyone is in a hurry," or is "concerned with making it" and is "so self-centered." Chicago's long dreary winters are blamed for creating their own unfriendliness as well as the standoffishness of others.

The warm weather of spring and summer seems to usher in a moratorium on distrust and aloofness (and, ironically, a simultaneous increase in forcible rapes, burglaries and other criminal acts). People emerge from indoors to bicycle through Chicago's extensive lake front parks, meander through shops, sunbathe at the beach and attend outdoor concerts. Not only do the seasons have a bearing on actual behavior, they are very much a part of the consciousness of these graduates. (Warm weather will be a time "when I'll find out who my neighbors are.")

Our data indicate, however, that despite this dramatic seasonal shift in casual street behavior—from stares and averted eyes to smiles—only rare encounters develop beyond a quick "hi." Only one male respondent followed up a street meeting by asking the girl out, and in this instance both persons recognized each other as tenants of the same building. The few relationships that had evolved from casual neighborhood meetings—in shops or laundromats or through a street encounter—were viewed as eventful because they were so atypical. Unlike the college community where it is tacitly assumed that socioeconomic background and social motives converge, in the city one has only the appearance of youth as a common bond, and even that may be highly suspect.

Making a Living

For the most part males appear to have a solid cultural understanding and acceptance of work, the preparation necessary for a lifetime work role and the behavior essential for successful on-the-job performance. Some educated women share this orientation, but many do not. Based on our data, females may be placed in three categories (with some overlap): 1) the career girl, that is, one who aspires to developing her work role into a career; 2) the female who views working as an "experience," who wants to gain satisfaction from her work and feel responsible, but who does not regard this role as an end in itself, that is, as a lifetime career. She is likely to consider it as either temporary (until she marries) or as a secondary commitment to her primary future role as wife and mother. The career-committed girl, on the other hand, tends to view the two roles as either comparable or complementary; 3) the girl who begrudges her work role. She would prefer not to have to work either because she envisions herself as a wife/mother and not a worker or simply because at present (and possibly for the rest of her life) she is not ready to settle down to the responsibility of a job. This category includes girls who have not yet decided what they want to do with their lives. They may seek jobs that prolong the freedom from decision-making which characterized their college years; they may, for example, work as waitresses or receptionists, earning enough to keep the body together.

The males in our sample also fall into three categories with regard to their work orientation: 1) the conventional career-oriented male who strives for success within the corporate world or who at least subscribes to the traditional definition of success as prestige and financial gain; 2) the man who consciously rejects traditional work options and values. Working at temporary jobs (cab driver, construction worker) that provide for minimal necessities, he most closely resembles the third female above. Also in this category are those young men who seek satisfaction in non-middle-class work situations, especially those involving craftsmanship—carpentry, mechanics, leatherwork and the like; 3) the male who straddles both worlds but belongs to neither. Typically craving material success, he lacks either talent, skill or motivation. This young graduate is most likely to be frustrated because the type of job he lands or can qualify for cannot begin to satisfy his material cravings.

The straddler's plight is shared, although to a lesser degree, by all of our young newcomers to the city, whether male or female. Some may be more, others less, concerned with "the freedom only money can buy," but quite soon after graduation, the majority confront the hard economic fact that a bachelor's degree is at best an admission card to, not a guarantee of, the fruits of upward mobility.

According to Ivar Berg's research reported in *The Great Training Robbery*, the typical college graduate is awakening to the fact that a great disparity exists between the number of educated persons in the United States and the number of jobs that make full use of their background. He discovers that although his undergraduate degree is not without value, his college experience with its relatively free and unstructured environment and its emphasis on creativity and responsibility did little to prepare him for a work world in which creative and responsible positions are the exception rather than the rule. This realization both challenges and threatens the ego of the more highly motivated graduates; it reveals above all the mediocrity of the rest. Attending college had been adequate testimony of personal worth; but simply going to work, on the contrary, often provides evidence of abject failure.

Finding far less satisfaction and/or challenge than he had hoped for and even expected, the young urban graduate (like his counterpart in blue-collar work) reports personal associations as the major source of job satisfaction. Involvement in the meeting-mating process, then, becomes an important compensating factor, both for ego gratification and as a diversion from workaday routine.

Friends and Dates

Based on the inordinate amount of attention devoted by the media to singles bars, one mistakenly assumes that the bar scene is the exclusive social setting for the casual relationships established by young unmarried graduates; here, we have been led to believe, lie the underpinnings of the "sexual revolution:" one-night stands in which liberated females display the same sexuality as males.

Our data indicate that the typical graduate frequents singles bars only one or two nights a week, if that often. These bars are usually noisy; sitting is actively discouraged by an arrangement of narrow counters and a dearth of seats; interaction especially during initial contact tends to be nonverbal. Attendance at such places appears to vary inversely with the amount of time one has lived in the city. One female commented, "I made the Rush Street scene at first, but it seemed so desperate;" another, "You head there in the beginning. What else is there to do?" It is a rare woman who, after six months in Chicago, continues to seek social contacts at singles bars. Certainly by the time she is approaching 25—the upper age point in this sample—the typical female has little use for this scene.

Males may continue to frequent swinging singles bars for a longer period of time. The rhetoric of the sexual revolution notwithstanding, it is the male who seeks sex or at least an environment which feeds his psychosexual fantasies. Although tending to marry at or above their social level, men are willing to have sex with females who are their social inferiors, for example, with the many high-school-educated habitués of swingers bars. In a complementary fashion such females appear to use the bar scene for husband-hunting probably with a very low chance of success. Swinging bars serve their purpose in the long run only if everyone is committed to swinging or—in the case of marriage-minded women—they aspire to a payoff from casual sex in the form of a more permanent relationship.

Sit-down style bars, which abound in the more northerly parts of Chicago's North Side singles area, draw more steady customers but receive less play in the media because the setting is not frankly sexual. Most of the women in our sample who reported frequenting one or more of these bars tended to define the crowd in terms of friends rather than potential dates. A place to talk is the main attraction for the many young graduates in groups, with a date or with a person of the same sex.

One could argue that both styles of bars offer a nostalgic re-creation of the college years in a peer-concentrated setting but unlike the undergraduate scene, the personal return is more in terms of a feeling of security rather than actual dating relationships. Such a feeling, however, is apt to elude those who visit the Rush Street bars where the ambience is one of contrived artificiality—interaction is forced and conviviality strained. "You watch people . . . they don't talk. Hell, they can't! The noise in the place is fantastic."

Each bar has its following and thus its in-group which is a kind of heterosexual fraternity. Among the regulars are persons with odd working hours—stewardesses and bartenders/waiters who maintain the fellowship of their clique in other settings, as for example, sunbathing during the week in "their" section of Lake Michigan's Oak Street beach. However, the nighttime regulars generally do not see each other socially outside of the bar setting. Describing this scene as a "meat market" and the bar clientele as "plastic," most graduates (accustomed to the informality of the college atmosphere where "making it" just happened or involved only minimal effort) find its requirements for survival and success totally repugnant.

If young urban graduates cannot establish dating relationships in the bars to any significant degree, where do they go? We have already discounted housing as a primary meeting-dating nexus. For a working person who spends his or her day at the office, interaction at home is likely to be restricted to the elevator or laundry room, the latter being the only facility in many buildings which could lend itself to this activity. But as one female graduate put it, "I could go down there with all the beautiful people, but I like to get my laundry done in a hurry; I want to get it over with." Furthermore, because singles are a transient population their chances for establishing lasting relationships in a building are reduced. But most significantly the majority of graduates consider home as a private and inviolate place; they do not welcome intrusions and they avoid making their apartments overly accessible. Many respondents reported that intrabuilding dating was "too close to home," that discontinued relationships could be awkward. More often they reported finding friends rather than dates at or near their home bases.

Similarly, organizations do not appear to be significant sources of dating relationships. Persons in this age group are not volunteers to any great degree; even those who were active in college find themselves unmotivated when it comes to seeking out organizations in the city. Comments such as "never get around to it" and "always seem to be busy" are common. Many perceive no great personal reward from such associations, especially when compared to the satisfactions gained in college from fraternities, student government and the like.

A kind of powerless alienation is frequently evident; many feel that organizational activity cannot duplicate the standing and involvement they enjoyed as members of the college community. More importantly, whereas participation in college activities brought instant peer recognition, no such immediate approval exists in the city where friends have scattered interests. Finally, formal voluntary organizations in a city like Chicago—be they political, cultural or environmental—tend to have a mixed membership including large numbers of married people; in short, they are not ideal ways to make dates and meet prospective mates.

Organizations—like apartment buildings and singles bars—do not provide the spontaneity that most young people require of a setting for meeting dates. The excitement which accompanies the American meeting-dating encounter seems centered on its accidental character. For the first 21 years of their lives these graduates have been surrounded by their age peers and have rarely been forced to seek companionship. To do so now would involve violating these values—a step that many are simply unprepared to take.

To illustrate, one male graduate commented on his recent visit to a "singles only" dance, the advertisement for which promised "over 300 young, single Chicagoans." "I tell you—there were greasers and very straight types, varnished hairdos, 45-year-old divorcées. Dance steps were five years out of date. I split after 15 minutes. It embarrassed me." Clearly such self-conscious seekings of companionship would force the graduate back into a junior high-school world of after-the-game dances and acute awkwardness.

In passing, we should mention that parties are seldom cited as a setting for meeting dates, partly because it takes time to establish enough contacts to guarantee invitations. But more important, the majority of the graduates, including those who have lived in the city for a period of time, either do not go to parties or find that they already know most of the people attending them. (The number of comments about Chicago's cliquishness simply underscores the patterned nature of urban social interaction.)

Having eliminated most of the possible ways to meet dates, we are left with only one major alternative—the work situation. Work was the most frequently cited institutional setting for making friends and (indirectly) meeting persons of the opposite sex. This should not be surprising since the average person spends most of his waking day at work, and it is also the setting most likely to facilitate familiarity and emotional intimacy. By no means, however, does work guarantee that the graduate will meet people; the work situation must be such that the graduate makes contact with persons who are not only close to his age but also single. Where the modal graduate finds himself in the exclusive company of coworkers who are older and/or married, he seldom is able to develop close friendships. Such is the predicament of stewardesses and along with their odd working hours, it may account for their patronage of singles bars.

The relationship between work and dating is frequently a two-stage process. Most graduates form friendships on the job (a pattern conforming to the view of the city as constellations of functionally rather than spatially interrelated people); generally, they do not date persons from the office because eligibles are in short supply and because they tend to avoid intimacy with people whom they must face every day whether the relationship succeeds or fails. The typical graduate, however, has dates arranged through office friends in a "friend-of-a-friend" pattern.

Two predominant themes emerge from our discussion of young single college graduates in the city. First, the popular image of the "swinging singles" spawned and nurtured by the media is clearly false. There is little in the bars to attract these people, especially the women. Most of them do not lead lives of wild sensual abandon. Their apartment buildings are not re-creations of coeducational dormitories without housemothers. They are people coping with the same problems we all face: finding a place to live, searching for satisfaction from their jobs and seeking friends, dates and ultimately mates in an environment for which they have been ill-prepared and which does not easily lend itself to the formation of stable human relationships. That they are coping at all is significant; that they are doing it as well as they are is a testimony to their resiliency in the face of considerable odds. These people are among those on the front line of urban existence, aspiring to the goals of middle-class America—financial security, mating and the like—but lacking many of the usual institutional supports for their activities.

Second, we must reorient our thinking about the city away from the housing environment and the neighborhood (the classic focus of many urban studies) and toward the world of work. It is the adjustment these graduates make to the world of work and their patterns of forming and dissolving friendships outside of work that provide their significant connections and sense of self in the urban milieu.

How
and
Why
America's
Sex Standards
are Changing

Ira L. Reiss

The popular notion that America is undergoing a sexual "revolution" is a myth. The belief that our more permissive sexual code is a sign of a general breakdown of morality is also a myth. These two myths have arisen in part because we have so little reliable information about American sexual behavior. The enormous public interest in sex seems to have been matched by moralizing and reticence in scholarly research—a situation that has only recently begun to be corrected.

What *has* been happening recently is that our young people have been assuming more responsibility for their own sexual standards and behavior. The influence of their parents has been progressively declining. The greater independence given to the young has long been evident in other fields—employment, spending, and prestige, to name three. The parallel change in sexual-behavior patterns would have been evident if similar research had been made in this area. One also could have foreseen that those groups least subject to the demands of old orthodoxies, like religion, would emerge as the most sexually permissive of all—men in general, liberals, non-churchgoers, Negroes, the highly educated.

In short, today's more permissive sexual standards represent not revolution but evolution, not anomie but normality.

My own research into current sexual behavior was directed primarily to the question, Why are some groups of people more sexually permissive than other groups? My study involved a representative sample of about 1500 people, 21 and older, from all over the country; and about 1200 high-school and college students, 16 to 22 years old, from three different states. On the pages that follow, I will first discuss some of the more important of my findings; then suggest seven general propositions that can be induced from these findings; and, finally, present a comprehensive theory about modern American sexual behavior.

Are Race Differences Rooted in Class?

A good many sociologists believe that most of the real differences between Negroes and whites are class differences—that if Negroes and whites from the same class were compared, any apparent differences would vanish. Thus, some critics of the Moynihan

Report accused Daniel P. Moynihan of ignoring how much lower-class whites may resemble lower-class Negroes.

But my findings show that there are large variations in the way whites and Negroes *of precisely the same class* view premarital sexual permissiveness. Among the poor, for instance, only 32 percent of white males approve of intercourse before marriage under some circumstances—compared with 70 percent of Negro males. The variation is even more dramatic among lower-class females: 5 percent of whites compared with 33 percent of Negroes. Generally, high-school and college students of all classes were found to be more permissive than those in the adult sample. But even among students there were variations associated with race. (See Table I.)

TABLE I—Percent Accepting Premarital Sex

	Lower-class adults*	Lower-class students**
White men	32% of 202	56% of 96
Negro men	70% of 49	86% of 88
White women	5% of 221	17% of 109
Negro women	33% of 63	42% of 90

* From National Adult Sample
** From Five-School Student Sample

The difference between Negro and white acceptance of premarital intercourse is not due to any racial superiority or inferiority. All that this finding suggests is that we should be much more subtle in studying Negro-white differences, and not assume that variations in education, income, or occupation are enough to account for all these differences. The history of slavery, the depressing effects of discrimination and low status—all indicate that the Negro's entire cultural base may be different from the white's.

Another response to this finding on sexual attitudes can, of course, be disbelief. Do people really tell the truth about their sex lives? National studies have revealed that they do—women will actually talk more freely about their sex lives than about their husbands' incomes. And various validity checks indicate that they did in this case.

But people are not always consistent: They may not practice what they preach. So I decided to compare people's sexual attitudes with their actual sexual behavior. Table II indicates the degree of correspondence between attitudes and behavior in a sample of 248 unmarried, white, junior and senior college-students.

TABLE II—Sexual Standards and Actual Behavior

Current Standard	Most Extreme Current Behavior			Number of Respondents
	Kissing	Petting	Coitus	
Kissing	64%	32%	4%	25
Petting	15%	78%	7%	139
Coitus	5%	31%	64%	84

Obviously, the students do not *always* act as they believe. But in the great majority of cases belief and action do coincide. For example, 64 percent of those who consider coitus acceptable are actually having coitus; only 7 percent of those who accept nothing beyond petting, and 4 percent of those who accept nothing beyond kissing, are having coitus. So it is fairly safe to conclude that, in this case, attitudes are good clues to behavior.

Guilt Is No Inhibitor

What about guilt feelings? Don't they block any transition toward more permissive sexual attitudes and behavior? Here the findings are quite unexpected. *Guilt feelings do not generally inhibit sexual behavior.* Eighty-seven percent of the women and 58 percent of the men said they had eventually come to accept sexual activities that had once made them feel guilty. (Some—largely males—had never felt guilty.) Seventy-eight percent had *never* desisted from any sexual activity that had made them feel guilty. Typically, a person will feel some guilt about his sexual behavior, but will continue his conduct until the guilt diminishes. **Then he will move on to more advanced behavior**— and new guilt feelings—until over that; and so on. People differed, mainly, in the sexual behavior they were willing to start, and in how quickly they moved on to more advanced forms.

The factor that most decisively motivated women to engage in coitus and to approve of coitus was the belief that they were in love. Of those who accepted coitus, 78 percent said they had been in love—compared with 60 percent of those who accepted only petting, and 40 percent of those who accepted only kissing. (Thus, parents who don't want their children to have sexual experiences but do want them to have "love" experiences are indirectly encouraging what they are trying to prevent.)

How do parents' beliefs influence their children's sexual attitudes and conduct?

Curiously enough, almost two-thirds of the students felt that their sexual standards were at least similar to those of their parents. This was as true for Negro males as for white females—although about 80 percent of the former accept premarital intercourse as against only about 20 percent of the latter. Perhaps these students are deluded, but perhaps they see through the "chastity" facade of their parents to the underlying similarities in attitude. It may be that the parents' views on independence, love, pleasure, responsibility, deferred gratification, conformity, and adventurousness are linked with the sexual attitudes of their children; that a similarity in these values implies a similarity in sexual beliefs. Probably these parental values, like religiousness, help determine which youngsters move quickly and with relatively little guilt through the various stages of sexual behavior. Religiousness, for the group of white students, is a particularly good index: Youngsters who rank high on church attendance rank low on premarital coitus, and are generally conservative.

Despite the fact that 63 to 68 percent of the students felt that their sexual standards were close to their parents' standards, a larger percentage felt that their standards were even closer to those of peers (77 percent) and to those of very close friends (89 percent). Thus, the conflict in views between peers and parents is not so sharp as might be expected. Then too, perhaps parents' values have a greater influence on their children's choice of friends than we usually acknowledge.

The Importance of Responsibility

This brings us to another key question. Are differences in sexual standards between parents and children due to changing cultural standards? Or are they due to their different roles in life—that is, to the difference between being young, and being parents responsible for the young? Were the parents of today that different when they courted?

My findings do show that older people tend to be less permissive about sex—but this difference is not very marked. What is significant is that childless couples—similar to couples with children of courtship age in every other respect, including age—are much more willing to accept premarital intercourse as standard (23 to 13 percent). Furthermore, parents tend to be *less* sexually permissive the *more* responsibility they have for young people. Now, if the primary cause of parent-child divergences in sexual standards is that cultural standards in general have been changing, then older people should, by and large, be strikingly more conservative about sex. They aren't. But since parents are more conservative about sex than nonparents of the same age, it would seem that the primary cause of parent-child divergences over sex is role and responsibility—the parents of today were *not* that different when courting.

Being responsible for others, incidentally, inhibits permissiveness even when the dependents are siblings. The first-born are far less likely to approve of premarital intercourse (39 percent) than are the youngest children (58 percent).

Another intriguing question is, How do parents feel about the sexual activities of their boy children—as opposed to their girl children? The answer depends upon the sex of the parent. The more daughters a white father has, the more strongly he feels about his standards—although his standards are no stricter than average. The more sons he has, the less strongly he feels about his beliefs. White mothers showed the reverse tendency, but much more weakly—the more sons, the stronger the mothers' insistance upon whatever standards they believed in. Perhaps white parents feel this way because of their unfamiliarity with the special sexual problems of a child of the opposite sex—combined with an increasing awareness of these problems.

What explains these differences in attitude between groups—differences between men and women as well as between Negroes and whites? Women are more committed to marriage than men, so girls become more committed to marriage too, and to low-permissive parental values. The economic pressures on Negroes work to break up their families, and weaken commitment to marital values, so Negroes tend to be more permissive. Then too, whites have a greater stake in the orthodox institution of marriage: More white married people than unmarried people reported that they were happy. Among Negroes, the pattern was reversed. But in discussing weak commitments to marriage we are dealing with one of the "older" sources of sexual permissiveness.

The sources of the new American permissiveness are somewhat different. They include access to contraception; ways to combat venereal infection; and—quite as important—an intellectualized philosophy about the desirability of sex accompanying affection. "Respectable," college-educated people have integrated this new philosophy with their generally liberal attitudes about the family, politics, and religion. And this represents a new and more lasting support for sexual permissiveness, since it is based on a positive philosophy rather than hedonism, despair, or desperation.

In my own study, I found that among the more permissive groups were those in which the fathers were professional men. This finding is important: It shows that the upper segments of our society, like the lower, have a highly permissive group in their midst—despite the neat picture described by some people of permissiveness steadily declining as one raises one's gaze toward the upper classes.

Patterns of Permissiveness

All these findings, though seemingly diverse, actually fall into definite patterns, or clusters of relationships. These patterns can be expressed in seven basic propositions:

■ The *less* sexually permissive a group is, traditionally, the *greater* the likelihood that new social forces will cause its members to become more permissive.

Traditionally high-permissive groups, such as Negro men, were the least likely to have their sexual standards changed by social forces like church-attendance, love affairs, and romantic love. Traditionally low-permissive groups, such as white females, showed the greatest sensitivity to these social forces. In addition, the lower social classes are reported to have a tradition of greater sexual permissiveness, so the finding that their permissiveness is less sensitive to certain social forces also fits this proposition.

■ The more liberal the group, the more likely that social forces will help maintain high sexual permissiveness.

There was diverse support for this proposition. Students, upper-class females in liberal settings, and urban dwellers have by and large accepted more permissiveness than those in more conservative settings.

Indeed, liberalism in general seems to be yet another cause of the new permissiveness in America. Thus, a group that was traditionally low-permissive regarding sex (the upper class), but that is liberal in such fields as religion and politics, would be very likely to shift toward greater premarital permissiveness.

■ According to their ties to marital and family institutions, people will differ in their sensitivity to social forces that affect permissiveness.

This proposition emphasizes, mainly, male-female differences in courting. Women have a stronger attachment to and investment in marriage, childbearing, and family ties. This affects their courtship roles. There are fundamental male-female differences in acceptance of permissiveness, therefore, in line with differences in courtship role.

Romantic love led more women than men to become permissive (this finding was particularly true if the woman was a faithful churchgoer). Having a steady date affected women predominantly, and exclusiveness was linked with permissiveness. Early dating, and its link with permissiveness, varied by race, but was far more commonly linked with permissiveness in men than in women. The number of steadies, and the number of times in love, was associated with permissiveness for females, but was curvilinear for males— that is, a man with no steadies, or a number of steadies, tended to be more permissive than a man who had gone steady only once.

Such male-female differences, however, are significant only for whites. Among Negroes, male-female patterns in these areas are quite similar.

■ The higher the overall level of permissiveness in a group, the greater the extent of equalitarianism within abstinence and double-standard subgroups.

Permissiveness is a measure not only of what a person will accept for himself and his own sex, but of what behavior he is willing to allow the opposite sex. Permissiveness, I found, tends to be associated with sexual equalitarianism in one particular fashion: I found, strangely enough, that a good way to measure the *general* permissiveness of a group is to measure the equalitarianism of two subgroups—the abstinent, and believers in the double-standard. (Nonequalitarianism in abstinence means, usually, petting is acceptable for men, but only kissing for women. Equalitarianism within the double-standard means that intercourse is acceptable for women when in love, for men anytime. The nonequalitarian double-standard considers all unmarried women's coitus wrong.) In a generally high-permissive group (such as men), those adherents who do accept abstinence or the double-standard will be more equalitarian than will their counterparts in low-permissive groups (such as women). The implication is that the ethos of a high-permissive group encourages female sexuality and thereby also encourages equalitarianism throughout the group.

■ The potential for permissiveness derived from parents' values is a key determinant as to how rapidly, how much, and in what direction a person's premarital sexual standards and behavior change.

What distinguishes an individual's sexual behavior is not its starting point—white college-educated females, for instance, almost always start only with kissing—but how far, how fast, and in what direction the individual is willing to go. The fact is that almost all sexual behavior is eventually repeated, and comes to be accepted. And a person's basic values encourage or discourage his willingness to try something new and possibly guilt-producing. Therefore, these basic values—derived, in large part, from parental teaching, direct or implicit—are keys to permissiveness.

Since the young often feel that their sex standards are similar to their parents', we can conclude that, consciously or not, high-permissive parents intellectually and emotionally breed high-permissive children.

■ A youth tends to see permissiveness as a continuous scale with his parents' standards at the low point, his peers' at the high point, and himself between but closer to his peers—and closest to those he considers his most intimate friends.

The findings indicate that those who consider their standards closer to parents' than to peers' are less permissive than the others. The most permissive within one group generally reported the greatest distance from parents, and greatest similarity to peers and friends. This does not contradict the previous proposition, since parents are on the continuum and exert enough influence so that their children don't go all the way to the opposite end. But it does indicate, and the data bear out, that parents are associated with relatively low permissiveness; that the courtship group is associated with relatively high permissiveness; and that the respondents felt closer to the latter. Older, more permissive students were less likely to give "parental guidance" as a reason for their standards.

■ Greater responsibility for other members of the family, and lesser participation in courtship, are both associated with low-permissiveness.

The only child, it was found, had the most permissive attitudes. Older children, generally, were less permissive than their younger brothers and sisters. The older children usually have greater responsibility for the young siblings; children without siblings have no such responsibilities at all.

The findings also showed that as the number of children, and their ages, increased, the parents' permissiveness decreased. Here again, apparently, parental responsibility grew, and the decline in permissiveness supports the proposition above.

On the other hand, as a young person gets more and more caught up in courtship, he is progressively freed from parental domination. He has less responsibility for others, and he becomes more permissive. The fact that students are more sexually liberal than many other groups must be due partly to their involvement in courtship, and to their distance from the family.

Thus a generational clash of some sort is almost inevitable. When children reach their late teens or early 20s, they also reach the peak of their permissiveness; their parents, at the same time, reach the nadir of theirs.

These findings show that both the family and courtship institutions are key determinants of whether a person accepts or rejects premarital sexuality. Even when young people have almost full independence in courtship, as they do in our system, they do not copulate at random. They display parental and family values by the association of sex with affection, by choice of partners, by equalitarianism, and so on.

However, parental influence must inevitably, to some extent, conflict with the pressures of courting, and the standards of the courting group. Young people are tempted by close association with attractive members of the opposite sex, usually without having any regular heterosexual outlet. Also, youth is a time for taking risks and having adventures. Therefore, the greater the freedom to react autonomously within the courtship group, the greater the tendency toward liberalized sexual behavior.

Now, families are oriented toward the bearing and rearing of children—and for this, premarital sex is largely irrelevant. It becomes relevant only if it encourages marriages the parents want—but relevant negatively if it encourages births out of wedlock, or the "wrong," or no, marriages. Most societies tolerate intercourse between an engaged couple, for this doesn't seriously threaten the marital institution; and even prostitution gains some acceptance because it does not promote unacceptable marital unions. The conflict between the family and courtship systems depends on the extent to which each perceives the other as threatening its interests. My own findings indicate that this conflict is present, but not always as sharply as the popular press would have us believe.

Courtship pressures tend toward high-permissiveness; family pressures toward low-permissiveness. It follows that whatever promotes the child's independence from the family promotes high-permissiveness. For example, independence is an important element in the liberal position; a liberal setting, therefore, generally encourages sexual as well as other independence.

A Comprehensive Theory

To summarize all these findings into one comprehensive theory runs the risk of oversimplifying—if the findings and thought that went into the theory are not kept clearly in mind. With this *caveat,* I think a fair theoretical summary of the meaning of the foregoing material would be: How much premarital sexual permissiveness is considered acceptable in a courtship group varies directly with the independence of that group, and with the general permissiveness in the adult cultural environment.

In other words, when the social and cultural forces working on two groups are approximately the same, the differences in permissiveness are caused by differences in independence. But when independence is equal, differences come from differences in the socio-cultural setting.

There is, therefore, to repeat, no sexual revolution today. Increased premarital sexuality is not usually a result of breakdown of standards, but a particular, and different, type of organized system. To parents, more firmly identified with tradition—that is, with older systems—and with greater responsibilities toward the young, toward the family, and toward marriage, greater premarital sexuality seems deviant. But it is, nevertheless, an integral part of society—their society.

In short, there has been a gradually increasing acceptance of and overtness about sexuality. The basic change is toward greater equalitarianism, greater female acceptance of permissiveness, and more open discussion. In the next decade, we can expect a step-up in the pace of this change.

The greater change, actually, is in sexual attitude, rather than in behavior. If behavior has not altered in the last century as much as we might think, attitudes *have*—and attitudes and behavior seem closer today than for many generations. Judging by my findings, and the statements of my respondents, we can expect them to become closer still, and to proceed in tandem into a period of greater permissiveness, and even greater frankness. I do not, however, foresee extreme change in the years to come—such as full male-female equality. This is not possible unless male and female roles in the family are also equal, and men and women share equal responsibility for child-rearing and family support.

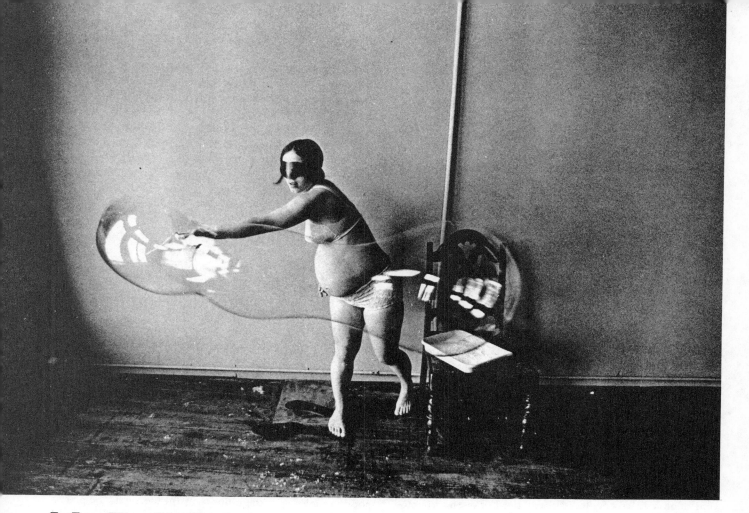

Hallelujah
the Pill?
Ruth B. Dixon

What do women want? Freud's famous question, for which he confessed he had no answer, is scarcely a mystery for many women today in the liberation movement. What women want, they say, is at the very least complete control over their own bodies, that is, their own reproductive behavior, thus ending involuntary pregnancy and compulsory motherhood. The second thing they want is a full range of choice among alternative life styles—career and home-making, bricklaying and engineering, marriage and mother-hood and so on into various permutations and combinations, all realized through a variety of true options, the

choice among them to be relatively free of pressure and coercion.

There is little doubt that in this country we are moving rapidly toward the ideal of "body control," toward the separation of sexual expression from pregnancy and child-birth. Consider that early in the century couples were being advised in manuals like *The Science of Eugenics and Sex Life* (1914) that "women are affectionate, and when they nestle close to a man, they excite sexual desire on the part of the man. Married couples will do well to sleep in separate beds. By this means, intercourse occurs less often, and health is preserved; for *opportunity* is the cause of much useless and injurious intercourse." Abstinence was the preferred method for avoiding pregnancy and for improving genetic quality. "Unfortunately for the race," writes one medical expert, "irresponsible sexual intercourse is so largely the rule among the married, that unwelcome, sickly and viciously inclined children are thrust into the world with no chance to make their own lives such as will be worth living."

But this is 1970. Gone are the days when women lived in terror of the sexual embrace because it meant still another pregnancy, still another year of sickness, still another child to care for. Gone are the days when separate bedrooms and locked doors were offered as solutions for the desperate. Technology has progressed, and with great rumblings the Mountain has given birth to—the Pill!

The Contracepting Society

Has the pill brought with it the emancipation of women, as so many have claimed? What *are* women doing with this revolutionary knowledge? Are they enjoying sex but declining marriage? Are they marrying their lovers but deciding against a future as merely wife and mother? Are they reluctant to bear children after one or two? Just what effect has the pill had on the timing and the number of marriages and births in recent years?

Recent national surveys indicate that the United States has indeed become a contracepting society. At least 90 percent of all married couples have practiced or intend to practice contraception at some point in their married lives, and when this figure is added to the 5 percent or so who know themselves to be sterile, there are very few who are willing simply to let the babies come willy-nilly. Contrasted with patterns in many less-developed nations where perhaps only 5 to 10 percent ever intentionally practice any form of birth control, and where most women profess to know of no method of preventing pregnancy, the achievement is startling. Contraception in the United States is being adopted earlier in marriage, and class, racial and religious differences are diminishing. The largest gains in birth control practices in the last 15 years or so have occurred among previously reluctant or unknowledgeable women, most notably among Catholics (especially the better educated), among the less educated in general, among younger women and among nonwhites, especially in the South. With the closing of these gaps, contraception is becoming truly universal.

To speak of a contracepting society is one thing; to explore just who does the contracepting and how effectively

is another. Class biases in the availability of services—especially those due to physicians they see as aloof or money-hungry, and to the inability of lower-class women to pay for safe abortions (either legal or illegal)—are still strong. Middle- and upper-middle-class women definitely come out ahead in the degree to which they are able to plan their pregnancies. They are more likely to know about a number of different kinds of contraception, to approve of them, to have access to them, to have used them and to have used medically sound and highly effective female methods. In this sense such women are indeed "liberated."

Among the poor, knowledge of contraception—often more folklore than truth in the first place—is rarely integrated into actual practice in an effective way. The knowledge somehow remains "out there," something that other people might find helpful or have some luck with, but not themselves. "I've heard about lots of ways, but I don't know if they're any good," says one man about birth control. A woman who says she douches "sometimes" adds, "I didn't know nothing when I got married. I never talked to no one about it. . . . Now I've talked around a little bit and I learned about the douche and my husband used a rubber once." But the whole effort is seen too quickly as futile when casual and sporadic attempts at birth prevention meet with repeated failure. One estimate for the years 1960 to 1965 is that approximately 40 percent of the children born to poor and near-poor couples were unwanted by one or both parents, compared to 14 percent of births to "non-poor" couples. Yet these unsuccessful users must be placed among the "contraceptors" in our society, those who have practiced birth control at some time in the past or intend to do so in the future.

Keeping in mind that being a user means very different things in different contexts, we can see that trends in the last few decades are nevertheless encouraging. We have witnessed not only a remarkable increase in the use of contraception and in attitudes favorable to its use but an interesting change in the methods most frequently employed. In the 1930s the most popular techniques were withdrawal, the condom and the douche; in the mid-fifties, the condom, diaphragm and rhythm. Then came the pill. First licensed for prescription in June 1960, the pill in five years had become by all odds the favorite method of birth control in the United States. A national sample survey in 1965 indicated that a third of the married women had tried the pill, and for a fourth it was the method they had used most recently (including one-fifth for Catholic wives). The old reliables—the condom, rhythm and especially the diaphragm—had dropped heavily out of favor. The intrauterine device (IUD), available generally only since 1964, is steadily growing in favor.

The implications of changing styles of contraception are important: there has been a definite transition from less effective methods and from those used by the male to highly effective female methods and, in the case of the pill and the IUD, to methods that the woman may use unbeknownst to her partner and without disturbing the spontaneity of the sexual act. This development is crucial. It means that women are for the first time truly able to control their own bodies in a *private* way, whether their mates agree or not.

This brings us to a moral dilemma that we might refer to as another dimension of Kate Millett's "sexual politics": should it be the responsibility, privilege or right of the woman to be in sole charge of marital fertility? Is it fair to leave her with the trump card? After all, not only is she then in a position deliberately to refuse her husband a child without his knowing (since the pill and IUD are invisible to him), she is also in a position to produce a child that he may not want and to blame the event on "contraceptive failure." Obviously neither outcome is desirable. But the husband on his part can do the same, although not so inconspicuously. A lower-class woman with five children who had wanted only two, when asked what method of contraception she was now using, complained, "That's the trouble, we don't use anything. I think my husband is going to put on a rubber and he don't half the time. . . . He is the one that is careless and goes in for too much fooling around. He doesn't have all the work and trouble!" In a secure relationship this dimension of sex normally remains latent or unconscious; the husband and wife mutually agree on what one or the other should do. But in a relationship tinged with resentment or mistrust, the political dimension becomes manifest. In this type of situation it would seem all the more important for a woman to be in charge of reproduction, since the consequences of conception will be primarily hers to bear. "He doesn't take care of the kids; *I* have to all the time," sighs one woman.

It is interesting that mutual agreement tends to be related to class. The lower in the social scale one goes, the more likely it is that couples find their sex life with each other unsatisfying and experience some conflict over the responsibilities of contraception. Too, lower-class wives are more likely than middle-class wives to want *fewer* children than their husbands: one-quarter of nonwhite women reported such a discrepancy of views in 1960. For these women, acquiring the means to resist their husband's empire-building impulses is crucial.

Now that women in every social group are increasingly taking the responsibility of birth control onto themselves and are acquiring knowledge of and access to methods they can use privately, the relevant question to ask is this: Just how emancipated are American women in their new role as charge d'affaires of their own reproduction?

The Pill is Not Enough

The answer is obvious: even though women are increasingly practicing efficient contraception, they are not even beginning to free themselves from their family-centered identities. Male-expressed fear that women on the pill would toss away their traditional wife-mother obligations have so far proved groundless. That this is so is apparent in three simple facts: American women still marry earlier on the average than in any other industrialized country, and almost all marry eventually; average family size is still higher than in most Western countries, with fewer women remaining childless or settling for only one child; and American women want for themselves, and consider ideal, higher numbers of children than in practically any other industrialized country. We are still a highly familistic society. The never-married woman and the childless wife are deviant.

Let us begin with marriage. It is true that marriage rates have fallen off slightly in recent years and that the average age at first marriage for females has slowed its long decline and taken a small turn upward. Earlier in the century women were marrying on the average in their 21st or 22nd year. Just after the end of World War II their median age at first marriage was 20.5 years, dropping to 20.1 years in 1956 and rising again to 20.3 in 1960 and up to 20.8 in 1969. But the single most popular time for getting married is the legal minimum, 18, and over one-quarter of American females marry at this age. This puts American brides, at least on the basis of 1960 figures, a full year younger on the average than those in Canada, Australia and New Zealand and from one to five years younger even than those in a number of highly traditional societies—Taiwan, Thailand, Ceylon, Hong Kong and the Philippines, among others—and certainly younger than those in Japan.

Not only do American women marry earlier but more of them get married. In this respect they are far more marriage-minded than in former years, for only 5.0 percent of women aged 35 to 44 in 1969 had never married and an even lower proportion of women aged 30 to 34 in 1967. Thus the slight tendency to postpone marriage at the younger ages since 1960 has been counteracted by a greater tendency to marry in the middle or late twenties, with the result that marriage is becoming more universal, not less. Compare these figures to those in Western Europe and the other English-speaking nations where one usually finds about one-eighth of all women passing through their childbearing years without marrying, and up to one-fifth in some cases.

The greatest differentiating factor in the timing and quantity of marriage for women is education; race and religion by themselves make little difference. Women with more education marry later, and more remain unmarried throughout their childbearing years (about one-tenth of college girls and one-quarter of those with some graduate education). Whether they remain unmarried voluntarily, however, is a moot point. One study exploring romanticism as a motivation for marriage uncovered these startling figures when American female college students were asked in the early sixties the question "Ideally, if it were up to you, would you like to get married?" only 1.4 percent said no. Compare this to 12.5 percent of female university students among the Singapore Chinese who said no, 18.6 percent in Burma and 28.2 in India!

Women also feel less and less compelled to remain in unsatisfactory marriages (as do men), for divorce rates are continuing to climb. In 1962 the United States surpassed Egypt to win the honor of having the highest divorce rate of any country in the world for which reliable statistics are available, but a sudden liberalization of Russian divorce laws in 1966 has put the United States in second place since then, with Egypt and several Eastern European nations next in line. Nevertheless, the high divorce rate apparently does not reflect a growing disenchantment with marriage in this country, for rates of *remarriage* among the divorced are also on the increase. Instead of deciding that marriage is not the inevitable solution to our personal problems we are simply jumping in and out of marriages at a faster rate.

Putting One's Mind To It

Then come the babies. It is unfair to compare reproductive behavior now to that in the depression when family size was necessarily small and when one-fifth of the women who had ever been married passed through their reproductive years without bearing children at all and another fifth bore only one. But we can take the depression years as an example of what American couples can do about their fertility when they really put their minds to it, and in this case they managed to keep their completed family size down to 2.4 children on the average. All this before the pill. In 1969, by contrast, the average family size of ever-married

women in their early forties was 3.1 children, and even women in their early thirties had already produced an average of 2.9 babies each. Only among the younger cohorts in the last five years are there signs that the baby boom of the fifties and early sixties is finally easing slightly. Analysis of this decline at younger years has shown that it is *not* due to the pill per se but to a greater determination among young couples to use *some* form of effective contraception, whatever it may be. However the total *numbers* of babies born will of course leap upward as 20 million baby boom daughters themselves enter their reproductive years, as they are now beginning to do.

The downward trend in the crude birthrate from its postwar peak in 1957 is easy to misinterpret. A couple of years ago when the birthrate had dropped to its lowest point since the depression, newspapers were full of expert "analyses" of the alleged growing reluctance of the American woman to have children. Many saw the two-child family coming back as a popular ideal. But the decline of the crude birthrate, which refers to the number of births per year per thousand persons, is largely an artifact of changes in the age composition of the population in which women of childbearing years make up a smaller proportion of the total population, and of changes in the timing of births and marriages. The drop in the birthrate since 1957 does not necessarily mean that married couples are having fewer children or that they are beginning to desire smaller families. As we pointed out, women in their early thirties in 1969 had already borne 2.9 children on the average, compared to 2.6 for women the same age in 1960 and 2.2 in 1954. Women under 30 have been reproducing slower, but whether they will continue their reduced fertility at older ages or make up the lost births at a future time remains an open question.

Family Size Desires

The actual reproductive behavior of the American woman tells only part of the story; perhaps more important to her future emancipation is the evidence on her *desired* and *ideal* fertility. This is where her consistently family-centered orientation truly reveals itself.

The ideal family size of American couples has not changed radically in the last several decades. Gallup polls from 1936 to 1966 show a low of 2.7 in 1943 and a high of 3.6 in 1966 when couples were asked the rather vague question, "What do you think is the ideal number of children for the average American family?" But the most frequently mentioned ideal has progressed from two children in 1940 to three children in 1945 to four children in 1960 and 1965, with both small and large families becoming less popular. In a large 1965 national survey *90 percent* of married women mentioned from two to four children as the ideal family size, 75 percent saying three or four. The homogeneity of family size ideals is amazing.

Personal desires (people don't necessarily consider the general norm ideal for themselves) are slightly less homogeneous, but even here 80 percent of the women questioned wanted from two to four children for themselves, and 70 percent expected to have this many. Only 4 percent wanted either no children or just one. However, women expect on the average to have *fewer* children than they would really like to have, or than they consider ideal for the average American family. In other words, if conditions were better, women would be having even more babies. In 1960 a national sample of women considered 3.4 children ideal but at the time of the interview wanted 3.3 children for themselves (or 3.7 if their life "could be relived") and expected to have 3.1. In 1965 the comparative figures were 3.3, 3.3 and 3.2.

Although actual fertility is an inverse function of occupation, education and income, desired fertility is quite another matter. One study showed virtually no variation by husband's income with a mean desired family size centering on 3.3 children; others show much less of a variation in desired family size than in actual fertility. This means that actual fertility tends to be lower than desired fertility the higher one goes in the social scale; women with some college education desired 3.2 children in 1965 but expected to have 2.9. The reverse is the case among the poor. Nonwhite women who had less than a high school education wanted 3.5 children but expected 4.2.

Ideal, desired and expected family size are consistently higher for Catholic women than for non-Catholics, and it is the college-educated Catholic women who have the most "expansionist" desires of any group: 3.9 children in 1965 and 4.8 in 1960! Lowest fertility desires are found among college-educated black women who wanted 2.7 children in 1965.

Even women who work, who have worked for a number of years since their marriage and who work primarily because they enjoy it and not for financial reasons want on the average 3.0 children! They are just as fertility-minded as the next person, but their active participation in nonfamilial roles opens up options not available to other women, and their creativity apparently goes in several directions. Although these career women want on the average three children, they expect to have only two. Thus the stereotype that it is primarily unfeminine women who go into careers is obviously false; married women who are enthusiastic about working *do* have family interests and *do* want children, but they want other, often competing, things as well. Women in higher status occupations—the professions, managerial and advanced clerical work and crafts—are more likely to remain childless (about 20 percent do so) and to have smaller families when they become mothers than are women employed in sales, farm or service work (from 10 to 15 percent childless). Employed women are twice as likely to be childless as women not in the labor force. Among all occupational groups specified in the census it is the female social scientists who are the least fertile! In 1960 over one-third of ever-married white women aged 35 to 44 in this category were childless, and the whole group averaged only 1.35 children each.

There are two kinds of emancipation—or shall we say the lack of it—implicit in the figures we have been discussing. The first is the problem of excess fertility, of having more children than one wants to have either through ignorance about contraception or through its inefficient practice. This is an important factor in the high fertility of the poor. Although we have been talking of the fertility of the married, the problem also holds for the unmarried. Women can become emancipated only when the threat of unwanted pregnancy ending either in adoption or forced marriage or illegitimate motherhood is gone, and this is possible only when a young girl or woman does not have to depend on the casual interest of her partner for contraceptive care.

Yet there is another kind of emancipation—a kind that we apparently have not even begun to approach. This is the emancipation from family life, from the primary identity of a woman in her role as wife and mother. Childless marriages are such a statistical rarity that one must assume that *voluntary* childlessness is almost nil. The one-child family is fast disappearing. Practically every married woman now has at least two children, and although she compensates for her increasing propensity to have this many by stopping after three or four, she is establishing herself in the service of a family as firmly as she knows how. According to the information we have on her desires and ideals she would do so even more freely if it were not for certain constraints on her reproductive behavior, primarily the cost of educating her children. At the same time, even with the increase in contraceptive knowledge and practice among the young, illegitimacy is on the increase, and one can only assume that many of these pregnancies are wanted and intended. A recent report from the National Center for Health Statistics estimated that one-third of all firstborn children in the United States are premaritally conceived, although most of course are legitimized by a hasty marriage before they are born. If these births are involuntary, women are victimized by their lack of control over their own bodies. If they are voluntary, women are in many cases "victimized" by their desire to rush into marriage and childbearing in order to gain an identity for themselves, in order to be adults and participate in a narrowly defined adult world. The pressures in our society to marry and to have children are almost impossible to resist.

What the statistics show us and what common sense supports is that the pill, which we have used here as a symbol of what contraception can do, is nothing but an instrument of the will of the user. It doesn't act by itself to reduce the birthrate. It doesn't free women who have no real desire to be, in this sense, free. What it does is to permit them to have their children when they want them, to stop having them when they want to stop and to settle down in their three- or four-child households in the secure and happy knowledge that things worked out exactly as they had planned. The pill brings one form of emancipation, but it does not bring the other. And that is where the real work needs to be done.

The Case for Demographic Diversity

Trends in marriage and motherhood since the 1930s tell a story that is both hopeful and discouraging. The discouraging part is that women are marrying earlier and more are getting married than in any other Western industrialized nation or previously in this country. Too, marriages are taking place in a more concentrated span of years in the life of each cohort. Transformed into real-life experience, this means that when women reach the age of 19 or 20 they discover that their female friends all seem to be getting married at once, and, anxious to avoid being the odd-one-out in a rapidly dwindling minority, they latch onto the first reasonably acceptable partner in order to retreat into a safe, recognized slot in the community structure. The same thing is happening to motherhood. Along with the larger desired family size—four is now most popular—one finds a telescoping of desires into the two-to-four child range and a telescoping of the timing of childbearing. When marriage rates and family size desires are as high and as uniform as they are in the United States, can they reflect real freedom of choice? As it stands now, conformity to social norms encouraging and glorifying family life appears to be the order of the day.

Although conformity is a difficult phenomenon to measure, there is general agreement that it plays an important role in shaping decisions about whether to have children and about how many are appropriate. The widely accepted norm is that one should have as many children as one can afford—no more, no less. One study found that most wives wanted to have about the same number of children as they said they thought their married friends of the same age would have. Married couples who want no children are considered highly deviant. As one woman seeking treatment for sterility put it, "I openly say now that we want children because I can remember in the very beginning I used to act like it didn't matter and I remember overhearing one girl saying something about our not wanting any children and it hurt very much to think they thought we were just being real selfish and didn't want any family." Even those who want only one or two are considered selfish or else too poor to have more. Parents of many children are said to be loving, generous and prosperous. One should *want* many children, but one should not have more than are financially feasible.

There is an encouraging underside to the story of the last few decades that may provide some real hope for the future, however. First, the low marriage rates and small families of the depression years were more a function of hardship than of real desire. When times were better couples went back to fulfilling their "natural" inclinations to marry earlier and to have more babies. Our reproductive behavior is now less constrained by financial worries than it was, and the potential for fulfilling our individual wants is greater. There is after all, nothing admirable about a society with high proportions of single and childless married women when this condition arises solely from the fact that many want to marry and have children but few can afford to do so. The low birthrates of Eastern European countries may make it appear as though women are more emancipated from traditional roles than they are here, but closer inspection reveals that their reduced fertility is necessary because wives *must* work if they wish to live in reasonable comfort, and they simply cannot manage a household with more than one or two children.

Second, we may also find hope in the growing homogeneity of marital and fertility behavior and desires in the United States because it means that class, racial, religious and other group differences are breaking down and that marriage and motherhood are not the privileged prerogative or the unwished destiny of one group more than another.

We noted that desired family size varies little by social class although actual fertility varies inversely. As poor and less-educated women are increasingly able to bring their fertility in line with their desires, they come closer to the goal of achieving maximum control over their own bodies—a goal that upper-middle-class women have already achieved. Surely this is a good thing.

Now, having reached the point where marriage and motherhood are financially feasible for most groups, unlike the depression years, and having reached the point where women are almost universally able—if they wish—to decide on the timing and the number of their children for themselves, we are ready to move on to the next stage—a stage of demographic diversity of a new sort.

Obviously this new freedom cannot come without first providing women with alternative sources of financial support, recognition, companionship, security, sexual fulfillment and a sense of belonging, or without providing alternative outlets for creativity, ambition and love. New forms of work, new forms of communal living are needed if we are to break away from our dependence on the isolated nuclear family for emotional sustenance. Minor alterations of the present structure will not do the trick because we will still be left with our pervasive need for *closeness*—a need that in the present system can be satisfied only in the private nests of our miniature and separate worlds. Thus we cannot expect that the high value now attached to family life and to children among all social classes will simply vanish as soon as other opportunities for women are available. The data on the family size desires of working women and highly educated women make this quite clear. Marriage and children satsify special needs and provide special pleasures that are not offered in any other sphere, the way our society is now constituted.

But with meaningful work and meaningful communal life the compulsion to seek private solutions to loneliness and alienation would be reduced. We could visualize a new era in which demographic patterns become an accurate reflection of *individual* needs, talents and predispositions instead of a reflection of strongly conformist social and economic group pressures induced by the lack of alternatives. Instead of living in a society where three out of four women get married between the ages of 18 and 23 and in which 19 in 20 have married by the time they reach 40, we could look forward to a society in which some marry young, others marry in their thirties or forties or choose not to marry at all. Instead of concentrating our childbearing in the mid-twenties and producing the socially appropriate three or four children, more women could remain childless, more could have just one, and the rest could spread out according to individual temperament. We could even begin to share each other's children. Instead of *having* to search out our own small burrows each with its mother and father and babies, some could choose such a private world freely and others choose larger and more fluid "families" of men and women and children, or of single friends or whatever.

As choices expand it is doubtful that more women would marry and have children since this is the universal pattern now, although some might well decide to have more children than they do. But certainly many would choose the opposite if the rewards of remaining single and childless were increased, or at least if the severe penalties that women in these positions now experience were lifted. Values can change. Only then, only when control over reproduction can be used to choose freely a life style uniquely suited to individual qualities, will women be able to say fully and truthfully, "Hallelujah the Pill!"

Abortion Laws and Their Victims

Alice S. Rossi

Millions of Americans have been personally involved in illegal abortions—the women who undergo the operations, their sex partners, and the close confidantes who share the burdens of their experiences, in most cases illegal ones. Despite this widespread personal experience, there has too long been a conspiracy of silence on the subject of abortion.

There are signs that public discussion is increasing—mass media articles, network television programs, popular movies such as "Blue Denim" and "Love with the Proper Stranger," proposals for law reform by various legal and medical bodies. But the focus of public attention is on the most dramatic, though least frequent, situations leading to the desire for abortion—conception through rape or incest, and threats to pregnancies from disease or drugs. Too little attention is paid to the overwhelming number of women who seek abortions, legal or illegal, because they do not want to give birth to an unwelcome or unexpected child.

Also, it is important to note, public discussion comes mainly from professional experts such as gynecologists, obstetricians, public health officials, and specialists in law, demography, family planning, and psychiatry. With rare exception too little is heard from the women directly concerned—those who have undergone the abortion.

Well-publicized abortion cases (such as that of Mrs. Sherry Finkbine who was eventually aborted of a deformed fetus in Europe) involve exposure to German measles during the first trimester of pregnancy or the use of thalido-

mide early in pregnancy, with its associated high probability of defect in the fetus. But few women who seek abortions have been exposed to German measles or taken thalidomide and hence fear a deformed fetus; few have serious heart or liver conditions that constitute a threat to their life if they carried the pregnancy to term; fewer still have been raped by a stranger or by their own father.

The majority of the women who seek abortions do so because they find themselves with unwelcome or unwanted pregnancies; abortion is a last-resort birth control measure when preventive techniques have failed or have not been used.

It is the situation *of not wanting a child* that covers the main rather than the exceptional abortion situation. But this fact is seldom faced. I believe many people are unwilling to confront this fact because it goes counter to the expectation that women are nurturant, loving creatures who welcome every new possibility of adding a member of the human race. To come to grips with the central motivation that drives women to abortion, *that they do not want the child,* requires admitting that the traditional expectation is a gross oversimplification of the nature of women and the complex of values which determine their highly individuated response to the prospects of maternity.

When a woman is anxious to conceive a child, there is nothing to match the joy that attends a confirmation that she is pregnant, except the actual birth of the baby. If we take 30 years as the fertility span of a woman, there are approximately 360 "chances" that she may become pregnant. If she wants and has three children, there will be some 325 months, or about 90 percent of her potentially fertile menstrual months, in which she does not have joyous anticipation of a pregnancy, but rather an undercurrent of feelings ranging from vague unease to considerable fear that she may be pregnant. These feelings are not completely allayed by cognitive confidence in her contraceptive technique. This is true even for women whose contraceptive practices are highly efficacious; for women who use no contraception, the apprehension is understandably more acute. Thus, one would think there would be less resistance to the idea that many women have a dread of pregnancy and, when they find themselves with an unwanted one, may seek an abortion.

Public Attitudes to Abortion

Are America's laws on the subject of abortion in line with the thinking of its citizens? Before we examine the varying legal patterns—and both the campaign for reform and its opponents—let's look at the way the people view the matter.

Until very recently, there were no organized groups in the United States supporting abortion reform to match the very vigorous opposition to such reform. So legislators had no way of knowing whether the public would greet a revision in the law negatively or with a response of "it's about time." Fortunately, there are now indicators available.

A representative sample of 1,484 adult Americans were asked their views on the conditions under which it should be possible for a woman to obtain a legal abortion, in a survey conducted by the National Opinion Research Center in December 1965. These adults were asked the following question:

"Please tell me whether or not you think it should be possible for a pregnant woman to obtain a legal abortion . . ."

They were presented with six varying circumstances, ranging from impairment of the mother's health, to that of a married woman who did not want any more children. The survey results (see the table) show the majority of the American population support the view that women should be able to obtain a legal abortion under the following circumstances:

■ 71 percent if the woman's own health is seriously endangered by the pregnancy.

■ 56 percent if she became pregnant as a result of rape.

■ 55 percent if there is a strong chance of serious defect in the baby.

When Catholics were compared to Protestant respondents, there was very little religious group difference. Although official Catholic doctrine makes no allowance for abortions in the event of high probability of deformity in the fetus or for pregnancies following sexual assault, close to a majority of Catholic men and women were in favor of legal abortion to cover such situations. Thus, there was no tendency to take an overall doctrinal stand against abortion among Catholics; instead, the range of support they gave varied by situation in precisely the same way that it did among Protestant or Jewish respondents.

Furthermore, the slight tendency for Protestants to be more liberal than Catholics was found to be largely a reflection of differential church attendance, not religious affiliation solely. Frequent church attenders are less likely to take a liberal stand on abortion than those who attend church less frequently *among both groups;* only because Catholics show generally higher church attendance (74 percent) than Protestants do (51 percent) was there any difference in liberal stand on abortion. The data further suggested that education has a "liberalizing" effect on the attitudes of Protestants but not of Catholics—there were no differences in attitudes among poorly educated Protestants and Catholics, but an increasing contrast as educational attainment increased.

Legislators will continue to be exposed to pressure against liberalization of the abortion laws from spokesmen of various religious faiths, but there is a clear support among the electorate from the major religious groups for revision of the existent statutes to cover not merely the life, but also the health, of a pregnant woman or serious risk of deformity in the fetus.

The study also showed that attitudes toward abortion cut across both political orientation and party lines. People with a liberal political orientation who are independent of any political party affiliation, show the most liberal attitudes toward abortion (mean of 51 percent on all six items). But at the next level of liberal views on abortion are Republicans of both liberal (47 percent) and conservative (46 percent) persuasion, and liberal Democrats (42 percent). Those least sympathetic to abortion law reform are conservative Democrats (36 percent) and those who are either politically uncommitted or apolitical.

What the American public clearly does *not* support, however, are abortions in situations which all studies indicate to be the predominant circumstances for women who seek abortions. Support for legal abortions in the remaining three situations is as follows:

■ 21 percent if the family has a very low income and cannot afford any more children.

■ 18 percent if she is not married and does not want to marry the man.

■ 15 percent if she is married and wants no more children.

Attitudes Toward Sex

The analysis showed no differences between Catholics and Protestants on these grounds. What mattered more was education, sex, and general attitude toward sex. Men with at least some college education, for example, are far more likely to approve legal abortions in the case of an unmarried pregnant woman (33 percent) than are women who have had some college training (19 percent) or men (19 percent) and women (9 percent) who have never gone beyond elementary school.

Restrictive attitudes toward premarital sex bear a decided relationship to opposition to legal abortion for every one of the six conditions we specified. Men and women who oppose premarital intercourse between an engaged couple are considerably less likely to approve a legal abortion than those who have a permissive or ambivalent attitude toward premarital intercourse—even where maternal health is endangered or the woman has been sexually assaulted. It is of interest that there are no attitude differences about abortion between men and women among those who hold *restrictive* views toward premarital sex relations; but among those with *permissive* attitudes, men are much more inclined than women to support legal abortions as birth control measures.

Overall then, there is clearly majority support for abortion as a safeguard of maternal health or a prevention of the anguish associated with bearing a deformed child. But any suggestion of abortion as a last-resort means of birth control is firmly rejected by the majority of American adults in the NORC sample. It does not seem to matter what the circumstances are—a poor family for whom an additional child would represent an economic hardship, a single woman who does not wish to marry the man with whom she had sex relations, or a married woman who does not want any more children. The American population approves family planning by means of acceptable contraceptive techniques, but any failure of traditional birth control measures should be followed not by an abortion, but by an acceptance of the pregnancy.

The fact that the last condition—of a married woman who has the number of children she wants—has been the experience of millions of living American women, has not affected public judgment that abortion is "wrong" and should not be legally allowed. The suggestion is strong, therefore, that Americans disapprove of any legitimate institutionalization of a widespread practice if the practice runs counter to the traditional social and religious norms surrounding sex and maternity.

The Legal Barriers

Let us turn now to the law. The perspective of a sociologist and a woman may, it is hoped, contribute to keeping the complex legal and medical considerations from deflecting our attention from the central problem at stake—what society should do for a woman facing an unwanted pregnancy.

State laws vary in the language used and whether the focus is on the mother alone or the mother and the child. In 32 states abortions are unlawful unless they are necessary to "save" or "preserve" the life of the mother. In nine states the preservation of life covers the mother or her child. In only five states and the District of Columbia does the letter of the law go beyond the restriction to saving a life; in Colorado and New Mexico abortions are permitted to preserve the mother's life or prevent "serious bodily injury"; in Alabama, Oregon, and the District of

ATTITUDES TOWARD LEGAL ABORTION—(1482 Respondents)

"Please tell me whether or not you think it should be possible for a pregnant woman to obtain a legal abortion . . ."	YES	NO	DON'T KNOW
If the woman's own health is seriously endangered by the pregnancy	71%	26%	3%
If she became pregnant as a result of rape	56	38	6
If there is a strong chance of serious defect in the baby	55	41	4
If the family has a very low income and cannot afford any more children	21	77	2
If she is not married and does not want to marry the man	18	80	2
If she is married and does not want any more children	15	83	2

Columbia, the law exempts abortions designed to preserve the life or "health" of the mother. Only in Maryland is the legal phrasing more general: the state law exempts abortions which would "secure the safety of the mother."

These statutes come under the criminal code. The goal of abortion reform groups has been concentrated on seeking a change in this penal code. Revision proposals are most frequently based on the Model Penal Code recommended by the American Law Institute in 1959. The clauses relevant to abortion extend exemption from criminal prosecution to cases in which the continuance of the pregnancy involves "substantial risk that mother or child will suffer grave and irremediable impairment of physical or mental health" or where the pregnancy "resulted from forcible rape." Thus, if there is a high probability of defect in the fetus or serious physical or psychological impairment of the mother should she carry the fetus to term, and if the presence of these circumstances is certified by at least two physicians, then a legal abortion will be possible under this revised code, and the doctors involved have a justifiable affirmative defense.

It is this revised penal code clause which has received rather widespread endorsement. Variations of it have been reviewed and hearings held in the legislatures of several states—Illinois, Minnesota, New Hampshire, California, and New York. In no case has reform yet succeeded. So too, the recommendation of the Committee on Human Reproduction of the AMA favoring law reform was turned down by the House of Delegates of the AMA, which referred the problem back to the Board of Trustees with a recommendation that the problem be explored "in depth with other interested groups."

Opposition to Change

Where illegal abortion is concerned, the estimated range of operations is from 250,000 to somewhat over 1,000,000 per year in the United States. We are on somewhat firmer ground in gauging the incidence of legal abortions conducted in hospital settings, particularly when they are based on statistics from municipalities in which such abortions are required to be justified and recorded. The most recent estimate for the United States is somewhere between 8,000 and 10,000.

Yet, to many people opposed to law reform this is not a "significant" problem because there is no agreement on exactly how extensive the incidence of illegal abortion is. Further, many persons refuse to believe even the lower limit of the estimated range, on the grounds that they personally know of no woman who has had an illegal abortion.

Also, they say, there is no need to change the law because abortion is declining, as contraceptive practices become more widespread and more effective.

Is the incidence rate a proper basis for deciding whether this is a major social problem or not? Medical researchers do not avoid attempts to find a cure for a rare disease because the chances are it will cripple or kill only 10,000 people a year. We do not consider unemployment a minor social problem because more than 90 percent of the labor force is employed. We do not rest content with educational attainment of American youth because the majority now complete a high school education.

The same reasoning should apply to the abortion problem. Those who argue with the incidence estimates, or resist change in our abortion laws on the grounds that it is not an extensive social problem, are either deluding us or themselves as to what is really at the heart of their disclaimers: they do not wish to see any liberalization of abortion laws because they are opposed to abortion per se; or they have little or no empathy for the women who want to obtain one; or they consciously or unconsciously believe the psychologically punishing and medically and legally risky experience of securing an illegal abortion is deserved —it is a *punishment* for becoming pregnant if you are poor or unmarried or already have a large family.

Legal Abortions

Who has abortions—both legal and illegal?

There is enormous variation from hospital to hospital, city to city, one physician to another in the ratio of therapeutic abortions to deliveries. One doctor may perform one abortion to every four or five deliveries, while another performs one abortion to every 2,000 deliveries. A private hospital with financially well-off patients, may perform one legal abortion in every 36 deliveries, while another hospital, one which treats clinic patients, has a record of no legal abortions in 24,417 deliveries.

The grounds justifying legal therapeutic abortions have changed over the years. Psychological justification has increased as strictly medical considerations of physical health have declined. Doctors have shown a gradual broadening of their conception of "health" to include many nonphysical factors in the woman's condition, a reflection of the slow penetration of psychoanalytic theory into medical training and medical thinking. The decline in abortions for medical reasons is also a reflection of medical progress: as tuberculosis declined in the population at large, so it declined as justification for legal abortions. As knowledge is acquired about the effect of radiation, rubella, or thalidomide upon the probability of defect in the fetus, new grounds for legal abortion enter the picture.

Following the model of the Scandinavian countries, there has been a marked trend in the United States since the 1950's toward the establishment of hospital abortion boards to review potential cases of abortion. Studies have shown that hospitals following this committee device have lower therapeutic abortion rates than hospitals without such committees; the establishment of the committees can be interpreted as a self-protecting response on the part of the medical profession against the trend toward an increasing number of legal abortions for psychological reasons.

The effect of liberalization of abortion laws upon subsequent patterns of live births and abortion rates can be gleaned by analysis of data from other countries. One pattern is clear: the birth rate declines more rapidly following such abortion liberalization than by any comparable measure such as contraceptive campaigns. This is nowhere more dramatically shown than in Japan since the passage of the Eugenic Protection Law in 1948. This act comes closer to abortion-on-demand than any abortion legislation anywhere in the world. The success of this policy in halting the skyrocketing population increase in Japan can be seen by comparing the rate of live births and of legal abortions in the year following the passage of the act, 1949, and comparable rates for 1962: the rate of live births per 1,000 population declined from 33.2 in 1949 to 17.0 in 1962, while the rate of legal abortions per 1,000 population increased from 3.0 to 10.4. This rapid increase in abortions during the 1950's was due mainly to older women aborting pregnancies after they already had a number of children.

Much the same story applies to countries in Eastern Europe. In Hungary, for example, which introduced interruption of pregnancy "on-request" in 1956, the number of legal abortions increased rapidly; by 1961 abortions exceeded the number of live births by more than one-fifth. The fact that the birth rate declined in East European countries which have liberalized abortion laws, but did *not* decline in the two countries which did not legalize abortion (Albania and East Germany) is strong evidence that the legalization of abortion depressed the birth rate.

It may be, incidentally, that the most dramatic birth rate reduction, in countries whose population is growing at alarming rates, would result from a two-part program:

liberalization of abortion laws which women will respond to (pregnancy being primarily "women's concern"), and contraceptive campaigns aimed at the men (sex being "men's concern").

Illegal Abortions

What is known about the pattern of *illegal abortion* cases is necessarily on less confident grounds:

■ Roughly one in five of the women in the Kinsey study who were ever married reported induced abortions. While this sample is not completely representative of the American population, somewhat greater confidence can be placed in the Kinsey picture of subgroup variations in the proportion reporting induced abortions. They found that induced abortions increase with the number of pregnancies terminated in marriage, testimony to the fact that women resort to abortion for pregnancies which occur after they have reached the family size they desire. The relationship shown by age and education is similarly interesting for the social pattern it suggests: among poorly educated women, the highest rate of induced abortion is among the older women; among well-educated women, the highest rate is among the younger women. What this suggests is that poorly educated women who become pregnant, either have illegitimate children (particularly if they are Negro), or marry and have the first child within wedlock, and abort their later pregnancies. Well-educated women abort their premarital pregnancies, marry later and use more reliable contraceptive techniques with more cooperative husbands to control their family size.

■ The abortion rate, like the fertility rate, is responsive to the economic cycle in the society. By comparing the rate of reported induced abortions with the age when they were performed, Paul Gebhard shows that abortions were probably greater during the depression and declined in the 1940's and 1950's.

The Right to Be Born

The official Catholic position on abortion has held simply that nothing may be done which would involve any direct killing of the fetus. The only exception is the application of the Catholic rule of "double effect" or "indirect killing." Catholic obstetricians may remove an ectopic pregnancy or a cancerous pregnant uterus because these operations have the primary purpose of saving the life of the mother, not the killing of the fetus, which is secondary.

Whatever the position of the church, the actual behavior of Catholics is quite another matter. Countries with predominantly Roman Catholic populations actually show high abortion rates, as they do of illegitimacy. In a recent survey of Roman Catholic Chile, for example, 27 percent of the women reported they had had induced abortions. In Roman Catholic France, the annual number of abortions equals the annual number of live births.

A religious group is free to characterize abortion as a sin if it sees fit to do so and to punish its members for this by some appropriate ecclesiastical censure if it wishes. The rest of the society should, however, enjoy the right to control their own reproductive lives in accordance with their conception of morality and human dignity.

Apart from the fine points of theology and ethical consideration, there is a quality of sentimentality about the defense of the right of the fetus to be born that strikes at least this feminine ear as alien to the ways and the feelings of women one has known or studied. I have never heard a woman wax sentimental about 300 or so ova which are never fertilized, nor have I heard remorse expressed for a two-month-old fetus that is spontaneously aborted. It is not the loss of a particular fetus a woman grieves over, but the loss of her potential maternity and potential baby. In a similar way, despite all claims to the contrary, there is no evidence that women who have had induced abortions are typically stricken with guilt and remorse as an aftermath. The few cases of women who do feel such regret must be weighed against the human price in bitterness, economic hardship, and psychological stress that is paid by the woman, her family, and the unwanted child if she does *not* obtain an abortion.

It would appear to be a matter of time and the continued and extended efforts of men and women who work for abortion reform, until American law will undergo some degree of liberalization. It is still an open question, however, how widespread the trend will be in various states to remove abortion from coverage by the criminal law (no other medical procedure is regulated by criminal law) and to place it under either civil statutes bearing on the licensing of physicians, or, more positively, statutes bearing on the regulation of hospitals. Either of these latter two changes would clearly and firmly shift responsibility to the medical profession.

But if we rest content with goals limited to the penal code revision that is most likely to be passed, we shall scarcely have helped many women in the United States. Nor will such passage of a revised code be followed by any significant increase in legal abortions and decrease in illegal abortions, since the law will not cover most of the women who now have abortions illegally. Married women who do not want to have a third or fourth child (or an unmarried woman who does not want to marry the man by whom she has conceived, or who does not want to marry her) will still be faced with a cruel choice between deceitful lying in order to get a legal abortion, or being honest about her motivation and seeking an illegal one.

Facing the Alternatives

Let us take, as an example, the plight of an unmarried woman who becomes pregnant. What alternatives does our society offer her, and what is the consequence for the woman and for the society?

■ *Marry the man by whom she conceived.* The price?— a high-risk marriage. There is no period for the mutual exploration of each other and adjustment to marriage itself, but a double task of adjusting to pregnancy and anticipated maternity while also adjusting to spouse, sex, and obligations of home maintenance. The outcome—a high probability of divorce and separation, a couple cheated of the joy and adventure and independence of the pre-parenthood stage of marriage, more children reared in fatherless homes, and strained relations between the woman and her parents, who are so often firmly insistent on the daughter's marriage as the solution to her pregnancy out of wedlock.

■ *Go through with the pregnancy and put the child up for adoption.* There are few writers in the literature on abortion who have stressed what many women in this situation feel deeply—the cruelty and sadism that is involved when her doctor, parents, minister, lawyer, or social worker suggest that she carry the child to term and then hand it over, never to see it again, to someone else to raise. It is a heartless recommendation, and psychiatrists inform us it creates far more difficult and extensive therapeutic problems than with patients who have an abortion early in pregnancy.

■ *Have the child illegitimately and rear it herself.* The price? Ask those engaged currently in trying to break the vicious cycle of poverty in the lower working class of our large cities: women with double responsibility as breadwinner and mother working at jobs for which they do not receive equal pay for equal work; encounters with men who do not want to assume responsibility for another man's child; children who often suffer from neglect to outright maternal rejection.

■ *Have an abortion*—if she has the good fortune to contact a physician courageous enough to recommend her for a legal abortion, or refer her to another physician for an illegal abortion.

To withhold the possibility of a safe and socially acceptable abortion for unmarried women is to start the chain of illegitimacy and despair that will continue to keep poverty, crime, and poor mental health high on the list of pressing social problems in the United States. Finally, it is expecting entirely too much of human frailty and the complex motivations underlying human sexual behavior to think abortions will no longer be necessary when contraceptive techniques are perfected and universally used. One has only to observe carefully the adaptive role the woman plays in sex in Mirra Komarovsky's *Blue Collar Marriage* or Lee Rainwater's *Workingman's Wife* and *And the Poor Get Children* to understand some of the limitations upon the consistent use of contraceptives by large numbers of American women. Furthermore, not all women can take the pill, nor be fitted with a ring, and pregnancies even occur in both types of birth control.

Social approval is extended to the woman who plans her family size and child spacing well by using the best contraceptive technique available and suitable for her, but if these measures fail, the only alternative is acceptance of pregnancy she does not want, or the unsafe and traumatic experience of an illegal abortion. Any woman, whether married or not, should be able to secure a safe abortion, upon her own request, at a reasonable fee, in a licensed hospital by a licensed and competent physician.

The Salutation of Mary *Lu 1.*

And the Angel came in unto her and said, Hail thou that art highly favoured. The Lord is with thee, Blessed art thou among Women. v. 28. And when she saw him she was troubled at his saying etc. Verse 29.
London 172?

The Male Maternal Instinct
Una Stannard

Women have the babies, but men have the maternal instinct.

If the maternal instinct is defined as an innate tendency to want children, and to love, cherish, nurture and protect children, then history reveals that men have had more of a maternal instinct than women.

For who, according to the Bible, was the first mother? It was a man—Adam. God put him to sleep and delivered a female from his rib cage. And, for that matter, wasn't a man, God the Father, the sole progenitor of Adam himself? He created Adam out of dust in His own image, just as in Greek myth Prometheus created man out of earth in the image of the gods. Similarly, Hephaestus created Pandora out of earth, and he also acted as a midwife for Zeus, splitting his head open with an ax to facilitate the delivery of Athena. Zeus also had another baby. When Semele prematurely gave birth to Dionysus, Zeus snatched up the child and sewed him into his thigh and carried him there to term. Myths you say, but they are myths written by men and expressing the male's deep desire to be a mother.

Little boys (as well as little girls) express their desire to have a baby even more directly than the ancient gods did. They walk around with their bellies stuck out and like to play with dolls. They would undoubtedly engage in such imitative play more if it were not sternly repressed in our culture, for in primitive societies the male desire to have babies is fully played out.

In many primitive societies, when the wife is having the baby the father takes to his bed and groans and cries out like a woman in labor. After delivery the baby is sometimes placed in his arms, and the man, dressed in his wife's clothes, is the one who receives congratulations. The wife goes back to work, but the father remains in bed for days, fasting or undergoing other rituals to assure the child's welfare. Couvade, which is what this widespread custom is called, is by no means the only way in which men reveal their desire for maternity. Among the Arapesh of New Guinea, the phrase "to bear a child" can be used for either a man or a woman because the father is believed to be as necessary as the mother in the physical and spiritual creation of babies. During the first weeks of pregnancy the father is required to deposit a great deal of semen into the womb because the baby is thought to be made equally of the mother's blood and the father's semen. Immediately after the baby is born, the father must lie down next to it and the mother so that the baby can receive its life-soul (which may come from the father or the mother). When the father is lying there, he is said to be "in bed having a baby." Furthermore, both the father and the mother must sleep with the baby for a year, for unless both do, it is believed that the baby cannot live. The father participates equally in feeding the baby, cleaning it and supervising it. Among the Arapesh, if one comments on the good looks of a middle-aged man, someone is likely to say that you should have seen him before he bore all those children.

Male Desire

The male desire to be like a woman is also seen clearly in the initiation ceremonies that boys have to undergo in most primitive societies. The circumcisions or subincisions that were often performed seem to have been meant to make boys like women. For example, among the Azande of the Belgian Congo, the word for circumcision and midwife are the same, and the prepuce and umbilical cord are believed to have identical medicinal properties. Subincision (slitting the penis the whole length of the urethra), which was universally practised among the central tribes of Australia, makes the penis resemble a vulva, and the subincision wound was sometimes actually called a vagina or a penis womb. Since boys with subincisions lose control of the flow of urine, they must, like women, squat when urinating. The blood that is shed in circumcision and subincision is believed to be analogous either to the blood of defloration or to menstrual blood (or occasionally to mother's milk, which is believed to be white blood). Boys of the Arunta tribe regularly open their subincision wounds and cause them to bleed again, an obvious imitation of menstrual periodicity. After circumcision, boys in many East African tribes are dressed in female clothes; others, like the Qatu of the New Hebrides, are secluded the way girls are at first menstruation.

Without these feminizing initiation ceremonies it was thought, paradoxically, that boys could not achieve the status of men. Seemingly even more paradoxical, these "man-making" ceremonies were in many ways symbolic of rebirth. The initiation houses were often called wombs or birth enclosures and the exit door resembled a gaping vagina. After initiation, the adult males who were in charge treated the boys as if they had been newly born, giving them new names, milk to drink, not allowing them to speak and carrying them on their shoulders as if they couldn't walk. The boys were now born again as men. Since a boy could only thus become a man, it is as if the men were saying that though women give birth to boys, only men can give birth to men; and the boys having been ritually transformed into women could in their turn give birth to the next generation of men.

There was another custom widely prevalent in early societies which gave men control not merely over the birth of men but of all life. Immediately after the birth of an Arapesh child, the midwife calls out the baby's sex to the father, who calls back either "Wash it" or "Don't wash it." If he commands the latter, the baby is killed. Similarly, in Roman times when a baby was born it was placed on the ground; only if the father raised it was it allowed to live. (Our phrase "to raise a child" derives from this custom.) We are familiar with the right of the Greek father to expose his newborn child and with the Chinese custom of killing female babies. One might think that such customs revealed, not a maternal impulse, but the male's hatred of maternity, yet the father's life and death rights over a newborn child made him the one who actually gave the baby life.

The primitive male's imitation or appropriation of women's reproductive functions would certainly not make it unfair to conclude that "womb envy" used to be widespread. In a deeper sense than men can now realize, that envy was justified, for the male's role in procreation was during man's early history not understood. We are not born knowing the relationship between sex and conception, and since the first signs of pregnancy do not occur until sometime after conception and since most acts of intercourse do not lead to conception, it is not surprising that it took man centuries to make the discovery. E.S. Hartland, in the two volumes of his *Primitive Paternity*, has collected a massive amount of evidence that indicates that early man regarded impregnation not as a physiological process but as a supernatural one. Impregnation was believed to occur at quickening, the moment when the woman feels the fetus move. It was thought that at that moment a spirit had entered the woman, either from the wind, stars, water, moon (the father of albino children), trees, lizards, birds, food, or whatever happened to be near the woman at quickening. (The story that used to be told to children, that the stork brings the baby, may have its origins in such beliefs.)

Spiritual Impregnation

It is of great significance that in most early cultures only the word mother means procreator, father meaning merely elder man or provider. It was only woman who could procreate, which meant that woman was the superior sex, and not merely because it was upon her that mankind depended for its continuance but because it was woman alone in whom the spirits chose to reside. In a sense, in most early primitive societies, every child is the Christ child in that he is believed to be a child got without intercourse, the embodiment of a Spirit. The belief that it was only women whom the spirits entered may be why it was later thought that women were more likely than men to become witches; as the fifteenth-century authors of *Malleus Maleficarum* (a textbook on witchcraft) put it: "Women are naturally more impressionable, and more ready to receive the influence of a disembodied spirit." And perhaps that is also why women are still believed to be more intuitive than men, to gain their knowledge without effort but seemingly all at once from some mysterious source.

Because woman was the sex who was in most intimate contact with the spirits, early religions tend to be Mother Goddess religions, and even when the male's role in procreation was understood, Mother Goddess religions continued to predominate and the male's role was perfunctory or ancillary. The male whom the Divine Mother chose to be her consort was necessary only to impregnate her, after which he was killed, like the male bee who succeeds in impregnating the queen bee only at the cost of his own life. In many mother religions men who wished to be priests happily wore female clothes and castrated themselves so that they could become one with the Goddess and share her life-bearing powers. At the festival of Ariadne in Cyprus, the priest lay in bed imitating the groans of a woman in labor. Among the Yakut of Siberia, male shamans were believed to be actually capable of having children. Far from being the almighty rod of male power, the penis was often thought to be the simple instrument of the womb. In a drawing in the Egyptian *Book of the Dead* a male with a huge erect phallus is arching himself up from the earth, eager to receive the woman who is hovering over him. The huge phalli that are so common in ancient art may not be evidence of the male's belief in his sexual superiority but rather evidence of his eagerness to lure the female. Procreate with me, the phalli seem to be saying, use me, let my seed be the one you give life to.

Sowers of Seed

For men to feel superior they apparently had to do more than discover the potency of semen, that is, that it was the male sex in whom the Spirit of Life resided; they also had to belittle woman's role as child-bearer, which was commonly done by regarding the womb as the mere nest where the baby grows. Among the Pilaga of South America, it was believed that in ejaculation the male delivers a minuscule baby into the womb, which is merely the place where it stays until it is big enough to come out. In Aeschylus' *The Eumenides*, Apollo explains to Orestes that the mother is not the "true life-begetter" of the child, but merely a "nurse of live seed. 'Tis the sower of the seed alone begetteth." Apollo offers proof for his theory by citing the example of Zeus who had Athena with no female help whatsoever. The ancient Egyptians (and other early peoples) felt free to use females captured in war as concubines because they believed the resulting offspring would have no taint of foreign blood since woman was merely the earth in which their seed was sown.

The early Christians went further than the ancient Greeks and Egyptians in belittling woman, but did so, interestingly enough, by having the Church and/or God the Father preempt woman's former role both as sole life-giver and as nurturer. The first way they preempted woman's role was by disregarding physical motherhood; unlike virtually all other societies and religions, the early Christians had no ceremonies associated with birth. Physical birth was not celebrated; it was ignored. Even the birth of Christ was originally ignored. Mark, the earliest of the gospels, begins with story of Christ's life with his baptism. Until late in the fourth century only Christ's baptism was celebrated (6 January, Epiphany), and in fact the date of his birth was unknown. (The 25th of December was later arbitrarily chosen because it was the day of the pagan celebration of Saturnalia.) Christ's physical birth, and that of all early Christians, was believed to be unimportant except that it enabled one to undergo baptism, one's real, one's spiritual birth. Baptism, a ceremony that was originally only for adults, was what gave a person true life, eternal, immortal life. Just as a Roman baby could not be said to have life until its father raised it from the ground, so an early Christian did not receive life, an immortal soul, until through baptism he became the child of God.

Milk of the Word

"The birth of Christians is in baptism," said Cyprian in a letter written in 256. Baptismal water was called the "Water of Life" (cf. amniotic fluid). As Clement of Alexandria put it, "He [Christ] generated us from our mother—the water" (*The Stromata*, Book IV, ch. 25). After baptism one was called a "newborn babe," a "babe in Christ," "an infant," and often received a new name and drank milk and honey. Moreover, the new babes in Christ, just like boys after initiation ceremonies, were supposed to imitate children—according to Papias, to be as frank and guileless as a child; according to Clement, to be as simple, tender, joyous and sensually pure. The custom among early Christians of "speaking in tongues," uttering ecstatic gibberish, was also in part an imitation of childish babbling.

The early Church became *Mater Ecclesia*. Woman was no longer our mother, the source of life, the Church was. The Church, said Paul in Galations (4:26), is "the mother of us all." The Church is "the true mother of the living . . . the second Adam," said Tertullian (*De Anima*, Ch. 43). And not only was the Church the true mother, it was also the only true nourisher. "The Lord Christ," said Clement, "did not pronounce the breasts of women blessed, nor selected them to give nourishment; but when the kind and loving Father had rained down the Word, Himself became spiritual nourishment." Clement compared seeking Christ to sucking: "for to those babes that suck the Word, the Father's breasts of love supply the milk." (*The Instructor*, Book I, Ch. 6). In the eighth *Ode of Solomon*, (an anonymous series of Christian odes from about 2nd Century) God says: "My own breast I prepared for them; that they might drink my holy milk and live thereby." Or as Peter put it, Christians are fed not by mother's milk but by "the milk of the word."

The early Christians would have liked to reject the mother entirely. They loved to point out that Adam, a male, was created first, and that Adam, not a woman, was the first mother. "The man is not of the woman, but the woman of the man," said Paul in Corinthians 11:8. Some early Christians bewailed the fact that after Adam all men had to be physically born of women. To save Christ from this taint, a sect like the Docetes denied that Christ was born of a woman. Mary, as the mother of Christ, was ignored for two centuries, and it was not until the fourth century that she was officially recognized as Theotakis (God-bearer), and then only after denying her sexuality by making her a virgin supernaturally impregnated by the Holy Spirit in the form of a dove.

But Mary was not celebrated as the supernatural procreator; she exists in the Church not as a goddess of fertility but as a symbol of the Church's nonsexual love of its children. Christians are still believed to be the true children of the Church, not of woman. According to the *Book of Common Prayer*, baptism supplies the child with "that thing which by nature he cannot have," that is, at baptism, the child is "born anew of Water and the Holy Ghost," given the only life that counts—immortal life.

The early Christian church further degraded woman as mother by regarding her as the producer of mere flesh. Woman gives us base fleshly life; the mother-father Church gives us nonmaterial, immortal life. The woman's breasts help us to grow physically; the Church's breasts give us "the milk of the word," spiritual nourishment. The flesh was unimportant, the spirit all important. The New Testament version of the creation in John is "In the beginning was the Word . . . and the Word was God" because for Christians life was nonphysical, abstract, of the spirit. God the Father, our spiritual procreator, is our true procreator. Woman is flesh, the material that the male seminal principle gives life to.

The early philosophers and scientists who studied procreation took the way of the New Testament, the way of spirit. Unlike the Pilaga of South America or the early Greeks, they could not think of semen as containing microscopic babies; that was too fleshly, too physical, too female a function. Semen became spiritualized; it was the Vital Spark, the First Cause that turned the inert constitutive matter of the female into a living being. For Thomas Aquinas (as it had been for his mentor Aristotle) "the power of the female generative virtue provides the substance but the active male virtue makes it into the finished product." Thomas Fienus, a seventeenth-century scientist, called semen "the rational soul" that enters the uterus and gives the shapeless material it finds there a form. Or as Buffon, the eighteenth-century naturalist, put it: "The male semen is the sculptor, the menstrual blood is the block of marble, and the foetus is the figure which is fashioned out of the combination."

Buffon believed in the spiritual role of semen even though spermatazoa had been discovered. In 1677 Leeuwenhoek put semen under the powerful microscope he had developed and saw the wriggling "animalcules." He immediately thought he had discovered the male's babies. Like the Pilaga Indians he believed the semen contained homonculi, complete men or women-in-little (he thought he could distinguish the sex of the animalcules), and that these minute babies were delivered into the female for nurturing. Other scientists immediately saw what Leeuwenhoek did and actually drew pictures of the babies men carried in their semen. But most scientists refused to regard the sperm as the male's babies; for them the male's role in generation continued to be the more exalted spiritual one.

Whether embryologists believed that the semen actually delivered the baby into the womb or ignited the Vital Spark of Life, they were almost all certain that the male was the essential giver of life, that the female merely supplied the raw material and/or nourishment for that life. A child's resemblance to its mother was generally explained as the effect on the seed of the soil it grows in. However, at times one does find a scientist, like Maupertuis, who theorized that both male and female must contribute equally to the child's heredity. But until the mid-19th century such scientists were usually a minority, and of those who did argue that male and female must contribute equally in the generation of a child, most nevertheless tended to give the male the more important, the vital role. For example, scientists who believed that the embryo was formed by the mixture of male and female semen (vaginal secretions) assumed that the male semen was the spiritual seed that activated, the female semen the material seed that nourished. Other scientists who presumably believed in sexual equality in generation declared that semen produced the fetus, the ovum, the placenta. Even the "ovists," those who believed that the embryo was preformed in the ovum, not the sperm, regarded the embryo as inert until the male's semen, like God breathing into Adam's nostrils, transformed it into a living soul.

Inner Space

The ovists were not popular; for centuries scientists, in spite of their knowledge of the existence of eggs in other female animals, denied the existence of the mammalian ovum. So eminent a physiologist as Harvey was among them. In 1672 when de Graaf discovered the ovarian follicles, many scientists refused to believe that they had anything to do with procreation; one scientist contended that they were vestigial testes of no more functional value than the male's nipples. De Graaf himself believed that the ovum had only a nutritive function and could not escape from the follicles until it had been activated by semen. This almost universal belief may explain why the mammalian ovum (although visible to the unaided eye) was not discovered until 1827. Scientists were looking for it at the wrong time—after copulation. Yet even its discoverer, von Baer, believed that the ovum needed semen to give it life and that its role in generation was wholly nutritive. The belief in the purely material or ancillary function of the ovum persisted until well into the nineteenth century. That a woman could have more than a passive nutritive role in generation was too much for the male maternal instinct.

It was not until 1861 that it was realized that the ovum was more than a source of nourishment for the embryo but was the female sex cell, and it was not until 1875 that the actual union of the female and male gametes was observed. Mendel's discovery of the absolutely equal contribution of the sexes to the heredity of the child ought to have been the final blow to the male's illusion that he was the lord of creation.

It ought to have been, but it was not. Even today scientists who really know better can't help talking as if they believed the male was the sole creator, the woman merely the nest. For example, so learned a psychoanalyst as Erik Erikson finds himself speaking of woman's "inner space" destined to bear the offspring of chosen men, a formulation that is no more sophisticated than that of the man in the street who refers to his wife as "the mother of my children," or the wife who dutifully echoes, "I bore his children," and when the children ask where babies come from tells them that daddy plants a seed in mummy.

Moreover, in spite of our knowledge of the equal role of the sexes in generation, the law still continues to act as if the father were the sole parent: all legitimate children must by law be named after the father. In several states the father is still regarded as the sole natural guardian of the children. Less than a century ago, of course, the father and the father only was the guardian of the children in virtually all countries. Upon divorce, the father was routinely granted custody of the children; the mother had absolutely no rights over them. Not until 1886 in England could a woman get custody of the children, and then only if the father was guilty of gross misconduct. The father as sole progenitor had "sacred rights."

It is perhaps because men were believed to be mothers in the original sense of sole procreator that they were and still are so anxious to have sons. We tend to think that men prefer sons because men are regarded as the superior sex, or because men somehow feel that they can prove their manliness only by generating a man. Other men say they want sons because they want to have their names carried on. But only male children carry on the father's name because only males were believed to be the continuers of the father's life. For a female was not believed to have seeds of life within her; she was the mere brooder of man's life. That was why it was so important for kings to have male heirs, or why men were allowed to divorce a wife who had produced no male descendants or why the Chinese would count as their children only their sons and would kill female infants. This custom seems less cruel when one realizes that only males were believed to be capable of giving life; the female was the inessential sex, the mere nest for a man's babies, and any nest would do.

Abortions and Virgins

The traditional male opposition to abortion also makes sense in the light of man's faulty knowledge of procreation. When a woman is believed to be merely the nurturer of life, then it makes sense that she should have no life and death rights over that life. For the child is the man's; it is his property, and the woman can be said only to be taking care of that property until she can deliver it safely into the man's arms. The Greeks and Romans approved of abortion and infanticide only when it was believed that the child would be or was imperfect property. For example, Plato thought that a woman who was impregnated after the age of 40 ought to be aborted because the chances of her having a defective child were high. On the same principle, all defective children were killed or exposed, and it was the man's right to kill the children or have them aborted because they were his sole property, not the woman's. A woman who had an abortion without her husband's permission was executed. Cicero approved of the custom because the woman had killed the man's life, his means of carrying on his name and the race. Christians disapproved of abortion for the same reason except that the real father of the child was God. As Lactantius argued in the fourth century, since it was God who gave the child life, only God could take that life away. In other words, the Divine Life that had been implanted in a woman was not hers; therefore she could not destroy it.

The male had a proprietary interest in assuring not only that the life he had created was not destroyed by abortion but that it was in fact his own seed of life the woman was carrying. The sexual double standard exists so that a man can be sure of his motherhood, that it is his child, not another man's, that the woman is bearing. It is men who require virginity in women in order to make sure the children are their own. Virginity originally had nothing to do with chastity or unchastity. A virgin was an independent woman, one who was not united with a man; virgins were often religious prostitutes and mothers. When women were believed to be the sole progenitors and the relationship between sex and children was not understood, virginity in the modern sense could have no value. On the contrary, men valued a woman who had proved her fertility. It was only when men considered themselves as the sole progenitors that virginity came to be highly regarded, for a man can never be absolutely sure it is his child a woman is carrying. To make sure, man has severely restricted woman's sexual and social life, demanding that women be virgins and making marriage the only way a woman can have legal children.

A legal child is a construct of men, a way of validating parenthood. Men invented the concept of illegitimacy. Where women are believed to be the sole generators of children there can of course be no illegitimate children, for there are no fathers (not human ones, at any rate). Where fathers are believed to be the sole mothers, a child without a legal father becomes taboo, worse than taboo. Under Roman law an illegitimate child was *filius nullius*, not a son, nothing, for the law recognized no relationship between the mother and child. In the light of the physiological knowledge of the time there was none, since women were merely, as Napoleon later said, machines by which children were manufactured. Therefore, since the child's real procreator was unknown, he had no relations, he was illegitimate, outside the law, a social outcast. Not only were illegitimate children declared to be legally nonexistent, so in a sense were their mothers. A woman who bore an illegitimate child was virtually excommunicated from society, or to use the Victorian phrase, she suffered "social death."

Since the woman who bore an illegitimate child made both herself and the child social outcasts, it should not be surprising that many a mother destroyed her illegitimate children. The sewers and rivers in medieval Rome used to be clogged with their bodies. In 1633 an act was passed in England "to prevent the Destroying and Murthering of Bastard Children," apparently to no effect. In 1713 Joseph Addison commented that "there is scare an assizes where some unhappy wretch is not executed for the murder of a child." In 1777 Frederick the Great wrote to Voltaire that the largest number of executions occurring in Germany were of girls who had killed their illegitimate infants.

Woman's maternal instinct was apparently not great enough to withstand the taboo of a patriarchal society that forbade a woman to have a child on her own. Yet that same patriarchal society, by forcing women to repudiate such children, enabled men to manifest their maternal instinct in another way, for the unhappy victims of the fate men had in the first place imposed upon them were rescued by male compassion. In 787 Archbishop Datheus of Milan opened a foundling hospital where women could secretly leave their illegitimate children instead of throwing them into the sewers and rivers. Similarly, in 1204 Innocent III, appalled by the number of dead infants fishermen found in their nets, opened a section of the hospital at Rome for illegitimate children. Again, in 1720, Thomas Coram, having been upset in his frequent walks to London by seeing infants abandoned on dunghills or on the sides of the road, "sometimes alive, sometimes dead, and sometimes dying," conceived the idea of a foundling hospital, a place where fallen women could have an alternative to killing or abandoning their infants.

Men, not women, have historically shown the most compassion for children. It was women chiefly who killed children, and not just illegitimate children. Few children used to survive infancy. Although women had always had the opportunity to observe infants and were presumably supplied with a maternal instinct to guide them, they had not learned how to take care of them. It is estimated that in the mid-eighteenth century 74.5 percent of all children died before they were five years old. They had always died in such great numbers and disease was not the chief killer; it was maternal ignorance and neglect. The "maternal instinct" had taught women to feed newborn infants such foods as butter, black cherry water and roast pig. They then dipped the babies in cold water and wound them tightly in swaddling bands, which were not changed more than once a day (if that often), for it was believed that changing and washing babies "robbed them of their nourishing juices." Restless babies were fed opium and alcohol. The use of opiates to quiet infants can be dated as far back as ancient Egypt and continued to be used throughout the nineteenth century. In Hogarth's *March To Finchley* we see infants sucking on gin bottles. The use of gin or other alcohol to calm infants was so common in England that when Coram's Foundling Hospital was finally established, the Board of Governors wrote to the College of Physicians to ask them if the infants in the hospital should be given alcohol as a pacifier.

Nor did the maternal instinct incline women to breast feed their babies. In Greek and Roman times among the upper classes, it was not fashionable to suckle one's own children; slaves were wet nurses. But it wasn't only the rich who were reluctant. It is estimated that in the eighteenth century in England only 3 percent of children in towns were nursed by their own mothers; poor mothers regularly hired wet nurses because they were obliged to work. And to put a baby out to nurse, which generally meant sending the baby to a woman in the country, was virtually to sentence it to death, for these baby farms, as they were called, were notorious for neglecting babies to death.

It must be said in exoneration of these mothers and nurses that the love of children as we now understand it developed late in civilized societies. There was no special interest in methods of child rearing. Childhood was despised as a period of inferiority and deficiency, and children were forced into adult roles as rapidly as possible. It was quite common for them to begin their work lives at the age of three; and the law treated them pretty much like adults: in 1831 a nine-year-old boy was hanged for setting fire to a house. Concern for the child's welfare, interest in understanding childhood as a unique and admirable period of life, in short the modern love of children, did not begin to flourish until the mid-eighteenth century.

Baby Doctors

Again, of course, it was not women who began to show an increased concern for children. Our cultural maternal instinct was manifest first in men. Dr. William Cadogan in 1748 wrote a pamphlet on the *Nursing and Management of Children from their Birth to Three Years of Age*—a pamphlet which, because it was based on the "observation and experience" of a man, began to rescue children from woman's maternal instinct. Dr. Cadogan was largely responsible for freeing infants from swaddling clothes, for letting them be washed and not fed pork at birth. His pamphlet became the bible of the Foundling Hospital, the nurses there being required to follow his recommendations. This 18th-century "Dr. Spock" went through ten editions and was used by mothers and physicians.

In that and the next century men continued their efforts to supply women with a maternal instinct. Physicians like Cadogan established pediatrics as a special branch of medicine, thus teaching women how to take better physical care of their children. Because of male philosophers and child psychologists women today know what they do about child rearing. In 1690 Locke wrote a book about education advising parents to play their children into learning; Rousseau urged mothers to breast feed their children and to let them run about freely; learned men such as Thomas Reid and Joseph Priestley had a heated controversy (based on the careful observation of both) over whether sucking was instinctive or learned; Richard Edgeworth devoted most of his life to supervising the education of his children (he had 22) in order to try to understand how the minds of children operate; while Bronson Alcott (the father of Louisa May Alcott) in the 1830s devoted several years to observing the minutiae in the daily lives of his children and making voluminous notes. It was because of these early child psychologists and their followers G. Stanley Hall, Freud,

Piaget, Gesell—all of whom studied children intensively—that women take better care of their children. Today, the new mother acquires a maternal instinct by buying a copy of the chief repository of the maternal instinct in the twentieth century—Dr. Spock. And even before she has the baby, the mother-to-be learns how to give birth, naturally, from men—Drs. Grantly Dick Read and Fernand Lamaze.

If there is a maternal instinct, history reveals that it is men who have it, not women. For who were feeding their children roast pig at birth? Who were refusing to breast feed their children? Who doped infants with opium and gin? Who tossed illegitimate babies into sewers? Whose ignorance and neglect saw to it that most babies died? Who whenever possible hired servants to take their children off their hands? Who in the early years of this century were agitating for birth control? Who at the present time are clamoring for free abortions and child-care centers? Women.

And who so longed to be a procreator that he recorded in the Bible that he was the first mother? Who described God the Father as suckling his children? Who decreed that children were his and only his by sealing all of them with his own name? Who declared illegal all 'fatherless' children? Who refused to let women be anything but machines for producing men's babies and who studied the medical problems of babies so that most of them could live? Who therefore are responsible for the present overpopulation of the world? Who were so certain of their maternity that our knowledge of procreation was retarded for centuries? And who studied the psychology of infancy and childhood so that whatever society knows about children is due to them? Men.

If there is a maternal instinct, an innate drive to have children and to concern oneself with them, obviously men have it. It may be that the male maternal instinct is so potent because as the biologist Earl W. Count has said, "'parental solicitude' primitively is a male function rather than a female." When parental care began, it was the male sex that was in our sense of the word the mother. Among lampreys, a primitive fish, it is the male who builds the nest and prepares for the babies. In a higher order of primitive fish, the stickleback, the male is fully the mother. As N. Tinbergen's close observations have shown, it is the male stickleback who builds a nest, then changes color from gray to red to attract a female and, having lured her into his nest and helped her lay her eggs, dismisses her. She, like the human male, has done her job and is no longer necessary. The male stickleback then completely takes over: he fertilizes the eggs, guards the nest from predators, sees to it that the eggs get a daily supply of oxygen and watches over the babies when they emerge until they are old enough to be on their own. Again, among the most primitive order of birds, it is the male who tends the young and even incubates the eggs.

Men will object that they are not primitive fish or birds, and they object rightly. For when fertilization became internal, that is, when the female's body became the nest, parental solicitude passed to the female, and a built-in coded tape that programs child rearing does exist in lower forms of female animal life. But recent studies have shown that is not innate in female primates. According to George Schaller, zoo apes who have never seen another female handling an infant ignore their own newborn babies or are afraid of them. Similarly, Harry Harlow's studies of monkeys reveal that monkeys brought up without a mother want nothing to do with their own babies; they refuse to look at them; they flick the baby off their back as if it were a bothersome fly. Even when monkeys grow up in monkey society, that is, observing mothers tending children, experience is important: female langurs take much better care of their second child than they do of their first.

Yet though it is now conceded that female primates do not innately know how to take care of their infants, it is still believed that female human beings do have such instinctive knowledge. His compendium of instructions notwithstanding, Dr. Spock's first piece of advice to mothers is to trust their instincts: what they instinctively feel like doing for their babies, he says, is usually best. Nor are girls required to take courses in child care in high school; most men and women think that merely by virtue of being female a woman will know how to take care of a baby. Furthermore, there is a widespread belief that a woman's most fundamental drive is biological, that she is programmed by nature to want, more than anything else in her life, babies and nurturance.

It is interesting that those who at present speak most categorically about women's maternal drive are men whose own lives have been dominated by children. For example, Bruno Bettelheim, who has spent more than half his life working with children and who wrote a book *Symbolic Wounds* about the primitive male's unconscious longing to have babies, insists that "as much as women want to be good scientists or engineers, they want first and foremost to be womanly companions of men and to be mothers." Erik Erikson believes that a woman's "somatic design," her "inner space," makes the fulfillment of children a biological and psychological necessity of her nature; yet he himself, though he lacks an "inner space," filled many years of his life studying children. Dr. Spock himself, who, like the Madonna, is forever associated in our minds with a child, believes that "biologically and temperamentally . . . women were made to be concerned first and foremost with child care." Is Dr. Spock really a woman?

Why is it that these intelligent men insist that women have a maternal drive and cannot see it in themselves? Why is it that, all scientific evidence to the contrary, women are still believed to have a maternal instinct? One reason is that in regard to women, men are conservative traditionalists who cling to old ways of thinking. Bettelheim, Erikson and Spock are no different from the nineteenth-century writer in the *Westminster Review* who said that "the maternal instinct is, with the average woman, the ruling instinct of her whole nature;" or from Robert Browning, who said that "womanliness means only motherhood;" or from Jean Paul, who remarked that "nature sent women into the world that they might be mothers and love children." And modern men are saying what medieval theologians used to imply when they debated such questions as: "Is not woman a higher type of animal put on earth like other animals for man's use?" Men seem to have always reduced woman to an animal, defining her by the purely biological function of reproduction.

One Flesh

Man has always looked at woman as a womb, but originally he did so in envy. He felt himself inferior, incomplete because he lacked the animal function of reproduction, and he tried to complete himself by amalgamating woman. The story is told in chapter 2 of Genesis, in which man reveals not only that his desire to give birth was so great that to do so he was willing to sacrifice a rib (penis?) but that what he wished to give birth to was not a son but a woman. Woman, says the Bible, means "taken out of Man." The woman that was taken out of Adam was the womb primitive man felt deprived of. Adam had womb envy. At any rate, as soon as woman is taken out of Adam, he proceeds to put her back in again by making her bone of his bone, flesh of his flesh. It is man, Genesis says, who must leave his father and mother and cleave unto his wife so they become one flesh. "Cleave" means both to split asunder and to adhere. Adam attaches to himself what he felt was sundered from him. In chapter 2 of Genesis, Adam feels inferior; he needs help, a mate to complete himself. To complete himself, Adam becomes womanized, just as in some primitive tribes boys are called "incomplete beings" until after the initiation ceremonies which symbolically feminize them. In other early religions we see the same desire of man to complete himself by becoming one with women. In the Eleusinian

mysteries, the male initiate is supposed to identify himself, become one with Demeter, the goddess of fertility. The purpose of Taoism was to teach the male to complete himself by assimilating the female principle. And according to the Midrashim (Jewish commentaries on the Scriptures), a man who is not married is "hardly a complete man"

In chapter 2 of Genesis we learned how man became complete by leaving his father and mother and cleaving to the woman (=womb) he felt was taken out of him. In chapter 3 we learn how man became complete by becoming head of household. He gained that dominant position by knowledge. For wasn't the apple woman eats knowledge of the male's role in procreation? Which was why it was a snake (the penis) that leads woman to that knowledge. When Adam assimilates that knowledge—eats the apple—Adam no longer feels he has to cleave to woman. Why should he? For isn't he the great creator of life? The husband, God now decrees, rules over the woman, and her desire must be the man's. Man used to try to complete himself by cleaving to woman; now man completes himself by making woman cleave to him. Or, as Blackstone graphically put it in his *Commentaries* (1765-69): at the time of marriage "the very being or legal existence of the woman is suspended . . . or at least is incorporated and consolidated into that of the husband."

Man's Womb

Feminists always bridle when they read this law of coverture in Blackstone, believing that it reveals the male's belief in the female's inferiority. But it also reveals the male's belief in his own inferiority, his feeling of incompletion until he has incorporated a woman. It is men who decided that upon marriage a being is created called Mrs. John Smith, who is not a man but a woman. If the woman loses her identity by acquiring a man's name, the man's name, his identity, is feminized. Mrs. John Smith is John Smith, woman incorporated.

But man has not incorporated the whole woman. He has completed himself by taking from woman only those parts that he himself lacks—womb and breasts. It is significant that it is only when woman becomes subordinate to Adam that her name is changed to Eve, which the Bible says means "the mother of the living." Woman is allowed to become mother only when Adam becomes dominant, that is, when Adam becomes the head, woman becomes his reproductive and nutritive parts. A woman loses her identity upon marriage because she no longer is a complete being: she becomes a man's womb.

Ideal Servants

To make himself the one complete sex, that is, to make

woman his womb, man has virtually cut off woman's head and as much as possible crippled her limbs. Man in a sense has decapitated woman by not permitting her to develop her intellectual capacities, and man has so shackled woman physically that her strength has deteriorated. In primitive societies the difference in strength between the two sexes is much less marked than it is in civilized societies. But when woman became man's womb, what need did she have of great strength, or even of legs? As time passed, man increasingly curbed woman's strength by not allowing her to do heavy physical labor, discouraging young girls from participating in muscle-building sports, preferring to marry "delicate" women and literally hobbling women's legs by means of encumbering skirts or high heels or, most obviously in China, foot binding (which actually did so cripple women that they could not walk unassisted). By crippling woman's legs and physical strength, man was crippling woman's aggression, which he of course also accomplished by not letting her use her head. All a woman was allowed to develop was her womb and breasts; she could produce only babies, and she could do only those physical tasks associated with babies and homemaking.

It is because man is the head, woman his lower parts, that man insists that woman keep her place, never leave the humble sphere she has been put in. That is why the ideal womanly virtues have always been those proper to a subordinate ("subordinate," by the way, literally means to order under): obedience, modesty, patience, submissiveness, compliance, passivity, silence, gentleness, selflessness, conformity, timidity, deference, willingness to do humble tasks, eagerness to please. For men the good woman has all the attributes of the good servant. And woman is the ideal servant because she can't quit.

Having been reduced to a womb and breasts, woman has become dependent upon man. All she can do is stay in a man's home and have his babies. (And, as we have seen, she isn't legally allowed to have babies unless she has so established her dependency.) "Depend" etymologically means to hang from, be attached to. Man by forcing woman to depend upon him turned her into a leech, a parasite. He did so out of his need to feel that he was the one complete sex. Nevertheless, he refuses to be conscious of what he has done, that it was his own sense of deprivation at not having a womb that made him reduce woman to her reproductive parts and thus force her to be dependent upon a man for her existence. Woman is a parasite because of man's desire for a womb.

Letting Go

Man has been able to be unconscious of his womb envy

because he has created a society whose customs and laws incorporate it. The male maternal instinct is not innate; it is built into the culture, the product of man's original and perennial womb envy. For each generation repeats the psychic history of the race: boys and girls continue to be born ignorant of the facts of reproduction and have to learn how mama has a baby and that the male sex, all obvious evidence to the contrary, does play a role in reproduction. The little boy has a natural and conscious womb envy which, however, the culture demands that he repress; yet the boy grows up in a society that has customs and laws that allow him to express his womb envy. Boys are taught that women are inferior incomplete beings created to serve as a man's womb, marriage being the magic ceremony that attaches a "womban" to a man, or to use legal terminology, husband and wife are one and that one is the husband. The children of that union are all named after the man, as if he were the only parent. Thus, merely by being conventional, by obeying the customs and laws of society, men can, without being conscious of it, act out their womb envy. In our male dominant society, man-made customs and legal fictions make men "the mother of us all."

Male womb envy runs like a fault beneath our culture. Often where it seems least apparent it is closest to the surface, for example, in the traditional male reluctance to participate in the physical care of children and the guiltless ease with which many fathers abandon their children. But if men were to tend babies their womb envy would be in danger of becoming conscious. Men therefore do what others consumed with envy do—disparage what they envy, classify child-rearing as lowly woman's work beneath the august capacities of men. For modern man, like his primitive forebears, continues to think of himself as the "spiritual" father of the race. Male machismo means the ability to make a woman pregnant and thus prove a man's potency, his life-creating powers, woman's role merely being to give embodiment to male life and to perform the physical labor subsidiary to the male's initial creative act. In our culture, when men do let themselves be interested in babies, their interest is scientific, abstract: they observe babies in laboratories; they do not change diapers.

Men will continue to be afraid of taking care of children so long as they are dominated by womb envy, that is, so long as their womb envy remains unconscious. For our unconscious drives dominate us until knowledge frees us of their grip. Unconscious male womb envy, the male maternal instinct, has not only deprived men and children of fatherly care, it has distorted society's general concept of love. The reduction of female human beings to wombs has made mature love between the sexes almost impossible. Man, having identified woman with womb, regards loving a woman as a return to the womb, as dependence, clinging, the bliss of uterine life, for which reason he is afraid of love, regards it as unmanly, a weakness, and compensates by taking a woman aggressively. Only thus can he simultaneously possess and escape from the womb, rape being the base expression of male sexual psychology. Yet even ideal love in our male culture is an affair of the womb, being most often described as mutual need, completion through another, symbiotic parasitism, not the free companionship of two equal independent beings.

The womb pattern not only has had a harmful effect on man's love life, it may also have damaged his creative life. For man can't seem to stop thinking of physical creation as the norm of creation. He is forever describing his mental creations in terms of birth. Socrates compared his method of teaching to that of a midwife; Francis Bacon equated the "images" of men's minds with those of their bodies; male writers like to call their books their children and when they finish one complain that they are suffering from postpartum depression; the terminology of astronauts is full of words like abort, umbilical. Implicit in such comparisons is man's unconscious feeling that physical procreation is superior to mental creation. Men are like blacks trying to prove they are as good as whites. But more important, it may well be that the male tendency to think of creation in terms of procreation has cut him off from other unimagined forms of creativity not modelled on physical birth. At any rate, we do know that man's unconscious maternity has in some ways crippled him mentally. It was because embryologists were so sure that the male was the real creator of life that they could not see what was in front of their eyes, misinterpreted what they did see and for centuries were incapable of asking the right questions. It was because Freud had to keep repressed the woman within him that he overstressed penis envy and thus failed in many ways to understand much of male as well as female psychology.

If Homo sapiens is ever to use his full mental and emotional power, man must free himself of his womb envy, which means that he must finally give birth to woman. He must let her go, let her exist in her own right as an independent being. Only when woman is no longer encapsulated in man will man be able to stop confusing mental creation with procreation, love with womblike dependence; only then will man no longer have to project the so-called tender attributes onto woman and be able to absorb them into his bloodstream and become whole again. And only then will woman regain the use of her head and limbs, of her mental and aggressive powers, and herself become a whole human being. ■

3. middle and old age in the family life cycle

Most of the young people whom we have followed in this book through the socialization, mating and procreation phases of the family life cycle eventually find that their life has settled down. Although small crises still occur, major ones are often avoided with the help of simple experience, modern medicine and growing economic means. The husband has increasingly turned his attention to his work and his hopes of fulfilling the American dream of success, unless he sees no future in it or is distracted by competing roles. The money he brings home from his job is converted into objects, purchased outside the home but made usable for its individualistic needs by the housewife's contribution in the last stages of the production process. These material goods facilitate various degrees of "the good life" and the insurance of a "nice funeral," even a better life for the next generation.

Despite many indications that some Americans are questioning economic values, money must not be ignored as an important component of the life style of families in the 1970s. In a word, we call it consumption. In fact, for many Americans the job itself is so unrewarding that the money and its use after working hours are the *only* incentives for continuing one's work role. The years since World War II have brought many incomes, in the present and in the mortgaged future, to such a level as to guarantee a car, a private house, and mechanical means of maintaining the household such as washing machines, refrigeration and television as well as other objects for recreation. Both car and house provide not only comfort but externally visible signs of success, reassurance that one is living the good life and some kind of guarantee for the way one's children will grow up. Ever since the post-World War II housing boom, moving to the fringes of the city, particularly to the suburbs, has been the aim of most families. The justification for such a move is that it is "good for the children," but there are many other benefits for adults, who gain community feeling and the security of a relatively homogeneous neighborhood, easing the strain of upward mobility. The new suburbs are particularly helpful in solving some of the social isolation and loneliness problems of young households. There is, of course, a growing proportion of urbanites, at all stages of the life cycle, who are truly cosmopolitan, enjoying the heterogeneity and stimulation of urban centers and refusing to limit their and their children's contact to people similar in occupation, income, color, ethnic identity and other characteristics currently considered a source of security. They may be the trend of the future, but they do not comprise significant numbers today.

At this time, however, rising costs of private housing, together with the desire of Americans to leave time for leisure instead of being tied to a constant round of home maintenance, have produced new experiments in housing units, including mushrooming condominiums with grass cutting, snow shoveling and similar services. The number of isolated privacy-demanding households, then, may decrease in the 1970s, as reflected by builders' advertisements guaranteeing freedom from loneliness and a round of fun activities on the new "community" grounds.

The fact that people at different ages have different housing needs is reflected by the clustered age distribution in metropolitan areas. The centers of our cities have been inhabited, since the war, by the old, the post-parental couples, the young marrieds, the singles, and the middle-aged who are insufficiently successful to move because of poverty and/or discrimination. In some cases housing units are small, housing costs limited and public transportation is available to those without a car. In other cases, as in "gold coast" buildings, single people mix with older but prosperous former suburbanites who want the conveniences of city life. Recent years have seen a partial reversal of housing patterns, as urban renewal efforts clear large tracts near the center of the city of their slum-like housing and replace them with expensive high rises.

With the exception of high-rise or private-dwelling communities devoted to the pre- or post-retirees, however, the average age of residents in most suburbs is low, because of the presence of young parents and young children. Whole towns are organized around these segments of the American population. Schools, playgrounds, shopping centers with large parking lots abound. Often there are few activities for the older teen-agers, as they are assumed to be busy with high school affairs or away at college. Suburbia is usually symbolized in terms of family life, with barbecues, neighboring, gardening and couple-companionate recreation. On Friday, and particularly on Saturday evenings, few couples above the lower class stay home alone; they entertain, visit or go to public places with other couples. Finding a baby-sitter is a major problem, sometimes solved by cooperative exchanges.

This pattern is so prevalent that the person who becomes divorced or widowed is completely out of place in most suburbs. Women find that they are no longer invited to join their couple-companionate friends of the past, so that they must either become isolated or make new friends with people of similar marital status. Even then, they may remain lonely for their former round of activities. The death or absence of a husband for any reason is particularly troublesome for the middle-class or upper-class woman, because so much of her identity and life lay in her marriage. The husband was someone toward whom she felt strong sentiments: he was a contributor in many activities, a partner in many roles, not only as parent but as couple-companionate friend, church co-member and so forth. He was someone who felt and expressed many sentiments toward his wife, in many kinds of interactions, making her an important person. In both middle-class and lower-class homes, a wife misses her husband because his presence organized time and work and because it prevented the house from being empty. He was also the "other half" in the division of labor. In divorce, the problems, including anger, guilt, shame—the whole unpleasant aftermath of the process of breaking up a marriage—are faced in different ways by the man and the woman. Widowhood is statistically more apt to happen to women, and the few men whose wives die before them face less social rejection and often remarry quickly.

Although widowhood is sometimes easier for women residing in urban centers, because of the heterogeneity of the population and the resources provided by larger communities, the age at which it occurs varies the experience. Women whose husbands die while most of their friends are still married report greater problems and frustrations than those widowed later. Part of this is due to the difficulties of converting a multidimensional social involvement which included the husband into a completely different life style, and part is due to rejection by prior associates. How a widow or divorced woman rebuilds her life depends on such factors as her age; the ages of her children; support systems of the society, such as governmental financial assistance or professional consultation and/or kin contributions; the availability of alternative roles such as a job; dating and remarriage opportunities; characteristics such as income, health, education and skills developed over a lifetime; her degree of dependence upon her former husband and her consequent ability to initiate action; location in the community in terms of involvement in its life; ease of transportation and communication and so forth.

Many women in the rapidly urbanizing and changing communities are so limited in their resources as to end up living very restricted lives, with a minimum of social engagement. They do not have the skills necessary for locating, entering and keeping a job. The family of orientation becomes dispersed. Old friends move away, and they discover that they lack the resources and the self-confidence to build new relations or enter new social roles.

The tragic fact about social isolation wherever there is no automatically immersing social group is that people cannot be healthy without primary relations, as Robert Weiss conceptualizes in "The Fund of Sociability." People need many different kinds of relations and these take time to build. No one can really replace a dead spouse, former work associates, the old friend who moved away, or small children in the home after they are grown. On the other hand, many people—and hopefully the proportion is growing, as people become better educated and urbanized into sequences of relations building skills—*are* able to rebuild social engagement after changes disrupting past patterns. They reenlist the qualities of interaction, reformulating and repackaging intimacy, social integration, the opportunity for nurturant behavior, reassurance of work and assistance through services into new support systems.

Even married Americans who do not experience widowhood or undertake desertion, separation or divorce may modify their relations with each other and with the rest of the world. Some, though at present a small minority, engage in what Charles and Rebecca Palson call "Swinging in Wedlock." The term "swinging" has gained popularity in recent years, but the behavior is so new that few researchers have yet studied it. Exchanging marital partners for sexual encounters, whether for one night or for repeated contacts, is an unusual variation on the traditional custom of having an "affair." As Morton Hunt pointed out in *The Affair* (1968), sexual outlets outside of marriage have a history as old as recorded life. Prostitution, the promiscuous offer of sexual privileges for a fee or material benefits, involves a complicated social circle and a definite location, be it a house managed by a "madame" and containing other prostitutes or a private apartment as in the case of streetwalkers or call girls, as well as some means of contacting potential clients. In societies in which prostitution is illegal, it requires the cooperation of police, public officials, landlords and medical personnel. Affairs have other requirements. They may involve an economic exchange whereby one partner, traditionally but not necessarily the male, supports the other, paying rent and/or other expenses. A woman is usually a mistress to only one man at a time. The partners are expected to feel a certain level of emotional attachment for each other and to interact in more than sexual exchanges. Recent freedom in sexual behavior given to or obtained by women has affected not only marriages but extramarital relations. There appears to be an increase in the number of affairs which lack an economic base, with neither partner supporting the other or with costs being shared equally.

"Swinging" has a different character in that husband and wife are aware of each other's sexual behavior and agree on partners. The Palsons believe that the basic love arrangement between a husband and wife who participate in swinging is positively affected, or at least that it is less damaged than by other forms of extramarital sexual encounters, but there is as yet insufficient research to document this conclusion.

Whatever the changes occurring in women's lives today due to education and increased egalitarianism, the tradition of "the double standard" still hangs on, according to Inge Powell Bell, who here analyzes its various forms and consequences. The middle years, she states, are the ones in which the burden of restricted choice of action is particularly heavy. No longer needed by small children, the housewife in a household containing a work-oriented husband and older children busy with their own affairs, or the housewife experiencing the first phase of the "shrinking circle" stage when the children have already started their own households, often feels functionless at a time when her energy and desire for engagement are high. As we noted in the Prologue, the average woman at age 46 has no children to care for, leaving her fifteen years with only her husband in the house and another fifteen or sixteen years in the second phase of the "shrinking circle," when she is alone. Psychologist Bernice Neugarten has undertaken several studies which indicate that women's supposed menopausal depression in the latter middle years is more a result of this functionless position than of any biological factors. Pauline Bart's essay, "Portnoy's Mother's Complaint," supports this view.

As the years go by, women solve the problems of the shrinking circle within the home in a variety of ways. In fact, the greatest range of life styles among American women begins to appear at the stages following confinement with small children. Full-time homemaking, participation in leisure-focused voluntary associations, charitable work, entrance into or increased attention to a job or career, involvement in the husband's activities, active engagement in the role of grandmother while the mother is engaged elsewhere and travel are some of the alternatives for women who still have time and energy for a choice and who are no longer constricted by the traditionally primary role of mother.

The husband's life, too, can develop along several alternative lines. Many men realize in middle years that they will not or do not want to continue trying to reach the heights of success they chose as goals twenty years earlier. Others have accomplished what they want and can rest on their laurels, while a third group continues to climb. Some become routinized, losing sight of the goal but continuing the ritual originally designed to move them toward one. Others turn their attention back to marriage and the family, while an increasing number start a new love relationship. The divorce rate among the middle aged has increased in recent years, either because marriage was found empty or because a "nice young thing" came along. The wives left behind in these situations are at a disadvantage, because men can marry down in age while women generally cannot, and also because there are fewer and fewer men each year, due to the disproportionately early male death rate.

The aging couple still in their first marriage, the remaining spouse, or the older remarrieds, begin to feel, and to see reflected in others, that old age is closing in. How it affects them depends on a variety of factors. The process is gradual and is highly influenced, particularly in urbanizing, industrializing and rapidly changing societies, by social definitions. As Irving Rosow explains in "And Then We Were Old," there is a marked loss of status upon retirement for men, due to the high stress on the economic institution and location within it. Unemployment and retirement are especially hard for people who have absorbed a marketing mentality; these events are "proof" that society no longer finds them worth anything in that it refuses to pay them for the use of their talents. Even being a sage is no longer possible in a culture which changes so rapidly and is so youth oriented.

Social scientists, observing aging people in American society during the 1950s, concluded that there is a natural process of voluntary withdrawal of the older person and of the society from each other until the final separation in death. The theory of social disengagement even became a popular justification for ignoring the elderly on the part of social agencies, community builders and even families. Simultaneously there has grown a realization that many of the problems of social withdrawal by the elderly may be not so much the result of age as of other characteristics of these historical generations (there is, after all more than one generation within the group lumped together as the elderly). The elderly tend to be people who have had little formal education and have experienced great and repeated life disorganization through migration to and within cities, and from the rate of social change around them. The combination of urban residence with village skills has contributed to their social isolation, each blow to the past life fabric and each new problem of adjustment reducing the social life space.

The successful alternative life styles of people beyond middle-age are evidence of developed flexibility. People who have had a relatively easy career, due to advantages of better health, education, finances and the whole package labeled "life chances" are able to turn the stage of "empty nest" or "shrinking circle" into a new life style. The success

of Leisure World, Sun City, Youngstown and other organized communities of the elderly in St. Petersburg, Pasadena and elsewhere are evidence that, given the resources and self-confidence, many people can build new sets of relations. Irving Rosow (1967) found that, even in the Middle West, a high density of people in similar life circumstances increases the "social integration of the aged," and new research indicates that people approaching old age from a better positioned middle age are increasingly aware of the fact that there is no necessity to restrict their social engagement just because of approaching years.

But regardless of how the life cycle is spent, whether in full enjoyment of both stable and changing social relations and activity, or in a fearful and a restricted social life space based on fear of change and a wish for the "good old days," there comes a time for death. The reality of facing death—the death of one's self and of significant others—is a major problem of aging. As Elizabeth Markson explains in "A Hiding Place to Die," and as many researchers who are finally studying the whole process of dying after years of scientific neglect find, people are less and less likely today to die at home. Like birth, death has been removed from the normal flow of life. We have prolonged the span of living through medicine, and now we push death out of the home, pretending it does not exist or that it will not affect us. This attitude toward dying has made the subject so taboo that Geoffrey Gorer (1965) refers to "the pornography of death." Hospitals make it as unobtrusive as possible. Medical personnel often avoid a terminal case, and families pretend not to know how ill a relative is—so that the patient has no one with whom he or she can work out his own grief over having to leave the world and its significant others. Also, modern culture does not allow the survivors sufficient time and opportunity to do "grief work," as Eric Lindemann calls the process by which the sentiments and memories of the past are worked out and new relations made possible. The bereaved need to talk, to cry, to sanctify the deceased, to explain how they themselves are now suffering and to broach experimentally the subject of the future.

While the life of one person is ending, the next generation, or even a third one, is being socialized to repeat the cycle, with changes. The children of the elderly are now functioning as adults—watching with trepidation whether their offspring will "turn out all right," select the right mate (or at least one who does not negate all parental values), and fulfill the dreams of success held by parents who have invested so much of their own egos and sentiments in them. New family units are formed and dissolved, increasingly experimental and increasingly analytical of family roles and relations.

The Fund of Sociability

Robert S. Weiss

Why do people require relationships with one another? What needs are being expressed? We recognize constantly, sometimes with surprise, how important relationships are to us. Newly divorced individuals are distressed by loneliness, even as they congratulate themselves on having ended a conflict-laden marriage. Individuals who work alone, such as writers, complain of isolation, even as they prize their autonomy. Travelers on shipboard, separated from their network of friends, may find themselves greeting with enthusiasm an acquaintance from their home town who, in other circumstances, they might have barely acknowledged. In all these ways social needs express themselves. What can be their nature?

In trying to find answers to this question, people have generally taken two lines of argument. One, associated with some schools of sociology, has been to assert that relationships which are close, so close they may be called primary, provide the individual with his understandings of reality, his moral values, his goals, even his sense of self. Relationships are important because through them the society organizes the individual's thinking and acting. Essentially, the society teaches its members what they want.

The second view, associated more with psychology than with sociology, has been that people have a number of needs or requirements which only relationships can satisfy, and that without appropriate relationships the individual will suffer. These needs are intrinsic to the individual, and are not formed by the society in which he lives. They may include needs for recognition, for affection, for power, for prestige, for belonging, and many more.

How can we move from these fairly general theoretical positions to a testable formulation of why people require relationships? Perhaps the simplest hypothesis we can phrase, one which would seem to be an implication of the first view but not of the second, is that of the "fund of sociability." According to this idea individuals require a certain amount of interaction with others, which they may find in various ways. They may with equal satisfaction have a few intense relationships or have a large number of relationships of lesser intensity. They would experience stress only if the total amount of relating to others was too little or too great.

The "fund of sociability" idea seemed to us to be a useful starting point in our effort to learn more regarding the assumptions, content, and functions of social ties. The research strategy that seemed to us a promising way to test this hypothesis was to seek out a group of individuals, all of whom had lost an important relationship but who also had the opportunity for unlimited sociability. It might then be seen whether increased sociability in some way compensated for the loss of the relationship.

For about a year, a colleague and I attended meetings of the Boston chapter of Parents Without Partners, a national organization of people who have children but who are living alone because of separation, divorce, or the death of their spouse. By listening to discussions of their past and current problems, and also from interviews with a good many members and former members, we hoped to be able to specify the nature of the losses sustained by these men and women with the end of their marriages, and the way in which membership in Parents Without Partners was useful to them.

We found that most members had joined simply because they were lonely, although there may well have been other reasons, including concern for their children or the desire to help others. The loneliness resulted directly from the absence of the marital relationship, rather than from such secondary factors as change in social role.

According to the "fund of sociability" hypothesis, we should expect to find members reporting that they had been lonely and restless after the dissolution of the marriage, but that interaction with others in Parents Without Partners had made up some part of that loss. We found, however, that although Parents Without Partners offered its members help with a host of difficulties, the sociability of belonging did not particularly diminish the sense of loneliness. Dating helped a good deal, but friendship did not. Although many members, particularly among the women, specifically mentioned friendship as the main contribution they received from Parents Without Partners, and these friendships sometimes became very close and very important to the participants, they did not compensate for the loss of the marriage. Friends and activities (discussion groups were perhaps the best) made the loneliness easier to manage, but they did not end it or even appreciably dimish it. One woman said, "Sometimes I have the girls over, and we talk about how hard it is. Misery loves company, you know."

Simple Sociability Not Satisfactory

Clearly the social needs satisfied in marriage, and, apparently, in dating, were not satisfied by simple sociability, no matter how much of it there was. But this raised the question of whether friendship was simply inadequate to supply the kind of interaction required, or whether friendship supplied something quite different, something that might not be found in marriage.

It seemed to us that friendship did offer something distinct from what marriage provides. But how to test this? We needed to find people who were married, but without friends. If friendships met social needs distinct from those met by marriage, then people without friends should be in distress, even though married. However, if friendship provided only a kind of time-filling sociability, then married people without friends should get along almost as well as married people with friends.

We began with a pilot study of six couples who had moved to the Boston suburbs from at least two states away. Our respondents were all middle-class and they had moved to Boston because of the husband's job.

Soon after the move, all but two of the wives were seriously unhappy; they were feeling a sense of social isolation similar in intensity (albeit shorter in duration) to the sense of emotional isolation that seemed to follow the dissolution of a marriage in others. The problem appeared to be that the housebound wife had no one with whom she could share the concerns of her daily life. Husbands could not really discuss with interest the dilemmas of child care nor the burdens of housework, and though they sometimes tried, they simply could not function properly as a friend. They might even compound the difficulty by saying they couldn't understand what was happening to their wives, and sometimes be downright unsympathetic because of what they felt were their own more serious problems of proving themselves on the new job. They were not troubled by the lack of people with whom they could share common interests, because at work they found men to talk to about the things that concerned them; the job, politics, sports, the local driving patterns, and the like. Two of the men with whom we worked listed for us the people they talked with during the day, and the number was impressive.

Meanwhile, the newcomer wives were likely to become painfully bored. In the absence of anyone with whom they could share their interests, they found housework and child care increasingly unrewarding. One wife who had been socially active and had considered herself reasonably happy in her former home began to drink heavily. Another wanted her husband to give up the promotion that had brought him to the Boston area, and to return to her parents' home town.

Of the two wives who did not seem to suffer from newcomer blues, the first was a woman who had no children and who immediately solved the problem of social isolation by going to work. The other was married to a man who in a previous move had bought a house in an old and settled neighborhood where friendships were well-established. To escape social isolation, she began taking night-school classes, and as her husband said when he talked with us, he hardly saw her except when they passed each other in the driveway. This time the husband moved into a new development where other homes were also owned by newcomers to the region, and spent his first weekend making friends with the new neighbors.

It now appeared clear to us that just as friendships do not provide the functions ordinarily provided by marriage, neither does marriage provide the functions ordinarily provided by friendship. Our current work on the nature of marriage suggests that marriages may vary in this, but nevertheless we believe that even in the most companionate of marriages, some important interests will not be shared within the marriage, and for women in the social group of the newcomer sample and even to a greater degree among poorer women the concerns of managing a family are not shared with the husband.

At this point, the hypothesis of a "fund of sociability" could be confidently rejected. It was clear that there were different kinds of relationships, providing different functions. The question then arose, how many relationships seemed to be necessary, and what functions did they seem to provide?

On the basis of further work with Parents Without Partners, we have been led to develop a theory that might be characterized as "the functional specificity of relationships." We believe that individuals have needs which can only be met within relationships, that relationships tend to become relatively specialized in the needs for which they provide, and as a result individuals require a number of different relationships for well-being.

Although there are many variations in the way people organize their lives, one can in general say that relations with kin seem to be reliable as sources of help, but not as sources of companionship; friends offer companionship, but not intimacy; and marriage or a near-marital relationship offers intimacy, but rarely friendship. We are not sure why this specialization develops. Undoubtedly, much has to do with underlying cultural definitions of the relationship. If wholehearted commitment between friends is difficult—and this seems the case in adult American life—then it will be possible for friends to share interests, but extremely difficult for them to develop the level of trust which would permit emotional intimacy.

The marriage relationship may be an exception to the generalization that relationships are specialized in function. In marriage each spouse provides for the other a degree of emotional integration, and also provides collaboration in managing the mechanics of life. But even here there may be conflicts between the way of relating to one another that is associated with the one function, and that associated with the other. In terms of the collaborative relationship, for example, it may be reasonable for a wife to criticize her husband's capacity to earn, but since she is also a source of emotional integration, her criticism can be devastating.

The specialization of relationship is probably always incomplete. Undoubtedly every friendship involves some emotional exchange and has the potential for more. Yet going beyond the understood assumptions of the relationship can endanger it. When it happens, for example, that one partner in a friendship seeks to move the relationship to one in which there is an assumption of unbounded trust, the more usual assumptions of the friendship may be temporarily flooded out. The consequence is likely to be uneasiness when the friends later find it necessary to return to the old basis. Generally there is so much resistance to changes of definition of a relationship that if a person loses the relationship that provided a particular function—as through the death of a spouse—he will be able only temporarily to alter his remaining relationships to fill the gap. Among members of Parents Without Partners, for example, we found a good deal of bitterness that stemmed from the failure of their friends to respond to their new relational needs.

Five Categories of Relationships

On the basis of our material we believe we can identify five categories of relational functions, each for the most part provided by a different relationship. All these functions seem to us to be necessary for well-being.

1) *Intimacy,* for want of a better term, is used to characterize the provision of an effective emotional integration in which individuals can express their feelings freely and without self-consciousness. It seems to us that this function of relationships prevents the individual from experiencing the sense of emotional isolation that is expressed in the term "loneliness." For a relationship to provide intimacy, there must be trust, effective understanding, and ready access. Marriage provides such a relationship and so, often, does dating, at least for a time. Occasionally a woman may establish a relationship of this kind with a close friend, her mother, or a sister. And under some circumstances a man may establish a relationship of this sort with a friend.

It may be noted, parenthetically, that the relationship between sexual involvement and emotional intimacy, when the individuals concerned are potentially appropriate sexual partners, is quite complex and may well vary by social group and by circumstance. Certainly sex and intimacy are not necessarily associated. Still, rather fragmentary evidence suggests that in the groups we have worked with, individuals who are potentially appropriate partners may find it difficult to maintain a non-sexual emotionally intimate relationship. Where individuals are not appropriate sexual partners there is no apparent difficulty in maintaining such a relationship.

2) *Social integration* is provided by relationships in which participants share concerns, either because of similar situations ("we are in the same boat") or because they are striving for similar objectives (as in relationships among colleagues). Such relationships allow a good deal of sharing of experience, information, and ideas. They provide the basis for exchange of favors, and sometimes for more substantial help (though not for help continued over time). Among women this function is usually provided by friendships; among men, by relations with colleagues, as well as by friendships. The absence of this relationship may be experienced as a sense of social isolation and will, we suspect, be accompanied by feelings of boredom.

3) *Opportunity for nurturant behavior* is provided by relationships in which the adult takes responsibility for the well-being of a child. Our impression, based on experience with Parents Without Partners, is that men seem able to act as foster fathers to children not their own, but that it is much more difficult for women to act as foster mothers. The conditions for the expression of nurturance—and the nature of nurturance—may be different in men and women. We suspect that absence of this function may be signaled by a sense that one's life is unfulfilled, meaningless, and empty of purpose.

4) *Reassurance of worth* is provided by relationships that attest to an individual's competence in some role. Colleague relationships, and the social support and mutual respect they imply, can do this for some men, particularly

those whose work is difficult or highly valued. Successful family life may function in this way for other men, competence or worth here depending not on particular skills, but on the ability to support and defend a family. Women who work may also find their employment a source of reassurance of worth. Women who do not work must look to relationships with husbands, children, and acquaintances for recognition of their competence in making and managing a home. The loss of any system from which recognition of work, value, or competence may be gained will, we believe, result in decreased self-esteem.

5) *Assistance* through the provision of services or the making available of resources, although a primary theme in kin relationships, may be provided by a number of other relationships as well, including friendships and relationships with neighbors. However it seems to be only among close kin that one may expect assistance that is not limited in time and extent. It is the importance of this function for the poor that leads to the development of relational patterns in which kin ties are of primary importance. We suspect that the absence of any relationship providing the assurance of assistance if needed would be reflected in a sense of anxiety and vulnerability.

In addition, there seems to be a sixth function which can be provided by relationships that some people find important. This function might be characterized as *guidance,* and may be provided by mental-health professionals such as social workers or psychiatrists, or by ministers and priests, among others.

Undoubtedly there are individual differences in capacity to withstand the absence of one or another of the functions without giving way to restlessness and to the development of such symptoms as loneliness and boredom. On the basis of accounts of individuals who have successfully weathered long periods of isolation, one might suspect that individuals who have more rigid character structures might be better able to forego the absence of some relational functions. One device that seems to have helped these men and women was to establish a detailed daily routine from which they did not deviate.

It is difficult at this point to say that any one of the relational functions is more important than another. The absence of intimacy can clearly be disorganizing for many individuals, and for most it would be accompanied by painful loneliness, but we are not able at this time to say that it is a more serious deficit than the absence of opportunity for nurturance. I have known childless couples to be as downcast by difficulties in adopting a baby as a lonely person might be by difficulties in finding love. It seems as though the absence of any relational function will create some form of dissatisfaction, accompanied by restlessness and occasional spells of acute distress.

This theory, like any theory of human nature, has implications for the way in which we might deal with individuals in difficult situations. We might consider two possible areas of application of these ideas: to the problem of relational loss, and to the problem of aging.

There are many forms of relational loss. There is the loss of friends that comes with moving from one area to another, the loss of colleagues that accompanies retirement, the loss of newly adult children from home, the loss of a spouse through death or divorce. Each of these losses would seem to have two aspects: first, the trauma that accompanies the damage to the individual's life organization; and, second, the deficit in the individual's life that is a result of the continuing absence of the functions once provided by the now-lost relationship. When individuals move from one area to another, the trauma aspect may be nothing more than sadness at leaving old friends and old associations, and not especially serious. The primary problem of relocation is that of deficit in the wife's relationships, the absence of new friends in the new situation. In conjugal bereavement, the loss by death of a spouse, the pain of loss is ordinarily very great and, for a good while, the trauma of the loss will be the primary source of distress. Yet even when this has been resolved, the life of the widow or widower is apt to continue to be unsatisfactory because of problems of relational deficit. It can be helpful to a widow or widower to recognize these two consequences of loss and to acknowledge that loneliness may be an unavoidable response to an unsatisfying situation rather than an inability to resolve the disruption of loss. Being able to identify what is wrong makes it easier to find remedies.

To turn to aging, the theory alerts us to the disturbances of social relationships that come with time. These include departure of children, retirement, possibly the loss of spouse, and, as a result of all the preceding, painful and sometimes bewildering reorientation of central life concerns.

When their children leave, the older couple may find a freedom they have not known for decades, but they also lose their opportunity for nurturance. They may continue to help their now-grown children, and they may be able periodically to indulge their grandchildren, but they probably will never again have the sense of being essential to someone else, which is at least one of the functions small children seem to provide for their parents.

Retirement Removes Important Basis for Self-Esteem

Retirement varies in its implications, but for many men, as Eugene A. Friedmann and Robert J. Havighurst have shown, it removes from their lives an important basis for self-esteem. The parallel, for a woman, would be the loss of a home to keep up. This too can occur in time, but usually at a considerably later point in a woman's life than retirement occurs in a man's. It must be said, though, that the loss of children from the home may constitute a partial retirement for women.

With bereavement, the aged person may have no access to intimacy, and despite remaining relationships with grown children, other relatives, and friends, may begin to experience chronic loneliness. The absence of an intimate tie, we suspect, makes it difficult for an individual to maintain an even emotional balance. Since his emotional responses are not communicated and responded to, they go unchecked, uncorrected by another's perceptions. The result may be distortions either in the direction of pathological distrust or in the direction of depression which are difficult to interrupt.

The aged will lose friends through death, including old friends with whom so much is shared that the relationships are irreplaceable. But they also may give up friends because the interests and concerns that were central to the friendship no longer have meaning for them. Losing her husband may change a woman's life so much that she may no longer have anything in common with her married friends. Retirement may make irrelevant a man's relationships with former colleagues. And at the same time these bases for former friendships are lost, the afflictions of age—sickness, limited income, dependence—may produce new central life concerns which can be shared by few others. The aged who become seriously ill, or crippled, or have a chronic condition that requires frequent medical care, cannot share with anyone their feelings about these physical problems, even though they may well find them the central concerns of their lives. Small wonder, then, if an aged person who is ill seeks out a doctor just to talk about his condition, even at the risk of being thought a hypochondriac.

The aged, therefore, are vulnerable to relational losses that bring in their wake feelings of loneliness, boredom, and worthlessness, and a sense that they are no longer of critical importance to anyone else. These feelings, taken together, have sometimes been characterized as a psychological syndrome that accompanies age. A simpler explanation is that these feelings are normal reactions to relational deficits, reactions that would be found in any group similarly afflicted.

This appraisal suggests that the social and emotional distresses that accompany age can be remedied, but only by relationships that supply the required functions. It gives us a guide to the sort of relationships that may help and the sort that probably will not. For the retired, activities that clearly benefit others, or display competence in an important or valued way, may substitute for employment; but a make-work task, a hobby, or just keeping busy will not.

The appraisal also suggests that relational losses can be repaired. Should loss take place, and this is almost inevitable with age, then the view taken here suggests that it would be better to advise such people that they attempt to establish new relationships that will provide the same functions, rather than "gracefully" accept constriction.

But this recommendation could be made universally. Beyond a certain point we cannot limit our relations with others without incurring serious loss. Just as it is bad advice to tell a widow to live for the children, or to tell someone who is aged to accept the inevitable losses, it is bad advice to tell a young person to forego intimacy for a time while he concentrates on his studies.

Swinging in Wedlock

Charles and Rebecca Palson

Since the later 1960s, an increasing number of middle-class couples have turned to mate swapping or "swinging" as an alternative to strictly monogamous marriage. That is, married couples (or unmarried couples with an apparently stable relationship) willingly and knowingly relinquish sexual rights to their own mates so that others may temporarily enjoy these rights. This phenomenon, which is fairly recent in its openness and proportions, provides an opportunity of testing, on a large scale, the traditional theories about the consequences of extramarital sexual activity. It has often been assumed that sexual infidelity, where all the concerned parties know of it, results to some

degree in jealousy. The intensity of jealousy is thought to increase in proportion to the amount of real or imagined emotional involvement on the part of the unfaithful member of the couple. Conversely, the more "purely physical" the infidelity, the less likely that there will be any jealousy. Thus it is often hypothesized that where marital stability coexists with infidelity, the character of the extramarital involvement is relatively depersonalized.

In the film *Bob and Carol and Ted and Alice*, Bob finds Carol, his wife, entertaining another man in their bedroom. Although he had previously told her that he was having an affair, and they had agreed in principle that she too could have affairs, he is obviously shaken by the reality. Nervously trying to reassure himself, he asks, "Well, it's just *sex*, isn't it? I mean, you don't *love* him?" In other words, Bob attempts to avoid feelings of jealousy by believing that Carol's affair involves only depersonalized sex in contrast to their own relationship of love.

In his book, *Group Sex*, Gilbert Bartell offers the same hypothesis about those people he calls "organization swingers:"

> They are terrified of the idea that involvement might take place. They take comfort from the fact that if they swing with a couple only once or at most twice, the chances of running into a marriage-threatening involvement are small.

These swingers, who can be described as organizational only in the sense that they tend to use swinger magazines or special swinging nightclubs to make their contacts, are mostly beginners who *may* act in ways that approximate Bartell's description. Near the end of the book, however, he mentions some couples he interviewed whom he calls dropouts. These people either had never desired depersonalized swinging or had passed through a depersonalized stage but now preferred some degree of emotional involvement and long-term friendship from their swinging relationships. Bartell does not explain how these couples continue to keep stable relationships and can remain free of jealousy, but the fact that such couples exist indicates that depersonalization is not the only way to jealousy-free swinging.

Our involvement with the subject has been partly a personal one, and this requires some introductory explanation. In September 1969, we read an article about swinging and became fascinated by the questions it raised about sex and the American family. Did this practice signal the beginning of the breakup of the family? Or was it a way to inject new life into marriage as the authors of the article suggested? How do people go about swinging and why? We contemplated these and many other questions but, not knowing any swingers, we could arrive at only very limited answers. It seemed to us that the only way to find out what we wanted to know was to participate ourselves. In one way this seemed natural because anthropologists have traditionally lived with the people they have studied. But our curiosity about swinging at that time was more personal than professional, and we knew that ultimately our participation would have personal consequences, although we had no idea what their nature might be. We had to decide whether exploration of this particular unknown was worth the risk of changing the perfectly sound and gratifying relationship which we had built during the previous three-and-a-half years. Finally, our misgivings gave way to curiosity and we wrote off to some couples who advertised in a national swinger's magazine.

Although, like most beginners, we were excited about swinging, we were nervous too. We didn't know what swinging in reality was like or what "rules" there were, if any. In general, however, we found those first experiences not only enjoyable from a personal point of view, but stimulating intellectually. It was then that we decided to study swinging as anthropologists. But, like many anthropologists who use participant observation as a method of study, we could never completely divorce ourselves from the personal aspects of our subject.

The method of participant observation is sometimes criticized as being too subjective. In an area such as sex, where experiences are highly individual and personal, we feel that participant observation can yield results even more thorough and disciplined than the more so-called objective methods. Most of our important insights into the nature of swinging could only have been found by actually experiencing some of the same things that our informants did. Had we not participated, we would not have known how to question them about many central aspects of their experience.

This article presents the results of our 18-month, participant observation study of 136 swingers. We made our contacts in three ways. First, we reached couples through swinger magazines. These are magazines devoted almost exclusively to ads placed by swingers for the purpose of contacting other interested couples and/or singles. Many, although not all, of the couples we contacted in this way seemed to be beginners who had not yet found people with whom they were interested in forming long-term relationships. Second, we were introduced to couples through personal networks. Couples whom we knew would pass our name on to others, sometimes explicitly because they wanted our study to be a success. Third, some couples contacted us as a result of lectures or papers we presented, to volunteer themselves as informants. It should be noted that we did not investigate the swingers' bars, although second-hand reports from couples we met who had used them for making contacts seem to indicate that these couples did not significantly differ from those who do not use the bars. Our informants came from Pennsylvania, New Jersey, New York, Massachusetts, Louisiana, California, Florida and Illinois. They were mostly middle class, although ten could be classified as working class.

Usually we interviewed couples in very informal settings, and these interviews were often indistinguishable from ordinary conversation that swingers might have about themselves and their activities. After each session we would return home, discuss the conversation and write notes on our observations. Later several couples volunteered to tape interviews, enabling us to check the accuracy of the field notes we had taken previously.

In spite of our efforts to find informants from as many different sources as possible, we can in no way guarantee the representativeness of our sample. It should be emphasized that statistics are practically useless in the study of swingers because of insurmountable sampling problems. We therefore avoided the statistical approach and instead focused the investigation on problems of a nonstatistical nature. The information we obtained enabled us to understand and describe the kinds of cultural symbols—a "symbolic calculus," if you will—that swingers must use to effectively navigate social situations with other swingers. This symbolic calculus organizes widely varying experiences into a coherent whole, enabling swingers to understand and evaluate each social situation in which they find themselves. They can thereby define the choices available to them and the desirability of each. Our research goal, then, was to describe the symbols that infuse meaning into the experiences of all the swingers that we contacted.

Unlike Bartell, we had no difficulty finding couples who either wanted to have or had succeeded in having some degree of emotional involvement and long-term friendship within a swinging context. In fact, many of them explained to us that depersonalization simply brought them no satisfaction. In observing such couples with their friends it was evident that they had formed close and enduring relationships. They host each other's children on weekends, celebrate birthdays together, take vacations together and, in general, do what close friends usually do. It should be noted that there is no way of ascertaining the numbers of couples who have actually succeeded in finding close friends through swinging. In fact, they may be under-represented because they tend to retreat into their own small circle of friends and dislike using swinger magazines to find other couples. Thus they are more difficult to contact.

In order to see how swingers are able to form such relationships it is necessary to understand not how they avoid jealousy, but how they deal with its causes. Insecurity and fear of being replaced are the major ingredients in any experience with jealousy. An effective defense against jealousy, then, would include a way to guarantee one's irreplaceability as a mate. If, for example, a wife knows that she is unlike any other woman her husband has ever met or ever will meet, and if they have a satisfying relationship in which they have invested much time and emotion, she can rest assured that no other relationship her husband has can threaten her. If, on the other hand, a woman feels that the continuance of her marital relationship depends on how well she cooks, cleans and makes love, jealousy is more likely to occur, because she realizes that any number of women could fill the same role, perhaps better than she.

Similarly, a man who feels that the continuance of his wife's loyalty depends on how well he provides financial security will be apt to feel more jealousy because many men could perform the same function. To one degree or another, many swingers naturally develop towards a more secure kind of marital relationship, a tendency we call *individuation*. Among the couples we contacted, individuation was achieved for the most part at a level that precluded jealousy. And we found that, to the extent that couples did not individuate, either jealousy occurred or swinging had to take other, less flexible forms in order to prevent it.

We found evidence of individuation in two areas. First, we found that patterns of behavior at gatherings of swingers who had passed the beginning stages were thoroughly pervaded by individuation. Second, we found that by following changes in a couple's attitudes toward themselves, both as individuals and as a couple and toward other swingers, a trend of increasing individuation could be observed.

Individuating Behavior at Gatherings

When we first entered the swinging scene, we hypothesized that swinging must be characterized by a set of implicit and explicit rules or patterns of behavior. But every time we thought we had discovered a pattern, another encounter quickly invalidated it. We finally had to conclude that any particular swinging gathering is characterized by any one of a number of forms, whatever best suits the individuals involved. The ideal, as in nonswinging situations, is for the initiation of sexual interaction to appear to develop naturally—preferably in a nonverbal way. But with four or more people involved and all the signaling and cross-signaling of intentions that must take place, this ideal can only be approached in most cases. The initiation may begin with little or no socializing, much socializing with sex later on as a natural outgrowth of the good feelings thus created, or some mixture in-between. Socializing is of the variety found at many types of nonswinging gatherings. The sexual interaction itself may be "open" where couples participate in the same room or "closet" where couples pair off in separate rooms. In open swinging, a "pretzel," "flesh pile" or "scene" may take place, all terms which signify groups of more than two people having sex with each other. Like Bartell, we found that females are much more likely to participate in homosexuality—probably near 100 percent— while very few men participate in homosexuality. Younger people tend to be much more accepting about the latter.

All of this flexibility can be summed up by saying that swingers consider an ideal gathering one in which everyone can express themselves as individuals *and* appreciate others for doing the same. If even one person fails to have an enjoyable experience in these terms, the gathering is that much less enjoyable for everyone.

An important consequence of this "do your own thing" ethic is that sexual experiences are talked about as a primarily personal matter. Conversely they are not evaluated according to a general standard. Thus one hears about "bad experiences" rather than "bad swingers." This is not to say that swingers are not aware of general sexual competence, but only that it is largely irrelevant to their appreciation of other people. As one informant said:

Technique is not that much. If she's all right, I don't care if she's technically terrible—if I think she's a beautiful person, she can't be that bad.

Beginners may make certain mistakes if they do not individuate. They may, for example, take on the "social director" role. This kind of person insists that a party become the materialization of his own fantasies without regard for anyone else's wishes. This can make the situation very uncomfortable for everyone else unless someone can get him to stop. Or, a nervous beginner may feel compelled to look around to find out what to do and, as a result, will imitate someone else. This imitation can be disturbing to others for two reasons. First, the imitator may not be enjoying himself. Second, he may be competing with someone else by comparing the effects of the same activity on their different partners. In either case, he is not involved with perceiving and satisfying the individual needs of his own partner. This would also be true in the case of the person who regularly imitates his or her own previous behavior, making an unchanging formula for interaction, no matter who he is with. Swingers generally consider such behavior insensitive and/or insincere.

Modification of Attitudes

Beginners tend to approximate the popular stereotype of sex-starved deviates. A 50-year-old woman described one of her beginning experiences this way:

It was one after another, and really, after a point it didn't make any difference *who* it was. It was just one great big prick after another. And I *never* experienced anything like that in my whole life. I have never had an experience like that with quite so many. I think in the course of three hours I must have had 11 or 12 men, and one greater than the next. It just kept on getting better every time. It snowballed.

The manner in which she describes her experience exemplifies the attitudes of both male and female beginners. They are not likely to develop a long lasting friendship with one or a small number of couples, and they focus much more on sex than the personalities involved. Frequently, they will be more interested in larger parties where individual personality differences are blurred by the number of people.

Simple curiosity seems to be the reason for this attitude. As one beginner told us, "Sometimes, we get titillated with them as people, knowing in the long run that it won't work out." It seems that because the beginner has been prevented so often from satisfying his curiosity through sexual liaisons in "straight" life, an important goal of early swinging is to satisfy this curiosity about people in general. This goal is apt to take precedence over any other for quite some time. Thus, even if a couple sincerely hopes to find long-lasting friendships, their desire to "move on" is apt to win out at first.

Bartell has asserted that both personality shallowness and jealousy are always responsible for this focus on sex and the search for new faces. For the most part, neither of these factors is necessarily responsible. First, the very same couples who appear shallow in fact may develop friendships later on. Second, as we shall see below, some couples who focus almost exclusively on sex nevertheless experience jealousy and must take certain precautions. On the other hand, some swingers *do* couple-hop because of jealousy. The Races, for example, dislike swinging with a couple more than once or twice because of the jealousy that arises each time. Very often only one member is jealous of the other's involvement but the jealousy will be hidden. Pride may prevent each from admitting jealousy for quite some time. Each partner may feel that to admit jealousy would be to admit a weakness and instead will feign disinterest in a particular couple to avoid another meeting.

This stage of swinging eventually stops in almost all cases we know of, probably because the superficial curiosity about people in general is satisfied. Women are usually responsible for the change, probably because they have been raised to reject superficial sexual relationships. Sometimes this is precipitated by a bad experience when, for example, a man is particularly rough or inconsiderate in some way. Sometimes a man will be the first to suggest a change because of erection problems which seem to be caused in some cases by a general lack of interest in superficial sexual contacts. In other words, once his general curiosity is satisfied, he can no longer sustain enough interest to be aroused.

The termination of the curiosity stage and the beginning of a stage of relative selectivity is characterized by increasing individuation of self and others. Among men this change manifests itself in the nature of fantasies that give interest to the sexual experience. The statement of one male informant exemplifies the change:

Now, I don't fantasize much. There's too much reality to fantasize, too much sex and sex realities we've experienced. So there is not too much that I *can* fantasize with. I just remember the good times we've actually had.

Instead of fantasies being what one would wish to happen,

they are instead a kind of reliving of pleasant past experiences with particular people. Also, some informants have noticed that where their previous fantasies had been impersonal, they eventually became tied to specific people with whom pleasant sexual experiences had been shared.

Increasing individuation is also noticeable in beginners' changing perceptions of certain problems that arise in swinging situations. Many male swingers have difficulty with erections at one time or another. Initially, this can be quite ego shattering. The reason for this trauma is not difficult to understand. Most Americans believe that the mere sight of a nude, sexually available woman should arouse a man almost instantly. A male who fails to be aroused may interpret this as a sign of his hitherto unknown impotency. But if he is not too discouraged by this first experience he may eventually find the real reasons. He may realize that he does not find some women attractive mentally and/or physically even though they are sexually available. He learns to recognize when he is being deliberately though subtly discouraged by a woman. He may discover that he dislikes certain situational factors. For example, he may find that he likes only open or only closet swinging or that he cannot relax sufficiently to perform after a hard day's work. Once a swinger realizes that his physical responses may very well be due to elements that inhere to the individual relationship rather than to an innate sexual inadequacy, he has arrived at a very different conception of sexual relationships. He is better able to see women as human beings to whom he may be attracted as personalities rather than as objects to be exploited for their sexual potential. In our terms, he can now more successfully individuate his relationships with women.

Women must cope with problems of a slightly different nature when they begin to swing. Their difficulties develop mostly because of their tendency to place decorum above the expression of their own individual desires in social situations. This tendency manifests itself from the time the husband suggests swinging. Many women seem to swing merely because their husbands want to rather than because of their own positive feelings on the matter. This should not be interpreted to mean that wives participate against their will, but only that as in most recreational activity, the male provides the initial impetus that she can then choose to go along with or reject. Her lack of positive initiative may express itself in the quality of her interaction. She is apt to swing with a man not because he manifests particular attributes that she appreciates, but because he lacks any traits that she finds outright objectionable. One woman describes one of her first experiences this way:

As I recall, I did not find him particularly appealing, but he was nice, and that was OK. He actually embarrassed me a bit because he was so shy and such a kind of nonperson.

This is not to say that women do not enjoy their experiences once they begin participating. The same woman remarks about her first experience in this way:

Somehow, it was the situation that made the demand. I got turned on, although I hadn't anticipated a thing up to that point. In fact, I still have a hard time accounting for my excitement that first time and the good time which I did actually have.

In fact, it sometimes happens at this stage that women become more enthusiastic about swinging than men, much to the latter's embarrassment.

Their enjoyment, however, seems to result from the same kind of psychology that is likely to propel them into swinging in the first place, the desire to please men. Hence, like her nonswinging counterparts, a woman in swinging will judge herself in terms of her desirability and her attractiveness to men much more than thinking about her own individuality in relation to others.

After swinging for awhile, however, her wish to be desired and to satisfy can no longer be as generalized because it becomes apparent that she is indeed desired by many men, and thus she has no need to prove it to herself. In order to make the experience meaningful, she arrives at a point where she feels that she must begin to actually refuse the advances of many men. This means that she must learn to define her own preferences more clearly and to learn to act on these preferences, an experience that many women rarely have because they have learned to rely on their husbands to make these kinds of decisions in social situations. In short, a woman learns to individuate both herself and others in the second stage of swinging.

Another change that swingers mention concerns their feelings towards their mates. They say that since they started swinging they communicate better than they did before. Such couples, who previously had a stable but uninteresting or stale marriage ("like brother and sister without the blood"), say that swinging has recreated the romantic feelings they once had for each other. These feelings seem to find concrete expression in an increasing satisfaction with the sexual aspects of the marital relationship, if not in an actual increase in sexual intercourse. This is almost always experienced by older couples in terms of feeling younger.

An explanation for this change, again, involves the individuation process. Marriage can grow stale if a couple loses a sense of appreciation of each other's individuality. A husband may look too much like an ordinary husband, a wife like an ordinary wife. This can happen easily especially when a couple's circumstances (job, children and so forth) necessitate a great deal of routinization of their life together. Such couples find in swinging the rare opportunity to escape from the routine roles that must be assumed in everyday life. In this setting individual differences receive attention and appreciation and, because of this, married couples can again see and appreciate their own distinct individuality, thus reactivating their romantic feelings for each other.

It is interesting to note that, those couples who do not answer in this way almost always experience jealousy, not romanticization, as a result of swinging. This is the case with one couple we interviewed, each of whom insists that the other is "better than anyone else," although it was clear by their jealousy of each other that neither was entirely confident of this.

Individuation, then, pervades the swinging scene and plays an important role in minimizing jealousy. But it alone cannot guarantee the control of jealousy—because there is always the possibility that a person will appreciate and be equally attracted to two unique individuals. Clearly, individuation must be complemented with something more if the marriage is to be effectively distinguished from other extramarital relationships.

This "something else" is compatibility. Two individuals who perceive and appreciate each other's individuality may nevertheless make poor living mates unless they are compatible. Compatibility is a kind of superindividuation. It requires not only the perception and appreciation of uniqueness, but the inclusion of this in the solutions to any problems that confront the relationship. Each partner must have the willingness and the ability to consider his or her mate's needs, desires and attitudes, when making the basic decisions that affect them both. This is viewed as something that people must work to achieve, as indicated by the phrase, "He failed in his marriage."

Unlike swinging, then, marriage requires a great deal of day-to-day giving and taking, and an emotional investment that increases with the years. Because such an investment is not given up easily, it provides another important safeguard against jealousy.

The dimension of marital compatibility often shows itself in swinging situations. If and when serious problems are encountered by one marriage partner, it is expected that the other partner will take primary responsibility for doing what is necessary. One couple, for example, was at a gathering, each sitting with their swinging partners. It was the first time they had ever tried pot, and the wife suddenly became hysterical. The man she was with quickly relinquished his place to her husband, who was expected to take primary responsibility for comforting his wife, although everyone was concerned about her. Another example can occur when a man has erection problems. If he is obviously miserable, it is considered wrong for his wife to ignore his condition, although we have heard of a few cases where this has happened. His wife may go to his side and they will decide to go home or she may simply act worried and less than completely enthusiastic, thus evincing some minimal

concern for her husband. In other words, the married couple is still distinguished as the most compatible partners and remains therefore the primary problem-solving unit.

The importance of compatibility also shows up in certain situations where a couple decides that they must stop swinging. In several cases reported to us, couples who had been married two years or less found that swinging tended to disrupt their marital relationship. We ourselves encountered three couples who had been married for under one year and had not lived together before marriage. All three had difficulties as a result of swinging, and one is now divorced. These couples evidently had not had the time to build up the emotional investment so necessary to a compatible marriage.

It is clear, then, that to the degree that couples individuate and are compatible, jealousy presents no major problems. Conversely, when these conditions are not satisfied, disruptive jealousy can result.

There are, however, some interesting exceptions. For a few couples who seem to place little emphasis on individuation, marital compatibility is an issue which remains chronically unresolved. Compatibility for them is a quality to be constantly demonstrated rather than a fact of life to be more or less taken for granted. Hence, every give-and-take becomes an issue.

These couples focus on the mechanics of sexual competence rather than on personal relationships. These are the people who will talk about "good swingers" and "bad swingers" rather than good and bad experiences. One of these husbands once commented:

Some people say there's no such thing as a good lay and a bad lay. But in my experience that just isn't true. I remember this one woman I went with for a long time. She was just a bad lay. No matter what I did, she was just lousy!

In other words, his bad lay is everyone's bad lay. One of his friends expressed it differently. He didn't understand why some swingers were so concerned with compatibility; he felt it was the sex that was important—and simply "having a good time."

Because they do not consider individuation important, these couples tend to approximate most closely the popular stereotypes of swingers as desiring only "pure sex." Swinging for these couples is primarily a matter of sexual interaction. Consequently, they are chiefly interested in seeing how sexually competent a couple is before they decide whether or not to develop a friendship. Competence may be defined in any or all of a number of ways. Endurance, size of penis, foreplay competence—all may be used to assess competence during the actual sexual interaction whether it be a large open party or a smaller gathering.

It is clear, then, that such couples perceive sex in a way

that individuators find uncongenial or even repugnant. When we first observed and interviewed them, we interpreted their behavior as the beginning stage of promiscuity that new couples may go through. But when we asked, we would find that they had been swinging frequently for a period of two years, much too long to be considered inexperienced. How, we asked ourselves, could such couples avoid jealousy, if they regularly evaluated sexual partners against a common standard? It seemed to us that a husband or wife in such a situation could conceivably be replaced some day by a "better lay," especially if the issue of marital compatibility remained somewhat unresolved. Yet these couples did not appear to experience any disruptive jealousy as a result of swinging. We found that they are able to accomplish this by instituting special, somewhat less flexible arrangements for swinging. First, they are invariably exclusive open swingers. That is, sexual interaction must take place in the same room. This tends to reduce any emotional involvement in one interaction. They think that closet swinging (swinging in separate rooms) is "no better than cheating." They clearly worry about the possibility of emotional infidelity more than individuators. An insistence on open swinging reduces the possibility of emotional involvement, and with it, the reason for jealousy. Second, they try to control the swinging situation as much as possible. So, for example, they are much more likely to insist on being hosts. And they also desire to state their sexual preferences ahead of time, thereby insuring that nothing very spontaneous and unpredictable can happen. Third, the women are more likely to desire female homosexuality and more aggressively so. This often results in the women experiencing more emotional involvement with each other than with the men, which is more acceptable because it does not threaten the marital relationship.

Conclusion: The Social Significance of Swinging

A full explanation of the reasons for the rise in popularity of swinging cannot be made adequately within the space of this article. But we would like to sketch briefly some of our findings in order to apply a corrective to the rather optimistic view which swingers have of swinging, the view which we have presented in this article.

A glance at the recent history of Western civilization reveals the locus of an adequate explanation. In the U.S.A. during this century, an increase in sexual freedom has always been followed by periods of relatively greater sexual repression. The flappers of the 1920's were followed by the more conservative women of the 1930's, and the freer female role of World War II was superseded by a wave of conservatism that sent women flocking back to the home. And, finally, in the 1960's, Americans have witnessed unprecedented heights of sexual freedom in this country. In its level of intensity, this last period is most analogous to what occurred in Germany during the 1920's and early 1930's. The interesting thing about these ebbs and flows in sexual freedom is that they correlate quite closely with certain kinds of economic developments. In these cases, where sexual freedom appears as a general trend in the population, it is clearly a function of factors which are beyond the immediate control of individuals. Such factors as investment flows, limited resources, fluctuations in world markets, and so forth, all events that seem isolated from the arena of intimacy which people carve for themselves, are in fact very much a part of their most personal relationships.

Three questions present themselves. First, what is the nature of the social conditions which surround swinging? Second, what is the relationship between those conditions and the consciousness of individual swingers? And finally, why should the two have anything to do with each other?

Taking last things first, for a moment, it is important to consider swinging as a social event which seems appropriate to the participants. By "appropriate" we mean that it makes sense to them in terms of how they see their relationships to other people, in terms of their conceptions of social reality, and in terms of their notions about value. These ideas appear rational only in so far as they seem to address themselves to the objective realities which people face in their day to day existence.

An interesting example of the relationship between objective reality and morality is the effect which Germany's great inflation during the 1920's had on the morality of the Berlin middle class. Otto Freidrich in his book *Before the Deluge* interviews a woman who vividly describes the effect of this economic development:

Yes, the inflation was by far the most important event of this period. The inflation wiped out the savings of the entire middle class, but those are just words. You have to realize what that *meant*. There was not a single girl in the entire German middle class who could get *married* without her father paying a dowry. Even the maids—they never spent a penny of their wages. They saved and saved so that they could get married. When money became worthless, it destroyed the whole system for getting married, and so it destroyed the whole idea of remaining chaste until marriage.

The rich had never lived up to their own standards, of course, and the poor had different standards anyway, but the middle class, by and large, obeyed the rules. Not every girl was a virgin when she was married, but it was

FIVE TYPES OF SWINGING COUPLES:
The Eversearches, the Closefriends, the Snares, the Races and the Successes

The following are composite case histories of five swinging couples. Although each case history is closely tied to one couple whom we knew fairly well, the case itself is more generalized to represent at least a few couples we have met. To check the accuracy of our perceptions of these different types of couples, we showed these case histories to five couples. All recognized other swinging couples whom they had also met.

Two problems present themselves here—the representativeness of the individual cases and the comprehensiveness of the five cases taken as a whole. In regard to the former, there is no way to know what proportion of swingers represent each case. In fact, to judge proportions from our sample might very well be misleading. This is because couples such as the Eversearches use swinging media and are therefore more visible and easier to contact, while couples like the Closefriends are very difficult to locate because they stay within their own circle of close friends. Hence, even though the Eversearches probably represent a higher proportion of our sample, this in no way tells us about the actual proportion of Eversearch types. In regard to the question of comprehensiveness, these case histories are only meant to intuitively represent the possible range of types. Many couples may better be seen as a mixture of types, and some types of couples may not be represented at all.

Jack and Jeanine Eversearch

Jack and Jeanine grew up in the same small town. They went to the same schools and the same church. In their sophomore year of high school they began to go steady. Just before she was to graduate, Jeanine, to her dismay, became pregnant, and her parents, experiencing a similar reaction, finally decided on abortion. They wanted her to go to college, enlarge her experiences, and perhaps find some other marriage prospect than the rather placid Jack.

At college, however, the two continued to see each other frequently. Jeanine occasionally went out with other men, but never felt as comfortable with them as she did with Jack. Jack never went out with anyone but Jeanine, mainly because his shyness prevented him from meeting other girls. It was predictable that the two would marry the June they graduated.

Five years and two children later, Jack and Jeanine were living much as they always had, in a new suburban home, close to their families. Life had become a routine of barbecues and bridge parties on weekends and children to get ready for school during the week, marked by occasional special events like a church social or a ride in the country. To all appearances, they seemed to have a model marriage.

But their marriage had actually changed, so gradually that the shift was almost imperceptible. Like most married couples, they had experienced a waning of sexual interest from time to time. But in their case, the troughs had lengthened until sex had become a perfunctory gesture, something they did just because they were married. As Jeanine said, "We didn't fight, because there was nothing to fight about. We just felt the inevitability of being together for the rest of our lives—something like brother and sister without the blood."

They had used the church before in a social way; they turned to it now for inspiration. Their congregation had recently acquired a new pastor, a sincere and intelligent man, whom almost everyone liked.

But the home situation continued to disintegrate. Jeanine, on her own there most of the day, found the situation intolerable and decided to seek help from the pastor:

I knew something was wrong but it was too vague to talk about very clearly. I just kept stammering about how . . . things weren't what they used to be. But I couldn't say exactly why. In fact, I was so fuzzy that I was afraid he'd misunderstand me and that instead of advice I'd get a lecture about how God is the source of all meaning in life or something like that. So, when he started telling me about the problems that he and his wife had, I was quite surprised but also delighted.

They continued to meet as friends, and it became apparent that the pastor needed Jeanine for personal comfort and support as much as she needed him. This led to an affair, which lasted until Jack came home unexpectedly early from work one day three months later.

After the initial shock faded, Jack was left with a feeling of total inadequacy:

I guess I thought that if Jeanine wanted to sleep with someone else, that meant I had disappointed her. I felt that my inability to rise in the company reflected on our marriage and on her choice of me as a husband—which didn't do my ego any good.

The episode proved fortunate, because it provided them with a reason to talk about their problems, and with the channels of communication open once more, their marriage began to seem fulfilling again. Their sexual interest in each other returned:

We started doing things in bed that we'd always been curious about but had never bothered to try or had been too embarrassed to mention. There were many nights when we couldn't wait to get into bed.

About a year after Jeanine's affair ended, they started discussing the possibility of swinging. But when they thought of it seriously, they realized that not one other couple they knew would be willing partners. Jack had heard of swingers' magazines, gave the local smut peddler a try, and brought one home.

They examined the magazine for hours, wondering about the people who had placed the ads and looking at the pictures. Finally, caution gave way to curiosity, and they answered four of the more conservative ads. Within a few weeks they had received encouraging answers from all four.

Jack and Jeanine found their first swinging experience very pleasant. They felt nervous at first when they were greeted at the door by the other couple because they did not know what to expect. Nevertheless, they enjoyed themselves enough to agree to swing when it was suggested by their hosts. Having their fantasies and desires come true in the bedroom was intensely pleasurable to them both, and when they returned home they longed to share their elation with someone else, but could think of no one who would not be shocked. So they called the other couple back and told *them* what a good time they'd had.

Encouraged by this first happy experience, the Eversearches began to swing with practically every couple they could contact. Lately, they have become more selective, but they still devote some time to contacting and meeting new people.

Looking back, both feel that swinging has changed them. Before, Jack had always gone along with the men he knew, accepting, at least verbally, their values, attitudes and behavior:

It bugs me now that I have to play some kind of he-man role all the time. I never used to notice it. You know how guys are always talking about this girl and how they would like to get her in bed? Well . . . I'm not interested in just sex anymore—I mean, I want to have someone I like, not just a writhing body.

Jeanine feels similarly:

All of a sudden it seems I have more insight into everybody, into how they interact with each other. Maybe because we've met so many different kinds of people. And I have to be very careful that I don't express some of my liberal views. Sometimes, I really want to tell our nonswinging friends about our new life—but then I'm sure they wouldn't understand.

Mike and Maryann Closefriend

Mike and Maryann are 30 and 25 years old and have been married five years. They originally met when Mike, then an advanced graduate student, gave a lecture about inner-city family structure to a group of volunteer social workers. Maryann was in the audience and asked several penetrating questions. After the talk, she approached him to find out more. They were immediately attracted to each other and started going out frequently. After about six months they rented an apartment together, and when Mike got his Ph.D. in social science a year later, they married and moved to the East Coast, where he had obtained a teaching post.

Their early life together seemed an experience of endless enjoyment. They went camping on weekends, took pottery classes, and were lucky in meeting several people whose outlook on life was similar to theirs, with whom they developed close relationships. These friends have helped not only in practical things, such as moving or house painting, but in emotional crises. When, for example, Mike and Maryann seemed to be on the verge of breaking up about two years ago, their friends helped to smooth things over by acting as amateur psychologists.

The Closefriends don't remember exactly how they started swinging. Mike says it was "just a natural consequence of our friendship—our feeling for our friends." They remember some nudity at their parties before they swung, mostly unplanned. People took off their clothes because of the heat or just because they felt more comfortable that way. Sometimes they engaged in sexual play of various kinds, and this led to intercourse as a natural part of these occasions. Sometimes just two people felt like swinging, and sometimes everyone. If the former was the case, people could just watch, or if the couple wanted privacy, they went to another room. And sometimes no one felt like swinging, and the subject was never brought up.

For the Closefriends, swinging seems to be a natural outgrowth of the way they approached marriage and friendship, and the way they feel about and relate to people in general. As Maryann puts it:

I guess it has to do with our basic belief in the totality of sharing and the kind of dialogue that we have with each other. Our no-holds-barred, no secrets kind of relationship produces such a lovely kind of glow that we just naturally like to share it with our friends. Our having close relationships with people is actually like having a second marriage. Not that we would all want to live together, although that might be possible some day. Some of the men, for example, couldn't live with me—we would be incompatible—but that doesn't make us any less desirable to each other.

Paul and Georgia Snare

When Paul met Georgia, he had been married about a year and was beginning to find his wife Serita both boring and demanding. A handsome young man, Paul had led an exciting life as a bachelor and found the daily routine of marriage very depressing:

I felt awfully trapped. . . . It just got worse and worse until I couldn't see going home anymore. I bought a motorcycle and joined up with a bunch of guys pretty much like me. We'd ride around all night so we wouldn't have to go home to our old ladies.

Georgia was a salesgirl in the drugstore next door to the camera shop where Paul worked. He used to drop by daily for cigarettes and a chat, and they became friendly. Paul even made a few passes, but Georgia knew he already had a wife and refused his attentions. Unused to this kind of treatment, Paul took her refusals as a challenge and became quite serious in his efforts to persuade her to go out with him. Finally, when Paul and Serita got a formal separation, Georgia accepted his invitations, and they began to date steadily.

Georgia became pregnant about three months before Paul's divorce was due to come through, so they were married the week after the decree became final. At first things went well. Georgia stayed home and took care of the small house in the suburbs that Paul had bought for her, and the marriage ran smoothly for about six months, until the baby came. Then Paul began to feel trapped again, "going to work every day, coming home to dinner and going to bed. I didn't want it to happen again but it did."

Paul resorted to outside affairs, but found them unsatisfactory because they took too much time and money, and "it just wasn't worth all the lying." He suggested to Georgia the possibility of swinging with some friends of theirs, pointing out that he loved her but that "every man needs a bit of variety." Georgia initially thought the idea was crazy, but Paul persisted and finally persuaded her to try it.

Persuading their friends, however, was another matter. They didn't want to come right out and proposition them, so they decided on seduction as the method of persuasion. They would

"date" a couple each weekend, and go dancing to provide an excuse for body contact. Paul would get increasingly intimate with the wife, and if the husband followed his example, Georgia would accept his advances.

They decided their first couple would be their old friends Bill and Jean. Everything went as planned for a while until Bill became suspicious and asked Paul to explain his attentions to Jean. When Paul did so, the couple became upset and left almost immediately.

Somewhat depressed by the loss of their friends, Paul and Georgia tried another couple they knew, but this time they enacted their plan more slowly. It took about six months, but it worked, and they continued to swing with the couple exclusively for about a year, until they discovered swinging magazines and began making new contacts through them.

Neither of the Snares have any problems with jealousy, and agree that this is because "we are so good in bed with each other that no one could really compete." From time to time Paul even brings home girls he has met; Georgia doesn't get jealous "just so long as he introduces them to me first and they do their thing in my house." For her part, Georgia has discovered that she likes women too and regularly brings home girls from a nearby homosexual bar. "Men," she says, "are good for sex, but it isn't in their nature to be able to give the kind of affection a woman needs." Georgia's activities don't worry Paul a bit:

A woman couldn't provide the kind of support I do. They just don't know how to get along in the world without a man. A lot of these lesbians she meets are really irresponsible and would never be able to take care of the kid.

Swinging has affected Georgia's self-confidence as well as changing her sex habits. She now feels much more confident in social situations, a change that occurred after she began making

her own choices about whom she would swing with. At first, she had let Paul make all the decisions:

If he liked the woman, then I would swing with the man. But it got so I couldn't stand it anymore. I had to make it with so many creeps! I just got sick of it after a while. Paul kept getting the good deals and I never found anybody I liked. Finally, I just had to insist on my rights!

Paul agrees that this is good and points out that one swinger they know constantly forces his wife to swing with men she has no desire for, and as a result their marriage is slowly disintegrating. He credits swinging with saving his own marriage with Georgia and thinks that, had he known about it before, it could have saved his first marriage too.

Frank and Helen Race

Frank and Helen met at a well-known West Coast university where both were top-ranked graduate students in biochemistry. Both were from Jewish backgrounds, strongly oriented toward academic achievement.

Frank, largely because of his parents' urging, had excelled in high school, both academically and in extracurricular activities. After high school, he enlisted in the marines, was commissioned after OCS training and commanded one of the best units on his base. Ultimately, he became dissatisfied with the life of a marine officer and left to attend college, where he finished his bachelor degree in three years, graduated with honors and went on to graduate school.

As a child, Helen had experienced much the same kind of pressure. Her father, an excellent musician, dominated the family and drove her endlessly. She began piano lessons at age four and remembers that he was always at her shoulder to scold her when she made a mistake. She was able to end music lessons only because she attended a college where no facilities were available, leaving her free to devote all her time to the study of biochemistry, which she much preferred.

Helen and Frank married during their third year of graduate school. It seemed a perfect match—two fine scholars with identical interests, who could work as a team. For the next four years they did work closely together on their respective Ph.D. dissertations, which were published and became well known in the field. Despite this success, however, they could not find jobs with prestige schools and had to take posts at a less well known institution.

They settled into their professional lives, both publishing as much as possible in the hope of eventually gaining positions at a more prestigious university. They worked together closely, constantly seeking each other's help and proffering severe criticisms. If either published more than the other during the year, the "underpublished" one would experience intense jealousy. Realizing this disruptive competition was a serious threat to their marriage, they sought help from a psychotherapist and from group therapy sessions.

The most important thing Frank and Helen learned about themselves in therapy was that by making their relationship competitive they had forfeited their appreciation of each other as individuals. They also discovered another element in their lives, which Frank links directly to their decision to take up swinging:

I told Helen that I missed terribly the experiences that other men had as kids. I was always too busy with school to ever have a good time dating. I only had a date once in high school, for the senior prom, and I had only had one girl friend in college. I felt that a whole stage of my life was totally absent. I wanted to do those things that I had missed out on—then maybe I'd feel more able to cope with our

problems. Much to my surprise, Helen felt she too had missed out.

Like the Eversearches, the Races met their first couple through an ad in a swinger publication. Their first meeting, however, was somewhat unpleasant. Frank felt jealous because he feared the man might be sexually better than he. He did not tell Helen this, however, but simply refused to return, on the grounds that he had not enjoyed the woman. Helen suspected Frank was in fact jealous, and many arguments ensued.

The Races have been swinging for about three years and average one contact every two or three months, a rate of frequency considerably lower than usual. Both agree that they have a lot of difficulty with jealousy. If, for example, they meet a couple and Helen is very attracted to the man, Frank will invariably insist he does not find the woman desirable. They have come to realize that the one who exercises the veto is probably jealous of the good time the other has had or is about to have and thus insists on breaking off the threatening relationship. They also realize that swinging may not be the best way to use their leisure time—but somehow they can't give up the hope that they may find the experiences they missed as young people.

Glen and Andrea Success

Glen and Andrea were married shortly before the end of the war, immediately after Glen graduated with a Ph.D. in biology. Because he felt that teaching at a university would be financially limiting, he found a job with a medical supply manufacturing company, which promised him a high-ranking executive position in the future. He has stayed with the company for nearly 20 years, rising to positions of increased responsibility.

Five years after he had begun work, Andrea and Glen were able to afford a luxurious suburban home. Well settled into their house and community, they

started their family. Andrea enjoyed motherhood and raised her two boys and a girl as model children:

There wasn't a thing we couldn't do. Glen and I traveled all over the States and Europe. We even went to Australia. We had bought ourselves a lovely house, we had a fine marriage and wonderful, healthy children. We had many fine friends too.

Glen claims it was this unusual good luck that eventually turned them to swinging. About seven years ago, they began to feel they had achieved everything that people usually want and anything else would be anticlimactic:

We knew one couple with whom we could talk about anything and everything, and we did! One conversation especially, I think, led to our considering swinging. We were talking about success and trying to define exactly what it meant. Andrea and I thought it was something like having all the money you need and a good marriage. They said that if that was true, then we already had everything we would ever want. ... Later on, when I thought about what he'd said, I got a funny kind of hollow feeling. Forty-five, I said to myself, and at the end of the line.

In this state of mind Glen got the idea that swinging might be a way out. He and Andrea spent about a month discussing the possibility and finally decided to try it out. Their first meeting with another couple was disturbing for them both, but they continued to look for more satisfactory people. If the second meeting had been equally bad, they probably would have given up the whole idea. But it ended pleasantly in a friendship that lasted about three years.

At first they had to rely on contacts from the *National Enquirer,* but about a year after they started swinging their local newspaper began running ads on the lines of "Modern couple interested in meeting the same. Box 1023." About ten of these ads appeared during the brief period before the paper found out what they were for and ceased to accept any more. By then Glen and Andrea had contacted all the couples who had advertised. These people, in turn, knew other swingers whom they had either met through national publications or had initiated themselves. Soon a large network began to form.

Glen applied his organizational talents to the swinging scene and was soon arranging parties for couples he felt would be compatible, spending his own money to rent halls for get-togethers. Many couples started coming to

him with their problems, and to help them out, he arranged for a doctor to direct group discussions dealing with typical swinging problems. He even contacted lawyers whom he knew personally to protect "his swingers," as he was beginning to call them, should they have any difficulties with the law. In fact, the Successes knew so many couples that other swingers began to rely on them as a kind of dating service that could arrange for either quiet evenings or major parties.

The Successes feel that in swinging they have finally found an activity which offers lasting interest and stimulation. Says Andrea:

Glen and I have done everything—I don't just mean sex. Just doing

things doesn't really appeal to us anymore. But swinging has managed to hold our attention for a long time. If you give me a choice between going to South America, nightclubbing or swinging, I think swinging is the most satisfying and interesting.

Why? Glen says:

I think it's because in swinging you can see people for who they really are—as individuals, without the masks they have to wear most of the time. In a way, I guess I never knew people before, and I'm amazed at the variety. Maybe that's why swinging holds my interest—everybody is different, a challenge to get to know.

---

generally accepted that one *should* be. But what happened from the inflation was that the girls learned that virginity didn't matter any more. The women were liberated.

It may seem odd to think of a person confronting his system of values and suddenly finding it obsolete, but that is exactly what happened to many of the swingers we talked to. This was reflected not only in their comments to us but in their approach to swinging as beginners. Couples who seemed otherwise very cautious and conservative would often persist through one, two, or as many as six perfectly horrendous initial experiences, absolutely determined to find a compatible couple. Such tenacity is remarkable in that these couples, like many middle class Americans, were prone to form strong opinions on the basis of their own personal experience. In addition to persistence, another important indicator of swingers' needs to modify their value systems is their stated satisfaction with swinging as a new life style. Generally, these couples feel that swinging benefits them not only as a form of entertainment but as an activity which boosts their self confidence, enlarges their understanding of others, and helps them shed their "hypocritical" attitudes.

The fact that swingers say they feel better about themselves as a result of swinging indicates that swinging and the ideology that goes along with it are more appropriate to the present conditions of their existence than were the values which these couples held previous to swinging. The question is, what were these new "facts of life" which the middle class had to deal with in the middle sixties?

Two related developments occurring during this period which affected practically every member of this society were rising inflation and increased speculation. By speculation we refer to the massive shift in investments away from increasingly productive capacity into such areas as land speculation, conglomerate building, defense production, and insurance and various other "service industries."

Where inflation did not result in outright cuts in the real, disposable income of the middle class, it at least generated considerable anxiety. Many women were forced onto the job market in order to help maintain their familial standard of living, abruptly threatened by the unexpectedly high cost of buying or keeping up a home, of financing a college education, or of paying taxes. Many young couples began to restrict the size of their families because they feared that they would not be able to provide adequately for their children. These couples felt that under such circumstances child rearing would prove a singularly unrewarding experience, both for themselves and their children.

This movement away from traditional forms of adulthood, which included marriage and a family, was exacerbated by the speculative trend in the economy which made it necessary. Far from causing anxiety, the new life styles were often viewed as being desirable. For they expressed the kind of human relationships inherent in a society where the economy runs on speculation and non-productive enterprise. In such an atmosphere, all social forms associated with production begin to seem less and less appropriate.

Swinging as an ideology addresses itself to the new conditions which the middle class faces as the result of economic stagnation. Before swinging, the nature of relations between husband and wife had more or less reflected the role of the family as an important biological and social reproductive unit of society. That is, the ideal of monogamous sexual relationships, realized even in the institution of cheating, reflected the notion that the family unit existed not only for rearing children but for the maintenance of the sexual division of labor. Husband and wife formed an interdependent productive whole that was crucial to the continuance of the society. Swinging breaks with the past in that it does not reflect any productive relation to society whatsoever. Sex within the context of swinging at its best merely symbolizes a loosely defined friendship. As one swinger told us, "It's all a lot of fun, but it sure is irrelevant to anything." This notion of "sex for fun" as many have called it does not confine itself to swinging, however. The trend towards a revivification of marriage through romance essentially returns fun and adventure to the marriage, replacing or dominating the old productive functions.

In essence, swinging helps a couple adjust their self conceptions so that they are more in tune with the surrounding conditions generated by social breakdown and decay. As a successful adaptation, however, swinging can in no way address itself to solving those problems.

The Double Standard

Inge Powell Bell

There is a reason why women are coy about their age. For most purposes, society pictures them as "old" ten or 15 years sooner than men. Nobody in this culture, man or woman, wants to grow old; age is not honored among us. Yet women must endure the specter of aging much sooner than men, and this cultural definition of aging gives men a decided psychological, sexual and economic advantage over women.

It is surely a truism of our culture that, except for a few kinky souls, the inevitable physical symptoms of aging make women sexually unattractive much earlier than men. The multimillion dollar cosmetics advertising industry is dedicated to creating a fear of aging in women, so that it may sell them its emollients of sheep's fat, turtle sweat and synthetic chemicals which claim, falsely, to stem the terrible tide. "Did you panic when you looked into the mirror this morning and noticed that those laugh lines are turning into crow's-feet?" "Don't let your eyes speak your age!" "What a face-lift can do for your morale!"

A man's wrinkles will not define him as sexually undesirable until he reaches his late fifties. For him, sexual value is defined much more in terms of personality, intelligence and earning power than physical appearance. Women, however, must rest their case largely on their bodies. Their ability to attain status in other than physical ways and to translate that status into sexual attractiveness is severely limited by the culture. Indeed, what status women have is based almost entirely on their sexuality. The young girl of 18 or 25 may well believe that her position in society is equal to, or even higher than that of men. As she approaches middle age, however, she begins to notice a change in the way people treat her. Reflected in the growing indifference of others toward her looks, toward her sexuality, she can see and measure the decline of her worth, her status in the world. In Simone de Beauvoir's words:

> she has gambled much more heavily than man on the sexual values she possesses; to hold her husband and to assure herself of his protection, and to keep most of her

jobs, it is necessary for her to be attractive, to please; she is allowed no hold on the world save through the mediation of some man. What is to become of her when she no longer has any hold on him: This is what she anxiously asks herself while she helplessly looks on the degeneration of this fleshly object which she identifies with herself.

The middle-aged woman who thickly masks her face with makeup, who submits to surgical face and breast lifting, who dyes her hair and corsets her body is as much a victim of socially instilled self-hatred as the black person who straightens his hair and applies bleaching creams to his skin.

The most dramatic institutionalization of different age definitions for men and women is the cultural rules governing the age at which one can marry. It is perfectly acceptable for men to marry women as much as 15 or 20 years younger than they are, but it is generally unacceptable for them to marry women more than four or five years older. These cultural rules show up very plainly in the marriage statistics gathered by the Department of Health, Education and Welfare. At the time of first marriage the age differential is relatively small; the groom is on the average 2.2 years older than his bride. When widowers remarry, however, the gap is 8.3 years; and when divorced men do, the gap is 4.5 years.

These age differentials put the woman at a disadvantage in several ways. First, whatever may be the truth about age and sexual performance, our culture defines the young as sexually more vigorous and desirable. Thus, the customary age differential means that the man gets the more desirable partner; the woman must settle for the less desirable.

More important, the divorced or widowed woman is severely handicapped when it comes to finding another marital partner. Let us take, for example, a couple who divorce when both are in their thirties. What is the difference in the supply of future marriage partners for the man and for the woman? The man can choose among all women his own age or younger. This includes all those women below 25, many more of whom are as yet unmarried. The woman, by contrast, is limited by custom to men her own age or older. She has access only to age brackets in which most people are married. She is thus reduced to the supply of men who come back on the marriage market as a result of divorce or widowerhood or to those few who have not yet married. It is easy to see which of the two will have an easier time finding companionship or a marriage partner. It is also easy to surmise that the awareness of this difference makes divorce a much more painful option for women than for men and thus puts many women at a continuous disadvantage within a strained marriage.

Statistics bear out our supposition that women have a harder time remarrying than men: see table at right It has been estimated that, while three-quarters of divorced men remarry, only two-thirds of divorced women ever do. In a study of widows and widowers done in 1948, Paul Glick found that half the men who had been widowed during the five years preceding the study had remarried, but three-quarters of the women were still alone. Among those who had been widowed from five to 14 years, two-thirds of the men had remarried, but only one-third of the women had.

Only a small proportion of these discrepancies is due to the shorter life expectancy of men and thus their relative scarcity in the upper-age brackets. For example, in the age brackets 45-64, there are a little over three times as many widowed and divorced women without mates as there are single widowed and divorced men. Yet in the total population the ratio of women to men in that age bracket is only 1.05 to 1. In the over-65 age bracket there are over three and a half times as many divorced and widowed women still alone; yet in the population as a whole, the ratio of women to men in this age bracket is only 1.2 to 1.

Still, the difference in life expectancy between the two sexes does work to a woman's disadvantage in another way. The gentleman in the ad below is making explicit an expectation which is made implicitly by most men:

RECENTLY DIVORCED, 53, affectionate, virile, tall, good-looking, yearns for the one utterly feminine, attractive, loving woman in her 30s, 40s with whom he can share a beautiful new life.

At age 50, this gentleman had a life expectancy of 23 years. (It is a little less now.) If he finds a woman of 35, her life expectancy will be 41.27. In other words, he is affectionately offering her a statistical chance of 18 years of widowhood. And she will be widowed at an age when men of her own age will be looking for women in their thirties and forties. At best, he may live to a ripe old age. When he is 75 she will be 57.

Now let us consider the case of a much larger group: women who have husbands. As middle age approaches, many of these married women find that they, too, are vulnerable to the difficulties posed by the different definitions of age in men and women. For them, however devoutly they may wish it as they tidy their homes, take care of their teen-aged children or play bridge, sexual adventure is usually out of the question. This is not just because of the more restrictive mores that bind them to fidelity; their age has already disqualified them for anything else. Not so for the husband. If he is a successful man, his virility will be seen as still intact, if not actually enhanced, and the affair becomes very much the question. Indeed, if he is engaged in a middle-class occupation, he is almost inevitably surrounded by attractive, young females, many of whom—the receptionist, the cocktail waitress at the downtown bar, the airplane hostess—have been deliberately selected to flatter his ego and arouse his fancy. In addition, many of the women hired to fulfill more ordinary functions—the secretaries, typists and the like—find the older man desirable by virtue of his success and wealth. Thus, the middle-aged wife, unless she is one of the statistically few whose husband is truly happy and faithful, is put into competition with the cards stacked against her. And even if her husband doesn't leave her for a younger woman or begin having affairs, she will probably experience anxiety and a sense of diminished self-esteem.

The mass media glamorize and legitimate the older man-younger woman relationship. Successful actors continue to play romantic leads well into their fifties and sometimes sixties (vide Cary Grant). Frequently they are cast opposite actresses at least half their age, and the story line rarely even acknowledges the difference. They are simply an "average" romantic couple. The question of whether the 20-year-old heroine is out of her mind to marry the greying 55-year-old hero isn't even raised.

The Prestige Loss

Occupation is man's major role, unemployment or failure in his occupational life the worst disaster that can befall him. The question "What do you do?" is seldom answered, "Well, I'm married and a father...," But because men draw their self-esteem and establish their connections to others very largely through their jobs, retirement is a time of psychic difficulty and discomfort for most men. The wo-

man faces a similar role loss much earlier. Her primary role in life is that of mother: her secondary role is that of homemaker, and her tertiary that of sexual partner. We have already seen that the role of sexual partner, and sexually desirable object, is impaired for many women as middle age approaches. Now we must contemplate the additional fact that the woman's primary role—that of mother—also disappears during middle age.

Indeed, with decreasing family size and increasingly common patterns of early marriage, women are losing their mother role much earlier than formerly. In 1890 the average woman took care of children until her mid-fifties. Today most women see their children leave home when they are in their late forties. Whereas in 1890 the average woman lived 30 years after her last child had entered school and 12 years after her last child married, today, with longer life expectancy, the average woman lives 40 years after her last child enters school and 25 years after her last child marries. Thus, women lose their major role long before the retirement age arrives for men.

Loss of sexual attractiveness and the maternal role comes at a time when the husband is likely to be at the peak of his career and deeply involved in satisfying job activities. Bernice Neugarten, in describing how people become aware of middle age, says:

Women, but not men, tend to define their age status in terms of timing of events within the family world, and even unmarried career women often discuss middle age in terms of the family they might have had . . .

Men, on the other hand, perceive the onset of middle age by cues presented outside the family context, often from the deferential behavior accorded them in the work setting. One man described the first time a younger associate helped open a door for him; another, being called by his official title by a newcomer in the company; another, the first time he was ceremoniously asked for advice by a younger man.

Little research has been done on the prestige accorded men and women in different age brackets. The few studies available point to older women as the lowest prestige group in society. In a projective test asking middle-aged persons to make up a story about a picture which showed a young couple and a middle-aged couple in conversation, Neugarten found that the older woman was seen as more uncomfortable in her role than any of the others and was the only figure who was as often described in negative as in positive terms. Mary Laurence found that respondents tended to rate women as having more undesirable personality traits than men through all age ranges, but the age group rated

How many men and women in different age groups remarry? (Number of marriages per 1000)

Widowed	Women	Men
45–64	16.2	70.1
65 and over	2.0	17.4
Divorced		
25–44	179.0	306.6
45–64	45.2	89.5
65 and over	9.7	26.5

most severely was women over 40.

A study of characters in American magazine fiction from 1890 to 1955 found a decline in the number of older women appearing as characters. By 1955 there were none at all. The middle-aged woman almost never sees herself and her problems depicted in print or on the screen. When they are, she sees mostly negative stereotypes. Her dilemma is very similar to that of the black ghetto child who finds in the "Dick and Jane" first reader a world that is irrelevant at best, invidious at worst. To have oneself and one's experiences verified in the mythology and art of one's culture is a fundamental psychological need at every stage of the life cycle.

Women's own attitudes toward aging are shown in the interesting finding that, in the listings of the Directory of the American Psychological Association, women are ten times as likely to omit their age as men. Thus, even professional women, who presumably have roles which extend undamaged into middle age, are much more likely than men to feel that their advancing age is a serious impairment.

On the question of whether middle-aged women are actually unhappier or more maladjusted than middle-aged men, the evidence is conflicting and inconclusive. A few studies by various researchers found little or no difference between middle-aged and old men and women on such factors as personality change, engagement with life and reported satisfaction with life. One study found older women more satisfied than older men.

One problem with these efforts, though, is that some of them lump together the middle-aged group with persons past retirement age. Some of the findings may therefore be due to the fact that the retirement age is far more stressful and acute for men than for women. Women have never invested much in careers and have been adjusting to role loss for many years. In old age an additional factor works in favor of women. Women are closer to relatives and thus more sheltered from complete isolation.

The studies present another problem in that the respondents themselves judged how happy or satisfied they were. The trouble with this is that subordinated groups learn to expect less and therefore to be satisfied with less. A middle-aged woman whose husband has had several affairs may report that her marriage has been satisfying because society has taught her to expect infidelity from her husband. A man whose wife had behaved in similar fashion would be less likely to regard his marriage as satisfying. Indeed, social conditioning would probably dictate a more painful crisis for the cuckolded husband. Moreover, measuring the satisfaction levels of people who are already so thoroughly "socialized" doesn't take into account the wife's feelings the first time she saw her own mother experience such treatment from her father and realized that a similar fate was in store for herself. It does not measure the emotional cost of adjusting to the expectation of abuse. In fact, if we were to confine our evidence to degrees of self-reported satisfaction, we might conclude that a great variety of social inequities create no emotional hardships for the subjugated. Elsewhere in this issue, however, Pauline Bart shows that middle age is much more stressful for women than for men and this finding corroborates the work of Judd Marmor who has reported that middle-aged women manifest psychiatric disorders three to four times as frequently as middle-aged men.

The Economic Loss

Discrimination against older women in employment is important because of the large number of people affected. The number of older women in the labor force has been growing rapidly in recent decades. In 1965, 50.3 percent of women in the age range of 45 to 54 and 41.4 percent of those 55 to 64 were employed. These percentages had risen sharply from 1940, when they were 24.5 percent and 18 percent respectively. In 1960, 40 percent of the total female work force was over 45 years old.

Discrimination against older workers of both sexes in industry is well documented. A 1965 Department of Labor survey concluded that half the job openings in the private economy are closed to applicants over 55 years of age, and one-fourth are closed to applicants over 45. Women are particularly disadvantaged by this discrimination because, as a result of their typical work and child-rearing cycle, many women come back on the labor market after a long period of absence (and are perhaps entering the market for the first time) during precisely these years. There is very little evidence on the question of whether older women are relatively more disadvantaged than older men. Edwin Lewis states that age is a greater detriment to women than to men but cites no evidence. A Department of Labor publication on age discrimination in employment claims that men are slightly favored, but the evidence is very incomplete. The study found that, compared to the percentage of unemployed older men and women, women were hired in somewhat greater numbers. But unemployment rates are based on self-reporting and are notoriously influenced by the optimism of a given group about the prospects of finding employment. Older women, many of whom are married, are less likely to report themselves as seeking work if they are pessimistic about the possibilities of getting any. The study also surveyed the employment practices of 540 firms and found that, although differences were slight, men were disadvantaged in a larger number of occupational categories. But in clerical work, in which 24 percent of women over 45 are engaged, discrimination against women was decidedly greater.

The problem of discrimination against older men and women is complicated by the fact that a study would have to take into account whether discrimination was practiced because of expected lack of physical strength, long training or internship programs or physical attractiveness. The former two considerations figure much more frequently in the case of men and certainly have more legitimacy as grounds for discriminating than the factor of physical attractiveness, which usually arises solely because the woman is seen as a sex object before she is seen as a productive worker. As long as this is the employer's orientation, it will probably do little good to cite him the studies proving that middle-aged women office workers are superior to young women in work attendance, performance and ability to get along agreeably with others. It would also be necessary to see how much relative discrimination there is within occupational categories. There is little discrimination in certain low-paid, undesirable jobs because the supply of workers in these categories is short. Women tend to be predominantly clustered in precisely these job categories.

A check of one Sunday's *Los Angeles Times* want ads yielded a count of 1,067 jobs advertised for women and 2,272 advertised for men. For both sexes specific upper-age limits or the term "young" were attached to less than 1 percent of the job listings, and there was almost no difference between men and women. However, 97 (or 9 percent) of the female ads used the term "girl" or "gal," while only two of the 2,272 male ads used the term "boy."

To check out my hunch that "girl" is an indirect way of communicating an age limitation, in a state where discrimination by age is supposedly illegal, I called five employment agencies in southern California and asked an interviewer who handles secretarial and clerical placement what he or she thought the term "girl" meant from the employer's side and how it would be interpreted by the average job seeker. Four of the five employment interviewers stated that the term definitely carries an age connotation for employer and job seeker alike. They defined the age implied variously as: "under 30"; "under 35—if we were looking in the 35-45 category we would use the term 'mature'; over 45 we don't say anything"; "It means a youngster. I certainly don't think a 45-year-old would go in if she saw that ad"; "It does mean age, which is why we always use the term 'women' in our company's ads (although we may use the term 'girl' on a specific listing)." The last person would not state a specific age because she was obviously worried about being caught in violation of the law, to which she frequently alluded. Only one of the five replied in the negative, saying "to me 'girl' is just another word for 'woman.' You can hardly use the term 'woman' in the wording of an ad." Everyone I questioned agreed that the term "girl Friday" (a tiny proportion of our cases) carries no age connotation. Several, however, mentioned that the terms "trainee," "recent high school grad" and "high school grad" were used to communicate an age limitation.

Along with the term "girl," a number of ads use physical descriptions—almost entirely lacking in men's ads. "Attractive gal for receptionist job" is typical. More specific are the following excerpts from the columns in the *Los Angeles Times*: "Exciting young atty seeks a sharp gal who wants a challenge"; "Young, dynamic contractor who is brilliant but disorganized needs girl he can depend on completely"; and one headlined "Lawyer's Pet" which goes on to say "Looking for a future: want challenge, 'variety,' $$$? Young attorney who handles all phases of 'law' will train you to become his 'right hand.'" Few women over 30 would consider themselves qualified to apply for these jobs.

The use of the term "girl" and the reaction of one employment agency interviewer who considered this as the only proper way to connote "woman" in a want ad underscores the extent to which women's jobs are still considered young girls' jobs, that is, the relatively unimportant work that a girl does before she gets married. One employment agency interviewer stated that his agency frequently had requests for a certain age level because companies want to keep the age range in a certain department homogeneous for the sake of congeniality. It is significant that he mentioned only the "twenties" or "thirties" as examples of such desirable age ranges.

One is tempted to make a comparison between the term "girl" and the insulting racist use of "boy" for all blacks, regardless of age. In both cases, the term indicates that the species under discussion is not considered capable of full adulthood. In both cases, blacks and women are acceptable and even likable when very old, as "uncle" and "grandmother," but somehow both are anachronistic as mature adults.

Given the scarcity and conflicting nature of the data, it is impossible to say with certainty that older women suffer more from discrimination than older men. The question certainly merits further and more systematic exploration.

Caste and Class

The division of this article into sexual, prestige and economic loss was taken from John Dollard's analysis of the sexual, prestige and economic gains of whites at the expense of blacks in his classic study, *Caste and Class in a Southern Town*. The choice was not an accident; spokesmen of women's liberation have often drawn heavily on the analogy between the problems of blacks and of women. Yet equally often one hears objections to the analogy. Blacks are, as a group, isolated in the lowest economic strata and physically ghettoed into the worst parts of town, while women, being inextricably connected to men through familial ties, do not share a drastic, common disability. It has also been suggested that to compare the plight of women with that of blacks is to belittle the importance of the need for black liberation. Most of these critics care as little for black liberation as for the liberation of women and need not be taken seriously.

Yet the intellectual objections to the analogy should be discussed. The argument actually rests on the assumption that middle-class status cushions all of life's shocks and that middle-class women are always comfortably imbedded in middle-class primary groups. It assumes further that the woes of lower-class women are all essentially class-connected rather than specifically sexconnected. The loneliness of widowhood, the anguish of a woman losing her husband to a younger woman, the perplexity of the woman whose children have left home and who finds herself unwanted on the labor market—these are real hurts, and they go deep, even in the middle class. Further, the notion of the individual as being deeply rooted in his primary groups certainly reflects a partial and outmoded view in a highly individualistic society where the nuclear family, usually the only long-lasting primary group, has become extremely unstable. In our society, men and women are expected to get through life essentially alone. This is true even of the woman who is able to maintain good family ties throughout her life. It is even truer for those who suffer the more common fate of having these ties weakened by discord or severed by death or separation. For the lower-class woman, of course, these difficulties are harsher and more unrelieved, but in every class the woman must bear them alone.

The differential definition of age in men and women represents a palpable advantage to men at the expense of women. It multiplies the options for emotional satisfaction on his side while it diminishes them on hers. It raises his prestige and self-esteem at the expense of hers. All men in our society benefit to some degree from this custom, while not a single woman who lives into middle age escapes bearing some of the cost. If we are ever to restructure this society into one of true equality for both sexes, this is one of the crucial points at which we must begin.

Portnoy's Mother's Complaint

Pauline Bart

A young man begs his mother for her heart, which a betrothed of his has demanded as a gift; having torn it out of his mother's proffered breast, he races away with it; and as he stumbles, the heart falls to the ground, and he hears it question protectively, "Did you hurt yourself, my son?"

Jewish folktale

Mrs. Gold is a young-looking Jewish housewife in her forties. A married daughter lives about 20 miles away. Her hyperactive brain-damaged 13-year-old son has been placed in a special school even farther away. After his departure

she became suicidally depressed and was admitted to a mental hospital. I asked her how her life was different now, and she answered:

It's a very lonely life, and this is when I became ill, and I think I'm facing problems now that I did not face before because I was so involved, especially having a sick child at home. I didn't think of myself at all. I was just someone that was there to take care of the needs of my family, my husband and children, expecially my sick child. But now I find that I—I want something for myself, too. I'm a human being, and I'm thinking about myself.

She was dissatisfied with her marriage; their mutual concern for their son held the couple together, but when their son entered an institution this bond was loosened, although they visited him every Sunday.

My husband is primarily concerned with only one thing, and that is making a living. But there's more to marriage than just that [pause] you don't live by bread alone.

Mrs. Gold states that she is not like other women for whom divorce is simple. She is considering divorcing him if their relationship does not improve. Yet, another patient whom I interviewed later told me Mrs. Gold had cried all night after her husband came to tell her he was divorcing her.

Although she believes her life was "fuller, much fuller, yes, much fuller" before her children left, she used to have crying spells:

But in the morning I would get up, and I knew that there was so much dependent on me, and I didn't want my daughter to become depressed about it or neurotic in any way, which could have easily happened because I had been that way. So I'm strong-minded and strong-willed, so I would pull myself out of it. It's just recently that I couldn't pull myself out of it. I think that if there was—if I was needed maybe I would have, but I feel that there's really no one that needs me now.

Her inability to admit anger toward her children and her perfectionist demands on herself is shown in the following remark: "It was extremely hard on me, and I think it has come out now. Very hard. I never knew I had the amount of patience. *That child never heard a raised voice.*"

While she is proud of her daughter and likes her son-in-law, there is an element of ambivalence in her remarks.

Naturally as a mother you hate to have your daughter leave home. I mean it was a void there, but, uh, I know she's happy . . . I'm happy for my daughter because she's happy.

Since she had used her daughter as a confidante when the daughter was a teen-ager, she lost a friend as well as a child with her daughter's departure. Mrs. Gold said she didn't want to burden her daughter with her own problems because her daughter was student teaching. The closeness they had now was "different" since her daughter's life "revolved around her husband and her teaching, and that's the way it should be." They phone each other everyday and see each other about once a week.

Like most depressives (Mrs. Gold is in the hospital for treatment of depression) she feels inadequate: "I don't feel like I'm very much." Between the day of her son's departure and her hospitalization she spent most of her time in bed and neglected her household, in marked contrast to her former behavior.

I was such an energetic woman. I had a big house, and I had my family. My daughter said, "Mother didn't serve eight courses. She served ten." My cooking—I took a lot of pride in my cooking and in my home. And very, very clean. I think almost fanatic.

She considers herself more serious than other women and couldn't lead a "worthless existence" playing cards as other women did. She was active in fund raising for the institution her son was in, but apparently, without the maternal role—the role that gave her a sense of worth—fund raising was not enough. Formerly her son "took every minute of our lives" so that she "did none of the things normal women did—nothing."

I can pardon myself for the fact [that he was placed in a school] that I did take care of him for 12 years and he was hyperactive. It was extremely hard on me, . . . I never knew I had that amount of patience.

Like most women interviewed, Mrs. Gold is puritanical and embarrassed about sex.

I think anything that gives you pleasure or enjoyment, anything like that. It's just that I'm not that kind of woman.

Mrs. Gold's problem, psychologically and sociologically, is, perhaps most dramatically apparent in her response when I asked her to rank seven roles available to middle-aged women in order of importance. She listed only one role: "Right now I think *helping my children*, not that they really need my help, but if they did I would really try very hard." Thus she can no longer enact the role that had given her life meaning, the only role she considered important for her. Her psychiatrist had told her, and she agreed, that a paying job would help her self-esteem. But what jobs are available for a 40-year-old woman with no special training, who has not worked for over 20 years?

Mrs. Gold has most of the elements that are considered by clinicians to make up the pre-illness personality of involutional depressives: a history of martyrdom with no payoff (and martyrs always expect a payoff at some time) to make up for the years of sacrifice, inability to handle aggressive feelings, rigidity, a need to be useful in order to feel worthwhile, obsessive compulsive supermother, superhousewife behavior and generally conventional attitudes.

Why Study Mrs. Portnoy and Her Complaints

Some of my friends have asked me what I am doing studying depressed middle-aged women. The question, implying that the subject is too uninteresting and unimportant to be worth studying, is itself evidence for the unfortunate situation these women find themselves in. But a society's humanity may be measured by how it treats its women and its aged as well as by how it treats its racial and religious minorities. This is not a good society in which to grow old or to be a woman, and the combination of the two makes for a poignant situation. In addition, there are practical and theoretical reasons why such a study is important. Practically speaking, women today live longer and end their childbearing sooner than they did in the last century. They are more likely now to reach the "empty nest" stage or the postparental stage (a term used by those investigators who do not consider this life cycle stage especially difficult). Moreover, in clinical terms, depression is the most common psychiatric symptom present in adults but, like middle age, it, too, has been generally ignored by sociologists.

Problems of middle age are important theoretically for several reasons. In the first place, there is contradictory evidence on the question of whether middle age is in fact a problem for women. After a study of middle age in 35 different cultures, for example, I found that most women in most of these cultures do not think of middle age as being a particularly stressful time. This would seem, at the very least, to refute such biological determinists as Hubert Humphrey's physician adviser, who, in a celebrated exchange with Representative Patsy Mink, declared that women ought to be barred from positions of serious responsibility because of the "raging hormonal influences" that overwhelm them at menopause. Nevertheless, it is a fact that many women in American society do undergo a painful period with the onset of middle age, and it is also a fact that some of these women collapse in a state of clinical depression, like Mrs. Gold.

This raises some serious questions. Why is it that one woman whose son has been "launched" says, "I don't feel like I've lost a son; I feel like I've gained a den," while another mother reports that the worst thing that ever happened to her was

> When I had to break up and be by myself and be alone, and I'm just—I really feel that I'm not only not loved but not even liked sometimes by my own children . . . they could respect me. If—if they can't say good things, why should they, why should they feel better when they hurt my feelings and make me cry and then call me a crybaby or tell me that I—I ought to know better or something like that. My worst thing is that I'm alone, I'm not wanted, nobody interests themselves in me . . . nobody cares.

Role and Self

The role one has in life and one's image of himself are intimately interconnected. When people are given the "Who Are You?" test, they usually respond by naming their various roles—wife, doctor, mother, teacher, daughter and the like. As a person goes from one stage of life to another, however, or from one step in a career to another, he or she must change his self-concept because the relevant or significant others, the people with whom he interacts, change. A loss of significant others can result in what Arnold Rose called a "mutilated self." One woman put it to me this way:

> I don't-I don't,—I don't feel like—I don't feel that I'm wanted. I don't feel at all that I'm wanted. I just feel like nothing. I don't feel anybody cares, and nobody's interested, and they don't care whether I do feel good or I don't feel good. I'm pretty useless . . . I feel like I want somebody to feel for me, but nobody does.

Another woman stated:

> I don't feel like I'm doing anything. I feel just like I'm standing still, not getting anywhere.

The traditional woman bases her self-esteem on a role, motherhood, that she must finally relinquish. Some do this with ease; some others, especially those with inflexible personalities, cannot. But the problem is not hers alone; society has provided no guidelines for her, no rites of passage. There is no bar mitzvah for menopause. The empty nest, then, may prompt the extreme feelings of worthlessness and uselessness that characterize depressives. One can think of these women as overcommitted to the maternal role and then, in middle age, suffering the unintended consequences of this commitment.

But there is more to it than that. Ideally, a mother should be flexible enough to stop mothering adult children, but if her personality is rigid, as depressives' usually are, she can't, and she can't expect them to stop acting like dependent children either. When the children do not act this way, she may feel resentful. But since a women is not "allowed" to be hostile to her children, she may turn the resentment inward and become depressed.

Moreover, a woman who overplays her role as mother may consciously or unconsciously want to place her children morally in her debt. Dan Greenberg's best-selling satire, *How To Be a Jewish Mother*, refers to guilt as the mother's main method of social control. It is no accident that his second book, *How To Make Yourself Miserable*, begins with the sentence, "You, we can safely assume, are guilty." It is the "supermother" who feels she can legitimately expect her children to be more devoted to her, more considerate of her, bring her more satisfaction than would otherwise be the case. Furthermore, in this situation, there may even be some payoff in the depressive collapse. When that happens, once again she gets the attention, sympathy and control over her children she had before they left.

I should make clear at this point why I have been quoting so extensively from Jewish empty nest mothers, women, moreover, who had been hospitalized for clinically defined depression. The most obvious reason is that in terms of the larger study I have done on the problems of middle-aged women cross-culturally, Jewish women in America occupy a pivotal place.

The literature on the Jewish mother is practically unanimous in painting her as "supermother" especially vulnerable to being severely affected if her children fail to meet her needs, either by not making what she considers "good" marriages, not achieving the career aspirations she has for them or even by not phoning her everyday. Not only is the traditional Jewish mother overinvolved with or over-identified with her children but the children are viewed as at the same time *helpless* without the mother's directives and as *powerful,* being able to kill the mother with "aggravation." As one depressed empty nest woman says, "My children have taken and drained me." In a sentence completion test, she filled in the blank after the words "I suffer" with "from my children."

Now, the theory governing my larger study of middle-aged women can be stated plainly enough. First, depression in middle-aged women is not due to the hormonal changes of the menopause, as is implied, for example, in the psychiatric diagnosis of "involutional melancolia." Rather, it is due to sociocultural factors that drastically reduce a woman's self-esteem. Second, depression is linked to actual or impending loss of a significant role; therefore, depression in middle-aged women will be linked with maternal role loss. Third, certain roles and attitudes toward them increase the effect of loss. For example, "supermothers" will have a higher rate of depression than normal mothers, and full-time housewives will have a higher rate than working women.

Obviously, one of the things that this theory would lead you to expect to find in "real life" is a higher rate of depression among Jewish mothers than among Anglos or among blacks. For, as everyone knows, the stereotypical Jewish mother is almost by definition an exaggerated version of the "supermother." Moreover, again according to the theory, one would expect to find that Jewish women would be more prone to depression than to other mental

TABLE 1

Jewish mothers are more depressed than mothers of other groups

Ethnicity	Percent Depressed	Total No.
Jews	84	122
Anglos	51	206
Blacks	22	28

The percent depressed among all non-Jews was 47 percent. Further investigation at one of the five hospitals showed 67 percent (six) of Jewish women with native-born mothers and 92 percent (thirteen) of Jewish women with European-born mothers to be depressed. Although the cases are few, the findings are suggestive.

illnesses and that European-born Jewish women, being presumably more traditional, would have higher rates of depression than American-born Jewish women.

Patients

These were my suppositions; to test them out I examined the records of 533 women between the ages of 40 and 59 who had had no previous hospitalization for mental illness. The women were in hospitals, ranging from an upper-class private hospital to the two state hospitals that served people from Los Angeles County. I compared women who had been diagnosed "depressed" (using the following diagnoses: involutional depression, psychotic depression, neurotic depression, manic-depressive depression) with women who had other functional (nonorganic) diagnoses.

I made every effort to overcome diagnostic biases on the part of the doctors and myself. First, the sample was drawn from five hospitals. Second, "neurotic depressives" were merged with the "involutional" and "psychotic depressives" and "manic-depressives" since I suspected that patients who would be called neurotic depressed at an upper-class hospital would be called involutional depressed at a lower-middle-class hospital—a suspicion that was borne out. Third, I used a symptom check list and found that depressed patients differed significantly from those given other diagnoses for almost all symptoms.

Fourth, a case history of a woman with both depressive and paranoid features was distributed to the psychiatric residents at the teaching hospital for "blind" diagnosis. In half the cases, the woman was called Jewish and in half Presbyterian. The results showed no difference in number of stigmatic diagnoses between the "Jews" and "Presbyterians" since the most and least stigmatic diagnoses (neurotic depression and schizophrenia) were given to "Presbyterians." Fifth, 39 MMPI (personality) profiles at one hospital were obtained and given to a psychologist to diagnose "blind." He rated them on an impairment continuum. The results supported the decision to combine psychotic, involutional and neurotic depressives, because the ratio of mild and moderate to serious and very serious was the same for all these groups.

Next, I conducted 20 intensive interviews at two hospitals to obtain information unavailable from the patients' records, using questionnaires already used on "normal" middle-aged women. I also gave them the projective biography test—a test consisting of 16 pictures showing women at different stages in their life cycle and in different roles. These interviews provided an especially rich source of information. I did not read their charts until *after* the interviews so as to leave my perception unaffected by psychiatrists' or social workers' evaluations.

Maternal role loss was recorded when at least one child was not living at home. I considered an overprotective or overinvolved relationship to be present when the record bore statements, such as "my whole life was my husband and my daughter" or if the woman entered the hospital following her child's engagement or marriage. Ratings of role loss, relationship with children and with husbands were made from a case history which omitted references to symptomatology, ethnicity or diagnosis, and high intercoder reliability was obtained for these variables. (Jewish coders were more likely to call a parent-child relationship unsatisfactory than non-Jewish coders. Categories were refined to eliminate this difference.) A woman was considered Jewish if she had a Jewish mother and regardless of profession of faith. The attitudes and values I am discussing need not come from religious behavior. For example, Mrs. Gold didn't attend religious services and was unsure of her belief in God. But she taught her daughter that "we just don't date Gentile boys" and considers herself very Jewish, "all the way through, to the core."

You Don't Have to be Jewish to be a Jewish Mother

My suppositions were confirmed: Jews have the highest rate of depression, Anglos an intermediate rate and blacks the lowest rate (see table 1). Jewish women are roughly twice as likely to be diagnosed depressed as non-Jewish women. Moreover, the very small group of Jewish women whose mothers were born in the United States had a rate of depression midway between that of Jewish women with European-born mothers on the one hand and Anglo women on the other. The low rates for black women suggest that their family structure and occupational roles tend to prevent depression. However, when I controlled the data, holding patterns of family interaction constant, the difference

between Jews and non-Jews sharply diminishes (Table 2). To be sure, overprotection or overinvolvement with children is much more common among Jews than among non-Jews. But it is clear that you don't have to be Jewish to be a Jewish mother. For example one divorced black women, who had a hysterectomy, went into a depression when her daughter, her only child, moved to Oregon. The depression lifted when the woman visited her and recurred when she returned to Los Angeles. Yet these results may simply reflect a greater unwillingness to hospitalize depressed black women in the Black community. Depressives are not likely to come to the attention of the police unless they attempt suicide. Therefore, if the woman or her family do not define her condition as psychiatric, she will remain at home. Only a prevalence study can fully test the hypothesis about the Black family.

Any doubts about the validity of my inferences from the hospital charts were dispelled by the interviews.

Even though they were patients and I was an interviewer and a stranger, one Jewish woman forced me to eat candy, saying, "Don't say no to me." Another gave me unsolicited advice on whether I should remarry and to whom, and a third said she would make me a party when she left the hospital. Another example of extreme nurturant patterns was shown by a fourth women who insisted on caring for another patient who had just returned from ECT (shock) while I was interviewing her. She also attempted to find other women for me to interview. The vocabulary of motives invoked by the Jewish women generally attributed their illness to their children. They complained about not seeing their children often enough. Non-Jewish women were more restrained and said they wanted their children to be independent.

Two of the Jewish women had lived with their children, wanted to live with them again, and their illness was precipitated when their children forced them to live alone. However, in another study I did, even women who lived with their children were all depressed. As one such woman complained:

> Why is my daughter so cold to me? Why does she exclude me? She turns to her husband . . . and leaves me out. I don't tell her what to do, but I like to feel my thoughts are wanted.

All the mothers, when asked what they were most proud of, replied, "My children." Occasionally, after this, they mentioned their husbands. None mentioned any accomplishment of their own, except being a good mother. This was reflected also in the ranked answers to the question of what was most important to them: being a homemaker, taking part in church, club and community activities, being a companion to one's husband, helping parents, being a sexual partner, having a paying job or helping children. Needless to say, "helping children" was most frequently ranked first or second by these postnest mothers. Since it is difficult to help children who are no longer home, women who value this behavior more than any other are in trouble. (Interestingly, "helping parents" was ranked first by only one. No woman listed "being a sexual partner" first, and three married women did not even include it in the ranking.)

TABLE 2

Over involved mothers who lose their maternal role are the most depressed group.

Condition	Percent Depressed	Total No.
Role Loss	62	369
Maternal Role Loss	63	245
Housewives with Maternal Role Loss	69	124
Middle-Class Housewives with Maternal Role Loss	74	69
Women with Maternal Role Loss Who Had Overprotective or Over involved Relationships with Their Children.	76	72
Housewives with Maternal Role Loss Who Have Overprotective or Over-involved Relationships with Their Children	82	44

Those interviewed were also given the projective biography test—16 pictures showing women in different roles and at different ages. The clinical psychologist who devised the test and analyzed the protocols without knowing my hypothesis noted they were "complete mothers." One of the pictures, showing an old woman sitting in a rocking chair in front of a fireplace, got overwhelmingly negative reactions. As one put it:

And this scene I can't stand. Just sitting alone in old age by just sitting there and by some fireplace all by herself [pause] turning into something like that. And to me this is too lonely. A person has to slow down sometime and just sit, but I would rather be active, and even if I would be elderly, I wouldn't want to live so long that I wouldn't have anything else in life but to just sit alone and you know, just in a rocking chair.

Another woman who was divorced and had both her children away from home said, "This could look very much like me. I'm sitting, dreaming, feeling so blue." When she chose that as the picture not liked, she said, "Least of all, I don't like this one at all. That's too much like I was doing—sitting and worrying and thinking." Two women even denied the aging aspects of the picture: "Here she is over here sitting in front of the fireplace, and she's got her figure back, and I suppose the baby's gone off to sleep, and she's relaxing." This woman interpreted every picture with reference to a baby.

What is to be Done

It is very easy to make fun of these women, to ridicule their pride in their children and concern for their well-being. But it is no mark of progress to substitute Mollie Goldberg for Stepin Fetchit as a stock comedy figure. They are as much casualties of our culture as are the children in Harlem whose IQs decline with each additional year they spend in school. In their strong commitment to and involvement with their children, they were only doing what they were told to do, what was expected of them by their families, their friends and the mass media. If they deviated from this role, they would have been ridiculed (ask any professional woman).

Moreover, what I am really talking about here is what happens to women who follow the cultural rules, who buy the American Dream, who think there is a payoff for good behavior, who believe in justice and who therefore suffer depression, a loss of meaning, when they discover that their lives have not turned out the way they expected. We even find the same syndrome in men. Men who have involutional psychosis are usually in their sixties, the retirement age. I would predict that these are men whose occupational roles were "props." Like the women who derive their identity almost exclusively from their role as mothers, there are men whose identity is completely wrapped up in their work. With retirement, then, one could expect to find symptoms of depression. And in fact, the director of admissions at the teaching hospital where I worked reported that it was not unusual for army officers to suffer involutional depressions on retirement. And a 1965 study on involutional depression in Israel found loss of meaning a factor among old pioneers who believed "that the values so dear to them were fast disappearing. Current ideals and expectations were now alien to them and the sense of duty and sacrifice as they knew it seemed to exist no longer. They felt different, isolated and superfluous."

But the cases of these women tell us something else that

is important. Two psychoanalysts, Therese Benedek and Helene Deutsch, state that menopause is more difficult for "masculine" or "pseudomasculine" women. The former describes this woman as one whose "psychic economy was dominated—much like that of a man's—by strivings of the ego rather than by the primary emotional gratifications of motherliness." Deutsch states that "feminine, loving" women have an easier time during climacteric than do "masculine, aggressive ones." However, my data shows that it is the women who assume the *traditional* feminine role—who are housewives, who stay married to their husbands, who are not overtly aggressive, in short who accept the traditional norms—who respond with depression when their children leave. Even the MMPI, masculine-feminine scores for women at one hospital were one half a standard deviation *more* feminine than the mean.

Until recent years, a common theme of inspirational literature for women, whether on soap operas or in women's magazines, has been that they could only find "real happiness" by devoting themselves to their husbands and children and by living vicariously through them. If one's sense of worth comes from other people rather than from one's own accomplishments, it follows that when such people depart, one is left with an empty shell in place of a self. If, however, a woman's sense of worth comes from her own interests and accomplishments, she is less vulnerable to breakdown when significant others leave. This point is obscured in much of the polemical literature on the allegedly dominant American female who is considered to have "lost" her femininity. It is, after all, *feminine* women, the ones who play the traditional roles, not the career women, who are likely to dominate their husbands and children. This domination, however, may take more traditional female forms of subtle manipulation and the invoking of guilt. If, however, a woman does not assume the traditional female role and does not expect to have her needs for achievement or her needs for "narcissistic gratification," as psychiatrists term it, met vicariously through the accomplishments of her husband and children, *then* she has no need to dominate them, since her well-being does not depend on their accomplishments. It is unreasonable to expect one sex in an achievement-oriented society not to have these needs.

The Women's Liberation movement, by pointing out alternative life styles, by providing the emotional support necessary for deviating from the ascribed sex roles and by emphasizing the importance of women actualizing their own selves, fulfilling their own potentials, can help in the development of personhood, for both men and women.

And Then We Were Old
Irving Rosow

The old are with us, but not of us.

More than 17,000,000 persons over sixty-five live in America today, making up almost nine percent of the population; but this is not why they are a problem. They increase ever more rapidly—one million every three years; nor is this why they are a problem.

They trouble us precisely because we are such an affluent society. They have become a standing embarrassment, a mute reproach to social conscience. Our productivity makes the sheer cost of meeting such social problems of secondary importance; we can view them against larger national goals and the kind of society we want to become. The price of social change is not a critical economic issue—it is basically a moral concern and a value choice.

The old lack money and they lack medical care.

But even if these needs were met, their problem would still not be solved. We must not confuse provision for material needs with a general solution. Although many specific needs are involved, the old in America suffer primarily from lack of function and status. And this will not be changed until the younger groups themselves change, so that the old can have self-respect and honor among us. But before younger people can change, many of our institutions and values must first alter—so we are caught in a major dilemma.

How do other cultures handle their aged? What conditions support the social position of old people—their prestige, status, or power? What fosters their social integration?

Leo Simmons has studied this problem among almost a hundred primitive societies represented in the Yale cross-cultural files. Others, such as Conrad Arensberg and Solon Kimball, provide supplemental data on more recent nonindustrial cultures as well. Taken together, they cover all stages of pre-industrial development, from the simplest food-gathering groups to advanced agricultural economies with complex systems of private property.

These studies show that the welfare of the aged varies according to seven factors which involve the resources that old people command, the functions they perform, and the state of social organization. Their position in their society is relatively stronger if:

■ They own or control property on which younger people are dependent. In this way they maintain their own independence while simultaneously governing the opportunities of the young. In rural Ireland, for instance, a son may not succeed to his inheritance before his fifties, and he may be deferential to his parents almost into their senility.

■ Their experience gives them a vital command or monopoly of strategic knowledge of the culture, including the full range of occupational skills and techniques, as well as healing, religion, ritual, warfare, lore, and the arts. As the principal bearers and interpreters of cultures in which there is little change and no science, the old have a strategic function in transmitting this knowledge to younger people.

■ They are links to the past and to the gods in tradition-oriented societies. In classical China, for example, old age was honorific and revered on religious as well as other grounds; and when the old died they were worshipped as ancestors.

■ The extended family is central to the social structure. A clan can and will act much more effectively to meet crises and dependency of its members than a small family. Mutual obligations between blood relatives—specifically including the aged—are institutionalized as formal rights, not generous benefactions.

■ The population clusters in relatively small, stable communities in which the governing values are sacred rather than secular; community structure is fairly clear cut, with formal age-grading and definite roles linked to different ages; almost all contacts between group members are face-to-face and personal; and an individual relates to the same group of people in many different contexts instead of many diverse groups—one at home, a second at work, and a third in church, for example.

The final two factors are rather surprising. They show that the relative welfare of the old person in his group improves to the extent that:

■ The productivity of the economy is low and approaches the ragged edge of starvation. The greater the poverty and the struggle to survive, the *relatively* better off old people are by the standards of their group. With low marginal productivity and a primitive division of labor, labor may be cheap, but the contribution of each additional pair of hands to the small gross product is valued.

To be sure, in such primitive economies extremely dependent old people are not sentimentally cared for indefinitely. Their fates are determined by the balance between what they put in and take out of the system. But, so long as an old person's productivity exceeds his consumption, including the time and effort required for his care, the culture retains and makes a place for him. However, when the balance shifts and his dependency threatens the group, then he tends to be expelled. Although the particular form of this fate may vary, swift death is common. The Masai of Africa unceremoniously throw the old dependent outside the village *bwoma* and forget about him, while the Polar Eskimos rather sorrowfully "put him out on the ice" —in both cases to die. But when his needs impose a severe strain on the group's resources, his *social* death precedes the physical.

■ Finally, there is high mutual dependence within a group. The great interdependence among members promotes mutual aid in meeting survival problems. Here the aged are benefactors as well as beneficiaries of reciprocity.

A range of studies indicate that even in America, old people are relatively better off and accepted when they own family farm land, live in small communities, are members of racial or ethnic minorities with extended kinship obligations, or belong to unskilled, working class groups where interdependence and mutual aid are standard conditions of survival. These findings argue well for the generality of the seven principles.

However, social change is systematically weakening these principles, regardless of local variations.

Property ownership. This has spread broadly through the population during the past generation. But it has been attended by an important separation between capital ownership and management in which control is *not* particularly centered in the hands of older people. Further, the growth of the economy has created many new jobs, but mainly for younger people. At the same time, changes in higher education have opened the gates of the universities to many more of them.

These developments have increased young people's opportunities and reduced their dependence. While an old property owner may be financially independent, he no longer has significant control over the life chances of the young; and they have less need to defer to him.

Strategic knowledge. Old people's skills, experience, and knowledge are no longer critical factors in our culture and seldom make them authorities. The speed and pervasiveness of social change now transform the world within a generation, so that the experience of the old becomes largely irrelevant to the young. The lifetime of a seventy-five-year-old person spans man's leap from the horse and buggy to the hydrogen bomb and space travel. Occupational and other skills are now taught through formal education rather than informally. The young and middle-aged learn attitudes and life styles largely from age mates and the mass media. Nor have the old solved the problems of the world successfully enough to inspire respect and confidence. Therefore, they are considered neither strategic agents of instruction nor founts of wisdom.

Religious links. Our society has never venerated the aged as peculiarly sacred links to ancestors, gods, or the past. The old are not protected by religious tradition.

Kinship and extended family. Kinship and family ties have been weakened in this century by occupational demands and frequent moving. Shifting job markets require flexibility of movement at the same time that urban homes have shrunk in size. The smaller isolated family has become the norm, and responsibility to one's spouse and children now takes clear priority over obligations to parents. Although children still do help aged parents, especially in the working classes, the major responsibility for old people has shifted to the government and other organizations.

Community life. Urbanization and residential mobility have also seriously weakened local community ties. Changing neighborhoods, turnover of residents, and urban impersonality have undermined those stable neighborhood structures which used to accommodate older people.

Productivity. Clearly, by any conceivable index, our productivity is tremendously high and growing. Because of automation, there is widespread displacement and no general labor scarcity outside of selected occupations. Since old people do not appreciably command skills in those occupations where labor is short, they are in little demand on the labor market. Except under special conditions, such as boom or war, they are not important to the work force.

Mutual dependence. Our economic growth and the drastic rise in living standards have undermined our mutual dependence. Greater income and opportunity have extended the range of personal choice and the freedom of action. Many goals can now be achieved with comparatively little reliance on other individuals, but this independence has been bought at the expense of solidarity and reciprocity. Except for the civil rights movement, it is a far cry indeed from the collective action of industrial unionization in the thirties.

Therefore, those factors which reinforce the position of old people in less advanced societies undermine the aged in America. We are too wealthy as a nation and too prosperous as individuals to *need* the old person. He can do little for us that we cannot do ourselves.

Younger groups have the power. And they tie help for the aged to need—and to political weight—rather than to right. By contrast a number of foreign nations, notably the Scandinavian and Low Countries, but including England, France, Germany, and Israel, have various programs for older people which are far more comprehensive, taken for granted, and self-regulating than ours.

THE HIGH COST OF AGING

Some features of American life are positively *inimical* to old people. We are youth-oriented, so that children and the young persons have a prior claim on our resources. We view this as an investment in the future rather than in the past, and it reflects pragmatism if not equity.

Also, though it has traditionally been difficult for men over forty to get employment, occupational obsolescence is occurring at steadily younger ages. Moreover, technological development affects not only the manual and less skilled workers, but is now reaching relentlessly into higher professional and managerial ranks and into the most advanced, complex levels of science.

In many fields, the fund of human knowledge doubles in about ten years, and as new ideas and techniques are introduced, experience counts for less and less. Consequently, the electronics engineer will eventually step aside for the solid-state physicist. Because of reluctance and the decline in learning ability as people grow older, we cannot expect easy retraining in new skills during middle age or later. Actually, advances in knowledge will result in a shorter work life and a younger retirement age in the future. By the end of the century the twenty-five hour week and retirement at fifty may well be commonplace—and these are conservative estimates.

While older workers can still make some contribution, their productive capacity and quality are generally lower at sixty-five than at thirty or forty. They may be kept productive if they are placed in carefully selected jobs, but it is another question whether they can be kept working at com-

petitive costs. Beyond sheer obsolescence lie two *other* obstacles to their continued employment:

■ Less productive older workers involve higher direct and indirect costs. Therefore, employers are asked to subsidize the aged either by absorbing higher expenses or by lowering profit margins. In either case, we expect them to assume the costs, and in our economy, their lack of enthusiasm for this is scarcely surprising.

■ The second obstacle to continued employment is the "efficiency" norm of large scale enterprises. Routine personnel procedures in recruitment, hiring, and job placement aim to eliminate inefficient individual processing. But the optimum assignment of old workers requires custom job-tailoring and personal attention. In other words, sheer bureaucratic pride in "running a taut ship" itself militates against individual treatment.

Thus changes in technology, the occupational system, urbanization, residential mobility, and the family have all been harmful to old people. The aged have been shorn of their major functions and supports; they have lower social status and no incentive to accept old age as rewarding. Consequently, to avert the stigma of age, they systematically deny that they are declining or getting old. To admit to being old is the final surrender.

How can they preserve the illusion of youth, of keeping age at bay? In general only by maintaining those factors that integrate an old person into society. But can their middle age patterns be continued into old age?

■ *Property and power.* We have seen earlier that old people cannot easily retain the bases of power, and that property may give them independence, but little control over or deference from others.

■ *Group memberships.* People are integrated into society not only by the resources they command and the functions they perform, but also through their social networks. Here the picture for the old is equally clear. Data on their associations show that participation in clubs and organizations declines steadily with age as low income, widowhood, and illness increase. Their informal relationships similarly diminish as neighborhoods change, families separate when children marry and pursue jobs, relatives and friends move away or die. More of their time is spent at funerals than ever before. In other words, old people progressively lose their group supports as networks of relatives, friends, and neighbors wither away through time.

231

What possible substitutes exist for these deteriorating social ties? One is the formation of new friendships with younger people nearby. However, younger age groups tend to be indifferent to or reject the old. This is trenchantly expressed in Joyce Cary's novel, *To Be a Pilgrim*:

Love is a delusion to the old, for who can love an old man? He is a nuisance; he has no place in the world. The old are surrounded by treachery, for no one tells them truth. Either it is thought necessary to deceive them, for their own good, or nobody can take the trouble to give explanation or understanding to those who will carry both so soon into a grave. They must not complain of what is inevitable; they must not think evil. It is unjust to blame the rock for its hardness, the stream for its inconstancy and its flight, the young for the strength and the jewel brightness of their passage. An old man's loneliness is nobody's fault. He is like an old fashioned hat which seems absurd and incomprehensible to the young, who never admired and wore such a hat.

It is consistent with this that research shows small chance of success for the development of friendships between old and young. Younger people have negative stereotoypes about the old; and their attitudes do *not* change as a result of contact, exposure to, or experience with them. For example, my own studies of local friendship patterns show that in a large apartment building with old and young residents, less than four percent of friendships in the building were between the age groups. There is an effective social barrier between older and younger people which proximity does not destroy. The aged, incidentally, are the only group for which this is true. Contact and exposure do break down invidious stereotypes about other groups; but not about old people. This is not only because age is devalued, but also because different age groups seldom are peers sharing a common role, similar life experiences, and a common fate.

■ *Major social roles*. People are also defined and located in society according to their major role attributes, such as marital status, work, income, and health. To the extent that an older person can maintain his middle-age characteristics in this respect, his later years pose few serious problems. But if these change, old age becomes strained, problematic, and demoralized. Older people are relatively well off and socially integrated if they are: (a) married and living with spouse; (b) still at work; (c) have no major loss of income; and (d) are in good health. But they are apt to be in serious difficulty if they are widowed, retired, have

suffered a large drop in income, and are in poor health.

What chances have they of showing up favorably on these four factors?

Marital status. As expected, the aged show more marital disruption than any other age group. Of those over sixty-five, only about 45 percent are still married and living with spouses. One-fourth of the men and more than one-half of the women are widowed.

But even these overall figures conceal the sharp rise in marital dissolution with increasing age. Each ten-year period after sixty-five finds an additional 20 percent widowed. For example, 15 percent of the men 65-69 are widowed compared to 58 percent of those over 85. For women, widowhood increases from 41 percent of those 65-69 to 83 percent of those 85 or older. Widowhood affects more women than men and probably has a harder impact on them. This will probably continue because women are generally younger than their husbands, they have lower mortality rates at every age, and their life expectancy rises ever faster. For example, in 1920, there were about equal numbers of men and women over sixty-five; in 1940, there were almost eleven women for every ten men; by 1950, there were fully twelve women for every ten men. The surplus of older women will presumably increase—and so will the strains of widowhood.

Work. The proportion of people over sixty-five in the labor force has declined steadily for the past sixty years. Two-thirds of the men were working in 1900 compared to scarcely one-third today, only about half of them full-time.

More important, of those men still working, almost one-half are *self-employed,* but precisely in those sectors of the economy where the independent operator is steadily giving way. The family farmer and small businessman are losing out to corporations; and professionals are increasingly entering business or government as salaried employees. Thus, the economy itself is steadily undermining the possibilities for self-employment.

What about the remaining older workers, those on wages? Except for a minority protected by effective seniority and flexible retirement provisions, they are very vulnerable. On the free labor market, older workers are in the traditionally marginal position of Negroes—the last hired and first fired. Apart from illness and a few atypical industries, one overriding factor governs whether older people work: when labor is scarce, old people have jobs; when labor is abundant, they do not. It is as stark as that. And in an era of automation, labor shortages promise to be ephemeral and localized.

Income. So long as older people continue to work, their income holds up reasonably well. Indeed, if their health is good, they may even be better off than earlier because their homes are usually paid off, their children independent, and their own needs more modest. But for the two-thirds who are retired, income is chopped to approximately *half* of their former earnings. Furthermore, despite steady increases in social security benefits from the early 'fifties, retirees have not received a *pro rata* share of our growing productivity. Between 1940 and 1960, all workers' *real* income after taxes rose by 51 percent while real social security benefits increased by only 17 percent, or one-third as much.

For the aged as a whole, income figures are appalling, and one cannot conceive how many of them manage to keep body and soul together at today's prices. It is perhaps a tribute to human resilience and adaptability. According to the Social Security Administration, among persons over sixty-five in 1960, about one-fourth of the women had no income at all, almost three-fourths had less than $1,000 per year, and fewer than one in ten had as much as $2,000 annually. The situation of men was not quite so bad, but it was bad enough. More than one-fourth had less than $1,000, one-third between $1,000 and $1,999, and about 40 percent had $2,000 or more per year. Fewer than one person in four had an income approaching $40 per week. Try to imagine an old couple or even a single person subsisting on less than this at recent price levels!

Health. Modern medicine has reduced infectious diseases so that the aged suffer mostly from chronic illness. Older people generally expect more aches, pains, and creaks in their daily lives, and they accept this as normal so long as they are still able to get around and function independently. For the most part, they do manage. Only about 15 percent have serious loss of mobility or capacity to function.

The foregoing losses do not affect persons over sixty-five uniformly. A major dividing line occurs at seventy-five. Significantly more people over seventy-five are widowed, retired, have low incomes, and are in very poor health.

STAYING IN THE RACE

We suggested earlier that old people are still fairly well integrated in society if their earlier social characteristics remain unchanged—if they are married and living with spouse, are still working, have adequate income, and tolerable health. But, what are the purely statistical chances that a person over sixty-five will show up favorably in *all four* respects? For the moment, we can arbitrarily take $2,000

per year as a minimum adequate income. Then, if we combine the individual probabilities of a favorable rating on each of the four separate role factors—marital status, work, income, and health—we find these results: the chances of a man over sixty-five having a favorable rating on *all* four items is only about 7 percent, and of a woman, less than 1 percent. This means that, on the average, only about seven men in a hundred and fewer than one woman in a hundred have a *good* chance of preserving the major bases of their social integration. The odds are somewhat better for those 65-69 and are drastically worse in each successive older group as illness, retirement, and widowhood exact their toll. Thus, the chances of retaining roles and, therefore, social integration are poor for the age group as a whole and steadily deteriorate with increasing age.

If the forces which protect the position of the aged are weak, could the old at least safeguard their material interests through organized political action? Do they have the potential power to wrest a larger, more equitable share of what our society has to offer? Obviously, politicians think that potential political strength is there, among old people and their families, and they are bidding for votes.

The basic problems are whether older people can relinquish their younger self-images, accept the negative implications of age, and mobilize politically to redress their deprivations. Can they admit that they have low status and act publicly on this basis? Or will pride, apathy, or wishful thinking prove stronger than their collective interests? Can the usual determinates of voting behavior and political action—social class, occupation, ethnicity, religion, region, and rural-urban residence—be overcome to weld together diverse groups on the basis of age? Can ingrained political alignments be uprooted and mobilized into an effective new political force?

Possibly, if two conditions can be met—if political goals center on immediate material benefit; and if the aged are also organized in stable *non-political* groups, each having a common identity *not* related to age. Thereby, action around collective interests could be encouraged by other group supports.

The overall picture is fairly bleak. It indicates that our values and institutions undermine the position of the aged. Our society makes little meaningful place for them, and current trends are further shrinking even that little room. The historical changes, particularly technological and economic, which victimize the aged cannot easily be reversed. And sheer hortatory pleas are unavailing. These are cold, bitter facts; but they are the realities.

BEYOND SECURITY

These are no simple answers to the question, "What is the solution to the problems of the aged?" for the question itself has different levels; it can refer to symptoms or to causes. Some limited, practical measures are possible—even though they only ameliorate symptoms. After all, if we try to make terminal cancer patients as comfortable as possible, we can do at least as much for the aged.

We might consider two alternatives. First, we can provide adequately for old people's material welfare and security. This means assuring them of all the medical care they need without quibbling about their eligibility or whether it will cost two billion or three billion dollars and without burying the patient, the doctor, or the hospital in paperwork. This is possible. It also means assuring all older people of a genuinely adequate income and decent standard of living, again without quibble or cavil. This would require major revision of the entire social security program and its income provisions. But this too is possible. One often wonders how pressing old people's problems would be if their income were simply doubled or tripled and they had the freedom of action which they are now denied. In the long run, how willingly and generously we approach such material needs may be as significant as what we do.

Second, we must consider how best to insulate old people from the social insults of age; specifically how to ease their loss of status and the indifference of younger people. Isolation and other problems grow as the aged lose their roles and their contacts, but these demoralizing pressures might slacken if the aged had ready access to other old people of similar background. Similarity of life experience and a common fate are a firm basis of communication, mutual understanding, and group formation. We are not advocating the formal segregation of the aged; but insofar as potential friends are found in the immediate environment, this might insulate them from the rebuffs of society, increase the prospect of new social ties, and partially revitalize their lives. Environments which integrate old people into local groups warrant careful study, and some research on this is being completed.

But we must not concentrate only on symptoms—particularly if we are successful in treating them. There is little doubt that some important concessions will be made, whether willingly or grudgingly, to the material needs of the aged, especially medical care and income. These must not be neglected; but we may still be barely scratching the surface of the problem.

More fundamental answers must be sought to the status issue. Basic solutions will be almost impossible unless our material values shift and our institutions change. We will have to place a higher value on our human resources, on social rights, on truth and beauty, not because they are practical but for their own sake. This is necessary before a life of genuine dignity and respect will be possible for older people—or for the young.

Actually, the crucial people are *not* the aged, but the *younger* groups. It is *we* who determine the status and position of the old. The problem is that of alienation—not only the alienation of old from young, but of the young from each other, and of man from man. No real way out of this dilemma exists without a basic reworking of our national aspirations and values. Anything less than this will see us treating only symptoms, nibbling at the tattered edges of our social problems without penetrating to their heart.

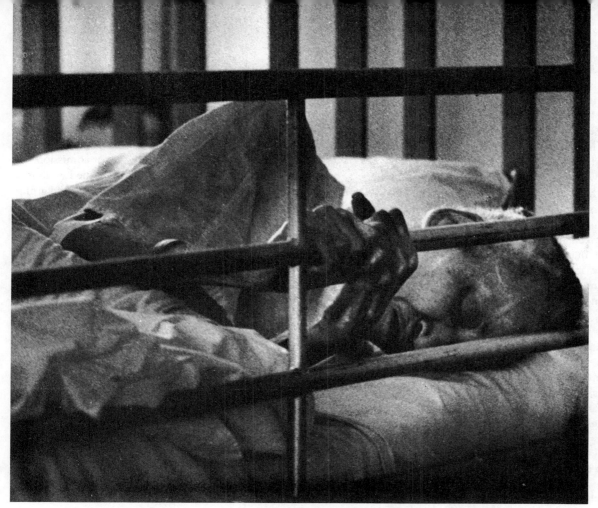

A Hiding Place to Die

Elizabeth Markson

Francis Bacon said, "Men fear death as children fear to go in the dark; and as that natural fear in children is increased with tales, so is the other." Much of this fear of death is valuable for survival, but it has also tended to obscure the actual conditions under which people die. Death has either been romanticized, the Victorian solution, or minimized, as in the United States today. The elaborate American funeral rituals described in Evelyn Waugh's *The Loved One* and Jessica Mitford's *The American Way of Death* are not contradictory evidence on this point, for the actual *act of dying* is shunned and much of the ceremony seems designed to deny that death has really occurred.

Few tales of death have been told by anyone, including social scientists, but the recent work of Barney G. Glaser and Anselm L. Strauss in *Awareness of Dying* and *Time for Dying* and other studies marks the opening of this area of inquiry. The study reported on here supports the idea, first suggested by Glaser and Strauss, that the anathema of dying is not only a problem for lay people, but also for health professionals, and describes one way in which professionals attempt to avoid the dying. Their success in doing so, it appears, depends on the relative status of the dying person.

There is a norm, subscribed to by at least some professionals, that old people should be allowed to die at home, but in fact most people die in hospitals or other institutions. It is suggested here that though it is desirable to die at home, for it is more comfortable, such comfortable deaths are a privilege accorded only to higher status people. Put another way, the lower the status of the dying person, the less likely are those around him to want to participate in his death.

It is well known that older patients who enter state mental hospitals have an excessive death rate. It has been suggested that this is because they are already dying when they are sent there, the early signs of impending death having been mistaken for insanity. Data gathered in New York State reveal, moreover, that older people tend to have higher death rates in both the state mental hospitals and county infirmaries than they do in any other kind of psychiatric treatment facility. Even those older people who are being treated in general hospital emergency rooms are less likely to die within six months of treatment than are those entering state and county hospitals.

These findings tend to confirm the idea put forward by a number of students of death that the old are sent to lower status institutions, particularly mental hospitals, to die. The following study of deaths of the aged at a state mental hospital will postulate the processes by which both the laity and professionals make the decision to send patients to mental hospitals when they are not mentally ill, but are simply taking too long to die.

This study of whether those who send geriatric patients to state mental hospitals know of the excessive risk of death is founded on an examination of the medical records of 174 elderly patients who were admitted to Fairview State Hospital during an eight-month period in 1967. The hospital serves two boroughs of New York City and their suburbs and is located near a suburban community. During the period studied, the hospital admitted all patients who applied. The medical and nursing staff supported this open-door policy on the grounds that denial of admission to any geriatric patient would be a disservice to both the patient and the community.

The physical illnesses of the 174 patients detected at the post-admission physical examination (Table l) make it clear that elderly people with a multiplicity of serious physical illnesses, primarily heart and circulatory diseases, either alone or in combination with other disorders, were being sent to the hospital. Indeed, 44 of the 174 (25 percent) died within 30 days of admission. Those patients with one or more severe physical illnesses included proportionately more of those who died within one month than of those who survived, and this difference is statistically significant.

The old people in this study were not only physically ill, but also grossly impaired. Less than half the group were able to walk without assistance. One quarter were described as "feeble," 11 percent were in wheelchairs and 19 percent were on stretchers, including 6 percent who were comatose. Those patients who were mobile were strikingly less likely to die than those who were feeble or worse at admission. Of the mobile group, only 9.1 percent had died within a month of admission; the figure for the incapacitated group was 38.9 percent.

While it seems evident that moribund patients were being sent to this hospital for the mentally ill, it is possible that these patients were referred to psychiatric care because their behavior mimicked mental illness, as suggested earlier. It might be expected that the dying would resemble at least a portion of those who have an organic brain syndrome but do not die, for both have symptoms of organic origin. To test this hypothesis, the reasons for referral recorded by Fairview's admitting psychiatrists were examined. Virtually all the complaints made about these patients by their families or others interested in having them committed concerned either senile behavior alone or in combination with such major psychiatric symptoms as delusions, hallucinations or depression, but this was equally true of those who died within a month and those who survived with one exception: the ten comatose patients who could not be examined by the psychiatrist. Six of the eight men and one of the two women in this group died shortly after admission.

In sum, it appears that no premonitory or prodromal signs of death that could be distinguished from psychiatric symptoms were detected among this group of old people, even in psychiatric examination. This is particularly interesting in view of Morton Lieberman's finding that specific personality changes occur among old people several months prior to death. Lieberman was studying a nursing home population, however, which may have differed considerably from the group of elderly mental hospital patients studied here. Further, since our data are drawn from case reports, personality differences associated with either dying or psychosis may have been obscured by inadequate descriptions.

Psychiatric diagnosis at the hospital was apparently routine and cursory. Organic brain syndrome with psychosis was the designation given 114 patients in our study. In more than 88 percent of the cases, this diagnosis differed in either degree or kind from that made by the referring hospital. Follow-up data on patients who survived more than a month showed that more than one third of those

236

TABLE 1   PHYSICAL DISEASES AND DEATHS

Diseases	All Ad-mitted	All Dying Within Month	Dying of Detected Disease
Cancer, all types	7	4	3
alone	2	1	0
with heart and/or circulatory diseases	3	3	3
with digestive and/or genitourinary diseases	2	0	0
with respiratory diseases	0	0	0
Heart and circulatory diseases, all types	85	24	17
alone	58	13	7
with respiratory diseases	8	6	6
with digestive and/or genitourinary diseases	13	2	1
with respiratory and digestive or genitourinary diseases	6	3	3
Respiratory diseases	5	1	1
alone	4	1	1
with digestive and/or genitourinary diseases	1	0	0
Digestive and/or genito-urinary diseases alone	15	6	0
None of the above	62	9	0

The two major causes of death listed on death certificates were heart and circulatory disease and respiratory diseases. There is general agreement that such illnesses are often related.

The totals given for each broad disease type, with the exception of cancer, do not include everyone with that disease, since combinations are given. Thus, the table shows 88 patients with heart disease, 85 in that category plus 3 who also have cancer.

---

diagnosed at admission as suffering organic brain syndrome with psychosis were found to have had no symptoms whatsoever, or to have been only apathetic, with no impairment of memory or confusion. Thus, it might be said that prodromal signs of death were missed in these cursory examinations, perhaps because the examining psychiatrists were aware that psychiatric treatment for the aged was less important than providing a place to die. Granting these reservations, however, the present data suggest that most patients were known or thought to be dying when referred to Fairview.

What seems crucial is that little effort was made to

TABLE 2   PHYSICAL IMPAIRMENT AND DEATHS

Impairment	All Admitted	All Dying Within Months N	%
None, walked without help	77	7	9.1
Feeble	43	12	27.9
In wheel chair	19	10	52.6
On stretcher	33	15	45.5
Not ascertained	2	0	—
All patients	174	44	25.3

The difference in death rates between patients on stretchers and those in wheelchairs is not statistically significant. It is possible that some patients who might otherwise have been on stretchers were propped up in wheelchairs for convenience in moving them.

TABLE 3   PRESSURE FOR ADMISSION AND DEATHS

Agents referring patients for admission	All Admitted	All Dying Within Month N	%
Male	69	24	34.8
Formal agents only	19	5	26.3
Informal agents	34	16	47.1
Family only	28	13	46.4
Family and/or community agents	6	3	50.0
Formal and informal agents	11	2	18.2
Agents unknown	5	1	20.0
Female	105	20	19.1
Formal agents only	18	4	22.2
Informal agents	70	13	18.6
Family only	58	10	17.2
Family and/or community agents	12	3	25.0
Formal and informal agents	17	3	17.7
Agents unknown	0	0	—
All patients	174	44	25.3

distinguish between symptoms reflecting an acute physical condition as opposed to chronic disorders of aging.

Some psychiatric hospitals have geriatric treatment programs aimed at helping patients get the most out of life, but Fairview's programs were marked by a fatalism that suggests that old people are expected to do nothing more than die. No physical examinations prior to admission were required, although elsewhere in the state such examinations have been shown to reduce inappropriate admissions. In fact, at the time of the study, deaths of those admitted *as well as those refused admission* at a sister hospital with a stringent screening program were only half as great as those at Fairview. This suggests that those responsible for referring the elderly for psychiatric care had learned where to send their dying patients. •

Death As a Career

The Fairview program structured the patient's career as one of dying rather than of active physical or psychiatric treatment. While the post-admission physical examination is routinely performed, almost all geriatric patients are classified as being of "failing status because of age and general debility." This designation seems to be applied almost automatically. It certainly is not associated with the presence of physical illness, ability to walk or chronological age. The role of the physician on Fairview's geriatric wards appeared to be to regularize the patients' deaths by tacitly legitimating the actions of the referring hospital. Thus, the high death rate among old people admitted to the hospital is made to seem part of the "natural" process of dying.

The physical disabilities of those who died within a month of admission are so similar to those of the survivors that the mental disability of *most* of the old people admitted may reflect physical problems. In other words, the admission of *most* of the elderly people to Fairview was probably inappropriate; instead they should have been receiving medical treatment or terminal care for their physical disorders in a general hospital ward.

As for the argument that a sick, confused person is easily mistaken for a mentally ill person, it is significant that young patients are never sent to state hospitals in the moribund condition described above. Patients aged 35, on stretchers, in comas or with intravenous tubes running are unlikely to be found applying for admission to Fairview. Yet such patients exist and often display toxic confusions similar to those of the older patients. The older patient is selected for transfer to the state mental hospital because he is considered in hopeless condition by family and physicians, because of the extreme pressure for hospital beds and because he has compounded the low status of old age with illness, and often poverty. The evidence for these conclusions is reported below.

The pressure that ends with an elderly person being sent to a state mental hospital seems to be begun by the family. Old people coming to Fairview were usually first defined as physically or mentally ill by their families or other community members, usually after a specific health crisis. The patient was either sent directly to the state hospital, or taken first to a medical hospital or nursing home for treatment, depending on available facilities and the attitudes of those in close contact with him.

Among the elderly sent to Fairview, the dying men are somewhat younger than women. The median age for men at death was 74.5; for women it was 78.7. This was not particularly surprising, given the greater life expectancy of women in general. What is surprising, however, is that men whose families have pressed for their admission are more likely to die within a month than men referred only by formal agents such as a nursing home or those referred both by their families and such formal agents. For elderly women, however, this does not seem to be true. There are two factors which may explain this difference. First, there is some reason to believe, from other work I've been doing, that elderly men consistently overrate their health and independence, while elderly women tend to underrate themselves—perhaps a last holding on to the remnants of an instrumental "fit," able-bodied role by the men; women, having greater expressive latitude, can legitimately complain more. Following this line of reasoning, elderly men would perhaps try to compensate and conceal their illness until it became very serious; women, on the other hand, would complain earlier. As soon as complaints become frequent, the family responds by sending the patient to a hospital; men, complaining later, would be in more risk of dying than the female early complainers.

A second factor is differences in family structure. Only 36 percent of the men in the study were still married, but 54 percent of the men who died were married. Women in the study were most likely to be widowed (61.9 percent) and of those who died, 55 percent were widows. Put differently, dying men are most likely to be admitted to Fairview when they become ill and are a burden to their wives who have themselves limited physical (or emotional) strength to deal with an old sick husband who requires nursing care or constant attention. Women, on the other hand, generally outlive their husbands and are most likely to be sent to mental hospitals when they present any kind of management problem, not just terminal illness, to children, other relatives, or to an institution.

Where Are The Children?

It has been observed that having one or more children tends to insulate old people against illness and relatively early death. It might also be expected that parenthood might protect the aged from commitment to a mental hospital for terminal care. This did not prove to be the case at Fairview. While 40 percent of the men and 30 percent of the women admitted had no living children, the likelihood of death within one month was the same for this group as for the group having one or more living children. Nor did the number of children living change the odds. This may mean that once a family has decided to send the patient to the hospital, their contact with him is reduced by distance. Or, the decision to send him to the hospital may result from previous difficulty in getting along with the patient, unusual family relationships or other situations reducing the basis for close ties with the old person. At any rate, in such situations the power the children might have had to postpone their aging parent's death is dissipated. The patient is already socially dead. Only his physical death is lacking.

Most patients did not arrive at Fairview from their own homes, however. Five of six came there from other institutions, most often hospitals. A hospital that is being fully utilized is always in the process of an informal review of patients, seeking out those who can be sent home or referred elsewhere. Combined with this pressure is a feeling, shared by the general public, that general hospital beds are expensive while mental hospitals beds are cheap. Whatever the source of this reasoning, it does not apply to these patients. They are suffering serious, often terminal, illnesses; the care they need will cost the same in any setting that shares the same labor market.

Of the patients sent to Fairview from other hospitals, about half were referred by receiving hospitals, that is, general hospitals with psychiatric service designated as reception centers for the mentally ill. Receiving hospitals in New York City have been the traditional route into state mental hospitals. They are overcrowded and there is considerable pressure to make a quick disposition of patients without concern for the refinements of the individual patient's situation. This may be particularly true for the elderly, whose physical condition is often ignored when a disposition is made. For example, one elderly male patient in the study had been taken to a receiving hospital in the city by his daughter, who stated that he urinated in the hallway and that she "could no longer care for his needs." He was sent to Fairview on a stretcher from the receiving hospital, which had neither admitted nor even examined him. According to the admitting psychiatrist's report, the patient had bedsores, indicating that his problems were long-standing. The psychiatrist observed:

He did not indulge in any spontaneous acts . . . . The

eyes were open and vision was intact as he blinked when fingers were brought close to his eyes. He showed fixed gazing and his eyes did not follow any moving object . . . . Patient showed no response to demands and showed no withdrawal from pain . . . . He retained food in his mouth and wet and soiled. He was mute and only made sounds in his throat.

Seventeen days after admission to Fairview, this patient died of bronchopneumonia. This not atypical case illustrates that many old people are sent away without adequate social and medical histories from receiving hospitals and in such impaired physical condition that it is difficult to determine whether or not they are mentally ill.

The remainder of the patients admitted to Fairview from hospitals have been in the medical wards of general hospitals. Like those from receiving hospitals, they often appear to have been sent to Fairview because they failed to respond to treatment or failed to die within a short period after being put on terminal care. For example, a 74-year-old man with an indwelling catheter was transferred from a medical ward to Fairview on a stretcher. The admitting psychiatrist reported:

He was transferred from . . . General Hospital on a health officer's certificate because of increasing obtundation (dullness). The patient was noted to be . . . breathing heavily and in some distress . . . . He was able to respond only to pain and contact with the patient was impossible.

This patient's physical examination after admission indicated merely that he was dehydrated. Five days after admission, he died of congestive heart failure and bronchopneumonia.

Geriatric patients with their numerous medical complaints and limited future are not the favored patients of general hospital personnel, as has been shown by Glaser and Strauss and others. There are, however, institutions like nursing homes specializing in the care of terminal patients. Only five women and five men in the group studied had been sent to Fairview from nursing homes. The cause, ordinarily, was some kind of disruptive behavior. One elderly man who died within a month of arriving at Fairview was admitted from a nursing home with lung cancer and malignant lesions of the brain and bones. While the nursing home had had no difficulty in giving him minimal physical care and controlling his pain, they became upset and turned to Fairview when he threatened to commit suicide. (Upon checking with an internal medical specialist, I was assured that this patient was *under*medicated for pain—dosage limited to prevent addiction in a dying patient! Motive for suicide?)

Unlike the general hospital, the nursing home does not seem to be concerned with freeing beds occupied by old people. Nor does the threat of death seem to concern them, but rather deviance. They do not like any threat to orderly and routine dying. For example, nursing home patients who survived more than a month of Fairview often had been sent for similar reasons: One female paraplegic cancer patient had been referred because she had tried to set her bed on fire.

It seems obvious that this state hospital functions as a geriatric house of death to which the elderly are relegated because of the despair of their families and the pressure on general hospital beds. There seem to be three elements that establish the pattern of withdrawal of interest and abandonment of the aged to a state mental hospital. One of these is old age itself. The old are already socially dying through relinquishment of roles; as they have little future before them, their lives are considered to have little social worth. But being old in itself is not enough; most old people do not die in state mental hospitals.

The second element is the high probability of dying, though this alone does not automatically lead to Fairview. Young patients who have terminal illnesses are more likely to be sent home for short periods of time and to return to die in the hospital.

The third element is low social status and lack of power. It has often been shown that the poor and powerless of any age are generally considered to have less moral worth than those with more money or those with access to the ear of those with money. The patients in this study were not only seriously ill and old, they were also from mostly working-class and lower-class backgrounds. Only five had had professional occupations and only 29 had a tenth-grade or better education. When old age and relatively low socio-economic status are merged, the person is doubly worthless for he is neither productive nor does he have the reputation for past productivity. A combination of great age, powerlessness *and* terminal illness makes one despised by medical and lay people alike and, unless death comes on schedule, suggests transfer to a state mental hospital. Here the old are hidden away, or taken away, from all that is familiar to them and left to await death. Death here, as Rilke observed, is "factory-like, of course. Where production is so enormous, an individual death is not so nicely carried out, but then that doesn't matter. It is quantity that counts."

Death Rights

The general lack of concern for the way old, sick people die is clearly a disavowal of any right to a death in stable and comfortable surroundings where opportunities for physical, psychological and spiritual comfort are protected. To some extent this is changing. All mental hospitals in New York State, for instance, have recently introduced geriatric screening programs designed specifically to exclude those patients who are dying or whose physical condition is the prime reason for their referral. These screening programs have already enabled some geriatric services to become active psychiatric treatment centers rather than houses of death. But where the old, sick, powerless people who might have died at Fairview will die now remains unresolved.

The statement that family life styles are strongly influenced by, if not dependent upon, other spheres of life in the society means more than just that the locations of residence and work are dependent upon the presence or absence of cities and factories. Everything that a society does, economically, politically, recreationally, educationally and religiously, affects the family, directly or indirectly. If the society enters war, young men are taken away to the armed forces. The laws governing the nation affect parent-child relations, inheritance, the status of women, divorce, etc. Whether young people stay home and help with the family work or leave daily to go to school depends on whether the society provides schools and insists on attendance. Birth, death and the care of the ill must be carried on in the home if there are no hospitals, clinics, doctors, nursing homes, funeral parlors and so forth. The pre-industrial family, as we have seen, was able to teach children everything they needed to know to carry on adult roles. It presented them with models of the next stage of growth and led them through increasing participation in the different institutionalized areas of life. The family was the main production, distribution and consumption unit, so that it contained the main economic roles. It was often the main religious unit, even when churches and religious training programs could be found. Recreational activities were carried out within its confines, often interwoven with work rather than segregated into a separate sphere of life.

But urbanization, industrialization and increasing societal complexity have brought major changes in the relations between the family and other societal institutions. Gradually the major functions of existence have been diversified, each becoming the domain of a special group, each located in a separate building, each concentrating on a segmentalized function and requiring segmentalized involvement by society's members. Schools, museums,

Part Four
The Family and Other Institutions

courts, jails, factories, office buildings, railroad stations, hospitals, city halls and other specialized places have emerged to meet the needs of a vast population—needs often created by the system itself (you don't need a post office if the only people with whom you want to or must communicate all live in your village).

To exist in this complex system, to voluntaristically engage in the extensive variety of roles and groups, and to utilize the resources available to their members, people need a vast amount of knowledge. If a democracy is to function on the basis of wise decisions about representatives and issues, society cannot afford ignorant members, not because of altruism but out of basic necessity. Few jobs can use illiterates, and the number of such jobs is decreasing rapidly. Even religion has become rationalized, requiring the ability to reason intellectually. For these reasons, modern societies have moved education out of the home into specialized buildings and shifted from concrete training by observation and example to ideational transmission of abstracted symbols. All children are judged to need this schooling, not just the elite or the males. Parents, older siblings and even grandparents have been deemed too limited in their knowledge to train the young. In fact, no one human being is judged competent to educate youth in every area of knowledge needed to function in the larger society. Teachers, themselves specially trained in one or a number of disciplines, take turns instructing youth. The school accepts children at an age when they are assumed to be sufficiently socialized and mature to stand the rigors of many hours of discipline and to have a sufficient foundation to absorb the information transmitted by methods judged effective for their age level, for it is assumed that learning is best organized by age. Children who are labeled deficient in learning ability or too handicapped for the standard methods are sent to special training centers.

But the fact that education takes place basically outside the home does not mean that the family can wash its hands of it. There is continual interaction between home and school. The family must not only continue to socialize children in acceptable behavior and to develop such abilities as speech, but it must continue to provide facilities for learning. Upper- and middle-class families generally manage to do what professional educators recommend, providing children with plenty of food in a balanced diet and sufficient sleep to insure a reservoir of energy and attention for the work demanded in schools. They provide privacy and quiet during study hours. They clothe children adequately, so that they can go to school regardless of weather. They accumulate cultural items which are believed to increase intelligence, as measured by tests of the manipulation of abstract concepts. They provide books and museum trips. Not surprisingly, the children of families which offer these basic educational essentials—that is, of families above the lower-class level—do better in schools than do children who, inadequately fed and clothed, live in crowded, noisy, non-intellectual homes which view the school as a foreign and strange element of life.

Not only do the children of the top social classes enter the school daily with a better chance of success due to background factors, but the school itself is so organized as to further their opportunities for success while diminishing those who enter with handicaps. Founded in a traditional class system, at a time when the ideal of behavior was middle-class, bordering on the elite, the schools were designated to convert children of the masses into young adults able to move up the socio-economic ladder. As Norman Denzin forcibly states in "Children and their Caretakers" the labeling and tracking systems of most schools are based on pre-established stereotypes of who is educable to what extent. Thus the educational institution effectively reflects the stratification system outside of the school walls. It does not take long before the child of a lower class family finds himself cooled out sufficiently to turn to other sources of success and satisfaction.

The American school system is based on several assumptions dating back to its European background of centuries, in spite of a superimposed democratic ideology and much recent research which shows that basic educational functions are not being met through its procedures. As Gunner Myrdal, a Swedish sociologist brought to America to study "the Negro problem," concluded in 1944 after extensive analysis, the underlying difficulty is "an American Dilemma" facing both whites and blacks. We are a nation wishing to democratize while simultaneously trying to preserve our traditional class prerogatives. Interestingly, the desire to preserve prerogatives is strong at all class levels: those who make it up to the next step of the high ladder want careful protective devices to prevent everyone else moving up with them. Status counts only if there are people with less status—as well as, of course, those who have more.

The school system reflects this dilemma. While professing faith that the schools can wipe out the effects of unevenly developed "life chances," it protects itself against failure to do this by assuming that uncontrollable biological factors prevent success with many children. The tracking system takes certain behaviors as symptoms of an underlying ability to be educated, labels, and then places the child into an appropriate track. The assumption behind the system is one of closed human potential. This traditional view of the human mind pictures it as being like a pitcher. Different people are born with different-sized pitchers, and there is no sense trying to fill a small pitcher with too much knowledge, because it will simply overflow. This ideological justification of the failure of schools to develop human potential to an extent offsetting the limitations of background and concurrent home influences has had the effect of a self-fulfilling prophecy. Children labeled as unable to learn because they do not respond to standardized teaching methods are so treated by the school system and end up justifying the predictors by not learning at desired rates and to desired levels. A convenient "proof" of the school's justifications for failure to educate whole categories of children has been the misused IQ test. As J. McVicker Hunt points out, in "Black Genes—White Environment," modern science has shown that IQ tests measure not inborn ability but what develops out of a vast store of potential during the child's socialization and education. In fact, no one is quite sure how much potential is the natural inheritance of each child. We do know that most people do not develop more than a limited amount of their ability. A basic reason is, of course, that most people do not have the time or energy to build up knowledge and skills to be a professional baseball player, a doctor, a lawyer, and another type of specialist all at the same time. But an additional reason is the whole set of limitations imposed on the child during his or her growing and learning period by the people and objects in the environment. Family and early childhood experiences either provide a knowledge base, self-confidence, and a desire for exploring the world which will enable the child to utilize the resources of education, or they thwart the child's natural curiosity. Of course, the effects of the socialization process are seldom extreme; most children are able to develop some areas and levels of their human potential sufficiently to function in modern society, though the participation varies considerably by educational achievement. According to most researchers, the degree of potential which is being developed, even through adequate schooling, has increased over the centuries and recent decades, in that more people are developing more abilities than in the elite-dominated past.

At best, the home, the neighborhood, the school, and ever widening environments provide the bases and attitudes facilitating the growth of intelligence and creativity in the young. As Michael A. Wallach and Nathan Kogan found in their research on creativity and intelligence in children's thinking, a major contributor to creativity is an atmosphere encouraging "playful contemplation." This atmosphere must exist not only in the home but also in the school, since the child uses both as sources of knowledge content and tools. At worst, the home and the school combine to create a problem situation such as that described by Charles Witter in "Drugging and Schooling." The school system as it has evolved up to now is dependent upon children's willingness to obey its rules, to sit and listen, to absorb the information given and to return it intact upon request. With only one teacher in the classroom for twenty, thirty or forty students, no schooling can take place without the cooperation of all or most of them. Where this cooperation is lacking, as in many ghetto schools, the classroom becomes a madhouse and the teacher is converted into a warden or passive onlooker. The need to control behavior then serves as a justification for the practice of drugging students which Witter and others have found so shocking and which is so much contrary to the ideology of democratic education because it results in passivity rather than active learning.

The child's education is not limited to the family and the school. The supposedly ideal situation is when the content and sentiments of the home, the school, the neighborhood, the peer group and all people and places into which the child ventures support each other to produce positive self- and other-feelings and a desire to be socialized along the ways described by the society as "good." All too often, such is not the situation. The child who is frustrated by his lack of meaningful and self-expanding experiences at home and at school may turn to the streets and to a peer group for his identification and definitions of the world. Gerald Suttles shows us the "anatomy of a Chicago slum" in which youth does exactly that—turns to antisocial groups of the street corner or the club house. Although not all gangs, or clubs formed by the young in slum and similar neighborhoods, actually engage in criminal behavior, much of the activity connected with "hanging around" the streets and clubs can get youth into trouble with society. According to Paul Lerman, in "Child Convicts," those young people who are branded "juvenile delinquents" and incarcerated for their acts often did not commit crimes in the adult sense of the law. For both girls and boys, the major reason for being rejected by society is trouble with their families or with school. Girls are additionally subject to brushes with law enforcement officials for not keeping their sexual activities private. Thus, society does not leave it up to the family alone to teach and enforce moral codes, norms and attitudes but, as the various essays in this Part emphasize, allows school and law enforcement groups to impose essentially middle-class stereotypes and judgments on the young.

Of course, the current trend of blaming the parents for the problems of youth fails to recognize the basic fact that the failure is due not to any unwillingness to be a good mother or a good father but the utter inability to be so. Parents are limited by their own resources, the abilities they have or have not developed, their fears and anxieties and their lack of power over the environment within which their children operate during the majority of their waking hours. As Harris Chaiklin, Paul H. Ephross and Richard Sterne note in "The Effects of Violence on Inner City Families," lower-class mothers are not revolutionaries, supporting the use of violence to meet anti-discrimination goals. Living in highly limited lifespace, surrounded by violence they fear and cannot control, they welcome all means of keeping peace and providing security. Even those cases in which parents turn their own children over to law enforcement agencies arise out of a desperate desire to prevent harm to the off-spring, combined with a total lack of private resources for doing so.

Traditional society depended not only on the family, the school and the neighborhood to insure that youth became socialized appropriately, but also, and sometimes primarily, on religious groups. It was the church and its ideology which was expected to prevent immoral acts through its system of socialization and social control. Into religious beliefs and norms are woven many items of the family institution and vice versa, as a glance at the *Bible*, the *Koran* or any other sacred book will prove. Religion traditionally reinforced the family in all situations in which the two systems, so to speak, "grew up together." It is only where a foreign religion is superimposed on the ongoing life that conflicts emerge, and one or usually both of the institutions must be modified.

Nathan Gerrard points out that people who are active in the serpent-handling religions of West Virginia still exist in an environment in which the religious institution dominates the socialization process. Gerrard shows the effects of this religion upon the personalities of its members, as well as upon their family identification and conformity. Church services form a major part of the lives of all generations. Unlike the situation of the Chicago slum, here the various areas of life and social contacts are woven together around a single set of beliefs and practices. The author concludes that these religions enable the members to adjust to the numerous problems they face by encouraging hedonistic

impulsiveness, focusing on short-term gratification. The value system is so strong as to prevent youth from absorbing values which might facilitate upward and outward mobility. The people are poor, but religious attitudes prevent them from using schools and other societal resources to decrease poverty.

This is an example of an institutional tie-in which controlled European and American families for centuries and still controls the lives of many people all over the world. They are locked into their style of life by a powerful ideological and behavioral system which prevents the growth of new knowledge and long-range, rational plans of action. The constraints of such a religion have insured continued marginal existence by preventing social change of a planned, organized and expanding form. The conclusion that social change can be prevented or slowed down by a strong ideology which encourages passive adaptation to existing conditions was reached by a famous sociologist, Max Weber, as early as 1891. Gerrard shows how the system operates to stabilize people at a lower-class level in the case of the serpent handling religions, while pointing out that other churches in the same communities foster attitudes facilitating economic success, much as did the Protestant revolution by contributing to the shift of European attention from religion to the economic institution. In a society in which so much of the change in family life is due to upward mobility, descriptions of the pervasiveness of institutions which delay such mobility, such as those of an Appalachian hollow, a Chicago slum or a pervasive religion, help explain deviations from the pattern.

Few observers of the American scene would argue that the schools, as they have existed in the past and as they continue to function, have succeeded in educating all members of society for full participation in the system. This failure, conjoined with others is reflected in the indices of personal and family disorganization discussed in the Prologue. Abundant America contains people who are clearly unable to maintain themselves and who, without society's help, would literally die or allow their children to die. Historically, there have been many social groups which have allowed, or have not prevented, the death of unsuccessful or isolated members. The American value system, however, does not allow death through neglect, even of its old and sick. But it does not systematically insure that people who cannot maintain themselves in society are helped in ways which are judged satisfactory by everyone involved. The essay on the history of the welfare movement by Frances Fox Piven and Richard Cloward is instructive in this regard. In agriculturally-based societies, people who needed help in times of crisis, such as at the death of a husband or illness of a wife, obtained it from the extended kin group of the community, who pitched in to redistribute the goods others produced until the family got back on its feet. Whole communities starved and vanished when their isolated plight was unknown outside, or when there was no cooperative system connecting them to larger social units. The class structure of the manor and the plantation usually necessitated a "lady bountiful" or a lord who would take responsibility for the welfare of the slaves or peasants on his land. The philosophy was "noblesse oblige."

Eventually, however, the burden of caring for the impoverished and those suffering temporary crises became too heavy for the upper classes and the churches, and class relations became sufficiently depersonalized to decrease both knowledge of needs and feeling of obligation. Societies became too large to warrant personal charity, yet the ideals of humanitarianism were too pervasive to permit neglect. Urbanization and industrialization deprived people of the opportunity for growing their own foodstuffs, and money became necessary for survival. Money comes from work in paid jobs, from activities not available to those who are unemployable because of lack of skills, handicaps, old age or the demands of other roles such as that of full-time mother. So society began to assume responsibility for maintaining people who could not get enough money from other sources, not without resentment but out of necessity.

Resentment is usually felt by those whose taxes cover the costs and by the residents of the cities and states in which unemployable migrants have relocated. Traditional ideals of "independence" are often cited as justifications for irritation at having to support other people whose situation is a product of the failure of a large social system to provide each family with a way of surviving. Any mismatch between a person's present abilities and the requirements of the economic world is overlooked. Some of the key attitudes concerning this topic are documented in the arguments over daycare centers, currently a major issue. As Gilbert Steiner documents in his essay on "Day Care Centers: Hype or Hope?" the history of this controversy reflects middle-class biases which prohibit the development of such centers as an alternative solution to paying a woman welfare money to keep her at home caring for her children. Although Americans do not object to taking children from the home between the ages of five and eighteen, and although they supply nursery schools for much younger children whose parents can pay to have them "enriched," the creation of publicly supported centers for children of the impoverished meets strong objections.

Frustration over welfare programs is also felt by the recipients, who resent the label of failure which it brings. The vicious cycle, as Myrdal called it, continues with each new group of migrants: inadequate education produces people who are incapable of getting good jobs in urban centers (or any jobs, in many cases), unable to earn sufficient income to prevent health and housing problems and tensions which result in individual and family disorganization, and at a loss to create an environment in which children can gain enough education to break out of the cycle. The agriculturally-reared immigrants from many nations and continents have gone through this cycle. Some break out of it faster than others because of one or more key social factors: degree of discrimination, cultural differences from the dominant middle-class American culture, physically desirable features (inherited or acquired through the culture), size of the migrant group, length of time it has been in the area of settlement, manner of settlement (scattered or in ethnic communities), desire for assimilation, ability to create a relatively self-sufficient community and so forth.

The chances of attaining a middle-class life style and of maintaining one's self within it, even in old age, are least likely for blacks who have recently moved from the rural South with its substandard schools to the urban North, for Puerto Ricans, for Mexicans, and for Amerindians. These people now inhabit the ghettos previously occupied by Poles, Italians, Irish and other Europeans. Their families are more likely to require help from the society than are families who have learned to live in the city through generations of experience.

While arguments continue about those who are unable to support themselves through working at a job for pay, the majority of men and, increasingly, of women participate in the labor market. They come into it prepared in varying degrees for a variety of occupations. The United States Labor Bureau lists 21,741 job titles. There are problems, however, in matching the job and the person, in preparing people to be qualified participants in specific occupations, and in bringing people and jobs together. Much job choice is haphazard: personal referral, chance glances at newspaper ads, political pull. Only the more highly trained or enlightened utilize the rapidly growing intermediary service of employment agencies.

A basic characteristic of the world of work is its set of assumptions restricting entry to certain people. Consciously or not, the employer has an image of the ideal, or at least the acceptable, employee. If he assumes that only white Anglo-Saxon males of middle years (but not over 45) are sufficiently competent for or able to learn the job, then he will not look for or accept an application from a woman, a black, a Hungarian or even an older Anglo-Saxon male. He certainly does not want someone with "too long" hair, a college dropout, or a handicapped person. The list of rejects for any job is usually long. In many employment situations in America, the least likely to be considered for an "important" occupation or position are the black male and the white female.

On the other hand, employers do not want high-status people in low-status jobs. There must be an "appropriate" match between the person's status, as measured by social class indices of background and current life style, and the status of the job for which he or she is applying. The criteria for all these complex and subtle judgments are often buried in the distant past of the world of work, rather than being an outgrowth of the actual job and the ability of applicants. Marijean Suelzle documents many of these problems in "Women in Labor," showing them to be the consequence of traditional stereotypes concerning what women "are," "should" be and "should" do. Prevalent assumptions concerning women restrict the occupations which they are allowed or encouraged to enter, the training they receive, the timing of their work experiences and their pay. The data that Suelzle have collected explode many myths concerning the work histories and attitudes of American women.

The relation of women and men to the world of work is heavily dependent, then, upon the education they obtain. Modern society demands that people decide on a profession or occupation very early in their eight decades of life. In most cases the choice is more limited than apparent, since the resources for becoming President of the United States, a doctor, a top business executive and so forth are simply not available to most people. Guidance counselors remind the female high school junior of areas she should not even consider. "After all, you are a girl and will get married, so there is no sense in taking too much mathematics and chemistry . . . ," as my daughter was told not long ago by a "well-meaning" principal. Women are not expected to become deeply involved in their work or to be career oriented, on the assumption that strong commitment in this direction would interfere with their interest in their basic function: reproduction. Usually it is the present or potential role of mother which is mentioned when the employment of women is discussed. This is one often cited excuse for the inadequacy of pay to women, the segregation into "women's work," and the restriction of women to the lower echelons of the work hierarchy. As mentioned during the discussion of retirement, the subject of pay is particularly significant in American society, with its emphasis on the economic institution, because the paycheck has many symbolic qualities. Not only does it facilitate a certain style of life, but its total size tells the receiver, and the world at large if its amount is known, what the person is worth to society. The "marketing mentality," as Fromm described the use of the paycheck to determine human worth, puts qualitative meaning on quantitative sums. You are a more worthy, more valuable person to society if you make a comparatively large amount of money on the job. It is this attitude which led Betty Friedan to urge women who are trying to break out of the "feminine mystique" to get out of the unpaid role of housewife into paid employment. It is also a major influence in Edward E. Lawler's essay, "How Much Money Do Executives Want?"

At the conclusion of this Part, we shall have finished our examination of past and present family life, leaving us with a final section—that concerned with the future, as indicated by trends from the past and the present.

Children and Their Caretakers Norman K. Denzin

Schools are held together by intersecting moral, political and social orders. What occurs inside their walls must be viewed as a product of what the participants in this arena bring to it, be they children, parents, instructors, administrators, psychologists, social workers, counselors or politicians. A tangled web of interactions—based on competing ideologies, rhetorics, intents and purposes—characterizes everyday life in the school. Cliques, factions, pressure groups and circles of enemies daily compete for power and fate in these social worlds.

Children and their caretakers are not passive organisms. Their conduct reflects more than responses to the pressures of social systems, roles, value structures or political ideologies. Nor is their behavior the sole product of internal needs, drives, impulses or wishes. The human actively constructs lines of conduct in the face of these forces and as such stands over and against the external world. The

human is self-conscious. Such variables as role prescription, value configurations or hierarchies of needs have relevance only when they are acted on by the human. Observers of human behavior are obliged to enter the subject's world and grasp the shifting definitions that give rise to orderly social behavior. Failing to do so justifies the fallacy of objectivism: the imputing of motive from observer to subject. Too many architects of schools and education programs have stood outside the interactional worlds of children and adults and attempted to legislate their interpretation of right and proper conduct.

Such objectivistic stances have given schools a basic characteristic that constitutes a major theme of this essay. Schools are presently organized so as to effectively remove fate control from those persons whose fate is at issue, that is, students. This loss of fate control, coupled with a conception of the child which is based on the "underestimation fallacy" gives rise to an ideology that judges the child as incompetent and places in the hands of the adult primary responsibility for child-caretaking.

Schools as Moral Agencies

Schools are best seen, not as educational settings, but as places where fate, morality and personal careers are created and shaped. Schools are moral institutions. They have assumed the responsibility of shaping children, of whatever race or income level, into right and proper participants in American society, pursuing with equal vigor the abstract goals of that society.

At one level schools function, as Willard Waller argued in 1937, to Americanize the young. At the everyday level, however, abstract goals disappear, whether they be beliefs in democracy and equal opportunity or myths concerning the value of education for upward mobility. In their place appears a massive normative order that judges the child's development along such dimensions as poise, character, integrity, politeness, deference, demeanor, emotional control, respect for authority and serious commitment to classroom protocol. Good students are those who reaffirm through their daily actions the moral order of home, school and community.

To the extent that schools assume moral responsibility for producing social beings, they can be seen as agencies of fate or career control. In a variety of ways schools remind students who they are and where they stand in the school's hierarchy. The school institutionalizes ritual turning points to fill this function: graduations, promotions, tests, meetings with parents, open-houses, rallies and sessions with counselors. These significant encounters serve to keep students in place. Schools function to sort and filter social selves and to set these selves on the proper moral track, which may include recycling to a lower grade, busing to an integrated school or informing a student that he has no chance to pursue a college preparatory program. In many respects schools give students their major sense of moral worth—they shape vocabularies, images of self, reward certain actions and not others, set the stage for students to be thrown together as friends or enemies.

Any institution that assumes control over the fate of others might be expected to be accountable for its actions toward those who are shaped and manipulated. Within the cultures of fate-controlling institutions, however, there appears a vocabulary, a rhetoric, a set of workable excuses and a division of labor to remove and reassign responsibility. For example, we might expect that the division of labor typically parallels the moral hierarchy of the people within the institution, that is, the people assigned the greatest moral worth are ultimately most blameworthy, or most accountable. Usually, however, moral responsibility is reversed. When a teacher in a Head Start program fails to

raise the verbal skills of her class to the appropriate level she and the project director might blame each other. But it is more likely that the children, the families of the children or the culture from which the children come will be held responsible. Such is the typical rhetorical device employed in compensatory education programs where the low performances of black children on white middle-class tests is explained by assigning blame to black family culture and family arrangements. Research on the alleged genetic deficiences of black and brown children is another example of this strategy. Here the scientist acts as a moral entrepreneur, presenting his findings under the guise of objectivity.

What is a Child?

Any analysis of the education and socialization process must begin with the basic question, "what is a child?" My focus is on the contemporary meanings assigned children, especially as these meanings are revealed in preschool and compensatory education programs.

In addressing this question it must be recognized that social objects (such as children) carry no intrinsic meaning. Rather, meaning is conferred by processes of social interaction—by people.

Such is the case with children. Each generation, each social group, every family and each individual develops different interpretations of what a child is. Children find themselves defined in shifting, often contradictory ways. But as a sense of self is acquired, the child learns to transport from situation to situation a relatively stable set of definitions concerning his personal and social identity. Indeed most of the struggles he will encounter in the educational arena fundamentally derive from conflicting definitions of selfhood and childhood.

Child Production as Status Passage

The movement of an infant to the status of child is a socially constructed event that for most middle-class Americans is seen as desirable, inevitable, irreversible, permanent, long term in effect and accomplished in the presence of "experts" and significant others such as teachers, parents, peers and siblings.

For the white middle income American the child is seen as an extension of the adult's self, usually the family's collective self. Parents are continually reminded that the way their child turns out is a direct reflection of their competence as socializing agents. These reminders have been made for some time; consider this exhortation of 1849:

> Yes, mothers, in a certain sense, the destiny of a redeemed world is put into your hands; it is for you to say whether your children shall be respectable and happy here, and prepared for a glorious immortality, or

whether they shall dishonor you, and perhaps bring you grey hairs in sorrow to the grave, and sink down themselves at last to eternal despair!

If the child's conduct reflects upon the parent's moral worth, new parents are told by Benjamin Spock that this job of producing a child is hard work, a serious enterprise. He remarks in *Baby and Child Care*:

> There is an enormous amount of hard work in child care—preparing the proper diet, washing diapers and clothes, cleaning up messes that an infant makes with his food . . . stopping fights and drying tears, listening to stories that are hard to understand, joining in games and reading stories that aren't very exciting to an adult, trudging around zoos and museums and carnivals . . . being slowed down in housework . . . . Children keep parents from parties, trips, theaters, meetings, games, friends . . . . Of course, parents don't have children because they want to be martyrs, or at least they shouldn't. They have them because they love children and want some of their very own . . . . Taking care of their children, seeing them grow and develop into fine people, gives most parents—despite the hard work—their greatest satisfaction in life. This is creation. This is our visible immortality. Pride in other worldly accomplishments is usually weak in comparison.

Spock's account of the parent-child relationship reveals several interrelated definitions that together serve to set off the contemporary view of children. The child is a possession of the adult, an extension of self, an incompetent object that must be cared for at great cost and is a necessary obligation one must incur if he or she desires visible immortality.

These several definitions of childhood are obviously at work in current educational programs. More importantly, they are grounded in a theory of development and learning that reinforces the view that children are incompetent selves. Like Spock's theory of growth, which is not unlike the earlier proposals of Gesell, contemporary psychological theories see the child in organic terms. The child grows like a stalk of corn. The strength of the stalk is a function of its environment. If that environment is healthy, if the plant is properly cared for, a suitable product will be produced. This is a "container" theory of development: "What you put in determines what comes out." At the same time, however, conventional wisdom holds that the child is an unreliable product. It cannot be trusted with its own moral development. Nor can parents. This business of producing a child is serious and it must be placed in the hands of experts who are skilled in child production. Mortal mothers and fathers lack these skills. Pressures are quickly set in force to move the child out of the family into a more "professional" setting—the preschool, the Head Start program.

Caretaking for the Middle Classes

Preschools, whether based on "free school" principles, the Montessori theory, or modern findings in child development, display one basic feature. They are moral caretaking agencies that undertake the fine task of shaping social beings.

Recently, after the enormous publicity attendant to the Head Start program for the poor, middle income Americans have been aroused to the importance of preschool education for their children. "Discovery Centers" are appearing in various sections of the country and several competing national franchises have been established. Given names such as We Sit Better, Mary Moppit, Pied Piper Schools, Les Petites Academies, Kinder Care Nursery and American Child Centers, these schools remind parents (as did the Universal Education Corporation in the *New York Times*) that:

> Evaluating children in the 43 basic skills is part of what the Discovery Center can do for your child. The 43 skills embrace all the hundreds of things your child has to learn before he reaches school age. Fortunately preschoolers have a special genius for learning. But it disappears at the age of seven. During this short-lived period of genius, the Discovery Center helps your child develop his skills to the Advanced Level.

Caretaking for the middle classes is a moral test. The parent's self is judged by the quality of the product. If the product is faulty, the producer is judged inadequate, also faulty. This feature of the socialization process best explains why middle-class parents are so concerned about the moral, spiritual, psychological and social development of their children. It also explains (if only partially) why schools have assumed so much fate control over children; educators are the socially defined experts on children.

The children of lower income families are often assumed to be deprived, depressed and emotionally handicapped. To offset these effects, current theory holds that the child must be "educated and treated" before entrance into kindergarten. If middle income groups have the luxury of withholding preschool from their children, low income, third-world parents are quickly learning they have no such right. Whether they like it or not, their children are going to be educated. When formal education begins, the culturally deprived child will be ready to compete with his white peers.

What is Cultural Deprivation?

The term "culturally deprived" is still the catchall phrase which at once explains and describes the inability (failure, refusal) of the child in question to display appropriate conduct on I.Q. tests, street corners, playgrounds and classrooms. There are a number of problems with this formulation. The first is conceptual and involves the meanings one gives to the terms *culture* and *deprived*. Contemporary politicians and educators have ignored the controversy surrounding what the word *culture* means and have apparently assumed that everyone knows what a culture is. Be that as it may, the critical empirical indicator seems to be contained in the term *deprived*. People who are deprived, that is, people who fail to act like white, middle income groups, belong to a culture characterized by such features as divorce, deviance, premarital pregnancies, extended families, drug addiction and alcoholism. Such persons are easily identified: they tend to live in ghettos or public housing units, and they tend to occupy the lower rungs of the occupation ladder. They are there because they are deprived. Their culture keeps them deprived. It is difficult to tell whether these theorists feel that deprivation precedes or follows being in a deprived culture. The causal links are neigher logically or empirically analyzed.

The second problem with this formulation is moral and ideological. The children and adults who are labeled culturally deprived are those people in American society who embarrass and cause trouble for middle income moralists, scientists, teachers, politicians and social workers. They fail to display proper social behavior. The fact that people in low income groups are under continual surveillance by police and social workers seems to go unnoticed. The result is that members of the middle class keep their indelicacies behind closed doors, inside the private worlds of home, office, club and neighborhood. Low income people lack such privileges. Their misconduct is everybody's business.

The notion of cultural deprivation is class based. Its recurrent invocation, and its contemporary institutionalization in compensatory education programs reveals an inability or refusal to look seriously at the problems of the middle and upper classes, and it directs attention away from schools which are at the heart of the problem.

Herbert Gans has noted another flaw in these programs. This is the failure of social scientists to take seriously the fact that many lower income people simply do not share the same aspirations as the middle class. Despite this fact antipoverty programs and experiments in compensatory education proceed as if such were the case.

Schools are morally bounded units of social organization. Within and from them students, parents, teachers and administrators derive their fundamental sense of self. Any career through a school is necessarily moral; one's self-image is continually being evaluated, shaped and molded. These careers are interactionally interdependent. What a teacher does affects what a child does and vice versa. To the extent that schools have become the dominant socializing institution in Western society it can be argued that experiences in them furnish everyday interactants with their basic vocabularies for evaluating self and others. Persons can mask, hide or fabricate their educational biography, but at some point they will be obliged to paint a picture of how well educated they are. They will also be obliged to explain why they are not better educated (or why they are too well educated), and why their present circumstances do not better reflect their capabilities (e.g., unemployed space engineers). One's educational experiences furnish the rhetorical devices necessary to get off the hook and supply the basic clues that will shore up a sad or happy tale.

The School's Functions

I have already noted two broad functions served by the schools: they Americanize students, and they sort, filter and accredit social selves. To these basic functions must be added the following. Ostensibly, instruction or teaching should take precedence over political socialization. And indeed teaching becomes the dominant activity through which the school is presented to the child. But if schools function to instruct, they also function to entertain and divert students into "worthwhile" ends. Trips to zoos, beaches, operas, neighboring towns, ice cream parlors and athletic fields reveal an attempt on the part of the school to teach the child what range of entertaining activities he or she can engage in. Moreover, these trips place the school directly in the public's eye and at least on these excursions teachers are truly held accountable for their class's conduct.

Caretaking and babysitting constitute another basic function of schools. This babysitting function is quite evident in church oriented summer programs where preschools and day-care centers are explicitly oriented so as to sell themselves as competent babysitters. Such schools compete for scarce resources (parents who can afford their services), and the federal government has elaborated this service through grants-in-aid to low income children.

Formal instruction in the classroom is filtered through a series of interconnected acts that involve teacher and student presenting different social selves to one another. Instruction cannot be separated from social interaction, and teachers spend a large amount of time teaching students how to be proper social participants. Coaching in the rules and rituals of polite etiquette thus constitutes another basic function of the school. Students must be taught how to take turns, how to drink out of cups and clean up messes, how to say please and thank you, how to take leave of a teacher's presence, how to handle mood, how to dress for appropriate occasions, how to be rude, polite, attentive, evasive, docile, aggressive, deceitful; in short, they must learn to act like adults. Teachers share this responsibility with parents, often having to take over where parents fail or abdicate, though, again, parents are held accountable for not producing polite children. Because a child's progress through the school's social structure is contingent on how his or her self is formally defined, parents stand to lose much if their children do not conform to the school's version of good conduct. When teachers and parents both fail, an explanation will be sought to relieve each party of responsibility. The child may be diagnosed as hyperactive, or his culture may have been so repressive in its effects that nothing better can be accomplished. Career tracks for these students often lead to the trade school or the reformatory.

Another function of the schools is socialization into age-sex roles. Girls must be taught how to be girls and boys must learn what a boy is. In preschool and daycare centers this is often difficult to accomplish because bathrooms are not sex segregated. But while they are open territories, many preschools make an effort to hire at least one male instructor who can serve as male caretaker and entertainer of boys. He handles their toilet problems among other things. Preschool instructors can often be observed to reinterpret stories to fit their conception of the male or female role, usually attempting to place the female on an equal footing with the male. In these ways the sexual component of self-identity is transmitted and presented to the young child. Problem children become those who switch sex roles or accentuate to an unacceptable degree maleness or femaleness.

Age-grading is accomplished through the organization of classes on a biological age basis. Three-year-olds quickly learn that they cannot do the same things as four-year-olds do, and so on. High schools are deliberately organized so as to convey to freshmen and sophomores how important it is to be a junior or senior. Homecoming queens, student body presidents and athletic leaders come from the two top classes. The message is direct: work hard, be a good student and you too can be a leader and enjoy the fruits of age.

It has been suggested by many that most schools centrally function to socialize children into racial roles, stressing skin color as the dominant variable in social relationships. Depictions of American history and favored symbolic leaders stress the three variables of age, sex and race. The favored role model becomes the 20 to 25-year-old, white, university-educated male who has had an outstanding career in athletics. Implicitly and explicitly students are taught that Western culture is a male oriented, white-based enterprise.

Shifting from the school as a collectivity to the classroom, we find that teachers attempt to construct their own versions of appropriate conduct. Students are likely to find great discrepancies between a school's formal codes of conduct and the specific rules they encounter in each of their courses and classes. They will find some teachers who are openly critical of the school's formal policies, while at the same time they are forced to interact with teachers who take harsh lines toward misconduct. They will encounter some teachers who enforce dress standards and some who do not. Some teachers use first names, others do not, and so on. The variations are endless.

The importance of these variations for the student's career and self-conception should be clear. It is difficult managing self in a social world that continually changes its demands, rewards and rules of conduct. But students are obliged to do just that. Consequently the self-conception of the student emerges as a complex and variegated object. He or she is tied into competing and complementary worlds of influence and experience. Depending on where students stand with respect to the school's dominant moral order, they will find their self-conception complemented or derogated and sometimes both. But for the most part schools are organized so as to complement the self-conception of the child most like the teacher and to derogate those most unlike him or her. And, needless to say, the moral career of the nonwhite, low income student is quite different from the career of his white peer.

I have spelled out the dimensions around which a student comes to evaluate himself in school. Classrooms, however, are the most vivid stage on which students confront the school, and it is here that the teacher at some level must emerge as a negative or positive force on his career. While the underlife of schools reflects attempts to "beat" or "make-out" in the school, in large degree the student learns to submit to the system. The ultimate fact of life is that unless he gets through school with some diploma he is doomed to failure. Not only is he doomed to failure, but he is socially defined as a failure. His career opportunities and self-conceptions are immediately tied to his success in school.

Schools, then, inevitably turn some amount of their attention to the problem of socializing students for failure. Indeed, the school's success as a socializing agent in part depends on its ability to teach students to accept failure. A complex rhetoric and set of beliefs must be instilled in the students. Children must come to see themselves as the school defines them. They are taught that certain classes of selves do better than other classes, but the classes referred to are not sociological but moral. A variation of the Protestant ethic is communicated and the fiction of equality in education and politics is stressed. Students must grasp the fact that all that separates them from a classmate who goes to Harvard (when they are admitted to a junior college) are grades and hard work, not class, race, money or prestige. Schools, then, function as complex, cooling out agencies.

Two problems are created. School officials must communicate their judgments, usually cast as diagnoses, prescriptions, treatments and prognoses, to students and parents. And second, they must establish social arrangements that maximize the likelihood that their judgments will be accepted, that is, submission to fate control is maximized, and scenes between parents and students are minimized.

Fate Control

The most obvious cooling out agents in schools are teachers and counselors. It is they who administer and evaluate tests. It is they who see the student most frequently. In concert these two classes of functionaries fulfill the schools' functions of sorting out and cooling out children. Their basic assignment is to take imperfect selves and fit those selves to the best possible moral career. They are, then, moral entrepreneurs. They design career programs and define the basic contours around which a student's self will be shaped.

A basic strategy of the moral entrepreneur in schools is co-optation. He attempts to win a child's peers and parents over to his side. If this can be accomplished, the job is relatively easy. For now everyone significant in the child's world agrees that he is a failure or a partial success. They agree that a trade school or a junior college is the best career track to be followed.

Another strategy is to select exemplary students who epitomize the various tracks open to a student. Former graduates may be brought back and asked to reflect on their careers. In selecting types of students to follow these various paths, schools conduct talent searches and develop operating perspectives that classify good and bad prospects. Like the academic theorist of social stratification, these officials work with an implicit image of qualified beings. They know that students from middle and upper income groups perform better than those from lesser backgrounds. They know that students who have college educated parents do better than those whose parents dropped out of high school. They learn to mistrust nonwhites. In these respects schools differ only slightly from medical practitioners, especially the psychiatrist who has learned that his trade works best on persons like him in background. Teachers too perpetuate the system of stratification found in the outside world.

Student Types

Schools can cool out the failures in their midst. They have more difficulty with another type of student, the troublemakers or militants. Troublemakers, as would be predicted, typically come from low income white and nonwhite ethnic groups. Forced to process these children, school systems developed their own system of stratification, making low status schools teach troublemakers. This has become the fate of the trade school or the continuation high school. Here those who have high truancy or arrest records, are pregnant, hyperactive or on probation are thrown together. And here they are presented with white

middle-class curriculums.

Militants and troublemakers refuse to accept the school's operating perspective. To the extent that they can band together and form a common world view, they challenge the school's legitimacy as a socializing agent. They make trouble. They represent, from the middle-class point of view, failures of the socializing system.

In response to this, schools tend to adopt a strategy of denial. Denial can take several forms, each revealing a separate attempt to avoid accountability. Denial of responsibility takes the form of a claim that "we recognize your problem, but the solution is outside our province." The need for alternative educational arrangements is recognized, but denied because of reasons beyond control. Private and public guilt is neutralized by denying responsibility and placing blame on some external force or variable such as the state of the economy.

When some resource is denied to a social group, explanations will be developed to justify that denial. My earlier discussion has suggested that one explanation places blame on the shoulders of the denied victim. Thus the theory of cultural deprivation removes blame, by blaming the victim. Scientific theory thus operates as one paradigm of responsibility.

Another form of the strategy is to deny the challengers' essential moral worth. Here the victim is shown to be socially unworthy and thereby not deserving of special attention. This has been the classic argument for segregation in the South, but it works only so long as the victim can be kept in place, which has lately in that part of the world involved insuring that the challenger or victim is not presented with alternative self models. Shipping black instructors out of the South into northern urban ghettos represents an attempt to remove alternative self models for the southern black child.

The Victim's Response

Insofar as they can organize themselves socially, victims and challengers may assume one of three interrelated stances. They may condemn the condemner, make appeals to higher authorities or deny the perspective that has brought injury. In so doing they will seek and develop alternative scientific doctrines that support their stance.

Condemning the condemner reverses the condemner's denial of moral worth. Here the school or political and economic system is judged hypocritical, corrupt, stupid, brutal and racist. These evaluations attempt to reveal the underlying moral vulnerability of the institution in question. The victim and his cohort reverse the victimizer's vocabulary and hold him accountable for the failures they were originally charged with (for example, poor grades or attendance records).

These condemnations reveal a basic commitment to the

present system. They are claims for a just place. They are a petition to higher authority. Democratic ideology is proclaimed as a worthy pursuit. The school is charged with failure to offer proper and acceptable means to reach those goals. Here the victims' perspective corresponds with dominant cultural ideologies.

Denial of perspective is another stance. Best seen in the Nation of Islam schools, the victim now states that he wants nothing the larger system can offer. He leaves the system and constructs his own educational arrangements. He develops his own standards of evaluation. He paints his own version of right and proper conduct. (Private educational academies in the South, partly a function of the Nixon administration, serve a similar function for whites.)

Denials of perspective thus lead to the substitution of a new point of view. If successfully executed, as in the case of the Nation of Islam, the victims build their own walls of protection and shut off the outside world. In such a setting, one's self-conception is neither daily denied nor derided. It is affirmed and defined in positive terms.

Lower self-conceptions would be predicted in those settings where the black or brown child is taught to normalize his deficiencies and to compensate for them. This is the setting offered by Head Start and Follow-Through. The victim accepts the victimizers' judgments and attempts to compensate for socially defined flaws.

Americans of all income levels and from all racial groups, including white, are troubled over the current educational system. They are demanding a greater say in the social organization of schools; they are challenging the tenure system now given teachers; they feel that schools should accept greater responsibilities for the failures of the system. (A Gallup Poll in late 1970 showed that 67 percent of those surveyed favor holding teachers and administrators more accountable for the progress of students.) Accordingly it is necessary to consider a series of proposals that would bring education more in line with cultural and social expectations.

From this perspective education must be grounded in principles that recognize the role of the self in everyday conduct. The child possesses multiple selves, each grounded in special situations and special circles of significant others. Possessing a self, the child is an active organism, not a passive object into which learning can be poured.

Conventional theories of learning define the child as a passive organism. An alternative view of the social act of learning must be developed. George Herbert Mead's analysis provides a good beginning. Creativity or learning occurred, Mead argued, when the individual was forced to act in a situation where conventional lines of conduct were no longer relevant. Following Dewey's discussion of the blocked act, Mead contended that schools and curricula must be organized in ways that challenge the child's view of the world. Standard curricula are based on an opposite view of the human. Redundancy, constant rewards and punishments, piecemeal presentation of materials, and defining the child as incompetent or unable to provoke his own acts best characterizes these programs. Course work is planned carefully in advance and study programs are assiduously followed. The teacher, not the child, is defined as the ultimate educational resource. Parents and local community groups, because they tend to challenge the school's operating perspective, are treated only ritualistically at P.T.A. meetings, open houses, school plays, athletic contests. Their point of view, like the child's, is seldom taken seriously. They are too incompetent. Taking them seriously would force a shift in existing power arrangements in the school.

Mead's perspective proposes just the opposite view of parents, children and education. Education, he argued, is an unfolding, social process wherein the child comes to see himself in increasingly more complex ways. Education leads to self-understanding and to the acquisition of the basic skills. This principle suggests that schools must be socially relevant. They must incorporate the social world of child and community into curriculum arrangements. Cultural diversity must be stressed. Alternative symbolic leaders must be presented, and these must come from realistic worlds of experience. (Setting an astronaut as a preferred "self model" for seven-year-old males as a present text book does, can hardly be defined as realistic). Problematic situations from the child's everyday world must be brought into the classroom. Mead, for example, proposed as early as 1908 that schools teach sex education to children.

Children and parents, then, must be seen as resources around which education is developed and presented. They must be taken seriously. This presupposes a close working relationship between home and school. Parents must take responsibility for their children's education. They can no longer afford to shift accountability to the schools. This simple principle suggests that ethnic studies programs should have been central features of schools at least 50 years ago. Schools exist to serve their surrounding communities, not bend those communities to their perspective.

Redefining Schools

If this reciprocal service function is stressed, an important implication follows. Schools should educate children in ways that permit them to be contributing members in their chosen worlds. Such basics as reading, writing and counting will never be avoided. But their instruction can be made relevant within the worlds the child most directly experiences. This suggests, initially at least, that black and brown children be taught to respect their separate cultural heritages. Second, it suggests that they will probably learn best with materials drawn from those cultures. Third, it suggests that they must be presented with self models who know, respect and come from those cultures—black teachers must not be removed from southern schools.

To the extent that schools and teachers serve as referent points for the child's self-conception it can be argued that it is not the minority student who must change. But instead it is the white middle-class child who must be exposed to alternative cultural perspectives. Minority teachers must be made integral components of all phases of the educational act.

Mead's perspective suggests, as I have attempted to elaborate, that the classroom is an interactive world. Research by Roger G. Barker and Paul V. Gump on big schools and little schools supports this position and their findings suggest an additional set of proposals. Briefly, they learned that as class and school size increases student satisfaction decreases. Teaching becomes more mechanized, students become more irrelevant and activities not related to learning attain greater importance, social clubs, for example. In short, in big schools students are redundant.

Classroom size and school size must be evaluated from this perspective. If schools exist to serve children and their parents, then large schools are dysfunctional. They are knowledge factories, not places of learning or self-development. Culturally heterogeneous, small-sized classes must be experimented with. Students must have opportunities to know their teachers in personal, not institutional terms. Students must be taught to take one another seriously, not competitively. Small, ecologically intimate surroundings have a greater likelihood of promoting these arrangements than do large-scale, bureaucratically organized classes.

At present, standardized, state and nationally certified tests are given students to assess their psychological, emotional, intellectual and social development. Two problems restrict the effectiveness of these methods, however. With few exceptions they have been standardized on white middle-class populations. Second, they are the only measurement techniques routinely employed.

A number of proposals follow from these problems. First, open-ended tests which permit the child to express his or her perspective must be developed. These tests, such as the "Who Am I?" question, would be given to students to determine the major contours of their self-conceptions. With this information in hand teachers would be in a better position to tailor teaching programs to a child's specific needs, definitions, intentions and goals.

Second, tests such as "Who is Important to You?" could be given students on a regular basis to determine who their significant others are. It is near axiomatic that derogation of the people most important to one leads to alienation from the setting and spokesman doing the derogation.

Teachers must learn to respect and present in respectful terms those persons most important to the child.

A third methodological proposal directs observers to link a student's utterances, wishes and self-images to his or her day-to-day conduct. Written test scores often fail to reflect what persons really take into account and value. In many social settings verbal ability, athletic skill, hustling aptitudes, money and even physical attractiveness serve as significant status locators. I.Q. tests often do not. Furthermore, a person's score on a test may not accurately reflect his ability to handle problematic situations, which is surely a goal of education. Observations of conduct (behavior) in concrete settings can provide the needed leads in this direction.

Methodological Implications

A critic of these proposals might remark that such measures are not standardized, that their validity is questionable, that they cannot be administered nationally, and that they have questionable degrees of reliability. In response I would cite the ability of Roger Barker and colleagues to execute such observations over time with high reliability (.80-.98 for many measures). But more to the point I would argue that conventional tests are simply not working and it is time to experiment with alternative techniques, perspectives and theories.

This defense suggests that schools of education must begin to consider teaching their students the methodologies of participant observation, unobtrusive analysis and life history construction. These softer methods have been the traditional province of sociologists and anthropologists. Members of these disciplines must consider offering cross-disciplinary courses in methodology, especially aimed for everyday practitioners in school settings. Graduate requirements for teaching credentials must also be reexamined and greater efforts must be made to recruit and train minority students in these different approaches.

These proposals reflect a basic commitment. Schools should be organized so as to maximize a child's self-development and they should permit maximum child-parent participation. It is evident that my discussion has not been limited to an analysis of compensatory education programs. This has been deliberate. It is my conviction that education, wherever it occurs, involves interactions between social selves. Taking the self as a point of departure I have attempted to show that what happens to a preschool child is not unlike the moral experiences of a black or brown 17-year-old senior. But most importantly, both should find themselves in schools that take them seriously and treat them with respect. Schools exist to serve children and the public. This charge must be also taken seriously.

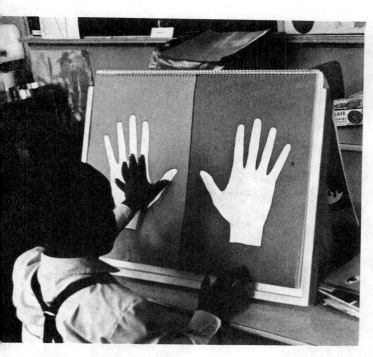

Black Genes— White Environment

J. McVicker Hunt

What determines human intelligence? What determines the competence of people? Is it fixed and immutable at a child's birth? Or does it change with time and circumstance? If it does, then what circumstances will best foster its maximum growth?

These questions once agitated only a small group of scholars and scientists. No longer. Today they have acquired urgent social and political significance. The fates of vast programs and many a career may hinge on the conclusions of the most recondite social-psychological study. A scholarly paper, a thicket of statistical tables, becomes an object of burning interest for journalists, politicians, and others concerned to find "the" answer to why the children of the poor don't seem to learn as much in school as their own children do.

I had thought, though, that at least in the years since World War II we had learned something about most of these matters. I had thought we had learned that it was no longer tenable to conceive of intelligence tests as indicators of fixed capacity or innate potential in children. I had thought we had learned that it was quite wrong to think we could predict an adult's intellectual competence from his score on a test taken as a child without specifying the circumstances he would encounter in the interim.

In fact our political and educational leaders do seem to have gotten this message. The circumstances that affect a child's experiences in the course of growing up *are* believed to play an important role in affecting intelligence and the motivation for achievement and competence. This notion has been used in formulating solutions to the crisis of the cities created by the heavy migration of the poor from the South. Only a little imagination and goodwill has been needed to infer that the children of lower socioeconomic backgrounds, once very widely considered to be innately stupid and lazy, may instead be viewed as children who have been cheated of that equality of opportunity which our forefathers considered to be the birthright of all.

Unfortunately, however, these changing conceptions of intelligence and growth appear to have reached the leaders even before they have been fully appreciated among those of us trained in the psychological sciences. I say "unfortunately" because the newer conceptions may have led to excessive hopes among politicians and the administrators of our educational systems. Too many of them have a tendency to confuse the perfectly justifiable expectation that there can be significant improvement in the competence of the children of the poor with the basic scientific know-how required to carry out, or even to plan, the broad educational programs needed to do the job. What I am worried about is that the confusion and excessive hopes may have created an "oversell" that will now be followed by an "overkill" of support for the efforts to develop and deploy effective educational programs. One has only to recall the recent vicissitudes of the Head Start program.

Moreover, the possibility of an overkill is made all the more dangerous by the revival of interest and belief in the notion that races differ in inherited potential for competence. People so persuaded are far from extinct. We all witnessed the great flurry of attention given by the national press to Arthur Jensen's recent paper on the relative immutability of the I.Q. Although one cannot with certainty rule out the possibility of racial differences in potential for competence, the whole issue is of very little import so long

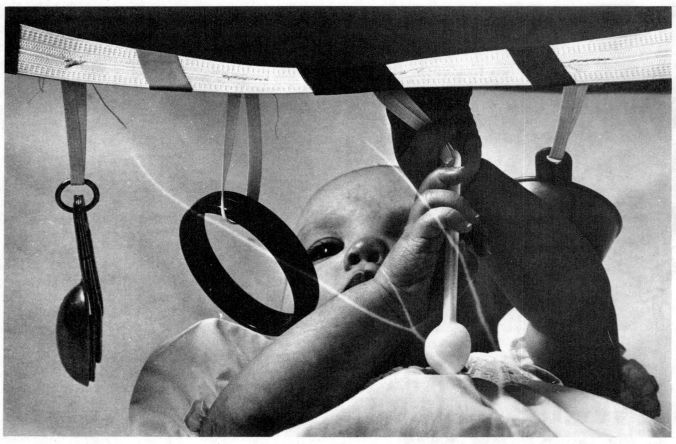

Until 1957 locomotor development in infants was considered predetermined. But new evidence shows that it too depends on circumstances of environment.

as the great majority of black, Puerto Rican, and Indian children grow up in poverty with extremely limited opportunities to acquire the language and number abilities and the motivation that underlie full participation in our society.

But I am no less fearful that the failure of some of our most expensive and publicized efforts to improve dramatically the learning potential of poor children may lead to an unjustified discouragement on the part not only of politicians but of the public that must pay for these efforts. I am afraid that our ignorance of how to proceed effectively may now deprive us, for an indefinite period, of the opportunity to do what I am confident ultimately can be done to meet these challenges. What we need is the opportunity to innovate and evaluate, to fail, to correct our misinterpretations and our failures, and gradually to de-

velop programs of educational technology, beginning even at birth, that *are* effective in fostering development.

It is these concerns that have prompted me to review here the evidence for the crucial importance of life's circumstances for the development of the cognitive skills and the attitudes that comprise competence.

Intelligence Test Scores Not Indicators of Capacity or Potential

It should have been obvious from the beginning that scores on tests of intelligence could not possibly serve as indicators of hereditary capacity or potential. It is a truism to say that one's genetic endowment sets limits on intellectual potential and also that it greatly influences what happens when we encounter any given series of circumstances. As a scientific statement, however, this is basically meaningless, as Alfred Binet, the developer of the most widely used I.Q. test, recognized as early as 1909 when he struck out against

". . . some recent philosophers [who] appear to have given their moral support to this deplorable verdict that the intelligence of an individual is a fixed quantity . . . we must protest and act against this brutal pessimism . . . (for) a child's mind is like a field for which an expert farmer has advised a change in the methods of cultivation, with the result that in the place of a desert land, we now have a harvest. It is in this particular sense, the one which is significant, that we say that the intelligence of children may be increased. One increases that which constitutes the intelligence of a school child, namely the capacity to learn, to improve with instruction."

Although the complex tests of Binet and Theodore Simon remained pre-eminent in the intelligence-testing movement, the conceptual framework built up around their use was developed by the students of Francis Galton and G. Stanley Hall, rather than by Binet. This framework emphasized from the beginning the role of heredity as a fixer of intelligence and a pre-determinant of development in the interpretation of test scores.

Moreover, throughout more than the first four decades of this century, American textbooks on genetics tended to emphasize the work of Gregor Mendel on the hereditary transmission of traits and to neglect the work of Walter Johannsen on the crucial role of the interaction of the *genotype* (the constellation of genes received by an organism from its progenitors) with the environment in determining the *phenotype* (the observable characteristics of an organism).

To be sure, some of the early evidence did seem to confirm the notion of intelligence tests as indicators of adult capacity. For instance, the I.Q.s of groups of children showed great constancy (which was a consequence of the way the tests were constructed) and also considerable individual constancy once a child got into school. Moreover, efforts at training children directly on the intellectual functions tested turned out to have but short-lived effects. Furthermore, the I.Q.s of persons closely related to a child proved to be more similar than the I.Q.s of persons less closely related or unrelated.

Since World War II, however, evidence has been accumulated that is so out of keeping with the belief that the tests indicate fixed innate capacity or potential that the belief is no longer tenable.

Perhaps the most incontrovertible of this evidence is that of rising intelligence in the face of predicted deterioration. The prediction of deterioration came from combining two observations. First, it has been obvious since the 17th century that poor families have more children than families of the middle and upper classes. Second, many studies have shown that people from low socioeconomic background typically average about 20 points of I.Q. below people in the upper-middle class. In 1937, R. B. Cattell multiplied the number of people at each I.Q. level by the reproduction rate at that level and computed the new mean to estimate the I.Q. of the next generation. From this procedure, he estimated a drop of a little over three points a generation, or about one point a decade. This he characterized as a "galloping plunge toward intellectual bankruptcy."

But Cattell's dire prediction has been repeatedly contradicted by rising I.Q.s in those populations where the children of a given age have been tested and retested after intervals of a decade or more. Thirteen years after his own forecast, Cattell himself published a study comparing ten-year-old children living in the city of Leicester, England in 1949 with the ten-year-old children living in that same city in 1936. In the place of the predicted drop of something slightly more than one point in I.Q., Cattell actually found an increase of 1.28 points. Although small, this increase was highly significant from the statistical standpoint.

In other studies, the predicted drop in I.Q. has been proven wrong by gains substantially larger than these. S. Smith reported a growth of around 20 points between the scores of children in various Honolulu schools in 1924, and the scores of children in those same schools in 1938. Lester Wheeler reported a 10-point increase in the mean I.Q. of children from a single group of families in the ten-year period before and after the great changes brought about in that community by the Tennessee Valley Authority. When Frank Finch compared the I.Q.s of all students in a sample of high schools in the 1920's and again in those same high schools in the 1940's, he found the average gains ranging between 10 and 15 points. But perhaps the most dramatic evidence of an upward shift came when the test performances of soldiers in World War II were compared with those of World War I soldiers. Clearly, if the tests measure fixed intellectual capacity or innate potential, and if the majority of each new generation comes from parents in the lowest third in·tested intelligence, something very, very strange is happening.

I.Q. Tests Are Like Achievement Tests

It has long been customary to differentiate intelligence tests from achievement tests. Some differences do exist. All are differences in degree, however, rather than in kind.

First, intelligence tests tend to tap a wider variety of experience, both in and out of school than do achievement tests. Most achievement tests are closely tied to specific courses of study. Intelligence tests are not. School experience still contributes, however, to performance on more broadly based tests of intelligence. Moreover, experiences in the home and in social groups contribute to performance on achievement tests. Second, achievement tests are aimed at relatively new learning, while intelligence tests depend typically on older learning.

Intelligence tests and achievement tests, then, are measures of current capacity depending directly upon previously acquired skills and information and motivation. Binet saw this at the turn of the century, but he had escaped the "advantages" of the tutelage of men with strong theoretical beliefs in intelligence fixed by heredity.

A Case of Misplaced Concreteness

Semantics can often have unfortunate consequences. The terms "dimension" and "scale" when applied to such matters as intelligence are a case in point. These terms were borrowed from measurement in the physical world where scales are instruments for measuring unvarying dimensions. When these terms are applied to the behavior of people, we tend also to apply notions of concreteness and constancy derived from the world of physical objects. Thus, calling intelligence a *dimension* of behavior and speaking of tests as *scales* tends to obscure reality. This becomes especially unfortunate when the semantics sap the motivation of teachers to change their approaches to promote increased development in children who resist their standard approaches and curricula.

Development

Let me turn next to those propositions concerning development that I believe are no longer tenable and that I believe are highly unfortunate in their influence upon those working in programs of early childhood education.

FALLACY: THE RATE OF DEVELOPMENT IS PREDETERMINED

I am confident that belief in a predetermined rate of human development is quite untenable. In the history of our thinking about psychological development, the constant I.Q. was the epitome of this notion. But it got support from the widely cited work of G. E. Coghill in the 1920's which related developmental sequences in the behavior of salamander larvae from head to tail and from trunk to limbs to microscopic histological evidences of neuromuscular maturation. Support also came from various other observations that I cannot take time to review here. Suffice it to say that maturation and learning were seen as two distinctly separate processes with maturation predetermined by heredity and learning controlled by the circumstances encountered.

Evidence contradicting the notion of a predetermined rate of development also appeared. Wendell Cruze reported that chicks allowed to peck for only 15 minutes a day failed to improve in the accuracy of their pecking. Moreover, the early longitudinal studies of intellectual development in children uncovered individual growth curves with changes in I.Q. as large as 60 points. Several students in the 1930's found increases in the I.Q.s of young children associated with nursery schooling.

At the time, however, the credibility of these observations of change in the rate of development was questioned by other observers who posited differing inherited patterns of growth or found methodological weaknesses in the studies. Differences of more than 20 points of I.Q. were found between identical twins reared apart under differing kinds of circumstances, but, because such instances were rare, they were considered to be merely examples of errors of measurement.

One of the most impressive of the early studies to cast doubt on the notion of a predetermined rate of development is that of Harold M. Skeels and Murlon H. Dye. This study was prompted by a "clinical surprise." Two residents of a state orphanage, one aged 13 months with a Kühlmann I.Q. of 46 and the other aged 16 months with an I.Q. of 35, were committed to an institution for the retarded. After six months there, where the mentally retarded women doted on them, these two children showed a remarkably rapid rate of development. Coupled with change from apathy to liveliness was an improvement of 31 points of I.Q. in one and 52 points in the other. After this, a group of 13 infants—ranging in age from 7 months to 30 months and in I.Q.s from 36 to 89, with a mean of 64 —were transferred from the orphanage (but not committed) to these wards for moron women. After being there for periods ranging from 6 months for the seven-month-old child to 52 months for the 30-month-old child, every one of these infants showed a gain in I.Q. The minimum gain was 7 points; the maximum was 58 points, and all but four showed gains of over 20 points.

On the other hand, 12 other infants—ranging in age from 12 to 22 months and in I.Q. from 50 to 103, with a mean I.Q. of 87—were left in the orphanage. When these infants were retested after periods varying from 20 to 43 months, all but one of them showed decreases in I.Q. that ranged from eight to 45 points, and five of the decreases exceeded 35 points. These findings suggested strongly that the effects of these two institutional environments differed greatly, but the idea that children's I.Q.s had been improved by moving them from an orphanage to a school for the mentally retarded was merely ridiculed, and the ridicule deprived the findings of their highly suggestive import.

In the light of the evidence accumulated since World War II, this study of Skeels and Dye has acquired the status of a classic, and the notion of a predetermined rate of development has become almost incredible.

FALLACY: MATURATION IS INDEPENDENT OF CIRCUMSTANCES

Locomotor development has long been considered to be predetermined, but in 1957 Wayne Dennis discovered an orphanage in Tehran where 60 percent of those infants in their second year were still not sitting up alone and where 84 percent of those in their fourth year were still not walking. When one considers that nearly all family-reared infants are sitting alone at eight months and nearly all such infants are walking alone by 20 months of age, it becomes clear that locomotor development cannot be independent of circumstances.

In the 1940's, the theorizing of Donald Hebb prompted investigators to rear animals under circumstances varying in complexity, especially in perceptual complexity. In the first such study, Hebb himself found the adult ability of rats reared as pets to be superior in solving maze problems to that of litter-mates reared in laboratory cages. Other investigators have found that dogs reared freely in complex environments are better as adults at learning mazes than their litter-mates reared in the monotony of laboratory cages.

The neuropsychological theorizing of Hebb and the theorizing of Holger Hydén, a Swedish biochemist, have prompted investigators to rear animals in the dark and in environments of various levels of complexity to determine the effects of such variations in rearing on both behavioral development and neuroanatomical maturation. Dark-reared chimpanzees, cats, rabbits, rats and mice have all shown deficiencies of both nerve cells and glial cells of their retinal ganglia when compared with animals or litter-mates reared in the light of laboratory cages. More recent investigations have extended these neuroanatomical deficiencies associated with dark-rearing to the appropriate nuclei of the thalamus and even to the striate area of the occipital lobe of the brain. These highly exciting finds indicate that even neuroanatomical maturation can no longer be considered to be independent of the circumstances in which animals develop.

FALLACY: LONGITUDINAL PREDICTION IS POSSIBLE

Despite such an accumulation of evidence as I have indicated (and there is much more), the belief in a constant I.Q. has given us the habit of thinking of the validity of tests in longitudinal terms. We have used and still use the scores based on the performances of children on tests administered at one age to predict what their school or test performances will be at later ages.

Yet, if even neuroanatomic maturation can be influenced by circumstances, and if psychological development is as plastic as this evidence implies, *longitudinal prediction is impossible from test scores alone.* The plasticity that appears to exist in the rate at which human organisms develop renders longitudinal prediction basically impossible unless one specifies the circumstances under which this development is to take place. In fact, trying to predict what a person's I.Q. will be at 20 on the basis of his I.Q. at age one or two is like trying to predict how heavy a two-week-old calf will be when he is a two-year old without knowing whether he will be reared in a dry pasture, in an irrigated pasture, or in a feed lot.

To be sure, longitudinal prediction improves with age. This results from the fact that test-retest validities involve part-whole relationships. Thus, if one is predicting I.Q. at 20, the older the child is at the time of the initial test, the larger becomes the predictor part of the criterion *whole.* Moreover, in actual situations, individuals tend to remain within sets of social, economic, and educational circumstances that are relatively stable. Thus, a very large share of whatever constancy individual I.Q.s have had can be attributed to a combination of the increasingly congruent part-whole relationship and with the sameness of circumstances.

Belief in a predetermined rate of development and in the possibility of predicting performance over time has had very unfortunate consequences for educational practice. When children fail to learn and are found to have low scores on intelligence tests, teachers are prompt to feel that "these children are doing as well as can be expected." Such an attitude dampens any inclination teachers may have to alter their approach to such children. Consequence? The tutelage that the child encounters remains essentially stable, and the child continues in his rut of failure.

An important corollary of the finding that the rate of development depends upon the circumstances encountered is a needed change in the conception of "readiness." The notion that children are ready for certain kinds of experiences and not for others has validity. On the other hand, the notion that this "readiness" is a matter of predetermined maturation, as distinct from learning or past encounters with circumstances, is basically wrong and potentially damaging. What is involved is what I have been calling "the problem of the match." If encountering a given set of circumstances is to induce psychological development in the child, these circumstances must have an appropriate relationship to the information and skills already accumulated by the child. This is no easy matter. Ordinarily, the best indicators of an appropriate match are to be found, I now believe, in emotional behavior. They are evidences of **interest and of mild surprise. If the circumstances are too** simple and too familiar, the child will fail to develop and he is likely to withdraw into boredom. If the circumstances demand too much of a child, he will withdraw in fear or explode in anger. So long as the child can withdraw from the circumstances without facing punishment, loss of love, fear of disapproval, or what-not, I believe it is impossible to over-stimulate him. The challenge in such a conception of "readiness" as that involved in the "problem of the match" is basically the problem of preparing the environment to foster development. We are a long way from solid knowledge of how to do this, but I believe we do have some sensible suggestions about how to proceed.

Developmental Order and Predeterminism

One more point about development and its implications. Order has always been obvious in behavioral development. In locomotor development, for instance, it is obvious that the infant is at first rooted to a given spot, that he learns to wheel and twist even before he sits up, that he sits up alone before he can creep, that he creeps or scoots before he stands, that he stands before he cruises, that he cruises while holding on to things before he toddles, that he toddles before he walks, and that he walks before he runs. Arnold Gesell and his collaborators at Yale devoted their total normative enterprise to describing the order in the various domains of behavioral development that take place with advancing age. Jean Piaget and his collaborators have also been concerned with describing the order in intelligence and in the construction of such aspects of reality as object permanence, as constancy of quantity, of shape, and of color, and causality, space, and time. Ina Uzgiris and I have been using these orderly landmarks in development as a basis for our ordinal scales of psychological development in infancy. In short, order in development is an obvious fact.

Although Gesell gave occasional lip service to the interaction between child and environment in behavioral development, all but one of his various principles of growth (that of "individuating maturation") described predetermined processes. Moreover, in 1954 Gesell explicitly said that "the so-called environment, whether internal or external, does not generate the progressions of development. Environmental factors support, inflect, and specify; but they do not engender the basic forms and sequences of ontogenesis."

Similarly, Mary Shirley saw evidence of Coghill's head-to-tail principle when she wrote that "motor control begins headward and travels toward the feet beginning with the eye muscle and progressing through stages in which the head and neck muscles are mastered, arms, and upper trunk come under control . . . the baby at last achieves mastery of his whole body. . . ."

Yet such an interpretation is not a necessary implication of the observed fact of orderliness in development. While Piaget, like Gesell, has found order in psychological development, he, unlike Gesell, has emphasized the role of interaction. According to Piaget, development occurs in the course of adaptive interaction between the child and the environment. This interaction involves two complimentary and invariant processes: *assimilation* and *accommodation*. Piaget conceives these processes as basically common to the physiological as well as the psychological domain. Assimilation occurs whenever an organism utilizes something from the environment and incorporates it into its own structures. Accommodation, the complement of assimilation, operates whenever encounters with the environment evoke a change in the existing structure of the central processes that mediate the interpretation of events and control action. Thus, accommodation is another term for adaptive learning.

Although I cannot here go into Piaget's ideas, they have definitely influenced my own thinking about learning. Attempting to understand them has opened my own eyes to the fact that circumstances influence development in ways quite other than those within the traditional rubrics under which we have studied learning.

Implications

LEARNING IN POVERTY

As I have already noted, the factors controlling the development of competence in early childhood are no longer purely an academic topic. These factors have acquired both social and political significance from the fact that our advancing technology is rapidly decreasing the economic opportunities for those without linguistic and mathematical abilities, the motivation to solve problems, and the inclination to carry social responsibility, and from the fact that a large number of black people, coming from a background of poverty and limited opportunity, lack these skills and motives. In the light of these challenges, what are the implications of the foregoing argument?

The intellectual capacity that underlies competence in substantial part is not fixed. In this connection, various lines of evidence suggest strongly that being reared in conditions of poverty and cultural deprivation deprives a child of opportunities to learn. The children in poor families have typically encountered many fewer kinds of objects than children of the middle class. As infants, the children of poverty often have inadequate diets and they live in crowded circumstances which expose them to a continuous vocal racket to which they become habituated. This habituation may account for the inadequacies in hearing other people speak that was found by Cynthia Deutsch and by Deutsch and Brown. Too often, the verbal interaction of children of the poor with their elders is limited to commands to stop whatever the child is doing without explanations as to why. Seldom are these children invited to note what is going on around them or to formulate their observations in their own language. These children are especially unlikely to learn the syntactical rules of the standard language. Seldom is their ingenuity rewarded except when they learn to avoid the punishment that comes when they get caught at something arbitrarily prohibited. In such circumstances, the low test scores repeatedly observed in the children of poverty are to be expected.

With respect to motivation, moreover, the children of poverty, black or white, have little opportunity to learn to take initiative, to give up present satisfactions for larger satisfactions in the future, or to take pride in problem-solving achievement. Seldom have the poor acquired such motives. Thus, their response to their children's demands are dictated largely by their own immediate impulses and

needs, not the children's. To these parents, a good child is typically a quiet child who does not bother them.

Regarding conduct, finally, these children of the poor are exposed to circumstances and standards that are hardly those prescribed by the demands of the dominant society. The models of behavior for these children often make them unfit for adaptation to either schools or marketplace. So long as a large percentage of black people are reared in poverty under these conditions of childrearing it is not tenable to attribute to race the existing deficiency in competence as measured by intelligence tests.

From such evidence as has been accumulating on the matter of class differences in child-rearing, it is becoming clearer and clearer that the accident of being born in poverty serves to deprive children of that equality of opportunity which our founding fathers considered to be the right of all Americans.

WHAT IS TO BE DONE?

These relatively new findings concerning the role of circumstances in the development of competence suggest that corrective efforts should be focused upon the young, and preferably upon the very young—even beginning with birth. These findings suggest that early childhood education can have tremendous social significance if we learn how to do it effectively. It is a long step, however, from justifiable hopes to the development of the educational technology in workable form and to its broad-scale deployment in America. The question is, can we extend these findings into programs of early childhood education fast enough?

Project Head Start was a fine step in the right direction. The danger is that it may have been taken with hopes too high before an adequately effective technology of early childhood education for the children of the poor had been developed. All too often, the Head-Start programs have merely supplied poor children with an opportunity to play in traditional nursery schools that were designed chiefly to exercise large muscles and to enable middle-class children to escape from their overly strict and solicitous mothers. Such opportunities are unlikely to be very effective in overcoming the deficient skills and motives to be found in the children of the poor.

Nursery schools were invented originally for the purposes of compensatory education. Shortly after the turn of the century, Maria Montessori developed a program for the poor children of the San Lorenzo district of Rome which appeared to be highly successful. She provided a practical solution to what I am calling the "problem of the match" by breaking the lock-step in education and permitting each child to follow his own interests in working with a variety of materials that she had found to be stimulating to children. She arranged these materials in sequences that would lead to conceptual skills. Moreover, in her classes she combined children ranging in age from three to six and thereby provided the younger with a graded series of models for imitation and the older ones with opportunities to learn by helping to teach the younger. Somewhat later, Margaret McMillan established her nursery schools in the slums of England to give these children, whom she considered to be environmentally handicapped, an opportunity to learn many of the abilities and motives that children of the middle class learn spontaneously. When the nursery schools were brought to the United States, however, it was only the well-to-do who could pay for them. Our traditional belief that class differences in ability are the inevitable consequence of heredity left Americans with little inclination to provide nursery schools for children of the poor. Thus, the schools got adapted to what were conceived to be the needs of the middle-class children. When the decision to mount Project Head Start was made, only these programs were widely available for deployment on a large scale. It should be no surprise, then, if the success of Project Head Start in improving the future academic success of children of the poor is highly limited.

In consequence of this unfortunate history, we have no ready-made technology of compensatory early childhood education designed to foster in children of the poor those abilities and motives underlying competence in the dominant society which circumstances prevented their acquiring.

This is beginning to be recognized. With the recognition is coming a tremendous explosion in new curricula for young children. My impression is that these achieve little unless they focus on the fostering of the ability to handle language and number concepts, and, with regard to motivation, on extending the time interval in which these children operate psychologically, and on developing pride in achievement. I see no substitute for a painstaking investigation of what works and what does not work coupled with a theoretical synthesis calculated to give us a more accurate picture of the various kinds of deficits to be found in children of the slums and more effective ways either to compensate for these deficits or to prevent them.

I am inclined to believe that we shall have to extend our programs to include children of ages less than four. I believe we shall have to involve the help of parents in these programs. Attempts to influence the child-rearing of parents of the lowest socioeconomic status by means of psychotherapy-like counseling have regularly failed. On the other hand, involving parents first as observers and then as aids in nursery schools, where they get an opportunity to see the effects of new (to them) ways of dealing with children and where these techniques are explained and tried out first in school and then in home demonstrations, all this appears to be highly promising. Here the investigations of Rupert Klaus and Susan Gray and their colleagues at the George Peabody College for teachers in Nashville, Tennessee, of Ira Gordon at the University of Florida, of Professor Merle Karnes at the University of Illinois, and of David Weikart at Ypsilanti, Michigan appear to be showing the way. In a summer nursery school for children of poverty in Nashville, for instance, Klaus and Gray have developed a curriculum that aimed at teaching language and number skills and the attitudes and motives required to cope with elementary schools. Home visitors brought each mother to observe and later to participate in the teaching at the nursery school. The home visitors interpreted for the mothers what they saw the teachers doing. Then, during the period between summer sessions of the nursery school, the home visitors saw each of the mothers every other week. During these visits, they demonstrated for the mothers such matters as how to read a story with enthusiasm, how to reinforce children for new abilities, and how to talk with children about such homemaking operations as peeling potatoes while in the process.

This effort has been evaluated by means of gains in scores on standard tests of intelligence and will be evaluated in terms of the later progress of these children in the schools. Tests given before and after the summer nursery school have shown spurts in scores of the nursery schoolers that do not appear in the test performances of the children who did not go to the nursery school.

The test results of this program also show two other highly promising phenomena. First, the younger siblings of the children going to nursery school whose mothers saw the home visitors regularly have turned out to be significantly superior in test performance to the younger siblings of four-year-old children in two contrast groups who got neither nursery school nor the home visits. This finding suggests that the mother must have been learning something about child-rearing that generalized to their management of their younger children.

Second, the younger children of the mothers in the contrast group who lived in the same neighborhood as those receiving the home visits got higher test scores than did the children of mothers in a contrast group living some 60 miles away. This finding suggests that mothers who learn new child-rearing practices from their observations at the nursery school and from the home visitor were somehow communicating them to their neighbors with whom they had face-to-face relationships.

The evidence is highly promising from these new efforts in compensatory education. But after Head Start we should beware of the flush of too-high hopes. I fear that the very limited success to be expected from the deployment of nursery schools designed chiefly for the children of the middle class may lead to an unjustified discouragement on the part of both political leaders and the public. I fear

a fading out of support for efforts in the domain of early childhood education. At this stage of history, it is extremely important that both political leaders and voters understand the limited nature of our knowledge about how to foster competence in the young, that they understand the basis for our justified hopes, and that they comprehend the need for the continued support of fundamental research and of the process of developing an adequate technology of early childhood education. Only with continued support for research and development in this domain can we expect to create effective means of compensating for and/or preventing the deficiencies of early experience required to meet the twin challenges of racial discrimination and poverty.

Creativity and Intelligence in Children's Thinking

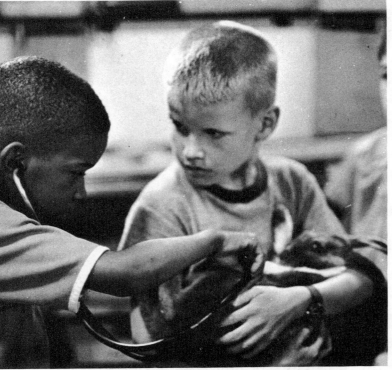

Michael A. Wallach and Nathan Kogan

While there has been a great deal of discussion in recent years concerning the importance of fostering "creativity" in our children, there is little solid evidence to support the claim that creativity can be distinguished from the more familiar concept of intelligence. To be sure, the word "creativity" has caught the fancy of the culture—frequent reference is made to creativity in contexts as diverse as education, industry, and advertising. Time and time again, how-

ever, the "proof" offered to support the existence of a type of cognitive excellence different from general intelligence has proven to be a will-o-the-wisp.

The logical requirements for such a proof can be put as follows. The psychological concept of *intelligence* defines a network of strongly related abilities concerning the retention, transformation, and utilization of verbal and numerical symbols: at issue are a person's memory storage capacities, his skill in solving problems, his dexterity in manipulating and dealing with concepts. The person high in one of these skills will tend to be high in all; the individual who is low in one will tend to be low in all. But what of the psychological concept of *creativity?* If the behavior judged to be indicative of creativity turns up in the same persons who behave in the ways we call "intelligent," then there is no justification for claiming the existence of any kind of cognitive capacity apart from general intelligence. We would have to assert that the notion of greater or lesser degrees of *creativity* in people simply boils down, upon empirical inspection, to the notion of greater or lesser degrees of general *intelligence.* On the other hand, in order to demonstrate that there are grounds for considering creativity to be a kind of cognitive talent that exists in its own right, another kind of proof would be required. It would be necessary to demonstrate that whatever methods of evaluation are utilized to define variations in creativity from person to person result in classifications that are different from those obtained when the same individuals are categorized as to intelligence.

When we reviewed the quantitative research on creativity, we were forced to conclude that these logical requirements were not met. Despite frequent use of the term "creativity" to define a form of talent that was independent of intelligence, examination of the evidence indicated that the purported measures of creativity tended to have little more in common with each other than they had in common with measures of general intelligence. If one could do about the same thing with an IQ measure as one could with the creativity measures, (regarding who should be considered more creative and who should be considered less creative) it was difficult to defend the practice of invoking a new and glamorous term such as "creativity" for describing the kind of talent under study.

While varying conceptions of the meaning of creativity had been embodied in the measures used, they all shared one thing in common: they had been administered to the persons under study as *tests.* From the viewpoint of the person undergoing assessment, the creativity procedures, no less than an intelligence test, carried the aura of school examinations. They were carried out with explicit or implicit time limits in classroom settings where many students underwent the assessment procedures at the same time. Indeed, we even found that the creativity procedures had been described to the students as "tests" by the psychologists who gave them.

We were suspicious that such a test-like context was inimical to the wholehearted display of cognitive characteristics which could be correctly referred to as being involved in creativity. Hence we believed that creativity had not yet been given a fair chance to reveal itself as a different form of excellence than intelligence. These suspicions were reinforced when we considered what creative artists and scientists have said concerning creative moments in their own work.

Their Creative Elders

In their introspections one finds an emphasis upon the production of a free flow of ideas—the bubbling forth of varieties of associations concerning the matter at hand. Einstein, for example, refers to the need for "combinatory play" and "associative play" in putting ideas together. Dryden describes the process of writing as involving "a confus'd mass of thoughts, tumbling over one another in the dark." Poincaré talks about ideas as having "rose in crowds" immediately prior to his obtaining a significant mathematical insight. These associations, moreover, range with high frequency into the consideration of unique, unusual possibilities, but ones which are nevertheless relevant to the issue rather than just bizarre. When we look into the conditions under which an abundant flow of unique ideational possibilities has been available, the artists and scientists indicate that the most conducive attitude is one of playful contemplation—if you will, of permissiveness. Creative awareness tends to occur when the individual—in a playful manner—entertains a range of possibilities without worry concerning his own personal success or failure and how his self-image will fare in the eyes of others.

With this in mind we formulated a research program that involved the extensive study of 151 fifth-grade children. They were of middle-class socio-economic status, and boys and girls were about equally represented in our sample. The work, which was supported in part by the Cooperative Research Program of the United States Office of Education, has been described in detail in our book, *Modes of Thinking in Young Children: A Study of the Creativity-Intelligence Distinction* (Holt, Rinehart and Winston, 1965).

From the introspections of scientists and artists arose some ground rules concerning what creativity might rightfully signify if in fact it constitutes a type of excellence different from intelligence. These ground rules might be put in terms of the following two injunctions:

■ First, study the flow of ideas—consider how unique and how abundant are the kinds of ideas that a child can provide when contemplating various sorts of tasks. One is talking here, of course, about relevant ideas, not about ideas that might earn the status of being unique only because they are so bizarre as to have no relevance at all to the task.

■ Second, provide an atmosphere that convinces the child that he is not under test—that the situation is one of play rather than one where his intellectual worthiness is under evaluation by others. This second injunction may be a particularly difficult one to fulfill on the American educational scene, where testing and the feeling of undergoing personal evaluation are ubiquitous. Yet if our considerations were correct, it obviously was essential to fulfill it if creativity was to receive a fighting chance to display itself.

Accordingly, we mustered every device possible to place the assessment procedures in a context of play rather than in the typical context of testing with which the children were all too familiar. There were no time limits on the procedures. They were administered to one child at a time rather than to groups of children seated at their classroom desks. The adults who worked with the children, moreover, had already established relationships in the context of play activities. We even took pains to avoid the customary vocabulary of tests and testing in connection with the research enterprise as a whole—in our talk with the children we described the work as oriented to the study of children's games for purposes of developing new games children would like.

The procedures involved such matters as requesting the child to suggest possible uses for each of several objects, or to describe possible ways in which each of several pairs of objects are similar to each other. For example, in one procedure the child was to suggest all the different ways in which we could use such objects as a newspaper, a cork, a shoe, a chair. "Rip it up if angry" was a unique response for "newspaper," while "make paper hats" was not unique. In another, he was to indicate similarities between, for example, a potato and a carrot, a cat and a mouse, milk and meat. "They are government-inspected" was a unique response for "milk and meat," while "they come from animals" was not unique. In yet another, he was to indicate all the things that each of a number of abstract drawings might be—such as the drawings shown in the illus-

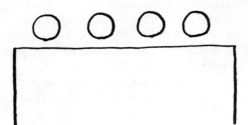

Left: Unique: "Foot and toes"
     Common: "Table with things on top"

Right: Unique: "Three mice eating a piece of cheese"
     Common: "Three people sitting around a table"

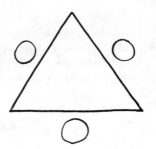

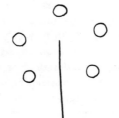

Left: Unique: "Lollipop bursting into pieces"
     Common: "Flower"

Right: Unique: "Two haystacks on a flying carpet"
     Common: "Two igloos"

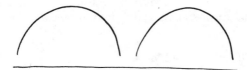

trations. For the triangle with three circles around it, "three mice eating a piece of cheese" was a unique response, while "three people sitting around a table" was not unique. For the two half-circles over the line, "two haystacks on a flying carpet" was a unique response, while "two igloos" was not unique.

Our interests were in the *number* of ideas that a child would suggest, and the *uniqueness* of the suggested ideas— the extent to which a given idea in response to a given task belonged to one child alone rather than being an idea that was suggested by other children as well. In addition, we used a variety of traditional techniques for assessing general intelligence with the same children.

When the results of the creativity assessment procedures were compared with the results of the intelligence measures, a definite divergence was obtained—the kind that had not been found in earlier studies. They had already shown, and so did our study, that a child who scores at the high intelligence end of one intelligence test will tend to score that way in other intelligence tests as well. In addition, however, our research revealed two further facts which tended to be different from earlier studies:

■ The various measures of creativity that we utilized had a great deal in common with one another: a child who scored at the high creativity end of one of our creativity measures tended to score at the high creativity end of all the rest of these measures.

■ Of particular importance, the indices of creativity and the indices of intelligence tended to be independent of each other. That is to say, a child who was creative by our measures would just as likely be of low intelligence as of high intelligence. Likewise, a child who was relatively low in creativity by our measures would as likely be of high intelligence as of low intelligence.

In short, the obtained facts *did* support the view that in school children creativity is a different type of cognitive excellence than general intelligence. Such an outcome was especially striking in light of the fact that our procedures for assessing creativity of necessity called upon the child's verbal ability in some degree—and verbal ability is known to contribute substantially to performance on IQ tests. Despite this possible source of commonality, the chances that a child of high intelligence would also display high creativity by our measures were no more than about 50-50.

What are some of the characteristics, then, of children in our four categories: intelligent and creative; neither intelligent nor creative; intelligent but low in creativity; and creative but low in regard to intelligence? The composite pictures that emerged from the experiments and observations that we carried out are composites in the sense that some portions of the evidence upon which they are based were more clear for the boys, while other parts of the evidence were more clear for the girls. However, the general pictures that emerged for the two sexes tended to suggest the same underlying characteristics.

High Creativity—High Intelligence

In many respects these children earn the most superlatives of any of the four groups. For example, when they are observed in the classroom they tend to be particularly high in degree of attention span and concentration upon academic work. At the same time, their academic bent does not put them at a social disadvantage. Quite to the contrary, they are observed to be the most socially "healthy" of the four groups: they have the strongest inclination to be friends with others, and others also have the strongest inclination to be friends with them. (These observations were made during play periods as well as during class sessions.)

These children, in addition, are the least likely of all four groups to behave in ways that suggest disapproval or doubt concerning oneself, one's actions, and one's work. However, this isn't merely a question of behaving in a manner most in harmony with the society's expectations, for these children also demonstrate a strong inclination to engage in various sorts of disruptive activities in the classroom. It's as if they are bursting through the typical behavioral molds that the society has constructed.

What are some of the underpinnings of the general behaviors just described for this group? For one thing, they are likely to see possible connections between events that do not have too much in common. The members of this group, in other words, are more willing to posit relationships between events that are in many respects dissimilar. For another thing, these children are particularly good at reading the subtle affective or expressive connotations that can be carried by what goes on in the environment. These two matters are not entirely separate—a sensitive, aesthetic "tuning" to the possible expressive meanings conveyed by human gesture or by abstract design forms involves seeing possible linkages between quite different kinds of objects and events. The children high in both creativity and intelligence seemed to be most capable of all the groups regarding this kind of aesthetic sensitivity.

To illustrate how we studied the child's ability to read subtle expressive connotations, consider the following example. We confronted the child with a picture of a straight line and asked him to imagine that he was looking down from above at a path that someone had made. The child

was to tell us what sort of person made this trail. Our interest was in determining whether the child's response conveyed information about the kinds of emotional experience that might characterize the person in question, or on the other hand conveyed information only about the superficial character of what the person did. An example of a response showing sensitivity to possible expressive meanings was: "Someone very tense; because if he were relaxed he might wander all over; somebody mad." On the other hand, here is an example of a response that did not show expressive sensitivity: "Man was traveling on a highway; he met people in a huge car; it had a lot of people and it was crowded; they traveled together and got food in restaurants; when they got where they were going, they had a nice vacation."

Turning finally to the way these children describe their own feeling states, we find a tendency for them to admit to experiencing some anxiety, some disturbance—neither a great deal nor very little. It may be that experiencing some anxiety serves an energizing function for them: it is not so much anxiety as to cripple them, and not so little anxiety as to leave them dormant. Also, their total mode of adaptation does not minimize the experience of anxiety for them.

Low Creativity—High Intelligence

In what respects are the children who are high with regard to general intelligence but low in creativity different from those who are high in both? Let us return first to behavior observed in classroom and play settings. While the high intelligence-low creativity children resembled the high creativity-high intelligence children in possessing strong capacities for concentration on academic work and a long attention span, in other respects they were quite different. Those of high intelligence but low creativity were least likely of all four groups to engage in disruptive activities in the classroom and tended to hesitate about expressing opinions. In short, these children seemed rather unwilling to take chances.

Parallel behavior was observed in their social relations with other children; while others had a strong inclination to be friends with them, they in turn tended to hold themselves aloof from interaction with other children. The high intelligence-low creativity children, therefore, seemed to be characterized by a coolness or reserve in relations with their peers. Others would seek out the high intelligence-low creativity children for companionship, possibly because of this group's high academic standing. The children in question, however, tended not to seek out others in return. Perhaps this group felt themselves to be on top of the social mountain, as it were—in a position where they could receive homage from others without any need for requital.

The observations regarding a tendency toward caution and reserve on the part of the high intelligence-low creativity children receive further corroboration in other areas of their functioning. For example, when asked to make arrangements and groupings of pictures of everyday objects in whatever ways they considered most suitable, they preferred to make groupings that were more conventional in nature. They tended to avoid making free-wheeling, unconventional arrangements in which there would be greater free play for evolving unique combinations of objects. For instance, a more conventional grouping would be assembling pictures of a lamppost, a door, and a hammer, and calling them "hard objects." A more unconventional grouping, on the other hand, would be putting together pictures of a comb, a lipstick, a watch, a pocketbook, and a door, and describing them as items that concern "getting ready to go out." It is as if a greater fear of error characterizes these children, so that when left to their own devices, they tend to gravitate toward ways of construing the world that are less open to criticism by others.

We also found out that if you *request* these children to try to behave in a manner that involves establishing more free-wheeling linkages among objects, they are capable of doing so. It is not that they lack the ability to look at the world in this manner, but the inclination. When an adult in their environment comes along and makes it clear that they are expected to consider unusual and possibly bizarre ways in which objects can be linked, they are able to conform to this task demand with skill. But most of the time, their environment tells them that the more unconventional ways of proceeding are more likely to lead them into error and be criticized as wrong. Since the possibility of error seems particularly painful to these children, their typical behavior is to proceed in a manner that is less likely, on the average, to bring them criticism.

Another example of the same sort of process is provided when we consider how the high intelligence-low creativity group reads the possible affective meanings that can be possessed by the behavior of others. As in the case of arranging objects into groups, one can contrast more conventional, expected ways and more unconventional, unusual ways of construing what the behavior of others may signify. For example, an angry figure can be described as "angry" with little risk of error. It requires acceptance of unconventional possibilities, on the other hand, for the child to ad-mit the idea that this figure might be "peaceful" or might be "searching." It turns out that the group in question is least likely to entertain the possibility of the more unconventional, unusual kinds of meanings. They seem locked, therefore, in more conventional ways of interpreting their social world as well as their physical world. Again, fear of possible error seems to be at work.

Since the high intelligence-low creativity children seem to behave in a manner that should maximize correctness and minimize error, we can expect them to be in particularly good standing in their classroom environment. Given their apparent tendency to conform to expectations, their mode of functioning should be maximally rewarding and minimally punishing for them. In short, there should be a high degree of fit between customary environmental expectations and their way of conducting themselves. We find, in fact, that this group admits to little anxiety or disturbance when asked to describe their own feeling states. Their self-descriptions indicate the lowest levels of anxiety reported by any of the four creativity-intelligence groups. Since this group behaves in a manner that should minimize worry or concern for them, their minimal level of reported anxiety probably represents an accurate description of how they feel. But at a cost, as we have noted, of functioning in a constricted manner.

High Creativity—Low Intelligence

Turning to the group characterized by high creativity but relatively low intelligence, we find, first of all, that they tend to exhibit disruptive behavior in the classroom. This is about the only respect, however, in which their observable conduct in the usual school and play settings resembles that of the group high in both creativity and intelligence. Of all four groups, the high creativity-low intelligence children are the least able to concentrate and maintain attention in class, the lowest in self-confidence, and the most likely to express the conviction that they are no good. It is as if they are convinced that their case is a hopeless one. Furthermore, they are relatively isolated socially; not only do they avoid contact with other children, but in addition their peers shun them more than any other group. Perhaps, in their social withdrawal, these children are indulging fantasy activities. At any rate, they are relatively alone in the school setting, and in many respects can be characterized as worse off than the group low in both creativity and intelligence.

It should be borne in mind that the high creativity-low intelligence children nevertheless give evidence of the same kind of creative thinking capacities as are found in the high creativity-high intelligence group. Again, for example, we find a greater likelihood of seeing possible connections between events that do not share much in common. The high creativity children, whether high or low regarding intelligence, are more willing to postulate relationships between somewhat dissimilar events.

Apparently, the kinds of evaluational pressures present in the case of intelligence and achievement testing as well as in the typical classroom environment serve to disrupt cognitive powers which can come to the fore when pressure is reduced. An interesting complementarity seems to exist with regard to the psychological situations found for the high creativity-low intelligence group and the low creativity-high intelligence group: while members of the former seem to perform more effectively when evaluational pressures are absent, members of the latter seem to work more adequately when evaluational pressures are present. It is as if the former children tend to go to pieces if questions of personal competence and achievement enter the picture, while the latter children have difficulty if they are denied a framework of standards within which they can evaluate what is required of them if they are to seem competent in the eyes of adults.

Low Creativity—Low Intelligence

While the children in this group show the greatest cognitive deprivation of the four groups under study, they seem to make up for it at least to some degree in the social sphere. From observations of their behavior in school and at play they are found to be more extroverted socially, less hesitant, and more self-confident and self-assured than the children of low intelligence but high creativity. The members of the low-low group are particularly poor regarding the kinds of aesthetic sensitivity that were mentioned earlier —for example, they show the weakest tendencies to respond to the possible expressive meanings that abstract line forms may convey. Despite such deficiencies, however, this group does not seem to be the maximally disadvantaged

group in the classroom. Rather, the low-low children seem to have worked out a *modus vivendi* that puts them at greater social ease in the school situation than is the case for their high creativity-low intelligence peers.

The Motivational Hurdle

Now that we have characterized the four groups of children, let us finally consider the implications of the relative roles played by ability and by motivational factors in a child's thinking. The only group that looks like it is in difficulty with regard to ability—and even in their case we cannot be sure—is the group low in both intelligence and creativity. In the cases of the two groups that are low regarding one cognitive skill and high regarding the other— the low intelligence-high creativity group and the high intelligence-low creativity group—our evidence suggests that, rather than an ability deficiency, the children in question are handicapped by particular motivational dispositions receiving strong environmental support. For the low intelligence-high creativity children, the difficulty seems to concern excessive fear of being evaluated; hence they perform poorly when evaluational standards are a prominent part of the setting. For the high intelligence-low creativity children, on the other hand, the difficulty seems to concern a fear of not knowing whether one is thought well of by significant others. The possibility of making mistakes, therefore, is particularly avoided. Further, if evaluational standards are not a clear part of the setting, so that the child does not know a right way of behaving in order to fulfill the expectations of others, performance will deteriorate because the problem of avoiding error becomes of prime importance.

In theory, at least, these kinds of motivational hindrances could be rectified by appropriate training procedures. If one could induce the low intelligence-high creativity children to be less concerned when evaluational standards are present, and the high intelligence-low creativity children to be less concerned when evaluational standards are absent, their thinking behavior might come to display high levels of both intelligence and creativity.

Drugging and Schooling

Charles Witter

Minimal brain dysfunction (MBD), one of at least 38 names attached to a subset of learning disabilities, can significantly hinder a grammar school student of average or above-average intelligence from achieving his full potential. Hyperactive, often loud and demanding and little responsive to the feelings of others (or himself), the MBD child can be seen as the very model of the uncontrollable student. Then, 30 years ago, it was discovered that amphetamines, stimulants and/or tranquilizers could calm the hyperactive child who was so often disruptive in class or at home. Amphetamines and stimulants such as Ritalin have a "paradoxical effect" in the prepubescent child: instead of being "speed," they actually slow him down, make him more tractable and teachable and permit calm to be restored for the harassed parent and overburdened teacher.

Such was the conventional wisdom on 29 September 1970 when Congressman Cornelius E. Gallagher (D-New Jersey) convened a hearing of his House Privacy Sub-committee. This article is a critique of the hearing and an urgent appeal for social scientists to assert humanist concern in a world increasingly reliant on biochemical manipulation.

For the child who is very carefully tested by a team of neurologists, pediatricians, psychologists and educators, the symptoms of MBD can be masked by drugs in as high as 80 percent of the cases, according to some authorities. Others say 50 percent, while dissenters state that the good results are either the result of increased personal attention received by the child or the magical properties the child ascribes to the drug. A careful reading of Department of Health, Education, and Welfare (HEW) testimony at the Gallagher hearing suggests that 200,000 children in the United States are now being given amphetamine and stimulant therapy, with probably another 100,000 receiving tranquilizers and antidepressants.

All the experts agree, however, that the use of medication to modify the behavior of grammar school children will radically increase—"zoom" was the word connected with the man most responsible for the promotion of the program at the National Institute of Mental Health (NIMH). Already specialists in this therapeutic method state that at least 30 percent of ghetto children are candidates, and this figure could run as high as four to six million of the general grammar school population. The authoritative *Journal of Learning Disabilities* puts it bluntly: "Disadvantaged children function similarly to advantaged children with learning disabilities."

Not all children with the ill-defined, perhaps indefinable, syndrome are likely to be treated with medication, but it must be recognized that drugs are a cheap alternative to the massive spending so obviously necessary to revitalize the public school system. Lest there be any doubt about whether leadership in America would be reluctant to embrace quick, inexpensive answers to social problems, consider the plan of the president's former internist, Dr. Arnold Hutschnecker, who would give all six-to eight-year-olds in the nation a predictive psychological test for their criminal potential. Those who flunked these tests—which have been shown to provide successful individual prognosis slightly over 50 percent of the time—would be sent to rehabilitation centers "in a romantic setting with trees out West," as Hutschnecker phrased it. This late, unlamented proposal was sent on White House stationery to the secretary of HEW with a request for suggestions on how to implement it. Once again, Mr. Gallagher's was the only congressional voice raised in opposition, and he branded those camps "American Dachaus." After hearings were threatened, HEW reported unfavorably, and the White House dropped the idea. Many other plans have gone forward, but the Hutschnecker proposal is important because of its high-level endorsement and encouragement, and the distressing impact it would have had on virtually every American family.

The National Institute of Mental Health, which studied the Hutschnecker plan for some three months, has granted at least $3 million to study drug therapy. The clearest statement on the reality of minimal brain dysfunction, however, has come from Dr. Francis Crinella, a grantee of the Office of Education. He said that MBD "has become one of our most fashionable forms of consensual ignorance." No simple medical examination or even an electro-encephalogram can disclose the presence of the disorder; "soft" neurological signs seem to be the only physical manifestation.

Passing the Buck

Dr. John Peters, director of the Little Rock Child Study Center of the University of Arkansas, testified that the only way to separate the active child from the hyperactive one was to have had his long experience in seeing thousands of normal and "deviant" children and then making a personal judgment. In Omaha, where the drugging was first discovered by the *Washington Post's* Robert Maynard, the doctors are not even that confident. How else does one explain the lines, reported also by Nat Hentoff, from the *Bulletin of the Omaha Medical Society*: "The responsibility of the prescription was not that of the doctor, but rather of the parent. The parent then vests responsibility in the teacher."

Wow! One could say with equal validity that the facts in a book are not the responsibility of the author; rather, he has vested responsibility in the researcher, who in turn has relied solely on secondary sources.

The conclusion must be that it is behavior and behavior alone that creates the diagnosis of MBD, and this behavior can only be found in the classroom or at home. Mark Stewart, who received NIMH support, wrote in the July 1970 *Scientific American*: "A child who has been described by his mother as a demon may be an angel when he comes to a psychiatrist's office. Most hyperactive children tend to be subdued in a strange situation and to display their bad behavior only when they feel at home. The explanation may lie in a stress-induced release of norepinephrine in the brain cells. Thus, *a state of anxiety may produce the same effect as a dose of amphetamine—through exactly the same*

mechanism" (emphasis added). With relentless logic, Stewart then discusses the behavior of lobotomized monkeys.

Two points on the physical aspects of drugs demand emphasis. First, John Oates of Vanderbilt University has found that "chronic use of amphetamine in small doses may produce symptoms which very closely resemble paranoid schizophrenia." Second, Stewart discredits the alleged "paradoxical effect" by pointing out that "it has been found that amphetamine has a somewhat similar effect on the performance of normal adults who are assigned a boring or complex task."

Would it then be unduly provocative and aggressively argumentative to phrase the question: "Does a long-term dosage of amphetamine and/or Ritalin induce stress in the bored child, producing a perfect student, whose anxiety-ridden behavior may be paranoid schizophrenic and resemble that of a lobotomized monkey?"

It was to speak to a considerably less loaded version of that question that Gallagher invited the provocative educator John Holt. Holt's contempt for orthodox teaching is well known; he compares today's schools to maximum security prisons. Gallagher had phrased his concern, "I fear there is a great temptation to diagnose the bored but bright child as hyperactive, prescribe drugs, and thus deny him full learning during his most creative years," and he introduced Holt's testimony as putting the discussion in the most important context, that of the child.

Holt's response did nothing to lower the issue's hyperbolic content:

We take lively, curious, energetic children, eager to make contact with the world and to learn about it, stick them in barren classrooms with teachers who on the whole neither like nor respect nor understand nor trust them, restrict their freedom of speech and movement to a degree that would be judged excessive and inhuman even in a maximum security prison, and that their teachers themselves could not and would not tolerate. Then, when the children resist this brutalizing and stupefying treatment and retreat from it in anger, bewilderment and terror, we say that they are sick with "complex and little-understood" disorders, and proceed to dose them with powerful drugs that are indeed complex and of whose long-run effects we know little or nothing, so that they may be more ready to do the asinine things the schools ask them to do.

Unfortunately, there are those of us who have either forgotten our own grammar school experiences or who think that only an in-depth, scholarly, jargonized study can yield an accurate description of reality. As a result, Holt's testimony needs reinforcement. This was made distressingly clear to me when, during the weeks prior to the hearing, I would describe our witness list and state: "John Holt, a former grammar school teacher." Invariably, the reply would be, "Yes, but what are his credentials?"

Among the abundance of supportive evidence of Holt's findings is that contained in Charles Silberman's recently published *The Crisis in the Classroom*. This study, commissioned by the prestigious Carnegie Corporation, found today's schoolrooms to be "grim" and "joyless." Could we not then wonder if the predicted "zoom" in hyperkinetic diagnosis and its concomitant drug therapy will not be used against precious childhood joy? Has Hutschnecker become institutionalized within the medical-educational complex? Have we put the Dachaus in the pill and then put the pill in the kid?

Dr. Rada Dyson-Hudson of Johns Hopkins University begins a letter to Gallagher: "As an anthropologist with a background in genetics and biology who is also the parent of a hyperactive son," and goes on to describe how her family moved to a rural setting to avoid being mangled by urban society. Based on her own personal observations, she says, "Where there are important, tiring or responsible physical jobs to do, a hyperactive child is a joy to have around." But a hyperactive child is no joy in overcrowded city classrooms or to the modern housewife.

Dyson-Hudson's professional judgment is also fascinating. She suggests that the prevalence of MBD in the population could mean that it is an inherited trait, has a selective advantage and, therefore, should not be regarded as pathological. She says that the selective advantage must be quite large, in order to counterbalance the higher mortality rate in hyperactive children. This is confirmed in dozens of letters to Gallagher that describe the MBD child as a mass of bandages and stitches, and Mark Stewart finds that many of the children he has studied have been victims of accidental poisoning.

On the other side, a recent New Jersey report states that in 80 children studied, four times as many children who show learning disabilities are adopted than those not adopted. But Dyson-Hudson's point demands further extensive research for two reasons.

First, pediatricians, psychiatrists and educators, particularly school administrators, contend that parents of hyperactive children are excitable, have a history of alcoholism and instability and fail to provide the child with a warm and loving upbringing. (This point is directly denied by hundreds of letters disclosing a real agony in parents who must finally go to drugs as a last resort.) With that sort of finding buttressing the experts' faith in themselves, it is easy automatically to write off the complaints of a child's parents and to coerce them into acquiescing to or embracing drug therapy.

Second, it is fair to speculate that hyperactivity may well be a considerable advantage for children, especially for ghetto kids. The latter truly have no childhood; they are instantly forced to match wits with hustlers, gang leaders, police and antipolice violence and an entire milieu where the prize of physically growing up goes to the toughest and the shrewdest. Theodore Johnson, a black chemist from Omaha, testified to the problems of coming of age in the ghetto and listed causative agents that could produce MBD-like behavior. In the school, he mentioned racist attitudes among teachers and administrators, inferior and outdated textbooks, irrelevant curriculum and inadequate facilities; and for the child, he found malnutrition, broken rest patterns, unstable home environment and physical fatigue.

On a larger social plane, it is possible to speculate that the use of drugs to make children sit perfectly still and reproduce inputs may once have had some functional purpose. Schools formerly trained the vast majority of students to become effective cogs in giant factories, and they were designed so that assembly line learning would result in assembly line production during working years. Yet, it is now obvious that service-oriented businesses are rapidly replacing manufacturing as the major source of employment. It is not unreasonable to suggest that children no longer need to be preconditioned for the rigid regimentation involved in earning a livelihood; an inquiring mind in an inquiring body is now marketable.

There would be far less need for many additional McLuhanesque probes into MBD drug medication if we could rely on the testimony of the Department of Health, Education, and Welfare before the Gallagher Privacy Subcommittee. If that testimony could stand up under informed scrutiny and if it reflected a conscientious effort to understand and to disclose all the facts, this article would also be unnecessary.

When the federal government sends officials to the Congress to defend a program of such impact, one has a right to expect that rigorous research and rigid control have gone into the decision. In my judgment, both were lacking, and several examples will illustrate my conviction that this massive technological incursion into the sanctuary of the human spirit operated on intelligence just as faulty as that surrounding last winter's Laotian sanctuary incursion.

First, with $3 million from NIMH alone, and with at least 300,000 children and 30 years' experience in the program, it could be expected that hundreds of studies could be cited to show the long-term effect on the children who have been given drugs. Yet, only in 1970 had funds been granted for this essential study, and the man selected to follow up on 67 children was Dr. C. Keith Conners. The HEW witnesses bristled when Gallagher offered the comment that Conners was engaged in evaluating "his own thing," but it is a fact that, prior to the grant for evaluation of these specific children, Conners had been given $442,794 in grants beginning in 1967 to test the effectiveness of drugs on children. Those studies were cited by HEW witnesses as confirming the validity of the treatment.

Wanted: Scientific Dedication

So, as we zoom up to and beyond six million grammar school children on drugs, we are offered a study of 67 cases that was begun in 1970, is now only in its preliminary data-gathering phase and is being carried out by a man whose professional career has been spent proving how effective the therapy is. One can scarcely imagine the cries of rage that would greet any mayor or governor proposing to evaluate road construction in this manner, but one can only assume that scientific research rises above such petty considerations as conflict of interest. In fairness to the selection of Connors, Ronald Lipman, Ph.D. (chief, Clinical Studies Section, National Institute of Mental Health), pointed out at the hearings: "I think one of the reasons why there have been so few followup studies is that they are so very difficult to do. They involve going back into medical records that are very difficult to come by. They involve tracking down people after a period of 20 years. This is very difficult logistically. *It requires a certain kind of scientific dedication that you just don't find too many people have*" (emphasis added).

Other testimony confirmed Lipman's pessimistic view of his colleagues. Dr. Dorothy Dobbs, director of the Food and Drug Administration's Division of Neuro-pharmacological Drug Products, and HEW's chief witness, Dr. Thomas C. Points, deputy assistant secretary for health and scientific affairs, both testified that they had conducted "cursory" investigations of the administration of these drugs in Omaha and that nothing was wrong. Later in the hearing it was disclosed that Dr. Byron Oberst, the program's primary proponent in Omaha, was unaware that the Food and Drug Administration (FDA) had listed two of the drugs he was using as "not recommended for use in children under 12." Dr. John Peters, director of the Little Rock Child Study Center, was found to be equally in the dark about FDA guidelines on one of the drugs he dispensed. (It must be mentioned that FDA has no authority to insist that drugs not be used; it has a formal mechanism that permits just about anything to be administered under a doctor's prescription.)

Two points are crucial, however: 1) the HEW witness did not volunteer the information that the department had communicated with Oberst pointing out his oversight; and 2) leading practitioners of drug therapy were unaware of FDA's recommendations.

Moreover, while the HEW witnesses cited some 40 studies conferring validity on the use of drugs to mask hyperactive behavior, they did not refer to Crinella's Office

of Education study referred to earlier—"one of our most fashionable forms of consensual ignorance" is a line certainly worth repeating—nor did they mention HEW's own studies by John Oates and Mark Stewart. But perhaps most compellingly, we heard nothing of the June 1970 statement of the American Academy of Pediatrics Committee on Drugs. In light of the supposedly wide support within the medical community for the efficacy of drugs, the academy's words are particularly significant:

An accurate assessment of the effectiveness of the chemotherapeutic approach poses enumerable difficulties. These stem from factors such as 1) the lack of uniform terminology, 2) marked variability in methodology for evaluation, 3) the absence of standardized requirements for precise diagnosis and classification of the symptomatology constituting learning impediments, and 4) the paucity of long-term, properly controlled studies. As a result, a valid evaluation of response and objective comparison of the effectiveness of drugs administered in an attempt to mitigate or lessen learning impediments becomes impossible.

Finally, the HEW testimony dismissed any possible connection between children relying on drugs during grammar school and the incredible problem of drug abuse in high schools and in the rest of society. The hearing ran for approximately eight hours, and Gallagher hammered away all day long on this most obvious "paradoxical effect," but it was only during the questioning of Sally Williams, chief of the School Nurse Division of the National Education Association, that a glimmer appeared. She had strongly supported the use of behavior modification drugs (controlled, naturally enough, by the school nurse), but, almost as an afterthought, she disclosed that ten students at her school were now on Ritalin at their own discretion. Her exact testimony is most revealing: "They were taken off the medication and they still came back to the 'springs inside,' the inability to control their behavior. So the doctor has put it on a PRN, which means when necessary, so because they are senior high school students they come up to the health office and come to me and say, 'I think I need my Ritalin now.' "

Apparently, the administration shared some of these doubts, because two short weeks after the hearing, the director of the Office of Child Development at HEW announced his intention to form a "blue ribbon" panel to consider the problem. Dr. Edward F. Zigler's statement of 12 October is very different from the tone of the HEW testimony of 29 September: he said the panel would "inform educators that perhaps it is as much a problem of the kind of schoolroom children have to adjust to rather than what is wrong" with the nervous systems of the children. On 10 March 1971 the panel issued its report, and Gallagher commended it for approximately one-half of his remarks in the *Congressional Record* of that day. He singled out two sentences:

> It is important to recognize the child whose inattention and restlessness may be caused by hunger, poor teaching, overcrowded classrooms, or lack of understanding by teachers and parents . . . . Variations in different socio-economic and ethnic groups must be considered in order to arrive at better definitions of behavior properly regarded as pathological.

In light of the evidence we gathered that drug company salesmen were huckstering their products' wonder-working capabilities at PTA meetings and at professional educational society gatherings, Gallagher also praised this stern warning: "These medicines should be promoted ethically and *only* through medical channels" (emphasis in original).

Unfortunately, the second half of Gallagher's statement was not reflected in media reports. He was sharply critical of the panel's failure to do any independent investigation; they had only produced a compendium, in layman's terms, of existing studies. Moreover, while the report reiterated many of the criticisms surfaced by the Privacy Sub-committee, the report made no comment on the desirability of having a mechanism within the federal establishment to encourage sensible caution at the local level. Gallagher said that "the suspicion still exists that these programs will be used to modify the behavior of black children to have them conform to white society's norms," and that "as admirable as the recommendations in the report are, they will be nothing but high sounding platitudes unless supervision of local schools can assure that they are given the attention I think they deserve." He called for the Office of Child Development to become the mandated overseer of the increasing nationwide use of behavioral modification drugs.

Assumption of this responsibility became absolutely essential when the Privacy Subcommittee was abolished by its parent Committee on Government Operations on 31 March 1971. Along with a special panel under Congressman Benjamin Rosenthal (D-New York) that had a remarkably effective record of protecting the consumer, the new committee chairman, Chet Holifield (D-California), decreed, as was his right with subcommittees without direct jurisdiction over specific federal agencies, that these issue-oriented studies were outside the committee's ambit. (Holifield has been either chairman or vice-chairman of the Joint Committee on Atomic Energy since its inception. At the risk of being labeled hyperactive myself, it is disquieting that the man who now says there is no valid reason for concern over privacy or consumer matters in the House has consistently stated that there are no dangers from nuclear power plants.)

It would be possible to continue to discuss privacy generally and behavior modification therapy specifically at a length only slightly less than that of the collected works of Dickens, but a brief reference to the National Education Association (NEA) is essential. It has become one of the most effective lobbies in the legislative and executive ambits in Washington, and its proposals often quickly turn into public policy. For that reason, it is important to find out just what it has in mind for future generations of American children. A particularly relevant example comes from the *NEA Journal* of January 1969 in an article entitled "Forecast for the 1970's." Two professors of education at Indiana University point to a radically altered school environment, but one of their statements says it all: "Biochemical and psychological mediation of learning is likely to increase. New drama will play on the educational stage as drugs are introduced experimentally to improve in the learner such qualities as personality, concentration, and memory. The application of biochemical research findings, heretofore centered on infra-human subjects, such as fish . . . . "

Fish? Fish! Gallagher has long been concerned with the privacy-invading aspects of credit bureaus, electronic surveillance, the computer and psychological testing, and he has said that the Age of Aquarius will become the Age of Aquariums, in which all our lives are lived in a fish bowl. His assumption, up until the investigation of drugging grammar school children, was that there would still be ordinary water in those aquariums; now the concern must be that human rights will be drowned in an exotic brew of biochemical manipulators, stirred and watched by an untouchable medical-educational complex.

The implications and ramifications to our future were well expressed in June 1970 by America's most highly placed social critic. Social scientists would do well to take action on the words of the former president of the Baltimore County Parent-Teacher Association, Spiro T. Agnew: "We as a country have hardly noticed this remarkable phenomenon of legal drug use, but it is new, it is increasing, and the individual and social costs have yet to be calculated."

Anatomy of a Chicago Slum
Gerald D. Suttles

In its heyday, the Near West Side of Chicago was the stronghold of such men as Al (Scarface) Capone and Frank (The Enforcer) Nitti, and served as the kindergarten for several figures still active in the underworld. For convenience, I will call this part of Chicago the Addams area —after Jane Addams, who founded Hull House there. The name is artificial, since it is never used by the local residents.

The Addams area is one of the oldest slums in Chicago, and researchers have invaded it almost as often as new minority groups have. Like most slums, it remains something of a mystery. In some ways it is easiest to describe the neighborhood by describing how its residents deviate from

the public standards of the wider community. The area has, for example, a high delinquency rate, numerous unwed mothers, and several adolescent "gangs." It is tempting to think that the residents are simply people suffering from cultural deprivation, unemployment, and a number of other urban ills. And if the residents insist upon the irrelevance of the standards of the wider community and the primacy of their own, this can be dismissed as sour grapes or an attempt to make of necessity a virtue.

Seen from the inside, however, Addams area residents require discipline and self-restraint in the same way as the wider community does. Conventional norms are not rejected but emphasized differently, or suspended for estab-

275

lished reasons. The vast majority of the residents are quite conventional people. At the same time, those who remain in good standing are often exceptionally tolerant of and even encouraging to those who are "deviant."

Certainly the social practices of the residents are not just an inversion of those of the wider society, and the inhabitants would be outraged to hear as much. Nor is the neighborhood a cultural island with its own distinct and imported traditions. The area's internal structure features such commonplace distinctions as age, sex, territoriality, ethnicity, and personal identity. Taken out of context, many of the social arrangements of the Addams area may seem an illusory denial of the beliefs and values of the wider society. But actually the residents are bent on ordering local relations because the beliefs and evaluations of the wider society do not provide adequate guidelines for conduct.

In anthropology, territorial grouping has been a subject of continued interest. Most anthropological studies begin by focusing upon social groupings that can be defined by their areal distribution. In turn, many of the social units singled out for particular attention—the domestic unit, the homestead, the tribe, and so forth—frequently have locality as one of their principles of organization. And where locality and structural forms do not coincide, anthropologists have regarded this discrepancy as a distinct problem that raises a number of theoretical and methodological issues.

The most obvious reason for focusing on locality groups is that their members cannot simply ignore one another. People who routinely occupy the same place must either develop a moral order that includes all those present or fall into conflict. And because almost all societies create a public morality that exceeds the capabilities of some of its members, territorial groups are always faced with the prospect of people whose public character does not warrant trust. In the United States a very large percentage of our population fails to meet the public standards we set for measuring someone's merit, trustworthiness, and respectability.

Many groups have avoided compromising these ideals of public morality by territorial segregation. More exactly, they have simply retreated and left valuable portions of the inner city to those they distrust. Obviously, this practice has its limits—it tends to aggregate those who are poor, unsuccessful, and disreputable in the same slum neighborhoods. These people must compromise the ideals of public morality or remain permanently estranged from one another.

In slum neighborhoods, territorial aggregation usually comes before any common social framework for assuring orderly relations. After all, ethnic invasion, the encroachment of industry, and economic conditions constantly reshuffle slum residents and relocate them around new neighbors. Since the residents lack obvious grounds for assuming

mutual trust, a combination of alternatives seems to offer the most promising course:

■ Social relations can be restricted to only the safest ones. Families can withdraw to their households, where they see only close relatives. Segregation by age, sex, and ethnicity are maneuvers that will prevent at least the most unfair and most likely forms of conflict and exploitation. Remaining close to the household cuts down on the range of anonymity and reduces the number of social relations. The general pattern, then, should be a fan-shaped spatial arrangement, with women and children remaining close by the house while males move progressively outwards, depending on their age.

■ Slum residents can assuage at least some of their apprehensions by a close inquiry into one another's personal character and past history. Communication, then, should be of an intimate character and aimed toward producing personal rather than formal relations. In turn, social relations will represent a sort of private compact in which particular loyalties replace impersonal standards of worth.

Neither of these patterns will immediately produce a comprehensive framework within which a large number of slum residents can safely negotiate with one another. The segregation by age, sex, and territorial groups, however, does provide a starting point from which face-to-face relations can grow and reach beyond each small territorial aggregation. The development of personal relations furnishes both a moral formula and a structural bridge between groups. Within each small, localized peer group, continuing face-to-face relations can eventually provide a personalistic order. Once these groups are established, a single personal relation between them can extend the range of such an order. Thus, with the acceptance of age-grading and territorial segregation, it becomes possible for slum neighborhoods to work out a moral order that includes most of their residents.

The Addams area actually consists of four different sections, each occupied predominantly by Negroes, Italians, Puerto Ricans, and Mexicans. And each of these sections falls into a somewhat different stage in its development of a provincial order.

Despite this difference and others, all four ethnic sections share many characteristics and seem headed along the same social progression. The overall pattern is one in which age, sex, ethnic, and territorial units are fitted together like building blocks to create a larger structure. I have termed this pattern "ordered segmentation" to indicate two related features: (1) the orderly relationship between groups; and (2) the order in which groups combine in instances of conflict and opposition. This ordered segmentation is not equally developed in all ethnic sections but, in skeletal outline, it is the common framework within which groups are being formed and social relations are being cultivated.

My own experiences within the Addams area and the presentation of this volume are heavily influenced by the ordered segmentation of the neighborhood. I took up residence in the area in the summer of 1963 and left a little fewer than three years later.

Methodology

Gerald D. Suttles spent three years in the Near West Side of Chicago making a study of a multiethnic community that includes Italians, Mexicans, Negroes and Puerto Ricans. He took up residence in the area in the summer of 1963 and did not leave until almost three years later. It took him a year or more to acquire friends and enter the private worlds of families, social-athletic clubs and other groups. The findings of his study are published in *The Social Order of the Slum* from which *Trans*-action has taken excerpts—chiefly from materials on the Italian population. The book in its entirety shows that there are broad structural similarities between all the ethnic groups—Italian, Mexican, Negro and Puerto Rican, although this structure is more clearly developed among the Italians. The excerpts draw on some of Suttles' more general observations rather than his detailed empirical findings.

As I acquired friends and close informants, my own ethnicity became a serious problem. A few people worked over my genealogy trying to find some trace that would allot me to a known ethnic group. After close inquiry, one old Italian lady announced with peals of laughter, "Geraldo, you're just an American." She did not mean it as a compliment, and I remember being depressed. In the Addams area, being without ethnicity means there is no one you can appeal to or claim as your own.

Only after a year or more in the Addams area was I able to penetrate the private world of its families, street-corner groups, and insular establishments. These are the groupings within which Addams area residents are least cautious and most likely to expose themselves. In large part my experience with these groups is limited to many adolescent male street-corner groups and my own adult friends, who formed a group of this type.

By far the most striking contrast is between the Negro and the Italian sections. For instance, almost all the Negroes live in public housing; the Italians usually control both their households and commercial establishments. The Negroes have very similar incomes and almost no political power; among the Italians, there *is* some internal differentiation of income and political power. Such differences draw the Italians and Negroes apart and generate radically different styles of life.

In most ways, the Puerto Rican section is the least complex of those in the Addams area. There are no more than 1100 Puerto Ricans in the section and, within broad age ranges, most of them know one another. Until 1965, no named groups had emerged among the Puerto Ricans.

The Mexicans are more numerous, and several named groups have developed among the teenagers. Unlike the Italians, however, the Mexican groups have not survived into adulthood. The Mexicans seem to have much in common with the Italians, and frequently their relationships are congenial. What gives the Mexicans pause is the occasional necessity to divide their loyalties between the Italians and the Negroes.

Although one must not overemphasize the extent of differences between all these ethnic sections, such differences as do occur loom large in the Addams area. The residents are actively looking for differences among themselves. The ethnic sections in the area constitute basic guidelines from which the residents of each section can expect certain forms of reciprocity, and anticipate the dangers that may be in store elsewhere.

The portion of the Addams area now controlled by the Italians is only a residue from the encroachments of the three other ethnic groups. But in total land space, it is the largest of any controlled by a single ethnic group. In population, it is not exceptionally big, though, and throughout the section an unusually high percentage of Mexicans have been accepted by the Italians as neighbors.

What the Italians lack in numbers, they often make up for by their reputation for using sheer force and for easy access to "influence" or "connections." It is said, for example, that many of the Italians are "Outfit people," and that many more could rely on mobsters if they needed help. Also, it is the general view that the Italians control both the vice and patronage of the First Ward, a political unit that includes the spoils of the Loop—downtown Chicago.

There are some very famous Italians in the Addams area, and they frequently get a spread in the city newspapers. There are many others not nearly so prominent but whose personal histories are still known in the neighborhood. At least five Italian policemen live in the area, and a few more who grew up there are assigned to the local district. The other ethnic groups have not a single resident or ex-resident policeman among them. Most of the precinct captains are also Italian; and, outside the projects, the Italians dominate those jobs provided by public funds. There are a number of Italian businessmen, each of whom controls a few jobs. It is also widely believed that they can "sponsor" a person into many of the industries of the city —the newsstands in the Loop, the city parks, the beauty-culture industry, a large printing company, and a number of clothing firms.

While there is some substance to this belief in Italian power and influence, it is actually quite exaggerated. Many of the Italian political figures seem to have little more than the privilege of announcing decisions that have been made by others. In most of the recent political actions that have affected the area, they have remained mute and docile. When the Medical Center was built and then extended, they said nothing. The Congress and the Dan Ryan Expressways were constructed with the local politicians hardly taking notice. Finally, when the University of Illinois was located at Congress Circle, the politicians, mobsters, and—indeed—all the male residents accepted it without even a show of resistance. In fact, only a group of Italian and Mexican housewives took up arms and sought to save some remnant of the neighborhood.

The Italians' notoriety for being in the rackets and having recourse to strong-arm methods is also a considerable exaggeration, or at least a misinterpretation. The majority of the local Italians are perfectly respectable people and gain nothing from organized crime. Yet, many of the common family names of the area have been sullied by some flagrant past episode by a relative. And in the area, family histories remain a basis for judging individual members and are extended to include all persons who share the same name. In another neighborhood, this information might be lost or ignored as improper; in the Addams area, it is almost impossible to keep family secrets, and they are kept alive in the constant round of rumor and gossip.

The local Italians themselves contribute to their reputation—because on many occasions they find it advantageous to intimate that they have connections with the Outfit. For example, outsiders are often flattered to think that they are in the confidence of someone who knows the underworld. Also, it is far more prestigious to have other people believe that one's background is buried in crime and violence than in public welfare. In America, organized crime has always received a certain respect, even when this respect had to be coerced. A recipient of public welfare is simply dismissed as unimportant. And during the Depression many of the Italians went on welfare.

"Right People" Can Protect Them

In addition, some of the Italians feel that a reputation of being in with the "right people" can in some circumstances ensure them against victimization. They often hint about their connections with the Outfit when facing the members of another ethnic group under uncertain odds, or when in an argument among themselves. Yet with friends and relatives, the Italians often complain bitterly of how they are maligned by the press and by their neighbors.

Ironically, the Italians are cautious in their dealings with one another; more than any other group, they are intimidated by the half-myth that is partly of their own creation. And indirectly this myth gives them considerable cohesion, and a certain freedom from the judgments and actions of the wider society. It is almost impossible to persuade one of them to make a complaint to the police, for instance, because of their fear of the Outfit; indeed, they shun all public sources of social control. They handle grievances, contracts, and exchanges in a very informal manner, usually limited to the immediate parties. If in need, they exact aid in the form of favors and generally ignore sources available to the general public. As a result, the Italians have been able to sustain among themselves the image of an independent, powerful, and self-confident people.

Behind the Scenes Bargaining

Yet the cohesion and solidarity of the Italians are very limited. They are based primarily on the suspicion that social arrangements are best made by private settlements. This suspicion, in turn, is based on the assumption that recourse to public means can do little more than excite retaliation and vengeance. These same suspicions and doubts undermine the possibilities of a unified and explicit stance by the Italians toward the wider community and political organization. First, very few of them believe that the others will cooperate in joint efforts unless it is to their personal advantage or they are under some dire threat. Second, the Italians simply fear that a united public stand will elicit a similar posture on the part of their adversaries and eliminate the opportunity for private negotiations. Accordingly, the Italians either shun public confrontations or slowly draw away, once so engaged. In retrospect, the spirit of *omerta* seems ineffectual when it confronts the explicit efforts of the wider community. (Literally, *omerta* means a conspiracy between thieves. The Italians use it to mean any private agreement that cannot be safely broached before the general public.)

The inability of the Italians to accept or engage in public appeals leaves them somewhat bewildered by the Negroes' civil-rights movement. By the Italians' standards, the Negroes are "making a federal case" out of something that should be handled by private agreement. Indeed, even those who accept the justice of the Negroes' cause remain perplexed by the Negroes' failure to approach *them* in some informal manner. Throughout the summer of 1964, when demonstrators were most active, the Italians always seemed aggrieved and surprised that the Negroes would "pull such a trick" without warning. The Negroes took this view as a "sham" and felt that the Italians had ample reason to anticipate their demands. To the Italians this was not the point. Of course, they knew that the Negroes had many long-standing demands and desires. What struck the Italians as unfair about the Negroes' demonstrations was their tactics: sudden public confrontations, without any chance for either side to retreat or compromise with grace.

Ultimately, both the Italians and Negroes did take their differences behind closed doors, and each settled for something less than their public demands. The main bone of contention was a local swimming pool dominated by the Italians and their Mexican guests.

In the background, of course, was the oppressive belief that the benefits of social life make up a fixed quantity and are already being used to the maximum. Thus, even the most liberal Italians assume that any gain to the Negroes must be their loss. On their own part, the Negroes make the same assumption and see no reason why the Italians should give way without a fight. Thus, whatever good intentions exist on either side are overruled by the seeming impracticality or lack of realism.

The Italians' career in the Addams area has been shaped by a traditional world view that relies heavily on a belief in "natural man." For example, it is felt to be "natural" for men to be sexual predators; for mothers to love their children, regardless of what their children do; for girls to connive at marriage; for boys to hate school; for a businessman to cheat strangers; and for anyone to choose pleasure in preference to discipline and duty. Implicit in the concept of natural man is the conviction that moral restraints have little real power in a situation in which they contradict man's natural impulses. Civilization is a mere gloss to hide man's true nature.

Often, although not always, man's natural impulses are at odds with his moral standards. Indeed, otherwise there would be no need for the church, the police, the government, and all other bodies of social control. But it is not always possible for these external bodies of social control to keep track of what people are doing. Inevitably, then, there will be occasions when people are free to choose between acting naturally and acting morally. For their own part, the Italians may have considerable conviction of their personal preferences for morality. In their dealings with other people, however they have little faith in this thin thread of individual morality. Correspondingly, to them their own personal morality becomes utterly impractical and must be replaced by whatever amoral expedient seems necessary for self-defense.

The general outcome seems to be an overwhelming distrust of impersonal or "voluntary" relationships. The other side of the coin is an equally strong tendency to fall back on those relationships and identities where one's own welfare is guaranteed by "natural inclinations." For the most part these are kin relations, close friendship, common regional origins (paesani), joint residential unity, and sacred pledges like marriage, God, parenthood, etc. Thus, the Italians in the Addams area have tended to turn in upon themselves and become a provincial moral world.

Actually, many of the Italians are quite "Americanized." Frequently, though, these people lead something of a double life. During the daytime they leave the neighborhood and do their work without much thought of their ethnicity. When they come home in the evening, they are obliged to reassume their old world identity. This need not be so much a matter of taste as necessity. Other people are likely to already know their ethnicity, and evasions are likely to be interpreted as acts of snobbery or attempts at deception. Moreover, members of the other three ethnic groups refuse to accept such a person's Americanization, no matter how much it is stressed. To others, an attempt to minimize one's ethnicity is only a sly maneuver to escape responsibility for past wrongs or to gain admission into their confidence. Finally, there are still many old-timers in the neighborhood, and it would be very ill-mannered to parade one's Americanism before them. Thus, within the bounds of the local neighboorhood, an Italian who plays at being an "American" runs the risk of being taken as a snob, phony, opportunist, coward, or fink.

Among the Italians themselves, notions of ethnicity are particularly well-elaborated. For the most part, these internal subdivisions are based on regional origins in Italy. By contrast, the other ethnic groups have very little internal differentiation. The Negroes make only a vague distinction between those raised in the South and those raised in the North. Among the former, Mississippians are sometimes singled out for special contempt. However, none of these divisions lead to cohesive social unities. But among the Italians their *paesani* (regional origins) take on great importance, and it remains the first perimeter beyond the family within which they look for aid or feel themselves in safe hands. Most *paesani* continue to hold their annual summer picnics and winter dance. Some have grown into full-scale organizations with elected officers, insurance plans, burial funds, and regular poker sessions.

Of all the ethnic groups in the Addams area, the Italians still have the richest ceremonial life. Aside from the annual *paesani* dances and picnics, there are parades, *feste,* and several other occasions. In the summer, their church holds a carnival that duplicates much of the Italian *feste.* On Columbus Day there is a great parade in the Loop, exceeded in grandeur only by the one held by the Irish on St. Patrick's Day. During Lent there are several special religious events and afterwards a round of dances, parties, and feasts. Throughout the summer a local brass band periodically marches through the streets playing arias from Puccini and Verdi. Sidewalk vendors sell Italian lemonade, sausages, and beef sandwiches. Horsedrawn carts go about selling grapes during the fall winemaking season, tomatoes when they are ready to be turned to paste, and fruit and vegetables at almost any time of the year.

Communal Ceremonies and Festivities

Even weddings, communions, funerals, and wakes maintain some of their communal nature. Weddings are usually known of beforehand and often attract a number of onlookers as well as those invited. Afterwards the couple and their friends drive around the neighborhood in decorated cars, honking their horns at one another and whomever they recognize on the streets. Parochial-school children usually receive first communion as a group and attract a good deal of attention. Wakes are also open to almost anyone, and funeral processions often tour a portion of the neighborhood. On this sort of occasion, the Mexicans follow much the same practice, although they lack full control of a local church where they can carry out these affairs to the same extent as the Italians. Among the Negroes and Puerto Ricans, weddings, funerals, and religious events tend to be quite private affairs, open through invitation alone.

The Italians are also favored by the relatively long period over which many of them have been able to know one another and to decide upon whom they can or cannot trust. Over time, a considerable amount of information has been accumulated on many people, and this circulates in such a way as to be available to even a fairly recent resident. Moreover, the intertwining of social relations has become so extensive that contact with one person often opens passage to many others. In this sense, "getting acquainted" is almost unavoidable for a new resident.

The forms of social organization in the Italian section are far more extensive and complicated than those of the other ethnic groups. At the top are two groups, the "West Side Bloc" and the "Outfit," which share membership and whose participants are not all from the Addams area. The West Side Bloc is a group of Italian politicians whose constituency is much larger than the Addams area but which includes a definite wing in the area. Generally its members are assumed to belong to or to have connections with the Outfit. A good deal of power is attributed to them within the local neighborhood, city, state, and nation. The Outfit, more widely known as the Syndicate, includes many more people, but it is also assumed to reach beyond the Addams area. Locally, it is usually taken to include almost anyone who runs a tavern or a liquor store, or who relies on state licensing or city employment. A few other businessmen and local toughs are accredited with membership because of their notorious immunity to law enforcement or their reputed control of "favors."

Indirectly, the Outfit extends to a number of adult social-athletic clubs (s.a.c.'s). These clubs invariably have a store-front where the members spend their time in casual conversation or drink, or play cards. A few of their members belong to the Outfit, and a couple of these clubs are said to have a "regular game" for big stakes. Each group is fairly homogeneous in age, but collectively the groups range between the late 20's up to the late 60's.

Below these adult s.a.c.'s are a number of other s.a.c.'s that also have a clubhouse, but whose members are much younger. As a rule, they are somewhat beyond school age, but only a few are married, and practically none have children. To some degree, they are still involved in the extra-familial life that occupies teenagers. Occasionally they have dances, socials, and impromptu parties. On weekends they still roam around together, attending "socials" sponsored by other groups, looking for girls or for some kind of "action." Within each young man's s.a.c., the members' ages cover a narrow range. Together, all the groups range between about 19 and the late 20's. They form a distinct and well-recognized age grade in the neighborhood because of their continuing involvement in those cross-sexual and recreational activities open to unmarried males.

Nevertheless, these young men's s.a.c.'s are somewhat outside the full round of activities that throw teenagers together. A good portion of their time is spent inside their clubhouse out of sight of their rivals or most bodies of social control. Most members are in their 20's and are able to openly enjoy routine forms of entertainment or excitement that the wider community provides and accepts. When they have a dance or party, it is usually restricted to those whom they invite. Being out of school, they are not forced each day to confront persons from beyond their neighborhood. Since many of them have cars, they need not trespass too much on someone else's domain.

These s.a.c.'s are not assumed to have any active role in the Outfit. At most, it is expected that they might be able to gain a few exemptions from law enforcement and an occasional "favor," e.g., a job, a chance to run an illegal errand, a small loan, someone to sign for their clubhouse charter (required by law), and the purchase of stolen goods or of anything else the boys happen to have on hand. It is assumed that they could solicit help from the Outfit if they got into trouble with another group, but very rarely are they drawn into this type of conflict. Almost invariably the opponent is a much younger "street group" that has encroached on what the s.a.c. considers its "rights"—e.g., tried to "crash" one of their parties, insulted them on the streets, made noise nearby, or marked up their clubhouse. Even at these times, their actions seem designed to do little more than rid themselves of a temporary nuisance. Once rid of their tormentors, they usually do not puruse the issue further, and for good reason. To charter such a club requires three cosigners, and these people may withdraw their support if the group becomes too rowdy. Also, they have a landlord to contend with, and he can throw them out for the same reason. Finally, they cannot afford to make too many enemies; they have a piece of property, and it would be only too easy for their adversaries to get back at them. Unlike all the groups described in the other three sections, they have a stake in maintaining something like law and order.

All the remaining Italian groups include members who are of high-school age. While they too call themselves s.a.c.'s, none of them have a storefront. All of them do have an established "hangout," and they correspond to the usual image of a street-corner group.

While the street groups in this section of the area often express admiration for the adult s.a.c.'s, they seldom develop in an unbroken sequence into a full-fledged adult s.a.c. Usually when they grow old enough to rent a storefront they change their name, acquire new members from groups that have been their rivals, and lose a few of their long-term members. Some groups disband entirely, and their members are redistributed among the newly formed s.a.c.'s. Of the 12 young men's and adult s.a.c.'s, only one is said to have maintained the same name from the time it was a street-corner group. Even in this case some members have been added and others lost. Together, then, the Italian street-corner groups make up the population from which future young men's s.a.c.'s are drawn, but only a few street-corner groups form the nucleus of a s.a.c.

Conceptually, the Italian street groups and the older s.a.c.'s form a single unity. In the eyes of the boys, they are somewhat like the steps between grammar school and college. While there may be dropouts, breaks, and amalgamations, they still make up a series of steps through which one can advance with increasing age. Thus, each street group tends to see the adult s.a.c.'s as essentially an older and more perfect version of itself. What may be just as important is their equally strong sense of history. Locally, many of the members in the street groups can trace their group's genealogy back through the Taylor Dukes, the 40 game, the Genna Brothers, and the Capone mob. Actually, there is no clear idea of the exact order of this descent line; some people include groups that others leave out. Moreover, there is no widespread agreement on which specific group is the current successor to this lineage. Nonetheless, there is agreement that the groups on Taylor Street have illustrious progenitors. On some occasions this heritage may be something of a burden, and on others a source of pride. In any case, it is unavoidable, and usually the Italian street group preface its own name with the term "Taylor." Among the younger groups this is omitted only when their name is an amalgam made up from a specific street corner or block. Only the adult s.a.c.'s regularly fail to acknowl-

edge in their name the immediate territory within which they are situated.

Direct Line of Succession from the Outfit

Since they see themselves in a direct line of succession to groups reputed to be associated with the Outfit, these street-corner groups might be expected to have a strong criminal orientation. In the Addams area, however, the Italian groups are best known for their fighting prowess, and their official police records show no concentration on the more utilitarian forms of crime. The fact is that, like the other adolescent groups in the area, the Italian boys are not really free to choose their own goals and identities. Territorial arrangements juxtapose them against similar groups manned by Negro and Mexican boys. If the Italian street-corner groups fail to define themselves as fighting groups, their peers in the other ethnic groups are certainly going to assume as much.

There is also considerable rivalry between Italian street-corner groups of roughly the same age. Commonly they suspect each other of using force to establish their precedence. In turn, each group seems to think it must at least put on a tough exterior to avoid being "pushed around." Privately there is a great deal of talk among them about the Outfit and about criminal activities, but it is academic in the sense that there is no strong evidence that their behavior follows suit.

It is interesting that the adult s.a.c.'s that actually have members in the rackets avoid any conspicuous claims about their criminal activities or fighting abilities. Their names, for example, are quite tame, while those of the street groups tend to be rather menacing. And their dances, leisure-time activities, and interrelationships are quite private and unpretentious. Unlike the street groups, they never wear clothing that identifies their group membership. The older men in the s.a.c.'s make no apparent attempt to establish a publicly-known hierarchy among themselves. Other people occasionally attribute more respect to one than another of them, but there seems to be little consensus on this. On their own part, the older groups seem to pay little attention to their relative standing and to be on fairly good terms. During my three years in the area, I never heard of them fighting among themselves.

Unlike the Negro and Mexican ethnic sections, there are no female counterparts to the named Italian street-corner groups. A very few Italian girls belong to two Mexican girls' groups that "hung" in the Mexican section. This, in itself, was exceptional; almost always the minority members in a street group are from a lower-ranking ethnic group. The Italian girls, however, are under certain constraints that may be lacking for those in the other ethnic groups. Naturally, their parents disapprove of such a blatant display of feminine unity. The Italian parents may gain stature by their power and precedence in comparison to the Negro and Mexican adults. Yet what seems far more significant is the general form that boy-girl relationships take among the Italians. On either side, the slightest hint of interest in the other sex is likely to be taken in the most serious way; as either a rank insult or a final commitment. Thus, any explicit alliance between a boys' and girls' group can be interpreted in only one of two ways: (1) all the girls are "laying" for the boys, or (2) they are seriously attached to each other. Neither side seems quite willing to betray so much and, thus, they avoid such explicit alliances.

This dilemma was quite evident on many occasions while I was observing the Italian boys and girls. The girls seemed extraordinarily coy when they were in a "safe" position—with their parents, in church, etc. When alone and on their own they became equally cautious and noncommittal. On public occasions, the boys seemed almost to ignore the girls and even to snub them. On Taylor Street, for instance, an Italian boys' group and an Italian girls' group used to hang about 10 feet from each other. Almost invariably they would stand with their backs to each other, although there were many furtive glances back and forth. During almost two years of observation, I never saw them talk. Later, I was surprised to learn that everyone in each group was quite well-known to the other. For either of them to have acknowledged the other's presence openly, however, would have been too forward. The boys are quite aware of this dilemma and complain that the girls are not free enough to be convenient companions. This, they say, is one reason why they have to go elsewhere to date someone. At the same time, they perpetuate the old system by automatically assuming that the slightest sign of interest by a girl makes her fair game. Out of self-defense, the girls are compelled to keep their distance. On private occasions, of course, there are many Italian boys and girls who sneak off to enjoy what others might consider an entirely conventional boy-girl relationship (petting, necking). In public, though, they studiously ignore each other. Throughout my time in the area I never saw a young Italian couple hold hands or walk together on the sidewalk.

The Barracudas were the first Mexican street-corner group to emerge in the Italian section. They first became a named group in the spring of 1964, and all members were Mexican.

Once established, the Barracudas installed themselves in the northwest corner of Sheridan Park. Virtually every Italian street group in the area makes use of this park, and several have their hangout there. Other people in turn refer to the Italian groups collectively as "the guys from the Park." The park itself is partitioned into a finely graduated series of more or less private enclosures, with the most private hangout going to the reigning group and the least private to the weakest group. The northwest corner of the park is the most exposed of any portion, and this is where the Barracudas installed themselves. Even in this lowly spot, they were much resented by the other groups. To the Italians the Park was almost a sacred charge, and the Mexicans' intrusion was a ritual pollution. The Barracudas were harassed, ridiculed, and insulted. On their own part, they became belligerent and vaunted all sorts of outrageous claims about themselves. Soon the situation deteriorated and the Italian groups became extremely harsh with the Barracudas. Since the Barracudas were no match for even some of the younger Italian groups, they removed themselves to one member's house.

Their new hangout placed them in an anomalous position. Ethnically they were identified as a Mexican group. Yet they were located in a part of the area that had been conceded to the Puerto Ricans. And individually most of them continued to reside in the Italian section. The general result seems to have been that the Barracudas were isolated from any of the other group hierarchies and placed in opposition to every group in the area. Within a year every white group was their enemy, and the Negroes were not their friends. The Barracudas responded in kind and became even more truculent and boastful. More than any group in the area, they openly embraced the stance of a fighting group. They wrote their name all over the neighborhood and even on some of the other groups' hangouts. In the meantime, they made a clubhouse out of a lean-to adjacent to a building on Harrison Street. Inside they installed a shield on which they wrote "hate," "kill," and other violent words. Carrying a weapon became almost routine with them, and eventually they collected a small arsenal. In time they had several small-scale fights with both the Italians from the Park and the Mexicans around Polk and Laflin. In due course, they acquired so many enemies that they could hardly risk leaving the immediate area of their hangout. At the same time, some of them began to go to Eighteenth Street, where they had "connections"—relatives. This only brought them into conflict with other groups in this neighborhood. By the summer of 1965, the Barracudas were as isolated and resentful as ever.

"Incognitos" and the "Pica People"

There are two other groups in the Italian section, the Pica People and the Incognitos. The groups' names are themselves an expression of their isolation. The Incognitos self-consciously avoided comparison with the other groups: They did not hang in the Park, hold socials, or become involved in any of the local sidewalk confrontations. About the same age as the Contenders, the Incognitos were notably different in their exclusion from the local round of praise and recriminations.

"Pica People" is a derisive name meant as an insult for five young men about 19 to 25 years of age. Although these five individuals associate regularly, they claim no group identity and become angry when called the Pica People. Unlike the Incognitos, the Pica People are well-known and often accused of some predatory display. They do not fight for group honor, but there is friction between them and all the other street-corner groups in the Addams area.

It was impossible to determine how these two groups came into existence. (I talked only twice with the Incognitos, who simply said they "grew up together." Local people started calling the Pica People by that name after a movie in which the "Pica People" were sub-humans. I knew some of the members of this group, but they became so angry at any mention of the name that I could not discuss it with them.) What is known of their composition may throw some light on why they were excluded from the structure of the other groups. All informants described the Incognitos as "good guys," still in school and no trouble to anyone. They were not considered college boys but, if asked, most informants said they thought some of them might go to college. Local youth agencies made no attempt to work with them, and the entire neighborhood seemed to feel they were not dangerous. Other street-corner groups in the Italian section did not look down on them, but they did exempt them from the ambitions that brought other groups into opposition.

The Pica People were just the opposite. All members were boastful of their alleged Outfit connections and their ability to intimidate other people. But the Pica People possessed so many personal flaws that they were rather useless to the Outfit. One member was slightly claustrophobic. Another was so weak that even much younger boys pushed him around. A third had an exceedingly unfortunate appearance. Under the circumstances, their pretensions became laughable.

Extremes of Street Corner Groups

The Incognitos and the Pica People seem to represent the extremes of a range in which the street-corner group is considered the normal adolescent gathering. Modest and well-behaved youngsters are excluded as exceptions, as are criminally inclined but unsuccessful young men. Both of these groups fell outside the range considered normal by the local residents and were thereby dissociated from the total group hierarchy.

The social context of the Italian street groups is somewhat different from that of the street groups in the other three ethnic sections. Among the Italians, the major share of coercive power still remains in adult hands. The wider community may not be very pleased with the form *their* power takes, but it is the only case where the corporate power of the adolescents is tempered by that of the adults. Also, since many of the same adults have an active role in distributing some of the benefits that are held in store by the wider community, their power is augmented. Perhaps the most obvious result of the adults' ascendency is that the adolescents do not simply dismiss them or adulthood as unimportant. A more immediate consequence is to give many of the adults the prerogative of exacting considerable obedience from the local adolescents. It is not all uncommon to see an Italian adult upbraid and humble one of the local youths. Not all adults have this privilege; but many do, and their example provides a distinct contrast to the other ethnic groups where similar efforts would be futile.

In the long run, the effectiveness of these coercive controls among the Italians may do little more than confirm their convictions that, outside of natural tendencies, there is no guarantee to moral conduct except economic and numerical strength. Within their own little world, however, such coercive measures constitute a fairly effective system of social control. Personal privacy and anonymity are almost impossible. In turn, each person's known or assumed connections dampen most chances at exploitation because of the fear of unknown consequences. Thus, the opportunities for immorality presented by transient relations and "fair game" are fairly rare. Within these limits, such an authoritarian system of social control will work. Outside their own section, of course, these conditions do not hold; and the Italian boys find themselves free to seize whatever advantages or opportunities present themself. Among themselves, they are usually only a rowdy and boisterous crowd. With strangers or in other parts of the Addams area, they become particularly arrogant and unscrupulous.

With these qualifications, it appears that well-established adolescent street-corner groups are quite compatible with strong adult authority and influence. In fact, judging from the Italian section, these adolescent street-corner groups seem to be the building blocks out of which the older and more powerful groups have originated. The younger groups continue to replenish the older ones and help maintain the structure within which adults are shown deference.

Moreover, the total age-graded structure of groups in the Italian section relates youngsters to the wider society both instrumentally and conceptually. The Italian street groups see themselves as replacements in an age structure that becomes progressively less provincial. At the upper age level, groups even stop prefacing their name with the term "Taylor"; and a few of their members have a place in the wider society through the Outfit and West Side Bloc. The relationship between these age grades also provides a ladder down which favors and opportunities are distributed. The wider community may hesitate at accepting the legitimacy of these transactions, but they are mostly of a conventional form. The "Outfit" and the "West Side Bloc" have a strong interest in maintaining a degree of social order, and the sorts of wanton violence associated with gangs do not at all fit their taste.

In Conclusion

The Addams area is probably a more orderly slum than many others, and it departs sharply from the common image of an atomized and unruly urban rabble. For all its historical uniqueness, the neighborhood does establish the possibility of a moral order within its population. The recurrence of the circumstances that led to its organization is as uncertain as the future of the Addams area itself. In spite of all these uncertainties, the Addams area shows that slum residents are intent upon finding a moral order and are sometimes successful in doing so.

Child Convicts

Paul Lerman

About 100 years ago, the state of New Jersey built a special correctional facility to save wayward girls from a life of crime and immorality. Over the years the ethnic and racial backgrounds of the institutionalized girls changed, the educational level of their cottage parent-custodians shifted upward, and the program of correction grew more humane. But the types of offenses that constitute the legal justification for their incarceration in the State Home for Girls have not changed, not appreciably.

The vast majority of the girls in the Home today, as in past years, were accused of misbehavior that would not be considered crimes if committed by adults. They were formally adjudicated and institutionalized as delinquents, but most of them have not committed real criminal acts. Over 80 percent of them in 1969 were institutionalized for the following misdeeds: running away from home, being incorrigible, ungovernable and beyond the control of parents, being truant, engaging in sexual relations, and becoming pregnant. Criminologists classify this mixture of noncriminal acts "juvenile status offenses," since only persons of a juvenile status can be accused, convicted and sentenced as delinquents for committing them. Juvenile status offenses apply to boys as well as girls, and they form the bases for juvenile court proceedings in all 50 states.

Most Americans are probably unaware that juveniles are subject to stricter laws than adults, and to more severe penalties for noncriminal acts than are many adults who commit felonies. This practice, so apparently antithetical to our national conceit of child-centeredness, began well before the Revolution. The Puritans of the Plymouth Bay Colony initiated the practice of defining and treating as criminal children who were "rude, stubborn, and unruly," or who behaved "disobediently and disorderly towards their parents, masters, and governors." In 1824, when the House of Refuge established the first American Juvenile correctional institution in New York City, the Board of Managers was granted explicit sanction by the state legislature to hold in custody and correct youths who were leading a "vicious or vagrant life," as well as those convicted of any crime. The first juvenile court statute, passed in Illinois in 1899, continued the tradition of treating juvenile status offenses as criminal by including this class of actions as part of the definition of "delinquency." Other states copied this legislative practice as they boarded the bandwagon of court reform.

My contention that juvenile status offenders are still handled through a *criminal* process will be disputed by many defenders of the current system who argue that the creation of the juvenile court marked a significant break with the past. They contend that juvenile courts were set up to deal with the child and his needs, rather than with his offense. In line with this benign aim, the offense was to be viewed as a symptom of a child's need for special assistance. The juvenile court was designed to save children—not punish them. Only "neglectful" parents were deemed appropriate targets of punishment.

Unfortunately, the laudable intentions of the founders of the court movement have yet to be translated into reality. The United States Supreme Court, in 1967, reached this conclusion; so, too, did the Task Force on Delinquency of the President's Commission on Law Enforcement and the Administration of Justice. Both governmental bodies ruled that juvenile court dispositions were, in effect, sentences that bore a remarkable resemblance to the outcomes of adult criminal proceedings. The Supreme Court was appalled at the idea that 15-year-old Gerald Gault could be deprived of his liberty for up to six years without the benefits of due process of law found in adult courts. The majority was persuaded that the consequences of judicial decisions should be considered, not just the ideals of the founders of the juvenile court.

From an historical perspective, the Supreme Court's ruling appears quite reasonable—although it was 70 years overdue. The juvenile court was grafted onto an existing schema for defining youthful misdeeds as illegal behavior. It was also grafted onto a correctional system that had begun separating youngsters from adults, and boys from girls, for many years before the first juvenile court was established.

Long before there was a juvenile court, the American predilection for utilizing legal coercion to control youthful behavior had been well established. The form of the jurisdictional mandate changed with the emergence of the juvenile court—but the substantive range and scope of youthful liability for noncriminal behavior has not really changed.

Since the Supreme Court ruling in *Gault v. Arizona*, there has been increased concern and debate over the introduction of legal counsel and minimal procedural rights in the operation of the juvenile court. The preoccupation with legal rights in the courtroom has, however, obscured the fact that the sociolegal boundaries of delinquency statutes were unaffected by *Gault*. Nevertheless, some revision of the laws has been undertaken by the states, at least since 1960 when the Second United Nations Congress on the Prevention of Crime and the Treatment of Offenders recommended that juveniles should not be prosecuted as delinquents for behavior which, if exhibited by adults, would not be a matter of legal concern.

One state, New York, even approached a technical compliance with the United Nations standard. In New York, juvenile status offenders are adjudicated with a separate petition alleging a "person in need of supervision" (PINS); traditional criminal offenses use a petition that alleges "delinquency." However, true to American tradition, both types of petitioned young people are locked up in the same detention facilities and reform schools. One of the most "progressive" juvenile court laws in the country was initially enacted with restrictions on mixing, but this was soon amended to permit the change to be merely semantic, not substantive. Besides New York, six other states have amended their juvenile codes to establish a distinctive labeling procedure to distinguish criminal and noncriminal acts. Each of these states (California, Illinois, Kansas, Colorado, Oklahoma and Vermont) has banned *initial* commitment to juvenile reformatories of children within the noncriminal jurisdiction of the court. Whether this ban will be continued in practice (and in the statutes) is uncertain. Meanwhile, young people can still be mixed in detention facilities, transfers to reformatories are technically possible, and subsequent commitments to delinquent institutions are apparently permitted. In addition, it is doubtful whether the public (including teachers and prospective employers) distinguishes between those "in need of supervision" and delinquents.

The Police as Dutch Uncles

If the letter and spirit of American juvenile statutes were rigorously enforced, our delinquency rates and facilities would be in even deeper trouble than they are today. For few American youth would reach adulthood without being liable to its stern proscriptions. However, mitigating devices are used to avoid further overcrowding court dockets and institutions, and to demonstrate that parents and enforcement officials can be humane and child-centered. Adult authorities are permitted to exercise discretionary behavior in processing actions by official petitions. The American system is notorious for its widespread use of unofficial police and judicial recording and supervision of juveniles, whether status offenders or real delinquents. As a matter of historical fact, the hallmark of the American system is the intriguing combination of limitless scope of our delinquency statutes and enormous discretion granted in their enforcement and administration. Our statutes appear to reflect the image of the stern Puritan father, but our officials are permitted to behave like Dutch uncles—if they are so inclined.

Discretionary decision making by law enforcement officials has often been justified on the grounds that it permits an "individualization" of offenders, as well as for reasons of pragmatic efficiency. While this may be true in some cases, it is difficult to read the historical record and not conclude that many juvenile status actions could have been defined as cultural differences and childhood play fads, as well as childhood troubles with home, school and sex. Using the same broad definition of delinquency, reasonable adults have differed—and continue to differ—over the sociolegal meaning of profanity, smoking, drinking, sexual congress, exploring abandoned buildings, playing in forbidden places, idling, hitching rides on buses, trucks and cars, sneaking into shows and subways and so forth. While many judgments about the seriousness of these offenses may appear to be based on the merits of the individual case, delinquency definitions, in practice, employ shifting cultural standards to distinguish between childhood troubles, play fads and neighborhood differences. Today, officials in many communities appear more tolerant of profanity and smoking than those of the 1920s, but there is continuing concern regarding female sexuality, male braggadocio and disrespect of adult authority. In brief, whether or not a youth is defined as delinquent may depend on the era, community and ethnic status of the official—as well as the moral guidelines of individual law enforcers.

National studies of the prevalence of the problem are not readily available. However, we can piece together data that indicate that the problem is not inconsequential. A conservative estimate, based upon analysis of national juvenile court statistics compiled by the United States Children's Bureau, indicates that juvenile status crimes comprise about 25 percent of the children's cases initially appearing before juvenile courts on a formal petition. About one out of every five boys' delinquency petitions and over one-half of all girls' cases are based on charges for which an adult would not be legally liable ever to appear in court.

The formal petitions have an impact on the composition of juvenile facilities, as indicated by the outcomes of legal processing. A review of state and local detention facilities disclosed that 40 to 50 percent of the cases in custody, pending dispositional hearings by judges, consisted of delinquents who had committed no crimes. A study of nearly 20 correctional institutions in various parts of the country revealed that between 25 and 30 percent of their resident delinquent population consisted of young people convicted of a juvenile status offense.

The figures cited do not, however, reveal the number of youths that are treated informally by the police and the courts. Many young people are released with their cases recorded as "station adjustments"; in a similar fashion, thousands of youths are informally dealt with at court intake or at an unofficial court hearing. Even though these cases are not formally adjudicated, unofficial records are maintained and can be used against the children if they have any future run-ins with the police or courts. The number of these official, but nonadjudicated, contacts is difficult to estimate, since our requirements for social bookkeeping are far less stringent than our demands for financial accountability.

One careful study of police contacts in a middle-sized city, cited approvingly by a task force of the President's Commission on Law Enforcement and the Administration of Justice, disclosed that the offense that ranked highest as a delinquent act was "incorrigible, runaway"; "disorderly conduct" was second; "contact suspicion, investigation, and information" ranked third; and "theft" was a poor fourth. In addition to revealing that the police spend a disproportionate amount of their time attending to noncriminal offenses, the study also provides evidence that the problem is most acute in low-income areas of the city. This kind of finding could probably be duplicated in any city—large, small or middle-sized—in the United States.

Legal Treatment of Delinquents without Crimes

A useful way of furthering our understanding of the American approach to dealing with delinquents without crimes is provided by comparing judicial decisions for different types of offenses. This can be done by reanalyzing recent data reported by the Children's Bureau, classifying offenses according to their degree of seriousness. If we use standard FBI terminology, the most serious crimes can be labeled "Part I" and are: homicide, forcible rape, armed robbery, burglary, aggravated assault and theft of more than $50. All other offenses that would be crimes if committed by an adult, but are less serious, can be termed "all other adult types" and labeled "Part II." The third type of offenses, the least serious, are those acts that are "juvenile status offenses." By using these classifications, data reported to the Children's Bureau by the largest cities are reanalyzed to provide the information depicted in the table. Three types of decisions are compared in this analysis: 1) whether or not an official petition is drawn after a complaint has been made; 2) whether or not the juvenile is found guilty, if brought before the court

Disposition of Juvenile Cases at Three Stages in the Judicial Process 19 of the 30 Largest Cities, 1965.

	Part I (Most Serious Adult Offenses)	Part II (All Other Adult Offenses)	Juvenile Status Offenses
% Court Petition after complaint	57% N=(37.420)	33% (52,862)	42% (33,046)
% Convicted — if brought into court	92% N=(21,386)	90% (17,319)	94% (13,857)
% Placed or Committed — if convicted	23% N=(19,667)	18% (15,524)	26% (12,989)

on an official petition; and 3) whether or not the offender is placed or committed to an institution, if convicted. The rates for each decision level are computed for each of the offense classifications.

The table discloses a wide difference between offense classifications at the stage of deciding whether to draw up an official petition (57 percent versus 33 percent and 42 percent). Part I youth are far more likely to be brought into court on a petition, but juvenile status offenders are processed at a higher rate than all other adult types. At the conviction stage the differences are small, but the juvenile status offenders are found guilty more often. At the critical decision point, commitment to an institution, the least serious offenders are more likely to be sent away than are the two other types.

It is apparent that juvenile justice in America's large cities can mete out harsher dispositions for youth who have committed no crimes than for those who violate criminal statutes. Once the petitions are drawn up, juvenile judges appear to function as if degree of seriousness is not an important criterion of judicial decision making. If different types of offenders were sent to different types of institutions, it might be argued that the types of sentences actually varied. In fact, however, all three offender types are generally sent to the same institutions in a particular state—according to their age and sex—for an indeterminate length of time.

Length of Institutionalization

If American juvenile courts do not follow one of the basic components of justice—matching the degree of punishment with the degree of social harm—perhaps the correctional institutions themselves function differently. This outcome is unlikely, however, since the criteria for leaving institutions are not based on the nature of the offense. Length of stay is more likely to be determined by the adjustment to institutional rules and routine, the receptivity of parents or

guardians to receiving the children back home, available bed space in cottages and the current treatment ideology. Juvenile status offenders tend to have more family troubles and may actually have greater difficulty in meeting the criteria for release than their delinquent peers. The result is that the delinquents without crimes probably spend more time in institutions designed for delinquent youth than "real" delinquents. Empirical support for this conclusion emerges from a special study of one juvenile jurisdiction, the Manhattan borough of New York City. In a pilot study that focused on a random sample of officially adjudicated male cases appearing in Manhattan Court in 1963, I gathered data on the range, median and average length of stay for boys sent to institutions. In New York, as noted earlier, juvenile status youth are called "PINS" (persons in need of supervision), so I use this classification in comparing this length of institutionalization with that of "delinquents."

The range of institutional stay was two to 28 months for delinquents and four to 48 months for PINS boys; the median was nine months for delinquents and 13 months for PINS; and the average length of stay was 10.7 months for delinquents and 16.3 months for PINS. Regardless of the mode of measurement, it is apparent that institutionalization was proportionately longer for boys convicted and sentenced for juvenile status offenses than for juveniles convicted for criminal-type offenses.

These results on length of stay do not include the detention period, the stage of correctional processing prior to placement in an institution. Analyses of recent detention figures for all five boroughs of New York City revealed the following patterns: 1) PINS boys and girls are more likely to be detained than are delinquents (54 to 31 percent); and 2) once PINS youth are detained they are twice as likely to be detained for more than 30 days than are regular delinquents (50 to 25 percent). It is apparent that juvenile status offenders who receive the special label of "persons in need of supervision" tend to spend more time in custodial facilities at *all* stages of their correctional experience than do delinquents.

Social Characteristics of Offenses and Offenders

The offenses that delinquents without crimes are charged with do not involve a clear victim, as is the case in classical crimes of theft, robbery, burglary and assault. Rather, they involve young people who are themselves liable to be victimized for having childhood troubles or growing up differently. Three major categories appear to be of primary concern: behavior at home, behavior at school and sexual experimentation. "Running away," "incorrigibility," "ungovernability" and "beyond the control of parental supervision" refer to troubles with parents, guardians or relatives. "Growing up in idleness," "truanting" and creating "disturbances" in classrooms refer to troubles with teachers, principals, guidance counselors and school routines. Sexual relations as "minors" and out-of-wedlock pregnancy reflect adult concern with the act and consequences of precocious sexual experimentation. In brief, juvenile status offenses primarily encompass the problems of growing up.

Certain young people in American society are more likely to have these types of troubles with adults: girls, poor youth, rural migrants to the city, underachievers and the less sophisticated. Historically, as well as today, a community's more disadvantaged children are most likely to have their troubles defined as "delinquent." In the 1830s the sons and daughters of Irish immigrants were over-represented in the House of Refuge, the nation's first juvenile correctional institution. In 1971 the sons and daughters of black slum dwellers are disproportionately dealt with as delinquents for experiencing problems in "growing up."

Unlike regular delinquents, juvenile status offenders often find a parent, guardian, relative or teacher as the chief complainant in court. Since juvenile courts have traditionally employed family functioning and stability as primary considerations in rendering dispositions, poor youth with troubles are at a distinct disadvantage compared to their delinquent peers. Mothers and fathers rarely bring their children to courts for robbing or assaulting nonfamily members; however, if their own authority is challenged, many parents are willing to use the power of the state to correct their offspring. In effect, many poor and powerless parents cooperate with the state to stigmatize and punish their children for having problems in growing up.

At least since *Gault*, the system of juvenile justice has been undergoing sharp attacks by legal and social critics. Many of these have pertinence for the processing and handling of juvenile status offenders. The current system has been criticized for the following reasons:

☐ The broad scope of delinquency statutes and juvenile court jurisdictions has permitted the coercive imposition of middle-class standards of child rearing.

☐ A broad definition has enlarged the limits of discretionary authority so that virtually any child can be deemed a delinquent if officials are persuaded that he needs correction.

☐ The presence of juvenile status offenses, as part of the delinquency statutes, provides an easier basis for convicting and incarcerating young people because it is difficult to defend against the vagueness of terms like "incorrigible" and "ungovernable."

☐ The mixing together of delinquents without crimes and real delinquents in detention centers and reform schools helps to provide learning experiences for the non-delinquents on how to become real delinquents.

☐ The public is generally unaware of the differences between "persons in need of supervision" and youths who rob, steal and assault, and thereby is not sensitized to the special needs of status offenders.

☐ Statistics on delinquency are misleading because we are usually unable to differentiate how much of the volume reflects greater public and official concern regarding home, school and sex problems, and how much is actual criminal conduct by juveniles.

☐ Juvenile status offenses do not constitute examples of social harm and, therefore, should not even be the subject of criminal-type sanctions.

☐ Juvenile institutions that house noncriminal offenders constitute the state's human garbage dump for taking care of all kinds of problem children, especially the poor.

☐ Most policemen and judges who make critical decisions about children's troubles are ill equipped to understand their problems or make sound judgments on their behalf.

☐ The current correctional system does not rehabilitate these youths and is therefore a questionable approach.

Two Unintended Consequences

In addition to the reasons cited, there are two unintended consequences that have not been addressed, even by critics. Analysis of the data presented earlier provides evidence that the current system is an unjust one. Youngsters convicted of committing the least serious offenses are dealt with more severely by virtue of their greater length of detention and institutionalization. Any legal system that purports to accord "justice for all" must take into account the degree of punishment that is proportionate to the degree of social harm inflicted. The current system does not meet this minimal standard of justice.

The recent ruling by the U.S. Supreme Court (Gault vs Arizona) found that the juvenile court of Arizona—and by implication the great majority of courts—were procedurally unfair. The court explicitly ruled out any consideration of the substantive issues of detention and incarceration. It may have chosen to do so because it sincerely believed that the soundest approach to insuring substantive justice is by making certain that juveniles are granted the constitutional safeguards of due process: the right to confront accusers and cross-examine, the right to counsel, the right to written charges and prior notice, and the right against self-incrimination. While this line of reasoning may turn out to be useful in the long run of history, adherence to this approach would involve acceptance of an undesirable system until the time that substantive justice could catch up with procedural justice. The likelihood that the injustice accorded to youth is not intentional does not change the current or future reality of the court's disposition. Nevertheless, the inclusion of juvenile status offenders as liable to arrest, prosecution, detention and incarceration probably promotes the criminalization of disadvantaged youth. Earlier critics have indicated that incorrigible boys and girls sent to reform schools learn how to behave as homosexuals, thieves, drug users and burglars. But what is the impact at the community level, where young people initially learn the operational meaning of delinquency? From the child's point of view, he learns that occurrences that may be part of his daily life—squabbles at home, truancy and sexual precocity—are just as delinquent as thieving, robbing and assaulting. It must appear that nearly anyone he or she hangs around with is not only a "bad" kid but a delinquent one as well. In fact, there are studies that yield evidence that three-quarters of a generation of slum youth, ages ten to 17, have been officially noted as "delinquent" in a police or court file. It seems reasonable to infer that many of these records contain official legal definitions of essentially noncriminal acts that are done in the family, at school and with peers of the opposite sex.

It would be strange indeed if youth did not define themselves as "bad cats"—just as the officials undoubtedly do. It would be strange, too, if both the officials and the young people (and a segment of their parents) did not build on these invidious definitions by expecting further acts of "delinquency." As children grow older, they engage in a more consistent portrayal of their projected identity—and the officials dutifully record further notations to an expected social history of delinquency. What the officials prophesy is fulfilled in a process that criminalizes the young and justifies the prior actions of the official gatekeepers of the traditional system. Our societal responses unwittingly compound the problem we ostensibly desire to prevent and control—real delinquent behavior.

In the arena of social affairs it appears that negative consequences are more likely to occur when there is a large gap in status, power and resources between the "savers" and those to be "saved." Evidently, colonial-type relationships, cultural misunderstandings and unrestrained coercion can often exacerbate problems, despite the best of intentions. Given this state of affairs, it appears likely that continual coercive intrusion by the state into the lives of youthful ghetto residents can continue to backfire on a large scale.

We have probably been compounding our juvenile problem ever since 1824 when the New York State Legislature granted the Board of Managers of the House of Refuge broad discretionary authority to intervene coercively in the lives of youth until they become 21 years of age—even if they had not committed any criminal acts.

Generations of reformers, professionals and academics have been too eager to praise the philanthropic and rehabilitative intentions of our treatment centers toward poor kids in trouble—and insufficiently sensitive to the actual consequences of an unjust system that aids and abets the criminalization of youth.

Sophisticated defenders of the traditional system are aware of many of these criticisms. They argue that the intent of all efforts in the juvenile field is to help, not to punish, the child. To extend this help they are prepared to use the authority of the state to coerce children who might otherwise be unwilling to make use of existing agencies. Not all acts of juvenile misbehavior that we currently label "status offenses" are attributable to cultural differences. Many youngsters do, in fact, experience troubles in growing up that should be of concern to a humane society. The fundamental issue revolves on how that concern can be expressed so as to yield the maximum social benefits and the minimum social costs. Thus, while the consequences of criminalizing the young and perpetuating an unjust system of juvenile justice should be accorded greater recognition than benign intentions, it would be a serious mistake to propose an alternative policy that did not incorporate a legitimate concern for the welfare of children.

New Policy Perspectives

The issue is worth posing in this fashion because of a recent policy proposal advanced by the President's Commission on Law Enforcement and the Administration of Justice. The commission suggested that "serious consideration should be given complete elimination from the court's jurisdiction of conduct illegal only for a child. Abandoning the possibility of coercive power over a child who is acting in a seriously self-destructive way would mean losing the opportunity of reclamation in a few cases."

Changing delinquency statutes and the jurisdictional scope of the juvenile court to exclude conduct illegal only for a child would certainly be a useful beginning. However, the evidence suggests that the cases of serious self-destructiveness are not "few" in number, and there is reason to believe that many adjudicated and institutionalized young people do require some assistance from a concerned society. By failing to suggest additional policy guidelines for providing the necessary services in a *civil* context, the commission advanced only half a policy and provided only a limited sense of historical perspective.

Traditional American practices towards children in trouble have not been amiss because of our humanitarian concern, but because we coupled this concern with the continuation of prior practices whereby disliked behavior was defined and treated as a criminal offense (that is, delinquent). Unfortunately, our concern has often been linked to the coercive authority of the police powers of the state. The problems of homeless and runaway youths, truants, sex experimenters and others with childhood troubles could have been more consistently defined as *child welfare* problems. Many private agencies did emerge to take care of such children, but they inevitably left the more difficult cases for the state to service as "delinquents." In addition, the private sector never provided the services to match the concern that underlay the excessive demand. The problem of the troublesome juvenile status offender has been inextricably linked to: 1) our failure to broaden governmental responsibility to take care of *all* child welfare problems that were not being cared for by private social agencies; and 2) our failure to hold private agencies accountable for those they did serve with public subsidies. We permitted the police, courts and correctional institutions to function as our residual agency for caring for children in trouble. Many state correctional agencies have become, unwittingly, modern versions of a poorhouse for juveniles. Our *systems* of child welfare and juvenile justice, not just our legal codes, are faulty.

The elimination of juvenile status offenses from the jurisdiction of the juvenile court would probably create an anomalous situation in juvenile jurisprudence if dependency and neglect cases were not also removed. It would be ironic if we left two categories that were clearly noncriminal within a delinquency adjudicatory structure. If they were removed, as they should be, then the juvenile court would be streamlined to deal with a primary function: the just adjudication and disposition of young people alleged to have committed acts that would be criminal if enacted by an adult. Adherence to this limited jurisdiction would aid the court in complying with recent Supreme Court rulings, for adversary proceedings are least suited to problems involving family and childhood troubles.

If these three categories were removed from the traditional system, we would have to evolve a way of thinking about a new public organization that would engage in a variety of functions: fact finding, hearing of complaints, regulatory dispositions and provision of general child care and family services. This new public agency could be empowered to combine many of the existing functions of the court and child welfare departments, with one major prohibition: transfers of temporary custody of children would have to be voluntary on the part of parents, and all contested cases would have to be adjudicated by a civil court. This prohibition would be in harmony with the modern child welfare view of keeping natural families intact, and acting otherwise only when all remedial efforts have clearly failed.

We have regulatory commissions in many areas of social concern in America, thereby sidestepping the usual judicial structure. If there is a legitimate concern in the area of child and family welfare, and society wants to ensure the maintenance of minimum services, then legally we can build on existing systems and traditions to evolve a new kind of regulatory service commission to carry out that end. To ensure that the critical legal rights of parents and children are protected, civil family courts—as in foster and adoption cases—would be available for contest and appeal. However, to ensure that the agencies did not become bureaucratic busybodies, additional thought would have to be given to their policy-making composition, staffing and location.

A major deficiency of many regulatory agencies in this country is that special interests often dominate the administration and proceedings, while affected consumers are only sparsely represented. To ensure that the residents most affected by proposed family and child welfare boards had a major voice in the administration and proceedings, they could be set up with a majority of citizen representatives (including adolescents). In addition, they could be decentralized to function within the geographical boundaries of areas the size of local elementary or junior high school districts. These local boards would be granted the legal rights to hire lay and professional staff, as well as to supervise the administration of hearings and field services.

The setting up of these local boards would require an extensive examination of city, county and state child welfare services to ensure effective cooperation and integration of effort. It is certainly conceivable that many existing family and child welfare services, which are generally administered without citizen advice, could also be incorporated into the activities of the local boards. The problems to be ironed out would of course be substantial, but the effort could force a reconceptualization of local and state responsibilities for providing acceptable, humane and effective family and child welfare services on a broad scale.

Citizen Involvement

The employment of interested local citizens in the daily operation of family and child welfare services is not a totally new idea. Sweden has used local welfare boards to provide a range of services to families and children, including the handling of delinquency cases. While we do not have to copy their broad jurisdictional scope or underrepresentation of blue-collar citizens, a great deal can be learned from this operation. Other Scandinavian countries also use local citizen boards to deal with a range of delinquency offenses. Informed observers indicate that the nonlegal systems in Scandinavia are less primitive and coercive. However, it is difficult to ascertain whether this outcome is due to cultural differences or to the social invention that excludes juvenile courts.

There exist analogues in this country for the use of local citizens in providing services to children in trouble. In recent years there has been an upsurge in the use of citizen-volunteers who function as house parents for home detention facilities, probation officers and intake workers. Besides this use of citizens, New Jersey, for example, has permitted each juvenile court jurisdiction to appoint citizens to Judicial Conference Committees, for the purpose of informally hearing and handling delinquency cases. Some New Jersey counties process up to 50 percent of their court petitions through this alternative to adjudication. All these programs, however, operate under the direct supervision and jurisdiction of the county juvenile court judges, with the cooperation of the chief probation officers. It should be possible to adapt these local innovations to a system that would be independent of the coercive aspects of even the most benign juvenile court operation.

Opposition to Innovation

Quite often it is the powerful opposition of special interest groups, rather than an inability to formulate new and viable proposals for change, that can block beneficial social change. Many judges, probation workers, correction officers, as well as religious and secular child care agencies, would strenuously oppose new social policies and alternatives for handling delinquents without crimes. Their opposition would certainly be understandable, since the proposed changes could have a profound impact on their work. In the process of limiting jurisdiction and altering traditional practices, they could lose status, influence and control over the use of existing resources. Very few interest groups suffer these kinds of losses gladly. Proponents of change should try to understand their problem and act accordingly. However, the differential benefits that might accrue to children and their families should serve as a reminder that the problems of youth and their official and unofficial adult caretakers are not always identical.

Experts' Claims

One proposal in particular can be expected to call forth the ire of these groups, and that is the use of citizens in the administration and provision of services in local boards. Many professional groups—psychiatrists, social workers, psychologists, group therapists and school guidance counselors—have staked out a claim of expertise for the treatment of any "acting out" behavior. The suggestion that citizens should play a significant role in offering assistance undermines that claim. In reply, the professionals might argue that experts—not laymen—should control, administer and staff any programs involving the remediation of childhood troubles. On what grounds might this kind of claim be reasonably questioned?

First, there is nothing about local citizens' control of child and family welfare activities that precludes the hiring of professionals for key tasks, and entrusting them with the operation of the board's program. Many private and public boards in the fields of correction and child welfare have functioned this way in the past.

Second, any claims about an expertise that can be termed a scientific approach to correction are quite premature. There does not now exist a clear-cut body of knowledge that can be ordered in a text or verbally transmitted that will direct any trained practitioner to diagnose and treat effectively such classic problems as truancy, running away and precocious sex experimentation. Unlike the field of medicine, there are no clear-cut prescriptions for professional behavior that can provide an intellectual rationale for expecting a remission of symptoms. There exist bits and pieces of knowledge and practical wisdom, but there is no correctional technology in any acceptable scientific sense.

Third, a reasonable appraisal of evaluations of current approaches to delinquents indicates that there are, in fact, no programs that can claim superiority. The studies do indicate that we can institutionalize far fewer children in treatment centers or reform schools without increasing the risks for individuals or communities; or, if we continue to use institutional programs, young people can be held for shorter periods of time without increasing the risk. The outcome of these appraisals provides a case for an expansion of humane child care activities—not for or against any specific repertoire of intervention techniques.

Fourth, many existing correctional programs are not now controlled by professionals. Untrained juvenile court judges are administratively responsible for detention programs and probation services in more than a majority of the 50 states. Many correctional programs have been headed by political appointees or nonprofessionals. And state legislatures, often dominated by rural legislators, have exercised a very strong influence in the permissible range of program alternatives.

Fifth, the professionalization of officials dealing with delinquent youth does not always lead to happy results. There are studies that indicate that many trained policemen and judges officially process and detain more young people than untrained officials, indicating that their definition of delinquency has been broadened by psychiatric knowledge. At this point in time, there is a distinct danger that excessive professionalization can lead to overintervention in the lives of children and their families.

Sixth, there is no assurance that professionals are any more responsive to the interests and desires of local residents than are untrained judges and probation officers. Citizens, sharing a similar life style and knowledgeable about the problems of growing up in a given community, may be in a better position to enact a *parens patrie* doctrine than are professionals or judges.

Seventh, in ghetto communities, reliance on professional expertise can mean continued dependence on white authority systems. Identification of family and child welfare boards as "our own" may compensate for any lack of expertise by removing the suspicion that any change of behavior by children and parents is for the benefit of the white establishment. The additional community benefits to be gained from caring for "our own" may also outweigh any loss of professional skills. The benefits accruing from indigenous control over local child welfare services would hold for other minority groups living in a discriminatory environment: Indians, Puerto Ricans, Mexicans, hillbillies and French Canadians.

Alternative Policy Proposals

The proposal to create family and child welfare boards to deal with juvenile status offenses may be appealing to many people. However, gaining political acceptance may be quite difficult, since the juvenile justice system would be giving up coercive power in an area that it has controlled for a long period of time. The proposal may appear reasonable, but it may constitute too radical a break with the past for a majority of state legislators. In addition, the interest groups that might push for it are not readily visible. Perhaps participants in the Women's Lib movement, student activists and black power groups might get interested in the issue of injustice against youth, but this is a hope more than a possibility. In the event of overwhelming opposition, there exist two policy proposals that might be more acceptable and could aid in the decriminalization of juvenile status offenses.

The two alternatives function at different ends of the traditional justice system. One proposal, suggested by the President's Task Force on Delinquency, would set up a Youth Service Bureau that would offer local field services and be operated by civil authorities as an alternative to formal adjudication; the second proposal, suggested by William Sheridan of the Department of Health, Education, and Welfare, would prohibit the mixing of juvenile status offenders and classic delinquents in the same institutions. The Youth Service Bureau would function between the police and the court, while the prohibition would function after judicial disposition. Both proposals, separate or in concert, could aid in the decriminalization of our current practices.

However, both proposals would still leave open the possibility of stigmatization of youth who had committed no crimes. The Youth Service Bureau would provide an array of services at the community level, but the court would still have ultimate jurisdiction over its case load, and any competition over jurisdiction would probably be won by the traditional court system. The prohibition of mixing in institutions would, of course, not change the fact that young people were still being adjudicated in the same court as delinquents, even though they had committed no crimes. In addition, the proposal, as currently conceived, does not affect mixing in detention facilities. These limitations are evident in the statutes of states that have recently changed their definitions of "delinquency" (New York, California, Illinois, Colorado, Kansas, Oklahoma and Vermont).

Both proposals deserve support, but they clearly leave the traditional system intact. It is possible that Youth Service Bureaus could be organized with a significant role for citizen participation, thus paving the way for an eventual take-over of legal jurisdiction from the juvenile court for juvenile status offenses (and dependency and neglect cases, too). It is conceivable, too, that any prohibitions of mixing could lead to the increased placement of children in trouble in foster homes and group homes, instead of reform schools, and to the provision of homemaker services and educational programs for harried parents unable to cope with the problems of children. Both short-range proposals could, in practice, evolve a different mode of handling delinquents without crimes.

The adaptation of these two reasonable proposals into an evolutionary strategy is conceivable. But it is also likely they will just be added to the system, without altering its jurisdiction and its stigmatic practices. In the event this occurs, new reformers might entertain the radical strategy that some European countries achieved many years ago—removal of juvenile status offenders from the jurisdiction of the judicial-correctional system and their inclusion into the family and child welfare system.

New Definitions

What is the guarantee that young people will be serviced any more effectively by their removal from the traditional correctional system? The question is valid, but perhaps it underestimates the potency of social definitions. Children, as well as adults, are liable to be treated according to the social category to which they have been assigned. Any shift in the categorization of youth that yields a more positive image can influence such authorities as teachers, employers, military recruiters and housing authority managers. For there is abundant evidence that the stigma of delinquency can have negative consequences for an individual as an adult, as well as during childhood.

It is evident, too, that our old social definitions of what constitutes delinquency have led us to construct a system of juvenile justice that is quite unjust. By failing to make reasonable distinctions and define them precisely, we not only treat juvenile status offenders more harshly but undermine any semblance of ordered justice for *all* illegal behavior committed by juveniles. Maintenance of existing jurisdictional and definitional boundaries helps to perpetuate an unjust system for treating children. That this unjust system may also be a self-defeating one that compounds the original problem should also be taken into account before prematurely concluding that a shift in social labeling procedures is but a minor reform.

We would agree, however, with the conclusion that a mere semantic shift in the social definition of children in trouble is not sufficient. The experience of New York in providing a social label of "person in need of supervision" (PINS)—without providing alternative civil modes for responding to this new distinction—indicates that reform can sometimes take the guise of "word magic." Children are often accused of believing in the intrinsic power of words and oaths; adults can play the game on an even larger scale.

We need alternative social resources for responding to our change in social definitions, if we are at all serious about dealing with the problem. Whether we are willing to pay the financial costs for these alternatives is, of course, problematic. One approach to this issue might be to identify funds currently spent for noncriminal youth in the traditional police, court, and correctional subsystems, and then reallocate the identified dollars into a new child welfare service. This reallocation strategy would not require new funding, but merely a financial shift to follow our new social definitions and intended responses. The choices would be primarily legal, political, and moral ones and not new economic decisions.

A second strategy for funding a new policy might be based on a more rational approach to the problem. We could attempt to assess the societal "need" for such services and then compute the amount of financial resources required to meet this newly assumed public responsibility. This approach could prove more costly than the reallocation strategy. Conceivably, the strategies of assessed need and reallocation could be combined at the same time or over the years. However, whether we might be willing to tax ourselves to support a more reasonable and moral social policy may turn out to be a critical issue. Perceived in this manner, the problem of defining and responding to children in trouble is as much financial as it is political, legal, and moral. But this, too, is an integral part of the American approach to delinquents without crimes.

Violence and Inner City Families

Harris Chaiklin,
Paul H. Ephross,
and Richard Sterne

Violence is endemic in American society, especially among the urban poor. In the past, frontier expansion and presumed cultural characteristics of immigrants were deemed sufficient explanations for periodic epidemics of violence, but the old shibboleths no longer fit our current social malaise. A new rationale for lawlessness has been found: violence is now considered part of the political value structure of Negro inner-city residents, our newest "immigrants."

In this new "official interpretation" a subtle but devastating shift has taken place in the stereotypical description of those who live in urban poverty. Depending on the social philosophy of the observer, the poor were formerly described as downtrodden, exploited and unhappy, or as irresponsible, unreliable and free spirits. Regardless of the vantage point of those who portrayed the moneyless, it was agreed that violence occurred frequently and that the "worthy poor" needed and wanted protection from the criminals in their midst. Today the urban poor, chiefly nonwhite, are pictured as bitter, resentful and hostile people who condone crime as an act of political liberation and praise violence as a means of forcing "the establishment" to meet their needs. The police are seen as agents of an occupying colonial power.

Our most prestigous public documents project this image. For example, the Kerner Commission reported that

> Negroes firmly believe that police brutality and harassment occur repeatedly in Negro neighborhoods. This belief is unquestionably one of the major reasons for intense Negro resentment against the police.

This "official" view is supported by and in part derived from the investigations and commentary of social scientists who study our social defects. For example, Richard R. Kern, who is usually a perceptive student of deviance, says in *Juvenile Delinquency*:

> Negro crime and violence within the ghetto divided the community against itself, and forced the law-abiding Negro into an uneasy alliance with the most visible symbol of white oppression, the policeman. But of late the alliance has been breaking down. By the 1960's the zealousness of white law enforcement had become a greater irritation than Negro crime.
>
> "Police brutality" had become a rallying cry which united the law-abiding with the law-violator in a common cause against a common oppressor.

Taken together these statements are a devasting and dismal view of the attitudes which poor people are supposed to have about violence. They also presume a remarkable degree of mass identification with the aggressor; the victims are now supposed to be pleased with being victimized.

Is this an accurate portrayal of the way most inner-city inhabitants respond to the violence around them? The Kerner Commission conclusion is presented without the customary cautions one expects in a generalization meant to apply to 24 million people. It is supported with a scattering of survey findings, obtained chiefly from nonprobability samples of young Negro males. Kern argues that Negro reaction against police brutality is so extreme that the entire community is willing to stand with its internal exploiters to dispose of its external tormentors.

Wherever there is extreme poverty young men commit

violent crimes and the police respond with counter-crimes often enough to allow both sets of participants in this macabre interaction to rationalize their actions, but this is not the constant nor predominant activity of either group. Still less is it the preoccupation of children, adult family heads and the aged, who are faced with the task of maintaining a coherent life in a dangerous environment.

The Kerner Commission, despite its estimate of Negro hostility towards the police, found that physical police brutality per se was not frequent. They concluded:

> In assessing the impact of police misconduct we emphasize that the improper acts of a relatively few officers may create severe tensions between the department and the entire Negro community.

Indeed they may. After each incident, community residents may be expected to express strong, negative feelings, but it does not follow that these are pervasive and enduring attitudes or that inner-city residents support all violent acts, even those directed against themselves. Yet, somehow the attitudes of a relatively few articulate and often self-appointed spokesmen have become accepted as the community's predominant view toward violence. Such attitudes have masked the real views and feelings of the majority who suffer from the lawlessness of inner-city life.

What are the majority attitudes of inner-city people toward the police and violence? As part of an evaluation of a welfare project we conducted a mail survey. The program had been designed to offer financial and service supplements to large inner-city AFDC families and was carried out by the Community Relations Division of the Baltimore City Department of Social Services.

Part of the survey developed a picture of the way welfare recipients view the world. The questionnaire was mailed from a university address. Mothers were promised anonymity and standard follow-up procedures were used. Of the 250 mothers in the program, 223 (89 percent) returned a questionnaire. Another seven (3 percent) were unable to complete the schedule because of sickness or other family problems.

The 89 percent response rate was achieved because of the positive attitudes the mothers had toward the program. The responses to an open-ended question indicate that mothers filled out the schedule because they wanted to do something for a program which had treated them like human beings. One mother put it very succinctly:

1. They were always willing to be helpful.
2. They would stand behind you, in times of trouble.
3. They let you voice your own opinion about matters concerning you and your family. They tried to awaken you to law, and your rights as a recipient. They should be allowed to stay instead of sending people to the moon.

The only concerns voiced about the mothers' willingness to cooperate came from the staff. At conferences held to discuss questionnaire form and content doubts were raised as to whether the mothers could understand the questions. The staff thought that there would be objections to questions on race and social attitudes, but the mothers had no such qualms. The care and attention that respondents gave to completing the questionnaire was remarkable. When poor mail service delayed delivery two mothers called us to complain because they thought they were being left out of the survey.

Table 1 shows the responses to the question "What is a policeman's job, mainly?" The attitudes of these female heads of large, Negro, welfare-receiving families toward the police was generally positive; only two responses fall in the negative categories.

TABLE 1

	Number	Percent
What is a policeman's job, mainly?		
To protect you	218	98
To keep an eye on you	1	—
To bother you	1	—
No answer	3	2
Total	223	100

TABLE 2

	Number	Percent
How do you feel when a police car comes into your neighborhood?		
I feel more secure	70	32
I feel curious	24	11
I feel afraid	1	—
I feel nervous	7	3
I don't notice	11	5
I get the feeling something's wrong	89	40
I'm not sure	20	9
No answer	1	—
Total	223	100

TABLE 3

In Baltimore, how would you say that the police treat blacks?	Number	Percent
Very well	21	9
Fairly well	95	43
Fairly badly	20	9
Very badly	22	10
Don't Know	63	28
No answer	2	1
Total	223	100

Table 2 shows the responses to the question, "How do you feel when a police car comes into the neighborhood?" The replies do not indicate great fear about the presence of the police, but for the most part reflect normal human concerns: when the police arrive something must be wrong, and if it is I feel better that they are here. Fear and nervousness accounted for only eight out of the 223 responses.

Table 3 shows responses to the direct question, "In Baltimore, how would you say that the police treat blacks?" There is no rousing enthusiasm for the police, but at least half the mothers were willing to say the police were treating Negroes fairly well. Even if the "don't know" responses are counted as negative, the picture is not one of a people whose only desire is to "off the pig."

The attitudes of these mothers toward the police are not strikingly different from those in any other segment of society. They know what a policeman should do; when he arrives they are ambivalent; and they think he treats people fairly well, though they have enough experience to know that he sometimes doesn't.

Have we obtained an honest and accurate picture of the way these women feel about the police? We think so, and the pattern of their responses to other attitudinal questions supports this interpretation.

These mothers have retained a belief in the American dream and the Protestant ethic. Eighty percent (177) feel that having to struggle for what you get in life is the best way to develop character. Seventy-six percent (170) feel that any able-bodied person who refuses a job should not receive assistance. Seventy-two percent (160) feel that except when there is a depression anyone can get a job if he tries. And they tend to be racial integrationists rather than separatists. When asked their preferred racial composition in a well-kept neighborhood only 6 percent (14) picked mostly black but 28 percent (63) picked half-and-half, and 58 percent (129) chose "no difference."

The mothers' strong support of the dominant American value system is matched by a realistic perception of the extent to which they do not participate in it. Only 12 percent (26) of the mothers describe their neighborhood as a good place to raise children. Sixty-one percent (131) definitely do not feel that they could get a job that would enable them to support their family adequately right now; and 30 percent (66) do not know whether they could get such a job. This estimate is backed up by a staff review for referral to the Work Incentive Program (WIN), which indicated that very few referrals could be made. Fewer than half of the 44 mothers (18 percent) who worked earned as much as 50 percent of the state grant standard for their family; i.e., $40 per person per month. Yet such is the belief in the work ethic that 52 percent (117) of the mothers feel that with job training they could support their family.

The mothers are optimistic about the world in general and about the future; 55 percent (122) think that things are getting better for poor people in Baltimore, and 78 percent (172) say that things will be better for them ten years from now. It is in the here and now that things are not so good; only 27 percent (59) described 1970 as a good year for their family.

There is little that is dramatic in the way these mothers look at the world. Their attitudes are conventional, and they are also poignant for they are pervaded by a realistic view of the extent to which they and their children cannot participate in what our society promises to all. This is reflected in the way one mother wrote about how she felt about the program:

> They brought my family and I from a long ways. They got me out of the geto. An all so gave pride I am able to feel like a person. Before I was ashamed for someone to come visit me all so I was shame for my children to play with other children as they had nice clothes and because of the family living all this has been granted to me. When this program go down I am wondering whats next. I wish I could explain how much it meant to me I thank you all so much. an god.

These mothers do not support violence of any sort. They can be indignant about specific instances of police brutality, but they are much more concerned about the realities of their day-to-day struggle to make ends meet. Burdened by poverty and its almost equally crushing counterpart, the relative deprivation which comes from living in an affluent society, they have not let their struggle to stay alive prevent them from internalizing basic social values.

These women do not see the police as enemies to be feared and distrusted and there is considerable evidence that this is the view of the overwhelming majority of inner-city residents. In a planning survey conducted by the University of Maryland Community Mental Health Center the police were always ranked second or third as the resource to be turned to if there were a disturbed member of the family. They never were mentioned as being among the most serious problems in the community, though various forms of crime were. And more police protection was ranked high on the list of outside resources needed for dealing with the community's problems.

Most major studies of inner-city life make relatively little mention of the police. Elliot Liebow identifies the crucial concerns of poor Negro men on Tally's Corner in Washington, D.C. as those common to all people: the need for sex and love in a loveless world; difficulty in maintaining family life and family roles; and economic deprivation. Liebow does not characterize the policeman as a significant part of the lives of Tally and his associates, nor does he attribute to them positive or negative feelings toward the police even when he describes members of a crowd viewing a particularly difficult arrest.

Camille Jeffers' participant observation study of the poor in a Washington housing project does not mention the police at all. She does reach a conclusion which is similar to ours:

If we see the low-income people who live in certain sections of our American cities as indigenous to a particular area or as bearers of a different culture (when it is highly doubtful that the areas or cultures are as different as usage and assertion indicate), we are committing, wittingly or unwittingly, descriptive and labelling errors that endanger our efforts to help urban poor people and to help them help themselves. . . . Another danger in the loose use of indigenous in contemporary settings where low-income families live is that it leads to false assumptions about what people want, and underestimations of their ability to assess accurately their needs, wants and what they get in promises and services.

What most of the poor want is help in being able to help themselves. One mother wrote:

Family living project has help many mother as far as getting things for their families. And it help mother to stand on their own feet and be just a little more independence as far as help to provide for their family. . . . I'm truly sorry that every mother in Baltimore would not receive these services. It should not end because of

the help it is to the family. And not just money wise but learning to become friends with your worker and understand that being poor is nothing to be ashamed of.

Most Negro poor people are not involved in the rhetoric of separatism and revolution which is projected as the prevailing need in the inner city. Donald Brieland, who investigated the racial preferences of low income Negroes for helping persons, concluded:

This study does *not* show that white helping persons are unwelcome in black neighborhoods. . . . The study also reinforces the importance of competence as the first requirement in selection of staff members. . . . As one person said, "Black awareness was clearly within the awareness of the subjects, but they did not let it get in their way in their quest for effective service."

The desire to be independent and to get competent help in achieving independence are the real concerns of the inner-city poor. Concern about police brutality does not loom large in their minds. What does is lack of protection and effective law enforcement. Even the Kerner Commission makes grudging admission of this:

The strength of ghetto feelings about hostile police conduct may even be exceeded by the conviction that ghetto neighborhoods are not given adequate police protection.

It is regrettable that the Commission did not provide a definitive answer to such a crucial question. There is, however, evidence about how the poor people feel about this. In a feature story on crime in Baltimore, *Life* magazine reported the results of a Louis Harris survey as follows:

High-crime area residents put more emphasis on increasing the *number* of police and improving antipoverty programs. Low-crime area residents put heavier emphasis on increasing the *authority* of police and cracking down on black militants.

In other words, the poor are asking for peaceful alternatives and the middle class want violent solutions to social problems.

Why, then, have some intellectuals—and some social scientists—distorted the attitudes towards violence to be found among poor, urban blacks? The reasons, we suggest, are to be found in the fears and misperceptions of the researchers. The middle class has helped to create a world it does not understand. William Braden has recently summarized his argument on this subject as follows:

There is a possibility that the Technological Juggernaut already is out of control — rumbling down a mountain while the managers oil its wheels. Nobody is really steering it. Not the Congress or the President or the merit-badge bureaucrats or anybody else.

Nobody is in charge. That is more frightening to contemplate than a competent dictatorship, benevolent or otherwise.

As it has become apparent that something is wrong and that past prescriptions will not cure current problems, some intellectuals have attempted to find a way to deal with their frustrations. One answer has been to create a new "noble savage," a man of violence who uses aggression as a political purification rite.

A new set of stereotypes has replaced the old picture of ghetto blacks as innocent, child-like, laughing (and always musical). Blacks in the ghetto are now thought to be angry, militant and gun-toting. They do not sing hymns, they shout slogans. The young intellectual who in his entire life has neither taken nor given a punch in anger can romanticize about the black militant and not be aware that he is stereotyping and dehumanizing just as surely and perhaps more destructively than the overt racist ever did. He gives cocktail parties to benefit those whose rhetoric is the most violent and seeks to force black people to illustrate his own fantasies. Albert Murray incisively describes the process:

As for those militant, and in truth somewhat envious black rhetoricians who (to the delight of white do-gooders and do-badders alike) accuse affluent black inhabitants of the "integrated" suburbs of having deserted the cause, they should take a more careful look. The minute a Negro moves into any integrated situation in the U.S. he becomes blacker than ever before. Ever so friendly white suburbanites almost always insist that their black neighbors identify themselves as a part of black suffering everywhere. White integrationists are far more likely to condemn and reject their clean-cut professionally competent black neighbors for not being black enough than to congratulate them or simply accept them for not being problems. "Man," said one middle aged black resident of Westchester County, a man who has spent his whole life working for better Negro education, job opportunities, and civil rights, "you go to one of those parties and fail to show the proper enthusiasm for Malcolm, Rap and Cleaver, and then some ofay millionaire and his wife will call you an Uncle Tom to your face! And you know who will back them up? Almost every establishment editor present. Man, its getting so that if you don't go in there pissing and moaning and making threats, they'll call you a moderate and drop your butt fifty times faster than Malcolm ever would. You got to cuss them out, or you're out of it, buddy. But damn, man, the minute you sound off you realize that they've tricked you into scat singing and buck dancing for them; because they are all crowding around like watching you masturbate, like they are ready to clap their hands and yell, 'Go man, go. Get hot, man. But Goddamnit you know what they really want you to be? A blind man with a guitar!' "

Out of such illusion-making exercises has grown the fantasy that there is general support for violence in all segments of the Negro community. That is not true. Those who reside in the inner city are the major victims of violence, whether from crime or riot. They do not see crime as an act of political guerrilla warfare. They see it as something to be feared and something from which they want protection and relief. In the face of the violence they live with, and despite middle-class fantasies, they have retained a faith in democracy. What they have trouble doing is getting a genuine response to their needs, feelings and aspirations.

The inner-city Negro family has enough to bear without being made to say that it loves its misery. Our new conventional wisdom about violence in the inner city says more about the perceivers than the perceived. The effects of violence on inner-city families are the same as they have always been: additional suffering for people whose lives are filled with misery. Middle-class frustration with the state of the world should not be allowed to replace old stereotypes with new ones that hide the real needs of the poor in our society.

The Serpent-Handling Religions of West Virginia

Nathan L. Gerrard

"... And these signs shall follow them that believe; In my name shall they cast out devils; they shall speak with new tongues; They shall take up serpents; and if they drink any deadly thing, it shall not hurt them; they shall lay hands on the sick, and they shall recover." *Mark* 16:17-18

In Southern Appalachia, two dozen or three dozen fundamentalist congregations take this passage literally and "take up serpents." They use copperheads, water moccasins, and rattlesnakes in their religious services.

The serpent-handling ritual was inaugurated between 1900 and 1910, probably by George Went Hensley. Hensley began evangelizing in rural Grasshopper Valley, Tenn., then traveled widely throughout the South, particularly in Kentucky, spreading his religion. He died in Florida at 70—of snakebite. To date, the press has reported about 20 such deaths among the serpent-handlers. One other death was recorded last year, in Kentucky.

For seven years, my wife and I have been studying a number of West Virginia serpent-handlers, primarily in order to discover what effect this unusual form of religious practice has on their lives. Although serpent-handling is outlawed by the state legislatures of Kentucky, Virginia, and Tennessee and by municipal ordinances in North Carolina, it is still legal in West Virginia. One center is the Scrabble Creek Church of All Nations in Fayette County, about 37 miles from Charleston. Another center is the Church of Jesus in Jolo, McDowell County, one of the most poverty-stricken areas of the state. Serpent-handling is also practiced sporadically elsewhere in West Virginia, where it is usually led by visitors from Scrabble Creek or Jolo.

The Jolo church attracts people from both Virginia and Kentucky, in addition to those from West Virginia.

Members of the Scrabble Creek church speak with awe of the Jolo services, where people pick up large handfuls of poisonous snakes, fling them to the ground, pick them up again, and thrust them under their shirts or blouses, dancing ecstatically. We attended one church service in Scrabble Creek where visitors from Jolo covered their heads with clusters of snakes and wore them as crowns.

Serpent-handling was introduced to Scrabble Creek in 1941 by a coal miner from Harlan, Ky. The practice really began to take hold in 1946, when the present leader of the Scrabble Creek church, then a member of the Church of God, first took up serpents. The four or five original serpent-handlers in Fayette County met at one another's homes until given the use of an abandoned one-room school house in Big Creek. In 1959, when their number had swelled several times over, they moved to a larger church in Scrabble Creek.

Snakebites, Saints, and Scoffers

During the course of our seven-year study, about a dozen members of the church received snakebites. (My wife and I were present on two of these occasions.) Although there were no deaths, each incident was widely and unfavorably publicized in the area. For their part, the serpent-handlers say the Lord causes a snake to strike in order to refute scoffers' claims that the snakes' fangs have been pulled. They see each recovery from snakebite as a miracle wrought by the Lord—and each death as a sign that the Lord "really had to show the scoffers how dangerous it is to obey His commandments." Since adherents believe that death brings one to the throne of God, some express an eagerness to die when He decides they are ready. Those who have been bitten and who have recovered seem to receive special deference from other members of the church.

The ritual of serpent-handling takes only 15 or 20 minutes in religious sessions that are seldom shorter than four hours. The rest of the service includes singing Christian hymns, ecstatic dancing, testifying, extemporaneous and impassioned sermons, faith-healing, "speaking in tongues," and foot-washing. These latter rituals are a part of the firmly-rooted Holiness movement, which encompasses thousands of churches in the Southern Appalachian region. The Holiness churches started in the 19th century as part of a perfectionist movement.

The social and psychological functions served by the Scrabble Creek church are probably very much the same as those served by the more conventional Holiness churches. Thus, the extreme danger of the Scrabble Creek rituals probably helps to validate the members' claims to holiness. After all, the claim that one is a living saint is pretentious even in a sacred society—and it is particularly difficult to maintain in a secular society. That the serpent-handler regularly risks his life for his religion is seen as evidence of his saintliness. As the serpent-handler stresses over and over, "I'm afraid of snakes like anybody else, but when God anoints me, I handle them with joy." The fact that he is usually not bitten, or if bitten usually recovers, is cited as further evidence of his claim to holiness.

After we had observed the Scrabble Creek serpent-handlers for some time, we decided to give them psychological tests. We enlisted the aid of Auke Tellegen, department of psychology, University of Minnesota, and three of his clinical associates: James Butcher, William Schofield, and Anne Wirt. They interpreted the Minnesota Multiphasic Personality Inventory that we administered to 50 serpent-handlers (46 were completed)—and also to 90 members of a conventional-denomination church 20 miles from Scrabble Creek. What we wanted to find out was how these two groups differed.

What we found were important personality differences not only between the serpent-handlers and the conventional church members, but also between the older and the younger generations within the conventional group. We believe that these differences are due, ultimately, to differences in social class: The serpent-handlers come from the nonmobile working class (average annual income: $3000), whereas members of

the conventional church are upwardly mobile working-class people (average annual income: $5000) with their eyes on the future.

But first, let us consider the similarities between the two groups. Most of the people who live in the south central part of West Virginia, serpent-handlers or not, have similar backgrounds. The area is rural, nonfarm, with only about one-tenth of the population living in settlements of more than 2500. Until recently, the dominant industry was coal-mining, but in the last 15 years mining operations have been drastically curtailed. The result has been widespread unemployment. Scrabble Creek is in that part of Appalachia that has been officially declared a "depressed area"—which means that current unemployment rates there often equal those of the depression.

There are few foreign-born in this part of West Virginia. Most of the residents are of Scottish-Irish or Pennsylvania Dutch descent, and their ancestors came to the New World so long ago that there are no memories of an Old World past.

Generally, public schools in the area are below national standards. Few people over 50 have had more than six or seven years of elementary education.

Religion has always been important here. One or two generations ago, the immediate ancestors of both serpent-handlers and conventional-church members lived in the same mining communities and followed roughly the same religious practices. Today there is much "backsliding," and the majority seldom attend church regularly. But there is still a great deal of talk about religion, and there are few professed atheists.

Hypochondria and the Holy Spirit

Though the people of both churches are native-born Protestants with fundamentalist religious beliefs, little education, and precarious employment, the two groups seem to handle their common problems in very different ways. One of the first differences we noticed was in the way the older members of both churches responded to illness and old age. Because the members of both churches had been impoverished and medically neglected during childhood and young adulthood, and because they had earned their livelihoods in hazardous and health-destroying ways, they were old before their time. They suffered from a wide variety of physical ailments. Yet while the older members of the conventional church seemed to dwell morbidly on their physical disabilities, the aged serpent-handlers seemed able to cheerfully ignore their ailments.

The serpent-handlers, in fact, went to the opposite extreme. Far from being pessimistic hypochondriacs like the conventional-church members, the serpent-handlers were so intent on placing their fate in God's benevolent hands that they usually failed to take even the normal precautions in caring for their health. Three old serpent-handlers we knew in Scrabble Creek were suffering from serious cardiac conditions. But when the Holy Spirit moved them, they danced ecstatically and violently. And they did this without any apparent harm.

No matter how ill the old serpent-handlers are, unless they are actually prostrate in their beds they manage to attend and enjoy church services lasting four to six hours, two or three times a week. Some have to travel long distances over the mountains to get to church. When the long sessions are over, they appear refreshed rather than weary.

One evening an elderly woman was carried into the serpent-handling church in a wheelchair. She had had a severe stroke and was almost completely paralyzed. Wheeled to the front of the church, she watched everything throughout the long services. During one particularly frenzied singing and dancing session, the fingers of her right hand tapped lightly against the arm of the chair. This was the only movement she was able to make, but obviously she was enjoying the service. When friends leaned over and offered to take her home, she made it clear she was not ready to go. She stayed until the end, and gave the impression of smiling when she was finally wheeled out. Others in the church apparently felt pleased rather than depressed by her presence.

Both old members of the conventional denomination and old serpent-handlers undoubtedly are frequently visited by the thought of death. Both rely on religion for solace, but the serpent-handlers evidently are more successful. The old serpent-handlers are not frightened by the prospect of death. This is true not only of those members who handle poisonous snakes in religious services, but also of the minority who do *not* handle serpents.

One 80-year-old member of the Scrabble Creek church—who did not handle serpents—testified in our presence: "I am not afraid to meet my Maker in Heaven. I am ready. If somebody was to wave a gun in my face, I would not turn away. I am in God's hands."

Another old church member, a serpent-handler, was dying from silicosis. When we visited him in the hospital he appeared serene, although he must have known that he would not live out the week.

The assertion of some modern theologians that whatever meaning and relevance God once may have had has been lost for modern man does not apply to the old serpent-handlers. To them, God is real. In fact, they often see Him during vivid hallucinations. He watches over the faithful. Misfortune and even death do not shake their faith, for misfortune is interpreted, in accordance with God's inscrutable will, as a hidden good.

Surprisingly, the contrast between the optimistic old serpent-handlers and the pessimistic elders of the conventional church all but disappeared when we shifted to the younger members of the two groups. Both groups of young people, on the psychological tests, came out as remarkably well adjusted. They showed none of the neurotic and depressive tendencies of the older conventional-church members. And this cheerful attitude prevailed despite the fact that many of them, at least among the young serpent-handlers, had much to be depressed about.

The young members of the conventional church are much better off, socially and economically, than the young serpent-handlers. The parents of the young conventional-church members can usually provide the luxuries that most young Americans regard as necessities. Many conventional-church youths are active in extracurricular activities in high school or are attending college. The young serpent-handlers, in contrast, are shunned and stigmatized as "snakes." Most young members of the conventional denomination who are in high school intend to go on to college, and they will undoubtedly attain a higher socioeconomic status than their parents have attained. But most of the young serpent-handlers are not attending school. Many are unemployed. None attend or plan to attend college, and they often appear quite depressed about their economic prospects.

The young serpent-handlers spend a great deal of time wandering aimlessly up and down the roads of the hollows, and undoubtedly are bored when not attending church. Their conversation is sometimes marked by humor, with undertones of cynicism and bitterness. We are convinced that what prevents many of them from becoming delinquent or demoralized is their wholehearted participation in religious practices that provide an acceptable outlet for their excess energy, and strengthen their self-esteem by giving them the opportunity to achieve "holiness."

Now, how does all this relate to the class differences between the serpent-handlers and the conventional-church group? The answer is that what allows the serpent-handlers to cope so well with their problems—what allows the older members to rise above the worries of illness and approaching death, and the younger members to remain relatively well-adjusted despite their grim economic prospects—is a certain approach to life that is typical of them as members of the stationary working class. The key to this approach is hedonism.

Hopelessness and Hedonism

The psychological tests showed that the young serpent-handlers, like their elders, were more impulsive and spontaneous than the members of the conventional church. This may account for the strong appeal of the Holiness churches to those members of the stationary working class who prefer religious hedonism to reckless hedonism, with its high incidence of drunkenness and illegitimacy. Religious hedonism is compatible with a puritan morality—and it compensates for its constraints.

The feeling that one cannot plan for the future, expressed in religious terms as "being in God's hands," fosters the widespread conviction among members of the stationary working class that opportunities for pleasure must be exploited immediately. After all, they may never occur again. This attitude is markedly different from that of the upwardly mobile working class, whose members are willing to postpone immediate pleasures for the sake of long-term goals.

Hedonism in the stationary working class is fostered in childhood by parental practices that, while demanding obedience in the home, permit the child license outside the home. Later, during adulthood, this orientation toward enjoying the present and ignoring the future is reinforced by irregular employment and the other insecurities of stationary working-class life. In terms of middle-class values, hedonism is self-defeating. But from a psychiatric point of view, for those who actually have little control of their position in the social and economic structure of modern society, it may very well aid acceptance of the situation. This is particularly true when it takes a religious form of expression. Certainly, hedonism and the associated trait of spontaneity seen in the old serpent-handlers form a very appropriate attitude toward life among old people who can no longer plan for the future.

In addition to being more hedonistic than members of the conventional church, the serpent-handlers are also more exhibitionistic. This exhibitionism and the related need for self-revelation are, of course, directly related to the religious practices of the serpent-handling church. But frankness, both about others and themselves, is typical of stationary working-class people in general. To a large extent, this explains the appeal of the Holiness churches. Ordinarily, their members have little to lose from frankness, since their status pretensions are less than those of the upwardly mobile working class, who are continually trying to present favorable images of themselves.

Because the young members of the conventional denomination are upwardly mobile, they tend to regard their elders as "old-fashioned," "stick-in-the-muds," and "ignorant." Naturally, this lack of respect from their children and grandchildren further depresses the sagging morale of the older conventional-church members. They respond resentfully to the tendency of the young "to think they know more than their elders." The result is a vicious circle of increasing alienation and depression among the older members of the conventional denomination.

Respect for Age

There appears to be much less psychological incompatibility between the old and the young serpent-handlers. This is partly because the old serpent-handlers manage to retain a youthful spontaneity in their approach to life. Then too, the young serpent-handlers do not take a superior attitude toward their elders. They admire their elders for their greater knowledge of the Bible, which both old and young accept as literally true. And they also admire their elders for their handling of serpents. The younger church members, who handle snakes much less often than the older members do, are much more likely to confess an ordinary, everyday fear of snakes—a fear that persists until overcome by strong religious emotion.

Furthermore, the young serpent-handlers do not expect to achieve higher socioeconomic status than their elders. In fact, several young men said they would be satisfied if they could accomplish as much. From the point of view of the stationary working class, many of the older serpent-handlers are quite well-off. They sometimes draw two pensions, one from Social Security and one from the United Mine Workers.

Religious serpent-handling, then—and all the other emotionalism of the Holiness churches that goes with it —serves a definite function in the lives of its adherents. It is a safety valve for many of the frustrations of life in present-day Appalachia. For the old, the serpent-handling religion helps soften the inevitability of poor health, illness, and death. For the young, with their poor educations and poor hopes of finding sound jobs, its promise of holiness is one of the few meaningful goals in a future dominated by the apparent inevitability of lifelong poverty and idleness.

The Relief of Welfare

Frances Fox Piven and Richard A. Cloward

Aid to Families with Dependent Children (AFDC) is our major relief program. It has lately become the source of a major public controversy, owing to a large and precipitous expansion of the rolls. Between 1950 and 1960, only 110,000 families were added to the rolls, yielding a rise of 17 percent. In the 1960s, however, the rolls exploded, rising by more than 225 percent. At the beginning of the décade, 745,000 families were receiving aid; by 1970, some 2,500,000 families were on the rolls. Still, this is not the first, the largest or the longest relief explosion. Since the inauguration of relief in Western Europe three centuries ago, the rolls have risen and fallen in response to economic and political forces. An examination of these forces should help to illuminate the meaning of the current explosion, as well as the meaning of current proposals for reform.

Relief arrangements, we will argue, are ancillary to economic arrangements. Their chief function is to regulate labor, and they do that in two general ways. First, when mass unemployment leads to outbreaks of turmoil, relief programs are ordinarily initiated or expanded to absorb and control enough of the unemployed to restore order; then, as turbulence subsides, the relief system contracts, expelling those who are needed to populate the labor market. Relief also performs a labor-regulating function in this shrunken state, however. Some of the aged, the disabled and others who are of no use as workers are left on the relief rolls, and their treatment is so degrading and punitive as to instill in the laboring masses a fear of the fate that awaits them should they relax into beggary and pauperism. To demean and punish those who do not work is to exalt by contrast even the meanest labor at the meanest wages. These regulative functions of relief are made necessary by several strains toward instability inherent in capitalist economics.

Labor and Market Incentives

All human societies compel most of their members to work, to produce the goods and services that sustain the community. All societies also define the work their members must do and the conditions under which they must do it. Sometimes the authority to compel and define is fixed in tradition, sometimes in the bureaucratic agencies of a central government. Capitalism, however, relies primarily upon the mechanisms of a market—the promise of financial rewards or penalties—to motivate men and women to work and to hold them to their occupational tasks.

But the development of capitalism has been marked by periods of cataclysmic change in the market, the main sources being depression and rapid modernization. Depressions mean that the regulatory structure of the market simply collapses; with no demand for labor, there are no monetary rewards to guide and enforce work. By contrast, during periods of rapid modernization—whether the replacement of handicraft by machines, the relocation of factories in relation to new sources of power or new outlets for distribution, or the demise of family subsistence farming as large-scale commercial agriculture spreads—portions of the laboring population may be rendered obsolete or at least temporarily maladjusted. Market incentives do not collapse; they are simply not sufficient to compel people to abandon one way of working and living in favor of another.

In principle, of course, people dislocated by modernization become part of a labor supply to be drawn upon by a changing and expanding labor market. As history shows, however, people do not adapt so readily to drastically altered methods of work and to the new and alien patterns of social life dictated by that work. They may resist leaving their traditional communities and the only life they know. Bred to labor under the discipline of sun and season, however severe that discipline may be, they may resist the discipline of factory and machine, which, though it may be no more severe, may seem so because it is alien. The process of human adjustment to such economic changes has ordinarily entailed generation of mass unemployment, distress and disorganization.

Now, if human beings were invariably given to enduring these travails with equanimity, there would be no governmental relief systems at all. But often they do not, and for reasons that are not difficult to see. The regulation of civil behavior in all societies is intimately dependent on stable occupational arrangements. So long as people are fixed in their work roles, their activities and outlooks are also fixed; they do what they must and think what they must. Each behavior and attitude is shaped by the reward of a good harvest or the penalty of a bad one, by the factory paycheck or the danger of losing it. But mass unemployment breaks that bond, loosening people from the main institution by which they are regulated and controlled.

Moreover, mass unemployment that persists for any length of time diminishes the capacity of other institutions to bind and constrain people. Occupational behaviors and outlooks underpin a way of life and determine familial, communal and cultural patterns. When large numbers of people are suddenly barred from their traditional occupations, the entire network of social control is weakened. There is no harvest or paycheck to enforce work and the sentiments that uphold work; without work, people cannot conform to familial and communal roles; and if the dislocation is widespread, the legitimacy of the social order itself may come to be questioned. The result is usually civil disorder—crime, mass protests, riots—a disorder that may even threaten to overturn existing social and economic arrangements. It is then that relief programs are initiated or expanded.

Western relief systems originated in the mass disturbances that erupted during the long transition from feudalism to capitalism beginning in the sixteenth century. As a result of the declining death rates in the previous century, the population of Europe grew rapidly; as the population grew, so did transiency and beggary. Moreover, distress resulting from population changes, agricultural and other natural disasters, which had characterized life throughout the Middle Ages, was now exacerbated by the vagaries of an evolving market economy, and outbreaks of turbulence among the poor were frequent. To deal with these threats to civil order, many localities legislated severe penalties against vagrancy. Even before the sixteenth century, the magistrates of Basel had defined twenty-five different categories of beggars, together with appropriate punishments for each. But penalties alone did not always deter begging, especially when economic distress was severe and the numbers affected were large. Consequently, some localities began to augment punishment with provisions for the relief of the vagrant poor.

Civil Disorder and Relief

A French town that initiated such an arrangement early in the sixteenth century was Lyons, which was troubled both by a rapidly growing population and by the economic instability associated with the transition to capitalism. By 1500 Lyons' population had already begun to increase. During the decades that followed, the town became a prosperous commercial and manufacturing center—the home of the European money market and of expanding new trades in textiles, printing and metalworking. As it thrived it attracted people, not only from the surrounding countryside, but even from Italy, Flanders and Germany. All told, the population of Lyons probably doubled between 1500 and 1540.

All this was very well as long as the newcomers could be absorbed by industry. But not all were, with the result that the town came to be plagued by beggars and vagrants. Moreover, prosperity was not continuous: some trades were seasonal and others were periodically troubled by foreign competition. With each economic downturn, large numbers of unemployed workers took to the streets to plead for charity, cluttering the very doorsteps of the better-off classes. Lyons was most vulnerable during periods of bad harvest, when famine not only drove up the cost of bread for urban artisans and journeymen but brought hordes of peasants into the city, where they sometimes paraded through the streets to exhibit their misfortune. In 1529 food riots erupted, with thousands of Lyonnais looting granaries and the homes of the wealthy; in 1530, artisans and journeymen armed themselves and marched through the streets; in 1531, mobs of starving peasants literally overran the town.

Such charity as had previously been given in Lyons was primarily the responsibility of the church or of those of the more prosperous who sought to purchase their salvation through almsgiving. But this method of caring for the needy obviously stimulated rather than discouraged begging and created a public nuisance to the better-off citizens (one account of the times describes famished peasants so gorging themselves as to die on the very doorsteps where they were fed). Moreover, to leave charity to church or citizen meant that few got aid, and those not necessarily according to their need. The result was that mass disorders periodically erupted.

The increase in disorder led the rulers of Lyons to conclude that the giving of charity should no longer be governed by private whim. In 1534, churchmen, notables and merchants joined together to establish a centralized administration for disbursing aid. All charitable donations were consolidated under a central body, the "Aumone-Generale," whose responsibility was to "nourish the poor forever." A list of the needy was established by a house-to-house survey, and tickets for bread and money were issued according to fixed standards. Indeed, most of the features of modern welfare—from criteria to discriminate the worthy poor from the unworthy, to strict procedures for surveillance of recipients as well as measures for their rehabilitation—were present in Lyons' new relief administration. By the 1550s, about 10 percent of the town's population was receiving relief.

Within two years of the establishment of relief in Lyons, King Francis I ordered each parish in France to register its poor and to provide for the "impotent" out of a fund of contributions. Elsewhere in Europe, other townships began to devise similar systems to deal with the vagrants and mobs cast up by famine, rapid population growth and the transition from feudalism to capitalism.

England also felt these disturbances, and just as it pioneered in developing an intensively capitalist economy, so it was at the forefront in developing nation-wide, public relief arrangements. During the closing years of the fifteenth century, the emergence of the wool industry in England began to transform agricultural life. As sheep raising became more profitable, much land was converted from tillage to pasturage, and large numbers of peasants were displaced by an emerging entrepreneurial gentry which either bought their land or cheated them out of it. The result was great tumult among the peasantry, as the Webbs were to note:

> When the sense of oppression became overwhelming, the popular feeling manifested itself in widespread organised tumults, disturbances and insurrections, from Wat Tyler's rebellion of 1381, and Jack Cade's march on London of 1460, to the Pilgrimage of Grace in 1536, and Kett's Norfolk rising of 1549—all of them successfully put down, but sometimes not without great struggle, by the forces which the government could command.

Early in the sixteenth century, the national government moved to try to forestall such disorders. In 1528 the Privy Council, anticipating a fall in foreign sales as a result of the war in Flanders, tried to induce the cloth manufacturers of Suffolk to retain their employees. In 1534, a law passed under Henry VIII attempted to limit the number of sheep in any one holding in order to inhibit the displacement of farmers and agricultural laborers and thus forestall potential disorders. Beginning in the 1550s the Privy Council attempted to regulate the price of grain in poor harvests. But the entrepreneurs of the new market economy were not so readily curbed, so that during this period another method of dealing with labor disorders was evolved.

Early in the sixteenth century, the national government moved to replace parish arrangements for charity with a nation-wide system of relief. In 1531, an act of Parliament decreed that local officials search out and register those of the destitute deemed to be impotent and give them a document authorizing begging. As for those who sought alms without authorization, the penalty was public whipping till the blood ran.

Thereafter, other arrangements for relief were rapidly instituted. An act passed in 1536, during the reign of Henry VIII, required local parishes to take care of their destitute and to establish a procedure for the collection and administration of donations for that purpose by local officials. (In the same year Henry VIII began to expropriate monasteries, helping to assure secular control of charity.) With these developments, the penalties for beggary were made more severe, including an elaborate schedule of branding, enslavement and execution for repeated offenders. Even so, by 1572 beggary was said to have reached alarming proportions, and in that year local responsibility for relief was more fully spelled out by the famous Elizabethan Poor Laws, which established a local tax, known as the poor rate, as the means for financing the care of paupers and required that justices of the peace serve as the overseers of the poor.

After each period of activity, the parish relief machinery tended to lapse into disuse, until bad harvests or depression in manufacturing led again to widespread unemployment and misery, to new outbreaks of disorder, and then to a resuscitation and expansion of relief arrangements. The most illuminating of these episodes, because it bears so much similarity to the present-day relief explosion in the United States, was the expansion of relief during the massive agricultural dislocations of the late eighteenth century.

Most of the English agricultural population had lost its landholdings long before the eighteenth century. In place of the subsistence farming found elsewhere in Europe, a three-tier system of landowners, tenant farmers and agricultural workers had evolved in England. The vast majority of the people were a landless proletariat, hiring out by the year to tenant farmers. The margin of their subsistence, however, was provided by common and waste lands, on which they gathered kindling, grazed animals and hunted game to supplement their meager wages. Moreover, the use of the commons was part of the English villager's birthright, his sense of place and pride. It was the disruption of these arrangements and the ensuing disorder that led to the new expansion of relief.

By the middle of the eighteenth century, an increasing population, advancing urbanization and the growth of manufacturing had greatly expanded markets for agricultural products, mainly for cereals to feed the urban population and for wool to supply the cloth manufacturers. These new markets, together with the introduction of new agricultural methods (such as cross-harrowing), led to large-scale changes in agriculture. To take advantage of rising prices and new techniques, big landowners moved to expand their holdings still further by buying up small farms and, armed with parliamentary Bills of Enclosure, by usurping the common and waste lands which had enabled many small cottagers to survive. Although this process began much earlier, it accelerated rapidly after 1750; by 1850, well over 6 million acres of common land—or about one-quarter of the total arable acreage—had been consolidated into private holdings and turned primarily to grain production. For great numbers of agricultural workers, enclosure meant no land on which to grow subsistence crops to feed their families, no grazing land to produce wool for home spinning and weaving, no fuel to heat their cottages, and new restrictions against hunting. It meant, in short, the loss of a major source of subsistence for the poor.

New markets also stimulated a more businesslike approach to farming. Landowners demanded the maximum rent from tenant farmers, and tenant farmers in turn began to deal with their laborers in terms of cash calculations. Specifically, this meant a shift from a master-servant relationship to an employer-employee relationship, but on the harshest terms. Where laborers had previously worked by the year and frequently lived with the farmer, they were now hired for only as long as they were needed and were then left to fend for themselves. Pressures toward short-term hiring also resulted from the large-scale cultivation of grain crops for market, which called for a seasonal labor force, as opposed to mixed subsistence farming, which required year-round laborers. The use of cash rather than produce as the medium of payment for work, a rapidly spreading practice, encouraged partly by the long-term inflation of grain prices, added to the laborer's hardships. Finally the rapid increase in rural population at a time when the growth of woolen manufacturing continued to provide an incentive to convert land from tillage to pasturage produced a large labor surplus, leaving agricultural workers with no leverage in bargaining for wages with their tenant-farmer employers. The result was widespread unemployment and terrible hardship.

None of these changes took place without resistance from small farmers and laborers who, while they had known hardship before, were now being forced out of a way of life and even out of their villages. Some rioted when Bills of Enclosure were posted; some petitioned the Parliament for their repeal. And when hardship was made more acute by a succession of poor harvests in the 1790s, there were widespread food riots.

Indeed, throughout the late eighteenth and early nineteenth centuries, the English countryside was periodically beseiged by turbulent masses of the displaced rural poor and the towns were racked by Luddism, radicalism, tradeunionism and Chartism, even while the ruling classes worried about what the French Revolution might augur for England. A solution to disorder was needed, and that solution turned out to be relief. The poor relief system—first created in the sixteenth century to control the earlier disturbances caused by population growth and the commercialization of agriculture—now rapidly became a major institution of English life. Between 1760 and 1784, taxes for relief—the poor rate—rose by 60 percent; they doubled by 1801, and rose by 60 percent more in the next decade. By 1818, the poor rate was over six times as high as it had been in 1760. Hobsbaum estimates that up to the 1850s, upwards of 10 percent of the English population were paupers. The relief system, in short, was expanded in order to absorb and regulate the masses of discontented people uprooted from agriculture but not yet incorporated into industry.

Relief arrangements evolved more slowly in the United States, and the first major relief crisis did not occur until the Great Depression. The inauguration of massive reliefgiving was not simply a response to widespread economic distress, for millions had remained unemployed for several years without obtaining aid. What finally led the national government to proffer aid was the great surge of political disorder that followed the economic catastrophe, a disorder which eventually led to the convulsive voting shifts of 1932. After the election, the federal government abandoned its posture of aloofness toward the unemployed. Within a matter of months, billions of dollars were flowing to localities, and the relief rolls skyrocketed. By 1935, upwards of 20 million people were on the dole.

The contemporary relief explosion, which began in the early 1960s, has its roots in agricultural modernization. No one would disagree that the rural economy of America, especially in the South, has undergone a profound transformation in recent decades. In 1945, there was one tractor per farm; in 1964 there were two. Mechanization and other technological developments, in turn, stimulated the enlargement of farm holdings. Between 1959 and 1961, one million farms disappeared; the 3 million remaining farms averaged 377 acres in size—30 percent larger than the average farm ten years earlier. The chief and most obvious effect of these changes was to lessen the need for agricultural labor. In the years between 1950 and 1965 alone, a Presidential Commission on Rural Poverty was to discover, "New machines and new methods increased farm output in the United States by 45 percent, and reduced farm employment by 45 percent." A mere 4 percent of the American labor force now works the land, signalling an extraordinary displacement of people, with accompanying upheaval and suffering. The best summary measure of this dislocation is probably the volume of migration to the cities; over 20 million people, more than 4 million of them black, left the land after 1940.

Nor were all these poor absorbed into the urban economic system. Blacks were especially vulnerable to unemployment. At the close of the Korean War, the national nonwhite unemployment rate leaped from 4.5 percent in 1953 to 9.9 percent in 1954. By 1958, it had reached 12.6 percent, and it fluctuated between 10 and 13 percent until the escalation of the war in Vietnam after 1964.

These figures pertain only to people unemployed and looking for work. They do not include the sporadically unemployed or those employed at extremely low wages. Combining such additional measures with the official unemployment measure produces a subemployment index. This index was first used in 1966—well after the economic downturns that characterized the years between the end of the Korean War and the escalation of the war in Vietnam. Were subemployment data available for the "Eisenhower recession" years, especially in the slum-ghettoes of the larger central cities, they would surely show much higher rates than prevailed in 1966. In any event, the figures for 1966 revealed a nonwhite subemployment rate of 21.6 percent compared with a white rate of 7.6 percent.

However, despite the spread of economic deprivation, whether on the land or in the cities, the relief system did not respond. In the entire decade between 1950 and 1960, the national AFDC caseload rose by only 17 percent. Many of the main urban targets of migration showed equally little change: the rolls in New York City moved up by 16 percent, and in Los Angeles by 14 percent. In the South, the rolls did not rise at all.

But in the 1960s, disorder among the black poor erupted on a wide scale, and the welfare rolls erupted as well. The welfare explosion occurred during several years of the greatest domestic disorder since the 1930s—perhaps the greatest in our history. It was concurrent with the turmoil produced by the civil-rights struggle, with widespread and destructive rioting in the cities, and with the formation of a militant grassroots movement of the poor dedicated to combating welfare restrictions. Not least, the welfare rise was also concurrent with the enactment of a series of ghetto-placating federal programs (such as the antipoverty program) which, among other things, hired thousands of poor people, social workers and lawyers who, it subsequently turned out, greatly stimulated people to apply for relief and helped them obtain it. And the welfare explosion, although an urban phenomenon generally, was greatest in just that handful of large metropolitan counties where the political turmoil of the mid- and late 1960s was the most acute.

The magnitude of the welfare rise is worth noting. The national AFDC caseload rose by more than 225 percent in the 1960s. In New York City, the rise was more than 300 percent; the same was so in Los Angeles. Even in the South, where there had been no rise at all in the 1950s, the rolls rose by more than 60 percent. And most significant of all, the bulk of the increase took place after 1965—that is, after disorder reached a crescendo. More than 80 percent of the national rise in the 1960s occurred in the last five years of the decade. In other words, the welfare rolls expanded, today as at earlier times, only in response to civil disorder.

While muting the more disruptive outbreaks of civil disorder (such as rioting), the mere giving of relief does nothing to reverse the disintegration of lower-class life produced by economic change, a disintegration which leads to rising disorder and rising relief rolls in the first place. Indeed, greatly liberalized relief-giving can further weaken work and family norms. To restore order in a more fundamental sense the society must create the means to reassert its authority. Because the market is unable to control men's behavior a surrogate system of social control must be evolved, at least for a time. Moreoever, if the surrogate system is to be consistent with normally dominant patterns, it must restore people to work roles. Thus even though obsolete or unneded workers are temporarily given direct relief, they are eventually succored only on condition that they work. As these adjustments are made, the functions of relief arrangements may be said to be shifting from regulating disorder to regulating labor.

Restoring Order by Restoring Work

The arrangements, both historical and contemporary, through which relief recipients have been made to work vary, but broadly speaking, there are two main ways: work is provided under public auspices, whether in the recipient's home, in a labor yard, in a workhouse or on a public works project; or work is provided in the private market, whether by contracting or indenturing the poor to private employers, or through subsidies designed to induce employers to hire paupers. And although a relief system may at any time use both of these methods of enforcing work, one or the other usually becomes predominant, depending on the economic conditions that first gave rise to disorder.

Publicly subsidized work tends to be used during business depressions, when the demand for labor in the private market collapses. Conversely, arrangements to channel paupers into the labor market are more likely to be used when rapid changes in markets or technology render a segment of the labor supply temporarily maladapted. In the first case, the relief system augments a shrunken labor market; in the other, its policies and procedures are shaped to overcome the poor fit between labor demand and supply.

Public work is as old as public relief. The municipal relief systems initiated on the Continent in the first quarter of the sixteenth century often included some form of public works. In England, the same statute of 1572 that established taxation as the method for financing poor relief charged the overseers of the poor with putting vagrants to work. Shortly afterwards, in 1576, local officials were directed to acquire a supply of raw goods—wool, hemp, iron—which was to be delivered to the needy for processing in their homes, their dole to be fixed according to "the desert of the work."

The favored method of enforcing work throughout most of the history of relief was the workhouse. In 1723, an act of Parliament permitted the local parishes to establish workhouses and to refuse aid to those poor who would not enter; within ten years, there were said to be about fifty workhouses in the environs of London alone.

The destitute have also sometimes been paid to work in the general community or in their own homes. This method of enforcing work evolved in England during the bitter depression of 1840–1841. As unemployment mounted, the poor in some of the larger cities protested against having to leave their communities to enter workhouses in order to obtain relief, and in any case, in some places the workhouses were already full. As a result, various public spaces were designated as "labor yards" to which the unemployed could come by the day to pick oakum, cut wood, and break stone, for which they were paid in food and clothing. The method was used periodically throughout the second half of the nineteenth century; at times of severe distress, very large numbers of the able-bodied were supported in this way.

The first massive use of public work under relief auspices in the United States occurred during the 1930s when millions of the unemployed were subsidized through the Works Progress Administration. The initial response of the Roosevelt administration was to appropriate billions for direct relief payments. But no one liked direct relief—not the president who called for it, the Congress that legislated it, the administrators who operated it, the people who received it. Direct relief was viewed as a temporary expedient, a way of maintaining a person's body, but not his dignity; a way of keeping the populace from shattering in despair, discontent and disorder, at least for a while, but not of renewing their pride, of bringing back a way of life. For their way of life had been anchored in the discipline of work, and so that discipline had to be restored. The remedy was to abolish direct relief and put the unemployed to work on subsidized projects. These reforms were soon instituted—and with dramatic results. For a brief time, the federal government became the employer of millions of people (although millions of others remained unemployed).

Quite different methods of enforcing work are used when the demand for labor is steady but maladaptions in the labor supply, caused by changes in methods of production, result in unemployment. In such circumstances, relief agencies ordinarily channel paupers directly into the private market. For example, the rapid expansion of English manufacturing during the late eighteenth and early nineteenth centuries produced a commensurately expanded need for factory operatives. But it was no easy matter to get them. Men who had been agricultural laborers, independent craftsmen or workers in domestic industries (i.e., piecework manufacturing in the home) resisted the new discipline. Between 1778 and 1830, there were repeated revolts by laborers in which local tradesmen and farmers often participated. The revolts failed, of course; the new industry moved forward inexorably, taking the more dependent and tractable under its command, with the aid of the relief system.

The burgeoning English textile industry solved its labor problems during the latter part of the eighteenth century by using parish children, some only four or five years old, as factory operatives. Manufacturers negotiated regular bargains with the parish authorities, ordering lots of fifty or more children from the poorhouses. Parish children were an ideal labor source for new manufacturers. The young paupers could be shipped to remote factories, located to take advantage of the streams from which power could be drawn. (With the shift from water power to steam in the nineteenth century, factories began to locate in towns where they could employ local children; with that change, the system of child labor became a system of "free" child labor.) The children were also preferred for their docility and for their light touch at the looms. Moreover, pauper children could be had for a bit of food and a bed, and they provided a very stable labor supply, for they were held fast at their labors by indentures, usually until they were twenty-one.

Sometimes the relief system subsidizes the employment of paupers—especially when their market value is very low—as when the magistrates of Lyons provided subsidies to manufacturers who employed pauper children. In rural England during the late eighteenth century, as more and more of the population was being displaced by the commercialization of agriculture, this method was used on a very large scale. To be sure, a demand for labor was developing in the new manufacturing establishments that would in time absorb many of the uprooted rural poor. But this did not happen all at once: rural displacement and industrial expansion did not proceed at the same pace or in the same areas, and in any case the drastic shift from rural village to factory system took time. During the long interval before people forced off the land were absorbed into manufacturing, many remained in the countryside as virtual vagrants; others migrated to the towns, where they crowded into hovels and cellars, subject to the vicissitudes of rapidly rising and falling markets, their ranks continually enlarged by new rural refugees.

These conditions were not the result of a collapse in the market. Indeed, grain prices rose during the second half of the eighteenth century, and they rose spectacularly during the Revolutionary and Napoleonic wars. Rather, it was the expanding market for agricultural produce which, by stimulating enclosure and business-minded farming methods, led to unemployment and destitution. Meanwhile, population growth, which meant a surplus of laborers, left the workers little opportunity to resist the destruction of their traditional way of life—except by crime, riots and incendiarism. To cope with these disturbances, relief expanded, but in such a way as to absorb and discipline laborers by supporting the faltering labor market with subsidies.

The subsidy system is widely credited to the sheriff and magistrates of Berkshire, who, in a meeting at Speenhamland in 1795, decided on a scheme by which the Poor Law authorities would supplement the wages of underemployed and underpaid agricultural workers according to a published scale. It was a time when exceptional scarcity of food led to riots all over England, sometimes suppressed only by calling out the troops. With this "double panic of famine and revolution," the subsidy scheme spread, especially in counties where large amounts of acreage had been enclosed.

The local parishes implemented the work subsidy system in different ways. Under the "roundsman" arrangement, the parish overseers sent any man who applied for aid from house to house to get work. If he found work, the employer was obliged to feed him and pay a small sum (6 d) per day, with the parish adding another small sum (4 d). Elsewhere, the parish authorities contracted directly with farmers to have paupers work for a given price, with the parish paying the combined wage and relief subsidy directly to the pauper. In still other places, parish authorities parcelled out the unemployed to farmers, who were obliged to pay a set rate or make up the difference in higher taxes. Everywhere, however, the main principle was the same: an underemployed and turbulent populace was being pacified with public allowances, but these allowances were used to restore order by enforcing work, at very low wage levels. Relief, in short, served as a support for a disturbed labor market and as a discipline for a disturbed rural society. As the historians J. L. Hammond and Barbara Hammond were to say, "The meshes of the Poor Law were spread over the entire labour system."

The English Speenhamland plan, while it enjoys a certain notoriety, is by no means unique. The most recent example of a scheme for subsidizing paupers in private employ is the reorganization of American public welfare proposed in the summer of 1969 by President Richard Nixon; the general parallel with the events surrounding Speenhamland is striking. The United States relief rolls expanded in the 1960s to absorb a laboring population made superfluous by agricultural modernization in the South, a population that became turbulent in the wake of forced migration to the cities. As the relief rolls grew to deal with these disturbances, pressure for "reforms" also mounted. Key features of the reform proposals included a national minimum allowance of $1,600 per year for a family of four, coupled with an elaborate system of penalities and incentives to force families to work. In effect, the proposal was intended to support and strengthen a disturbed low-wage labor market by providing what was called in nineteenth century England a "rate in aid of wages."

Enforcing Low Wage Work During Periods of Stability

Even in the absence of cataclysmic change, market incentives may be insufficient to compel all people at all times to do the particular work required of them. Incentives may be too meager and erratic, or people may not be sufficiently socialized to respond to them properly. To be sure, the productivity of a fully developed capitalist economy would allow for wages and profits sufficient to entice most of the population to work; and in a fully developed capitalist society, most people would also be reared to want what the market holds out to them. They would expect, even sanctify, the rewards of the market place and acquiesce in its vagaries.

But no fully developed capitalist society exists. (Even today in the United States, the most advanced capitalist country, certain regions and population groups—such as southern tenant farmers—remain on the periphery of the wage market and are only partially socialized to the ethos of the market.) Capitalism evolved slowly and spread slowly. During most of this evolution, the market provided meager rewards for most workers, and none at all for some. There are still many for whom this is so. And during most of this evolution, large sectors of the laboring classes were not fully socialized to the market ethos. The relief system, we contend, has made an important contribution toward overcoming these persisting weaknesses in the capacity of the market to direct and control men.

Once an economic convulsion subsides and civil order is restored, relief systems are not ordinarily abandoned. The rolls are reduced, to be sure, but the shell of the system usually remains, ostensibly to provide aid to the aged, the disabled and such other unfortunates who are of no use as workers. However, the manner in which these "impotents" have always been treated, in the United States and elsewhere, suggests a purpose quite different from the remediation of their destitution. These residual persons have ordinarily been degraded for lacking economic value, relegated to the foul quarters of the workhouse, with its strict penal regimen and its starvation diet. Once stability was restored, such institutions were typically proclaimed the sole source of aid, and for a reason bearing directly on enforcing work.

Conditions in the workhouse were intended to ensure that no one with any conceivable alternatives would seek public aid. Nor can there by any doubt of that intent.

313

Consider this statement by the Poor Law Commissioners in 1834, for example:

> Into such a house none will enter voluntarily; work, confinement, and discipline will deter the indolent and vicious: and nothing but extreme necessity will induce any to accept the comfort which must be obtained by the surrender of their free agency, and the sacrifice of their accustomed habits and gratifications. *Thus the parish officer, being furnished an unerring test of the necessity of applicants, is relieved from his painful and difficult responsibility: while all have the gratification of knowing that while the necessitous are abundantly relieved, the funds of charity are not wasted by idleness and fraud.*

The method worked. Periods of relief expansion were generally followed by "reform" campaigns to abolish all "outdoor" aid and restrict relief to those who entered the workhouse—as in England in 1722, 1834 and 1871 and in the United States in the 1880s and 1890s—and these campaigns usually resulted in a sharp reduction in the number of applicants seeking aid.

The harsh treatment of those who had no alternative except to fall back upon the parish and accept "the offer of the House" terrorized the impoverished masses in another way as well. It made pariahs of those who could not support themselves; they served as an object lesson, a means of celebrating the virtues of work by the terrible example of their agony. That, too, was a matter of deliberate intent. The workhouse was designed to spur men to contrive ways of supporting themselves by their own industry, to offer themselves to any employer on any terms, rather than suffer the degraded status of pauper.

All of this was evident in the contraction of relief which occurred in the United States at the close of the Great Depression. As political stability returned, emergency relief and work relief programs were reduced and eventually abolished, with many of those cut off being forced into a labor market still glutted with the unemployed. Meanwhile, the Social Security Act had been passed. Widely hailed as a major reform, this measure created our present-day welfare system, with its categorical provisions for the aged, the blind and families with dependent children (as well as, in 1950, the disabled).

The enactment of this "reform" signalled a turn toward the work-enforcing function of relief arrangements. This became especially evident after World War II during the period of greatly accelerated agricultural modernization. Millions were unemployed in agriculture; millions of others migrated to the cities where unemployment in the late 1950s reached extremely high levels. But few families were given assistance. By 1960, only 745,000 families had been admitted to the AFDC rolls. That was to change in the 1960s, as we have already noted, but only in response to the most unprecedented disorder in our history.

That families without jobs or income failed to secure relief during the late 1940s and the 1950s was in part a consequence of restrictive statutes and policies—the exclusion of able-bodied males and, in many places, of so-called employable mothers, together with residence laws, relative responsibility provisions and the like. But it was also—perhaps mainly—a consequence of the persistence of age-old rituals of degradation. AFDC mothers were forced to answer questions about their sexual behavior ("When did you last menstruate?"), open their closets to inspection ("Whose pants are those?"), and permit their children to be interrogated ("Do any men visit your mother?"). Unannounced raids, usually after midnight and without benefit of warrant, in which a recipient's home is searched for signs of "immoral" activities, have also been part of life on AFDC. In Oakland, California, a public welfare caseworker, Bennie Parish, refused to take part in a raid in January 1962 and was dismissed for insubordination. When he sued for reinstatement, the state argued successfully in the lower courts that people taking public assistance waive certain constitutional rights, among them the right to privacy. (The court's position had at least the weight of long tradition, for the withdrawal of civil rights is an old feature of public relief. In England, for example, relief recipients were denied the franchise until 1918, and as late as 1934 the constitutions of fourteen American states deprived recipients of the right to vote or hold office.)

The main target of these rituals is not the recipient who ordinarily is not of much use as a worker, but the able-bodied poor who remain in the labor market. It is for these people that the spectacle of the degraded pauper is intended. For example, scandals exposing welfare "fraud" have diffuse effects, for they reach a wide public—including the people who might otherwise apply for aid but who are deterred because of the invidious connotations of being on welfare. Such a scandal occurred in the District of Columbia in 1961, with the result that half of all AFDC mothers were declared to be ineligible for relief, most of them for allegedly "consorting with men." In the several years immediately before the attack, about 6,500 District of Columbia families had applied for aid annually; during the attack, the figure dropped to 4,400 and it did not rise for more than five years—long after that particular scandal itself had subsided.

In sum, market values and market incentives are weakest at the bottom of the social order. To buttress weak market controls and ensure the availability of marginal labor, an outcast class—the dependent poor—is created by the relief system. This class, whose members are of no productive use, is not treated with indifference, but with contempt. Its degradation at the hands of relief officials serves to celebrate the virtue of all work and deters actual or potential workers from seeking aid.

The Current Call for Reform

From our perspective, a relief explosion is a reform just because a large number of unemployed or underemployed people obtain aid. But from the perspective of most people, a relief explosion is viewed as a "crisis." The contemporary relief explosion in the United States, following a period of unparalleled turbulence in the cities, has thus resulted in a clamor for reform. Similar episodes in the past suggest that pressure for reform signals a shift in emphasis between the major functions of relief arrangements—a shift from regulating disorder to regulating labor.

Pressure for reform stems in part from the fiscal burden imposed on localities when the relief rolls expand. An obvious remedy is for the federal goverment to simply assume a greater share of the costs, if not the entire cost (at this writing, Congress appears likely to enact such fiscal reform).

However, the much more fundamental problem with which relief reform seeks to cope is the erosion of the work role and the deterioration of the male-headed family. In principle, these problems could be dealt with by economic policies leading to full employment at decent wages, but there is little political support for that approach. Instead, the historic approach to relief explosions is being invoked, which is to restore work through the relief system. Various proposals have been advanced: some would force recipients to report regularly to employment offices; others would provide a system of wage subsidies conditional on the recipient's taking on a job at any wage (including those below the federal minimum wage); still others would inaugurate a straight-forward program of public works projects.

We are opposed to any type of reform intended to promote work through the relief system rather than through the reform of economic policies. When similar relief reforms were introduced in the past, they presaged the eventual expulsion of large numbers of people from the rolls, leaving them to fend for themselves in a labor market where there was too little work and thus subjecting them once again to severe economic exploitation. The reason that this happens is more than a little ironic.

The irony is this: when relief is used to enforce work, it tends to stabilize lower-class occupational, familial and communal life (unlike direct relief, which merely mutes the worst outbreaks of discontent). By doing so, it diminishes the proclivities toward disruptive behavior which give rise to the expansion of relief in the first place. Once order is restored in this far more profound sense, relief-giving can be virtually abolished as it has been so often in the past. And there is always pressure to abolish large-scale work relief, for it strains against the market ethos and interferes with the untrammeled operation of the market place. The point is not just that when a relief concession is offered up, peace and order reign; it is, rather, that when peace and order reign, the relief concession is withdrawn.

The restoration of work through the relief system, in other words, makes possible the eventual return to the most restrictive phase in the cycle of relief-giving. What begins as a great expansion of direct relief, and then turns into some form of work relief, ends finally with a sharp contraction of the rolls. Advocates of relief reform may argue that their reforms will be long-lasting, that the restrictive phase in the cycle will not be reached, but past experience suggests otherwise.

Therefore, in the absence of economic reforms leading to full employment at decent wages, we take the position that the explosion of the rolls is the true relief reform, that it should be defended, and that it should be expanded. Even now, hundreds of thousands of impoverished families remain who are eligible for assistance but who receive no aid at all.

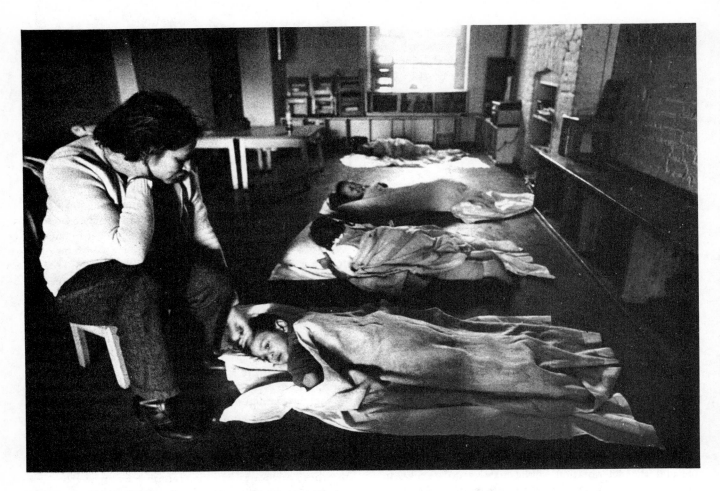

Day Care Centers

Hype or Hope?

Gilbert Y. Steiner

By the end of the 1960s it was evident that under the most prosperous of conditions, public assistance was not about to wither away. A considerable fraction of the population was still outside the sweep of social security's old age pensions, survivors' benefits, or disability insurance, and also outside the sweep of the country's prosperity. "It becomes increasingly clear," the *New York Times* editorialized after the overall level of unemployment in New York City declined to 3.2 percent of the civilian labor force while at the same time the number of welfare clients in the city climbed to one million, "that the welfare rolls have a life of their own detached from the metropolitan job market."

It is detached from the national job market as well. In 1961, when there were 3.5 million AFDC recipients, unemployment as a percent of the civilian labor force nationally was a high 6.7 percent. By 1968 the national unemployment figure was hovering around a record low 3.4 percent, and there was serious talk among economists about the possible need for a higher rate of unemployment to counteract inflation. But the average monthly number of

AFDC recipients in 1968 was up to 5.7 million, almost 4.4 million of whom were children. In 1969 the monthly recipient total averaged 6.7 million, and for the first six months of 1970 it was 7.9 million.

Public assistance also has a separate life outside the growth of the economy. The gross national product was $520 billion in 1961; in 1969 it was $932 billion. One of the things not expected to rise under those prosperous conditions was payments to relief recipients. Yet total payments in AFDC alone in 1961 were $1,149 million; in 1969 total payments were $3,546 million and rising rapidly.

To put all this another way, it is roughly accurate to say that during the 1960s the unemployment rate was halved, AFDC recipients increased by almost two-thirds, and AFDC money payments doubled. Whatever the relationship between workfare and welfare, it is not the simple one of reduced unemployment making for reduced dependency. How has government responded to this confounding news?

For the most part over the past ten years it has responded by tirelessly tinkering with the old welfare system. Special emphasis has been placed on preparing the welfare population emotionally and vocationally for participation in the labor market, thereby enjoying not only the economic security provided by employment itself, but also the unemployment insurance and survivors' insurance, if needed, which employment gives access to. The first such effort—the professional social service approach characterized by a stated plan emphasizing services over support and rehabilitation over relief—showed no progress after running its full five-year trial period from 1962 to 1967. And so, in 1967 a series of programs was invented in order to push relief clients to work. Work experience, work training, work incentives—whatever the titles and whatever the marginal differences in program content—were all designed, in the catch phrase often used, to move people off the relief rolls and onto the tax rolls. Each program assumed that the gulf between labor force participation with accompanying economic security benefits, on the one side, and relief status, on the other side, was bridgeable.

It was not until 1967, however, that it came to be perfectly acceptable to think of mothers with dependent small children as proper objects of the effort to get the very poor off the relief rolls and onto the tax rolls.

Agreement on this question resulted from the confluence of two separate concerns. One concern was with costs and criticisms. Representative Wilbur Mills, powerful leader of the crucial House Ways and Means Committee, viewed with alarm the costs of an unchecked public assistance program:

I am sure it is not generally known that about 4 or 5 years hence when we get to the fiscal year 1972, the figure will have risen by $2.2 billion to an amount of $6,731,000,000 . . . . If I detect anything in the minds of the American people, it is this. They want us to be certain that when we spend the amounts of money that we do, and of necessity in many cases have to spend, that we spend it in such a way as to promote the public interest, and the public well-being of our people.

Is it . . . in the public interest for welfare to become a way of life?

A different concern motivated an HEW task force, department officials, and some of Mills' legislative colleagues. The task force showed little worry over how many billions of dollars public relief was costing, but did concern itself with the turmoil and deprivation that beset recipients in depressed rural areas and in urban ghettos. Thus, to the Mills conclusion that the costs are prohibitive, there was joined a related HEW conclusion, shared by some members of Congress, that the quality of life on welfare was intolerable.

One congressman with such a view is the only lady member of the Ways and Means Committee, Martha Griffiths. Mrs. Griffiths was especially indignant over the conditions imposed on AFDC mothers.

I find the hypocrisy of those who are now demanding freedom of choice to work or not to work for welfare mothers beyond belief. The truth is these women never have had freedom of choice. They have never been free to work. Their education has been inadequate and the market has been unable to absorb their talents . . . .

Can you imagine any conditions more demoralizing than those welfare mothers live under? Imagine being confined all day every day in a room with falling plaster, inadequately heated in the winter and sweltering in the summer, without enough beds for the family, and with no sheets, the furniture falling apart, a bare bulb in the center of the room as the only light, with no hot water most of the time, plumbing that often does not work, with only the companionship of small children who are often hungry and always inadequately clothed—and, of course, the ever-present rats. To keep one's sanity under such circumstances is a major achievement, and to give children the love and discipline they need for healthy development is superhuman. If one were designing a system to produce alcoholism, crime, and illegitimacy, he could not do better.

Whatever the differing motivation, HEW's task force, Mills and Mrs. Griffiths all pointed in the direction of change from the status quo. And the change agreed upon was abandonment of the heretofore accepted idea that the only employable AFDC recipients were unemployed fathers.

In 1967 the Ways and Means Committee unveiled its social security and welfare bill at about the same time that HEW Secretary John Gardner unveiled his reorganization of the welfare agencies in his department. That reorganization merged the Welfare Administration, the Administration on Aging, and the Vocational Rehabilitation Service into a new agency called the Social and Rehabilitation Service (SRS). To run it, Gardner named Mary Switzer, a veteran commissioner of vocational rehabilitation who was aptly described by a local journalist as "a diligent disciple of work." This bit of tinkering was designed to send the message through the federal welfare bureaucracy that the secretary was receptive to policy change, apparently including a new work emphasis. The great drive to employ dependent mothers and provide day care for their children thus began both in the administration and in Congress two years before President Nixon discovered it anew.

Day Care

Despite an announcement by Miss Switzer in April 1969 that a reduction in the number of people on the welfare rolls is "a top priority of the Social and Rehabilitation Service" which she asked state welfare admistrators "to make yours as well," it was really beyond the power of either Miss Switzer or the state administrators to effect a big breakthrough in the AFDC problem. The key to moving some people off the rolls is employment for the AFDC employable parent. The rub is that even training for employment, a first step, requires an expensive new industry—day care—which now lacks organization, leadership, personnel and money for construction of facilities. Moreover, once the realities of work training and day care programs are examined, it becomes evident that there is not much incentive for a poorly educated AFDC mother to accept training for herself and day care service of uncertain quality for her children.

Training AFDC mothers for employment, actually finding jobs for them, and providing day care facilities for their children present formidable problems. A recent survey of the AFDC population found that 43 percent of the mothers had gone no further than the eighth grade, including 10.6 percent with less than a fifth grade education. Work training that leads to employment at wages adequate to support a family is likely to be prolonged, at best, for this undereducated group.

The realities of the coming crunch in day care are even more troublesome. Day care provisions accompanying the 1967 work incentive (WIN) legislation did not extend to the creation of a federal program authorizing funds for new facilities. There are approximately 46,300 licensed facilities caring for 638,000 children. If every place in every licensed day care facility in the United States were to be reserved for an AFDC child under the age of six, there would be more than one million AFDC children in that age group with no place to go. There would also be consternation among the thousands of non-AFDC mothers with children of that age level who are already in day care centers.

In short, there are not enough facilities—good, bad or indifferent—to accomplish the day care job envisioned by the congressional and administration planners who still talk of moving parents from welfare rolls to payrolls. Representative Fernand St. Germain was undoubtedly right in stating in 1969 that "costs of new facilities are too much for the states to bear alone; centers will only be built in numbers that have any relation to the critical need if federal assistance is forthcoming." No one seems to have foreseen this in 1967, however, and the point never got into the HEW program memorandum that influenced the employable mother discussions and proposals of the House Ways and Means Committee.

But the day care problem goes beyond the matter of adequate space to an important philosophical and political question regarding the appropriate clientele for the service.

There is no political conflict over the proposition that a young mother suddenly widowed and left dependent on social security survivors' benefits should be supported with public funds so that she can stay home and take care of her children. Nor is there congressional discussion or any HEW proposal for day care for those children. If 94.5 percent of AFDC dependency were attributable to death of the father, there would be no congressional interest in day care to speak of.

But, in fact, 94.5 percent of AFDC dependency is not attributable to death of the father; only 5.5 percent is. Most of the political conflict and a good deal of the interest in day care is over whether the public should subsidize those women whom Senator Russell Long once called "brood mares" to stay home, produce more children—some of them born out of wedlock—and raise those children in an atmosphere of dependency.

While medical authorities and professional social workers are still divided philosophically over how accessible day care should be and to whom, Congress in 1967 and President Nixon in 1969 simply embraced the possibility of putting day care to work in the cause of reducing public assistance costs. In other words, political attention has focused less on the practical limits of day care and more on its apparent similarities to baby sitting.

Day care was simply not ready to assume the responsibilities thrust on it by the welfare legislation adopted in 1967, and it was not ready for President Nixon's proposal to expand it in 1969. Whether day care is a socially desirable or even an economical way of freeing low income mothers with limited skills and limited education for work or work training still has not been widely considered. In the few circles where it has been considered, there is no agreement. Both the 1967 legislation and the Nixon proposal for escalation should have been preceded by the development of publicly supported, model day care arrangements that could be copied widely; by attention to questions of recruitment and appropriate educational training for day care personnel; by an inventory of available and needed physical facilities; by the existence of a high-spirited and innovative group of specialists in government or in a private association or both; and by enough experience to expose whatever practical defects may exist in day care as a program to facilitate employment of low income mothers. Instead of meeting these reasonable conditions for escalation, public involvement in day care programs for children, a phenomenon especially of the last ten years, remains unsystematic, haphazard, patchworky.

The Children's Bureau Approach

For many years before 1969, the HEW Children's Bureau ran the bulk of the federal day care program. It did not encourage an approach that would make day care readily available on demand. Stressing that day care can be harmful unless it is part of a broader program overseen by a trained social worker, the bureau defined day care as a child welfare service offering "care and protection." The child in need of day care was identified as one who "has a family problem which makes it impossible for his parents to fulfill their parental responsibilities without supplementary help." The social worker was seen as necessary to help determine whether the family needs day care and if so to develop an appropriate plan for the child, to place the child in a day care program, to determine the fee to be paid by the parents and to provide continuing supervision.

Change comes slowly to child welfare—as to other specialists. Those in the Children's Bureau found it difficult to adjust to the idea of day care available to all comers and especially to low income working mothers. On the one hand, the talk from the top of the bureau has been about the need to face reality in the day care picture—"when," as one bureau chief put it as early as 1967, "thousands of infants and young children are being placed in haphazard situations because their mothers are working." On the other hand, down the line at the bureau the experts continued to emphasize the importance of the intake procedure to insure that children placed in day care "need" the service.

With this approach it might be expected that while the day care expansion movement has ground along slowly, it has ground exceedingly fine. Day care undoubtedly is a risky enterprise. Every center should have a genuinely high-quality, sympathetic environment; no center should be countenanced without clear evidence that such an environment is being created, and all centers that do not give such evidence should be discouraged. The payoff, therefore, for what might seem to be excessive caution by the Children's Bureau could have been a jewel of a limited program and no second or third rate imitations. Then, when money and will were at hand, the jewel could be reproduced.

In fact, no day care activity was discouraged, whether of low quality or not. Caution on the subject of quantity did not work to guarantee quality. Whether or not there would be any day care activity depended on the states, and the federal agency was accommodating, both because it was hard to interest the states in day care at all, and because Congress provided money in fits and starts, rather than in a steady flow. When the money did come, there was an urgent need to spend it.

Funding

Between 1962 and 1965, HEW had only $8.8 million to parcel out to the states for day care. Moreover, it was never able to count on having anything from year to year, so that it is understandable that the federal agency was in no position to threaten the states about the quality of service. The 1962 law required that federal day care money go only to facilities approved or licensed in accordance with state standards. The law said nothing about minimum federal standards. In 1962 a number of states had no day care licensing programs at all; among the states that did, the extent of licensing and the standards used varied considerably. The Children's Bureau's own guidelines were little more than advisory. To raise the quality of day care nationally, the bureau had to fall back on persuasion and consultation, weak tools compared to money.

Licensing

One certain effect of the 1962 requirement that the available federal money go only to licensed facilities was to divert a substantial part of the funds into licensing activity itself and away from actual day care services. For fiscal 1965, for example, 43 percent of the $4 million appropriated for day care was spent on personnel engaged in licensing, while only 36 percent was used to provide day care services in homes or centers. This increased licensing activity has the effect of distorting the picture of growth of day care facilities. In 1960, licensed day care facilities had a reported total capacity of 183,332; in 1965 this had increased to 310,400; in 1967 the figure was up to 473,700; in 1968 to 535,200; and in 1969 to 638,000. There is universal agreement, however, that the growth figure is mostly illusory, a consequence of formerly unlicensed facilities now being licensed.

Moreover, there is more form than substance to licensing decisions. The fact that a day care facility is licensed cannot yet be taken to mean that its physical plant and personnel necessarily satisfy some explicitly defined and universally accepted standards. Like "premium grade" automobile tires, licensed day care facilities can differ sharply in quality—and for the same reason, the absence of industry-wide standards. Licensing studies by public welfare agencies are invariably assigned to new and untrained caseworkers. The results are unpredictable and there is no monitoring body able and authorized to keep a watchful eye on who is being licensed.

Even from those who accept the simplistic assumption that only the absence of child care services and of job or training opportunities preclude AFDC recipients from becoming wage earners, there is no suggestion that just any kind of child care will do. Yet the state of the art in day care is not sufficiently advanced to make it reasonable to expect that states can meet the requirement to provide day care services other than in makeshift, low quality programs. There is clear validity in the complaint of the National Committee for the Day Care of Children that the 1967 legislation was not designed to help children develop mentally and physically, but was "a hastily put together outline for a compulsory, custodial service which is not required to maintain even minimal standards of adequacy."

Challenge from Head Start

Only a month after taking office, President Nixon called for a "national commitment to providing all American children an opportunity for healthful and stimulating development during the first five years of life." A few weeks later secretary of HEW Robert Finch welcomed the delegation of the Head Start program to HEW as the occasion for a new and overdue national commitment to child and parent development. Finch indicated publicly that he was not inclined to put Head Start in the Children's Bureau and instead placed it in a new HEW Office of Child Development (OCD) where the Children's Bureau was also transferred. Social planners in HEW, the Bureau of the Budget and the White House envisioned a new era: day care programs for low income children would be modeled on Head Start; simple custodial arrangements would not be tolerated; parents would be involved. The way for this happy outcome had already been paved by issuance of the Federal Interagency Day Care Requirements, a joint product of HEW and OEO, approved in the summer of 1968.

Things have not worked out. Whatever Finch's initial intention, the day care programs operated by the Children's Bureau never made it to the OCD. In September 1969 a new Community Services Administration was created within the Social and Rehabilitation Service to house all service programs provided public assistance recipients under social security. The Head Start bureau of the OCD, according to the terms of the reorganization, was given some responsibility in Social Security Act day care programs—to participate in policy making and to approve state welfare plans on day care. But effective control of the money and policy in the day care programs remains with the Social and Rehabilitation Service. President Nixon's "commitment to providing all American children an opportunity for health-ful and stimulating development during the first five years of life" has so far produced more talk than money.

A High Cost Service

There has simply not been enough thinking about the benefits and costs of a good day care program to merit the faith political leaders now express in day care as a dependency-reducing mechanism. Federal day care program requirements are, for the most part, oriented to the idea of day care as a learning experience. They are, therefore, on a collision course with supporters of mass day care as an aspect of the struggle to reduce welfare costs. The high-quality program requirements reject simple ware-housing of children, but the prospects for meeting high standards are not good. It seems inevitable that there will be disappointment both for those who think of day care as a welfare economy and for those who think of day care for AFDC children as an important social and educational advance.

Consider the situation in the District of Columbia, which is reasonably typical of the day care problem in large cities. The District Public Welfare Department (DPW) in May 1969 was purchasing child care for 1,056 children, of whom about 400 were children of women in the WIN program. Of the total 1,056 children, 865 were in day care centers, 163—primarily infants too young to be placed in centers—were in family day care homes, and 28 were in in-home care arrangements, a service considered practical only for large families. The total anticipated day care load for the end of fiscal 1969 was 1,262. District day care personnel estimated that 660 AFDC mothers to be referred to WIN during fiscal 1970 (on the basis of 55 per month) would need, on the average, day care for 2 children. These additional 1,320 children would bring the likely number for whom the District would be paying for care to 2,582 by July 1, 1970. Budget requests for day care for fiscal 1970 totaled $3,254,300 in local and federal funds ($1,148,000 of local funds brings $2,106,300 in federal money). Of this amount, about $3 million is for purchase of care, the remainder for administrative expenses. If budget requests were met, the purchase cost of day care in the District would thus be expected to average almost $1,200 per child. Costly as that may seem to be, it represents only a little more than half the actual cost.

It is the beginning of day care wisdom to understand that it is an expensive mechanism and to understand that there are qualitative differences in the care provided. The elegantly stated effort of the DPW is to secure "in addition to good physical care, the kind of exceptionally enriched day care experience that is specifically designed and programmed to stimulate and promote the maximum in emotional, physical, and educational growth and development of the child." Alas, one-third of the centers with which the DPW contracts only "offer primarily custodial and protective care," a code phrase for warehousing. Fees paid day care centers by the District Welfare Department are supposed to be a function of the quality of services offered. Grade A centers are paid $4.00 a day, B centers $3.00 a day, and C centers $2.50 a day. The department's Standards for Day Care Centers say that it uses a fee schedule for two reasons: "to assure that proper value is received for each dollar spent and, secondly, to provide a monetary stimulus to contract day care facilities to up-grade the quality of their services to meet the Department's maximum expectations." Each center's "rating," known only to it and to the Welfare Department, is for "internal use" and is not revealed to the welfare mother because, according to department officials, it would not be fair to the center to do so. A more pertinent question is whether it is fair to the mother, since 25 of the 55 centers from which day care is purchased are graded B or C, and since half of all placements are in B or C centers.

All centers—whether A, B or C—must meet the Health Department's licensing requirements, as well as additional specific standards set down by the Welfare Department in the areas of educational qualifications of personnel, program content, and equipment and furnishings. Yet there are two problems with this seemingly tidy picture. The first is the insistence of close observers that while the Welfare Department's standards for centers look satisfactory on paper, they have not been put into practice very consistently. The second is that even the paper standards will not do when the federal interagency standards become effective July 1, 1971. Spokesmen for the National Capital Area Child Day Care Association (NCACDCA) and District Health Department licensing personnel are critical of the Welfare Department's day care operation. Both suggest there is a lack of awareness in the Welfare Day Care Unit of what constitutes good day care. That high ranking is reserved, in the judgment of these people, for the centers operated by NCACDCA. The critics complain that only the NCACDCA centers can legitimately meet the Welfare Department's own A standards and maintain that the other A centers simply do not meet them. They claim, for example, that one way these latter centers "meet" the educational qualifications for personnel is to list as a director an "absentee"—perhaps a kindergarten teacher in the District of Columbia school system or that of a neighboring county.

No one disputes that most centers in the District cannot meet the Federal Interagency Day Care Requirements—particularly the child-adult ratios and the educational qualifications for staff. Even a good number of the A centers do not meet the child-adult ratio requirements, and the B and C centers meet neither the staff educational qualifications nor the child-adult ratios of the federal requirements. If the day care centers have not met the federal standards by July 1, 1971, DPW cannot continue making payments on behalf of children for whom it receives federal matching funds. But in the District Welfare Department the view is that the requirements are unrealistic and that widespread complaints from private users who cannot afford the costs involved may result in a lowering of standards.

All the evidence suggests that day care is expensive whether the auspices are public, private or mixed. In a curiously chosen experiment, the Department of Labor decided in 1969 to fund an experimental day care program for its own employees at a time when emphasis was presumably being placed on supporting day care for the welfare poor. Its estimated budget for the first full year of care for 30 children was $100,000, one-third of which was for nonrecurring development costs, including renovation for code compliance, equipment and evaluation. Tuition from the group of working mothers involved amounted to only $7,300, leaving $59,600 of public funds necessary to provide care for 30 children—a subsidy of almost $2,000 per child without considering nonrecurring cost items. Doubling the number of children served the second year would require a budget of $100,000, resulting in an average annual per child cost over the two years of $1,850, or of $2,225, if the renovation and equipment items are not dismissed as readily as the department sought to dismiss them in its official explanation.

The National Capital Area Child Day Care Association estimates costs at almost $2,400 per child per 50-week year. Its standard budget for a 30-child center exceeds $71,000. Tight-fisted budget examiners might effect reductions, but they cannot be consequential unless the pupil teacher ratio is drastically revised. Morever, NCACDCA salary figures are unrealistically low. Head teachers for a 30-child center are hard to come by at $7,300. (See table.)

If these per child costs of desirable day care are projected nationally, the annual bill for all preschool AFDC children must be figured conservatively at $3 billion.

Client Arithmetic

Most women in the District of Columbia WIN program are being trained in clerical skills in anticipation that they will take jobs with the federal government as GS-2s. This is an optimistic view since most trainees have ninth to eleventh grade educations while a GS-2 needs a high school diploma or equivalency or six months' experience and the ability to pass a typing test. That problem aside, the District AFDC mother who completes work incentive training and is placed in a GS-2 job will be better off financially than the mother who stays on welfare. Her gain will be greater the smaller the size of her family. She will have fewer children to support on her fixed earnings, whereas the larger the family on AFDC, the larger the grant.

For many a female head of a family of four in the spring of 1970, however, the work and day care arithmetic was not encouraging as the following illustration shows. If the GS-2 mother has three children and claims four exemptions, about $39 of her monthly salary of $385 is deducted for retirement ($18.50) and for federal ($17) and local ($3.50) taxes, leaving a take home pay of about $346 a month. If two of the three children are in Welfare Department child care arrangements, placed there when the mother entered the WIN program, the mother would pay the department about $6.00 a week toward their care; if the mother had only one child in care, she would pay $5.50. Assuming two children in care, the mother's monthly cost would be about $26, lowering her net earnings to $320.

Suppose, however, that the woman stayed on AFDC. The average benefit for a four-person family on AFDC in the District would bring her $217 monthly. Both the welfare mother and the working mother would be eligible for Medicaid, but only the welfare mother would be eligible for food stamps. For $60 a month she could receive $106 in food stamps, a gain of $46. The welfare mother's child could also receive free lunches at school while the working mother's could not. (The working mother is considerably above the income scale used to determine eligibility for free lunches, although in cases where it is felt children are going hungry, exceptions to the income scale can be made.) A school lunch costs 25 cents in the District's elementary schools. If the welfare child took advantage of the free lunch the mother would save about $5 a month. Thus, the welfare mother would end up with a total of about $268 in welfare, food stamps and school lunches while the working mother would have about $320 a month. In addition, the 1967 welfare amendments allow a welfare mother to earn $30 per month without loss of benefits. The net gain for working full time compared to working only 19 hours a month at the minimum wage is thus reduced to $22. From this, the working mother would have expenses to cover such items as transportation and extra clothes for herself and might have to make some after school care arrangement for her third (school-aged) child.

City Arithmetic

How much work training and day care can save the District of Columbia will depend on how many trainees complete training successfully, get a job and keep it, and on how many children of trainees need child care. The Welfare Department will benefit financially by the AFDC mother's entering a training program and becoming employed as a GS-2 unless the mother has four or more children in day care—which would be most unusual. While it might give the

Standard Day Care Center Budget for Thirty Children for One Year

A. *Personnel*

3 Full-time teachers (head teacher, $7,300; teacher, $7,000; teacher assistant, $4,700)	$19,000
2 Full-time aides ($4,140 each)	8,280
1 Half-time clerk	2,400
Part-time maintenance help (cook, $2,610; janitor, $2,024)	4,634
Substitute (teacher aide, $4,300) and part-time student aide ($1,214)	5,514
Subtotal	$39,828
Fringe benefits (11 percent)	4,381
Total	$44,209

B. *Consultant and Contract Services*

Part-time social worker ($2,500), psychiatric consultant ($5,000), and educational consultant ($1,000)	$8,500
Dietitian	500
Dental and emergency medical service	450
Total	$9,450

C. *Space*

Rent ($1,800); custodial supplies and minor repairs ($1,800)	$3,600

D. *Consumable Supplies*

Office, postage, and miscellaneous (blankets, towels, etc.)	$450
Educational ($400) and health supplies ($30)	430
Food and utensils	4,674
Total	$5,554

E. *Rental, Lease, or Purchase of Equipment*

Children's furniture ($3,000) and office equipment ($200)	$3,200
Equipment: basic (easels, blocks, etc., $1,500); expendable (dolls, puzzles, books, etc., $700); outdoor, with storage ($1,000)	3,200
Total	$6,400

F. *Travel*

Staff ($240) and children's trips ($720)	$960

G. *Other*

Telephone ($36 a month; installation $50)	$482
Insurance (liability, property, and transportation liability)	$700
Total	$1,182
Total project cost	$71,355
Child cost per year	$2,378

Source: Derived from budget of National Capital Area Day Care Association, Inc., Washington, D.C., August 1968.

AFDC mother of three $217 each month, the department would pay only part of her day care cost once she begins working (the department pays all costs for the first three months). With an average cost to the department for day care of $17.50 per child per week, using our hypothetical

GS-2 mother with two children in day care and one in elementary school, the mother would pay $6 a week and the Welfare Department $29 a week for day care. This working mother thus represents a monthly saving to the department of about $56. If, however, the AFDC mother had four children in day care centers and one in elementary school, the mother would pay $6.50 a week toward their care (this figure is the same for three or more children) and the department $63.50. The department would thus spend $273 a month for child care—and save nothing compared to what it would have given her on AFDC to care for her own children at home.

Prospects

What are the prospects for success in turning day care into a program that will reduce the costs of AFDC? They hinge, first, on large numbers of AFDC mothers actually turning out to be trainable and able to be placed in jobs under any conditions and, second, on finding some cheaper substitute for traditional day care centers.

The difficulty in securing the physical facilities and staff needed to develop the traditional centers looked overwhelming to state welfare administrators examining the day care problem in 1967. They did, however, see some hopes for neighborhood day care, a kind of glorified, low income equivalent of the middle class baby-sitting pool. Stimulated by OEO's success in involving poor people in poverty programs, HEW early in 1967 started pushing neighborhood day care demonstration projects using welfare mothers to help care for other welfare mothers' children. This seemingly ideal solution has its own problems. One of them is sanitary and health requirements that, if enforced, disqualify the substandard housing used by many recipients. The unknown emotional condition of the AFDC mother is an equally important problem in this use of the neighborhood care idea. A spokesman for the Welfare Rights Organization warns:

Do not force mothers to take care of other children. You do not know what kind of problem that parent might have. You do not know whether she gets tired of her own children or not but you are trying to force her to take care of other people's children and forcing the parents to go out in the field and work when you know there is no job.

This is why we have had the disturbance in New York City and across the country. We, the welfare recipients, have tried to keep down that disturbance among our people but the unrest is steadily growing. The welfare recipients are tired. They are tired of people dictating to them telling them how they must live.

Not surprisingly, day care and work training through WIN are lagging as the hoped-for saving graces of public assistance. New York City's experience is instructive. In 1967 the City Council's finance committee concluded that an additional expenditure of $5 million for 50 additional day care centers to accommodate 3,000 additional children was warranted. "The Committee on Finance is informed," said its report, "that many (welfare) mothers would seek employment if they could be assured of proper care of their children while at work. We feel that expansion . . . on a massive scale is called for." The mayor's executive expense budget for day care was thereupon increased by about 60 percent and appropriations in subsequent years have continued at the higher level. But the New York City Department of Social Services—like the U.S. Department of Health, Education, and Welfare—lacks a program for such a rapid expansion of day care. Actual expenditures have lagged. In contrast to the anticipated 50 new centers caring for 3,000 additional children, it was reported in June 1969 that 19 new centers accommodating 790 children had been established.

The national figures resulting from the 1967 amendments are no more encouraging. Like New York City, the federal government has not been able to shovel out the available money. Consider the situation around the time of the Nixon family assistance message. Of a projected June 1969 goal of 102,000 WIN enrollees, only 61,847 were in fact enrolled by the end of that month. Of a projected 100,000 child care arrangements, only about 49,000 children were receiving care at the end of June 1969, and 50 percent of them were receiving care in their own homes. Thus, when President Nixon proposed 150,000 new training slots and 450,000 new day care places in his August 1969 welfare message, the Labor Department and HEW had already found that 18 months after enactment of the 1967 legislation they were unable to meet more than 60 percent of their modest work and training goals or more than 50 percent of their even more modest day care goals.

WIN Loses

The gap between original projections and depressing realities held constant into 1970. The Labor Department first estimated a WIN enrollment level of 150,000 at the close of fiscal 1970, later scaled the figure down to 100,000. And as of February 1970 the cumulative WIN data took the shape of a funnel:

Welfare recipients screened by local agencies for possible referral	1,478,000
Found appropriate for referral to WIN	301,000
Actually referred to WIN	225,000
Enrolled in WIN program	129,000
Employed	22,000

As for day care, 188,000 children were initially expected to be receiving "child care"—which includes care in their own homes by grandmothers or other relatives—on June 30, 1970. The target later was dropped to a more modest

78,000. In May 1970 there were just 61,000 reported in child care, and only about one-fifth of these children were really cared for in a day care facility. Approximately one-half were cared for in their own homes, one-tenth in a relative's home, and the last one-fifth were reported to have "other" arrangements—a category that actually includes "child looks after self."

By July 1970 the House Labor-HEW appropriations subcommittee was discouraged about the progress of work training-day care activity. "It doesn't sound too good," said Chairman Dan Flood (Democrat of Pennsylvania) after hearing the WIN program statistics. The committee proposed a reduction of $50 million from the administration's request for $170 million in 1971 work incentive funds. There was no confusion about either the purpose of the program or its lack of accomplishment:

The objective of the work incentives program is to help people get off the welfare rolls and to place them in productive jobs. While the committee supports the program, it has just not been getting off the ground for several reasons, such as poor day care standards for children.

Unfortunately, the sorry history and the limitations of day care and work training as solutions to the welfare problem could not be faced by the administration's welfare specialists in 1970 because all of their energies were directed toward support for the Nixon family assistance plan. But after a few years it will inevitably be discovered that work training and day care have had little effect on the number of welfare dependents and no depressing effect on public relief costs. Some new solution will then be proposed, but the more realistic approach would be to accept the need for more welfare and to reject continued fantasizing about day care and "workfare" as miracle cures.

Women in Labor

Marijean Suelzle

To read the newspapers one would think that the top jobs in public life are opening up for women and that our occupational status was rising generally: Interstate Commerce Commissioner Virginia Mae Brown became the first woman to head an independent federal administrative agency; Helen D. Bentley became chairman of the Maritime Commission; the first four female scientists explored the Antarctic; Barbara J. Rubin, a jockey, was the first woman to win a pari-mutuel race; and a 13-year-old girl, Alice De Rivera, integrated the all-male Stuyvesant High School in New York. While publicity on the "breakthroughs" does break down some psychological barriers, it exaggerates and misrepresents the real occupational changes. In order to find out what these real changes are, we must look at social trends that affect the changing profile of women in the labor force and at some myths and stereotypes that surround the working woman.

In 1920 the average woman worker in this country was 28 years old and single. Today she is 39 years old, married and living with her husband. In 1920 she was most likely to be a factory worker or other operative, but large numbers of women were also clerical workers, private household workers and farm workers. Her occupational choice was extremely limited. Today the average woman in the labor force is most likely to be a clerical worker, with other large numbers of women being service workers outside the home, factory workers or other operatives and professional or technical workers. She may be working in any one of 479 individual occupations, but most women are concentrated in a relatively small number of occupations.

Times of Life and Work

Caroline Bird has identified five factors influencing the changing profile of the woman worker. First, the vital statistics of birth, marriage and death have changed so that women have more years of life when they are not bearing or rearing children. One of the most important factors effecting the change is greater longevity, especially for women. The baby girl born in 1900 (that is, the grandmother of many women entering the labor force today) had a life expectancy of 48 years, whereas the baby girl born today has a life expectancy of 74 years, a figure that can be expected to go higher. About half today's women marry by age 20, and more marry at age 18 than at any other age. On the average, they will have had their last child by age 30 and will be in their mid-thirties by the time their youngest child is in school. The mother will have about 40 years, or one-half, of her life ahead of her, freed from child-rearing responsibilities.

A second important factor affecting the profile of the woman worker is education. Girls have consistently outnumbered boys among high school graduates, although the difference has narrowed. In 1900, girls were approximately 60 percent of all high school graduates, whereas recently the number of girls graduating from high school is only slightly higher than the number of boys—50.4 and 49.6 percent respectively in 1968. During this period, of course, the number of both girls and boys graduating from high school has been growing steadily. Each year more women enroll in and graduate from institutions of higher education, but women still lag behind men in pursuing education beyond high school, and, according to Dean Knudsen, the lag is *increasing*. Women earned 19 percent of the bachelor's or first professional degrees awarded in 1900, as against 41 percent in 1965; 19 percent of the master's degrees awarded in 1900, as against 32 percent in 1965; and 6 percent of the doctor's degrees awarded in 1900, as against 11 percent in 1965. But if we take the period 1940 to 1964 and asked what proportion of girls were enrolled for degree credit, Dean Knudsen has shown that the proportion of girls has declined by 5.5 percent.

A third factor is the experience of employment itself. In 1900, women were only 18 percent of all workers; in 1940, about 25 percent. The proportion reached a high of 36 percent during World War II, dropped back to 28 percent

with the return of male veterans to civilian jobs, before beginning to climb again to 37 percent today. The shift in production from home to factory has influenced the rise in the numbers and proportion of women in the labor force. The work ethic, self-fulfillment and the right of each individual to happiness have increasingly become associated with educational and career attainment, the paycheck and its rate of increase. Thus, the homemaker role as the only role capable of meeting the cultural ideals is called into question. Far from a shameful necessity reflecting the inadequacy of the husband as provider, earnings have become a point of pride for wives of men who are obviously able to "support" them adequately.

A fourth minor factor affecting the profile of the woman worker is the increasing desegregation of work. Sex-typing of jobs, however, remains the norm. The woman worker is concentrated in a relatively small number of occupations. One-third of all working women are employed in seven occupations—secretary, saleswoman, general private household worker, teacher in elementary school, bookkeeper, waitress and professional nurse. This can be contrasted to the scarcity of women in such professional positions as physician, engineer, and scientist despite the increased job openings created by the tremendous interest in research and development. Job channeling and labeling come about through custom, an unquestioning acceptance of certain assumptions about masculinity and feminity. The question asked is often "Is it fitting and proper?" rather than "Is she qualified?"

The fifth and final factor affecting the profile of the woman worker is a general desegregation of the sexes—in the professions, the church, education, recreation and public accommodation.

To the above five factors identified by Caroline Bird, a sixth can be added, that of an increasing awareness of and concern over the population explosion. Although population predictions are necessarily tentative, Dr. Richard S. Miller, a Yale University ecologist, projects the current doubling time of the world's human population as 36 years into the next century, 20 years beginning in 2000 and 16 years beginning in 2020. The total world population by his projection is 28 billion people in 2036, an obvious impossibility. Some women today are aware not only that motherhood is not enough but also that, for the first time in history, it is actually socially irresponsible to have as many children as one would like. The efforts of such social movements as Zero Population Growth, with their goal of one adult, one child, have already caused some women to report negative social reactions when they are expecting their third (or more) child. Such social criticism is leading many women to seek career alternatives rather than bearing more than two (or in some cases any) children.

Changing Profile of Women in the Labor Force

According to the U. S. Department of Labor Women's Bureau, there have been some startling changes in the profile of women in the labor force, as there have been in the profile of the woman who actually works. However, the changes have *not* all been unidirectional and do not bear out the "onward and upward ideology" reflected in the media. While the rate of labor force participation has expanded, earnings relative to males are down, as are the rates of women employed in most higher status occupations. Factors pushing and attracting women into the labor force are increasing while, at the same time, rewards for so participating are declining.

Fifty years ago, in 1920, less than one-fourth of all women 20 to 60 years of age in the population were workers

Women and Careers

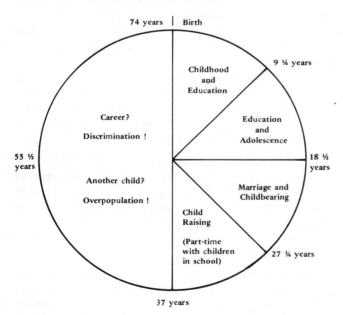

The baby girl born in 1970 has a life expectancy of 74 years. About half of today's women marry by age 20, and more marry at age 18 than at any other age. On the average, they will have had their last child by age 30 and will be in their mid-thirties by the time their youngest child is in school. The mother will have about one-half of her life ahead of her. If she decides to reenter the job market after a period of absence for childrearing, she will face difficulty in upgrading her skills and discrimination in an occupational structure geared to continuous (male) employment. At the same time, an increased concern with the population explosion will influence her not to have more than two children.

(23 percent). Today almost half of all women 18 to 64 years of age in the population are workers (49 percent). The age at which women were most apt to be working has remained the same over the last 50 years although the rate has changed. During both periods women were most apt to be working at ages 20 to 24; but only 38 percent were working in January 1920, as opposed to 56 percent in April 1969. The pattern of employment throughout the life cycle has also changed. In 1920 female participation in the labor force dropped off at age 25, decreased steadily with age, and by the time they were aged 45 to 54 only 18 percent were working. In contrast, female participation in the labor force today drops off at age 25 but rises again at age 35 to a second peak of 54 percent at ages 45 to 54. The changed pattern of employment throughout the life cycle reflects the different employment outlook of the 35-year-old woman in 1920. In 1920 less than one out of every five women 35 to 64 years of age was in the labor force. Today almost half the women at age 35 can expect to work 24 to 31 more years. More than one-half of today's young women will work full-time for 25 or more years. Today 37 percent of all workers are women.

As I mentioned earlier, women are concentrated in a relatively small number of occupations. The number of occupations in which 100,000 or more women were employed increased between 1950 and the present time by the addition of seven occupations—baby-sitter, charwoman and cleaner, counter and fountain worker, file clerk, housekeeper (apart from private household) and stewardess, musician and music teacher and receptionist—hardly impressive additions when one bears in mind the increased educational attainment of women during this period.

Another example of the clear sex-typing of (underpriced) "women's work" shows up if we examine sex ratios in the major occupational categories. In more than half of the 36 occupations in which 100,000 or more women were employed in 1960, at least three out of four workers were women; in at least one-third, nine out of ten were women.

Women have been gaining status in some sectors of the economy, but they have been losing it in others. For example, in the executive branch of the Federal Civilian Service, increasing numbers of young women are taking the Federal Service Entrance Examination and being appointed to professional positions at entrance levels. Their numbers have doubled between 1963 and 1967 (rising from 18 to 35 percent). In addition, 29 percent of those selected as management interns in 1967 were women, as compared to only 14 percent in 1965. At the same time, however, the proportion of women teachers at the college and university level has declined. Only 22 percent of the faculty and other professional staff in institutions of higher education were women in 1964, down from the proportion in 1940 (28 percent), 1930 (27 percent) or 1920 (26 percent).

When averages are computed separately for men and for women in the labor force, women are consistently shown to be the disadvantaged group. Women workers are concentrated in lower-paying jobs, they earn less than men in all kinds of jobs, and their unemployment rate is higher. Furthermore, the gap between the earnings of women and of men has been steadily widening since 1956 (see table). Thus, the status of women in the labor force relative to the status of men has been declining for at least the past 15 years. Furthermore, the areas in which women have been making positive occupational gains are more than being offset by those areas in which opportunities have been decreasing.

The increase in women's employment is a case of moving in, not up. Top positions for women are too few relative to their increased educational attainments over the past 50 years. There are many reasons for the pay and status differentials, most of them based on hoary stereotypes concerning women's work. But these attitudes and practices are fostered not only by the employer but the woman employee herself. For even though many of these myths have been shattered by serious investigation, there are few truths that make their way easily and quickly into public knowledge to become new myths. Some of the current myths are these:

Myth 1: Women naturally don't want careers, they just want jobs.

As a generalization about women entering or in the job market in 1970, the statement may or may not be accurate. It is a myth because of the "naturally." There is nothing natural about the low aspirations of women, any more than the low aspirations of ethnic minorities in public life. To assume that "ambition" is unfeminine is to admit no individual variability: it depends on the person, not the sex.

In a recent study Matina Horner administered a story completion test to female and male undergraduates. Women were asked to write a story based on the sentence "After first-term finals, Anne finds herself at the top of her medical-school class." (Men were given the same task, but with the word "John" replacing the word "Anne" in the sentence.) Over 65 percent of the girls told stories which reflected strong fears of social rejection, fears about definitions of womanhood or denial of the possibility that any mere woman could be so successful:

Anne is pretty darn proud of herself, but everyone hates and envies her.

Anne is pleased. She had worked extraordinarily hard, and her grades showed it. "It is not enough," Anne thinks. "I am not happy." She didn't even want to be a doctor. She is not sure what she wants. Anne says to hell with the whole business and goes into social work—not hardly as glamorous, prestigious or lucrative; but she is happy.

It was luck that Anne came out on top because she didn't want to go to medical school anyway.

In contrast, less than 10 percent of the boys showed any signs of wanting to avoid success. Rather, they were delighted at John's triumph and predicted a great career for him.

Generalized statements about women's ambivalence about ambition, based on findings such as the above, become part of a myth system when they are used to make predictions and decisions about individual women. It is always necessary to allow for individual differences no matter how true the generalization. Nearly 10 percent of the boys in Horner's study *did* show a tendency to avoid success. And nearly 35 percent of the girls *did not* as the following story indicates:

Anne is quite a lady—not only is she tops academically, but she is liked and admired by her fellow students— quite a trick in a man-dominated field. She is brilliant— but she is also a woman. She will continue to be at or near the top. And ... always a lady.

Especially pernicious is the tendency to take a generaliza tion beyond the level of description to make assumptions that the differences are biologically determined. This a- mounts to blindness to the statistical probability that most women will work for a large part of their adult lives.

Women's Image

At the present time there is an elaborate educational system designed to teach women to underestimate themselves. Society's expectations enter the teaching process before girls reach school, but once they do, school textbooks continue to keep a ceiling on the aspirations of little girls. A recent study of five social studies textbooks written for grades one to three revealed that men were shown or described in over 100 different jobs and women in less than 30. Almost all the women's jobs are those traditionally associated with women. Women are shown as having so few jobs of interest available to them that they might as well

"PAY GAP" BETWEEN MEN AND WOMEN GETS WIDER		
Median earnings per year, full-time workers		
1957	$3,008	$4,713
1958	$3,102	$4,927
1959	$3,193	$5,209
1960	$3,293	$5,417
1961	$3,351	$5,644
1962	$3,446	$5,794
1963	$3,561	$5,978
1964	$3,690	$6,195
1965	$3,823	$6,375
1967	$3,973	$6,848
1968	$4,150	$7,182
1969	$4,457	$7,664
(Latest available)		

Source: United States Department of Commerce.

UNEMPLOYMENT RATE: HIGHER FOR WOMEN THAN MEN		
Rate of unemployment, average for year		
1960	5.9%	5.4%
1961	7.2%	6.4%
1962	6.2%	5.2%
1963	6.5%	5.2%
1964	6.2%	4.6%
1965	5.5%	4.0%
1966	4.9%	3.2%
1967	5.2%	3.1%
1968	4.8%	2.9%
1969	4.7%	2.8%

Source: United States Department of Labor:

WOMEN EARN LESS THAN MEN IN ALL KINDS OF JOBS		
Median annual earnings, full-time workers		
Occupation	Women	Men
Scientists	$10,000	$13,200
Professional, technical	$6,691	$10,151
Proprietors, managers	$5,635	$10,340
Clerical workers	$4,789	$7,351
Sales workers	$3,461	$8,549
Craftsmen	$4,625	$7,978
Factory workers	$3,991	$6,738
Service workers	$3,332	$6,058

Source: United States Department of Labor, National Science Foundation Data for 1968.

MOST WOMEN WORKERS ARE IN LOWER-PAYING JOBS		
People Employed as:	% of all Women Workers	% of all Male Workers
Proprietors managers	4%	14%
Professional technical	15%	14%
Craftsmen	1%	20%
Factory workers	15%	20%
Clerks sales workers	42%	13%
Service workers	16%	7%
Household workers	6%	Less than 1%

Source: United States Department of Labor

stay home and have children. But even their work at home is downplayed. Women are not shown teaching or disciplining their children, baking complicated dishes or handling money in a knowledgeable way. Because the father is making money and therefore the more important member of the family, a house is where Mr. Brown "and his family live." Even pictures show men or boys seven times as often as women or girls.

Moreover, examination of any toy catalog will show page after page of dolls and household appliances for little girls, but no little girls' outfits for engineer, chemist, lawyer or astronaut. TV commercials (bear in mind the length of time the average American child spends before the TV set) endlessly show women helpless before a pile of soiled laundry until the male voice of authority overrides hers to tell how brand X with its fast-acting enzymes will get her clothes cleaner than clean.

If a woman desires or has to work, and if her early socialization hasn't "taken," then for the mature woman there are such venerable institutions as Dr. Spock to make her feel guilty for doing so, especially if she has children.

"Why can't a woman," asked Dr. Benjamin M. Spock, "be less like a man? . . .

"The absurd thing is that men go into pediatrics and obstetrics because they find them interesting and crea-

tive, and American women shun childbearing and childrearing because they don't. . . .

"Man is the fighter, the builder, the trap-maker, the one who thinks mechanically and abstractly. Woman has stayed realistic, personal, more conservative.

"Everybody can disprove me by saying these are culturally determined, but I can disprove them by saying that these are emotionally determined."

This type of rhetoric, reinforcing male vanity, has been used until recently to prevent Third World people from taking themselves seriously in occupational terms also, as the following paraphrase by Karen Oppenheim illustrates:

"Why can't a Negro," asked Dr. Benjamin M. Spock, "be less like a white? . . .

"The absurd thing is that whites go into agricultural science and overseeing because they find them interesting and creative, and American Negroes shun cotton picking and plant pruning because they don't. . . .

"Whites are the fighters, the builders, the leaders, the ones who think mechanically and abstractly. Negroes have stayed rhythmic, personal, more happy-go-lucky.

"Everybody can disprove me by saying these are culturally determined, but I can disprove them by saying that these are emotionally determined."

To the influence of textbooks, the media and books on child care we can add the fact that many young women have never had the experience of dealing with a woman in a responsible position of authority. School guidance counsellors assist in the cooling-out process by discouraging women from entering nontraditional fields of employment.

Myth 2: If women do pursue a career they tend to be more interested in personal development than in a career as a way of life.

Another form of this myth is "She will only get married, have children and drop out of the labor force anyway." Figures from the Women's Bureau show the fallacy in this line of reasoning. *One-tenth* of *all* women remain single, and these women work for most of their lives. In fact, those who enter the labor force by age 20 and remain unmarried will work 45 years on the average—*longer* than the 43-year average for men. In addition, *one-tenth* of all *married* women do not have children. If they enter the labor force by age 20, they will work 35 years on the average, eight years less than men. Although it is difficult to estimate the average time spent in the labor force by women with children (the tendency is to work, drop out when the children are small and then reenter), the average woman today will be in her mid-thirties by the time her youngest child is in school. If she reenters the labor force at age 35 and has no more children, she will average another 24 years of work. Women in the labor force who are widowed, separated or divorced at age 35 will work on the average another 28 years (17 percent of women in the population aged 16 or over were widowed or divorced in 1967; 15 percent of those were in the labor force).

Apart from those women who are single, widowed, divorced, married with no children or married with their youngest child in school, there are women with pre-school age children who are motivated to work either due to financial necessity or to the desire for a continuous career pattern. For all of these women it is not only (or perhaps not even primarily) their lack of motivation that prevents their career advancement so much as it is institutionalized assumptions concerning the normality of marriage, motherhood and the inevitability of withdrawal from the labor force. A striking example of this was reported by journalist Jane Harriman who wrote in a recent *Atlantic* article that she was fired from her job when she asked her boss to give her leave to have a baby. That the baby was to be illegitimate only underscores the assumptions and expectations that people have about motherhood. Why, for that matter, shouldn't there be paternity leaves, or paternity firings?

A related, equally serious, result of assuming women to be a marginal and uncommitted work force is the lack of adequate day care facilities. In 1965 the Census Bureau conducted a national study of women who had worked 27 weeks or more in 1964, either full- or part-time, and who had at least one child under 14 years of age living at home. The 6.1 million mothers surveyed had 12.3 million children under 14 years of age, of whom 3.8 million were under six years. But licensed public and private day care facilities available three years later could provide for only about half a million of those children!

The California Advisory Commission on the Status of Women, for example, had to report that the actual unmet need for children's center services was an unknown quantity. Most districts reported waiting lists from 50 to 100 percent of their present capacity. A two-year delay after being placed on a waiting list was not unusual. One out of every five poverty level residents not in the labor force, but who wanted a regular job, listed inability to obtain child care as the primary reason for not looking for work. Even the available facilities were found to be inadequate. The problems encountered in existing programs and services included obsolete and unsafe facilities, lack of a state-level child care coordinating council, staff shortages, lack of continuity of funding, segregation of children by economic class, lack of adequate licensing standards, transportation and lack of facilities for children under two, for school-aged children up to the age of 12 years and for sick children.

Myth 3: There will be a higher absenteeism and turnover rate amongst women than amongst men, due to the restrictions imposed by children on working mothers.

The third myth is used to rationalize discriminatory employment practices related to women. However, in a 1969 study the Women's Bureau found labor turnover rates more influenced by the skill level of the job, the age of the worker, the worker's record of job stability and the worker's length of service with the employer than by the sex of the worker. Indeed a study of occupational mobility of individuals 18 years of age and over showed that men changed occupations more frequently than women. Between January 1965 and January 1966, 10 percent of the men, as against 7 percent of the women, were employed in different occupations. Similarly, women on the average lose more workdays due to acute conditions than do men, but men lose more workdays due to chronic conditions such as heart trouble, arthritis, rheumatism and orthopedic impairment. Considering both conditions, during a one-year period, *women lost less time* than men because of illness or injury (5.3 days for women versus 5.4 days for men 17 years of age and over).

Myth 4: Women are only working for pin money, for extras.

The fourth myth is used to justify discrimination in employment when a job is given to a less qualified man because "she didn't need the money anyway." The Women's Bureau found 1.5 million female family heads—more than one-tenth of all families were headed by a woman in 1966—were the sole breadwinners for their families. Moreover, families headed by women were the most economically deprived: in 1967 almost one-third of such families lived in poverty, and they were the most persistently poor. Their median income was only $4,010 rising to $5,614 if the woman head was a year-round full-time worker. The income is substantially lower than the $8,168 median income of male-head families in which the male head worked full-time year-round but the wife was not in the labor force. Even where both husband and wife are working, the woman's income is often not for frivolous luxuries but means the difference between economic survival or not. In March 1967, 43 percent of those wives whose husbands' incomes were between $5,000 and $7,000 were in the labor force; 41 percent where husbands' incomes were between $3,000 and $5,000; 33 percent between $2,000 and $3,000; 27 percent between $1,000 and $2,000; and 37 percent when husbands' incomes were under $1,000.

At the state level, the California Advisory Commission on the Status of Women found nearly one in ten families in California headed by a woman. Similar to the national findings, in California economic need is the most compelling reason to work for the great majority of women with young children. The two factors most responsible for the need are the amount and the regularity of the husband's earnings. Women's earnings are not supplementary but basic to the maintenance of their family. Women comprise 35.7 percent of the California labor force, and the California economy depends significantly on women workers.

Myth 5: Women control most of the power and wealth in American society.

The inference that is supposed to be drawn from this notion is that women are "the power behind the throne," the major controllers of economic wealth even though they do not earn it. A weak form of the argument, for example, is that women are the major American stockholders. The argument is false. The Women's Bureau found 18 percent of the total number of shares of stock reported by public corporations were owned individually by women, 24 percent individually by men. The remaining 58 percent were held or owned by institutions, brokers and dealers. In estimated market value, stock registered in women's names was 18 percent of the total, in men's names 20 percent. A glance at the board of directors of public corporations will reveal an almost totally male membership, casting great doubt on how much social control women have, even over the stock they do own.

Women may spend a major portion of their husbands' earnings, but the expenditures are typically for the smaller consumer items. Major purchases such as those of a house or a car will be decided by the husband or by the husband and wife together, rarely by the wife alone. Most women do not even know the exact amount of their husbands' income, so it is he who has the ultimate power over how much of it she can spend. In any event, the amount of power over expenditure is nonexistent when the most important buying decision to be made is that between brand X and brand Y of detergent. Job discrimination, the inability to realize one's true potential, is a high price to pay for the dubious privilege of deciding what color socks he will wear.

Myth 6: It will be too disruptive to an efficient work orientation if women and men are permitted to mingle on the job.

Studies have repeatedly shown that traditional attitudes such as these are illogical, based on bias and prejudice, rather than on fact. With respect to the ego threat implied by a woman co-worker or supervisor, men are likely to report that they would feel their masculinity threatened, if they do not have a working wife or if they have never worked for a female supervisor. If they have had the experience, however, their view changes to the positive. Relevant here is the fact that it is much harder for women to get the title than to get the work. Too often, women end up in clerical dead-end jobs, keep getting assigned more and more authority and responsibility as their experience and competence increase, but with no corresponding title or salary increase. They may run the office, but it will be in the old "helpmate" pattern, in the private sense of adjunct to the boss rather than in the public sense of official recognition (social or economic) from others.

The problem of women entering male fields is similar, especially if the field is one of higher status than women are usually allowed to enter. Women and men work compatibly without disruptive sexual involvement as graduate students, laboratory technicians and bank tellers. The real problem with women entering the male-dominated trades or professions, or with men entering the clerical field, would seem to be the salaries. This would create the problem of women being paid "too much" and men "too little" for what has come to be defined as appropriate for women and men.

In brief, myths concerning sexuality on the job are mostly invoked when there is a danger of a crossing-over of female and male status and pay differentials on the job. Although the principle of "equal pay for equal work" is widely accepted and sometimes even legally enforced, great care is taken to ensure that women and men are not given the same job titles and corresponding opportunities for advancement.

Myth 7: Women are more "human-oriented," less mechanical, and they are better at tedious, boring or repetitive tasks than men are.

The myth embodies the dual notion that women's place is in the (human-oriented) home and that women are innately inferior to men in intellectual capacity. When feminists were demanding the right to an education in the last century, educators such as Dr. Edward H. Clarke in a book entitled *Sex in Education* published in 1873, expressed learned judgments that the demand for equality in education was physically impossible. A boy could study six hours a day, according to Dr. Clarke, but if a girl spent more than four the "brain or special apparatus will suffer ... leading to those grievous maladies which torture a woman's earthly existence, called leucorrhoea, amenorrhoea, dysmenorrhoea, chronic and acute ovaritis, prolapsus uteri, hysteria, neuralgia, and the like." While this quaint wording makes us smile at the ignorance of an earlier generation, it should be noted that Dr. Clarke was only painfully seeking a rationalization for making the value judgment that "what is" must inevitably, innately, biologically —and therefore logically—"continue to be so." Dr. Clarke was Professor of Materia Medica at Harvard from 1855 to 1872 and for five succeeding years an Overseer. He opposed the suggestion that women be admitted to Harvard College. Women were not educated equally with men; women could not be educated equally with men.

Yet few people today smile at the ignorance of today's generation in denying women equal access to a scientific education. The young woman who wants to be an engineer, astronaut, or scientist will be ridiculed out of her decision by her family, school counselors, textbooks, and teachers, and by her peers. The woman who wants a technical education will find many colleges and trade schools do not accept women in pre-employment apprenticeship courses in fields such as carpentry and electronics. The woman who works in a factory will find herself assigned to the tedious, repetitive, boring jobs, denied on-the-job training, placed on a separate seniority list than men (last hired, last promoted, first fired) and, of course, paid less. Women are not educated equally with men; women cannot be educated equally with men. The scientific and technical arena is the last hold out of Dr. Clarke's earlier philosophy. The woman who is unable to become an engineer or a carpenter and the woman who is assigned to the tedious factory position are both being discriminated against by the same myth.

Employers still advertise in separate male and female help wanted columns; unions still advertise for journeywomen and journeymen. The journeywoman is given less training, her promotional ladder is shorter or non-existent, and she is paid less. The woman in the factory, i.e., the woman at the lowest level in the hierarchy of this form of discrimination, suffers the greatest economic deprivation. She is the least educated, most unskilled, and often her job is necessary for her sheer physical survival. Union leadership is often absent or unresponsive to her plight. If she has a family to support or is a single head of household, she does not have the time to attend union meetings that a man, because he also has a wife who is his caretaker, does. The lack of opportunity for on-the-job training and her social education to a more passive role than her male counterpart also militate against her organizing in her own self-interest as long as her wages remain at the survival level, i.e., as long as she has something—anything—to lose.

As Marjorie B. Turner points out, we know nothing about the comparative propensity of women and men to join unions on an industry-wide basis. The Women's Bureau reports that 1 out of 7 women in the nation's labor force, but 1 out of 4 men workers, belonged to a union in 1966. Whether this is a reflection of sex labelling in jobs, discrimination, segregated locals, or difficulty or disinterest in organizing women is unknown.

The evidence regarding innate sex differences in mechanical and verbal aptitudes is sufficiently contradictory that no generalizations are warranted. Through the preschool and early school years, girls exceed boys in both verbal performance and ability with numbers. By high school, boys fairly consistently excel at mathematics. In addition, boys more accurately assess their abilities and performance by high school, whereas girls seem to show an earlier decline in tested performance. Such differences could, of course, be genetic. However, it seems equally or more plausible to

suggest that they are related to social pressures operating differently on women and men to mold them into the adult roles they are assigned by tradition to play. As children, girls are taught to be passive and submissive, and this is conducive to grade school performance. By high school, boys are taught to prepare for careers, and this is conducive to high school performance. The cultural interpretation is consistent with Matina Horner's findings regarding the stronger motive to avoid success in college women than in college men. Until a culture evolves in which both sexes are treated as *people* with equal opportunities and expectations, the question of genetic differences in intellectual functioning will have to remain moot.

Even granting that sex differences may have a genetic base, the statistical picture that emerges is still one of highly overlapping curves for women and men, rather than separate ones. We would be led to predict perhaps a 60:40 or smaller split in the sexes among certain occupations, but not one that is 100:0. Clearly, whether or not sex differences in mechanical aptitude are genetically determined, the current labor market certainly assumes that they are.

But evidence to support the opposite conclusion was provided by the demonstrated competence of women in a wide range of occupations during World Wars I and II. Even today, the Women's Bureau reports that by mid-1968 women were being or had been trained as apprentices in 47 skilled occupations. Many of the apprenticeships, such as that of cosmetologist or dressmaker, reflected traditional roles. But some women were being trained as clock and watch repairman, electronic technician, engraver, optical mechanic, precision lens grinder, machinist, plumber, draftsman, electrical equipment repairer, electronic subassembly repairer and compositor.

Women's entry into traditionally male apprenticeship fields illustrates the fallacy of the myth that women are better than men at tedious, boring or repetitive tasks. It is doubtful whether the boredom, repetitiveness or tediousness differs greatly between a clock and watch repairman (male) and a typist (female) or between a precision lens grinder (male) and a dental technician (female). As Caroline Bird has documented, women's work in one part of the world or at one historical period may be man's work in another part of the world or at another time. What doesn't change is that whatever men do is regarded as more important, and gets more rewards, than what women do. The boundaries are defined by status, not aptitude, for even in traditionally female fields the persons in the highest positions of authority are most likely to be male.

Myth 8: Women need to be "protected" because of their smaller size.

There is no question but that women are physically smaller on the average than are men, but the inferences drawn from, and the restrictions imposed by, the biological fact are socially determined. In other cultures and at other times it has been women who have pulled the plows or carried burdens on their heads because of their presumed superior physical strength. Today it is men who suffer from hernias, back troubles and a shorter life expectancy because of the heavier physical tasks they are expected to assume. The industrial revolution made most, if not all, heavy physical work unnecessary, providing employers are willing to invest in the necessary laborsaving equipment. As long as there is a marginal, exploitable, male labor force (as has been the case with Third World peoples in America), it is often cheaper for the employer to use manual labor than to provide the requisite equipment.

Protective laws with respect to lifting should be extended to cover all *people* not restricted to one sex. Where lifting is required, a person's physical ability to hold the job should be medically, not sexually, determined. There may be some jobs involving lifting which only a few women—or men—would be able to perform. At the present time there seems little inclination for women to enter such fields as professional football. (There is one exception, and she may truly prove the rule: she was squashed by an opposing guard.) There has, however, been much resistance to women jockeys, whose smaller size is a decided asset.

As long as there are protective laws governing women only, and not protective laws for workers in general, such laws can be used to perpetuate discrimination. A job requiring heavy lifting can be placed in the lower rung of a promotional hierarchy, even if experience at that job bears no relation to subsequent positions in the hierarchy. It has the effect of preventing women from entering *any* of the positions in the hierarchy because they are not allowed to enter the one with the weight-lifting restriction at the bottom.

With respect to restrictions on night work ostensibly concerning the safety of women going to and from their jobs, the rationalization only seems to occur when the overtime or shift work involved would place her in a higher status occupational category as well. As baby-sitter, as charwoman, as librarian, as telephone operator, as nurse, as keypuncher, the woman working at night is considered perfectly capable of looking after her own safety. It is well worth remembering that men often place women on pedestals only so they do not have to look us in the eye!

Vicious Circle

The myth systems that perpetuate sexual discrimination bring us round full circle. Women are stereotyped as lacking in aggressive and managerial qualities; if they do have the qualities or the opportunity to learn them, laws and customs are invoked to prevent their being used. Women and men are not judged as individuals based on demonstrated competence, but on the basis of sexual stereotypes. Moreover, women's underestimation of their own abilities combines with others' underestimation of their abilities to produce the declining status of women in today's labor force.

As Cynthia Fuchs Epstein points out, success is difficult for women because of the nature of informal channels of support and communication. Breaking a color, ethnic or sex occupational barrier means that the newcomers have not shared the same worlds as their colleagues. Casual chats, informal rituals, jokes, shared experiences—all become strained and serve to keep the newcomer in the psychological position of "the stranger."

It is true that women are becoming more emancipated, but it is an emancipation from the home and not towards higher status in the labor force. Although the mass media provide great fanfare for women as they become "firsts" in traditionally male fields, the publicity obscures the overall decline in women's status in the labor force. The Horatio Alger myth of American society was always a cruel hoax. Perpetuated with respect to women, it is simply laughable, when the average woman with five years of college can expect to earn the equivalent of a man with a high school education.

334

How Much Money Do Executives Want?

Edward E. Lawler, III

What are the most important rewards in an executive's life? To many businessmen the answer is simple and obvious: money. The expression "private enterprise," repeated so frequently and fondly, often means simply the chance to make money.

But behavioral science research and thought over the past several decades have put a host of modifiers onto this simple belief. We have learned that people work not only for salaries, but for less tangible returns such as self-realization, job satisfaction, independence, security, prestige, and to give meaning and companionship to their lives. Some researchers say that higher pay may not be

the most important of these motives; among higher level employees it may not be very important at all.

One of the results of the tendency of some researchers to stress non-financial incentives is that managers are not always sure what place, if any, money should have as a motivator of performance effectiveness. The myths that have grown up about management compensation as a result of this confusion are well illustrated in a study I conducted recently among 500 managers from all levels of management and from a wide variety of organizations. They were asked whether they agreed or disagreed with five statements that contained assumptions about the psy-

335

chological aspects of management compensation—assumptions with important implications for the administration of pay.

■ At the higher paid levels of management, pay isn't one of the two or three most important job factors (61 percent agreed).

■ Money is an ineffective motivator of outstanding job performance at the management level (55 percent agreed).

■ Information about management pay rates is best kept secret (77 percent agreed).

■ Managers are likely to be dissatisfied with their pay even if they are highly paid (54 percent agreed).

■ Managers are not concerned with how their salary is divided between cash and fringe benefits; the important thing is the amount of salary they receive (45 percent agreed).

As can be seen, better than 50 percent of managers participating in the study agreed with the first four assumptions, and almost that many agreed with the last.

Recently, research results have begun to accumulate which suggest that all of these assumptions may be partially or completely invalid. Let us therefore examine them more closely.

Importance of Pay to Managers

Historically, we have progressed from the view that man is primarily motivated by economic motives to one that stresses psychological and social needs. This is all to the good; but it may have gone too far. Those who have emphasized the importance of non-economic goods have tended to downgrade the continuing importance of pay. Either they have overlooked it altogether, or they imply that, in our time of general affluence, it is not as important as it used to be. Since experts in "human relations" have shown pay to be relatively unimportant, managers feel they are compelled to play it down too. When the managers in my study were asked how they thought the experts would reply to the statement that pay isn't a major job factor to the higher paid executives, 71 percent said they thought experts would agree. What of themselves? Fewer—but still a majority (61 percent)—of the managers also agreed.

Does this mean that pay should be dismissed as unimportant? I do not think the evidence justifies such a conclusion.

The belief that pay decreases in importance as one accumulates more and more has its roots in Abraham Maslow's theory of a hierarchy of needs. Briefly, Maslow's theory says that human needs are arranged in a hierarchy of decreasing urgency. At the bottom are survival and physical comfort. These are followed by social needs, esteem needs, and finally, needs for autonomy and self-actualization. According to Maslow, once the lower order needs are relatively well satisfied, they become unimportant as motivators, and people turn toward the higher order needs. If it is assumed (as most do who say pay is unimportant) that pay satisfies only lower level needs, then it becomes obvious that once a person's physical comforts are taken care of, his pay will become unimportant.

But I do not believe that pay satisfies only lower level needs. I contend that *pay is a unique incentive—unique because it is able to satisfy both the lower order physiological and security needs, and also higher needs such as esteem and recognition.* Recent studies show that managers frequently think of their pay as a form of recognition for a job well done and as a mark of achievement. The president of a large corporation has clearly pointed out why:

> Achievement in the managerial field is much less spectacular than comparable success in many of the professions . . . the scientist, for example, who wins the Nobel prize. . . . In fact, the more effective an executive, the more his own identity and personality blend into the background of his organization, and the greater is his relative anonymity outside his immediate circle.

One form of recognition that managers do receive that is visible and "spectacular" is pay. Pay has become an important indicator of the value of a person to an organization. Thus it is not surprising to hear that one newly-elected company president whose "other" income from securities approximated $125,000, nevertheless demanded a salary of $100,000. When asked why he did not take $50,000, and defer the rest until after retirement, at a sizable tax saving, he replied, "I want my salary to be six figures when it appears in the proxy statement."

It is precisely because pay satisfies higher order needs as well as lower order needs that it may remain important to managers regardless of how large their income is. For example, one recent study clearly showed that although pay is slightly less important to upper level managers (presidents and vice-presidents) than it is to lower level managers, it is still more important than security, social, and esteem needs for upper level managers. At the lower management level, pay was rated as more important than all but self-actualization needs. (See Figure 1)

We can turn to motivation theory to help explain further why pay continues to be important to many managers. Goals that are initially desired only as a means to an end can in time become ends in themselves—thus money may cease to be only a path to the satisfaction of needs and may become a need itself. For many managers, money and money-making have become ends. As one manager put it, "It is just like bridge—it isn't any fun unless you keep score." In summary, the evidence shows that although pay may be important to managers for different reasons as they rise, it remains important at all levels.

Pay as an Incentive

It is known that a number of incentive plans have failed to produce expected increases in productivity. Because of this, many have assumed that pay necessarily is an ineffective incentive for managers. This view is expressed well by a company president: "Wage systems are not, in themselves, an important determinant of pace of work, application to work, or output." Correspondingly, there has been a decline in the use of pay incentive systems. In a 1935 sample of companies 75 percent replied that they used wage incentive programs. By 1939 this had fallen to 52 percent, and by 1958 to 27 percent. These figures point up the general disillusionment; it is also reflected in my study, showing that 55 percent of the managers

sampled felt that pay is not a very effective incentive at the management level.

What has led to the failure and abandonment of so many incentive systems? I feel that many of the failures can be attributed to the use of pay as an incentive in a manner which does not agree with the theoretical basis for expecting pay to be a motivator. The logic is that if pay is tied to productivity, then productivity should increase with pay. This logic seems to be supported by the psychological law of effect, which states that if behavior (productivity) appears to lead to a reward (pay), it will tend to be repeated.

But do incentive schemes designed to relate pay to productivity really follow the law of effect? I believe they do not because typically they are not concerned with *whether the managers see their pay as tied to performance.* Top management is typically concerned only with whether *they* feel pay is tied to performance and not whether other employees feel this way. I have considerable evidence that many managers who work under systems that, according to top management, tie productivity to pay simply do not feel that better work will bring them higher pay.

I recently distributed a questionnaire to over 600 middle and lower level managers in a variety of organizations, all of which purported to use pay as an incentive. The man-

Figure 1—The importance of personal needs varies with the manager's level. *(Left-hand scale numbers are arbitrary.)*

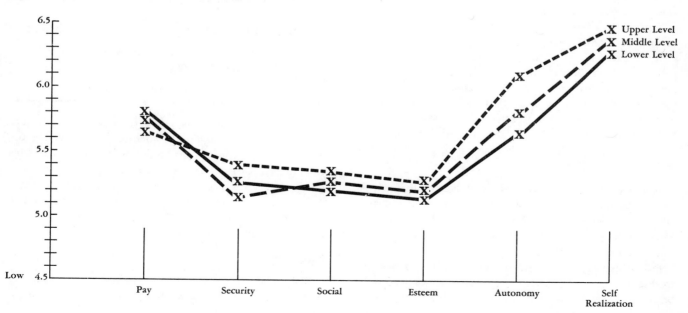

agers were asked what factors determined their pay. The consensus was that the most important ones were training and experience—*not* performance. A look at how their superiors rated them, and their pay, showed that they were correct. There was virtually *no* relationship between pay and rated job performance. How then could they believe in their organizations' incentive programs?

But other data from the same managers did show that pay can be an effective incentive. Those managers most highly motivated to perform their jobs effectively were characterized by two attitudes: (1) They said that their pay was important to them. (2) They felt that good job performance would lead to higher pay. For them the law of effect was in order—pay was a significant reward which they saw as contingent upon performance.

It is not enough therefore to have a pay plan *called* an incentive system. The people subject to the plan must *feel* that it is an incentive and this comes about only when they feel their pay is related to their performance.

In the companies I studied pay actually was not closely tied to performance, so it is not surprising that the managers doubted that it was. But there is still a question of whether actually tying pay to performance will guarantee that employees accept that the relationship holds for them. I feel it is not enough, although it probably is a necessary precondition. Indeed, there is considerable evidence that even workers on piece-rate plans are not convinced that their long-term economic good will be furthered by high productivity. One reason for this is that in order to believe that pay is tied to performance an employee, whether he is a manager or a worker, must have substantial trust in his superior and other members of the organization. Without a high degree of trust, the individual can hardly be expected to believe that his performance will be fairly evaluated and that his long-term economic good will be furthered by performing well. That such trust often is not present, and indeed, that it often is not deserved, is illustrated by the many cases of piece-rate changes and consequent quota restrictions that have occurred to workers in many organizations.

It also seems that for employees to believe that pay is tied to performance, there must be good communication about pay policies and actions. As we will see, secrecy often interferes with these necessary communications.

The unintended consequence of many stock option and bonus plans is to circumvent the problems of establishing trust and good relationships between superior and subordinate by establishing an automatic "objective" reward system. But my feeling is that even "objective" financial reward systems will never be effective under conditions of low trust and poor relationships. This also appears to be true for the many management compensation plans. Many of these management incentive plans (such as stock options) often do more to destroy the perception that pay is based upon performance than to encourage it. They pay off years after the behavior that is supposed to be rewarded has taken place; and the size of the reward given is often independent of the quality of performance.

Two other factors suggest that cash payments may be particularly appropriate now:

■ A recent study found that managers preferred cash payments to other forms of compensation.

■ New tax laws now make it possible to get almost as much money into the hands of the manager through salary as through stock options and other forms of deferred payment.

There is one other reason why incentive plans often fail. They are frequently set up in such a way that earning more money must be done at the expense of the satisfaction of other needs or desires. For instance, if managers are rewarded solely on the basis of the performance of subordinates, they are caught in a bind: on the one hand they want more production, no matter what it costs the total organization; on the other, they want to cooperate with managers in other parts of the organization. Thus, the pay incentive system may set up a conflict system for managers

---

"Highly paid foremen ($12,000 and above) were better satisfied than company presidents who received less than $50,000."

---

as a piece-rate system often does for blue collar workers.

In summary, the significant question is not whether pay is effective or ineffective as an incentive, but under what conditions it is most effective. Pay can potently motivate good job performance when managers understand that it is being deliberately used to reward, or to extend recognition for, good performance—and when other needs are also met by good and effective work.

Satisfaction With Pay

We frequently hear that, with money as with peanuts, no matter how much someone gets, he always wants more.

And indeed, as demonstrated earlier, pay does remain important, no matter what a man's income. But the conclusion, accepted by 54 percent of those in my study, that managers will remain dissatisfied even if highly paid, does not necessarily follow from this premise.

There is an important difference between how much someone wants to get and what he feels is fair for what he is doing. Individuals tend to strike a mental balance between what they put into their jobs (effort, skill, education, experience, time, new ideas) and what they receive in return (money, status, privileges, etc.). Dissatisfaction comes when an individual feels that what he puts out exceeds what he gets back in the form of pay. He judges the fairness of the balance by comparing it to what other employees, usually co-workers, put out and get back. Dissatisfaction will usually come when one man's pay is lower than that of someone he considers roughly equal or inferior in ability, job level, and performance. But when he gets pay that compares favorably, he will tend to be satisfied. This does not mean, of course, that he would pass up a chance to make more money; it simply means that he feels he is being fairly treated and is not dissatisfied.

A recent study of over 1,900 managers shows that managers can be, and in fact frequently are, satisfied with their pay. They were first asked to rate on a scale (from one to seven) how much pay they received for their jobs. Next they were asked to rate how much pay they *should receive.*

As can be seen from Figure 2, which presents the results for the presidents who participated in the study, those paid high in relation to other presidents were satisfied. For this group ($50,000 and over), there was no difference between what they said they received and what they thought they should receive. But those receiving less than other presidents said there was a substantial difference between what their pay should be and what it was. The same results were obtained at each level of management down to and including foremen. At each level the highly paid were quite satisfied; it was the low paid managers who were dissatisfied. In fact, highly paid foremen ($12,000 and above) were better satisfied than company presidents who received less than $50,000.

There is even evidence that some managers can and do feel that they receive too much pay for their positions. Of the 1,900 studied, about 5 percent said they got too much. They apparently reached this conclusion by comparing themselves with other managers. Although the percentage is small, the fact that this feeling exists at all is evidence that individuals do not always feel they deserve more and

more pay. It is also evidence that some organizations are not doing the best possible job of distributing their compensation dollars.

It may be wise for companies to consult subordinates and peers when considering pay raises for a manager. Giving a high salary to someone other employees consider a poor performer can have several bad results. First, it can cause dissatisfaction among other managers who are good performers but get no raise. Good performers will never be satisfied with their pay under such circumstances. Second, and most important, a raise to a poor performer is a signal to other managers that pay is not really based on merit—an attitude that can destroy any motivational impetus created by an otherwise well-administered compensation program.

Should Salaries Be Secret?

The most commonly accepted axiom of good personnel practice is that management pay should be kept secret. (77 percent of my sample accepted it.) Many organizations go to great lengths to maintain this secrecy. Information is frequently kept locked in the company safe, and the pay checks of top management may receive special handling so that the salaries are not known even to the personnel manager.

The reason typically given is that secrecy helps to reduce dissatisfaction: what managers don't know won't hurt them, since they can't make invidious comparisons. But this reasoning is false; they make the comparisons anyway. What has not been clear in the past is to what extent secrecy affects the accuracy of the guesses they make upon which to base their comparisons.

Trying to gather some evidence about the effects of secrecy, I recently conducted an attitude survey. The following specific questions were investigated:
—Is there a tendency for managers to feel that there is too large or too small a difference between their pay and that of their subordinates and that of their superiors?
—Is a manager's satisfaction with the size of the difference between his pay and that of his superior or subordinate related to his satisfaction with his overall pay level?
—Do managers have an accurate picture of the pay of other managers?

The questionnaire was distributed to 635 middle and lower level managers in four private companies and in three government organizations. Responses were received from 563 managers (response rate of 88.7 percent). The four private companies were in widely different industries. They had in common secrecy policies about management pay. The managers in the government organizations also had widely varied jobs, ranging from managing liquor stores to soil conservation. These government organizations did make some information about their general pay rates available to managers, but the salary of each was confidential. Because of the wide variety of organizations sampled, and because of the high response rate, the results of this study should have relevance for a great number and variety of organizations.

The questionnaire had two parts. One asked the managers to estimate average yearly salaries of managers in their organizations at their own level, one above, and one below. (Actual average salaries were revealed to me by the organizations.) The second part asked the managers to indicate how well satisfied they were with their own salaries. They were also asked whether there was too much or too little difference between their own pay and that of their superiors and their subordinates.

The results clearly showed that in addition to often feeling that their own pay was too low, these managers felt that the pay of both subordinates and superiors was too close to theirs. They apparently felt that the pay scales in their organizations are too compact—not enough separation existing between the salaries at different management levels. Thus, regardless of whether a manager looked up-

"Secrecy about salaries may lead to lower satisfaction with pay and to decreased motivation for effective performance."

ward or downward he would be dissatisfied with what he saw. (He was slightly more apt to be dissatisfied if he looked downward, feeling that his subordinates were too close behind him.) When he looked below, or alongside at those at his own level, he apparently felt that their high rates of pay showed he was not sufficiently appreciated.

Actually, however, he underestimated what his superiors were getting and overestimated the pay of subordinates and peers, thereby misunderstanding his own position in relation to them. One-third of the managers overestimated the annual pay of their subordinates by more than $1,000. The managers answering the questionnaire did not have a clear picture of the real situation—secrecy had kept them from it—and so much of their dissatisfaction was not only unnecessary but based on erroneous guesses. Interestingly, government managers were consistently more accurate than the private managers—because they had more accurate information.

Figure 2—Are company presidents satisfied with their pay? Yes, if they earn $50,000 or more per year. Otherwise, no. *(Left-hand scale numbers are arbitrary.)*

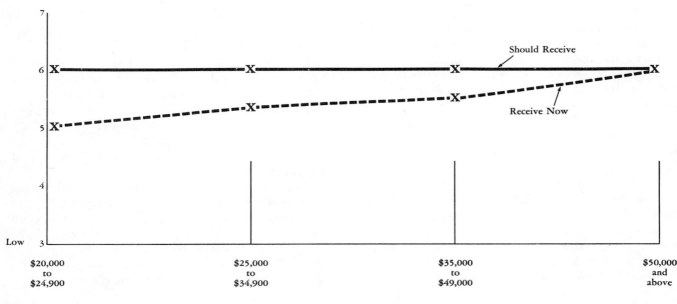

What were the effects of these distorted pictures on job performance and satisfaction? Since managers judge fairness by comparisons, and they estimated peer and subordinate pay too high, it followed that they felt their own salaries to be too low. Obviously, one effect of secrecy may be to increase dissatisfaction.

Secrecy may also contribute to dissatisfaction and lowered incentive when used by an executive to avoid telling subordinates what he really thinks of their work. Frequently a manager, distributing raises, gives some employees more than others because of greater improvement. However, if he tells each that he has given as much as he could, he implies that he is in general satisfied with their performances. The amount of increase is not tied in the subordinate's mind to the quality of his effort—the good worker is not sure he is getting more than the poor one, and the poor performer may feel his work is apparently good enough because he got a raise too.

There are other disadvantages to secrecy. Several studies have shown that accurate feedback about quality of work is a strong stimulus to good performance. People work better when they know how well they are doing—in relation to some meaningful standard. For a manager, pay is one of the most meaningful pieces of feedback information. High pay means good performance. Low pay is a signal that he is not doing well and had better improve. Our findings show that when managers don't really know what other managers earn, they can't correctly evaluate their own pay. Since they tend to overestimate the pay of subordinates and peers, the majority of them consider their pay as low—in effect, they receive negative feedback. Moreover, even when this feedback suggests they should change work behavior, it does not tell them what type of change to make. When managers are not doing their jobs well, negative feedback is undoubtedly what they need. But it gives a false signal to managers who are working effectively. Overall, it may be that because of the rumors and false information that inevitably circulate when pay is secret, then salary information must be public if managers are ever to believe that pay is based upon performance.

If secrecy policies cost so much in job satisfaction and in motivation for effective performance and promotion, it seems only sensible to abandon them. But what type of information *should* be given? Should managers be told what every other manager earns? Ultimately, I think this may be advisable. Initially, organizations that now have strict secrecy policies could start to move in this direction by giving out accurate information about the average or median salary at different levels and for different types of jobs. Managers could also be told the pay ranges for these jobs and they could be told the control points or similar devices that are used to determine their pay. But such limited information should only be a first step toward complete disclosure when the climate of the organization is prepared for it. There is no definitive reason why organizations cannot make salaries public information. It is far better to let managers know exactly how their pay compares with that of other managers than to have them make inaccurate and unfavorable comparisons based upon misinformation.

When Is a Dollar Not a Dollar?

When any organization is asked how much money it spends on compensation, it usually adds together money spent for salaries and fringe benefits. Union contracts are usually described as providing an x-cents-per-hour compensation "package." But is a dollar spent on cash salary really equal to a dollar spent on life insurance or other fringe benefits? Economically, and in terms of costs to the organization, it seems so; and this is probably why 45 percent of managers sampled believe that managers are not greatly concerned with how their pay is divided.

However, I do not believe that each manager actually regards the component parts of his own compensation this way. Several studies show that some benefits are valued more than others, even though the cost to the company is the same. For example, one study found that most employees strongly preferred hospital insurance to additional pension money, though both cost the organization the same.

The preferences of individuals for different benefits vary greatly, depending upon such factors as age, sex, marital status, and number of children. Older workers value pension plans much more than do younger workers, and unmarried men value a shorter work week more highly than married men, undoubtedly because different needs are salient for them. Managers in one location want certain things, in another they want others—which indicates that an organization may need different benefit packages in different locations. They may also have to design different packages for different groups. Indeed, it may be that the optimum solution is to adopt a "cafeteria" compensation program—that is, a plan that would allow every employee to divide his compensation dollars as he sees fit among the benefits offered. Previously, such a program would have been too difficult to be practical; but the computer now makes it feasible.

Cafeteria wage plans would appear to have a particularly bright future among managers who are unfettered by union contracts. Cafeteria wage plans have two additional benefits. First, they allow employees to participate in an important decision about their jobs. Even among managers, opportunities for actual participation (as contrasted with pseudo-participation for morale purposes) are rare enough so that in every situation where participation can be ligitimately and reasonably employed, it should be. Second, cafeteria-style wage plans help to make clear to the employees just how much money actually goes into their total compensation package. There are many reports of situations where employees do not even know of the fringe benefits for which their organizations are paying. With cafeteria wage plans this would be virtually eliminated.

Challenge for Management

What are the lessons to be learned from the recent research on the psychological aspects of compensation practices? I believe the following conclusions appear warranted:

■ Even at the higher paid levels of management, pay is important enough to be a significant motivator of good job performance. However, it will be a motivator only when seen by the managers themselves as tied to performance.

■ Managers can be, and in fact frequently are, satisfied with their pay when it compares favorably with that of other managers holding similar positions.

■ Secrecy policies have significant hidden costs attached to them. The evidence indicates that secrecy may lead to lower satisfaction with pay and to a decreased motivation for effective performance.

■ In order to get the maximum value for money spent on compensation, organizations may have to institute cafeteria-style wage payment systems to allow each manager to select the benefits and the amounts he wants.

Will organizations be willing to make these innovations? This question can be answered finally only five or ten years from now. However, there are at least two immediate reasons for believing that organizations will be slow to change.

First, as one critic has put it, most organizations seem intent on keeping their compensation programs up with but never ahead of the Joneses—in a "me too" type of behavior. Unfortunately, many organizations got badly "burned" when they tried to install piece-rate incentive wage schemes that ignored needs other than money. Once burned, twice shy.

Second, since none of the results of this group of studies offers a miraculous cure for present ills, slow movement may be desirable and necessary. These studies show that there are costs and risks involved. For example, it appears that if companies wish to make the most efficient use of pay as an incentive, they must be willing to improve communications about how pay is determined. They must develop an effective performance appraisal and measurement system. They must have a situation where high trust exists between superiors and subordinates. Finally, they must consider gradually eliminating secrecy about compensation.

Just the action of eliminating secrecy, no matter how well handled, will probably cause problems for some employees. In particular, openness will be difficult for the relatively low paid managers to handle. Others can, legitimately, believe their privacy has been violated.

The same point can be made about tying pay more clearly to performance, or about cafeteria-style wage plans. Any innovation entails costs; but the fact that top management continually questions present compensation systems suggests that innovation is needed and that eventually it will take place.

We have seen thus far, with the help of a variety of social scientists, the great range of existing family patterns at different stages of the family life cycle and their relations to the educational, political, economic, religious and recreational spheres of social organization. We can now turn to the critical question: What of the future? The question has been asked before, so that we can look at some of the answers already given, as well as to possibilities for alternative life styles that others have suggested, before summarizing predictions presented in prior essays and venturing some conclusions of our own.

One of the dramatic processes in United States history has been the "middle-classization," if we can coin such a term, of much of its population. Nevertheless, there are geographically and socially isolated islands in this society, such as the Amerindian reservation, a hill town out West, a tightly bordered ethnic community or a ghetto where the intertwining of institutions retaining a life style is so strong as to prevent that status decrystallization which is the first step of outward and upward mobility.

Most nations of the world, including the American and its parent "old country" societies, contained until recently three layers: a tiny elite, intermediary classes or caste sets of varying location in the social pyramid and of varying size in proportion to the total population, and, finally, an immense bottom layer. Urbanization, industrialization and increased societal complexity have shaken up this pyramid, necessitating and facilitating social mobility. Class and caste systems which were once strong enough to guarantee assignment on the basis of an inherited status role of royal family member, aristocrat, nobleman, artisan, merchant or peasant, have now become segmentalized into a variety of separate status hierarchies. The various criteria for social class placement in American society have be-

Part Five

Families of the Future

come separate from one another: educational achievement, including years, type of schooling, and prestige of school; occupation, with its complex internal stratification; income, including size and source; residence, specifically size, style, location and duration; association, including membership in formal groups and circles of informal socialization; consumer habits, including vacations, clothing, and recreation; minority identity, including definitions such as Negro, Jew, Pole, Mexican; ancestral traits, including the above listed traits of forefathers; and familial traits, including the above for spouse and children; and others. Children of serfs and peasants, of the urban unskilled workers and of minorities kept out of the system altogether, have been able to decrystallize their inheritance and achieve a variety of positions in the different status systems that have emerged. These upwardly mobile off-spring have used societal, family and self-developed resources to achieve positions in one or more status categories different from the ones their forebears held in the past, and they have reached a life style of a higher class. Although dramatic movement across several strata within one or two generations is still uncommon, the total process has had dramatic consequences not only on family life but on society in general.

Status decrystallization—and recrystallization at a new level, even downwardly—is often accompanied by geographical mobility. Such a resettling facilitates the break-up of old habits of thought, action, and interaction sufficiently to facilitate reorganization on a new level. This has been true of migrants from rural areas within the United States or from other countries, as sociologists Thomas and Znaniecki (1918–1920) found in their analysis of *The Polish Peasant in Europe and America*. Most of those whom they described had come to America between 1880 and 1914 and were highly disorganized by the time they were studied. Many of their descendants are now in the middle class in terms of education, occupation, income, residence, and life style, although some retain the habits of thought and attitudes of the immigrant culture. This is true, in fact, of most Americans. The young are more solidly middle class, with more choices and ideologies. But, as Annabelle Motz stresses, in "The Family as a Company of Players," the adults are so new to their social status as to be constantly anxious that their neighbors may disapprove of their behavior. This sense of unease faces the descendants of all ethnic and rural minorities who populate America's urban centers.

The process of middle-classization is documented by Lloyd H. Rogler's essay, "A Better Life: Notes from Puerto Rico." The family Rogler describes is in the process of moving upward: it has developed habits of long-range planning and has concentrated its resources on moving to a middle-class community. The family's background is lower-class, but it builds a more middle-class environment for the children, the father being willing to give up the traditional short-range hedonism of the "macho" style of life and turn his attention toward cooperative action within the family.

The decrystallization of the traditional lower class has continued to bring the whole working class closer to the middle class than was true in the past. The very bottom of the socio-economic pyramid is still occupied by what is now called the "under class," but the steady, blue-collar worker stands close in many respects to the white-collar worker life style, according to Gerald Handel and Lee Rainwater in "The Working Class—Old and New." (It is interesting to note that the name assigned this segment of the population implies that the rest of society is *not* working, an implication which Marx would have applauded). Thus, the under class is vanishing as a peasant-like aggregate. Individuals and families move up the social ladder, and society becomes urbanized. There is diffusion of higher-class cultural values through mass education and communication. And although slum schools fail in many ways to socialize and educate their pupils into middle-class morality and construction of reality, they succeed in transmitting some knowledge and in facilitating the escape of some students. The young today are better educated than their grandparents were, and we can assume that the trend, although painful and interrupted due to discrimination and a general lack of motivation to really change things, will continue.

What will happen to American society? Will we become a people mainly of the middle and upper classes? What changes in life styles will characterize the future of the family? Will stabilized, new generations abolish single-family dwelling units and return to communal living? Will homosexuality achieve sufficient societal approval or at least tolerance to become a viable alternative to heterosexual unions? Laud Humphreys documents many interesting changes in the attitudes and behaviors of male homosexuals in his "New Styles in Homosexual Manliness," including an expanding subculture which is more radicalized and virile than in the past but is diversified, allowing for internal variations.

Most social scientists do not expect a strong swing to extreme life styles external to family life, but rather variations on the themes of current interpersonal relations. Many of the aspects of the youth revolt often labeled as that of the "flower children" have become incorporated into new styles of intimate interaction. Fred Davis feels justified in saying that ". . . All of Us May Be Hippies Someday," from an analysis of values in the movement which has challenged traditionally rigid familial roles. Supported by sensitivity sessions and transactional analysis, the young and even the middle-aged today are examining the "games people play" when they want to avoid relating to each other directly because of anxiety. The security many people feel today functions to release energies for the examination of past values and attempts at new ways of developing fuller lives. As Richard Flacks found through much research, the "young intelligensia in revolt," are products of liberal, comfortably established, upper middle class households. Despite assumptions held by many Americans, social movements are developed and led by those who have had a stable background in the advantaged classes, a background fostering self-confidence, idealism and courage. Few ideational or value reformations are developed and disseminated by the ill-housed, ill-fed, ill-educated. Outbreaks of violence, sudden and impulsive or one-shot mass demonstrations do occur in poverty-ridden areas; but social movements, whether by youth, women, blacks or other historical categories of people, have been developed, expanded and sustained by the organizational efforts of educated, advantaged men and women.

And here is the crux of future change. As things stand in America at present, in terms of developmental socialization and increasingly open mass education in democratic principles, each person is predictably going to be more individuated, less responsive to mass behavior stimuli and authoritarian control, and more flexible. People will tend to build lives with long-range plans, after careful examination of the the conditions and resources on hand, and to weave complex systems of action in cooperation with others. Not driven, in the sense of compulsive striving with little gratification on the way, they are apt to be less neurotic and more in touch with a "joie de vivre" than their predecessors were. They will benefit from the hard work of prior generations which created a society of abundance for many, though they are apt to turn away from the value system of the Protestant ethic which made it ideologically possible.

Thus the immediate effect of changes in the family, brought about at first through changes in other social institutions but increasingly through purposeful reexamination of basic values and social relations, will be a greater emphasis on the interpersonal dynamics of the family. At least, this is what observers of the American scene such as Lee Rainwater predict for the 1984 benchmark. Harley Browning advises us to change "the timing of our lives" to fit the realities of lengthened span of existence in a complex and resource-abundant society. Margaret Mead predicts even more drastic changes in the matter of whether to enter family life at all in her "Future Family."

These and other authorities suggest the probability that increased security provided by changes in economic and technological institutions will lead to greater self-confidence and willingness to pursue purposive change. It seems likely that such changes will enrich the interpersonal dimensions of American lives, including family relations, with consequences devolving upon societal values and life styles.

The Family As a Company of Players

Annabelle B. Motz

All the world's a stage, and we are all players.

Erving Goffman in his *The Presentation of Self in Everyday Life* views our everyday world as having both front stage and back. Like professionals, we try to give a careful and superior performance out front. Back stage we unzip, take off our masks, complain of the strain, think back over the last act, and prepare anxiously for the next.

Sometimes the "on stage" performances are solos; sometimes we act in teams or groups. The roles may be carefully planned, rehearsed, and executed; or they may be spontaneous or improvised. The presentation can be a hit; or it can flop badly.

Picture a theater starring the family. The "stars" are the husband, wife, and children. But the cast includes a wide range of persons in the community—fellow workers, friends, neighbors, delivery-men, shopkeepers, doctors, and everyone who passes by. Usually husband and wife are the leads; and the appeal, impact, and significance of their performances vary with the amount of time on stage, the times of day and week, the circumstances of each presentation, and the moods of the audience.

Backstage for the family members is generally to be found in their homes, as suggested by the expression, "a man's home is his castle." The front stage is where they act out their dramatic parts in schools, stores, places of employment, on the street, in the homes of other persons; or, as when entertaining guests, back in their own homes.

My aim is to analyze the performances of family members before the community audience—their *front stage* appearances. This behavior conforms to the rules and regulations that society places upon its members; perhaps the analysis of the family life drama will provide insights into the bases of the problems for which an increasing number of middle-class persons are seeking professional help.

Many years ago, Thorstein Veblen noted that although industrialization made it possible for the American worker to live better than at any previous time in history, it made him feel so insignificant that he sought ways to call attention to himself. In *The Theory of the Leisure Class,* Veblen showed that all strata of society practiced "conspicuous consumption"—the ability to use one's income for non-essential goods and services in ways readily visible to others. A man's abilities were equated with his monetary worth and the obvious command he had in the market place to purchase commodities beyond bare necessities. Thus, a family that lives more comfortably than most must be a "success."

While conspicuous consumption was becoming an essential element of front stage performance, the ideal of the American as a completely rational person—governed and governing by reason rather than emotion—was being projected around the world. The writings of the first four decades of this century stress over and over again the importance of the individual and individual opinion. (The growth of unionism, the Social Security program, public opinion polling, and federal aid to education are a few examples of the trend toward positive valuation of each human being—not to mention the impact of Freud and Dewey and their stress on individual worth.) The desirability of rule by majority and democratic debate and voting as the best means of reaching group decisions—all these glorified rationality.

As population, cities, and industry grew, so also did anonymity and complexity; and rationality in organizations (more properly known as bureaucratization) had to keep pace. The individual was exposed to more and more people he knew less and less. The face to face relationships of small towns and workshops declined. Job requirements, duties and loyalties, hiring and firing, had to "go by the book." Max Weber has described the bureaucratic organization: each job is explicitly defined, the rights of entry and exit from the organization can be found in the industry's manual, and the rights and duties of the worker and of the organization toward the worker are rationally defined; above all, the worker acts as a rational being on the job—he is never subject to emotional urges.

With the beams and bricks of "front" and rationality the middle-class theater is built; with matching props the stage is set.

There are two basic scenes. One revolves about family and close personal relationships. It takes place in a well-furnished house—very comfortable, very stylish, but not "vulgar." The actors are calm, controlled, reasonable.

The other scene typically takes place in a bureaucratic anteroom cluttered with physical props and with people treated like physical props. The actors do not want the audience to believe that they *are* props—so they attract attention to themselves and dramatize their individuality and worth by spending and buying far more than they need.

What does this mean in the daily life of the family stars?

Take first the leading lady, wife, and mother. She follows Veblen and dramatizes her husband's success by impressing any chance onlookers with her efficient house management. How does one run a house efficiently? All must be reasoned order. The wife-housekeeper plans what has to be done and does it simply and quickly. Kitchen, closets, and laundry display department store wares as attractively as the stores themselves. The house is always presentable, and so is she. Despite her obviously great labors, she does not seem to get flustered, over-fatigued, or too emotional. (What would her neighbors or even a passing door-to-door salesman think if they heard her screaming at the children?) With minimal household help she must appear the gracious hostess, fresh and serene—behind her a dirty kitchen magically cleaned, a meal effortlessly prepared, and husband and children well behaved and helpful.

Outside the home, too, she is composed and rational. She does not show resentment toward Johnny's teacher, who may irritate her or give Johnny poor marks. She does not yawn during interminable and dull PTA programs (what would they think of her and her family?). At citizen meetings she is the embodiment of civic-minded, responsible, property-ownership (even if the mortgage company actually owns the property). Her supermarket cart reflects her taste, affluence, efficiency, and concern. At church she exhibits no unchurchly feelings. She prays that her actions and facial expression will not give away the fact that her mind has wandered from the sermon; she hopes that as she greets people, whether interested in them or not, she will be able to say the "right" thing. Her clothes and car are extremely important props—the right make, style, finish; and they project her front stage character, giving the kind of impression she thinks she and the other members of the family want her to give.

ENTER FATHER CENTER STAGE

The male lead is husband, father, and man-of-affairs. He acts in ways that, he hopes, will help his status, and that of his family. At all times he must seem to be in relaxed control of difficult situations. This often takes some doing. For instance, he must be both unequal and equal to associates; that is, he is of course a good fellow and very democratic, but the way he greets and handles his superiors at work is distinctly, if subtly, different from the way he speaks to and handles inferiors. A superior who arrives unexpectedly must find him dynamically at work, worth every cent and more of his income; an inferior must also find him busy, demonstrating how worthy he is of superior status and respect. He must always be in control. Even when supposedly relaxing, swapping dirty jokes with his colleagues, he must be careful to avoid any that offend their biases. He has to get along; bigots, too, may be able to do him good or harm.

Sometimes he cannot give his real feelings release until he gets behind the wheel—and the savage jockeying which takes place during evening rush may reflect this simultaneous discharge by many drivers.

The scene shifts back to the home. The other stars greet him—enter loving wife and children. He may not yet be ready or able to re-establish complete emotional control—after all, a man's home is his backstage—and the interplay of the sub-plots begins. If his wife goes on with her role, she will be the dutiful spouse, listening sympathetically, keeping the children and her temper quiet. If she should want to cut loose at the same time, collision will probably still be avoided because both have been trained to restrain themselves and present the right front as parents to their children—if not to each other.

Leisure is not rest. At home father acts out his community role of responsible family head. The back yard is kept up as a "private" garden; the garage as a showroom for tools on display. He must exhibit interest—but not too much enthusiasm—in a number of activities, some ostensibly recreational, retaining a nice balance between appearing a dutiful husband and a henpecked one. Reason must rule emotion.

The children of old vaudevillians literally were born and reared in the theater—were nursed between acts by mothers in spangles, trained as toddlers to respond to footlights as

347

other children might to sunlight. The young in the middle-class family drama also learn to recognize cues and to perform.

Since "front" determines the direction and content of the drama, they are supposed to be little ladies and gentlemen. Proper performances from such tyros require much backstage rehearsal. Unfortunately, the middle-class backstage is progressively disappearing, and so the children too must be prepared to respond appropriately to the unexpected—whether an unwanted salesman at the door who must be discreetly lied to about mother's whereabouts or a wanted friend who must not be offended. They are taught rationality and democracy in family councils—where they are also taught what behavior is expected of them. Reason is rife; even when they get out of hand the parents "reason" with them. As Dorothy Barclay says when discussing household chores and the child, "Appealing to a sense of family loyalty and pride in maturity is the tack most parents take first in trying to overcome youngsters' objections (to household chores). Offering rewards come second, arguing and insisting third."

"Grown-up" and "good" children do family chores. They want the house to look "nice"; they don't tell family secrets when visitors are present, and even rush to close closet and bedroom doors when the doorbell rings unexpectedly.

The child, of course, carries the family play into school, describing it in "show and tell" performances and in his deportment and dress. Part of the role of responsible parenthood includes participation in PTA and teacher conferences, with the child an important player, even if offstage.

To the child, in fact, much of the main dynamic of the play takes place in the dim realm of offstage (not always the same as backstage)—his parents' sex activities, their real income and financial problems, and many other things, some of them strange and frightening, that "children are not old enough to understand."

They early learn the fundamental lessons of front stage: be prepared; know your lines. Who knows whether the neighbors' windows are open? The parents who answers a crying child with, "Calm down now, let's sit down and talk this over," is rehearsing him in stage presence, and in his character as middle-class child and eventually middle-class adult.

Often the family acts as a team. The act may be rehearsed, but it must appear spontaneous. Watch them file in and out of church on Sunday mornings. Even after more than an hour of sitting, the children seem fresh and starched. They do not laugh or shout as on the playground. The parents seem calm, in complete control. Conversations and postures are confined to those appropriate for a place of worship.

Audience reaction is essential to a play. At church others may say, "What nice children you have!" or, "We look forward to seeing you next Sunday." Taken at face value, these are sounds of audience approval and applause; the performers may bask in them. Silence or equivocal remarks may imply disapproval and cause anxiety. What did they really mean? What did we do wrong? Sometimes reaction is delayed, and the family will be uncertain of their impression. In any case, future performances will be affected.

Acting a role, keeping up a front, letting the impressions and expectations of other people influence our behavior, does result in a great deal of good. Organized society is possible only when there is some conformity to roles and rules. Also a person concerned with the impression others have of him feels that he is significant to them and they to him. When he polishes his car because a dirty one would embarrass him, when his wife straightens her make-up before answering the door, both exhibit a sense of their importance and personal dignity in human affairs. Those who must, or want to, serve as models or exemplars must be especially careful of speech and performance—they are always on stage. When people keep up appearances they are identifying themselves with a group and its standards. They need it; presumably it needs them.

Moreover, acting what seems a narrow role may actually broaden experience and open doors. To tend a lawn, or join a PTA, social club, or art group—"to keep up appearances"—may result in real knowledge and understanding about horticulture, education, or civic responsibility.

For the community, front produces the positive assets of social cohesion. Well-kept lawns, homes, cars, clean children and adults have definite aesthetic, financial, and sanitary value. People relate to one another, develop common experiences. People who faithfully play their parts exhibit personal and civic responsibility. The rules make life predictable and safe, confine ad-libs within acceptable limits, control violence and emotional tangents, and allow the show to go on and the day's work to be done. Thus, the challenging game of maintaining front relates unique personalities to one another and unites them in activity and into a nation.

So much for the good which preoccupation with front and staging accomplishes; what of the bad?

First, the inhibition of the free play of emotion must lead to frustration. Human energies need outlets. If onstage acting does not allow for release of tension, then the escape should take place backstage. But what if there is virtually no backstage? Perhaps then the releases will be found in the case histories of psychiatrists and other counselors. Communication between husband and wife may break down because of the contrast between the onstage image each has of the other as a perfect mate and the unmasked actuality backstage. Perhaps when masks crumble and crack, when people can no longer stand the strain of the front, then what we call nervous breakdown occurs.

GROWING UP WITH BAD REVIEWS

And how does the preoccupation with front affect the growth and development of the child? How can a child absorb and pattern himself after models which are essentially unreal? A mother may "control" her emotions when a child spills milk on her freshly scrubbed floor, and "reason" with him about it; she may still retain control when he leaves the refrigerator open after repeated warnings; but then some minor thing—such as loud laughter over the funnies—may suddenly blow off the lid, and she will "let him have it, but good!" What can he learn from such treatment? To respect his mother's hard work at keeping the house clean? To close the refrigerator door? Not to laugh loudly when reading the comics? That mother is a crab? Or, she's always got it in for him? Whatever he has learned, it is doubtful it was what his mother wanted! Whatever it was it will probably not clarify his understanding of such family values as pride in work, reward for effort, consideration of other people, or how to meet problems. Too, since the family's status is vitally linked with the maintenance of fronts, any deviance by the child, unless promptly rectified, threatens family standing in the community. This places a tremendous burden on a child actor.

Moreover, a concentration on front rather than content must result in a leveling and deadening of values and feelings. If a man buys a particular hat primarily because of what others may think, then its intrinsic value as a hat—in fact, even his own judgment and feelings about it—become secondary. Whether the judgment of those whose approval he covets is good or bad is unimportant—just so they approve. Applause has taken the place of value.

A PTA lecture on "The Future of America" will call for the same attentive front from him as a scientist's speech on the "Effects of Nuclear Warfare on Human Survival." Reading a newspaper on a crowded bus, his expression undergoes little change whether he is reading about nuclear tests, advice to the lovelorn, or Elizabeth Taylor's marital problems. To his employer he presents essentially the same bland, non-argumentative, courteous front whether he has just been refused a much deserved pay raise or told to estimate the cost of light bulbs. He seems impartial, objective, rational—and by so doing he also seems to deny that there is any difference to him between the pay raise and the light bulbs, as well as to deny his feelings.

THE PRICE OF ADMISSION

What price does the community pay for its role as audience?

The individual human talents and energies are alienated from assuming responsibility for the well-being and survival of the group. The exaggerated self-consciousness of individuals results in diluted and superficial concern with the community at a time when deep involvement, new visions, and real leadership are needed. Can the world afford to have over-zealous actors who work so hard on their lines that they forget what the play is all about?

It is probable that this picture will become more general in the near future and involve more and more people—assuming that the aging of the population continues, that the Cold War doesn't become hot and continues to need constant checks on loyalty and patriotism, that automation increases man's leisure at the same time as it keeps up or increases the production of consumer goods, and that improved advertising techniques make every home a miniature department store. The resulting conformity, loyalty, and patriotism may foster social solidarity. It may also cause alienation, immaturity, confusion, and much insecurity when new situations, for which old fronts are no longer appropriate, suddenly occur. Unless people start today to separate the important from the tinsel and to assume responsibility for community matters that are vital, individual actors will feel even more isolated; and the society may drift ever further from the philosophy that values every person.

Tomorrow's communities will need to provide new backstages, as the home, work place, and recreation center become more and more visible. Psychiatrists, counselors, confessors, and other professional listeners must provide outlets for actors who are exhausted and want to share their backstage thoughts. With increased leisure, business men will probably find it profitable to provide backstage settings in the form of resorts, rest homes, or retreats.

The state of the world is such today that unless the family and the community work together to evaluate and value the significant and direct their energies accordingly, the theater with its actors, front stage, backstage, and audience may end in farce and tragedy.

A Better Life
Notes from Puerto Rico

Lloyd H. Rogler

All of the husbands and wives interviewed during a recent study of families in the *caseríos*—large housing projects in Puerto Rice—dreamed of buying a small house in the suburbs. They often described that dream house. But only one family had ever actually done anything about that dream—the Vilás.

Luis and Rosa Vilá have made a down payment on a house located in a mushrooming middle-class development on the outskirts of San Juan. Physically, the house is not a notable improvement over their present apartment, which is centrally located, has three bedrooms, living-dining room, kitchen, porches at front and back, and adequate closets. It is freshly painted and Mrs. Vilá keeps it immaculate.

By their own admission, the Vilás have never before lived in such physical comfort and the monthly rental is only $17.00. But nevertheless they are not happy. According to Mrs. Vilá:

> The neighbors are low-class, bad people. . . . They drink too much. . . . The neighbors upstairs throw scrub water and garbage out the window. . . . The husbands and wives insult each other. Some married women are having affairs with other men. I have a neighbor who is always kissing her boy friend in public. . . . They gossip a lot. . . . They have stolen some plants which I put outside to grow. . . . One of my neighbors belonged to the can-can gang (a group of notorious shoplifters).

Most of all, the Vilás do not believe it is a good neighborhood in which to raise children. "Hoodlums" frequently accost their daughters and "tell them nice things with bad intent." The Vilás do not mingle with their neighbors or allow their daughters to play outside. They yearn to assume a respectable position among persons and families who count socially.

The Vilás are no better off than the other families we studied. Luis Vilá, a self-employed, semiskilled upholsterer, earns $160 per month.

Clearly, Luis' family does not enjoy an advantage in income. If income does not propel them toward the middle class, what does?

Rosa Vilá is 36 years old, with a sixth grade education. She was born and raised on a farm, in a wooden shack with a corrugated zinc roof and an outdoor latrine and shower. Her father was a sharecropper, raising tobacco and several tropical fruits and vegetables. He went through the fourth grade, was barely able to read, and could not write. Her mother was illiterate. When Rosa was 14 years old, the parents came to San Juan with their ten children. Shortly afterward, her father abandoned them, lived with a mistress, and then returned to the farm.

Rosa's mother became a seamstress doing piecework at home, and Rosa left school to help sew blouses. The human misery which they experienced is deeply etched in Rosa's memory. She recalls how her mother lost control, became very nervous, had to be taken to the psychiatric hospital, and died without regaining her mental health. "After this," Rosa says, "I decided to marry a hard-working and reliable man, even though he might be poor. I wanted a man who would take care of me—who would provide for my family."

Rosa Vilá came to San Juan; but San Juan reached out to Luis Vilá. The farm on which he was born and raised was swallowed up by the city. Streets, homes, apartment houses, and a church now cover it.

As a boy he had worked with his father and helped supplement the family income with bootlegging. Both parents were illiterate. Luis completed the eighth grade. Now he regrets not having gone through high school. "My only serious complaint against my father is that he did not let me remain in school after the eighth grade. We had too much work on the farm." Otherwise he admired his father extravagantly. Emotionally, he still feels closer to him than to any member of his parental family. He remembers him as a man of impeccable morality, of service to his community, clean and orderly, and not mercenary. He sees these attributes also in himself. "Most of all, my father was a very hard worker and a responsible man. I am that way too."

After he left the farm he labored on a truck which carried heavy supplies to construction sites. He clerked in a warehouse, greased cars, and was helper to an auto mechanic. Four years ago he got a job installing seat covers in cars, and capitalized on this to learn the rudimentary skills he now employs in his own business.

Because his father's earnings from agriculture were supplemented by the bootlegging and the family was able to live moderately well, Luis believes his parents belonged to the middle class. Although by most social and economic standards he himself would be considered lower class, *he sees himself as middle class.* The move from *caserío* to private home will, to him, confirm that vision.

The move will also represent a triumph for Rosa and the children—a seventeen-year old boy and two daughters, fourteen and twelve. During the first years of marriage Luis was not as committed to their welfare as he is now. Although even then a hard worker, he was a casual husband and father, typical of the other husbands in our study. He was a thorough *macho*—the traditional he-man of Puerto Rican society. The husband who is a *macho* follows the dictum that "the woman belongs in the home, the man in the street." In the "street" the man proves his masculinity by sexual accomplishments; he continually describes them with great emphasis on his vigor and potency. A *macho* is physically strong and courageous; he does not retreat from a fight, display cowardice, or fear pain; if he is married, he does not allow his wife to govern him. In the early years of marriage, evening always found Luis in the local *cafetines.* Much of his income was spent on drinking and "women of the happy life." By Rosa's account, he had affairs with about fifty women: "Even when I was pregnant he was chasing women."

After several years of marriage, Rosa returned from a visit to her relatives to be told by a neighbor that Luis had a "girl friend." She was upset and angry but did not discuss it with him. She began to have violent attacks which frightened him. He reports that during an attack, ". . . she hurls herself on the floor and is almost unconscious for half-an-hour. She gestures wildly and her mouth is out of shape." One of our staff psychiatrists diagnoses Rosa's attacks as "hysterical hyperkinetic seizures." To the Vilás, however, the attacks have supernatural meaning. During them Rosa has revelations from the world of spirits. Luis believes it was the spirits who informed Rosa of his extra-marital affair:

My wife is a spiritualistic medium. She has revealed secrets that only I knew. At that time she told me that the spirits told her that I had a girl friend. She told me where and when I had been meeting the girl. She even told me what the girl looked like and the color of her skin. I believe that spirits can communicate through persons who have mental faculties.

Not only were Rosa's spirits potent enough to detect Luis's infidelities, but even his much-admired father has spoken to him through Rosa's mouth:

My father speaks through my wife to give me advice. He tells me to be kind to the children and not to lose my temper with them. He tells me to advise them, not to spank them. He tells me that I have a complete family, a good family, and a very good wife. He tells me that I ought not to make my wife suffer, to think things over.

As a result, nine years ago Luis quit being a *macho* and has been a model husband ever since.

Typically the lower-class Puerto Rican husband maintains close control over his earnings. The husbands spend freely without rendering an account, and the wives, ruled by the norm that they must accept things as they are, seldom question what they get for household expenses. But the Vilás decide together what is to be purchased, from groceries and furniture to the new house. The expenditures serve to benefit the family as a whole.

Typically also, lower-class Puerto Rican parents seldom discuss sex with their children, fearing disrespect and promiscuous behavior. But the Vilás have agreed that their daughters should get sex instruction from Rosa. Rosa tells them the details of sexual intercourse, but reminds them of the importance of chastity before marriage. Luis and Rosa also differ from other couples in their beliefs about child-rearing. They seldom use physical punishment, preferring to reprimand, discuss the nature of the wrong, and, in the extreme case, confine to a bedroom. Recently however, Luis lost his temper and slapped their son for dating a girl with a bad reputation. Rosa shared Luis' concern that their son might be forced to marry the girl. She did not openly dispute Luis's use of physical punishment, but afterward she talked to him in private, suggesting that the boy should be handled *a la buena* (with gentle persuasion). Luis agrees that this method is more effective.

After the third child was born, Rosa had herself sterilized because, "We did not want to have any more children. . . . We want to give our children the best. I knew that if we would have any more children we would not be able to give them the education they should have because we do not have much money." Both parents would like to have the children finish high school and attend college although they know that their eldest child, the son, is not interested in school and that their youngest daughter is not very intelligent. However, they have high hopes that the elder daughter will receive two years of college education. Despite the reservations the Vilás have about their oldest and youngest children, they spend many hours with all three, helping with homework. The strong involvement of the Vilás in the details of their children's education is most unusual. When other parents were questioned, most announced lofty educational aspirations for their offspring, but few are familiar with their children's educational experiences. Recently, Luis joined the Parent-Teachers Association in which few slum or *caserío* parents participate.

Luis Vilá brought to his marriage habits of hard work, a conviction that he belongs in the middle class, and a willingness to acquire higher skills. His mental health, drive, and vigor have enabled him to capitalize on his relatively limited resources. Rosa's desire for a stable family and a reliable and hard-working husband is so intense that she is not only willing to sacrifice, scheme, and fight for them, but a strong threat to them could throw her into attacks.

The Vilás started with a few advantages, not the least being the example and influence of Luis' much revered father. At present Luis has no particular advantage in education, occupation, or earnings over his neighbors; but the values, activities, and family relations of the Vilás separate them from the other families in ways that compel them to rise.

Their way has not been easy. Probably their greatest victory and lift upward occurred when Luis quit being the self-indulgent, Latin *macho* "he-man" to become the sober, faithful provider Rosa dreamed about. And this might very well have not been possible without a little timely help from the supernatural.

The Working Classes— Old and New

Gerald Handel and Lee Rainwater

In 1959 the United States Department of Labor heralded the near achievement of a classless society in the United States in a report that stated: "The wage-earner's way of life is well-nigh indistinguishable from that of his salaried co-citizens." This was welcome news not only to the Labor Department but to the business community. *Business Week* summarized the report in an article entitled "Worker Loses His Class Identity."

The Labor Department report, written by economists, raises an issue which concerns sociologists seeking to understand the structure of American society. Has the rise in working class income in the post-war years and the movement of working class people into suburbs been sufficient to transform working class people into middle class—or at least to set in motion a strong process of transformation?

The Labor Department says yes, and states, without much documentation: "The adoption of middle class attitudes, the change in what workers have come to expect . . . points to this great revolution in class relations."

We interviewed a sample of 298 working class couples and 101 lower middle class couples—husbands and wives being interviewed separately—distributed in five cities: Camden, New Jersey; Gary, Indiana; Chicago; Louisville; and Denver. They lived in apartments, in new and old city houses, and in new and old houses in the suburbs.

Three general conclusions emerged:

1. Certain behaviors and attitudes increasingly found in the working class have a surface similarity to those in the middle class, but they have a different meaning for the working class than they do for the middle class. They are caused by increased opportunity rather than by any change in basic working class outlook and are occurring primarily in education and housing.
2. In family life and social participation, the working class seems to be dividing into two main groups, "traditional" and "modern." In these areas the "modern" group comes closer to lower middle class values and behaviors.
3. As consumers, the working class resembles the middle class in spending for hard goods but not in other ways. This reflects persisting differences in working class and middle class life styles.

The pattern is complex, and reflects the interplay of many factors. Below are indications how these generalizations apply to specific life areas.

EDUCATION

Where once the working class could see little value in higher education, it is now commonplace for working class parents to want a college education for their children. Yet as we probe deeper it becomes clear that college education has quite different meanings for working class and middle class people. For instance, working class parents seldom aspire to a college education for their daughters. They are likely to regard a daughter's stay in college as wasted unless she completes the course and uses it in a job—school teaching is the occupation usually mentioned. Education is conceived quite narrowly as vocational training—a kind of entry card to employment.

While people in the lower middle class do not slight the importance of vocational preparation, they conceive education more broadly. They are likely to believe that education is valuable even if not put to direct use. They might regard a year or two of college for a girl valuable for making her a more "refined" person rather than a total waste of time and money. Middle class parents look on schooling not only as preparation for a job but as a means of enabling children to get more out of life. They also expect the school to teach their children "how to get along with other people."

A HOME IN THE SUBURBS

Like the middle class, working class people have been moving to new tract housing, both in suburbs and inside city limits. The attitudes that prompt these moves show

353

certain differences from those of the middle class, though there are also similarities. The working class couple is more often motivated by a desire to flee from subordination to a landlord. Living in an apartment carries to them something of the same meaning as working for a boss. The landlord can and often will tell them to keep their children from playing in the halls of the building, not to run water after 10 p.m., or not to be noisy. Owning one's own home means to the working class an escape from restriction.

To the middle class suburbanite, owning a house is an assertion of his rightful place in society. He is not fleeing from exploitation by property-owners; he *is* a property-owner, one in a neighborhood of similar responsible persons, and he has the house and deed to prove it.

The increasing respect for education by the working class and the increased interest in home owning involve attitudes and behavior that superficially resemble those of the middle class but have a quite different significance.

TRADITIONAL AND MODERN

In family behavior the changes are more varied. The modern working class pattern has more similarities to the middle class than it has with the traditional working class. The essential change is the increased importance given to the immediate family at the expense of the broad, extended family.

In the old-fashioned traditional working class, family relationships intertwine with economic relationships. Very often a young man will choose an occupation in which his father or some other close relative is already working. He will be "taken on" in the same factory or join a closely controlled union. In the modern working class, this link between family and occupation is broken. A young man is more likely to work where and at what he likes, or can get, regardless of family.

Living near parents, brothers and sisters, or other close relatives is highly valued in the traditional working class. Numerous studies have shown that working people are more likely than middle class to have most of their social activities with relatives. If they do not live near relatives, they may very well spend their vacations visiting them. In contrast, the modern working class couple is more likely to have unrelated couples as friends, and social activities with these friends are more important to them than activities with relatives.

In the traditional working class family, the wife thinks of herself as someone who does *for* her family. Her self conception as a wife centers around cooking, laundry, and cleaning house. She considers the kitchen the most important room in her house.

But the modern working class wife bases her self-regard on what she does *with* her family. Her image is broadened from servant of the family to sharer in family affairs. She considers the living room the most important room because that is the one where the family relaxes together.

LESS FOR SERVICES

The prosperity of the post-war years has resulted in increased working class purchases of houses, automobiles, and other durable items. At the same time, however, the American economy as a whole has shown a rapid increase in spending for services in which the working class has not shared proportionately. There are several aspects of working class life style that account for their low output for services.

Even though a larger percentage of working class children are going to college, the proportion is still lower than in the middle class. Further, the children are far more likely to go to publicly-supported junior colleges or state universities, where fees are lower, than to private schools. Expenditures for educational services, therefore, claim a smaller percentage of the working class income.

Working class men do a tremendous amount of their own home repairs and improvements. Expenditures for carpenters, plumbers, electricians, and painters are likely to be less than in middle class families.

For similar reasons, expenses for car repairs and car washing are also generally less.

Working class men buy fewer suits and spend less on dry cleaning.

Working class families are more likely to buy an automatic washer—or to use coin-operated laundromats—than to use a commercial laundry or diaper service.

They will more probably spend their vacations either at home or visiting relatives. Their hotel, motel, and transportation expenses will be lower than those for middle class people.

They do not eat in restaurants as often, though some working class women say they wish they could. Their meals away from home are more often picnics in the park, dinner with relatives, or stops at a drive-in.

In all of these areas, working class attitudes and life style keep down expenditures for services. The great growth in the service sector of the economy is a middle class phenomenon.

Is the working class becoming part of the middle class? There is no flat yes or no answer that will cover all aspects of life. In different areas, change proceeds at different rates, with different consequences—and all the factors are not yet known. But the obliteration of class lines heralded by the Labor Department report is a great exaggeration.

New Styles in Homosexual Manliness

Laud Humphreys

Near the heart of a metropolis on the eastern seaboard, there is a historic park where homosexuals have been cruising for at least a hundred years. As an aging man told me:

> Back around 1930, when I was a very young man, I had sex with a really old fellow who was nearly 80. He told me that when he was a youngster—around the end of the Civil War—he would make spending money by hustling in that very park. Wealthy men would come down from the Hill in their carriages to pick up boys who waited in the shadows of the tree-lined walks at night.

In our motorized age, I have observed car drivers circling this park and adjoining residential blocks for the same sexual purposes. On a Friday night, unless the weather is bitter cold, a solid line of cars moves slowly along the one-way streets of this area, bumper to bumper, from 9:00 P.M. until 5:00 in the morning. The drivers pause in their rounds only long enough to exchange a few words with a young man on the sidewalk or to admit a willing passenger. There is no need to name this park. A knowledgeable person can find such pickup activity, both homosexual and heterosexual, in every major city of the Western world.

Cruising for "one-night-stands" is a major feature of the market economy in sex. In *The Wealth of Nations* Adam Smith postulated the ideal form of human relationship as being specific, depersonalized, short-term and contractual. This capitalist ideal is realized in the sex exchange of the homosexual underworld perhaps more fully than in any other social group, and the cruising scene of the gay world may continue for another hundred years or more. There are indications, however, that in the affluent, highly industrialized centers of our civilization the popularity of this sort of activity is declining. No one, of course, could make an up-to-date count of all the participants in even a single segment of the sexual market, and no base is available from which to estimate variations in such activity over time. One can only depend on careful observers of the scene, chief among whom are the participants themselves. I can report, then, what respondents tell me, checking their observations against my own of the past six years.

Decline of Cruising

Even with this limited source of data, it is still possible to discern a trend away from the traditional cruising for pick-ups as the major activity of the homosexual market. Men still make sexual contracts with other men along the curb-stones of our cities and in the shadowy places of public parks, but at least three social factors are acting to alter and curtail those operations and to increase the popularity of other forms of sexual exchange.

The most obvious factor affecting the cruising scene along this nation's roadways is perhaps the least important: the matter of crime in the streets. As a criminologist, I am yet to be convinced that the streets are actually less safe than they were 10, 30 or 100 years ago. American streets have been the scenes of assaults and robberies for genera-tions. Slums expand into certain areas, making some streets more dangerous than they were; but slums also contract, leaving once dangerous streets more safe. I doubt, however, that it is any more dangerous to pick up a hitchhiker in 1970 than it was in 1940.

Moreover, anyone seeking deviant sex is engaged in a risky activity, and usually knows it. Indeed, risk in the pursuit of sex simply increases the appeal of the homo-sexual markets for millions of American men. The chances they take add an element of adventure to the gaming en-counters and, for many participants, serve as an aphro-disiac. In fact, of course, most of the moral risk—and much of the physical danger—encountered by homosexuals comes from vice squad operations. The mugger is no more to be feared than the violent policeman. When I interviewed him, the man I quoted above was still recuperating from a severe beating at the hands of a patrolman. Two years ago, an active member of the homophile movement was shot to

death by a vice squad detective in a Berkeley, California, park. But such attacks by police and youthful toughs are nothing new in homosexual marketplaces.

Nevertheless, crime in the streets is of importance in cur-tailing homosexual cruising, if only because it is perceived and publicized as being on the increase. It thus becomes more an excuse than a deterrent. Since the man who cruises for sex has always been vulnerable to such victimization, that alone does not serve as a major factor in his decision to switch to another form of sexual exchange. But, if he is driven by other social forces to a new market place, he may use the widely perceived threat of violence as an excuse for changing.

Another factor in contemporary society that does effec-tively turn men away from this sort of sexual liaison is the growing scarcity of time. To cruise for sex requires leisure. The successful cruiser must have plenty of time to devote to his favorite sport. As with fishing, one dare not be hur-ried. It takes a great deal of time to size up a trick, to convince him that you are a legitimate score, for both parties to signal their intentions and to effect a contract. More time is required to find a safe locale for the sexual act—an out-of-the-way place to park, an apartment or hotel room, a *pied-a-terre* maintained for this purpose. For cruis-ing, expressways and fast cars are scarcely more advanta-geous than cobblestone streets and carriages; in this as in so many things, technological advance represents no gain be-cause it has not been accompanied by increased leisure. The plague of anomie, caused by a people with too much time on its hands, has yet to descend on us.

The Swedish economist Staffan B. Linder discusses the actual fate of *The Harried Leisure Class*:

> We had always expected one of the beneficent results of economic affluence to be a tranquil and harmonious manner of life, a life in Arcadia. What has happened is the exact opposite. The pace is quickening, and our lives in fact are becoming steadily more hectic.

The clock on the cover of a paperback edition of Thor-stein Veblen's *The Theory of the Leisure Class* has no hands. But Veblen was careful to point out that he used the term "leisure" not to "connote indolence or quiescence. What it connotes is non-productive consumption of time." As Veblen indicated, it is consumption, not production, that is inefficient and time wasting. Indeed, so much time is consumed in our society, Linder says, that there is an in-creasing scarcity of it. The upper stratum of society that Veblen defined as the Leisure Class at the end of the nine-teenth century must now be defined as the Jet Set: "Superficial people in the rich countries [who] are often in a greater hurry than anyone else. They are enormously busy, even if it is sometimes difficult to see with what."

There was a time when a man of means could dally with a maid in a Victorian attic room or spend a leisurely afternoon with his mistress. He could afford to cruise for a pickup or manage a tryst in some sylvan glade. As Linder states, "To court and love someone in a satisfactory manner is a game with many and time-consuming phases." The pleasures of the bed are declining, he continues, in three ways: "Affairs, which by their very nature occupy a great deal of time, become less attractive; the time spent on each occasion of lovemaking is being reduced; the total number of sexual encounters is declining."

Among the evidence that tends to support Linder's hypotheses is that gathered in a recent study of the sexual behavior of Frenchmen. Jacques Baroche notes that the fabled Gallic lover is leaving his mistress and turning to the fleeting sex act. One man interviewed in the research states that "only one thing counts in love—it is the brief encounter."

Impersonalization

Cruising operations may have led to the ideal type of relationship for a laissez faire capitalist of a century ago, but the market economy has since produced social factors necessitating transformation of its own sexual adjunct. It is no longer sufficient for human relationships to be depersonalized, short-term and contractual, such as that which might be expected to result from a pickup on the streets. In the sexual sphere, at least, relationships must now be utterly impersonal, highly expedient, fleeting in nature. The capitalist criteria have become more demanding.

In my study of the impersonal sex that occurs in public rest rooms, *Tearoom Trade* I wrote:

What the covert deviant needs is a sexual machine—collapsible to hip-pocket size, silent in operation—plus the excitement of a risk-taking encounter. In tearoom sex he has the closest thing to such a device. This encounter functions, for the sex market, as does the automat for the culinary, providing a low-cost, impersonal, democratic means of commodity distribution.

The sexual encounter in the tearoom constitutes the epitome of libidinal enterprise for the contemporary, consuming society. An old man on the toilet stool, serving as habitual insertee in fellatio with a succession of commuters, could better meet the standards of Madison Avenue only if he were an antiseptic machine with a coin slot in his forehead and stereo speakers for ears.

Approaching the phenomena of impersonal sex from a psychoanalytic standpoint rather than a socioeconomic one, Rollo May says in "Love and Will:" "The Victorian person sought to have love without falling into sex; the modern person seeks to have sex without falling into love." My objection to May's analysis (other than his apparent ignorance of Steven Marcus' "Other Victorians") is its implication that modern man knows what he seeks. We pursue what we have been conditioned to seek, what is expedient for members of the consuming society. We are subject to the subliminal suggestion that love and sex are essentially indistinguishable and any distinctions irrelevant. As with Coca-Cola, things go better with sex.

The increasing scarcity of time has differing effects upon the various segments of American society. As Linder suggests, some men simply find it more expedient to take their sex at home. Millions of others, however, limited or lacking in the conjugal exchange of goods and services, are turning to market places of impersonal sex, such as the tearooms. For instance, my data indicate that Roman Catholic religious affiliation is a causal factor in tearoom participation, because that church's prohibition of the use of artificial contraceptives limits the sexual outlet in marriage. Of the married men in my sample of tearoom participants, 50 percent are Roman Catholic or married to a Roman Catholic, as compared to 26 percent of married men in the control sample. For some single men, primarily those with higher educational levels, masturbation provides a sufficiently expedient sexual outlet. Others must turn to impersonal sexual exchanges to meet these needs.

The overall effect is the increasing impersonalization of the sexual markets. Prostitutes are now offering five-minute "blow jobs" in the parking garages of major cities, while the free service of tearooms increases in popularity. As more "straight" men, those lacking in homosexual identity and self-image, turn to impersonal sexual outlets provided by the gay world, others who seek homosexual relationships find the tearooms more rewarding than cruising the streets. America's sexual answer to the increasing scarcity of time, tearoom activity, seems to counter Linder's prediction that "the total number of sexual encounters is declining." Perhaps Sweden is lacking in such facilities.

Virilization

If the scarcity of time in our society were the only factor influencing homosexual market operations, why aren't all men with homosexual interests crowding into the nation's public toilets to satisfy their growing demand for what can be found there? There is, however, another social factor

357

acting upon the gay world to produce a countertendency. The cruising scene, so familiar to those interested in the homosexual subculture, is yielding to attacks from two sides: it is not sufficiently impersonal and expedient for some, and too much so for others. Sexual exchanges in the gay underworld are experiencing a polarization, torn between a growing impersonalization on the one hand and increasing virilization on the other.

By virilization, I refer to the increasingly masculine image of the gay scene. Few gay bars are now distinguished by the presence of limp wrists and falsetto voices. Increasingly, these centers for the homosexual subculture are indistinguishable from other hangouts for youths of college age. Girls are now common among the patrons in gay bars. Beards, leather vests, letter jackets and boots have their place alongside the more traditional blue jeans and T-shirts. If any style predominates, it is that of the turned-on, hip generation.

As Tom Burke pointed out in *Esquire* a year ago, just when the public seemed ready to accept the sort of homosexual portrayed in *The Boys in the Band* that life style began to fade away: "That the public's information vis-a-vis the new deviate is now hopelessly outdated is not the public's fault. It cannot examine him on its own because, from a polite distance, he is indistinguishable from the heterosexual hippie." Although this "new homosexuality" is increasingly evident on both coasts, as well as on campuses across the country, it is just beginning to appear in the gay bars and coffeehouses of Denver, Omaha and St. Louis. The hip, masculine image for homosexuals is not yet as universal, the transformation not so dramatic, as Burke would have us believe. "The majority of contemporary homosexuals under forty," he claims, "are confirmed potheads and at least occasional acid-trippers." Such a statement makes good copy, but there is no evidence for it. My sample of tearoom participants included fewer drug users than the control samples indicates are in the nondeviant population. But my research subjects were, by definition, only those who seek the impersonal sex of tearooms. My current research in the homosexual ecology of a sample of cities throughout the nation indicates a far higher proportion of pot smokers, perhaps 20 percent, among the population who engage in homosexual activity than I encountered during my field research six years ago. Clearly, the youth counterculture with its attendant styles of dress and drug use has spawned a young, virile set to coexist with the effete martini sippers of the traditional gay world.

The new emphasis in the homosexual subculture, then, is upon virility: not the hypermasculinity of Muscle Beach and the motorcycle set, for these are part of the old gay world's parody on heterosexuality, but the youthful masculinity of bare chests and beads, long hair, mustaches and hip-hugging pants. The new generation in gay society is more apt to sleep with a girl than to mock her speech or mannerisms. Many of these young men (along with the older ones who imitate their style) frown upon an exclusive orientation to homosexual or heterosexual activity. The ideal is to be a "swinger," sensitive to ambisexual pleasures, capable of turning on sexually with both men and women.

In a crowded gay bar in Boston I recently watched this new facet of the subculture in action. Neither the young men nor the girls scattered throughout the room were at all distinguishable from any other college-age group in the taverns of that city. There were fewer women, to be sure, but the dress, appearance and conversations were typical of any campus quadrangle. A handsome youth in a denim jacket and pants introduced an attractive young girl to a group standing at the bar as his fiancee. One man remarked, with a grin, that he was jealous. The young man, whom I shall call Jack, placed an arm around the shoulders of his fiancee, and, pulling her head toward his, explained: "Tom here is an old lover of mine." "Aren't we all!" another member of the party added, upon which all within earshot laughed.

After the bar closed, I was invited, along with the young couple, to join a number of patrons for "some group action" in a nearby apartment. A rather common, two-room pad with little furniture but many pillows and posters, the apartment was illuminated by only a single lightbulb suspended from the kitchen ceiling. Once our eyes had adjusted to the darkness of the other room, we could see about a dozen men, stretched in a number of stages of undress and sexual activity over the mattress and floor at the far end of the room. Excusing himself, Jack joined the orgy. In a few minutes, I could discern that he was necking with one man while being fellated by another.

Having explained my research purposes on the way to the apartment, I sought to explore the girl's reactions to her lover's apparent infidelity. I asked whether it bothered her. "Does it arouse me sexually, do you mean?" she replied. "No. Like, does Jack's behavior upset you?" With a laugh, she answered, "No, not at all. Like, I love Jack for what he is. You know, like, he swings both ways. If that's his thing, I groove on it. He could have left me home, you know— that's what some guys do. They leave their chicks home and, like, feed them a lot of shit so they can slip out and get their kicks. One of the things I dig most about Jack is that he shares everything with me. Having secrets just leads to hangups." "But don't you feel even a bit jealous?" I probed. "Like, wouldn't you rather be making love to him than standing here rapping with me?" "Why should I?" she said. "Like, Jack and I'll go home and ball after this is over. He's a beautiful person. Being able to share himself with so many different people makes him more beautiful!"

Later, Jack and his fiancee left those of us who were bound for an all-night restaurant. Arm in arm, they headed for the subway and a pad in Cambridge. Their story, I think, is an accurate reflection of the morality of the youth counterculture, both in its easy acceptance of a variety of sexual expressions and its nondefensive trust that the deeper, personal relationships are the more important ones.

Subcultural Diversity

Like the scarcity of time, such norms of the counterculture have differing effects upon the sexual markets and life styles of the gay world, depending upon the permeability of various segments of the homosexual society. In order to outline and gauge these changes, it is necessary to construct a taxonomy of the homosexual community. Once we are able to consider its diverse segments in relation to each other, we can compare their reactions to some of the forces of contemporary society.

In my study of tearoom sex, I delineated four basic types of participants in these impersonal encounters: trade, ambisexuals, the gay and closet queens. These men are differentiated most clearly by the relative autonomy afforded them by their marital and occupational statuses. When one engages in sexual behavior against which the society has erected strong negative sanctions, his resources for control of information carry a determining relationship to his life style, as well as to his self-image and the adaptations he makes to his own discreditable behavior. An example of this principle of classification would be that married men who are bound hand and foot to their jobs have more to fear—and less to enjoy—from their clandestine encounters because they have relatively fewer means of countering exposure than men of greater autonomy.

I have chosen the word "trade" from the argot of the homosexual community because it best describes that largest class of my respondents, the married men with little occupational autonomy. In its most inclusive sense in the gay vocabulary, this term refers to all men, married or single, who think they are heterosexual but who will take the insertor role in homosexual acts. Except for hustlers, who will be discussed later, most of these men are married. As participants in homosexual activity, they are nonsubcul-

tural, lacking both the sources of information and the rationalization for their behavior that the gay circles provide. Generally, the trade are of lower-middle or upper-lower socioeconomic status. They are machinists, truck drivers, teachers, sales and clerical workers, invariably masculine in appearance, mannerisms and self-image. Single men, I have found, are generally less stable in sexual identification. Once they begin to participate in homosexual relations, therefore, their straight self-image is threatened, and they tend to drift into the less heterosexual world of the closet queens or gay bar crowd. Apart from an exclusive concern with tearoom operations, however, I think it preferable to allow for the inclusion of some single men in the trade classification.

Moving into the upper strata of society, it is difficult to find participants in homosexual activity who think of themselves as strictly heterosexual. Americans with the higher educational level of the upper-middle and upper classes tend to find literary justification for their ventures into deviant sexual activity. The greater occupational autonomy of these men enables them to join in friendship networks with others who share their sexual interests. If these men are married, they tend to define themselves as "ambisexual," identifying with a distinguished company of men (Alexander the Great, Julius Caesar, Shakespeare, Walt Whitman and a number of movie stars) who are said to have enjoyed the pleasures of both sexual worlds. In this classification are to be found business executives, salesmen with little direct supervision, doctors, lawyers and interior decorators.

College students join with artists, the self-employed and a few professional men to constitute the more autonomous, unmarried segment of the gay society. These men share enough resources for information control that they are unafraid to be active in the more visible portions of the homosexual subculture. In the tearoom study, I refer to them as "the gay," because they are the most clearly definable, in the sociological sense, as being homosexual. They are apt to have been labeled as such by their friends, associates and even families. Their self-identification is strongly homosexual. Because their subcultural life centers in the gay bars, coffeehouses and baths of the community, I will refer to them here as the "gay bar crowd."

The fourth type identified in my previous research are the "closet queens." In the homosexual argot this term has meanings with varying degrees of specificity. Occasionally, trade who fear their own homosexual tendencies are called closet queens. Again, the term may be used in referring to those in the subculture who feel that they are too good or proper to patronize the gay bars. In its most general sense, however, it is employed to designate those men who know they are gay but fear involvement in the more overt, bar-centered activities of the homosexual world. Because they avoid overt participation in the subculture, the married ambisexuals often receive the closet queen label from the gay bar crowd. I should like to maintain the distinctions I have outlined between ambisexuals and closet queens, however, because of the contrasting marital and socioeconomic statuses of the two groups. As I employ the term in my tearoom typology, the closet queens are unmarried teachers, clerks, salesmen and factory workers. Living in fear that their deviance might be discovered, they tend to patterns of self-hatred, social isolation and lone-wolf sexual forays.

There is a fifth type of man who is seldom found in tearooms, where money does not change hands, but who plays an important role in the homosexual markets. I mean the hustlers, homosexual prostitutes who operate from the streets, theaters and certain bars, coffeehouses and restaurants of the urban centers. The majority of these "midnight cowboys" share a heterosexual self-image. Indeed, since relatively few of them make a living from sexual activity, there is strong evidence that, for most hustlers, the exchange of money functions more to neutralize the societal norms, to justify the deviant sexual behavior, than to meet economic needs.

My observations suggest that there are at least three subdivisions among male prostitutes. One large, relatively amorphous group might properly be called "pseudo-hustlers." For them the amount of money received holds little importance, a pack of cigarettes or a handful of change sufficing to justify their involvement in the forbidden behavior, which is what they really wanted. Another large number of young men would be called "semiprofessionals." This type includes members of delinquent peer groups who hustle for money and thrills. Unlike the pseudo-hustlers, these young men receive support and training from other members of the hustling subculture. They are apt to frequent a particular set of bars and coffeehouses where a strict code of hustling standards is adhered to. Although a minority of these boys rely upon their earnings for support, the majority gain from their hustling only enough to supplement allowances, using their take to finance autos and heterosexual dates.

New to the sexual markets are the "call boys." Advertising in the underground papers of such cities as Los Angeles, San Francisco and New York as "models," these young men charge an average fee of $100 for a night or $25 an hour. I have seen a catalogue distributed by one agency for such hustlers that provides frontal nude, full-page photographs of the "models," complete with telephone numbers. In general, the call boys share a gay or ambisexual identity and take pride in their professional status. The appearance of these handsome, masculine youngsters on the gay scene is an important manifestation of the virilization of the homosexual market.

These five, basic types constitute the personnel of the gay world. The hustlers and trade, few of whom think of themselves as homosexual, are the straight world's contribution to the gay scene. Without their participation, the sex exchanges would atrophy, becoming stale and ingrown. The ambisexual enjoys the benefits of his status, with a well-shod foot firmly planted in each sexual world. He need not be as covert as either the closet queen or trade and, when out of town on a business trip, may become very overt indeed. The open, visible members of the homosexual community are the hustlers and those I have called, for the purposes of this taxonomy, the gay bar crowd. With this classification in mind, it is possible to see how the contemporary social forces are diffused and filtered through interaction with each class of persons in the gay community.

Polarization of Market Activity

As the growing scarcity of time drives an increasing number of American males from every walk of life into one-night-stand sexuality, the impersonalized sex exchange thrives. Rest stops along the expressways, older tearooms in transportation terminals, subways, parks and public buildings—all enjoy popularity as trysting places for "instant sex." The more expedient an encounter's structure and the greater the variety of participants, as is the case with tearoom sex, the less attractive are the time-demanding liaisons of the cruising grounds.

The trade and closet queens, in particular, find their needs met in the impersonal sex market of our consuming society. Here they can find sex without commitment, an activity sufficiently swift to fit into the lunch hour or a brief stop on the way home from work. The ambisexuals—many of them harried business executives—prefer the tearooms, not only for the speed and anonymity they offer, but also for the kicks they add to the daily routine.

Covert members of the gay society provide impetus to the impersonalization of the homosexual market. My study of tearoom participants revealed that trade, closet queens and ambisexuals share highly conservative social and political views, surrounding themselves with an aura of respectability that I call the breastplate of righteousness. In life style, they epitomize the consuming man of the affluent society. In tearooms, they fill the role of sexual consumers, exchanging goods and services in every spare moment they can wring from the demands of computerized offices and automated homes. At the same time, however, their conservatism makes them nearly impervious to the pressures of the youth counterculture.

On the overt side of the gay world, the virile influence of hip culture is having profound effects. Already poorly represented in the tearoom scene, the gay bar crowd is preconditioned to embrace some of the stronger norms of the flower people. At least in word, if not always in deed, these overt leaders of the gay community espouse the deeper, more personal type of relationship. Theirs is a search for lovers, for men with whom they may build abiding relationships. Moreover, like hippies, these men flaunt some of the more sacrosanct mores of the straight society. With the hustlers, they share a sense of being an oppressed minority. On the whole, they are happy to discard the effeminate mannerisms and vocabulary of low camp in return for the influx of the new blood, the turned-on generation.

Arrival of the new bold masculinity on the gay bar scene has made the bars more suitable for hustlers of drinking age. As recently as 1967, I have seen hustlers ejected from a midwestern bar that now plays host to many of them. In those days, they were too easily identified by their rough, masculine appearance that contrasted with the neat effeminacy of the other customers. On both coasts, and increasingly in other parts of the country, bars and coffeehouses are now replacing the streets as sexual markets for hustlers and their scores.

One might surmise that the meeting of hustlers and the gay bar crowd in the same branch of the sexual market would signify a countertendency to what I see as a personalization of sex on the more virile side of the sexual exchange. But this, I think, is to misunderstand prostitution, both heterosexual and homosexual. Hustling involves many deeply personal relationships, often accompanied by a sense of commitment. Admittedly with much futility, prostitutes generally seek love and hope for the lover who will keep them. Persons who lack knowledge of the tearooms and other scenes of thoroughly impersonal sex fall victim to the stereotype of the frigid prostitute who values the customer only for his money. In reality, prostitution is at the corner grocery end of the market economy spectrum. Tearoom sex ranks near the public utility extreme of the continuum.

The addition of the hip set with its virile, drug-using, ambisexual life style has transformed the gay bar into a swinging, far less inhibited setting for sexual contact. The old bar is familiar from gay novels: a florid, clannish milieu for high-pitched flirtation. Patrons of the new bars are justifiably suspicious of possible narcotics agents; but black, white, lesbian, straight women, heterosexual couples, old and young mix with an abandon unknown a decade ago.

Gay bathhouses, once little more than shabby shelters for group sex, although still active as sexual exchanges, are now becoming true centers for recreation. The underground press, along with homophile publications such as the *Los Angeles Advocate*, provide a medium for such facilities to compete in advertising their expanding services. Such advertisements, limited as they may be to underground newspapers, are distinctive marks of the new virilized sex exchanges. By advertising, bars, baths and even hustlers proclaim their openness. It is as if this overt portion of the homosexual community were announcing: "Look, we're really men! Mod men, to be sure, children of the Age of Aquarius; but we are real men, with all the proper equipment, looking for love." In the 1970s it will be very difficult for a society to put that down as deviant.

The new generation's counterculture has also had its impact on the homophile movement, a loose federation of civil rights organizations that reached adolescence about the same time as the flower children. Beginning with the Mattachine Foundation, established around 1950 in Los Angeles, the homophile movement has produced a history remarkably parallel to that of the black freedom movement. Frightened by the spirit of McCarthyism, its first decade was devoted primarily to sponsoring educational forums and publications, along with mutual encouragement for members of an oppressed minority.

During the sixties, with the leadership of attorneys and other professional men, it began to enlist the support of the American Civil Liberties Union in using the courts to assure and defend the civil rights of homosexuals. About the time ministers marched in Selma, clergymen (inspired, perhaps, by the stand of the Church of England in support of homosexual law reform in that nation) began to join the movement as "concerned outsiders." The National Council on Religion and the Homosexual was formed, and, with clergy as sponsors and spokesmen, members of the movement entered into dialogues with straights.

Activists Alliance, dedicated to nonviolent protest, has provided youthful leadership for homophiles of varying ideological persuasions in the campaign to reform that state's sodomy, fair employment and solicitation statutes. In both Albany and San Diego, organizations with reformist emphases have taken the name of Gay Liberation Front.

Although severe enough to confound social scientists who attempt to describe or analyze *the* homophile movement, the rift between homophile groups has yet to diminish their effectiveness. Much anger was generated when invading radicals disrupted the 1970 meetings of NACHO, but that organization has yet to enjoy what anyone would call a successful conference anyway. Meanwhile, the hotline maintained by the Homophile Union of Boston serves as a center of communication for the nine, varied homophile groups that have developed in that city during the past 18 months.

Three factors promote cooperation between the conservative, reform and radical branches of the homophile movement. First, instances of police brutality in such widely scattered cities as New York, Los Angeles, San Francisco and New Orleans have brought thousands of homosexuals together in protest marches during the past year. Nothing heals an ailing movement like martyrs, and the police seem pleased to provide them. Because a vice squad crusade is apt to strike baths and bars, parks and tearooms, all sectors of the homosexual market are subject to victimization in the form of arrests, extortion, assaults and prosecution. There is a vice squad behind every active homophile group in America. With a common enemy in plain clothes, differences in ideology and life style become irrelevant.

Second, the *Los Angeles Advocate* has emerged as the homosexual grapevine in print. With up-to-date, thorough news coverage rivaling that of the *Christian Science Monitor* and a moderate-activist editorial policy, this biweekly is, as it claims, the "Newspaper of America's Homophile Community." With communication provided by the *Advocate* and inspiration gained from the successes of the Women's Liberation Movement, the larger homophile organizations appear to be moving into a position best described as moderately activist.

Finally, a truly charismatic leader has appeared on the homophile scene. The Rev. Troy Perry, founder of the Metropolitan Community Church, a congregation for homosexuals in Los Angeles, was arrested during a fast in front of that city's Federal Building in June of 1970. The fast coincided with "Gay Liberation Day" marches of 2,000 persons in New York and 1,200 in Los Angeles. An articulate, moving speaker, Perry began to tour the nation for his cause. I have seen him honored by a standing ovation from an audience of a hundred main-line Protestant and Catholic clergy in Boston. Because he commands general respect from both gay libs and liberals in the movement, it is impossible not to draw a parallel between this minister and Martin Luther King. When I suggested that he was "the Martin Luther King of the homophile movement," he countered that "Martin Luther *Queen* might be more appropriate." As an evangelical religious movement spreads from the West coast, replacing drugs as a source of enthusiasm for many in the youth counterculture, Perry's position of leadership should increase in importance.

Just as the world of female homosexuals should benefit from the trend towards liberation of women, so the male homosexual world of the 1970s should thrive. Divisions of the movement may provide the advantages of diversification. The new blood provided by the Gay Liberation Front, alarming as it may be to some traditionalists, is much healthier than the bad blood that has existed between a number of NACHO leaders.

Concurrently, the same social forces that are dividing and transforming the homophile movement have polarized and strengthened the homosexual markets. By now, the consuming American should know that diversification in places and styles of exchange is a healthy indicator in the market economy. Both virilization and impersonalization will attract more participants to the market places of the gay world. At the same time, traditionalists will continue to cruise the streets and patronize the remaining sedate and elegant bars. When threatened by the forces of social control, however, even the closet queens should profit from the movement's newly-found militance.

Why All of Us May be Hippies Someday

Fred Davis

And thus in love we have declared the purpose of our hearts plainly, without flatterie, expecting love, and the same sincerity from you, without grumbling, or quarreling, being Creatures of your own image and mould, intending no other matter herein, but to observe the Law of righteous action, endeavoring to shut out of the Creation, the cursed thing, called Particular Propriety, which is the cause of all wars, bloud-shed, theft, and enslaving Laws, that hold the people under miserie.

Signed for and in behalf of all the poor oppressed people of England, and the whole world.

Gerrard Winstanley and others
June 1, 1649

This quotation is from the leader of the Diggers, a millenarian sect of communistic persuasion that arose in England at the time of Oliver Cromwell. Today in San Francisco's hippie community, the Haight-Ashbury district, a group of hippies naming themselves after this sect distributes free food to fellow hippies (and all other takers, for that matter) who congregate at about four o'clock every afternoon in the district's Panhandle, an eight-block strip of urban green, shaded by towering eucalyptus trees, that leads into Golden Gate Park to the west. On the corner of a nearby street, the "Hashbury" Diggers operate their Free Store where all—be they hip, straight, hostile, curious, or merely in need—can avail themselves (free of charge, no questions asked) of such used clothing, household articles, books, and second-hand furniture as find

their way into the place on any particular day. The Diggers also maintained a large flat in the district where newly arrived or freshly dispossessed hippies could stay without charge for a night, a week, or however long they wished —until some months ago, when the flat was condemned by the San Francisco Health Department. Currently, the Diggers are rehabilitating a condemned skid-row hotel for the same purpose.

Not all of Haight-Ashbury's 7500 hippies are Diggers, although no formal qualifications bar them; nor, in one sense, are the several dozen Diggers hippies. What distinguishes the Diggers—an amorphous, shifting, and sometimes contentious amalgam of ex-political radicals, psychedelic mystics, Ghandians, and Brechtian avant-garde thespians—from the area's "ordinary" hippies is their ideological brio, articulateness, good works, and flair for the dramatic event. (Some are even rumored to be over 30.) In the eyes of many Hashbury hippies, therefore, the Diggers symbolize what is best, what is most persuasive and purposive, about the surrounding, more variegated hippie subculture—just as, for certain radical social critics of the American scene, the hippies are expressing, albeit elliptically, what is best about a seemingly ever-broader segment of American youth: its openness to new experience, puncturing of cant, rejection of bureaucratic regimentation, aversion to violence, and identification with the exploited and disadvantaged. That this is not the whole story barely needs saying. Along with the poetry and flowers, the melancholy smile at passing and ecstatic clasp at greeting, there is also the panicky incoherence of the bad LSD trip, the malnutrition, a startling rise in V.D. and hepatitis, a seemingly phobic reaction to elementary practices of hygiene and sanitation, and—perhaps most disturbing in the long run—a casualness about the comings and goings of human relationships that must verge on the grossly irresponsible.

But, then, social movements—particularly of this expressive-religious variety—are rarely of a piece, and it would be unfortunate if social scientists, rather than inquiring into the genesis, meaning, and future of the hippie movement, too soon joined ranks (as many are likely to, in any case) with solid burghers in an orgy of research into the "pathology" of it all: the ubiquitous drug use (mainly marihuana and LSD, often amphetamines, rarely heroin or other opiates), the easy attitudes toward sex ("If two people are attracted to each other, what better way of showing it than to make love?"), and the mocking hostility toward the middle-class values of pleasure-deferral, material success, and—ultimately—the whole mass-media-glamorized round of chic, deodorized, appliance-glutted suburban existence.

The Hip Scene Is the Message

Clearly, despite whatever real or imagined "pathology" middle-class spokesmen are ready to assign to the hippies, it is the middle-class scheme of life that young hippies are reacting against, even though in their ranks are to be found some youth of working-class origin who have never enjoyed the affluence that their peers now so heartily decry. To adulterate somewhat the slogan of Marshall McLuhan, one of the few non-orientalized intellectuals whom hippies bother to read at all, *the hip scene is the message,* not the elements whence it derives or the meanings that can be assigned to it verbally. (Interestingly, this fusion of disparate classes does not appear to include any significant number of the Negro youths who reside with their families in the integrated Haight-Ashbury district or in the adjoining Negro ghetto, the Fillmore district. By and large, Negroes view with bewilderment and ridicule the white hippies who flaunt, to the extent of begging on the streets, their rejection of what the Negroes have had scant opportunity to attain. What more revealing symbol of the Negro riots in our nation's cities than the carting off of looted TV sets, refrigerators, and washing machines? After all, aren't these things what America is all about?)

But granting that the hippie scene is a reaction to middle-class values, can the understanding of any social movement—particularly one that just in the process of its formation is so fecund of new art forms, new styles of dress and demeanor, and (most of all) new ethical bases for human relationships—ever be wholly reduced to its reactive aspect? As Ralph Ellison has eloquently observed in his critique of the standard sociological explanation of the American Negro's situation, a people's distinctive way of life is never solely a reaction to the dominant social forces that have oppressed, excluded, or alienated them from the larger society. The cumulative process of reaction and counterreaction, in its historical unfolding, creates its own ground for the emergence of new symbols, meanings, purposes, and social discoveries, none of which are ever wholly contained in embryo, as it were, in the conditions that elicited the reaction. It is, therefore, less with an eye toward explaining "how it came to be" than toward explaining what it may betoken of life in the future society that I now want to examine certain facets of the Hashbury hippie subculture. (Of course, very similar youth movements, subcultures, and settlements are found nowadays in many parts of the affluent Western world—Berkeley's Telegraph Avenue teeny-boppers; Los Angeles' Sunset Strippers; New York's East Village hippies; London's mods; Amsterdam's Provos; and the summer *Wandervögel* from all over Europe who chalk the pavement of Copenhagen's main shopping street, the Strøget, and sun themselves on the steps of Stockholm's Philharmonic Hall. What is culturally significant about the Haight-Ashbury hippies is, I would hazard, in general significant about these others as well, with—to be sure—certain qualifications. Indeed, a certain marvelous irony attaches itself to the fact that perhaps the only genuine cross-national culture found in the world today builds on the rag-tag of beards, bare feet, bedrolls, and beads, not on the cultural-exchange programs of governments and universities, or tourism, or—least of all—ladies' clubs' invocations for sympathetic understanding of one's foreign neighbors.)

What I wish to suggest here is that there is, as Max Weber would have put it, an *elective affinity* between prominent styles and themes in the hippie subculture and certain incipient problems of identity, work, and leisure that loom ominously as Western industrial society moves into an epoch of accelerated cybernation, staggering material abundance, and historically-unprecedented mass opportunities for creative leisure and enrichment of the human personality. This is not to say that the latter are the *hidden causes* or tangible *motivating forces* of the former. Rather, the point is that the hippies, in their collective, yet radical, break with the constraints of our present society, are—whether they know it or not (some clearly do intuit a connection)—already rehearsing *in vivo* a number of possible cultural solutions to central life problems posed by the emerging society of the future. While other students of contemporary youth culture could no doubt cite many additional emerging problems to which the hippie subculture is, willy-nilly, addressing itself (marriage and family organization, the character of friendship and personal loyalties, the forms of political participation), space and the kind of observations I have been able to make require that I confine myself to three: the problems of *compulsive consumption*, of *passive spectatorship*, and of the *time-scale of experience*.

Compulsive Consumption

What working attitude is man to adopt toward the potential glut of consumer goods that the new technology will make available to virtually all members of the future society? Until now, modern capitalist society's traditional response to short-term conditions of overproduction has been to generate—through government manipulation of fiscal devices—greater purchasing power for discretionary consumption. At the same time, the aim has been to cultivate the acquisitive impulse—largely through mass advertising, annual styling changes, and planned obsolescence—so that, in the economist's terminology, a high level of aggregate demand could be sustained. Fortunately, given the great backlog of old material wants and the technologically-based creation of new wants, these means have, for the most part, worked comparatively well—both for advancing (albeit unequally) the mass standard of living and ensuring a reasonably high rate of return to capital.

But, as Walter Weisskopf, Robert Heilbroner, and other economists have wondered, will these means prove adequate for an automated future society in which the mere production of goods and services might easily outstrip man's desire for them, or his capacity to consume them in satisfying ways? Massive problems of air pollution, traffic congestion, and waste disposal aside, is there no psychological limit to the number of automobiles, TV sets, freezers, and dishwashers that even a zealous consumer can aspire to, much less make psychic room for in his life space? The specter that haunts post-industrial man is that of a near worker-less economy in which most men are constrained, through a variety of economic and political sanc-

tions, to frantically purchase and assiduously use up the cornucopia of consumer goods that a robot-staffed factory system (but one still harnessed to capitalism's rationale of pecuniary profit) regurgitates upon the populace. As far back as the late 1940s sociologists like David Riesman were already pointing to the many moral paradoxes of work, leisure, and interpersonal relations posed by a then only nascent society of capitalist mass abundance. How much more perplexing the paradoxes if, using current technological trends, we extrapolate to the year 2000?

Hippies, originating mainly in the middle classes, have been nurtured at the boards of consumer abundance. Spared their parents' vivid memories of economic depression and material want, however, they now, with what to their elders seems like insulting abandon, declare unshamefacedly that the very quest for "the good things of life" and all that this entails—the latest model, the third car, the monthly credit payments, the right house in the right neighborhood—are a "bad bag." In phrases redolent of nearly all utopian thought of the past, they proclaim that happiness and a meaningful life are not to be found in things, but in the cultivation of the self and by an intensive exploration of inner sensibilities with like-minded others.

Extreme as this antimaterialistic stance may seem, and despite its probable tempering should hippie communities develop as a stable feature on the American landscape, it nonetheless points a way to a solution of the problem of material glut; to wit, the simple demonstration of the ability to live on less, thereby calming the acquisitive frenzy that would have to be sustained, and even accelerated, if the present scheme of capitalist production and distribution were to remain unchanged. Besides such establishments as the Diggers' Free Store, gleanings of this attitude are even evident in the street panhandling that so many hippies engage in. Unlike the street beggars of old, there is little that is obsequious or deferential about their manner. On the contrary, their approach is one of easy, sometimes condescending casualness, as if to say, "You've got more than enough to spare, I need it, so let's not make a degrading charity scene out of my asking you." The story is told in the Haight-Ashbury of the patronizing tourist who, upon being approached for a dime by a hippie girl in her late teens, took the occasion to deliver a small speech on how delighted he would be to give it to her—provided she first told him what she needed it for. Without blinking an eye she replied, "It's my menstrual period and that's how much a sanitary napkin costs."

Passive Spectatorship

As social historians are forever reminding us, modern man has—since the beginnings of the industrial revolution—become increasingly a spectator and less a participant. Less and less does he, for example, create or play music, engage in sports, dance or sing; instead he watches professionally-trained others, vastly more accomplished than himself, perform their acts while he, perhaps, indulges in Mitty-like fantasies of hidden graces and talents. Although this bald statement of the spectator thesis has been challenged in recent years by certain social researchers—statistics are cited of the growing numbers taking guitar lessons, buying fishing equipment, and painting on Sunday—there can be little doubt that "doing" kinds of expressive pursuits, particularly of the collective type, no longer bear the same *integral* relationship to daily life that they once did, or still do in primitive societies. The mere change in how they come to be perceived, from what one does in the ordinary course of life to one's "hobbies," is in itself of profound historical significance. Along with this, the virtuoso standards that once were the exclusive property of small aristocratic elites, rather than being undermined by the oft-cited revolutions in mass communications and mass education, have so diffused through the class structure as to even cause the gifted amateur *at play* to apologize for his efforts with some such remark as, "I only play at it." In short, the cult of professionalism, in the arts as elsewhere, has been institutionalized so intensively in Western society that the ordinary man's sense of expressive adequacy and competence has progressively atrophied. This is especially true of the college-educated, urban middle classes, which—newly exposed to the lofty aesthetic standards of high culture—stand in reverent, if passive, awe of them.

Again, the problem of excessive spectatorship has not proved particularly acute until now, inasmuch as most men have had other time-consuming demands to fill their lives with, chiefly work and family life, leavened by occasional vacations and mass-produced amusements. But what of the future when, according to such social prognosticators as Robert Theobald and Donald Michael, all (except a relatively small cadre of professionals and managers) will be faced with a surfeit of leisure time? Will the mere extension of passive spectatorship and the professional's monopoly of expressive pursuits be a satisfactory solution?

Here, too, hippies are opening up new avenues of collective response to life issues posed by a changing socio-technological environment. They are doing so by rejecting those virtuoso standards that stifle participation in high culture; by substituting an extravagantly eclectic (and, according to traditional aestheticians, reckless) admixture of materials, styles, and motifs from a great diversity of past and present human cultures; and, most of all, by insisting that every man can find immediate expressive fulfillment provided he lets the socially-suppressed spirit within him ascend into vibrant consciousness. The manifesto is: All men are artists, and who cares that some are better at it than others; we can all have fun! Hence, the deceptively crude antisophistication of hippie art forms, which are, perhaps, only an apparent reversion to primitivism. One has only to encounter the lurid *art nouveau* contortions of the hippie posters and their Beardsleyan exoticism, or the mad mélange of hippie street costume—Greek-sandaled feet peeking beneath harem pantaloons encased in a fringed American Indian suede jacket, topped by pastel floral decorations about the face—or the sitar-whining cacophony of the folk-rock band, to know immediately that one is in the presence of *expressiveness* for its own sake.

In more mundane ways, too, the same readiness to let go, to participate, to create and perform without script or forethought is everywhere evident in the Hashbury. Two youths seat themselves on the sidewalk or in a store entranceway; bent beer can in hand, one begins scratching a bongo-like rhythm on the pavement while the other tattoos a bell-like accompaniment by striking a stick on an empty bottle. Soon they are joined, one by one, by a tambourinist, a harmonica player, a penny-whistler or recorder player, and, of course, the ubiquitous guitarist. A small crowd collects and, at the fringes, some blanket-bedecked boys and girls begin twirling about in movements vaguely resembling a Hindu dance. The wailing, rhythmic beating and dancing, alternately rising to peaks of intensity and subsiding, may last for as little as five minutes or as long as an hour, players and dancers joining in and dropping out as whim moves them. At some point—almost any—a mood takes hold that "the happening is over"; participants and onlookers disperse as casually as they had collected.

Analogous scenes of "participation unbound" are to be observed almost every night of the week (twice on Sunday) at the hippies' Parnassus, the Fillmore Auditorium, where a succession of name folk-rock bands, each more deafening than the one before, follow one another in hour-long sessions. Here, amidst the electric guitars, the electric organs, and the constantly metamorphizing show of lights, one can see the gainly and the graceless, the sylph bodies and rude stompers, the crooked and straight—all, of whatever condition or talent, *dance* as the flickering of a strobe light reduces their figures in silhouette to egalitarian spastic bursts. The recognition dawns that this, at last, is dancing of utterly free form, devoid of fixed sequence or step, open to all and calling for no Friday after-school classes at Miss Martha's or expensive lessons from Arthur Murray. The sole requisite is to tune in, take heart, and let go. What follows must be "beautiful" (a favorite hippie word) because it is *you* who are doing and feeling, not another to whom you have surrendered the muse.

As with folk-rock dancing, so (theoretically, at least) with music, poetry, painting, pottery, and the other arts and crafts: expression over performance, impulse over product. Whether the "straight world" will in time heed this message of the hippies is, to be sure, problematical. Also, given the lavish financial rewards and prestige heaped upon more talented hippie artists by a youth-dominated entertainment market, it is conceivable that high standards of professional performance will develop here as well (listen to the more recent Beatles' recordings), thus engendering perhaps as great a participative gulf between artist and audience as already exists in the established arts. Despite the vagaries of forecasting, however, the hippies—as of now, at least—are responding to the incipient plenitude of leisure in ways far removed from the baleful visions of a Huxley or an Orwell.

The Time-Scale of Experience

In every society, certain activities are required to complete various tasks and to achieve various goals. These activities form a sequence—they may be of short duration and simple linkage (boiling an egg); long duration and complex linkage (preparing for a profession); or a variety of intermediate combinations (planting and harvesting a crop). And the activity sequences needed to complete valued tasks and to achieve valued goals in a society largely determine how the people in that society will subjectively experience *time*.

The distinctive temporal bent of industrial society has been toward the second of these arrangements, long duration and complex linkage. As regards the subjective experience of time, this has meant what the anthropologist Florence Kluckhohn has termed a strong "future orientation" on the part of Western man, a quality of sensibility that radically distinguishes him from his peasant and tribal forebears. The major activities that fill the better part of his life acquire their meaning less from the pleasure they may or may not give at the moment than from their perceived relevance to some imagined future state of being

or affairs, be it salvation, career achievement, material success, or the realization of a more perfect social order. Deprived of the pursuit of these temporally distant, complexly modulated goals, we would feel that life, as the man in the street puts it, is without meaning.

This subjective conception of time and experience is, of course, admirably suited to the needs of post-18th century industrial society, needs that include a stable labor force; work discipline; slow and regular accumulation of capital with which to plan and launch new investments and to expand; and long, arduous years of training to provide certain people with the high levels of skill necessary in so many professions and technical fields. If Western man had proved unable to defer present gratifications for future rewards (that is, if he had not been a future-oriented being), nothing resembling our present civilization, as Freud noted, could have come to pass.

Yet, paradoxically, it is the advanced technology of computers and servo-mechanisms, not to overlook nuclear warfare, that industrial civilization has carried us to that is raising grave doubts concerning this temporal ordering of affairs, this optimistic, pleasure-deferring, and magically rationalistic faith in converting present effort to future pay-off. Why prepare, if there will be so few satisfying jobs to prepare for? Why defer, if there will be a superabundance of inexpensively-produced goods to choose from? Why plan, if all plans can disintegrate into nuclear dust?

Premature or exaggerated as these questions may seem, they are being asked, especially by young people. And merely to ask them is to prompt a radical shift in time-perspective—from what *will be* to what *is,* from future promise to present fulfillment, from the mundane discounting of present feeling and mood to a sharpened awareness of their contours and their possibilities for instant alteration. Broadly, it is to invest present experience with a new cognitive status and importance: a lust to extract from the living moment its full sensory and emotional potential. For if the present is no longer to held hostage to the future, what other course than to ravish it at the very instant of its apprehension?

There is much about the hippie subculture that already betokens this alteration of time-perspective and concomitant reconstitution of the experienced self. Hippie argot— some of it new, much of it borrowed with slight connotative changes from the Negro, jazz, homosexual, and addict subcultures—is markedly skewed toward words and phrases in the active present tense: "happening," "where it's at," "turn on," "freak out," "grooving," "mind-blowing, "be-in," "cop out," "split," "drop acid" (take LSD), "put on," "uptight" (anxious and tense), "trip out" (experience the far-out effects of a hallucinogenic drug). The very concept of a happening signifies immediacy: Events are to be actively engaged in, improvised upon, and dramatically exploited for their own sake, with little thought about their origins, duration, or consequences. Thus, almost anything—from a massive be-in in Golden Gate Park to ingesting LSD to a casual street conversation to sitting solitarily under a tree—is approached with a heightened awareness of its happening potential. Similarly, the vogue among Hashbury hippies for astrology, tarot cards, I Ching, and other forms of thaumaturgic prophecy (a hippie conversation is as likely to begin with "What's your birthday?" as "What's your name?") seems to be an attempt to denude the future of its temporal integrity—its unknowability and slow unfoldingness—by fusing it indiscriminately with present dispositions and sensations. The hippie's structureless round-of-day ("hanging loose"), his disdain for appointments, schedules, and straight society's compulsive parceling out of minutes and hours, are all implicated in his intense reverence for the possibilities of the present and uninterest in the future. Few wear watches, and as a colleague who has made a close participant-observer study of one group of hippies remarked, "None of them ever seems to know what time it is."

It is, perhaps, from this vantage point that the widespread use of drugs by hippies acquires its cultural significance, above and beyond the fact that drugs are easily available in the subculture or that their use (especially LSD) has come to symbolize a distinctive badge of membership in that culture. Denied by our Protestant-Judaic heritage the psychological means for experiencing the moment intensively, for parlaying sensation and exoticizing mundane consciousness, the hippie uses drugs where untutored imagination fails. Drugs impart to the present—or so it is alleged by the hippie psychedelic religionists—an aura of aliveness, a sense of union with fellow man and nature, which—we have been taught—can be apprehended, if not in the afterlife that few modern men still believe in, then only after the deepest reflection and self-knowledge induced by protracted experience.

A topic of lively debate among hippie intellectuals is whether drugs represent but a transitory phase of the hippie subculture to be discarded once other, more self-generating, means are discovered by its members for extracting consummatory meaning from present time, or whether drugs are the *sine qua non* of the subculture. Whatever the case, the hippies' experiment with ways to recast our notions of time and experience is deserving of close attention.

The Hippies' Future

As of this writing, it is by no means certain that Haight-Ashbury's "new community," as hippie spokesmen like to call it, can survive much beyond early 1968. Although the "great summer invasion" of émigré hippies fell far short of the 100,000 to 500,000 forecast, the influx of youth from California's and the nation's metropolitan suburbs was, despite considerable turnover, large enough to place a severe strain on the new community's meager resources. "Crash pads" for the night were simply not available in sufficient quantity; the one daily meal of soup or stew served free by the Diggers could hardly appease youthful appetites; and even the lure of free love, which to young minds might be construed as a substitute for food, tarnished for many—boys outnumbered girls by at least three to one, if not more. Besides, summer is San Francisco's most inclement season, the city being shrouded in a chilling, wind-blown fog much of the time. The result was hundreds of youths leading a hand-to-mouth existence, wandering aimlessly on the streets, panhandling, munching stale doughnuts, sleeping in parks and autos and contracting virulent upper-respiratory infections. In this milieu cases of drug abuse, notably involving Methedrine and other "body-wrecking" amphetamines, have showed an alarming increase, beginning about mid-summer and continuing up to the present. And, while the city fathers were not at first nearly so repressive as many had feared, they barely lifted a finger to ameliorate the situation in the Haight-Ashbury. Recently, however, with the upcoming city elections for Mayor and members of the Board of Supervisors, they have given evidence of taking a "firmer" attitude toward the hippies: Drug arrests are on the increase, many more minors in the area are being stopped for questioning and referral to juvenile authorities, and a leading Haight Street hippie cultural establishment, the Straight Theatre, has been denied a dance permit.

It has not, therefore, been solely the impact of sheer numbers that has subjected the new community to a difficult struggle for survival. A variety of forces, internal and external, appear to have conjoined to crush it. To begin with, there is the hippies' notorious, near-anarchic aversion to sustained and organized effort toward reaching some goal. Every man "does his own thing for as long as he likes" until another thing comes along to distract or delight him, whereupon the hippie ethos enjoins him to drop the first thing. (Shades of the early, utopian Karl Marx: ". . . in the communist society it [will be] possible for me to do this today and that tomorrow, to hunt in the morning, to fish in the afternoon, to raise cattle in the evening, to be a critic after dinner, just as I feel at the moment; without ever being a hunter, fisherman, herdsman, or critic." From *The German Ideology*.) Even with such groups as the Diggers, projects are abandoned almost as soon as they are begun. One of the more prominent examples: An ongoing pastoral idyll of summer cultural happenings, proclaimed with great fanfare in May by a group calling itself the Council for the Summer of Love, was abandoned in June when the Council's leader decided one morning to leave town. Add to this the stalling and ordinance-juggling of a city bureaucracy reluctant to grant hippies permits and licenses for their pet enterprises, and very little manages to get off the ground. With only a few notable exceptions, therefore, like the Haight-Ashbury Free Medical Clinic, which—though closed temporarily—managed through its volunteer staff to look after the medical needs of thousands of hippies during the summer, the new community badly failed to provide for the hordes of youth drawn by its paeans of freedom, love, and the new life. Perhaps there is some ultimate wisdom to "doing one's own thing"; it was, however, hardly a practical way to receive a flock of kinsmen.

Exacerbating the "uptightness" of the hippies is a swelling stream of encounters with the police and courts, ranging from panhandling misdemeanors to harboring runaway minors ("contributing to the delinquency of a minor") to, what is most unnerving for hip inhabitants, a growing pattern of sudden mass arrests for marihuana use and possession in which as many as 25 youths may be hauled off in a single raid on a flat. (Some hippies console themselves with the thought that if enough middle-class youths get "busted for grass," such a hue and cry will be generated in respectable quarters that the marihuana laws will soon be repealed or greatly liberalized.) And, as if the internal problems of the new community were not enough, apocalyptic rumors sprung up, in the wake of the Newark and Detroit riots, that "the Haight is going to be burned to the ground" along with the adjoining Fillmore Negro ghetto. There followed a series of ugly street incidents between blacks and whites—assaults, sexual attacks, window smashings—which palpably heightened racial tensions and fed the credibility of the rumors.

Finally, the area's traffic-choked main thoroughfare, Haight Street, acquired in the space of a few months so carnival and Dantesque an atmosphere as to defy description. Hippies, tourists, drug peddlers, Hell's Angels, drunks, speed freaks (people high on Methedrine), panhandlers, pamphleteers, street musicians, crackpot evangelists, photographers, TV camera crews, reporters (domestic and foreign), researchers, ambulatory schizophrenics, and hawkers of the underground press (at least four such papers are produced in the Haight-Ashbury alone) jostled, put-on, and taunted one another through a din worthy of the Tower of Babel. The street-milling was incessant, and all heads remained cocked for "something to happen" to crystallize the disarray. By early summer, so repugnant had this atmosphere become for the "old" hippies (those residing there before—the origins of Hashbury's new community barely go back two years) that many departed; those who remained did so in the rapidly fading hope that the area might revert to its normal state of abnormality following the expected post-Labor Day exodus of college and high-school hippies. And, while the exodus of summer hippies has indeed been considerable, the consensus among knowledgeable observers of the area is that it has not regained its former, less frenetic, and less disorganized ambience. The transformations wrought by the summer influx—the growing shift to Methedrine as *the* drug of choice, the more general drift toward a wholly drug-oriented subculture, the appearance of hoodlum and thrill-seeking elements, the sleazy tourist shops, the racial tensions—persist, only on a lesser scale.

But though Haight-Ashbury's hippie community may be destined to soon pass from the scene, the roots upon which it feeds run deep in our culture. These are not only of the long-term socio-historic kind I have touched on here, but of a distinctly contemporary character as well, the pain and moral duplicity of our Vietnam involvement being a prominent wellspring of hippie alienation. As the pressures mount on middle-class youth for ever greater scholastic achievement (soon a graduate degree may be mandatory for middle-class status, as a high-school diploma was in the 1940s), as the years of adolescent dependence are further prolonged, and as the accelerated pace of technological change aggravates the normal social tendency to intergenerational conflict, an increasing number of young people can be expected to drop out, or opt out, and drift into the hippie subculture. It is difficult to foresee how long they will remain there and what the consequences for later stages of their careers will be, inasmuch as insufficient time has passed for even a single age cohort of hippies to make the transition from early to middle adulthood. However, even among those youths who "remain in" conventional society in some formal sense, a very large number can be expected to hover so close to the margins of hippie subculture as to have their attitudes and outlooks substantially modified. Indeed, it is probably through some such muted, gradual, and indirect process of social conversion that the hippie subculture will make a lasting impact on American society, if it is to have any at all.

At the same time, the hippie rebellion gives partial, as yet ambiguous, evidence of a massiveness, a universality, and a density of existential texture, all of which promise to transcend the narrowly-segregrated confines of age, occupation, and residence that characterized most bohemias of the past (Greenwich Village, Bloomsbury, the Left Bank). Some hippie visionaries already compare the movement to Christianity sweeping the Roman Empire. We cannot predict how far the movement can go toward enveloping the larger society, and whether as it develops it will—as have nearly all successful social movements—significantly compromise the visions that animate it with the practices of the reigning institutional system. Much depends on the state of future social discontent, particularly within the middle classes, and on the viable political options governments have for assuaging this discontent. Judging, however, from the social upheavals and mass violence of recent decades, such options are, perhaps inevitably, scarce indeed. Just possibly, then, by opting out and making their own kind of cultural waves, the hippies are telling us more than we can now imagine about our future selves.

Young Intelligentsia in Revolt

Richard Flacks

Karl Marx expected that capitalist exploitation of industrial workers would lead them to oppose the culture of capitalism—that is, that workers would organize not only on behalf of their own interests but ultimately on behalf of human liberation. What now seems clear is that opposition to capitalist culture arose less in the working class than among tiny groups of artists and intellectuals. Obviously, such people were too few in number and too isolated from the productive process to have any historical significance in Marx's eyes. To the extent that he had any hope for a revolutionary contribution from them, it was that they would follow his example and join the working-class struggle, which of course few did.

What Marx could not anticipate, however, was that the antibourgeois intellectuals of his day were the first representatives of what has become in our time a mass intelligentsia, a group possessing many of the cultural and political characteristics of a class in Marx's sense. By intelligentsia I mean those engaged vocationally in the production, distribution, interpretation, criticism and inculcation of cultural values. Most of the occupations in which the intelligentsia work are located outside the capitalist sector of the economy, either as free professions or in nonprofit educational institutions or other public bureaucracies. If, as in the case of the mass media, they are coordinated by private corporations, the intelligentsia are often officially depicted as serving such values as pleasure, art and truth, rather than commercial values.

It is important to note that these occupations are among the most rapidly growing, numerically, of any in the society. This is due in part to increasing governmental investment in educational, scientific and social service activities, and in part to the increase in leisure time and the consequent demand for entertainment and recreation. But more fundamentally, it is a function of the need in advanced industrial society for people to do the work of planning, prediction, innovation and systematic training, and socialization that the system now requires for its survival and growth. In the past century, then, the intelligentsia has been transformed from a tiny group of marginal status to a fast-growing, increasingly organized mass playing a key role in the functioning of the system.

Several years ago, when some of us at the University of Chicago looked into the social backgrounds of New Left students, we found that our group of activists was distinct from other college students in the degree to which they aspired to be part of the intelligentsia. But we also found, after interviewing their parents, that there was a substantial continuity between basic values and aspirations of the two generations. Both the activists and their parents were hostile to the self-denying, competitive, status-oriented individualism of bourgeois culture, and both sought a way of life that emphasized self-expression, humanism, openness to experience and community. In addition, both the students and their parents were substantially disaffected from the political system—though the students, of course, were more thoroughly alienated than their parents. It seemed clear to us that the students, through their activism, were for the most part attempting to fulfill and extend an ideological and cultural tradition already present in their families, rather than rebelling against the values on which they had been raised.

The fact that there have been, in the United States and Europe, a number of previous examples of political and cultural movements, based in the intelligentsia, with parallel ideological overtones, suggests, as does the generational continuity within activists' families, that the current youth radicalism is an expression of a definite historical process. This process may be described as the effort by many in the ranks of the intelligentsia to articulate and implement values which would serve as alternatives to those prevailing in capitalist culture.

Intellectuals as a Class

Historically, the revolt against bourgeois culture has taken many, quite divergent, ideological forms, ranging from socialism on the left to romanticism on the right, and it was acted out in a variety of ways, from direct participation in revolutionary movements to withdrawal into bohemian communities. In the first years of this century,

371

however, a characteristically American intellectual radicalism began to emerge, which differed in important respects from the perspectives that prevailed in Europe. Like the Europeans, the new radical American intellectuals expressed their disaffection in a variety of ways: muckraking journalism, literary and social criticism in little magazines, realistic novels, avant-garde poetry and painting, salon conversation, scholarly radicalism, progressive politics, labor-organizing, the socialist movement. But unlike their European counterparts, American intellectuals tended to have a relatively optimistic and rationalist perspective. They believed that social, political and personal reforms were possible, especially if science and reason were brought to bear on pressing problems.

Significantly, the revolt of American writers and intellectuals coincided with the rise of the feminist movement. One consequence of the impact of feminism on the perspective of American intellectuals was a tendency for the boundaries between private and public issues to become blurred or obliterated. Political reform in the larger society was linked to reform of family life and individual character, with the result that many intellectuals emphasized conscious, deliberate and scientific reform of the socializing institutions, the family and the school in order to create new values and character types and thereby to facilitate social change.

Optimism of the Intelligentsia

The specific hopes of the early twentieth century radical intellectuals were largely abortive. But their assault on Victorianism, the Protestant Ethic and business values had a wide impact. Progressive education, social work, child psychology, psychotherapy—a host of new professions emerged which had their original impulse in the desire to cure the effects of the dominant culture and which embodied implicit or explicit criticism of it. An important result of these new ideas, when combined with the rising status of women, was to create a new kind of middle-class family—less authoritarian, less hierarchical, more child-centered, more democratic, more self-conscious in its treatment of children. In these ways, the criticism of capitalist culture by tiny groups of European and American intellectuals became rooted in American life and incorporated into the value system of large numbers of middle-class Americans who attended the universities or were influenced by university-centered thought.

Now it is not the case, of course, that the rising intelligentsia was predominantly radical politically or unconventional culturally. Rather, what has been characteristic of this class politically is its very substantial optimism about the direction of the society and a whole-hearted acceptance of the legitimacy of the national political system, coupled with a strong hostility to those aspects of politics and culture identifiable as reactionary and regressive. What supported their optimism was their faith in three interrelated instruments of change.

First, they believed that the federal government could be molded into a force for social amelioration, economic progress and equality. This hope was, of course, crystallized during the New Deal and solidified during World War II and the immediate postwar period. Second, they believed that the new vocations, the service, helping and educational professions they had entered, would be significant in curing and preventing social and psychological pathology, extending the possibilities for democracy and upward mobility and raising the intellectual and cultural level of the people. Third, they tended to believe that the values they held were best implemented through self-conscious efforts to create families and a personal life style embodying democratic, humanistic, egalitarian principles, in contradiction to the authoritarian, repressed, Victorian, anti-intellectual and acquisitive style of life they perceived as characteristic of other middle-class people.

These beliefs emerged most strongly in the twenties and thirties, and it was possible to maintain them all during the New Deal period and the forties when it appeared that there was a real chance for the welfare state actually to be realized. Moreover, the horrors of fascism and Stalinism permitted many of the educated to feel that the United States, whatever its flaws, was the major defender of democratic values. Post–World War II prosperity greatly raised living standards and cultural possibilities for this group and also seemed to be creating the conditions for social equality. Thus, the parents of the present generation of student activists, despite their antipathy to traditional capitalist culture, maintained a generally complacent view of American society when they themselves were young and in the years when their children were growing up.

By the late fifties, however, some of this complacency undoubtedly began to break down. The Eisenhower years were a period of political stagnation and anti-Communist hysteria in which it became evident that the drive toward a welfare state and social equality might not be inherent in American political institutions. It also became clear that America's international role was incongruent with humanist, democratic values and beliefs. At a more fundamental level, many of the educated, as they reached middle age, began to have some doubts about the moral worth of their own occupations and about the degree to which they too had participated in the pursuit of status and material comfort. The late 1950s was a period of increasing social criticism much of which revolved around the collapse of meaning in vocation and about the moral callousness of the American middle class.

By 1960, then, the development of the American intelligentsia as a class had come to this. Demographically, it had grown over several decades from small pockets of isolated, independent intellectuals to a substantial stratum of the population, including many in new white-collar vocations. Culturally, it had begun to develop a family structure and value system at odds with the traditional capitalist, Protestant Ethic, middle-class culture. Politically, it had passed through a period of optimistic reformism and seemed to be moving into a period of increasing disillusionment. The newest and largest generation of this stratum was thronging the nation's colleges, at just that point historically when the sustaining ideologies of industrial society—liberalism, socialism, communism—had reached exhaustion. At the same time, the cold war and anticommunism had ceased to be a workable framework for American international policy, and the colored population in the United States and around the world was breaking into active revolt.

Coming Together

In the decade since 1960, the offspring of the intelligentsia have become politicized and increasingly radicalized, despite the fact that, having been born to relatively high privilege and social advantage, they saw society opening ever wider vistas for personal success and enrichment. Why have they, in large numbers, refused to follow their fathers and mothers—adopting a stance of slightly uneasy acceptance of the prevailing social order while trying to establish a personal life on a somewhat different cultural basis?

In part, the disaffection of these youth is a direct consequence of the values and impulses their parents transmitted to them. The new generation had been raised in an atmosphere that encouraged personal autonomy and individuality. Implicitly and explicitly it had been taught to be skeptical about the intrinsic value of money-making and status and to be skeptical about the claims of established authority. It incorporated new definitions of sex

roles. Having seen their parents share authority and functions more or less equally in the family, and having been taught to value aesthetic and intellectual activity, these were boys who did not understand masculinity to mean physical toughness and dominance, and girls who did not understand femininity to mean passivity and domesticity. Moreover, they were young people—young people for whom the established means of social control were bound to be relatively ineffective (and here they were particularly different from the older generation). Growing up with economic security in families of fairly secure status, the normal incentives of the system—status and income—were of relatively minor importance, and indeed many of their parents encouraged them to feel that such incentives ought to be disdained.

In retrospect, it seems inevitable that young people of this kind should come into some conflict with the established order. Because of their central values, they, like the earlier generations of intellectuals, would necessarily be social critics. Because of their material security, they, like earlier generations of high status youth, were likely to be experimental, risk-taking, open to immediate experience, relatively unrepressed. Because of their character structure, they would very likely come into conflict with arbitrary authority in school and other situations of imposed restriction. Because of their values and sex role identifications, they would find themselves out of harmony with the conventional youth culture with its frivolity, anti-intellectualism and stereotypic distinctions between the sexes.

Furthermore, their impulses to autonomy and individuality, their relative freedom from economic anxiety and their own parents' ambivalence toward the occupational structure would make it difficult for them to decide easily on a fixed vocational goal or life style, would make them aspire to construct their lives outside conventional career lines, would make them deeply critical of the compromise, corruption and unfreedom inherent in the occupations of their fathers—the very occupations for which they were being trained.

Much of this had happened before, but the situation of the young intelligentsia of the sixties differed radically from that of their precursors. First, their numbers were enormously greater than ever before. Second, they faced, not a scarcity of jobs, but an abundance of careers—yet the careers for which they were being trained no longer held the promise of social melioration and personal fulfillment that their parents had anticipated. Third, these youth sensed not only the narrowness and irrationality of the prevailing culture but the deeper fact that the dominant values of bourgeois society, appropriate in an age of scarcity and entrepreneurial activity, had become irrelevant to a society which was moving beyond scarcity and competitive capitalism. Thus, by the late fifties, more youth were feeling more intensely than ever before a sense of estrangement from capitalist culture—an estrangement which could not be assuaged by the promise of material security the system offered.

The cultural crisis these youth experienced provided the ground for their coming together. But the transformation of cultural alienation into political protest, and eventually into revolutionary action, was due to more immediate and concrete pressures. It was the emergence of the southern civil rights movement which, more than any other single event, led the young intelligentsia in the early sixties to see the relevance of political opposition and social change to their own problems. The nonviolent movement showed, for one thing, how small groups of committed youth could undertake action that could have major historical impact. It demonstrated how such action could flow directly from humanistic values. But above all, it confronted these white students with the fact that all of their opportunities for personal fulfillment were based on white upper-middle-class privilege and that continued passivity in the face of racism meant that one was in fact part of the oppressive apparatus of society, no matter what one's private attitudes might be.

Hopes of SDS

Participation in the civil rights struggle seemed, however, to offer a way out of this dilemma, and civil rights protest helped to open the consciousness of many students to other political issues. It made them aware that there was more to their problems than the fact that the culture offered little support for their personal aspirations; it also threatened their existence. But at the same time numbers of students became rapidly sensitive to the fact that the nuclear arms race, the cold war and the militarization of society were not simply facts of life but deliberate, therefore reversible, policies. It was not long before the protest tactics acquired in the civil rights movement began to be applied to the demand for peace.

When one reads today the Port Huron Statement (June 1962) and other documents of the early Students for a Democratic Society (SDS) and the New Left, one is struck by the degree to which the early New Left conceived of itself largely as a political reform movement rather than in clearly revolutionary terms. While it's true, as Todd Gitlin has suggested, that the early new radicals of the sixties were filled with "radical disappointment" with the American way of life, it is also the case that they retained a good deal of optimism about the possibilities for change in the context of American politics. In particular, it was hoped that the labor movement, the religious community, the liberal organizations, the intellectual community, the civil rights movement all could eventually unite around a broad-based program of radical reform.

The role of the student movement was seen by the early SDS leaders as providing the intellectual skills needed for such a new movement and, somewhat later, as important for producing people who would help to catalyze grass root activities in a variety of places. Direct action such as the sit-ins, freedom rides and other forms of protest and civil disobedience was seen, on the one hand, as a vital tactic for the winning of reform and, on the other hand, as a method by which the more established institutions such as the labor movement could be induced to move in the direction of more vigorous action. In this early phase of the student movement, SDS and other New Left leaders were little aware of the possibility that a mass movement of students on the campus could be created and engaged in collective struggles against university authority. Rather the New Left's role on the campus was seen primarily as one of breaking through the atmosphere of apathy, educating students about political issues, so that they could begin to take a role off the campus in whatever struggles were going on.

But the early reformism of the New Left was soon abandoned. The failure of the established agencies of reform to create a political opposition and to mobilize mass support for political alternatives was most decisive in preventing the new movement of the young intelligentsia from becoming absorbed by conventional politics, thereby following in the footsteps of previous movements of American intellectuals. This collapse of the so-called liberal establishment thus marked a new stage in the consciousness of the American intelligentsia—beyond cultural alienation, beyond social reform, beyond protest—toward active resistance and revolution.

The emergence of the student movement in the sixties, then, signifies a more fundamental social change and is not simply a species of "generational conflict." The convergence of certain social structural and cultural trends has produced a new class, the intelligentsia, and, despite the apparent material security of many in this class, its trajectory is toward revolutionary opposition to capitalism.

This is because, first, capitalism cannot readily absorb the cultural aspirations of this group—aspirations that fundamentally have to do with the abolition of alienated labor and the achievement of democratic community. Second, the incorporation of this group is made more difficult by the concrete fact of racism and imperialism—facts which turn the vocations of the intelligentsia into cogs in the machinery of repression rather than means for self-fulfillment and general enlightenment. Third, the numerical size of this group and the concentration of much of it in universities make concerted oppositional political action extremely feasible. Finally, the liberal default has hastened the self-consciousness of students and other members of this class, exacerbated their alienation from the political system and made autonomous oppositional politics a more immediate imperative for them. Thus, a stratum, which under certain conditions might have accepted a modernizing role within the system, has instead responded to the events of this past decade by adopting an increasingly revolutionary posture.

In part, this development grows out of the antiauthoritarian impulses in the fundamental character structure of the individual members which provide much of the motivation and emotional fuel for the movement. But, as the history of the movement shows, there was an early readiness to consider whether established political alternatives were in fact viable. That such readiness has virtually disappeared is almost entirely due to the failure of the political system itself—a failure most manifest in the crises of race, poverty and urban life on the one hand and the international posture of the United States on the other.

Over the last decade the American government has consistently failed to enforce new or existing legislation guaranteeing civil rights. It has consistently failed to implement promised reforms leading to social and economic equality. It has demonstrated a stubborn unwillingness and/or incompetence in dealing with the deepening crises of urban life, and it has supported essentially repressive, rather than ameliorative, policies with respect to the black revolt.

Even more crucial in undermining the legitimacy of the system for young people was, of course, the war in Vietnam—the fact that the United States was unable to win the war; the fact that it dragged on endlessly to become the longest war in American history; the fact that the United States in Vietnam was involved in an effort to suppress a popular uprising; the fact that the United States in Vietnam committed an interminable series of atrocities and war crimes, especially involving the destruction of civilian life; the fact that the war was accompanied by a military draft and that alongside the draft a system involving the social tracking of all young males in America had grown up; the fact that the war in Vietnam was not simply an accident of policy but an essential ingredient of what became increasingly identified as a worldwide imperialist policy involving the suppression of popular revolution and the maintenance and extension of American political and corporate power throughout the Third World.

Moreover, alongside the growth of conventional and nuclear military power and the penetration of American institutions, including especially the universities, by military priorities, there grew up a paramilitary establishment which had attempted to control and manipulate organizations and events throughout the world and also at home. This development was perhaps best symbolized for students by the fact that the Central Intelligence Agency had subsidized the National Student Association and had extensive ties with American academics. Finally, the war continued and escalated despite vast expressions of popular discontent.

This, more than anything else, reinforced the New Left's disbelief in the efficacy of conventional political means of affecting policy. By the time of the Democratic Convention in 1968, a very large number of young people were convinced that only extreme action of a disruptive sort could have any substantial effect on major policy and that "working through the system" was a trap, rather than a means to effect change.

Obviously, many young people, fearing the consequences of a full-scale delegitimation of authority, continue to search for a more responsive political alternative within the system. But the stagnation of liberalism in these years along with the astonishing series of assassinations of spokesmen for its revitalization have made such hopes appear increasingly unrealistic. Thus the growth of revolutionary sentiment among the students proceeds apace. As the legitimacy of national authority declines, a process of delegitimation occurs for all in authoritative positions—for instance, university officials—and proposals for melioration and compromise are viewed with deepening suspicion. Political polarization intensifies, and those in the opposition feel, on the one hand, the imperative of confrontation as a means of further clarifying the situation and, on the other hand, that the entire structure of social control is being organized for the purpose of outright repression. And for American students confrontation is made more urgent by the moral pressure of the black liberation movement, which continuously tests the seriousness of their proclaimed revolutionary commitment.

New Front Line

The early New Left frequently criticized university life as well as the larger society, but it was also quite ambivalent toward the university as an institution. University authority was seen as paternalistic and as subservient to dominant interests in the society. University education was regarded as a contributor to student indifference towards social questions. At the same time, the Port Huron Statement and other early New Left writing viewed the university as a potential resource for movements for change, university intellectuals as potentially useful to such movements and the university as a relatively free place where political controversy could flourish provided it was catalyzed.

Prior to the fall of 1964, SDS leaders ignored the campus as a base of operation, persuading a considerable number of students to either leave school or to work off the campus in the efforts to organize the urban poor. In large measure, university reform campaigns were felt by the most committed activists to be both irrelevant and, in a certain sense, immoral, when people in the South were putting their bodies on the line. The Berkeley free speech movement of 1964 helped to change this perception of the campus. The police action at Berkeley, the first of numerous large-scale busts' of student protestors, suggested that a campus struggle could be the front line. And the political impact of Berkeley in California, and indeed internationally, suggested that there was nothing parochial or irrelevant about an on-campus struggle. Moreover, these events coincided with the turning away of portions of the civil rights movement, especially the Student Nonviolent Coordinating Committee, from efforts to work with white students. Further, Berkeley coincided with the escalation of the war in Vietnam and with the discovery, only dimly realized before, that the universities were major resources in the development of the military potential of the United States.

Beginning in the fall of 1966 attacks on military research installations, on ROTC, on connections between the university and military agencies, on military recruitment and recruitment by defense corporations became the prime activity of SDS and other student groups for a number of months. Every major confrontation mobilized hundreds of students for highly committed direct action and many thousands more for supportive action. Typically the is-

sues raised by the student movement on a campus were supported by as many as two-thirds of the student body, even though large numbers of students were unwilling to participate in disruptive actions as such. And as previously uncommitted students joined these actions, many were radicalized by the experience of participation in a community of struggle, by the intransigence and obtuseness of university administrators and by the violence of police repression of the protests. Institutional resistance was fostering student "class consciousness."

By the late sixties, the movement was no longer the exclusive property of those I've been calling the young intelligentsia. It was having a widening impact on students at nonelite campuses, in junior colleges and high schools, and on nonstudent youth in the streets and in the Armed Forces. To a great extent, the availability of larger numbers of young people for insurgent ideas and actions is rooted in the cultural crisis we alluded to at the outset of this paper. For all youth experience the breakdown of traditional culture, the irrelevance of ideologies based on scarcity. Vast numbers of youth in America today are in search of a less repressed, more human, more spontaneous life style.

The radicalization of youth is enhanced by the peculiar social position of high school and college students, who have achieved some degree of independence from family authority but are not yet subject to the discipline of work institutions. The high school and college situation is, on the one hand, extremely authoritarian but, on the other hand, functions to segregate young people, maintaining them in a peculiar limbo combining dependency with irresponsibility. The impact of the cultural crisis on the school situation is to make really vast numbers of young people ready for new and more liberating ideas, while they have the freedom and energy to spend time in examination and criticism of prevailing values and ideologies.

In addition, the situation of youth is exacerbated by the demands of the imperialist system for manpower and by the increasing bureaucratization of both education and vocation. More concretely, the draft is the reality that undermines the endless promises made to American youth. What the draft means is that one is not really free to pursue self-fulfillment, even though one has been taught that self-fulfillment is the highest goal and purpose of the system. Not only is that promise undermined by the necessity to serve in the army and die in the mud of some distant jungle, a fate reserved for relatively few young men, but the draft serves to facilitate control over the careers of all young men by serving explicitly as a means for tracking youth into occupations believed to be in the interest of the state. The result for school youth is postponement or avoidance of the military but subjugation to an educational system that reproduces many of the worst features of the larger society in terms of authoritarianism, competitiveness, individualism and dehumanization. The growth of a mass youth movement depended on the emergence of a group of young intelligentsia whose own socialization was particularly at odds with the dominant culture, but once such a circle of youth emerged, their expressions, both cultural and political, spread like wildfire.

Thus, the story of the student movement in the United States over the past decade has been one of continued self-transformation. Once student activism was characteristic of tiny groups of campus rebels, the offspring, as we have suggested, of the educated middle class, who faced severe value and vocational crisis, could find no moral way to assimilate into American society and so searched for a new basis for living in cultural avant-gardism and moralistic dedication to social reform. In the past decade, obviously, the movement has spread well beyond this original group. It has transformed itself from a nonideological movement for vague principles of social justice into a new radical movement in quest of a new social vision and a new framework for social criticism, and finally into a movement spearheaded by revolutionaries tending, more and more, to look to classical revolutionary doctrine as a guiding principle and to embody, more and more, classical models of revolutionary action as their own.

It is a movement that rejects and is at the same time entangled by its roots in what I have called the intelligentsia. Yet it has expressed most clearly the fundamental aspirations of the rising generation of that class for a new social order in which men can achieve autonomy and full participation in determining the conditions of their lives, in which hierarchy and domination are replaced by community and love, in which war, militarism and imperialism are obsolete and in which class and racial distinctions are abolished. It is a movement of surprising strength. It has touched the minds of millions and changed the lives of thousands of young people, both here and abroad. It has severely shaken the stability of the American empire and challenged the basic assumptions of its culture. But its most sensitive adherents have become increasingly despairing, as the movement has reached the limit of its possibilities. This despair is rooted first in the unresponsiveness of the political system to pressure for reform; second, in the narrow class base of the movement; third, in the seemingly overwhelming capacity of the authorities to manage social control. Out of this despair arises the sense that revolution is an urgent, if impossible, necessity, that the movement must transcend its social base, that it must make common cause with other enemies of the empire around the world.

Co-optation

Given this new consciousness, what can be said about the future of the movement? It seems to me that one can envision several possibilities. First, any student and youth movement has the potential of becoming a relatively insulated expression of generational revolt. This is not the explicit intention of very many spokesmen for the New Left, but it certainly appears to be the implicit expectation of many agencies of social control. A generational movement may be understood as a movement of cultural and social innovation whose impact has been contained within the framework of existing society. For agencies of social control, the ideal circumstance would be the opportunity to eliminate those elements in the movement that are most disruptive and destructive, while putting into effect some of the cultural, social and political innovations and reforms the movement advocates.

Accordingly, you put Yippies in jail but work out some means to legalize the use of marijuana. You put draft-resisters in jail or into exile while abolishing conscription. You expel SDS from the campus while admitting student representatives to the board of trustees. You deride and derogate the women's liberation movement while liberalizing abortion laws. You break up and harass hippie urban communities while providing fame and fortune to some rock music groups. This is all done with the aid of ideological perspectives that emphasize that what is going on is a generational revolt, that there is a generation gap, that the big problem is one of communication between the old and the young. The hope is that if reforms can be made that will liberalize the cultural and social atmosphere, particularly in relation to sex, drug use, art, music, censorship and so forth, the mass of youth will not become tempted by the message of the radical vanguard.

If the new political and cultural radicalism were to become channeled more fully in the direction of generational revolt, it would then be serving stabilizing and modernizing functions for the going system, and it would not be the first time that a radical movement in the United States ended up functioning this way. But from the point of view of New Left activists, such an outcome for the movement would represent profound failure, particularly if it meant, as it does now seem to mean, that the most active and militant of the participants of the movement would suffer, rather than benefit, from any social change that might be forthcoming.

There is a substantial likelihood, however, that the student movement and the New Left of the sixties will move in the direction we have just outlined. The most important fact supporting this outcome is that the movement has, in the ten years of its existence, failed very largely to break out of its isolation as a movement of the young, and particularly of the relatively advantaged young. There are reasons to think that this isolation could be broken in the near future, and we shall suggest some of these shortly, but it is important to recognize that most of the public understanding of what is happening has revolved around the generational problem, rather than the substantive political and social questions that the movement has raised. Most of the expressed sympathy for the movement on the part of the elders has been couched in terms of solving the problems of youth and liberalizing the cultural atmosphere, rather than in joining in the making of a social revolution.

At the same time, however, despite the very large-scale public discussion of the need for reform and innovation, the prevailing tendencies of the state and other dominant institutions do not seem to be primarily in this direction. Even such apparently unthreatening changes as liberalization of laws governing drug use, the 18-year-old vote, the involvement of students in direct participation in university government or the abolition of the draft meet very strong resistance and do not now seem to be on the agenda. Instead, what is in prospect is further tightening of drug laws, further restrictions and harassment of the communal outcroppings of the youth culture, further efforts at censorship, a continuation of the draft and a generally more hostile climate with respect to even the modest aspirations for change of most young people today. All of this, of course, could change in a relatively short period of time as those who are now young move into full citizenship and have the opportunity directly to influence public and institutional policies. But what happens in the intervening years is likely to be crucial.

Another reason for believing that the New Left has considerable capacity for resisting this kind of incorpora-tion into the culture is that the movement is profoundly suspicious of and sensitive to the dangers of co-optation. Most movement participants are aware at one level or another that the classic American pattern for controlling revolutionary and quasi-revolutionary movements is to destroy or isolate the most militant sections while implementing, at least on paper, the programmatic thrust of the movement. This is what happened in the labor movement. It is what is happening in the black liberation movement, and it is certainly what is being advocated for the student movement. In this way the American political system has served to contain the revolutionary thrust of movements that develop within it, while keeping these movements fragmented, preventing their outreach into sectors of the population beyond those that form the original constituency of the movement.

☐ By 1975 there will be well over 50 million adults born

As I say, new leftists wish to avoid at all costs the buying off of the movement through piecemeal reform. This is one reason why the movement is so hesitant to propose concrete reforms and to proclaim its interest in short-range goals. A greater danger, however, is that the movement has been unable to offset pressures, both internal and external, that maintain it as a movement of youth.

The future of the New Left depends now on its ability to break out of its isolation and to persuade the majority of Americans that their interests depend on the dismantling of imperialism and the replacement of capitalism with a fully democratized social order. The movement cannot afford to be encapsulated as a generational revolt. It cannot wait until the present young "take over." It cannot survive in a climate of repression and polarization unless large numbers of people are moving in a similar political direction. It cannot survive and ought not survive if it conceives itself to be an elite band of professional revolutionaries, aiming to "seize power" in the midst of social chaos and breakdown.

What are the structural conditions that might open up the possibility of the New Left transcending its present age and class base? Here are at least some:

☐ The class base of the movement is rapidly changing as the "youth culture" spreads to the high schools and junior colleges, to army bases and young workers. Along with this cultural diffusion, the mood of resistance spreads— protest is now endemic in high schools, it is evident in the armed forces, it is growing in the junior colleges.

☐ Inflation and high taxes have led to a decline in real

wages. Current fiscal policies generate rising unemployment. A new period of labor militance may have already begun. This situation converges with the influx of postwar youth into the labor force, with the militant organization of black caucuses in unions, with intensifying organization and militance among public employees and with the first efforts by former student radicals to "reach" workers. It may be that in spite of the Wallace phenomenon, racism and the alleged conservatism of the American working class a new radicalism is about to become visible among factory, government and other workers.

☐ The impoverishment and disintegration of public services, the systematic destruction of the natural environment, urban squalor, the tax burden—all are deeply felt troubles which are directly traceable to the profit system and the military priority. The sense of crisis and frustration that these problems generate throughout society offers the ground for the formulation and promulgation of radical program, action and organization.

☐ Political repression, although obviously dangerous for the survival of radicalism, can have the effect of intensifying rather than weakening insurgency. This would be particularly true if repression is seen as an assault on whole categories of persons, rather than on handfuls of "outside agitators." So, for instance, many participants in the youth culture now connect their own harassment by the police with the Chicago Conspiracy trial and other government attacks on radicals. Repression at this writing seems more likely to stiffen the mood of resistance among young people than it is to end attacks on "law and order."

☐ By 1975 there will be well over 50 million adults born since 1940. Most of these will have achieved political consciousness in the past decade. This fact alone suggests a major transformation of the political landscape by the second half of the seventies.

☐ In the next five years the proportion of the labor force definable as "intelligentsia" will have substantially increased. Current Bureau of Labor Statistics manpower projections for "professional, technical and kindred workers" are for a 40 percent increase in this category between 1966 and 1975, reaching a total of about 13 million in 1975. If my analysis in this essay is correct, this group should be a major source of radicalism in the coming period. The situation of these workers is now dramatically changing from one of high opportunity to relative job scarcity due to current federal and state budgetary policies. Thus one can expect that the radicalization of the intelli-

gentsia will continue to intensify in the years ahead.

One might suggest that these conditions provide the opportunity for a large-scale and successful "new politics" of liberal reform to assert itself. But the current exhaustion of political liberalism may well mean that a new "center-Left" coalition cannot be formed—that we have finally arrived in this country at the point where reformism is no longer viable.

An alternative possibility would be the emergence of a popular socialist party oriented to both "parliamentary" and "extraparliamentary" activity. Although this would certainly facilitate the transcendence of the New Left, there are as yet no signs that such a development is even incipient. In any case, the most important insight of the New Left is that political organization is not enough—the heart of revolution is the reconstruction of civil society and culture.

"The Long March"

It may well be that the singular mission of the new mass intelligentsia is to catalyze just such a transformation—to undertake what Rudi Dutschke called "the long march through the institutions of society." This march began in the universities. In coming years it may well continue through all significant cultural, educational, public service and professional institutions. It would have a double aim: to force these institutions to serve the people rather than the corporate system and the state and to engage cultural workers and professionals in struggles to control their work and govern the institutions that coordinate it and determine its use.

It is possible that such struggle by the intelligentsia could stimulate similar struggles in the primary economic institutions—to build a basis for workers' control and for the abolition of technologically unnecessary labor.

In addition to such institutional struggle, the reconstruction of civil society and culture requires the further development of self-organization of communities and especially of exploited and oppressed minorities. Such self-organization—of racial and ethnic minorities and of women—is necessary for any general cultural transformation. Struggle by communities for control of their own development and services prepares the basis for a decentralized and democratized civil society. It is obvious that all such developments have profound need for the services of professional, intellectual, cultural and scientific workers.

It is natural to assume that the development of political, civil and cultural struggle requires central, disciplined organization. My own feeling is that it requires something prior to, and perhaps instead of, the classical revolutionary party. What is really crucial is the organization of local "collectives," "affinity groups," "communes," "cells" of people who share a revolutionary perspective, a common locale of activity, a sense of fraternity, a willingness to bind their fates together. Each such group can be free to work out its priorities, projects and work style. What is necessary is that these groups generally conceive of themselves as catalysts of mass action rather than as utopian communities or elite terrorists. Most of the dramatic movements of the sixties occurred because small groups of friends undertook action that was catalytic or exemplary to larger masses. Most of the exciting cultural development in this period occurred in a similar way. Many of the problems the party is supposed to exist to solve can be coped with without centralization. Problems of communication can be handled by the underground media—which up to now have been the expression of a host of small collectives. National action projects can be coordinated by ad hoc coalitions and umbrella organizations. The generation of resources can be managed through movement banks and quasi foundations. There is no reason why collectives in different or similar milieus cannot meet together to exchange experience. If the purpose of a revolutionary movement is not to seize power but to educate the people to take it for themselves, then a maximally decentralized mode of work is appropriate. And in a period of tightening repression, a cellular rather than centralized mode of organization is obviously advantageous.

The revolution in advanced capitalist society is not a single insurrection. It is not a civil war of pitched battles fought by opposing armies. It is a long, continuing struggle—with political, social and cultural aspects inextricably intertwined. It is already underway. It is not simply a socialist revolution—if by that one means the establishment of a new form of state power that will introduce social planning and redistribute income. It is more than that. For it must be a revolution in which the power to make key decisions is placed in the hands of those whose lives are determined by those decisions. It is not, in short, a revolution aimed at seizing power but a revolution aimed at its dispersal.

It is possible that the New Left's current return to Old Left styles and models signifies that the kind of revolution of which I speak is premature, that the classes and groups that would be most active in producing it have not achieved full consciousness. We are not yet in an age of "postscarcity," and consequently the revolutionary visions appropriate to that age will have a difficult time establishing their reality. Perhaps, then, the New Left of the sixties is not destined to be the catalyst of the new revolution. I am personally convinced, however, that whatever the immediate destiny of the movement might be, the social and cultural changes that produced it and were accelerated by it are irreversible and cannot be contained within a capitalist framework. Once the material basis for human liberation exists, men will struggle against the institutions that stand in its way. The rise of the student movement in the United States and other industrial societies is a crucial demonstration of the truth of this proposition. For it is a sign that a revolutionary class consciousness appropriate to the era of monopoly capital, advanced technology and dying imperialism is in existence.

Post-1984 America

Lee Rainwater

The way of life of Americans changes constantly yet somehow over long periods of time is recognizably the same. Indeed, whether the life style of particular groups of Americans is seen as changing or stable is somewhat a matter of emphasis and purpose. Moreover, when predicting what life styles will be in a decade or so, the issue of change versus stability, of emergence versus repetition, is a complex one. Demographic and economic analysis shows that there will be striking changes in these objective indicators of socioeconomic position. On the other hand, during the past two or three decades—during which there have been similarly striking socioeconomic changes—the life styles of the various social classes have been remarkably stable despite all the technological innovation and socioeconomic progress.

Changes in life style and values in the future are likely to be subtle, or even superficial, in the sense that they represent adaptations to basic core values and patterns of interpersonal relationships to a new social, economic and ecological situation. The stability of life style is maintained in exactly this way—by constant reinterpretation of the meanings and use of particular products and services to make them consistent with the basic themes of various life styles.

The Next 15 Years

We are often misled into thinking about social problems by fastening too much on the present and the immediate past in developing the paradigms by which we seek to understand and control problems. As antidote for that let us look at what seems to be the most likely course of development of the broad segments of the American society over the period of the next 15 years.

The nation is now heavily urban in its pattern of settlement; by the mid-1980s it will be slightly more urban, the proportion of the population in metropolitan areas having increased from 68 percent to 71 percent. But there is another side to this increased urbanization. Because of the transportation revolution brought on by the automobile and the superhighway, within the urban areas the population is less and less densely settled—the population per square mile in urbanized areas will have decreased from 6,580 in 1920 to around 3,800 in 1985. And the proportion of the population living in the suburban areas will have increased from 39 percent to 45 percent. This is what suburbanization is all about; it is a trend that can be expected to continue into the future. This means that more and more land will be subject to the stresses of suburbanized development.

The population will grow, but current indications are that the growth will not be nearly as great as has been previously thought. The rate of population growth seems to be slowing down and some of the most experienced demographers believe that somewhat greater perfection of contraceptive technology will lead to zero population growth without any special need for exhortation. The population of the mid-1980s is likely to include some 240 million Americans—about 35 million more than today.

This growth is not particularly dramatic although it will certainly require a great deal in the way of new facilities. The most dramatic aspect of population change is the change in the age distribution. If the sixties and early seventies have been the generation of youth—of the teenager and early twenties adult—the late 1970s and 1980s will be the era of the young marrieds. The number of men and women between the ages of 24 and 34 will increase by 60 percent; the younger group will increase less than 10 percent. There will be a 37 percent increase in the number of adults between 35 and 45, a small decrease in the number 45 to 54, and a 27 percent increase at the over-65 level. The big demographic impact on the society, then, will be in the years of youthful maturity.

Most indications are that the economy will grow fairly steadily through the 1970s and 1980s. This will result in an increase in the size of the GNP from one to 1.7 trillion dollars. It is expected that the service sector of the economy will grow much more rapidly than the goods sector but the growth in the latter will not be inconsiderable.

In the daily life of members of the society the concomitant impact of this growth is a very large increase in personal income. The median income for families is expected to grow from around $10,000 to over $16,000 (in dollars of 1970 purchasing power).

However, there are no indications to suggest that this income will be distributed more equitably in the future

381

than it is at present. As has been true for the post-World War II period it seems likely that, although each income class will participate in the rising personal income, those at the bottom will not be increasing their share of the pie. That would mean that in the future as today the richest 20 percent of families would still be receiving over 40 percent of all of the personal income, and the poorest 20 percent would still be receiving less than 5 percent of the money income.

Of these various changes, two principal ones seem likely to have the greatest import for life style changes that have taken place over the past decades and that will take place (in all likelihood with increasing intensity) in the next two decades. The first of these is economic and the second cultural.

We are so used to the steady increase in affluence (despite occasional periods of two or three years of relative stagnation) and we adapt so rapidly to each successive level of affluence, that it is often difficult to realize how very large the shifts in personal income are. For example, the median income of families and unrelated individuals is projected to increase by $6700 from 1971 to 1985 (1970 dollars). One way of looking at this increase is to say that over a 17-year period median income will increase as much as it has over the previous 50 years. Thus, although the proportionate increase in income year by year, decade by decade is projected to be about the same over the next few years as it has been over the past half-century, the absolute increase is much larger because of the larger base on which the constant proportionate increase takes place. The result of these increases will be that by the mid-1980s half of the population will enjoy the level of living that characterized only the top 3 percent of the population in 1947 or the top 15 percent of the population in 1970. The very large bundle of goods and services that goes with this very large absolute increase in median income can be expected to have important interactions with the emerging life styles of the 1980s, both affecting and being affected by those styles. The table presents comparative data for 1968 and 1985.

Comparing Actual 1968 with Predicted 1985 Family and Individual Income in the United States.

Income levels	Families		Families and Individuals	
	1968	1985	1968	1985
Number (millions)	50.5	66.7	64.3	85.9
Percent	100	100	100	100
Under $3,000	10	4	19	9
$3,000 to $4,999	12	6	14	8
$5,000 to $9,999	38	18	34	19
$10,000 to $14,999	25	23	21	21
$15,000 to $24,999	12	33	10	29
$25,000 and over	3	16	2	15
Aggregate income (billions)	$486	$1,074	$544	$1,277
Percent	100	100	100	100
Under $3,000	2	1	4	1
$3,000 to $4,999	5	1	6	2
$5,000 to $9,999	29	8	30	9
$10,000 to $14,999	31	18	30	17
$15,000 to $24,999	23	37	21	35
$25,000 and over	10	35	9	36
Mean income	$9,600	$16,100	$8,500	$14,900
Median income	$8,600	$14,700	$7,400	$13,500

The median educational attainment of the population is expected to grow to only 12.6 years by 1985, and the proportion who attend college is projected to increase to 31.5 percent, with 18.8 percent completing college.

While these upward shifts in educational attainment are not particularly dramatic, the small increases there, in addition to numerous other forces expanding the knowledgeability of the population (and shifting its values and tastes in a more sophisticated and cosmopolitan direction) will combine to make important changes in the world view of consumers in the 1980s. The continuing urbanization of the population and the impact of modern communications have the effect of exposing the average citizen to a much wider range of information, and a much wider range of perspectives for interpreting that information, than has ever been true in the past. The citizen in the 1980s is therefore likely to be less insulated from national and worldwide trends in taste, style and innovation than has ever been true.

Life styles will increasingly be built out of a rapidly expanding multiplicity of choices—choices made possible by the interaction of affluence and cosmopolitanism. One of the most striking things about American society since World War II (or longer than that) has been the extent to which the lives of most Americans involve what they put together out of the choices available to them rather than to what they are constrained to do by their socioeconomic situation. Much of the conflict and turmoil in the society probably has as much to do with anxiety and uncertainty engendered by continuing massive increases in the range of choices available to people as with more frequently cited factors. Indeed the "oppression" that many of those who "protest" feel (aside from blacks and other minorities) is probably more the oppression of having many choices and not knowing how to choose among them than of being "forced" to do things one does not wish to do.

Out of the current ferment about life styles is very likely to come the institutionalization of a set of pluralistic standards which legitimate a far wider range of ways of living in American society than has previously been the case. From the various liberation movements (black, brown, red, women, gay men, gay women, youth) will probably come a more widespread ethic of pluralism in life styles. (And this will be more than toleration in that it will involve recognition of the legitimacy of different kinds of identities and life styles.)

The ability to pursue a life style more tailored to individual choice (and less constrained by standards as to what a respectable conforming person should be like) is tremendously enhanced by the increases in material affluence and cultural sophistication. Because of higher incomes one can afford to take up and put aside different styles of living without regretting the capital investment that each may take. The security about the future which goes with steady increases in prosperity allows for the deferral of more permanent life style choices to the future; without this kind of security individuals feel they must make the permanent commitments relatively early in life. To the extent that sanctions against what has been nonconforming behavior decline, individuals are paradoxically less likely to be fixed in nonconforming identities and styles once chosen, since the "road back" is not blocked by discrimination or the necessity to repent. And by the same token, the nonconforming life style can be pursued more fully and more vigorously because of less need for secretiveness if a respectable future is desired.

For the most part these shifts in opportunity for choice will not involve dramatic changes in life for the great bulk of Americans because their exercise of choice will tend to be in the direction of elaborating and perfecting the existing class-related life styles. However, given the resources available to them it is likely that their particular version of those life styles will become increasingly distinctive, increasingly tailored to the needs and identities which they bring to their life situation and which evolve out of its year to year development. It is likely that more and more individuals and families will find it possible to elaborate particular arenas in which they can indulge one or another special taste or interest in a major kind of way. As in the past the increasing level of affluence and sophistication will allow the great middle majority of the population to increase their psychological and financial investment in leisure time activities, and there will be a broadening range of the kinds of activities chosen by different families of equal resources for this kind of investment.

At the level above the middle majority, where the absolute dollar amounts of the increase are even greater, one can expect to find, as in the past, even more highly specialized interests and pursuits. The "class mass" will be in the vanguard of the development of new styles—styles which as time goes on will tend to filter down, be reinterpreted and assimilated to the ongoing middle majority styles.

More of the Same

In the post-World War II period the life styles of each of the major social classes have evolved in terms of a logic dictated by the values and needs of families in each class as these interact with the increasing resources and possibilities available. The dominant trends of each class can be expected to continue to be important as families from these respectability was not so apparent.) While respectability certainly continues to be a touchstone for the lower-white-collar way of life, it is increasingly taken for granted and decreasingly an issue of preoccupation for lower-middle-class men and women.

The growing economic affluence and the wider horizons that come from higher education and constant attention to the messages of the mass media have highlighted the striving after wider horizons as perhaps the central theme in the development of a modern lower-middle-class life style. Affluence allows the working-class family to turn in on itself since it no longer has to be so deeply enmeshed in a mutual aid network of community and peers. Affluence allows a lower-middle-class family to reach outward to experience and make use of a wider slice of the world outside the family. This is true both for lower-middle-class individuals who move toward expression of personal interests and for the lower-middle-class family as a whole, which is able to increasingly define as central to family interaction the experiences they have as individuals or together in the outside world. These wider horizons, however, are pursued from a very solid family-oriented base, and with the assumption that the experiences of the wider world will not change the members in any essential way or change their relationships to each other. Therefore the traditional base of family togetherness as a core goal of the lower-middle-class life style is not challenged. Thus lower-middle-class people come to have a wider range of experiences and possessions that have previously been considered characteristic of the upper-middle-class taste and way of life. Here too, however, the reinterpretation of new life style elements and the changes in the social class above them result in a continued distinctiveness about the life style.

In the upper-middle class the push out to the larger world is intensified. The central characteristics of the upper-middle-class orientation towards living have always been self-sufficiency and the pursuit of self-gratification. It is a more egocentric class in that the claims of respectability and of membership in diffusely obligating groups such as kindred are subordinated to personal goals and desires. Increasing resources and knowledgeability intensify the striving after exploration and fuller self-realization. This is particularly apparent among upper-middle-class youth where parental indulgence, current life situation and family resources combine to maximize the possibilities for fullest realization. At the level of older upper-middle-class persons the experimental approach to perfecting life styles is more subdued but is also often pursued with greater resources. Upper-middle-class people are in a position to afford, and are likely to have the knowledge to select, major new additions to their way of life—whether this be a vacation home and the frequent use of it to develop an alternative social world, or the development of a fairly systematic plan of vacation travel that, for example, allows one to see the U.S.A., then Europe, then Asia, with in-between excursions to the Caribbean and Latin America. Because of the extremely large absolute increase in income that will accrue to this group, one can expect a considerable strengthening in the 1980s of this propensity toward elaborate life style innovations. Thus while the median increase in family income projected for 1970 to 1985 is $6700, the median increase for the upper-middle class will more likely be on the order of $17,000 to $20,000. Such a large absolute increase obviously provides a very rich resource for upper-middle-class experimentation with new life styles without the necessity of sacrificing the material base that supports the more traditional life style.

In addition to the unfinished agenda of the social classes discussed above, one can expect life style changes in response to the changing circumstances that future developments will bring. In some cases (as in fertility) these changes represent a reversal of previous trends, in other cases simply an intensification of changes that have been taking place over a longer period of time.

Changes in Family Living

Adults will spend less time in the "full nest" stage of the family life cycle. This will come about through a later age at marriage and birth of the first child, an unchanging age at the birth of the last child and an unchanging or perhaps slightly declining age at which the child ceases to live at home.

As a lasting legacy of youth and Women's Liberation thinking we are likely to find that young people marry somewhat later than they have in the past. There is no evidence of a major revolution in the extent of premarital sexual relations—the Kinsey Institute study of college youth completed in the mid-1960s showed essentially no change over the first Kinsey study in the proportion of women who had had premarital relations. In both cases approximately half the women had had premarital sexual relations. However, there do seem to be important changes in the pattern of sexual relations for that portion of the female population that has premarital sexual relations at all. Sexual relationships are likely to be more frequent and more institutionalized, more open and more accepted within the peer group than was true in the 1930s. Since

there is reason to believe that the post-World War II trend toward earlier marriage in the middle class (the lower and working class had always married young) was in large part responsive to an effort on the part of young people to establish their maturity and adult status, the development of alternate modes of being "grown up" should mean less of a rush to marriage. The beginning of legitimation of premarital sexual relations in the context of youth peer group relations (rather than as furtive and hidden activities) should go a long way toward reducing pressure for marriage to establish legitimate adulthood. (For that matter the 18-year-old vote and the consequent courting by politicians may bring somewhat the same result.)

It seems likely that at the level of the class mass (as least the highly urban and more cosmopolitan portion of it) relationships that involve young couples living together will become fairly widespread. Under these circumstances marriage will come when the couple decide to settle down either to have children or to begin seriously to build incrementally a career and its related family base. For large numbers of other young men and women, less institutionalized patterns of heterosexual relationships may serve to allow a sense of adulthood without marriage. We have already seen the development in a few cities, particularly on classes use the resources that come to them to further accomplish their goals and aspirations.

For the working class the dominant theme has been the solidification of the nuclear family base. Traditionally the working class has been very much enmeshed in kinship, ethnic and peer group ties, and the nuclear family has tended to be relatively "porous" to influences from the outside. Already in the early 1960s the affluence of the post-World War II period had produced a modern working-class family in which husband and wife interacted in a closer and less rigid way, and in which they directed themselves together toward the goal of perfecting a secure, comfortable and pleasant home as the central focus of their lives. Their relationships, particularly the father's, with the children also reflected this sharp focus on the home as opposed to previous external ties. This development was central to the consumer goals of the modern working-class family which were strongly oriented toward investment in the home to perfect it as a secure, comfortable, cozy place. In many ways this modern working-class family seemed to be adopting the styles of the lower-middle class. But that class also was in the process of change.

The lower-middle class has traditionally centered its life style on a necessity to achieve and maintain respectability. (This has been a lesser point of elaboration for the working class. Even as the modern working class developed in ways that made it seem superficially similar to the lower-middle class in day-to-day life, the importance of the striving after the West Coast, of a wide range of singles institutions. One can expect this pattern to continue to spread across the country and to become more elaborate as the level of affluence of young adults permits this.

Social and heterosexual relationships of the kind sketched above (involving as a common, though not majority pattern, reasonably regular participation in sexual relationships) depend, of course, on a high possibility of preventing unwanted births. The continued development of more and more effective contraceptive devices (and in the 1980s a once-a-month technique such as the prostaglandins should be well established) means that the technical base for this pattern of social relationships will be available. Legalization of abortion on demand (which should be the case by the 1980s in the states with the great majority of the population) allows for the clearing up of "mistakes" which often currently precipitate marriages (apparently about one-quarter of all brides are pregnant at marriage). While there is ample evidence that the availability of contraception does not have much impact on women's willingness to give up their virginity, the willingness to establish a regular premarital sexual relationship is much more responsive to the possibility of effective and interpersonally simple contraception.

Of course the same contraceptive techniques and the availability of abortion which make possible lower rates of premarital fertility also allow couples to space births and to have exactly the number of children they want. Analysis of surveys already conducted suggests that if couples had only the children they chose to have—that is, if pregnancy was completely voluntary—the average completed fertility of married couples would be on the order of 2.6 children (whereas in fact average completed fertility has been running more on the order of 3.3 children).

We have almost no information as to why there seems to be a shift towards smaller family ideals during the past decade. There is no way of predicting with much assurance what fertility desires will be in the late 1970s and 80s. However, according to fertility survey data, even in a period of fairly high fertility a great deal of the expressed preference for medium and large families may well have been a rationalization of "accidents" and unplanned pregnancies. This makes it seem most reasonable to predict a continued trend toward lower fertility.

The results of these various changes in mating behavior are that women would be likely to complete their fertility in the late twenties as they do now, having (again on the average) started their families somewhat later than they do now. The children would be grown and old enough to leave home while the parents are on the average somewhat younger than they are now. For example, the median case might be one in which the mother marries at 22 or 23 and has 2 children. The last one is born when she is 27 or 28 and, the children leave home for college or a job and

"singles" living when the mother is not yet 50. Whereas the typical time period between the marriage and the last child leaving home is now between 25 and 30 years, given these patterns of marriage and fertility the more typical range in the 1980s might be 20 or 25 years. The life style elaborations both prior to marriage—the various "singles" styles—and those after the children leave home would loom larger than is presently the case.

Changing Role of Women

The new feminism seems to contain two strains of thought for women, one of which may very well have a pervasive effect and the other a more limited effect. The first involves a greater self-consciousness on the part of women about their subordinate status within the family and in the larger world, and a drive for more autonomy, self-respect and self-expression.

The second involves a challenge to the still established notion that a woman's place is (really) in the home. The implications of the new feminism are easy to misconstrue because of a peculiarity of the interests of the leaders versus the subjects of the movement. By definition women who seek leadership or elite positions within the Women's Liberation Movement are persons whose major identity goals are bound up with activities in the public world, and often also with career aspirations. Such interests, aspirations and the relevant skills are entailed in the elite roles. Therefore the leaders of the Women's Liberation Movement will probably consistently underplay the importance of equality goals and aspirations that do not relate in one way or another to the larger, more public, world. More specifically, the leaders will tend not to regard as legitimate the homemaker role as a major commitment on the part of women. The mass of the followers, however, will be much concerned with their ability to fulfill the homemaker role in a way that is personally gratifying, in a way that allows for the development of autonomy, self-respect, and a sense of valid identity within the narrower and more private worlds that they themselves construct. Even though they will often find the public level of discussion of feminine equality frustrating because it does not take these aspirations as fully legitimate, they probably will prove remarkably tenacious (as people do generally in such a situation) in pursuing their own interests by reinterpreting a great deal of the public ideology of the movement to support the actual roles that they play in their private worlds.

As quickly becomes apparent in any discussion between men and women on this subject, the liberation of women also involves a very significant change in attitudes on the part of men and in relationships between men and women. The kind of thinking that is apparent in the new feminism (except in its more radical version) clearly assumes the viability of marriage but points in the direction of greater equality between husbands and wives in their functioning. This amounts to a strengthening of trends apparent over the last several decades in the middle-class family towards more sharing of power and duties and a less sharply defined division of labor. It has in the past been a point of considerable ambivalence among middle-class women as to whether they are the servants of their families, the hidden bosses of their families, or persons of equal status whose duties happen to be those of keeping things running smoothly within the home. It is the latter definition which is likely to be strengthened by the new feminism.

As incomes rise, the need for the woman's management of the home, and the complexity of that activity of manager, purchasing agent and doer of tasks also rise. If more and more goods and services are brought into and used within the home the woman's work there becomes more valuable rather than less. Yet women have the problem that the values of the society do not define the wife's work as general manager of the home as productive and worthwhile in the same sense that paid-for labor is regarded as productive and worthwhile. Thus women can define themselves as oppressed and "underpaid" for their valuable work for other members of the family. Many women's first impulse is to get out of the home and to earn self-respect and respect from others by work in the labor market. Such work not only earns a clear-cut status, but the demands in jobs are more specific and less diffuse than are homemakers' tasks. Women sometimes find it easier to feel that they are doing a good job at those more specifically defined tasks than at home where a woman's work is never done—nor is it unambiguously judged. Yet with the rise in affluence and productivity in the commodity sector, the kinds of services that a woman might buy to take care of her home become increasingly expensive so that women will be loath to buy on the outside market much of the labor that will be necessary to maintain the home.

There may well be a class difference in response to the combination of affluence and a continuing emphasis on feminine equality. Very likely at the working- and lower-middle-class level, the two will combine to give women a greater sense of worth and to encourage them toward more autonomous functioning within the homemaker role. At the upper-middle-class level, however, there may be an increasing emphasis on career for purely self-expressive goals. (At all class levels there may be some increase in the proportion of women in the work force—because of the decline in fertility and the fewer years in which a woman has children in the home.) Upper-middle-class women have always included activities outside the home (either in voluntary activities or at jobs) as a central part of their role definition. They will certainly expect, as part of rising affluence, to be able to engage in these self-enhancing and self-validating activities more fully. This will put a strong premium on work organization and homemaking products which facilitate labor and timesaving. While on the one hand the home will be a more elaborate and complex place, on the other hand the woman will want to spend less time there. This will create a great demand for innovations which make homes easier to keep clean and neat, meals quicker to prepare and so forth.

Since families are smaller it is likely that there will be greater opportunities for the development of individual interests and activities on the part of all members of the family. The lesser burden of child care and rearing certainly enhances these possibilities for the mother, and for the father. The children too, because of greater resources available and a lessened tendency to treat the children as "a group," will be more likely to move in individualistic directions. (During the height of the large-family enthusiasm of the 1950s this potentiality was viewed negatively, as encouraging the "selfishness" of both parents and children.)

For the same reasons the family as a group becomes more "portable." The smaller family can more easily leave the home base for travel—both short-run travel as to a weekend cottage, and longer-run vacations. The heavy home-centeredness that was a concomitant of the large-family enthusiasm of the 1950s can be expected to decline as families feel themselves less space-bound.

Modern communications combined with the greater sophistication of the audience have the effect of bringing the world in on the average citizen in more and more forceful terms as the years go on. He reacts to what he sees in various ways—sometimes with fright and intimidation and other times with interest, approval and fascination. Both of these responses can be expected to be at least as characteristic of the 1980s citizen as of today's, assuming that all the world's problems are not solved between now and then. But the need to pull back, to disengage from exposure to the world's events (not just the large scale events seen on the evening news but also those observed and important in one's day-to-day life at work, on the street, in the local community and elsewhere) strengthens people's commitment to home as their castle, as well as encouraging them toward seeking to relax and vacation in other locales which are tranquil, isolated, private. The feeling that the world is too much with us leads to an interest in getting away from it all, getting "back to nature."

There Won't be Enough Time to Spend All the Money

People become busier the more affluent they are. Paradoxically, people whose affluence is increasing tend to make choices which result in their having less free or uncommitted time rather than more. There is considerable evidence to suggest that, with increasing affluence, workers do not choose greater leisure rather than more income; work hours tend either not to decrease at all or to decrease very slightly. None of the predictions made in the early 1950s concerning significantly shorter working hours seem to have held up. Indeed, in the few cases where unions have bargained for a short work week the slack seems to have been taken up for a fair number of the workers by more moonlighting. This makes good economic sense. After all, a man doesn't have to have anything extraordinarily interesting to do with his leisure time if his only choice is earning 50 cents an hour. On the other hand, at ten dollars an hour the leisure time needs to be pretty gratifying to cause him to forego his money.

With increasing affluence people are able to buy more and more goods and services, but then they run into the hard fact that the using of the products and services requires time. And the time available for consumption does not change. One cannot really buy time; all one can do is try to buy more efficient use of time. This fact has profound implications for life styles—many of these implications are discussed within the framework of economic theory by Steffan Linder in *The Harried Leisure Class* (Columbia University Press, 1970).

In general, when there are so many products to use and things to do and gratifications to be derived from both, people will tend to become impatient with routine, purely instrumental activities which seem to consume a great deal of time and effort relative to the gratification they produce. Similarly, people will tend to shift their commitments in the direction of activities that seem to provide more gratification per time unit and away from those which seem time-consuming in relation to the amount of gratification they provide.

The principal effect of this time/affluence dynamic is to make daily life more "commodity and service intensive." That is, people will tend to use more and more products and services in ways that maximize the satisfaction in a given period of time. Linder argues that with rising incomes pure leisure time (that is time in which you do nothing much) tends to decline because the degree of gratification that is available from goods and services, that were previously too expensive, is now greater than the gratification that is available from leisure and from one's own efforts to turn leisure into gratifying activity. Similarly, activities that are less productive of gratification tend to be given up or the time devoted to them sharply curtailed in favor of activities that are more productive and more expensive. The less time goods take per unit of satisfaction provided, the more in demand they will be. The cheapness of the product in terms of time becomes more and more important as the importance of their cheapness in terms of money declines. Individuals tend to give up relatively less

productive activities such as reading or taking long walks in familiar territory or leisurely engagement in lovemaking in favor of activities that require less time investment per unit of gratification. The same activities may be pursued in more exotic settings as a way of heightening satisfaction through the use of economic resources—thus the man who would hardly waste his time to view nature in the city park a few blocks away from his home may be ecstatic about the beauties of the Scottish countryside. People are notorious in not being tourists in their own cities because they are "too busy," but they will spend a great deal of money to visit a distant city and end up knowing more about its interesting sights than they do about the ones in their own home town.

These trends, coupled with the trends toward freeing women even more from their household duties, will tend to heighten awareness of the home as a "system" involving shelter, furnishings, production processes and their maintenance, a view in line with at least one economic theory of how households operate (Gary S. Becker, "A Theory of the Allocation of Time," *American Economic Review*, September, 1965). The home will become a more and more capital-intensive place as the cost of both externally supplied labor and household labor increases.

The Consumption of Services Will Grow and Broaden

A large segment of the multiplicity of choices that become available to people as their affluence rises has to do with the wide range of services which they can afford. People are able to buy expensive services which they previously had to forego (like regular medical care) or perform for themselves. As their own time becomes more and more valuable they are more willing to pay others to do things for them, if those others can perform the task more efficiently (often at the cost of possession of special equipment) or in a more satisfying way. This trend toward having others do work previously performed by household members is most dramatically evident in the rapid growth of franchise food operations. In the future one would expect an increase in the proportion of the family food budget used for meals away from home.

A second area in which a large expansion of services is likely has to do with the public sector. If the current national consensus toward disengagement from worldwide empire becomes a more or less permanent feature of the nation's stance towards the larger world, then one can expect an even greater rate of growth in public sector services than has been apparent over the last decade. The basis of support of demand for a broader and more fully developed range of public sector services is provided both by increasing affluence and by the broad exposure of most of the population to "informed opinion" through the mass media. Also, a higher proportion of the population attends college and is exposed there to welfare-oriented teaching which emphasizes public sector services of all kinds.

Future of the Underclass

So much for likely life style developments affecting the fortunate majority of Americans who are above the level of economic marginality. But what of the groups that have occupied so much of the public attention during the decade just finished—the poor and the oppressed minorities?

All of the income projections currently made predict no change in the distribution of income. Thus from 1947 (and very likely for much longer than that) through 1985 there is no present reason to imagine a major change in the distribution of income among families. In 1985, as at present and as in past decades, it is projected that slightly less than 20 percent of families will be living on incomes that are less than half of the median family income.

By 1985 the income that marks the top of the underclass will stand at $8,200 a year, an increase of $3,400—even larger than the absolute increase since 1947. However the constant dollar gap between the underclass income and that of the man in the mainstream also grows—from $2,800 in 1947 to $5,600 in 1971 to $8,400 in 1985.

There are obviously two ways to look at what happens to disadvantaged groups under these economic circumstances. If one focuses on the absolute changes, one can say that they are far better off than today. If one focuses on changes relative to the majority segments of the society, one can say that they are not at all or only slightly better off.

The people we would have called poor on the basis of an examination of their way of life in 1950 we would very likely call poor in 1970 because their way of life is much the same despite the fact that it includes slightly more in the way of material goods. Their affluence has increased somewhat but in absolute amounts the affluence of the bulk of the population has increased even more and they will find themselves further away from the going standard of American life now than they did in 1960. The issue of poverty then and the apparent progress toward eliminating it has concealed all along the issue of inequality and the fact of no progress toward eliminating it.

If membership is the key issue in the human's effort to find a meaningful life and if in affluent industrial societies membership can be achieved only through the command over the goods and services that are required for mainstream participation, then it follows that we will continue to have poor people and oppressed minorities so long as a significant proportion of Americans have incomes far removed from that of the average man. It follows that the underclass will be alive and well in 1985. And all of the

pathologies of the city which are generated by the oppression and deprivation which produce the underclass will also still be with us.

Just as there are reasons for predicting no change in the income distribution, there are good reasons for predicting only small changes in the relative incomes of white and black families by 1985. The 1960s saw a significant increase in black family incomes relative to whites—from around 53 percent of white income to around 63 percent of white income. However, there has been no improvement in that figure in the last couple of years—emphasizing again the crucial role of high unemployment rates in black economic oppression. Indeed, an economist, Harold W. Guthrie, has projected the comparative experience of white and non-white families from 1947 through 1968 into the future by calculating the number of years required for equality of family income between the two races under various employment conditions. His results suggest that at current unemployment rates equality of income between black and white families would take well over 100 years to achieve.

At the so-called full unemployment rate of 4 percent it would still require 30 years to achieve equality of income. Only with a sustained unemployment rate lower than 3½ percent would black and white incomes be equal by 1985. Given the kinds of swings in unemployment experienced in the 1960s we could perhaps expect black family incomes to increase to between 70 and 75 percent of white family income. At 75 percent of white family income, blacks would be enjoying the standard of living purchased by over $12,000 a year, significantly better than the median family income for whites today. Their incomes would have almost doubled. Yet relative to whites the absolute difference in income would be slightly larger than it is today.

As we have seen, without marked improvements in their economic situation the black underclass will continue to grow in numbers. Because the black migration from the rural South to the major metropolitan areas does not seem to be abating very fast, it is likely that the size of the urban ghettos will continue to grow, in some cities spilling over into the suburbs. In any case the ghettos will remain the locales of concentrated trouble and violence that they are today.

Because the underclass will still be there, and because of the much higher level of affluence, property crime rates will probably continue to increase, and crimes of violence will probably not decrease very much. There may or may not be recurrent periods of urban rioting—but then the riots are really less important to the day-to-day lives of people living in the ghetto than the more random and individual violence to which they are subjected. One can expect larger and larger areas of the city to deteriorate and become abandoned, and one can expect more no-man's-lands to develop in cities, areas where no one wants to go for any legitimate purpose, and which are abandoned to whatever use marginal persons may want to put them. Again, although the financial cost to individuals with whose commercial or residential investments in the areas of deterioration may be great, the net cost of the deterioration of the cities will continue to be fairly small relative to the general level of affluence, and relative to the opportunities that the expanding suburban and exurban rings provide.

Finally, while one can expect to see a very large growth in the "human service" industries—with perhaps a large part of that growth directed toward doing something about the problems of the underclass—it seems likely that these service-oriented programs will continue to prove to be failures. They will provide opportunities for middle-class professionals and hopefully for a few mobile persons from the underclass to earn a good and steady income but will not do much in fact to improve life for the "clients" of these services.

Only if there is a very major shift in the way Americans think about and cope with the problems of poverty, race, urban distress and the like is 1985 likely to appear much better to us in these respects than 1972.

Timing of Our Lives

Harley L. Browning

Only quite recently in his history has man been able to exercise any important and lasting influence on the control of his mortality. In Western Europe mortality declines have been documented for periods ranging up to several hundred years, but this accomplishment recently has been overshadowed by the spectacular drops in mortality in many developing countries. They are now accomplishing in a few decades what the European countries took many generations to achieve. In Mexico, to cite one remarkable example, male life expectancy at birth has nearly doubled within the span of a single generation (1930-1965). During this period, the life expectancy of Mexican men rose from 32 to 62 years.

Man's great leap forward in mortality control, which now permits so large a proportion of those born in advanced societies to pass through virtually all important stages in

the life cycle, must surely be counted among his most impressive accomplishments. Yet, there has been no systematic effort to follow out all the ramifications of this relatively new condition. If a Mexican boy born in 1965 can expect to live twice as long as his father born in 1930, can he not also expect to pass through a life cycle markedly different in quality and content from that of his father?

One would think that a man who had little chance of living beyond 35 would want to cram all the important stages of his life into a brief period. Conversely, one might expect that if given twice the time in which to live out his life cycle, an individual might plan and space out the major events in his life such as education, marriage, birth of his children and beginning of his work career and so on—to gain the optimal advantage of all this additional time. But, in reality, little intelligent use is being made of the extension of life expectancy in terms of the spacing of key events in the life cycle.

Here, for purposes of exploring the possibilities opened up by recent advances in mortality control, I want first to document the astonishing increase in life expectancy of recent times. From there we can examine some of the implications that can be drawn from it and consider the potential consequences of increased longevity in altering the timing of events in the life cycle. Finally, I shall comment on the feasibility of planning changes in the life cycle to better utilize the advantages of reduced mortality rates. Since my purpose is to set forth a perspective for the linking of life expectancy and life cycle, I have not attempted systematically to provide data for all of my generalizations. Therefore, my conclusions must be taken as exploratory and tentative.

In the investigation of the relationship of changes in life expectancy to changes in the life cycle, it is worthwhile to consider two groupings of countries—the developed countries, where life expectancy has been increasing over a considerable period of time, and the developing countries, with their recent and very rapid increases.

For the developing countries, an important question for which we have little evidence as yet is how much people are aware at all social levels of the dramatic change in life expectancy. Perhaps it is not generally "perceived" because the change has not had time to manifest itself in the lifetime of many persons. The fact that in Mexico there is now so great a generational difference in life expectancy that the son may expect to live almost twice as long as his father surely will have considerable impact upon the family and other institutions. But we can only know these changes for certain as the son passes through his life span,

well into the next century, a time when all of us will be dead.

Mexico is a striking case but by no means an isolated one. A number of other developing countries will achieve much the same record within a fifty-year period or less. Thus, for a substantial part of the world's population, the mortality experience of succeeding generations will differ markedly and to an extent unparalleled in any other historical period.

There are striking extremes between conditions in primitive and pre-industrial countries with unusually high death rates and the situation that many countries in Western Europe and Anglo-America either have already reached or are closely approaching. For instance, India between 1901 and 1911 represented the conditions of extremely high mortality under which mankind has lived during most of his time on this earth. A male child born in this period and locale had a life expectancy of slightly less than 23 years. Today such conditions are extremely rare. At the other extreme, a boy born in the United States in 1950, for example, could expect to live almost to age 74.

As is well-known, the greatest improvement in mortality control has come about through the reduction of deaths in infancy and early childhood. In India around 1901, nearly one-half of those born were lost by age five. By contrast, under the conditions prevailing in the United States in 1950, 98.5 per cent of male children were still living five years after birth.

For the purposes of relating life expectancy to life cycle, however, it is not the losses in the early years that are of the most importance. Death at any time, including the first few years of life, is of course a "waste," but the loss on "investment" at these ages for both parents and society is not nearly so great as for those persons who die at just about the time they are ready to assume adult responsibilities. This is when such significant events in the life cycle as higher education, work career, marriage and family take place. For this reason, the focus of this article is upon the fifty-year span from age 15 to 65. By age 15 the boy is in the process of becoming a man and is preparing himself either for college or entry into the labor force. Fifty years later, at age 65, the man is either retired or, if not, his productivity is beginning to decline noticeably in most cases.

But what are the consequences of these changes that have recently permitted a substantial part of the world's population for the first time to live what Jean Fourastie has called "a biologically complete life." What can be the meaning of death in a society where nearly everyone lives out his allotted threescore and ten years? Is death beyond the age of 65 or 70 really a "tragic" occurrence? The specter of early and unexpected death manifested itself symbolically in countless ways in societies with high mortality. Of France in the twelth century, Fourastie writes, "In traditional times, death was at the center of life, just as the cemetery was at the center of the village."

Not everyone believes that the great increase in life expectancy is entirely favorable in its consequences. Some argue that perhaps advanced societies now allow too high a proportion of those born into them to pass through to advanced ages. "Natural selection" no longer works effectively to eliminate the weak and the infirm. In other words, these people maintain that one consequence of improved mortality is that the biological "quality" of the population declines.

While we can grant that a number of individuals now survive to old age who are incapable of making any contribution to their society, the real question is how numerically important a group they are. My impression is that their numbers have generally been exaggerated by some eugenicists. The cost of maintaining these relatively few individuals is far outweighed by the many benefits deriving from high survivorship. In any event, the strong ethical supports for the preservation of life under virtually all conditions are not likely to be dramatically altered within the next generation or so.

Whatever the problems occasioned by the great rise in natural increase, no one would want to give up the very real gains that derive from the control of mortality man now possesses. One of the most interesting features is the biological continuity of the nuclear family (parents and children) during the period when childbearing and child-rearing take place. In most societies the crucial period, for men at least, is between ages 25 and 55. But only a little more than a third of the males born under very backward conditions survive from age 15 to age 55. By contrast, almost 94 percent in Europe and Anglo-America reach this age. The fact that until relatively recently it was highly probable that one or both parents would die before their children reached maturity had a profound effect upon family institutions. In "functional" terms, the survival of the society depended upon early marriages and early and frequent conceptions within those marriages. Andrew Collver has shown this very effectively in his comparative study of the family cycle in India and the United States:

In the United States, the married couple, assured of a

long span of life together, can take on long-term responsibilities for starting a new household, rearing children and setting aside some provisions for their old age. In India, by contrast, the existence of the nuclear family is too precarious for it to be entrusted entirely with these important functions. The joint household alone has a good prospect for continuity.

Not all societies with high mortality are also characterized by the importance of joint households. But all societies of the past in one way or another had to provide for children who were orphaned before they reached maturity. One largely uncelebrated consequence of greatly reduced mortality in Western countries, for example, has been the virtual disappearance of orphanages. In the United States, the number of complete orphans declined from 750,000 in 1920 to 66,000 in 1953. In this way a favorite theme of novelists a century or so ago has largely disappeared. Were Dickens writing today he would have to shift his attention from orphans to the children of divorced or separated parents. The psychological and economic consequences of whether homes are broken by divorce or separation rather than by the death of one or both parents obviously may be quite different.

I need not elaborate the obvious advantages of increased life expectancy both for the individual and his society in terms of advanced education and professional career. Under present conditions it is now possible for an individual realistically to plan his entire education and work life with little fear of dying before he can carry out his plans. In this respect, the developed countries have a considerable advantage over developing countries, for the former do not suffer many losses on their investments in the training and education of their youth. But under conditions that are still typical of a large number of countries, a third of those who have reached the age of 15 never reach age 45, the peak productive period of an educated person's life. In such countries, primary education for everyone may be desirable but a part of the investment will be lost for the substantial number who will die during their most productive period.

Another consequence, perhaps overlooked, of the improvement of life expectancy in advanced countries is the fact that while even the rich and powerful were likely to die at early ages in older societies, now everyone, including the poor, can expect to pass through most of the life span. Considerable attention in America is now concentrated on conditions of social inequality, and clearly very large differences exist for characteristics such as education, occupation, and income. But in a society where about eighty-five of every one hundred persons can expect to reach their 65th birthday, extreme differences in longevity among the social strata do not exist. This is not to say that mortality differentials do not exist; they do, but not nearly to the degree found for other major socioeconomic variables. For the poor, unfortunately, increased longevity may be at best a mixed blessing. Too frequently it can only mean a prolongation of ill health, joblessness, and dependency.

What is still not well-appreciated are the consequences of the prolongation of life for the spacing of key events in the life cycle. Obviously, wholesale transformation of the life cycle is impossible because most of the events of importance are to one degree or another associated with age. Retirement cannot precede first job. Nevertheless, the timing of such events or stages as education, beginning of work career, marriage and birth of first and last child is subject to changes that can have marked repercussions on both the individual and the society.

One of the difficulties of dealing with the life cycle is that it is rarely seen in its entirety. Specialists on child development concentrate only on the early years, while the period of adolescence has its own "youth culture" specialists, and so on.

But another important reason why changes in the life cycle itself have not received much attention is the lack of data. Ideally, life histories are required so that the timing of each event can be specified, but until quite recently the technical problems in gathering and especially in processing detailed life histories on a large scale were so great as to make the task unfeasible. Now, however, with the help of computers, many of these problems can be overcome.

Let's examine one particular instance—age at first marriage in the United States—in which one might expect increased life expectancy to have some effect either actual or potential on the life cycle. The data are reasonably good, at least for the last seventy years, and age at first marriage is an event subject to a fair amount of variation in its timing. More interestingly, age at first marriage can greatly affect the subsequent course of a person's life and is indicative of changes in social structure.

In the time period of concern to us, 1890-1960, the generational life expectancy in the United States at age 20 increased 13 years for males and 11 years for females. This is not so great an increase as is now occurring in developing countries but it is still an impressive gain. With an appreciable extension in his life expectancy, a person might reasonably be expected to alter the spacing of key events in his life cycle in order to take advantage of the greater "space" available. In particular, we might expect him to marry at a somewhat later age. But exactly the opposite has happened! Between 1890 and 1960 the median age at first marriage for males declined about four years, a very significant change. For females, the decline was only two years, but their age at first marriage in 1890 (22) already was quite low.

Isn't this strange? During the period of an important extension in life expectancy, a substantial decline in age at first marriage has occurred. Unquestionably, many factors go into an adequate explanation of this phenomenon. One of the reasons why age at first marriage was high around the turn of the century was the numbers of foreign-born, most of them from Europe where marriage at a later age was characteristic, even among the lower strata. Immigrants who arrived as single men had some difficulty finding wives and this delayed their first marriage. In addition, around the turn of the century, middle-class men were not expected to marry until they had completed their education, established themselves in their careers and accumulated sufficient assets to finance the marriage and a proper style of living.

The greatest drop in age at first marriage occurred between 1940 and 1960, especially for females. During this period a great many changes took place in society that worked to facilitate early marriages. "Going steady" throughout a good part of adolescence became accepted practice. Parents adopted more permissive attitudes toward early marriage and often helped young couples to get started. The reduced threat of military conscription after 1946 for married men with children was also a big factor along with a period of general prosperity and easy credit that enabled newlyweds to have a house, furnishings and car, all with a minimal down payment. And not only is marriage easier to get into, it is now easier to get out of; divorce no longer carries the stigma once attached to it.

Of course, many early marriages are not wholly voluntary and in a substantial number of cases the couple either would never have married or they would have married at a later age. David Goldberg has estimated, on the basis of a Detroit survey, that as high as 25 percent of white, first births are conceived outside of marriage, with a fifth of these being illegitimate. As he puts it:

We have been accustomed to thinking of the sequence marriage, conception and birth. It is apparent that for a very substantial part of the population the current sequence is conception followed by birth, with marriage intervening, following birth or not occurring at all. This may represent a fundamental change in marriage and fertility patterns, but historical patterns are lacking. An increase in illegitimate conceptions may be largely responsible for the decline in marriage age in the postwar period.

Unfortunately, there is no way to determine if the proportion of illegitimate conceptions has risen substantially since 1890.

The causes of early first marriage are not so important for the purposes of this article as their consequences for subsequent events of the life cycle. For one thing, age at first marriage is closely related to the stability of the marriage. The high dissolution of teenage marriages by divorce or other means is notorious. One may or may not consider this as "wastage" but there is no question about the costs of these unsuccessful unions to the couples involved, to their children and often to society in the form of greater welfare expenditures.

Not only has age at first marriage trended downward, especially since World War II, but family formation patterns have also changed. For the woman, the interval between first marriage and birth of her first child has diminished somewhat and the intervals between subsequent births also have been reduced. As a result, most women complete their childbearing period by the time they reach age 30.

Marriage, Work and Babies

The effects of these changes on the family cycle are as yet not very well understood. But the lowering of age at first marriage among men encompasses within the brief span of the early twenties many of the most important events of the life cycle—advanced education, marriage, first stages of work career and family formation. This is particularly true for the college-educated. Since at least four of every ten college-age males will have some college training, this is an important segment of the population. Each important stage of the life cycle requires commitment and involvement of the individual. If he crowds them together, he reduces both the time he can devote to each of them and his chances for success in any or all of them.

From our discussion of increased life expectancy and the timing of one particular aspect of the life cycle, age at first marriage, we might conclude that there is little relationship between the two. Man has been able to push back the threat of death both in developing and developed societies but he has not seen fit to make much use of this increased longevity. Must this be? Would not the "quality" of the populations in both developing and developed countries be improved by a wider spacing of key events in the life cycle? I believe a good argument can be made that it would.

First, take the situation in the developing countries. What would be the consequences of raising the age at marriage several years and of widening the interval between births? The demographic consequences would be very important, for, independent of any reduction of completed family size, these changes would substantially reduce fertility rates. Raising age at marriage would delay births as a short-run effect and in the long run it would lengthen the span of a generation. At a time when there is much concern to slow down the rate of population growth in most developing countries, this would be particularly effective when coupled with a concomitant reduction in completed family size.

A second effect of the raising of age at marriage and widening the spacing of births would be to allow these societies to better gear themselves to the requirements of a modernized and highly-trained population. A later age at marriage for women could permit more of them to enter the labor force. This in itself would probably result in lowered fertility. In most developing societies, the role and position of the woman *outside* of the home must be encouraged and strengthened.

Accommodating the Sex Drive

The case of the developed countries, particularly the United States, is somewhat different. I see very few advantages either for the individual, the couple or the society in the recent practice of squeezing the terminal stages of education, early work career and marriage and family formation into the period of the early twenties. There simply isn't time enough to do justice to all of these events. The negative effects are often felt most by the women. If a woman is married by age 20, completes her childbearing before 30 and sees her children leave home before she reaches 50, she is left with a long thirty years to fill in some manner. We know that many women have difficulty finding meaningful activities to occupy themselves. True, the shortening of generations will permit people the opportunity of watching their great-grandchildren grow up, but does this compensate for the earlier disadvantages of this arrangement? From the standpoint of the society, there are few if any advantages.

If an argument can be made that little intelligent use is being made of the extension of life expectancy in terms of timing key events in the life cycle, what can be done about it? In any direct way, probably very little. "Licensing" people to do certain things at certain ages is, to my mind, appropriate only in totalitarian societies. So far as I am aware, contemporary totalitarian societies have made relatively little effort to actively regulate the timing of events in the life cycle. The Chinese, for example, have only "suggested" that males defer marriage until age 30. But if the state is not to force people to do things at specified ages, at least it might educate them as to the advantages of proper spacing and also make them aware of the handicaps generated by early marriage and, particularly, early family formation. Both in developing and developed countries there probably is very little direct awareness of how spacing will affect one's life chances and how something might be done about it.

Obviously, if marriage is delayed, then something must be done to accommodate the sex drive. Fifty years ago the resolution of this problem was for men to frequent prostitutes while women had fainting spells, but neither alternative is likely to gain favor with today's generation. Perhaps Margaret Mead has once again come to our rescue with her proposal that two kinds of marriages be sanctioned, those with and those without children. Under her "individual" marriage young people could enter into and leave unions relatively freely as long as they did not have children. This, of course, would require effective contraception. Such a union would provide sexual satisfaction, companionship, and assuming the women is employed, two contributors to household expenses. This arrangement would not markedly interfere with the careers of either sex. Marriages with the purpose of having children would be made more difficult to enter into, but presumably many couples would pass from the individual into the family marriage. This suggestion, of course, will affront the conventional morality, but so do most features of social change.

Future Family
Margaret Mead

There was an article by an eminent psychologist in the *New York Times* recently, saying there wasn't any generation gap, because lots of parents got on with lots of children.

But the generation gap has not got anything to do with parents and children. The generation gap is between all the people born and brought up after World War II and the people who were born before it. It's not at all about children and getting on with parents.

If you happen to be a parent who was born and brought up before World War II, and you happen to have children at the moment, you're on one side of the generation gap and they're on the other. But this is an accident. In about 15 years there'll be parents and children on this side of the generation gap. And all the people on the other side will be at least grandparents.

What we're talking about as the generation gap only happened once. It isn't about parents not getting along with children, or children rebelling or changing styles of morality. It's simply that at the time of World War II the whole world became one, so that there is a complete difference between all young people and all older people.

In New Guinea, you have children who are studying medicine whose parents were cannibals. That's quite a gap. But whether it's more or less of a gap than the gap between a sophisticated cabinet member and his son, that's a question. Or between a professor of physics and his youngest student in college.

We've mixed this gap with conflict between parents and children and professors and college students at present because the oldest members of the new generation—the inhabitants of this new post-World War II world—are just 25 now. Five years ago, the oldest members were only 20, and they were all in college, and none of them were members of the establishment. So that it looked as if this was a battle between students and parents, and students and teachers, and everybody in college. But it wasn't.

Now the oldest are 25, and a lot of them are getting to be members of the faculty. They can't be treated as traitors any more.

At the moment, two things are happening that we have to take into account. One is the fact that we're having a revolt, a new kind of revolt, which is only partly connected with the generation gap. It's particularly characteristic of the Western industrialized society. In the past, most revolutions and revolts and rebellions have been by people who were being done evil to by other people. They were being enslaved, exploited, sent down in mines, treated terribly. It was perfectly clear they were rebelling against bad treatment.

Now, we're having a revolt of all the people that are being done good to. For the first time in history, children—all children, after all, are being done good to by their parents—pupils, students, mental patients, welfare mothers, and even people who are being rehabilitated in Federal prisons, are suggesting they take a share in what's going on.

This is the first time we have had this kind of rebellion, and students are included in it. In the past, the professors knew best, the doctors knew best, the social workers knew best, psychiatrists knew best. There were great numbers of professional people who knew best and did good. Then the beneficiaries were supposed to be appreciative. And they've now become extremely unappreciative. And they're all insisting on getting into the act.

Welfare mothers, after all the taxes we pay, are suggesting that they'd like to have shoes for their children in September, because school begins then and not in November. And some of them are saying that all the children in the family should have shoes; that's better than having to take turns wearing them.

Students get into this particular category too, because they've been done good to for a long time—for several hundred years. There was a period when the students found the professors; they presumably were doing good for the professors, at that point. But the professors soon got control. They've been doing good to the students all over the place; suffering, working for very poor salaries, dedicated and worn out. And now the students are saying "We'd like to take a hand in what's going on." Now, from that point of view, the students and the welfare mothers and the mental patients are all in the same position. This isn't entirely about the generation gap and it isn't only about students.

Whenever there is a period of upheaval in the world, somebody's going to do something to the family. If the family's being very rigorous and puritanical, you loosen it up. And if it's being very loose, you tighten it up. But you have to change it to really feel you're accomplishing something. If we go back into history we find over and over again, in moments of revolutionary change, that people start talking about the family, and what they're doing to it, and what's wrong with it. They even predict it's going to disappear altogether. It is in fact the only institution we have that doesn't have a hope of disappearing.

No matter how many communes anybody invents, the family always creeps back. You can get rid of it if you live in an enclave and keep everybody else out, and bring the children up to be unfit to live anywhere else. They can go on ignoring the family for several generations. But such communities are not part of the main world.

As one of my sophomore students wrote the other day, when I had asked them to say where they were going to be 15 years from now: "Fifteen years from now it may not be necessary to get married; but nevertheless I expect to live with the father of my children."

And that is, strictly speaking, where we are. Girls are going to live with the fathers of their children—if they can catch them. And on the whole, they're just as interested in catching them as they've been throughout history. But there will be a great deal of discussion, and a great deal of gloom, and a great deal of talk about the family falling to pieces. In fact, we've got more families per capita than we've ever had. We're more married than we've ever been, and we're more married than most peoples. We've a terribly overmarried society, because we can't think of any other way for anybody to live, except in matrimony, as couples.

It's very, very difficult to lead a life unless you're married. So everybody gets married—and unmarried—and married, but they're all married to somebody most of the time. And so that we have, in a sense, overdepended on marriage in this country. We've vastly overdone it.

At the graveside—you know, when a woman has just lost a husband that she's been happy with 20 years, the first thing people say is, "I do hope she marries again." They don't give her two minutes to grieve before they start marrying her off again. We also have had a form of marriage that is probably one of the most precarious and fragile forms of marriage that people have ever tried. That form—the Nuclear Family—was not named after the Bomb. It was just named after the physical analogy, but calling it the Nuclear Family is very good, because it is just about as dangerous as the bomb.

The Nuclear Family is a family consisting of one adult man and one adult woman, married to each other, and minor children. The presence of any other person in the household is an insult. The only people that can come in are cleaning women and sitters. In-laws become sitters—which means that when they come in, you go out, and you never have to see them. Furthermore, today, mothers are very uncomfortable with adolescent daughters in the house. So they push them out as rapidly as possible. If they're rich, they send them to Barnard, and if they're poor, they get them married, and they work at it, very hard, because there isn't room in the kind of kitchens we've had since 1945 for two women.

We have put on the Nuclear Family an appalling burden, because young couples were expected to move as far from both sets of relatives as they could, and they had to move, a great deal of the time.

Millions and millions of Americans move every year, moving miles from relatives or anybody that they know. We know now that the chances of a post-partum depression for a woman are directly proportional to the distance she is from any female relative or friend. When we put her in a new suburb all by herself, her chances of getting a post-partum depression go way up. There are millions of young families living in such suburbs, knowing nobody, with no friends, no support of any kind.

Furthermore, each spouse is supposed to be all things to the other. They're supposed to be good in bed, and good out of it. Women are supposed to be good cooks, good mothers, good wives, good skiers, good conversationalists, good accountants. Neither person is supposed to find any sustenance from anybody else.

Young people from Europe who wanted to come to the United States had to bring their spouses with them, and leave their parents behind or they'd never have gotten here. In India or Africa, when you have a great mass of very traditional relatives, the thing to do is to take your girl and leave, and go a long way off if you want to live the way you want to live.

So it's a good style of family for change, but it's a hazardous kind of family, nonetheless. And if it is hazardous enough in the city, it's a hundred percent more hazardous in the suburbs. There's a special kind of isolation that occurs in the suburbs. So the attack on the Nuclear Family is, I think, thoroughly justified.

There is a need to have more people around: more people to hold the baby, more people to pitch in in emergencies, more people to help when the child is sick, when the mother is sick, more children for other children to play with so you don't have to spend a thousand dollars sending them to nursery school, more kinds of adults around for the children to pick models from in case father or mother can't do the things they want to do. The communes aim to supply these. Real communes, of course, are more extreme—this country was founded by many forms of communes, and it's been so with them ever since—but the bulk of people don't live in communes. One of the things the communes are emphasizing is a lot of people sharing child-care, sharing bringing up the children again, so the children have more security, and don't have to think every day, "What if something happens to Mommy; what if something happens to Daddy? Will there be anyone

at all?" I think we're going to have a trend toward different kinds of living.

It will take quite a little while, because it means building new houses, on the whole—new kinds of apartments, closer together, places where you don't have to drive 15 miles to use somebody else's washing machine when yours breaks, and where people can get together more closely. We won't have this right away—but we're going to have it.

It means places where all the people can live somewhere near young people, and places where young married couples with children will be cherished and cared for and flanked on all sides by people who don't have children at the moment. Maybe they've had them before; maybe they haven't had them yet, maybe they don't want any. But it'll be a place where they, also, can find children, and won't be banished from children as they are at present. If today you don't have children of your own, you hardly ever see any. We banish our old people far away from any children at all, and the only thing we ask them to do is to live on in misery and smile, so their children won't feel guilty.

With the population explosion, the pressure on women to marry is going to be reduced, and the pressure to be mothers is going to be enormously reduced. For the first time in history we're not going to tell a woman that "Your principal glory is to be a wife and a mother."

By dint of telling women that their major job was to be wives and mothers, we told most men their major job was to be breadwinners and very much limited the number of men who could do the things they wanted to do most. We always talk about career women, and the wonderful careers they would have had, if they hadn't had those five children. But nobody looks at fathers and thinks what a life he'd have had if he hadn't had those five children.

He might have been able to paint instead of being a stock broker. Or a musician, instead of running a jewelry store he inherited. When you shut women up in a home and require wifehood and motherhood, you shut men up and require husbandhood and fatherhood at the same time. As we reduce the requirements for motherhood, we reduce the requirements for fatherhood. And we'll release a lot of people to be individuals and to make contributions as individuals, rather than as parents.

This isn't going to happen immediately, but we get a lot of funny forerunners. The members of the Women's Liberation Movement, in its extreme form, walk around saying how well they get on without men. We're quite prepared to have a lot of women get on without men now. It won't do a bit of harm. There're too many women, and if some of them would get on without men it would relieve the pressure.

Twenty years from now, we'll have many fewer families, but children will still be brought up in families because we don't know how to bring them up any other way. The family will be just as safe as it ever was, but everybody won't have to live in it all the time. We'll recognize that the family is the perfect place for children. It is just ideal for children, and doubtfully ideal for anybody else for the whole of their lives—except in very exceptional cases. Of course we'll also recognize that when we used to have the idea of lifelong marriage, the expectation of life was 37. When one spouse died and the other was left with a batch of little children they had to marry somebody else.

Today, the expectation of life is over 30 years after the last child leaves home. In terms of rapid change, it means the rate of change for both husbands and wives is very different than in the past. We may move to an ideal of marriage, which is an ideal of people staying married until the children are grown. At present, they have an ideal of staying together forever, but in fact they get divorced very often. If instead they have as an ideal staying together until the children are grown and not having children until they were ready to do that, not picking out somebody you'd like to spend the weekend with, parenthood will probably become much more solemn, and much more of a commitment. If it doesn't, of course, we're going to have some government putting contraceptives in the drinking water.

Some people are somewhat worried by the present notion of the young that they are not going to get married, but they're going to live "in sin." It's a very funny kind of sin—because you do it with the approval of the dean of women, your minister, and both sets of parents. We used to call it common law marriage—when people are generally known to tradesmen as living together. You could sue people to get part of their property when they died, and all that sort of thing. Well, what young people in general today call an "arrangement" is an absolutely public union.

When I proposed that there be a simple marriage ceremony, which would go with the stated intention of having no children,—they said "No." They're going to experiment with "arrangements"—public, virtuous, publicly proclaimed—and then, later, they're going to get married.

We've been cheating women when, in the last ten years, we wanted women to work. We were very short of cheap labor so we told them they needed to be fulfilled. The last source of educated cheap labor was women. So finally everybody discovered that it is very unfulfilling to stay at home, and a woman, of course, when she has her children, maybe she would stay at home for a few years and then she'd leave to be fulfilled. And the foundations gave money, centers were established to lure her out and get her re-educated.

But of course they weren't going to pay her like men, because after all she was more interested in her home, she wouldn't want to leave her children, and you know art lessons sometimes take up more time than little babies—and so she'd want a job from which she could get home early like being a clerk in a team-teaching outfit, instead of a teacher. Something like that—so she could go home when her children did. And of course she wouldn't want to be very ambitious, because all the strain would be bad; she'd want to keep something for home.

In the last ten years, women have been pretty well beguiled and bedazzled into becoming self-fulfilling, educated cheap labor. And I think it's not surprising if some of them are saying that they think they are exploited, and they don't want to be exploited any more.

At the end of World War II, when they wanted all the women that held jobs to go home so the men could get them back, women who'd done well in Washington were told they were overmature, overexperienced:—"Please go home."

I think we'll be bringing girls up with more sense of themselves as people, and that they're going to be people all the way through. If they choose parenthood, they'll choose it much more as they've chosen vocations, and much less as if it were just something the neighbors are doing.

The authors represented in Part Five, devoted to descriptions of alternate life styles toward which the families of the 1970s may be heading, are not the only social scientists who have illuminated this subject. Many harbingers of future change have been identified by others studying the past or the present. For it is the task of the social scientist to generalize knowledge of what is, into predictions of what else will or could be. Let us examine some of these predictions, in the order in which we discussed the families of the 1970s.

First, how can we expect the socialization process to change in the future? This volume indicates several trends. For one thing, as parents become more educated, they will utilize more developmental, rather than restrictive, approaches in child rearing. More confident and competent as human beings than were the more limited parents of prior generations, they are apt to provide better socializing milieu for their children. Less anxiety-ridden, less paranoid about the world, they will be able to provide their offspring with freedom to experiment within the limits of the child's, rather than only the parent's, needs. In a word, they will be better able to socialize their children into creativity and potential development than were the parents who concentrated their efforts on restricting experimentation because of their own fears and restrictions. Most readers of this book will be in the forefront of this movement of expanded parenthood.

A second change in the socialization of future Americans is an expected expansion in the flexibility of social roles for which the young can be prepared, with the help of the various liberation movements. Young women of today, becoming more and more aware of self- and other-limiting cultural patterns tied to traditional sex roles, will be more willing and able to encourage their daughters to try a variety of actions and social roles which never occurred to prior generations as "decent" or

Epilogue

realistic alternatives. In particular, we can expect encouragement by mothers of greater achievement orientation and occupational experimentation by girls, both in initial "playing at the role" in the home and in actual preparation to be doctors, ditch diggers, lawyers, scientists and tool-and-die makers. The socialization of boys can be expected to change less in the near future, until there develops a movement examining the limitations of current systems on men.

It is also probable that other identities, now neglected or negatively transmitted to the young, will become sources of more positive socialization in the future. The "black is beautiful" movement and its ethnic and religious counterparts are likely to succeed, as the more confident new generations, knowing they could melt past identities in the acculturation pot if they wished, decide to add individualistic aspects to their multidimensional selves. The less paranoic environment that they will simultaneously create will facilitate the blooming of a variety of new identities which can coexist with traditional identities without insisting that they are "better than" the identities of others. There must be ways of enjoying being white, male, Protestant and/or Anglo-Saxon without depriving blacks, women, and members of other religious and ethnic groups of the pleasure of their identities.

We can also expect the future to expand the number of socialization agents helping parents in their responsibilities at all stages of the child's development cycle, as the society increasingly realizes the dysfunctional aspects of isolated households. A variety of experimental methods will undoubtedly be attempted by a variety of people, with different degrees of satisfaction.

I agree with Harley Browning that we need to make much more flexible "the timing of our lives," and I predict that this will occur. Young people are now postponing marriage and childbearing; they are reentering the educational and labor fields at a variety of times, organizing their study-work-marriage-procreation sequence in more flexible ways. This trend is observable in both sexes, and in the relations of each with the other. Increased availability of symmetrical sexual outlets prior to marriage is making it less necessary to marry in order to guarantee partners for intercourse, thereby facilitating the expansion of attention to other social roles. Men are increasingly accepting the involvement of their wife or sexual partner in social roles away from the home, although some strains are evident in the process. In the future—not immediately, but over the long run—we can expect greater flexibility in the in-home and the out-of-home engagement by both sexes. Some couples will take

turns supporting one or the other in ventures in and out of home, school and work. Men will build their lives on two or three careers, rather than deciding early on one and being locked into it. Professional physicians often do this, moving, for example, from private practice to administration, then to a different type of practice (i.e., clinic or cooperative association with colleagues). We can expect such a movement to expand to other occupations. This means the cooperation of family members, as one person moves out of the labor market and, while being retrained, is economically supported by the other. Child bearing and child rearing will become only one of the careers a woman can have in her life, preceded and followed by other careers. The extended family or the society at large may financially support both mother and father during the early years of their children's lives, so that both mother and father can devote full time to their parental roles, as Margaret Mead and others predict.

With the growing flexibility of marriage, we can expect more alternatives, not as deviations but as acceptable styles. Undoubtedly, some people will want to maintain "traditional" families, with a strict sexual segregation of roles. Both matrifocal and patrifocal units, in which the husband or wife plays a minimal role, or is absent by choice, rather than by desertion, will continue, side by side with households containing more than one male or female—paired or in more complex combinations. More frequent and open homosexual unions may be an outgrowth of the "gay liberation" movement and the new styles of homosexuality described by Laud Humphreys. Most Americans, however, are likely to oppose the redefinition of homosexuality as a normal and acceptable sexual union in the near future. Few of the new parents of the next few decades will be able to deviate from their own backgrounds with sufficient ease to allow their children the opportunity to experiment with homosexual behavior and identities; so it is not likely to be the home which will socialize the young in that direction. The future can, however, contain more interracial and intergroup marriages and child adoptions of other combinations.

Whether divorce continues to be prevalent depends on many factors, a basic one being whether it is defined as a deviation or as an expected part of life. Definition of divorce as a failure in marriage can predictably lead to stronger attempts to prevent it. Alternative definitions could sanction serial marriages, as people's self- and other-definitions change. One mate might be selected for romantic love, another later for sharing parental roles, a third for mid-life and a final one for old age. The fact is that greater flexibility in life style is liable to result in experimentation not only with the structure and content of marriage, but with its acceptable duration. Marriages based on the economic or psychological dependence of women upon men in an asymmetrical relation are apt to be discontinued, when their need decreases with the greater financial and personality independence of the "second sex." Although some have predicted that this will decrease the desire for marriage, this seems unlikely simply because there are many reasons, beyond economic or psychological dependency, why people live together. If marriages are to be continued and sustained, they will have to provide both partners with satisfactions that no competing relations or roles can offer in a society of open choice. Such satisfactions may arise from a redefinition of human needs to include the need for a continued relation with another human being, of opposite sex and same peer status. It is possible that this redefinition will include the acceptance of additional sexual, companionate, recreational, partners besides the spouse, either throughout the marriage or at different stages of its life cycle. If not, then the redefinition of human needs and the socialization of children must convince people that they really do not need sexual variety or other types of close relations outside the marital unit.

In any case, the cry that people should no longer tolerate, but try to change, social relations based on exploitation is loud and clear. It comes not only from women, but from children, the poor, welfare clients, grandparents, husbands, workers, students, the aged, business executives and other members of American society who are rebelling against what they now label as past oppression. They want to define their situations for themselves, and they demand a voice in what others are doing for them. They want to be partners in the activity rather than passive recipients.

It is hard to predict what will happen with the aging and dying of our society, in spite of the many attempts to do so. We know that there are increasing numbers of people labeled "old" in America and that, with each new generation, these people become better educated and better able to draw back into their hands some of the status and power they have lost. It is possible, as several social scientists believe, that they will form a new political force which the rest of society will have to recognize. As recreation becomes a more acceptable style of life, with the decline of the Protestant work ethic, the elderly, who have more time to develop old and new leisure activities can again become sages for the less-trained adult and youth generations. We can expect the flexibility of life styles to extend to them, as some of them become consultants in work or in play; some may withdraw to same-age communities, not wanting to be bothered with assisting the younger generations, while others become foster grandparents. People may begin new careers not only at age 40 or 45, but at 50 and 60. There are, and can be, more and more occupations which have no age limit.

As the family becomes more stabilized in egalitarian and nonexploitative relations, or as people either reject or tire of experimentation and concern with this unit, they will turn their attention outwardly in a purposeful attempt to reform other social institutions in order to facilitate full human life. As mentioned in the Prologue, families, in cooperation with each other and through the activities of individual members, can be expected to reformulate the value system away from the economic institution toward greater emphasis on humanitarian and interpersonal relations.

For Further Reading

PROLOGUE

Two anthropological texts which generalize about the family from information on many societies are Paul J. Bohannan's *Social Anthropology* (Holt, Rinehart & Winston, 1963) and Melville Herskowitz' classic *Cultural Anthropology* (Alfred A. Knopf, 1955).

Theories of cultural change which contributed to my comments include Phillipe Ariès' *Centuries of Childhood* (Random House, Vintage Books, 1965), Eric Fromm's *Escape from Freedom* (Holt, Rinehart & Winston, 1941), William Ogburn's *Social Change* (Viking Press, 1922), David Riesman's *The Lonely Crowd* (Yale University Press, 1950), and Max Weber's *The Protestant Ethic* and *The Spirit of Capitalism* (Charles Scribner's Sons, 1958).

Background on changes in the life cycles of men and women is contained in Evelyn Duvall's *Family Development* (J. B. Lippincott, 1957).

The framework for role theory as applied here came from Florian Znaniecki's *Social Relations and Social Roles* (Chandler Publishing Co., 1965). I have applied it before in a book on the roles of wife, housewife, mother, friend, neighbor, and community member of nearly 1,000 women with a variety of life styles in the Chicago area in *Occupation Housewife* (Oxford University Press, 1971).

Any issue of *transaction,* or *Society* as it is now called, will show how subjects discussed in the present book are published together with essays on other topics in the social sciences, plus book reviews, comments on current research, and the like.

Psychology Today is also an interesting magazine, with a greater emphasis on the individual than *transaction/Society.*

The *Journal of Marriage and the Family* contains articles sociologists write for each other, as do *The American Journal of Sociology* and *The American Sociological Review.* Language in the *Review* tends to be more technical than that in the other periodicals mentioned.

PART ONE. PRE-INDUSTRIAL FAMILIES

Margaret Mead's *An Anthropologist at Work: Writings of Ruth Benedict* (Houghton Mifflin, 1959) provides insights into the training, experiences, and feelings of a well-known anthropologist. All of Mead's and Benedict's books are pertinent reading, especially Mead's *Coming of Age in Samoa* (William Morrow, 1928) and *Growing Up in New Guinea* (William Morrow, 1962) and Benedict's *Patterns of Culture* (Houghton Mifflin, 1934) and *The Chrysanthemum and the Sword: Patterns of Japanese Culture* (Houghton Mifflin, 1946).

Descriptions of life in other pre-industrial or essentially rural and agricultural societies include Arthur Phillips' *Survey of African Marriage and Family Life* (Oxford University Press, 1953), George Peter Murdock's *Social Structure* (Macmillan, 1949), and Harry M. Caudill's *Night Comes to the Cumberlands* (Little, Brown, 1963).

Kapluna Daughter (Briggs)

Book of the Eskimos by Peter Freuchen (Bramhall House, Crown, 1961) contains excellent insights into Eskimo ideas and attitudes about human relationships.

The Nunamiut Eskimos by Nicholas Gubser (Yale University Press, 1965).

Married Life in an African Tribe by I. Schapera (Sheridan House, 1941).

Land of the Good Shadows by Heliuz Washburne and Anauta (John Day, 1940) is an account of Eskimo life by an Eskimo woman.

Life in Appalachia (Coles)

Stinking Creek by John Fetterman (E. P. Dutton, 1967) describes one hollow, sensitively and honestly.

Yesterday's People by Jack A. Weller (University of Kentucky Press, 1965) contains a minister's social and cultural observations, along with some thoughtful and properly ambiguous conclusions.

"I Divorce Thee" (Rosen)

The Muslim Matrimonial Court in Singapore by Judith Djamour (The Athlone Press, University of London, 1966), although concerned with the other end of the Islamic world, is the only book by an anthropologist dealing with the actual workings of a contemporary Moslem divorce court.

World Revolution and Family Patterns by William Goode (Free Press, 1963).

The Family in Various Cultures by Stuart A. Queen and Robert W. Habenstein (J. B. Lippincott, 3rd edition, 1967).

PART TWO. FAMILIES IN TRANSITION

Among the many studies of immigrants in American cities, the classics are generally considered to be Herbert Gans' *Urban Villagers* (Free Press, 1962), W. I. Thomas and Florian Znaniecki's *The Polish Peasant in Europe and America* (Dover Publications, 1958) and Louis Wirth's *The Ghetto* (University of Chicago Press, 1928).

The influence of urbanization, industrialization, and increasing societal complexity upon the family and its members has also been described in Robert F. Winch and Rae Lesser Blumberg's "Societal Complexity and Family Organization," in Winch and Louis Wolf Goodman's edited collection, *Selected Studies in Marriage and the Family* (Holt, Rinehart & Winston, 1968); and in William Goode's *World Revolution and Family Patterns* (Free Press, 1963).

Even the Saints Cry (Lewis)

Five Families by Oscar Lewis (Basic Books, 1961).

Psychological Miscarriage (Morris)

The Battered Child edited by Ray E. Hefler and Henry Kempe (University of Chicago Press, 1968).

"Transition to Parenthood" by Daniel F. Hobbs, Jr. (*Journal of Marriage and the Family* 30: August 1968, 413–417).

Violence Against Children by David G. Gil (Harvard University Press, 1970).

Wednesday's Children by Leontine Young (McGraw-Hill, 1964).

Seminole Girl (Garbarino)

The Indian, America's Unfinished Business edited by William Brophy and Sophie D. Aberle (University of Oklahoma Press, 1966), part of the University's American Indian Series, treats the Indian and his problems from a statistical but sympathetic point of view.

Big Cypress: A Changing Seminole Community by Merwyn S. Garbarino (Holt, Rinehart & Winston, 1972).

The American Indian Today by Stuart Levine and Nancy Lurie (Everett Edwards, 1968) is a collection on problems facing contemporary Indians.

Genteel Backlash (Sennett)

Uses of Disorder: Personal Identity and City Life by Richard Sennett (Alfred A. Knopf, 1970) discusses at greater length the issues raised in this article.

"Urbanism As a Way of Life" by Louis Wirth (*American Journal of Sociology* 44: July 1938, 1–24).

The Suburban Community edited by William M. Dobriner (G. P. Putnam's Sons, 1958).

The Emerging City by Scott Greer (Free Press, 1962).

Families Against the City: Middle Class Homes of Industrial Chicago by Richard Sennett (Harvard University Press, 1970).

The Brutality of Modern Families (Sennett)

In the Country of the Young by John Aldridge (Harper & Row, Harper's Magazine Press, 1970) is a long essay on the "smothering" that has occurred in suburban families during the past two decades.

The Promised City by Moses Rischin (Harvard University Press, 1962) is a moving account of immigrant life in New York at the turn of the century.

The Levittowners by Herbert Gans (Pantheon Books, 1967) is an excellent community study of a suburb filled with people of immigrant background who are now lower-middle class. The issues of family and communal togetherness are treated here in a wholly different way than in the above references.

PART THREE. FAMILIES OF THE 1970s

The nineteenth-century French statesman and author Alexis de Tocqueville expressed serious doubt over the future of *Democracy in America* (Alfred A. Knopf, 1945) and of its consequences on the quality of social life.

1. SOCIALIZATION IN THE FAMILY LIFE CYCLE

Much of the theory in this section is drawn from the symbolic interaction approach to human socialization, of which the pioneer book is George Herbert Mead's *Mind, Self and Society* (University of Chicago Press, 1934). Mead's work is difficult to read, however, even for advanced students of sociology. Herbert Blumer, who most influenced sociologists to examine Mead's ideas, has a collection of essays which are easier to digest, in *Symbolic Interactionism: Perspective and Method* (Prentice-Hall, 1969).

The Swiss psychologist Jean Piaget has been researching the development of moral sentiments, perception of shapes, reasoning, and other abilities of children and reporting these processes in several books.

Margaret Mead has been documenting the strength of socialization in forming sexually "appropriate" behavior and personality since 1935, particularly in *Sex and Temperament in Three Primitive Societies* (William Morrow, 1935) and *Male and Female* (William Morrow, 1949).

The effects of socialization on blacks in America, in terms of restricting ability and personality growth, are only now being researched.

Two authors who have probably been most influential in causing American women to reexamine assumptions about the female personality are Simone de Beauvoir, primarily in her *The Second Sex* (Alfred A. Knopf, 1953) and Betty Friedan in *The Feminine Mystique* (W. W. Norton, 1963). There has been a recent outpouring of books and articles focusing on women's identity including Germaine Greer's *The Female Eunuch* (McGraw-Hill, 1971).

Why is a Smile? (Watson)

Attachment and Loss by J. Bowlby (Hogarth Press, 1969).

The Growth of Sociability by H. R. Schaffer (Penguin Books, 1971).

"Smiling, Cooing, and 'The Game'" by John S. Watson (*Merrill-Palmer Quarterly*, in press).

Threat and Obedience (Aronson)

The Self in Social Interaction, Vol. I, by Chad Gordon and Kenneth Gergen (John Wiley, 1968).

The Socialization of the Second Sex (Freeman)

"Current Patterns in Sex Roles: Children's Perspectives" (*Journal of the National Association of Women Deans and Counselors* 25: October 1961, 3–13) and "Sex-Role Identification: A Symposium"

(*Merrill-Palmer Quarterly* 10: 1964, 3–16), both by Ruth E. Hartley.

Roots of Black Manhood (Hannerz)

The Negro Family in the United States by E. Franklin Frazier University of Chicago Press, 1966).

Soulside: Inquiries into Ghetto Culture and Community by Ulf Hannerz (Columbia University Press, 1969).

The Myth of the Negro Past by Melville J. Herskovits (Beacon Press, 1958).

Urban Blues by Charles Keil (University of Chicago Press, 1966).

Tomorrow's Tomorrow: The Black Woman by Joyce A. Ladner (Doubleday, 1971).

Tally's Corner by Elliot Liebow (Little, Brown, 1967).

Behind Ghetto Walls by Lee Rainwater (Aldine-Atherton, 1970).

2. DATING, MATING, AND PROCREATING IN THE FAMILY LIFE CYCLE

James Coleman and his associates John W. C. Johnstone and Kurt Johassohn studied high schoolers in and around Chicago. Their findings are contained in *Adolescent Society* (Free Press, 1961).

Robert F. Winch discusses some functions of dating in *The Modern Family* (Holt, Rinehart & Winston, 3rd edition, 1971). A variety of articles on dating, sexual relations, and alternatives to marriage are contained in Jack and JoAnn DeLora's edited collection, *Intimate LIfe Styles: Marriage and Its Alternatives* (Goodyear, 1972). Ira L. Reiss ("How and Why America's Sex Standards Are Changing") and Robert Bell are two sociologists who have written extensively on the sexual behavior of Americans—premarital, marital, and extra-marital.

Gunnar Myrdal's *An American Dilemma* (Harper & Row, 1969) was one of the first and classic works to examine the complexity of racism as a justification for keeping blacks and whites apart, particularly during courtship years.

Lee Rainwater examines attitudes toward sexual relations and contraception among lower-class women in *And the Poor Get Children* (Quadrangle Books, 1960).

White Gangs (Miller)

Delinquency and Opportunity: A Theory of Delinquent Gangs by Richard A. Cloward and Lloyd E. Ohlin (Free Press, 1960) explains the existence of both gangs and major types of gangs. It has had a profound impact on American domestic policy.

Delinquent Boys: The Culture of the Gang by Albert K. Cohen (Free Press, 1955) is the first major attempt to explain the behavior of gang members with modern sociological theory.

Street Gangs and Street Workers by Malcolm W. Klein (Prentice-Hall, 1971) is a fascinating account of two projects aimed at reducing gang delinquency—one by increasing group cohesion, the other by dissolving it. The book contains an excellent review of major research findings bearing on types and activities of American street gangs.

Group Process and Gang Delinquency by James F. Short, Jr., and Fred L. Strodtbeck (University of Chicago Press, 1965) represents an empirical "test" of divergent theories of gangs and delinquency. It includes the first systematic application of statistical techniques and the first systematic application of the social-psychological conceptual framework to the study of gangs.

The Gang: A Study of 1313 Gangs in Chicago by Frederic M. Thrasher (University of Chicago Press, 1927) is the classic work on American youth gangs. Although published in the 1920s, it remains the most detailed and comprehensive treatise on gangs and gang life every written.

Teen-Age Interracial Dating (Petroni)

2, 4, 6, 8, When You Gonna Integrate? by Frank Petroni, Ernest A. Hirsch, and C. Lillian Petroni (Behavioral Publications, 1970).

Racially Separate or Together by Thomas F. Pettigrew (McGraw-Hill, 1971) is an excellent account of factors past, present, and future which have impeded and may continue to impede un-self-conscious interracial mixing.

Sororities and the Husband Game (Scott)

Courtship, Marriage, and the Family by Robert F. Kelley (Harcourt Brace Jovanovich, 1969).

Mate Selection by Robert F. Winch (Harper & Row, 1958).

Singles in the City (Starr and Carns)

Education and Jobs: The Great Training Robbery by Ivar E. Berg (Praeger Publishers, 1970) is an in-depth analysis of the actual relationship between education and opportunity in the United States.

Status Passage: A Formal Theory by Barney G. Glaser and Anselm L. Strauss (Aldine-Atherton, 1971) is a systematic study of changes in status including careers.

How and Why America's Sex Standards Are Changing (Reiss)

The Encyclopedia of Sexual Behavior edited by Albert Ellis and Albert Albarbanel (Hawthorn Books, 1961) is the most complete and authoritative source of its kind available, containing articles by approximately 100 authorities.

Journal of Social Issues—"The Sexual Renaissance in America"—(April 1966) contains contributions by many leading researchers: Robert Bell, Jessie Bernard, Carlfred Broderick, Harold Christensen, Paul Gebhard, Lester Kirkendall, Roger Libby, Lee Rainwater, Ira L. Reiss, Robert Sherwin, and Clark Vincent.

Sex in America edited by Henry A. Gruenwald (Bantam Books, 1964).

"Living Together: An Alternative to Marriage" by Judith L. Lyness, Milton E. Lipetz, and Keith E. Davis (*Journal of Marriage and the Family* 34: May 1972, 306–311).

Premarital Sexual Standards in America by Ira L. Reiss (Free Press, 1964).

The Social Control of Premarital Sexual Permissiviness by Ira L. Reiss (Holt, Rinehart & Winston, 1967).

The Family System in America by Ira L. Reiss (Holt, Rinehart & Winston, 1971).

The Sexual Behavior of Young People by Michael Schofield (Little, Brown, 1965) is a carefully executed study of English teenagers with much information that can be compared with American studies.

Abortion Laws and Their Victims (Rossi)

A Study of Abortion in Primitive Societies by George Devereux (Julian Press, 1955) views abortion as a cultural device for birth control.

Pregnancy, Birth and Abortion by Paul H. Gebhard, Wardell Pomeroy, Clyde Martin, and Cornelia Christenson (Harper & Row, 1958) contains excellent empirical studies of abortion.

"Abortion—or Compulsory Pregnancy" by Garrett Hardin (*Journal of Marriage and the Family* 30: May 1968, 246).

The Sanctity of Life and the Criminal Law by Granville Williams (Alfred A. Knopf, 1957) is a fine account of the legal and ecclesiastical history of abortion.

The Male Maternal Instinct (Stannard)

Womankind by Nancy Reeves (Aldine-Atherton, 1971).

3. MIDDLE AND OLD AGE IN THE FAMILY LIFE CYCLE

There is relatively little being written by social scientists about middle age, with the exception of Bernice Neugarten's work. See particularly her *Personality in Middle and Late Life* (Aldine-Atherton, 1964).

Sexual behavior in middle age is reported in *Intimate Life Styles* cited above. Although not a social scientist, Morton Hunt has written an interesting account in *The Affair* (World Publishing Co., 1969).

Old age has been a neglected subject among social scientists but is now drawing their attention. Two of the main books are Irving Rosow's *Social Integration of the Aged* (Free Press, 1967) and Elaine Cumming and William E. Henry's *Growing Old* (Basic Books, 1961).

Death has been newly "discovered" by sociological and psychological researchers. See, for example, Geoffrey Gorer's *Death, Grief and Bereavement* (Doubleday, Anchor Books, 1967) and Anselm Strauss and Daniel Glaser's *Awareness of Dying* (Aldine-Atherton, 1965).

The effects of death upon survivors were first analyzed in psychiatrist Eric Lindemann's "Symptomology and Management of Acute Grief" in Robert Fulton's *Death and Identity* (John Wiley, 1965).

Peter Marris studied widows in London for his *Widows and Their Families* (Routledge and Kegan Paul, 1958), and I have reported on Chicago area widows in *Widowhood in an American City* (Schenkman Publishing Co., 1972).

The Fund of Sociability (Weiss)

Kinship in an Urban Setting by Bert Adams (Markham, 1968) is an analysis of survey data dealing with the functioning of kin relationships for a sample of married adults living in Greensboro, North Carolina.

Husbands and Wives by Robert O. Blood, Jr., and Donald M. Wolfe (Free Press, 1960) is a report of a survey of married pairs living in Detroit which describes how the couples manage their joint enterprises of home and family, and in somewhat less detail how they maintain the more emotional aspects of their relationships.

Family and Social Network by Elizabeth Bott (Tavistock, 1957) is a study of different organizations of marital and social relationships which can serve to provide the same set of relational functions.

Human Nature and the Social Order by Charles Cooley (Charles Scribner's Sons, 1922).

The Meaning of Work and Retirement by Eugene Friedmann and Robert Havighurst (University of Chicago Press, 1954) is a collection of studies describing the meaning of work in various occupations.

"Loneliness: Forms and Components" by Helena Z. Lopata (*Social Problems* 17: Fall 1969, 248–262).

"Clique Contacts and Family Orientations" by Joel L. Nelson (*American Sociological Review* 31: October 1966, 663–672).

Sourcebook in Marriage and the Family by Marvin B. Sussman (Houghton Mifflin, 1963) is a good collection of articles on aspects of dating, marital relationships, parent-child relationships, and relationships with other kin.

Swinging in Wedlock (Palson and Palson)

Group Sex by Gilbert D. Bartell (New American Library, 1971).

The Double Standard (Bell)

Woman in a Man-Made World edited by Nona Glazer-Malbin and Helen Youngelson Waehrer (Rand McNally, 1972).

Portnoy's Mother's Complaint (Bart)

"Why Women's Status Changes in Middle Age; The Turns of the Social Ferris Wheel" by Pauline Bart (*Sociological Symposium*, Fall 1969).

Current Perspectives in Psychiatric Sociology edited by Paul Roman and Harrison Trice (Science House, in press).

And Then We Were Old (Rosow)

Old People in Three Industrial Societies by Ethel Shanas at al. (Aldine-Atherton, 1968).

"Structural Constraints on Friendships in Old Age" by Zena Blau (*American Sociological Review* 26: 1961, 429–439).

Employment, Income and Retirement Problems of the Aged edited by Juanita Kreps (Duke University Press, 1963).

Aging and Society, Vol. I, by Matilda Riley and Anne Foner (Russell Sage Foundation, 1968).

A Hiding Place to Die (Markson)

The Dying Patient by Orville Brim et al. (Russell Sage Foundation, 1970) is a collection of articles on death in its social context, including when, why, and where people die, how medical personnel and hospitals cope with death, and ethical, social, legal, and economic questions related to death.

Memento Mori by Muriel Spark (Avon Books, 1971) is an insightful novel about aging and impending death and the social responses to these phenomena.

Passing On by David Sudnow (Prentice-Hall, 1967) is a participant observation study of dying in two general hospitals, including descriptions of "worthy" versus "unworthy" patients and of handling the dying and the dead.

PART FOUR. THE FAMILY AND OTHER INSTITUTIONS

Probably the book most relevant to this Part is Robin William, Jr.'s *American Society* (Alfred A. Knopf, 3rd edition, 1970), which shows the interrelationships between various institutions within this larger unit.

Children and Their Caretakers (Denzin)

Big School and Small School by Roger Barker and Paul V. Gump (Stanford University Press, 1964) presents a convenient review of Barker's and Herbert Wright's perspective on schools and education. Their work challenges current positivistic methodologies and theories of children and education.

The Sociology of Teaching by Willard Waller (John Wiley, 1967), originally published in 1937 remains the best available analysis of life in schools as seen by teachers and students. It anticipates and goes beyond more recent critiques by Paul Goodman, Herbert Kohl, John Holt, and others.

Black Genes—White Environment (Hunt)

The Disadvantaged Child: Studies of the Social Environment and the Learning Process by Martin Deutsch (Basic Books, 1967) anthologizes many of the pioneering developments in early childhood education.

Studies in Cognitive Development: Essays in Honor of Jean Piaget edited by David Elkind and John H. Flavell (Oxford University Press, 1969) is an anthology primarily concerned with the investigations and theorizing of Piaget, whose work has inspired, at least in part, many recent developments in the field.

Experience, Structure, and Adaptability edited by O. J. Harvey (Springer Publishing Co., 1966) includes a variety of investigations of the role of early experience in the development of flexibility and adaptability.

Revolution in Learning: The Years from Birth to Six by Maya Pines (Harper & Row, 1967) is a non-technical survey of many developments in early childhood education.

Creativity and Intelligence in Children's Thinking (Wallach and Kogan)

Creativity and Intelligence: Explorations with Gifted Students by Jacob Getzels and Philip W. Jackson (John Wiley, 1962).

Guiding Creative Talent by E. Paul Torrance (Prentice-Hall, 1962).

Modes of Thinking in Young Children: A Study of the Creativity-Intelligence Distinction by Michael Wallach and Nathan Kogan (Holt, Rinehart & Winston, 1965).

The Talented Student by Michael A. Wallach and C. W. Wing, Jr. (Holt, Rinehart & Winston, 1969)

"Creativity" by Michael A. Wallach, in P. H. Mussen's edited collection, *Carmichael's Manual of Child Psychology*, Vol. I. (John Wiley, 3rd edition, 1970).

College Admissions and the Psychology of Talent by C. W. Wing, Jr., and Michael A. Wallach (Holt, Rinehart & Winston, 1971).

Drugging and Schooling (Witter)

Federal Involvement in the Use of Behavior Modification Drugs on Grammar School Children, of the Right to Privacy Inquiry (Hearings before a Subcommittee of the Committee on Government Operations, House of Representatives, Ninety-First Congress, Second Session, September 29, 1970) can be purchased from the Superintendent of Documents, U.S. Government Printing Office, Washington, D.C., 20402 for 65 cents (check or money order).

Anatomy of a Chicago Slum (Suttles)

Tally's Corner by E. Liebow (Little, Brown, 1967).

Child Convicts (Lerman)

Delinquency and Social Policy edited by Paul Lerman (Praeger Publishers, 1970) presents further evidence and discussion of injustice, ineffective correction, police discretion, and other topics relating to adult behavior vis-a-vis young people.

Borderland of Criminal Justice: Essays in Law and Criminology by Frances A. Allen (University of Chicago Press, 1964) was frequently cited by the U.S. Supreme Court in the *Gault* decision. This perceptive legal scholar examines legal and social consequences of the American predilection for attempting to criminalize social problems.

Children and Youth in America edited by Robert H. Bremner (Harvard University Press, 1970).

Juvenile Defenders for a Thousand Years: Selected Readings from Anglo-Saxon Times to 1900 edited by Wiley B. Saunders (University of North Carolina Press, 1970).

The Child Savers: The Invention of Delinquency by Anthony M. Platt (University of Chicago Press, 1969).

Children in Urban Society: Juvenile Delinquency in Nineteenth-Century America by Joseph M. Hawes (Oxford University Press, 1971).

Task Force Report: Juvenile Delinquency and Youth Crime and *Task Force Report: Corrections*, both by the President's Commission on Law Enforcement and the Administration of Justice (U.S. Government Printing Office, 1967).

Varieties of Police Behavior by James Q. Wilson (Harvard University Press, 1968).

Violence and Inner City Families (Chaiklin, Ephross, and Sterne)

The Age of Aquarius by William Braden (Quadrangle Books, 1970).

"Black Identity and the Helping Person" by Donald Brieland (*Children* 16: September-October 1969, 18).

Assimilation in American Life by Milton M. Gordon (Oxford University Press, 1964).

Living Poor by Camille Jeffers (University of Michigan, Ann Arbor Books, 1967).

Juvenile Delinquency edited by Richard R. Korn (Thomas Y. Crowell, 1968).

The Omni-Americans by Albert Murray (Outerbridge & Lazard, E. P. Dutton, 1970).

Report of the National Advisory Commission on Civil Disorders (Bantam Books, 1968).

Community Organizations and Services to Improve Family Living (University of Maryland School of Social Work and Community Planning, 1970).

The Serpent-Handling Religions of West Virginia (Gerrard)

They Shall Take Up Serpents by Weston LaBarre (University of Minnesota Press, 1962) is a psychological interpretation of serpent-handling and its history.

"Ordeal by Serpents, Fire, and Strychnine" by Berthold Schwarz (*Psychiatric Quarterly*, 1960, 405–429) reports on more than 200 instances of serpent-handling personally observed by the author.

The Small Sects in America by Elmert T. Clark (Abingdon Press, 1959) is an excellent account of the holiness movement, of which the serpent-handling sect is an offshoot.

Life and Religion in Southern Appalachia by W. D. Weatherford and Earl D. Brewer (Friendship Press, 1962) treats the role of religion in the life of the rural poor in Appalachia.

Racial and Cultural Minorities by George E. Simpson and J. Milton Yinger (Harper & Row, 3rd edition, 1965).

Beyond the Melting Pot by Nathan Glazer and Daniel P. Moynihan (M.I.T. Press, 1963).

The Relief of Welfare (Piven and Cloward)

The Village Labourer by J. L. Hammond and Barbara Hammond (Longmans, Green, 1948) contains evidence from English history on the relationship of economic change to the rise of disorder, and on the role of relief-giving in moderating disorder.

Captain Swing by E. J. Hobsbawm and George Rudé (Pantheon Books, 1968) is a detailed study of one series of English rural disorders in the 1830s.

Aid to Dependent Children by Winifred Bell (Columbia University Press, 1965) is the best account of this American relief program which has lately become so controversial.

Regulating the Poor by Frances Fox Piven and Richard A. Cloward (Pantheon Books, 1971).

Day Care Centers (Steiner)

The Employed Mother in America by F. Ivan Nye and Lois W. Hoffman (Rand McNally, 1963).

Women in Labor (Suelze)

Woman's Place: Options and Limits in Professional Careers by Cynthia Fuchs Epstein (University of California Press, 1970).

Neighborhood, City and Metropolis: An Integrated Reader in Urban Sociology edited by Robert Gutman and David Popenoe (Random House, 1970).

How Much Money Do Executives Want? (Lawler)

Men, Money and Motivation by A. Patton (McGraw-Hill, 1961) reviews many of the issues concerned with compensation.

Work and Motivation by V. H. Vroom (John Wiley, 1964) provides a good basis on which to answer questions about the motivational basis for pay operating as an incentive.

Money and Motivation by W. F. Whyte (Harper & Row, 1955) contains a number of engrossing case studies.

The Organization Man by William Whyte (Simon & Schuster, 1956).

PART FIVE. FAMILIES OF THE FUTURE

Probably the best-known recent book on the future is Alvin Toffler's *Future Shock* (Random House, 1970), which includes a chapter on the family. Toffler has also edited *The Futurists* (Random House, 1972). He has some very good points to make, but few social scientists would consider his work sufficiently grounded in verifiable fact. He builds a case, rather than examining all the evidence.

"Variant Marriage Styles and Family Forms" edited by Marvin B. Sussman is a special issue of a journal published by the National Council of Family Relations (*The Family Coordinator* 21: October 1972).

The Family As a Company of Players

"Appearance and Education in Marriage Mobility" by Glen H. Elder, Jr. (*American Sociological Review* 34: August 1969, 519–533).

A Better Life (Rogler)

Social Class in America by W. Lloyd Warner (Harper & Row, Torchbooks, 1960).

Social Stratification by Egon E. Bersel (McGraw-Hill, 1962).

The Working Classes (Handel and Rainwater)

Working Class Suburb by Bennett Berger (University of California Press, 1960).

New Styles in Homosexual Manliness (Humphreys)

Out of the Closets: The Sociology of Homosexual Liberation by Laud Humphreys (Prentice-Hall, 1972).

Tearoom Trade: Impersonal Sex in Public Places by Laud Humphreys (Aldine-Atherton, 1970).

The Harried Leisure Class by Steffan B. Linder (Columbia University Press, 1970).

Why All of Us May Be Hippies Someday (Davis)

It's Happening by J. L. Simmons and Barry Winograd (Marc-Laird Publications, 1966).

Looking Forward: The Abundant Society by Walter A. Weisskopf, Raghavan N. Iyer et al. (Center for the Study of Democratic Institutions, 1966).

The Next Generation by Donald N. Michael (Random House, Vintage Books, 1965).

The Failure of History by Robert J. Heilbroner (Grove Press, 1961).

Young Intelligentsia in Revolt (Flacks)

The New Radicalism in America by Christopher Lasch (Random House, 1965) illuminates the development of radicalism among the American intelligentsia in the early twentieth century.

Young Radicals by Kenneth Keniston (Harcourt Brace Jovanovich, 1968) vividly describes the family backgrounds and experience of a set of early new left activists.

The New Left Reader edited by Carl Oglesby (Grove Press, 1969) is a collection of important theoretical statements from the international New Left.

Youth and Social Change by Richard Flacks (Markham Publishing Co., 1971).

Toward a Rational Society by J. Haberman (Beacon Press, 1970).

Post-1984 America (Rainwater)

Rich Man, Poor Man by Herman P. Miller (Thomas Y. Crowell, 1971) projects income and consumption to 1985 and relates shifting consumption behavior to changes in the age distribution of the population.

The Future of Inequality by S. M. Miller and Pamela Roby (Basic Books, 1970) discusses unchanging patterns of inequality in American society and their implications for the future.

Timing of Our Lives (Browning)

From Generation to Generation by S. N. Eisenstadt (Free Press, 1956) sets forth the normative approach to the life cycle and its key events.

American Families by Paul Glick (John Wiley, 1957) represents the demographic approach to the family life cycle.

"The Life Cycle of the Social Role of the Housewife" by Helena Z. Lopata (*Sociology and Social Research* 51: October 1966, 5–22).

Future Family (Mead)

Man's World, Woman's Place by Elizabeth Janeway (William Morrow, 1971).

Street Kids by Larry Cole (Grossman Publishers, 1971).

The Contributors

Elliot Aronson

Pauline B. Bart

Inge Powell Bell

Jean L. Briggs

Harley L. Browning

ELLIOT ARONSON ("Threat and Obedience") is a social psychologist and professor of psychology at the University of Texas at Austin. The recipient of the annual award of the American Association for the Advancement of Science for creative research in social psychology in 1970, he is co-editor of *The Handbook of Social Psychology* (with Gardner Lindzey) and *Theories of Cognitive Consistency: A Sourcebook*, as well as editor of *Voice of Social Psychology* and author of *The Social Animal*. His current research interests include social influence, interpersonal attractiveness, and encounter groups.

PAULINE BART ("Portnoy's Mother's Complaint") is assistant professor of sociology in psychiatry at the University of Illinois' College of Medicine in Chicago. She recently co-authored "A Funny Thing Happened on the Way to the Orifice: Women in Gynecology Texts" and is chairperson for education for Sociologists for Women in Society. Her most recent book is *Society, Culture and Depression*.

INGE POWELL BELL ("The Double Standard") is associate professor of sociology at Pitzer College for Women in Claremont, California. Since she received her Ph.D. in 1964 she has worked mainly on a study of local-level right-wing leaders in Southern California.

JEAN J. BRIGGS ("Kapluna Daughter: Living with Eskimos") is associate professor in the Department of Sociology and Anthropology of the Memorial University of Newfoundland. Her research of Eskimo emotional patterns is an extension of that reported in her book *Never in Anger*.

HARLEY L. BROWNING ("Timing of Our Lives") is associate professor of sociology at the University of Texas at Austin and director of the Population Research Center. His major research interests are the modernization process, particularly urbanization and internal migration in Latin America, and explorations in social demography.

DONALD E. CARNS ("Singles in the City") is assistant professor of sociology at Northwestern University. He is co-editor with John Walton of *Cities in Change: A Reader in Urban Sociology.* His current research interests include change and extended kinship, young adults and lesbianism.

HARRIS CHAIKLIN ("Effects of Violence on Inner City Families") is professor in the School of Social Work and Community Planning at the University of Maryland at Baltimore. He is the author of numerous articles, research reports, professional papers and book reviews.

RICHARD A. CLOWARD ("The Relief of Welfare") is professor at the Columbia School of Social Work. He was a founder of Mobilization for Youth and is its director of research. His latest book is *Regulating the Poor: The Functions of Public Welfare*, co-authored with Frances Fox Piven.

ROBERT COLES ("The Case of Hugh McCaslin") is a research psychiatrist at Harvard University. He has worked in Appalachia and as a consultant to the Appalachian Volunteers. He has published widely in the field of child psychiatry and is the author of several books, including *Children of Crisis: A Study of Courage and Fear.*

FRED DAVIS ("Why All of Us May be Hippies Someday") is professor of sociology at the University of California, San Francisco. He is the author of *Passage Through Crisis, Polio Victims and Their Families* and is editor of *The Nursing Profession, Five Sociological Essays.* He is presently conducting research in the areas of youth culture and the spontaneous termination of deviant careers.

NORMAN K. DENZIN ("Children and Their Caretakers") is associate professor of sociology at the University of Illinois, Urbana. He has conducted participant observation studies of children between the ages of one and four and is preparing a book on this research entitled *Chilren, Society and Social Relationships.*

412

Donald E. Carns

Harris Chaiklin

Richard A. Cloward

Robert Coles

Fred Davis

Ruth B. Dixon

Paul H. Ephross

RICHARD L. FLACKS

He is author of *The Research Act* and editor of *Children and Their Caretakers*.

RUTH B. DIXON ("Hallelujah the Pill?") is assistant professor of sociology at the University of California, Davis. She is interested in population problems and policies in less-developed and industrial countries and has completed a dissertation on the determinants of variations in average age at first marriage and proportions never married of men and women in Western Europe and Asia.

PAUL EPHROSS ("Effects of Violence on Inner City Families") is associate professor in the School of Social Work and Community Planning at the University of Maryland at Baltimore. His major research interests center around program evaluation and interpersonal phenomena in daily life.

RICHARD FLACKS ("Young Intelligentsia in Revolt") is associate professor of sociology at the University of California in Santa Barbara. He has done considerable research and writing on the student movement and the New Left. He was a founder of Students for a Democratic Society. His latest book is *Youth and Social Change*.

JO FREEMAN ("The Socialization of the Second Sex") is working on her doctorate at the University of Chicago. She has been an organizer in the women's liberation movement and is also a free-lance writer and photographer. She has published about a dozen articles in magazines and anthologies on women.

MERWYN S. GARBARINO ("Seminole Girl") is associate professor of anthropology, University of Illinois at Chicago Circle. She is also a fieldworker in the Welfare and Family Services Department of the American Indian Center in Chicago. Until she began working at the Indian Center she was engaged in research on the Florida Seminole at Big Cypress Reservation. Her latest book is *Big Cypress—A Changing Seminole Community*.

NATHAN L. GERRARD ("The Serpent Handling Religions of West Virginia") is professor and chairman of the department of sociology, Morris Harvey College, Charleston, West Virginia. His research interests include the cultural and social patterns of the "hollows", the communities of non-farm rural poor in West Virginia.

Jo Freeman

Merwyn S. Garbarino

Nathan L. Gerrard

Ulf Hannerz

GERALD HANDEL ("The Working Classes") is associate professor of sociology at The City College of New York and the Graduate School of the City University of New York. The editor of *The Psychosocial Interior of the Family*, he is co-author of *The Child and Society* and of *Workingman's Wife: Her Personality, World and Life Style*. He is also associate editor of the *Journal of Marriage and the Family*.

ULF HANNERZ ("Roots of Black Manhood") of the Institute of Ethnography at Sweden's University of Stockholm, Sweden, has done field work among blacks in Washington, D.C. He is the author of *Soulside: Inquiries into Ghetto Culture and Community*.

LAUD HUMPHREYS ("New Styles in Homosexual Manliness") is associate professor of sociology at Pitzer College, Claremont, California. He is the author of *Out of the Closets: The Sociology of Homosexual Liberation*, and his research interests include deviant behavior, crime and delinquency.

J. McVICKER HUNT ("Black Genes—White Environment"), professor of psychology and of elementary education at the University of Illinois, is the author of over 100 articles in journals and anthologies. He has edited *Personality and the Behavior Disorders* and is the author of *Intelligence and Experience* and *The Challenge of Incompetence and Poverty: Papers on the Role of Early Education*.

NATHAN KOGAN ("Creativity and Intelligence in Children's Thinking") is professor and chairman, Department of Psychology, New School for Social Research. He is the author of *Risk Taking: A Study in Cognition and Personality*.

EDWARD E. LAWLER, III ("How Much Money Do Executives Want?") is professor of psychology and program director, Institute for Social Research, University of Michigan. Author of numerous articles and papers, his most recent book is *Motivation in Organizations*.

PAUL LERMAN ("Child Convicts") is associate professor of social work at the Graduate School of Social Work, Rutgers University, where he teaches courses on delinquency and social policy, social welfare policy and research. His major interest is in understanding societal responses to youthful deviance.

413

OSCAR LEWIS ("Even the Saints Cry") was professor of anthropology at the University of Illinois. He conducted family studies in Mexico, New York, Puerto Rico and Cuba. Among his books are: *Five Families, The Children of Sanchez; Pedro Martinez: A Mexican Peasant and his Family;* and *La Vida: A Puerto Rican Family in the Culture of Poverty—San Juan and New York.*

ELIZABETH W. MARKSON ("A Hiding Place to Die") is director of the Mental Health Research Unit of the New York State Department of Mental Hygiene. She has worked with the N.Y. Department of Social Services, and as a lecturer and sociologist at the State University at Albany. Her major research interests are medical sociology, the life cycle and deviant behavior.

MARGARET MEAD ("Future Family") is Curator Emeritus of Ethnology at the American Museum of Natural History. She holds over twenty honorary degrees, has held numerous positions and lectureships since 1925 and is renowned for her expeditionary work among South Seas peoples in Samoa and Bali. Among her numerous publications are *The Small Conference: An Innovation in Communication* (with Paul Beyers), *A Way of Seeing* (with Rhoda Metraux), *Culture and Commitment: A Study of the Generation Gap, Coming of Age in Samoa, Growing Up in New Guinea* and *Rap on Race* (with James Baldwin).

WALTER B. MILLER ("White Gangs") is senior research associate at the Joint Center for Urban Studies sponsored by Massachusetts Institute of Technology and Harvard University and is director of the Roxbury Delinquency Research Project. He has co-authored *Street Gangs and Street Workers.*

MARIAN GENNARIA MORRIS ("Psychological Miscarriage") holds graduate degrees in both nursing and social work and was research associate at Hahnemann Medical College and Hospital in Philadelphia. At Children's Hospital of Los Angeles, Department of Psychiatry, she has done work on abusive parents.

ANNABELLE B. MOTZ ("The Family as a Company of Players") is professor of sociology at American University, Washington, D.C. She is the author of articles that reflect her research interest in social psychology, social organization and family living.

414

Laud Humphreys

J. McVicker Hunt

Nathan Kogan

Edward E. Lawler, III

Paul Lerman

Oscar Lewis

Elizabeth Markson

Walter B. Miller

CHARLES PALSON ("Swinging in Wedlock") is a doctoral candidate in anthropology at the University of Chicago. He also teaches marriage and family relations at Immaculata College, Immaculata, Pennsylvania. He is national president of the Student Evaluation Project which publishes student evaluations of graduate departments of anthropology.

REBECCA PALSON ("Swinging in Wedlock") has studied anthropology and art. Co-author with her husband of several articles on culture of sex and the structure of swingers' relationships, she is working with him on a book, *Friends and Lovers: A Study in the Use and Meaning of Sex.*

FRANK A. PETRONI ("Teen-Age Interracial Dating") is assistant professor of sociology at the University of Arizona, Tucson. He was formerly a research sociologist with the Menninger Foundation, Topeka, Kansas. He is currently co-editing an anthology on labeling theory and social problems.

FRANCES FOX PIVEN ("The Relief of Welfare") is a political scientist teaching at Boston University, has authored many articles on urban politics, is currently working on a book titled *Recent Movements of the Poor and Why They Failed,* and is associated with the founding of the welfare rights movement.

LEE RAINWATER ("The Working Classes—Old and New," and "Post-1984 America") is professor of sociology in the Department of Sociology and John F. Kennedy School of Government at Harvard University. His major works include *Behind Ghetto Walls: Black Families in a Federal Slum; And the Poor Get Children: Sex, Contraception and Family Planning in the Working Class; Family Design: Marital Sexuality, Family Size and Contraception; Moynihan Report and the Politics of Controversy* (with William Yancey); *Workingman's Wife: Her Personality, World and Life Style* (with Gerald Handell) and *Soul.*

IRA L. REISS ("How and Why America's Sex Standards Are Changing") is professor of sociology and director of the Family Study Center at the University of Minnesota. He has served as associate director of the *American Sociological Review, Social Problems,* and the *Journal of Marriage and the Family.* His books include *Premarital Sexual Standards in America, The Social Context of Premarital*

Margaret Mead

Charles Palson

Rebecca Palson

Frank Petroni

Frances Fox Piven

Sexual Permissiveness, and *The Family System in America.*

LLOYD ROGLER ("A Better Life") is professor of sociology at Case Western Reserve University. Presently studying urbanization in Latin America, he was born and raised in Puerto Rico and has an interest in the psychiatric aspects of Puerto Rican family life both on the mainland and in Puerto Rico. His book on this subject is *Trapped: Families and Schizophrenia.*

LAWRENCE ROSEN ("I Divorce Thee") is a Russell Sage Foundation Resident in Law and Society at the University of Chicago where he is working for his J.D. degree. He spent the academic year 1970-71 at the Institute for Advanced Study in Princeton. His main interests are in the anthropology of the Middle East and comparative law.

IRVING ROSOW ("And Then We Were Old") is professor at the Langley Porter Neuropsychiatric Institute of the University of California at San Francisco. He is an authority on gerontology, and his major theoretical interest as a sociologist is in adult socialization. His most recent books are *Social Integration of the Aged* and *Socialization to Old Age.*

ALICE S. ROSSI ("Abortion Laws and Their Victims") is professor of sociology at Goucher College in Baltimore. Areas of research interest in which she has published include family sociology, career development, sex roles, reproductive behavior, and the history of feminism. She is currently editing two books, *American Women on the Move* and *Essential Works of Feminism.*

JOHN FINLEY SCOTT ("Sororities and the Husband Game") is associate professor in the Department of Sociology at the University of California at Davis. His published articles deal with kinship in complex societies and the role of norms in sociological theory.

RICHARD SENNETT ("Genteel Backlash: Chicago 1886" and "The Brutality of Modern Families"), assistant professor of sociology at Brandeis University and a fellow of the Cambridge Institute, is director of the Urban Family Study, a project exploring changes in white working-class family life. He is the author of *Families Against the City: Middle Class Homes of Industrial Chicago* and *The Uses of Disorder: Personal Identity and City Life.*

415

UNA STANNARD ("The Male Maternal Instinct") is the author of *The New Pamela,* a novel about a woman who tries to defy the double standard by opening doors for herself and asking men to bed. She is also the author of "The Mask of Beauty" in *Fifty-one Percent: The Case for Women's Liberation* and "Clothing and Sexuality" in *Medical Aspects of Human Sexuality.*

JOYCE R. STARR ("Singles in the City"), a doctoral candidate in sociology at Northwestern University, is currently a consultant for the Drug Abuse Council in Washington, D.C. Her main research interests are in evaluation research and young adult life style.

GILBERT Y. STEINER ("Day Care Centers") is senior fellow and director of the Government Studies Program at The Brookings Institution. He has long been a consultant to state and local governments and has written many books and articles, including *The Congressional Conference Committee, Legislation by Collective Bargaining, Social Insecurity: The Politics of Welfare* and *The State of Welfare.*

RICHARD STERNE ("The Effects of Violence on Inner City Families") is associate professor in the school of social work at the University of Minnesota. He has a great variety of publications, most recently "Pass/Fail: Pass or Fail?" (with Peter Chommie) and "Accountability and Payoff in the Social Services: An Overview."

MARIJEAN SUELZLE ("Women in Labor") is a doctoral candidate in the Department of Sociology at the University of California, Berkeley. Author of many papers, her recent research projects include a study of changing sex roles and attitudes towards women's liberation among Berkeley students, and a study of discrimination against nonacademic women at Berkeley.

GERALD D. SUTTLES ("Anatomy of a Chicago Slum") is author of *The Social Order of the Slum: Ethnicity and Territoriality in the Inner City.* He is a faculty member at the Depart-

Lee Rainwater

Ira L. Reiss

Irving Rosow

Alice S. Rossi

John Finley Scott

Richard Sennett

Una Stannard

Joyce R. Starr

Gilbert Y. Steiner

Richard Sterne

Michael A. Wallach

Marijean Suelzle

John S. Watson

Robert S. Weiss

Helena Lopata

ment of Sociology at the State University of New York at Stony Brook.

ARTHUR TUDEN ("Ila Slavery in Zambia") is associate professor of anthropology at the University of Pittsburgh. He has conducted extensive field research in Rhodesia and is currently working on the question of social stratification in Africa south of the Sahara.

MICHAEL A. WALLACH ("Creativity and Intelligence in Children's Thinking") is professor of psychology at Duke University and editor of the Journal of Personality. His recent articles consider the talented student and creativity. He is the author of *The Intelligence/Creativity Distinction* and co-author of *College Admissions and the Psychology of Talent.*

JOHN S. WATSON ("Why is a Smile?") is associate professor of psychology at the University of California, Berkeley. He is a developmental psychologist with special interests in the development of memory, learning and social behavior in human infants.

ROBERT S. WEISS ("The Fund of Sociability") is a lecturer in sociology in the Department of Psychiatry of the Harvard Medical School, working in its Laboratory of Community Psychiatry. His research centers on problems in social psychology and research methods.

CHARLES WITTER ("Drugging and Schooling") was educated at Stanford University. He was staff director for Congressman Cornelius E. Gallagher's Special Subcommittee on Privacy and is now staff consultant to the House Committee on Foreign Affairs. He is working on a book on privacy.

HELENA Z. LOPATA (editor of this collection) is director of the Center for the Comparative Study of Social Roles and professor in the Department of Sociology at Loyola University of Chicago. *Occupation: Housewife and Widowhood in an American City* are among her recent publications. Her interests in the sociology of women include cross-cultural research on widowhood.

Charles Witter